# FLOOD TIDE OF EMPIRE

*Spain and the Pacific Northwest, 1543–1819*

*by Warren L. Cook*

*New Haven and London: Yale University Press*

*1973*

*Published with assistance from the
Kingsley Trust Association Publication Fund
established by the Scroll and Key Society
of Yale College.*

*Copyright © 1973 by Yale University.
All rights reserved. This book may not be
reproduced, in whole or in part, in any form
(except by reviewers for the public press),
without written permission from the publishers.
Library of Congress catalog card number: 72–75187
International standard book number: 0–300–01577–1*

*Designed by John O. C. McCrillis
and set in Baskerville type.
Printed in the United States of America by
The Vail-Ballou Press, Inc., Binghamton, N.Y.*

*Published in Great Britain, Europe, and Africa by
Yale University Press, Ltd., London.
Distributed in Canada by McGill-Queen's University
Press, Montreal; in Latin America by Kaiman & Polon,
Inc., New York City; in Australasia and Southeast
Asia by John Wiley & Sons Australasia Pty. Ltd.,
Sydney; in India by UBS Publishers' Distributors Pvt.,
Ltd., Delhi; in Japan by John Weatherhill, Inc., Tokyo.*

*To my parents,*
*the late Silas Warren Cook,*
*and Amy Morris Jensen,*
*whose veneration for the history*
*of the Pacific Northwest is the*
*source from which this investigation*
*originally stems*

# Contents

# *Preface*

DESPITE scores of place names of Spanish derivation on maps of the Pacific coast as far north as Alaska, relatively few Americans know that, long before the Lewis and Clark expedition set forth, the red and yellow banner of Carlos III flew over the Pacific Northwest, exacting deference from other nationalities. Iberians discovered the Columbia River seventeen years before it was sighted by Captain Robert Gray, and they were the first to reconnoiter the coast of Oregon, Washington, and British Columbia—explorations culminating in a resounding international crisis in 1790 that profoundly affected not only the European powers but also the United States. That fledgling nation fell heir to Spanish achievements in the Northwest when Madrid withdrew, thereby gaining a vast realm that might under other circumstances have gone to Britain or Russia. The full historical import of Iberian participation in international rivalry for that area is still unappreciated.

Henry R. Wagner, who more than any other historian is associated with the investigation of Spanish voyages along the Pacific coast, devoted much of his life to assembling and annotating a prodigious volume of narratives related to the coastline from Mexico northward; but, as Lewis Hanke recently noted, Wagner was "more at home in the minutiae of bibliography than in the larger questions of history" (*HAHR* 48 [1968]: 695).

It would be difficult to surpass Wagner's monographs on the discovery and charting of the northwest coast, or William R. Manning's handling of the Nootka Sound controversy. Rather, *Flood Tide of Empire* seeks to portray Spanish interaction with the Indians, British, Russians, and Americans —five life styles competing for hegemony over the same territory. Spanish alternatives, choices, successes, and failures can be understood only in the context within which they acted. If this perspective seems anthropological, as well as diplomatic, it is because the outcome often hinged upon cultural differences, as much as on economic and political factors.

The chief obstacle to such an overview is the sheer volume of pertinent sources. Spanish officers visiting the Pacific Northwest were required to keep journals and submit written reports which, together with the orders to them, were copied and recopied for perusal by the viceroys in Mexico City and the ministry in Madrid. Countless carefully tied bundles of such material lie in Mexican and Spanish archives, and additional thousands of items have migrated to other countries. No one could aspire to mining all this evidence; much is owed to the spadework in those repositories by Bolton, Chapman, Ogden, Nasatir, Jackson, and others. Excerpts of Spanish sources in the pages that follow have been translated by the respective editors, unless otherwise credited. Those never published before in English are my own translations.

A debt of gratitude must be acknowledged to many persons and institutions for facilitating my research:

In Canada, France, and Great Britain: Willard W. Ireland, Provincial Archives of British Columbia, Victoria; Mr. and Mrs. Louis Holker, Victoria; Chief Ambrose Ma-kwee-na, Nootka; M. R. Monnier, Bibliothèque Nationale, Paris; and personnel of the British Museum, London.

In Mexico: J. Ignacio Rubio Mañé and Beatriz Arteaga, Archivo General de la Nación, Mexico City.

In Spain: personnel of the Archivo General de Indias, Seville; Archivo Histórico Nacional, Madrid; Museo de América, Madrid; Tomás Magallón, Biblioteca Nacional, Madrid; Miguel Maticorena Estrada, Escuela de Estudios Hispano-Americanos, Seville; Luís Navarro García, Universidad de Sevilla; Julio F. Guillén and Roberto Barreiro-Meiro, Museo Naval, Madrid.

In the United States: George P. Hammond and John Barr Tompkins, Bancroft Library of the University of California; Peabody Museum and Widener Libraries, Harvard University; John H. Pomfret, Henry E. Huntington Library, San Marino; Robert M. Sutton and Colette Wright, Illinois Historical Survey, University of Illinois, Urbana; Library of Congress, Washington, D.C.; Newberry Library, Chicago; Myra Ellen Jenkins, New Mexico State Records Center, Santa Fe; Alexander Walker, Tillamook County Pioneer Museum, Tillamook, Oregon; Bruce LeRoy, Washington State Historical Society Museum, Tacoma; Archibald Hanna and Charles Ludwig, Beinecke and Sterling Libraries, Yale University; the late Frederick William Beinecke, New York City; William H. Goetzmann, University of Texas; E. W. Giesecke, Olympia, Washington; Benjamin Lane, Manzanita, Oregon; Chief John Markishtum, Neah Bay, Washington; Irving W. Robbins, Jr., Atherton, California; Michael E. Thurman, Southern Methodist University, Dallas; and Iris Higbie Wilson, Long Beach College, Long Beach, California.

Donald Cutter, University of New Mexico, provided important leads and helpful criticism. Special acknowledgment must be extended to Samuel Flagg Bemis, Professor Emeritus of Diplomatic History, Yale University. His vast knowledge in fields which merge in this subject—Hispanic America, the American West, and international diplomacy—greatly benefited the conception and development of this investigation.

Appreciation is due my colleague Robert L. Patterson for helpful criticism of the manuscript. Edward Tripp, Ellen Graham, and Antoinette Blood of Yale University Press were of great help. My brother, Charles E. Cook, of Spokane, gave valuable photographic service at Nootka and Neah Bay. To my wife, Sandra, I owe assistance in so many ways as to make this labor of love partly hers.

W. L. C.

*Castleton State College, Vermont*
*April 1972*

# *Abbreviations*

Archival designations follow the National Union Catalogue.

| | |
|---|---|
| *AH* | *American Heritage* |
| AHA | American Historical Association |
| *AHR* | *American Historical Review* |
| *ASP* | *American State Papers* |
| AT | Author's translation |
| Aud. | *Audiencia* (a colonial jurisdictional division) |
| BCHA | British Columbia Historical Association |
| *BCHQ* | *British Columbia Historical Quarterly* |
| BCPAD | British Columbia Provincial Archives Department |
| CaBViPA | Provincial Archives of British Columbia, Victoria |
| CClH | Honnold Library, Pomona College, Claremont, California |
| *CHR* | *Canadian Historical Review* |
| *CHSQ* | *California Historical Society Quarterly* |
| CLU-WAC | William Andrews Clark Memorial Library, University of California in Los Angeles |
| C.O. | Records of the Colonial Office (UKLPRO) |
| Col. | *Colección* |
| CSmH | Henry E. Huntington Library, San Marino, California |
| Cuad. | *Cuaderno* (folder) |
| CtY-B | Beinecke Rare Book Library, Yale University, New Haven, Connecticut |
| CtY-BWA | Western Americana Collection (CtY-B) |
| CU-B | Bancroft Library, University of California, Berkeley, California |
| DLC | Manuscript Division, Library of Congress, Washington, D.C. |
| DNA | National Archives, Washington, D.C. |
| *EHR* | *English Historical Review* |
| FrBN | Bibliothèque Nationale, Paris |
| F.O. | Records of the Foreign Office (UKLPRO) |
| *GJ* | *Geographical Journal* |
| Guad. | *Audiencia de Guadalajara* (Sections in SpAGI and MxAGN) |
| *HAHR* | *Hispanic American Historical Review* |
| *HM* | *Historical Magazine* |

| | |
|---|---|
| ICN | Newberry Library, Chicago, Illinois |
| IU-H | Illinois Historical Society, University of Illinois, Urbana, Illinois |
| *JW* | *Journal of the West* |
| leg. | *Legajo* (bundle of documents) |
| Mex. | *Audiencia de México* (Section in SpAGI) |
| MHi | Massachusetts Historical Society, Boston, Massachusetts |
| MH-P | Peabody Museum, Harvard University, Cambridge, Massachusetts |
| MoHi | Missouri Historical Society, Columbia, Missouri |
| MxAGN | Archivo General de la Nación, Mexico City |
| MxBN | Biblioteca Nacional, Mexico City |
| MxMDN | Archivo de la Biblioteca, Ministerio de Defensa Nacional, Mexico City |
| MxMN | Museo Nacional, Mexico City |
| *NMHR* | *New Mexico Historical Review* |
| NmSRC | State Record Center and Archives, Santa Fe, New Mexico |
| *OHQ* | *Oregon Historical Quarterly* |
| *PAAE* | *Publications in American Archaeology and Ethnology* |
| *PAAS* | *Proceedings of the American Antiquarian Society* |
| Ph | Photostat or microfilm |
| *PHR* | *Pacific Historical Review* |
| *PHSSC* | *Publications of the Historical Society of Southern California* |
| *PNQ* | *Pacific Northwest Quarterly* |
| *SHQ* | *Southwestern Historical Quarterly* |
| SpAGI | Archivo General de Indias, Seville |
| SpAHN | Archivo Histórico Nacional, Madrid |
| SpBN | Biblioteca Nacional, Madrid |
| SpBP | Biblioteca de Palacio, Madrid |
| SpMA | Museo de América, Madrid |
| SpMBA | Museo de Bellas Artes, Madrid |
| SpMN | Museo Naval, Ministerio de Marina, Madrid |
| T | Transcript |
| TxU | University of Texas Library, Austin, Texas |
| UKLBM | British Museum, London |
| UKLPRO | Public Records Office, London |
| *WHQ* | *Washington Historical Quarterly* |

# *1  The Maritime Approach to the Northwest Coast, 1540–1650*

THE WESTERN EDGE of North America, north of Cape Mendocino, was the last temperate zone coastline to withhold its secrets from European explorers. In the elimination of that hiatus in knowledge, Iberian mariners played a principal role, carrying Spain's empire to a flood tide of expansion. Indeed, this was the high water mark of Madrid's effort to hold sway over vast dominions in America. But in the pursuit of this ambitious thrust, His Catholic Majesty's officials embroiled him in a confrontation with other imperial powers that, ultimately, had far-reaching and dire consequences for Spain, gravely undermining her strength and contributing to the eventual loss of most of her American empire.

Above San Francisco Bay the coastline of North America loses some of the ruggedness of the precipitous cliffs south of Monterey; the profile is softened by forests close to the shore, and at intervals the ceaseless attack of great combers upon the headlands is interrupted by occasional stretches of flat beach where a river meets the sea. Surf boils over shallow bars at the bay's mouth. North of the Golden Gate for a thousand miles there is hardly a cove to protect vessels daring to brave fog banks all too frequently blanketing the shore. But beyond the Strait of Juan de Fuca, the continental fringe alters remarkably. Countless fjords incise the coast, providing shelter within their reaches, legacy of a time when an ice cap, pushing seaward, carved vertical-walled gorges beneath its mighty weight. Coastal British Columbia and southern Alaska are labyrinths of islands and waterways. Sinuous channels separate a myriad of islands from the mainland. Cool, moist air masses rise over the coastal range, blanketing it with forest and crowning the peaks with glaciers. Sweeping clockwise across the northern Pacific, the Japan Current bathes the submarine slope with mineral-laden water from the depths—water which, upon nearing the surface, promotes abundant plankton, an inexhaustible source of sustenance for larger creatures. Ashore, alpine meadows host a variety of ruminants, and cascading streams abound with salmon and trout—a bountiful fare for bears and lesser furry mammals.

Millennia ago the first hunters crossing into America found ample provender on the northwest coast. While groups in nearby regions retained more rudimentary ways of life, the coastal tribes turned much of their attention to elaborating artifacts and patterns of behavior of great complexity. Intensely proud of their skill at slaying killer whales, the most ferocious inhabitants of their world, chiefs of the northwest coast jockeyed for social rank by demonstrating prowess as hunters. Pelts of the elusive sea otter, finest of all furs, were preferred raiment for a warrior of pretension. Sea otter robes, decorative blankets of mountain goat wool, and emblazoned sheets of hammered copper were choice presents in a potlatch, characteristic ceremony of the area whereby a leader sought to enhance his status by outdoing all rivals in extravagant gift-giving. Sea otter pelts, and native skill at securing them, were factors leading to the sudden irruption of Europeans into the North Pacific area and the consequent focus of international attention upon one of the last zones of cartographic and political vacuum on the globe.

### SPANISH SEARCH FOR A NORTHWEST PASSAGE

Iberian concern with the northwest coast of North America commenced over two centuries before the first historically documented voyages beyond northern California. Conquistadores reached the Pacific shore of New Spain in 1522, soon after Aztec power crumbled. Hernando Cortés, his appetite whetted for additional booty, immediately organized explorations northward along the coastline and consumed much of the fortune won in Mexico.

Europeans of many nationalities dreamed of finding a more direct route to the Orient than around Africa. In 1523 the Emperor Carlos (fifth of the Holy Roman Empire, first of Spain) sent Cortés instructions stressing the necessity of a search for the strait, said to lie somewhere in the north, connecting the Pacific and the Atlantic.[1] If such a passage existed, Carlos intended that it should be his subjects who would find it. This passage was originally thought to be a channel connecting the Pacific and the Arctic Ocean, or "North Sea," from which another strait led to the Atlantic. The earliest reference to it in print—by geographer Giacomo Gastaldi in 1562— called it the "Strait of Anián," a name derived perhaps from misplacing Marco Polo's "Aniá," or from Anus Cortereal, a Portuguese mariner who explored the Labrador coast about 1500.[2]

After journeying to Madrid expressly to obtain a royal grant of rights and privileges for conquest toward the northwest, in 1532 Cortés outfitted an expedition commanded by Diego Hurtado de Mendoza. It reached the Río Fuerte, on the Sinaloa coast, where all the members were slain by Indians. Undaunted, the Conqueror of Mexico equipped two more ships; but the *San Lázaro* turned back before accomplishing anything of importance, and the mutinous crew of the *Concepción* killed their captain,

1. Carlos V, Instructions to Cortés, Valladolid, June 26, 1523, in *Colección de documentos inéditos relativos al descubrimiento, conquista y colonización de las posesiones Española* (42 vols. Madrid, 1864–84), 23 : 353–56.

2. H. R. Wagner, "Apocryphal Voyages to the Northwest Coast of America," *PAAS*, n.s. 41 (1931) : 182; Ernest S. Dodge, *Northwest by Sea* (New York, 1961), p. 181.

Diego de Becerra. The *Concepción's* new leader, Basque pilot Fortún Jiménez, discovered Baja California in 1533. Jiménez and most of his companions met death at native hands, but a few survived to tell of gold and pearls on a great island. The news led Cortés himself in 1535 to the coast discovered by Jiménez. Extensive search yielded a few pearls but no gold or even food, and the searchers returned almost empty-handed.[3]

The pearls and reports of an "Island of Women" to the northwest spurred explorers toward the region called "Californias," a name derived from a fictional locality in a popular sixteenth-century novel of chivalry.[4] First applied to the "island" off Mexico's western coast, it was sometimes loosely used to indicate everything northward to the supposed Anián. When Spanish explorers reached Alaska in the eighteenth century, the northwest coast became the "Costa Septentrional de Californias" or "Costa del Norte de California" and, on occasion, "Nueva California."

Explorers in central Mexico heard vague accounts of additional indigenous nations toward the northwest, inciting fresh hopes of riches comparable to those of the Aztec and Inca. Alvar Núñez Cabeza de Vaca arrived in Mexico City in 1536 to relate a bizarre odyssey. Accompanied by three other naked, near-starved castaways he had wandered from the Texas coast to the Gulf of California. He told of finding emeralds and hearing accounts of pearls and other riches in settlements on the "South Sea," or Pacific coast of North America. Viceroy Antonio de Mendoza sent Franciscan Marcos de Niza, veteran of the conquest of Peru, to investigate. The credulous friar returned with impressive tales of "Cíbola"—gold, silver, emeralds, and "cities" beyond a golden *pueblo* which he claimed to have seen from a distance. Cortés, newly enthusiastic, lavished additional fortune in dispatching three more vessels northward, under Francisco de Ulloa, hoping to find the rumored cities by sea. In 1539–40 Ulloa explored to the head of the Gulf of California and rounded Cape San Lucas, at the tip of the peninsula, reaching Cabo del Engaño at 30° north latitude. His explorations showed the known portions of California to be a peninsula, and this fact was recorded in contemporary cartography, but by the close of the century the concept that California was separated from the mainland by a strait regained currency. The "island" of California prevailed on maps and globes until 1701, when Padre Kino rediscovered what Ulloa had ascertained.

Fabulous reports of Cíbola prompted Francisco Vásquez de Coronado's

3. H. R. Wagner, *Spanish Voyages to the Northwest Coast of America in the Sixteenth Century* (San Francisco, 1929), p. 6. This is the most important description, to date, of explorations northward up to 1603; it is supplemented by Maurice G. Holmes, *From New Spain by Sea to the Californias 1519–1668* (Glendale, Calif., 1963).

4. Garci Rodríguez de Montalvo, *Las Sergas de Esplandián* (Madrid, 1510); he may have derived the name from "Califerne" of the eleventh century *Canción de Rolando*. See Álvaro del Portillo, *Descubrimientos y exploraciones en las costas de California* (Madrid, 1947), p. 128.

expedition, which reached the pueblos of Arizona and New Mexico in 1540. Parties on extensive sidetrips discovered the Grand Canyon and penetrated onto the Great Plains. As maritime support for this campaign the viceroy sent three ships under Hernando de Alarcón. Reaching the head of the gulf, Alarcón ascended the Colorado some distance, searching in vain for the overland expedition. All this effort produced little but disappointment, and no tangible wealth of any quantity, dampening hopes of finding other civilizations in that direction.

Viceroy Mendoza ordered Francisco de Bolaños northward in 1541 to ascertain whether foreigners could enter the Pacific by the supposed strait to the north. Bolaños was turned back by a violent storm about halfway up the west coast of Baja California and contributed nothing significant to geographical knowledge. Pedro de Alvarado, conquistador of Guatemala and El Salvador, cherished hopes of duplicating the feats of Cortés and Pizarro. He organized an expedition with the viceroy as partner and João Rodrigues Cabrilho, a wealthy adventurer from Portugal, as associate. Alvarado died in 1541, but "Cabrillo" set out the following year with the *San Salvador* and the *Victoria* to become the first to reach Alta California. He traversed the Santa Barbara Channel, visiting coastal villages and naming many of the geographical features, but he failed to sight the entrance to San Francisco Bay, so camouflaged by islands as to prevent viewing its interior from the sea. Turned back by storms near Point Reyes, just north of the Golden Gate, the vessels put in at San Miguel Island, off Santa Barbara, where the commander died from the consequences of a fall. Command devolved upon the Levantine pilot of the *Victoria,* Bartolomé Ferrelo. Early in 1543 he sailed beyond Point Reyes, sighting Point Arena. Strong winds obliged him to head away from land, until the storm shifted to the southwest and he was forced to run before it, in danger of being thrown upon the coast, which was shrouded in the storm but judged to be not far off. Logs in the water heightened this fear and indicated a river nearby. It may have been the Eel River, or perhaps the Mad, near the present Eureka, just south of the California-Oregon border.[5] A shift to a northerly gale forced the *Victoria* southward. Discouraged by February storms and short of food, Ferrelo and his companions accepted the new direction gratefully and headed home.

The feats of Rodrigues Cabrilho and Ferrelo, high water marks of sixteenth-century exploration northward, were never mentioned in subsequent early accounts of California voyages. The explanation lies in deliberate Spanish policy. Place names bestowed by early explorers seldom endured and were supplanted by later expeditions, for Madrid considered it in her interest to keep geographic details as secret as possible, for protection from marauders. Sailing charts were never printed. For specified purposes the

5. Wagner, *Spanish Voyages,* p. 74.

Board of Trade allowed copies of limited portions of the *Padrón Real,* a master chart closely guarded in Seville. Maps from each new exploration were treated as state secrets and their data added to the master chart. The few that escaped destruction were filed away and remained inaccessible until they were encountered by modern historians.[6] Later expeditions set out without detailed knowledge of previous accomplishments.

### MANILA GALLEONS AND THE NORTHWEST COAST

Beginning in 1527 Spanish ships took advantage of the northeast trade-winds to cross from Mexico to the Philippines and Moluccas. Barred by the Portuguese from returning to Europe by way of the Indian Ocean, the Spanish were obliged to seek a route back to Acapulco and make an overland transit to reach the Atlantic and the motherland. Credit for establishing the return route in 1565 is given to Carmelite Fray Andrés de Urdaneta, a former sailor, who reasoned that the strong northward current off Japan would carry a vessel to California and New Spain.[7] With increased knowledge of the winds and currents, galleons traveling annually between Acapulco and Manila became a vital link in the network of communications and economy of the far-flung Spanish empire. That these vessels may have sighted the northwest coast, on one occasion at least, is tangibly demonstrated by the remains of a Manila galleon wrecked at Nehalem Beach in northern Oregon, an episode examined in the next chapter. Broad-beamed and low-waisted, with towering poop decks and often equally high forecastles adorned with elaborate woodcarving, the galleons were a majestic sight under full sail. But they were ungainly and deep of draft when fully loaded on their return trips from the Orient, and their excessive weight was an impediment to speed. They averaged four months from Acapulco to Manila, but took half again as long on the great arc across the North Pacific. Crammed to the gunwales with cargo, supplies, and passengers, with the deck a veritable barnyard for fresh meat, they were unusually prone to infestations of rats and other pests and were incubators for disease. A globe-trotting Italian apothecary depicted the mortifications he endured aboard a Manila galleon in 1697, conditions that prevailed aboard most vessels visiting the northwest coast until sanitary measures were instituted in the 1790s.

> There is hunger, thirst, sickness, cold, continual watching, and other sufferings: besides the terrible shocks from side to side, caus'd by the furious beating of the waves. I may further say they endure all the

6. This was a handicap recognized in the eighteenth century by historian Francisco Javier Clavigero and discussed at length in Holmes, *From New Spain,* pp. 129–30.

7. H. R. Wagner, "Urdaneta and the Return Route from the Philippine Islands," *PHR* 13 1944) : 313–16.

plagues God sent upon *Pharoah* to soften his hard heart; for if he was infected with leprosy, the galeon is never clear of an universal raging itch, as an addition to all other miseries. If the air then was fill'd with gnats, the ship swarms with little vermine, the Spaniards call *Gorgojos,* bred in the bisket; so swift that they in a short time not only run over cabins, beds, and the very dishes the men eat on, but insensibly fasten upon the body. Instead of locusts, there are several other sorts of vermin of sundry colours that suck the blood. Abundance of flies fall into the dishes of broth, in which there also swim worms of several sorts.[8]

On meat days he had contracted with the boatswain for a supplement of water buffalo jerky, so hard that it required pounding before becoming edible, "with no other sauce than water to wash it down." Nutritious, but notorious as a thirst-inducer, it would have aggravated the traveler's discomfort, and fresh water was always in short supply, doled out in tiny rations. The meal ordinarily provided he described as a concoction

in every mouthful whereof there went down an abundance of maggots, and *Gorgojos* chew'd and bruis'd. On fish days the common diet was rank old fish boil'd in fair water and salt; at noon we had *Mongos,* something like kidney beans, in which there were so many maggots, that they swam at the top of the broth, and the quantity was so great, that besides the loathing they caus'd, I doubted whether the dinner was fish or flesh. This bitter fare was sweetened after dinner with a little water and sugar; yet the allowance was but a small coco shell full, which rather increas'd than quench'd drought.[9]

Despite hardships and hazards, the galleons plied their route throughout the colonial period. The wealthy aristocracy of Spanish America clamored for oriental finery. From Acapulco galleons carried manufactured goods, cloth, tools, arms, and munitions, as well as Mexican silver. They brought back silks, fine china, porcelain, gold coins, cinnamon and other spices, candles, and beeswax in bulk, and other oriental products in demand in Spanish America. Manila was "commercially little more than a way-station between China and Mexico" until the latter half of the eighteenth century.[10]

An expedition organized by Álvaro de Medaña sailed westward from Peru to discover the Solomon Islands in 1568 and on the return made its first landfall off Alta California. The commander of Medaña's vessels, Pedro Sarmiento de Gamboa (better known as a chronicler of the Incas), would claim years later that on this occasion he sailed southward along the

8. Giovanni Francesco Gemelli Careri, "A Voyage Round the World," in Awnsham Churchill, *A Collection of Voyages and Travels* (London, 1746), 4 : 463–64.

9. Ibid.

10. William Lytle Schurz, *The Manila Galleon* (New York, 1939), pp. 26–32.

coast from 34° north latitude, the point reached by Ferrelo in 1543.[11] The voyages of Francisco de Gali (1584) and Pedro de Unamuno (1587), while listed among expeditions to the upper Pacific coast, were merely trips by two Manila galleons that visited California harbors of which accounts happened to survive. Unamuno and some of his men went ashore at to-day's Morro Bay, north of Santa Barbara. How many similar visits occurred but went unchronicled is beyond ascertaining.

### DRAKE'S CHALLENGE TO THE "SPANISH SEA"

Spain's veiling of her activities in the Pacific was based on an actual need. For decades, knowledge of the Manila galleons was kept from rivals. The slow vessels sailed without escort and carried no heavy armament. Thus they were easy prey to any attacker, and their main protection depended upon keeping the traffic and the route a secret. Inevitably, however, buccaneers were drawn to the Pacific by silver galleons plying the Peru-Panama route. "Francisco Draque" was a name that inspired terror on the Spanish Main. In 1578 Drake discovered a route around South America that avoided risking interception within the Strait of Magellan, and he commenced scourging ports in Chile and Peru, seizing vessels, and even keeping Lima and Panama City in a state of alarm. Off what is now Ecuador he overpowered the *Nuestra Señora de la Concepción,* laden with bullion, and from its charts obtained first knowledge of the Manila galleons and their route. He was making captures off Costa Rica by March of 1579 and seized a vessel bound for Panama carrying two pilots with experience on the Acapulco-Manila route. Their charts, sailing directions, and personal knowledge were of great utility. Behind him Drake could assume that every commander along the west coast of the Americas would be alert; ahead lay the enticing prospect of discovering the Strait of Anián.[12] He headed northward along the continental shore until discouraged by inclement weather. With the *Golden Hind* so laden with booty that its seaworthiness was doubtful, and after months of damage below the water line from the shipworm *Teredo navalis,* Drake dared not attempt a Pacific crossing and a return to England via the Cape of Good Hope without replacing worm-eaten planks. A sheltered cove was required, far from any area frequented by Spanish warships, and he turned southward in search of such a protected anchorage.

The northernmost point reached by Drake has been a topic of controversy. Henry Wagner's extensive study of the evidence (1926) suggests that

11. Wagner, *Spanish Voyages,* pp. 121–24.

12. That Drake's enterprise had among its original objectives the search for Anián and acts of possession leading to the creation of colonies is asserted by Eva G. R. Taylor, "The Missing Draft Project of Drake's Voyage of 1577–80," *GJ* 75 (1930) : 44–47. K. R. Andrews, "The Aims of Drake's Expedition of 1577–1580," *AHR* 73 (1968) : 724–41, believes Drake's actions "are explicable in terms of the events of the voyage" (p. 737).

he sailed not much beyond 42° to 43°, approximately the present California-Oregon boundary, and that the 48° asserted in a work published in 1628 was an unjustifiable interpolation for ulterior political motives.[13] As the site of Drake's thirty-six-day sojourn for repairs, fresh water, and firewood, Wagner made a case for Bodega Bay, forty-eight miles north of the Golden Gate. Drake is chronicled as performing an act of possession for Elizabeth I, calling the land "Nova Albion," and affixing to a tree a brass plate with an appropriate legend. In 1934 a plaque fitting the description was found at what traditionally had been called "Drake's Bay," twenty-eight miles north of San Francisco Bay. Basing his opinion on ethnological and linguistic evidence Robert Heizer suggests that the cove's traditional name is apt.[14]

Following his sojourn ashore, Drake landed on one of the Farallon Islands to kill seals for much-needed provisions. As had previous explorers, he passed close by the Golden Gate, unsuspecting. Assisted by captured charts, Drake crossed the Pacific successfully and became the first English circum-navigator. The *Golden Hind* dropped anchor at Plymouth after two years and ten months at sea, and Drake was acclaimed and knighted by his queen. His feat did much to give his compatriots greater confidence in their prowess at rivaling the Spanish Empire, and English colonizing schemes in the New World were stimulated. Drake's claim to "Nova Albion" involved not only a coastal strip but the entire western portion of North America beyond the area securely in Spanish hands, and subsequent royal grants along the Atlantic coast were confidently extended through to the Pacific as a consequence.[15] To Drake's effort can be attributed a considerable measure of the self-assuredness with which Britain challenged Madrid's pretensions to the northwest coast in the eighteenth century.

Soon after Drake's return, English maritime depredations and resentment over religious issues mounted to such a pitch that Elizabeth's erstwhile suitor, Felipe II, made his attempt with the "Invincible Armada" to dethrone the Virgin Queen. The persistence with which English sea rovers attacked Spanish vessels and possessions was a by-product of the profound hatred of all things associated with the "popish" ways that English Protestants had rejected. Isabella's successors took with deadly seriousness their responsibilities as defenders of the Faith, and the Western world had to reckon with the might of Spanish kings, derived from seemingly inexhaustible

13. H. R. Wagner, *Sir Francis Drake's Voyage Around the World: Its Aims and Achievements* (San Francisco, 1926), pp. 135–43.

14. For details of the plate's discovery, loss, and subsequent peregrinations, see R. B. Haselden, "Is the Drake Plate of Brass Genuine?" *CHSQ* 16 (1937) : 271–74; California Historical Society, *The Plate of Brass: Evidence of the Visit of Francis Drake to California in the Year 1579* (San Francisco, 1953). Robert F. Heizer, "Francis Drake and the California Indians, 1579," *University of California PAAE* 42 (1947) : 3, 251–301.

15. Adolph S. Oko, "Francis Drake and Nova Albion," *CHSQ* 43 (1964) : 148–49.

riches from domains around the globe. The Church created the Holy Inquisition for its own defense and purification, but to Englishmen, the Inquisition was synonymous with Spain, and in striking at Iberian shipping or sacking ports they committed merciless acts in "defense" of the Reformation. In turn, captive corsairs were sometimes burned as heretics in the next *auto de fé*. Such was the mutual hatred between England and Spain, even in peacetime, that plunder seized from captured vessels and pillaged settlements could be enjoyed by English corsairs and even the Crown itself without a qualm.

The *Golden Hind's* booty prompted imitation of its captain's exploits, and Thomas Cavendish set sail in 1586 with three heavily armed vessels to prey upon Spanish shipping in the Pacific. Some of his crew had been there with Drake. Elizabeth and Felipe II would soon be at war, and Cavendish took particular care to seize pilots and maps on captured vessels, as a means of pulling back the curtain of secrecy with which Spain had cloaked her realms. After sacking Paita, in Peru, en route toward Panama he overpowered a ship from whose pilot he gleaned sufficient information to position his vessels near Cape San Lucas at the proper time of year to intercept the next galleon from Manila. The heavily laden *Santa Ana* hove into sight on November 15, 1587, its crew and passengers exhausted after the voyage from the Philippines. Not anticipating an enemy encounter, the ship did not carry a single cannon for defense. Nevertheless, the battle lasted for two days, with the *Santa Ana* repelling four boarding attempts and enduring repeated broadsides until its decks and rigging were a shambles, and it had to surrender.[16] Among the booty were 122,000 pesos in gold—worth more than a million dollars today—and a treasure in pearls, silk, damask, and other luxuries. The galleon was taken to a nearby beach, 190 survivors set ashore, and a torch put to its battered hulk. From the two pilots Cavendish extracted information concerning the route to the Philippines, and he ended up taking one of them with him. Duplicating Drake's feat of circumnavigation, he arrived in Plymouth shortly after the armada's defeat.

### THE ABORTIVE SETTLEMENT AT MONTEREY

The *Santa Ana's* loss struck fear into the hearts of Spanish merchants and officials that such attacks would recur and lead to foreign encroachments to the northwest of New Spain, a coastline not yet under effective Iberian surveillance. Its uncharted, unguarded bays held a threat of watering places

16. Peter Gerhard, *Pirates on the West Coast of New Spain, 1565–1742* (Glendale, Calif., 1960), pp. 91–94. Tomás de Alzola captained the galleon; his chief pilot, Sebastião Rodrigues Cermenho, would play a major role in subsequent explorations. Manuel Fernández de Navarrete, "Introducción," p. liv(n) in *Relación del viage hecho por las goletas Sútil y Mexicana en el año de 1792*, by [José Cardero] (Madrid, 1802).

and lairs from which corsairs might prey upon galleons obliged to skirt the shores of Alta California. Aside from the foreign danger, there were other motives for improving knowledge of the northwest coast. The route from Manila was exceptionally long and hazardous. Some vessels had been lost and others severely damaged by storms. Delays from being becalmed in mid-Pacific meant that many aboard succumbed or were near death before reaching North America. Ignorance of the coast made many captains fearful of landing and facing unknown perils to obtain food and water. Once the well-known signs appeared—floating logs and branches, kelp beds, land birds, subtle changes in sea color—showing that they were nearing the American coast, pilots customarily headed southeast, hoping to make landfall near Cape San Lucas and arrive quickly in Acapulco. A southerly current along the coast could be depended upon to speed them along.

Cavendish's sortie triggered the next phase in exploration, for it led to suspicions that buccaneers had found the Strait of Anián. Luís de Velasco, viceroy from 1590 to 1595, exceeded his predecessors in zeal for discovering the legendary passage. Felipe II ordered that the search for it be furthered by the exploration and settlement of California. Velasco replied that, although the treasury lacked funds for such an effort, there were private individuals of sufficient wealth interested in undertaking the project in return for specific privileges to exploit whatever might be disclosed. He soon concluded an agreement with Sebastián Vizcaíno and a consortium to carry out explorations in California.[17]

It is against this background that Juan de Fuca's controversial voyage to the northwest coast in 1592 is alleged to have taken place. Evidence links Fuca with Vizcaíno and associates, but most historians withhold from Fuca's account the stamp of authenticity. The pros and cons will be examined at some length in the following chapter, together with those of several other voyages usually classed as apocryphal.

An associate of Vizcaíno, Sebastião Rodrigues Cermenho, set sail from Acapulco in 1594 to carry out the "new discovery" of Cape Mendocino and the coastline beyond in order to locate an adequate port in upper California. He proceeded first to Manila, returning in 1595 with the *San Agustín,* a crew of seventy, and 130 tons of cargo—in effect the Manila galleon for that year. First landfall occurred in November near Trinidad Head, some sixty-five miles south of the California-Oregon boundary. The rugged terrain, reefs, and breakers discouraged landing at that latitude, and he continued southward as far as Drake's Bay, just south of Point Reyes, where an Indian

17. Fernández de Navarrete, "Introducción," pp. lvii–lx; Viceroy Velasco to Felipe II, Mexico City, October 8, 1593, in Francisco Carrasco y Guisasola, ed., *Documentos referentes al reconocimiento de las costas de las Californias* (Madrid, 1882), pp. 15–16; "Asiento que tomó el Virrey de Nueva España con Sevastian Vizcaino," Mexico City, Nov. 16, 1593, SpMN (Col. Navarrete, 19 : 4).

came out to meet them paddling a reed *balsa* with a double-bladed oar. The following day four more natives visited the *San Agustín,* and Rodrigues Cermenho decided to take a party ashore for an official act of possession, naming the site "Bahía de San Francisco." A launch carried aboard ship for the purpose of charting the coastline in detail was put over the side. The boat proved their salvation after a storm arose from an unprotected quarter and drove the galleon ashore, where breakers battered it to pieces. Quantities of beeswax and chests of silk washed ashore but were useless to the castaways. A foraging party penetrated a short distance inland, finding nothing of note. The seventy-odd survivors embarked in the launch, hopefully christened *San Buenaventura.* In haste to reach port with the injured and ill, the commander could not accomplish his main objective of careful inspection of every bay along the coast to select the most appropriate site for a port.[18]

To fulfill the royal order for colonizing an adequate harbor on the California coast, Vizcaíno himself set out in 1596 with an expedition of three ships equipped for the purpose. He attempted a settlement at La Paz, on the east coast of Baja California, but aridity frustrated the project. An exploratory party up the east coast had to turn back after a skirmish with the natives in which nineteen expeditionaries were killed. Desperately short of provisions, Vizcaíno and his followers returned to the mainland, and the effort at La Paz was abandoned.

Gaspar de Zúñiga y Acevedo, conde de Monterey, who succeeded Velasco as viceroy in 1595, halted private expeditions of discovery, preferring to make them a royal prerogative financed by the viceregal treasury and closely controlled from Mexico City. He is on record as opposing discovery of the Strait of Anián lest it "awaken someone who was asleep" and invite foreign encroachments.[19]

Upon succession to his father's throne in 1598, Felipe III took a great personal interest in encouraging exploration of the North Pacific and the western coast of North America. A royal order for a new expedition to chart the coast from Cape Mendocino southward led the conde de Monterey to turn to Vizcaíno, whose previous experience recommended him for leadership of the effort. Unlike previous probes northward—all private enterprises—Vizcaíno's project was financed with royal funds. His instructions were to follow the coastline from Cape San Lucas to Cape Mendocino, charting every bay and estuary large enough for the entry of ships and

18. Velasco to Felipe II, Mexico City, April 6, 1594, in Carrasco, *Documentos Referentes,* p. 16; Sebastián Rodrigues Cermenho, "Derrotero y relación del descubrimiento que hizo el capitán y piloto mayor Sebastián Rz. Cermenho," April 24, 1596, SpAGI (Aud. Mex. 27).

19. Conde de Monterey to Felipe II, February 29, 1596, in Carrasco, *Documentos Referentes,* pp. 19–22; Henry Raup Wagner, *Cartography of the Northwest Coast of America to the Year 1800,* 2 vols. (Berkeley, 1937), 2 : 114.

locating spots where water, ballast, and firewood could be obtained near safe anchorage. If time, weather, and provisions permitted, he was to "make a reasonable effort to reconnoiter to Cape Blanco which is at 44° and if, as being an unknown, unseen coast, it is incorrect on the map and the coast beyond Cape Mendocino to Cape Blanco runs toward the west, you should reconnoiter 100 leagues and no more, and having examined them, although the weather be favorable, you shall not go any farther along, but return toward Cape San Lucas." [20] The order confirms the unaccountable appearance on Spanish maps at this time of "Cabo Blanco," beyond the farthest point reached by Ferrelo or Rodrigues Cermenho. Oregon's westernmost promontory, just short of 43° north latitude, preserves the name to this day.

Vizcaíno and some 200 persons sailed from Acapulco in May 1602 with the *San Diego,* the *Santo Tomás,* the *Tres Reyes,* and an unnamed longboat for examining narrow or shallow waterways. They carried supplies sufficient for a year. After charting San Diego Bay, the islands off Santa Barbara, and Monterey Bay (named after the viceroy), the *Santo Tomás* departed homeward with those too ill with scurvy to be of further use and whose lives would be sacrificed if they continued northward. In January 1603 the other vessels made an attempt to reach Cape Blanco. Favorable winds enabled them to reach a latitude estimated as corresponding to Cape Mendocino, but a violent change in weather brought a furious wind from the south, accompanied by such dense rain and fog that days seemed night, and the vessels became separated. With so many ill that only two sailors were able to go aloft and reef the sails, a junta of officers decided to be content with the latitude reached, for to go on would be courting death for everyone. Vizcaíno ordered the prow returned southward as soon as the gale permitted. Several days later they were able to take a reading of 41°, but a storm arose from the southwest that drove them toward the perils of an unknown coast. One night a giant wave struck the flagship as it beat southward against the wind, rolling it so far on the beam that many thought it would surely capsize. Sick and well alike were thrown from their bunks, and Vizcaíno fractured several ribs. The *San Diego* was carried to 42° before the torment ceased and the latitude ascertained. Land appeared in the distance—high, thickly forested mountains covered with snow to the water's edge. A prominent headland was named Cape San Sebastián, in honor of the commander's personal saint. When the wind altered to the northwest, they were grateful to hurry homeward.

Vizcaíno dared not await the *Tres Reyes* at Santa Catalina Island, as prearranged, for not enough hands were in sufficient health to raise the anchor,

20. Conde de Monterey to Vizcaíno. Mexico City, March 18, 1602, in Portillo, *Descubrimientos,* pp. 301–07, AT.

once lowered. The sick succumbed at an alarming rate and the bedridden clamored to hasten ahead. Scurvy made their mouths ulcerous, with gums so swollen that the scant rations of weevil-ridden chickpeas and spoiled pork could scarcely be swallowed. The ship was a floating infirmary; so acute was the situation that officers had to perform such menial tasks as manning the wheel, climbing to the yardarm to furl sails, and toiling in the galley to prepare meals for prostrate companions. Putting in briefly at the Mazatlán Islands they found a fruit, called "xocohuistle," which healed the mouths of the scurvy-ridden so that in a short time they could eat fresh food and were restored to health. Its virtues were not forgotten and two centuries later "tocoquixtle" syrup appeared among supplies of the first Spanish expedition to reach Alaska. Hardships of the expedition of 1602–03 took a toll of forty-eight lives before both vessels returned to home port. Only after reaching Mexico City did Vizcaíno receive news of the *Tres Reyes,* and to this day there are no known logs or journals written by anyone aboard, although summaries of its voyage are included in chronicles composed by persons accompanying the flagship. The consort vessel also surmounted Cape Mendocino, to an alleged 43° of latitude. Freezing cold and scurvy took a terrible toll. Captain Martín de Aguilar, his first pilot, and two ordinary seamen perished. Boatswain Estéban López took charge and brought the vessel southward, hugging the coast. According to Vizcaíno, López testified that:

at 41°, close to Cape Mendocino they found a large bay and into it on the north side entered a voluminous river which flows with such force of current that although they tried for an entire day, with a stern wind, to sail up it, they could not enter it more than two leagues. The river was in flood, bringing down many tree trunks and the land is one of giant pines and oaks and the coast runs from this spot north-south to Cape Mendocino and from there northwest-southeast to Cape Blanco.[21]

A more credible account says López claimed to have been carried by the storm to a latitude of 43° and that at 39° 15′ he discovered

a voluminous river and an island at the mouth of a very good and secure port and another great bay at a latitude of 40° 30′ in which another very large river entered and a great quantity of Indians came out to meet them in dugouts of pine and cedar. Since there were so many, the Spaniards didn't dare take the launch upriver, although the Indians invited them to do so, giving them a lot of fish, game, and differ-

21. "Relación que dió el Contra Maestre de la fragata *Los Tres Reyes* la cual me dió por escrito Sebastián Vizcayno," appendix to Gerónimo Martín Palacios, "Derrotero," SpMN (332), pub. in Portillo, *Descubrimientos,* p. 351, AT.

ent kinds of nuts and other things as an encouragement to come with them into the river.[22]

The largest river was named "Río de Martín Aguilar," in honor of the deceased captain. Since all accounts from the *Tres Reyes* are second hand, it is difficult to ascertain which rivers were sighted. Humboldt Bay, just north of Cape Mendocino, may correspond to the entrance noted. In 1615 Torquemada's *Monarchia Indiana* put this "Río de Martín Aguilar" at 43°, the *Tres Reyes*'s maximum latitude, inducing later generations to conceive it to be the western entrance to the Strait of Anián. It persisted on maps of western North America until the late eighteenth century.

Vizcaíno was blocked from further discoveries along the Pacific coast by the same obstacles previous explorers had run into. In trying to buck the prevailing current, fierce winds, and cold weather of the worst time of the year, he got no farther than Ferrelo or Rodrigues Cermenho had penetrated. His most important accomplishment was the disclosure of the qualities of Monterey Bay. His praise of it led the viceroy to advocate that it be colonized, but within the year the conde de Monterey was replaced by Juan de Mendoza y Luna, marqués de Montesclaros, who discredited plans for a settlement there. Montesclaros's criticisms have been attributed to spite, a desire for personal enrichment, and a negative attitude toward everything championed by his predecessor.[23]

Montesclaros annulled Vizcaíno's appointment as captain of a Manila galleon and named him *alcalde mayor* of Tehuantepec, which would have had the effect of removing him from the scene of action, but Felipe III gave specific orders that Vizcaíno be sent as commander of the galleon for 1607. On the return trip he was to search for the "Armenian's Islands" (*Islas del Armenio*), an archipelago reputed to lie in mid-Pacific. Afterward, Vizcaíno should survey Monterey Bay once again, with a view toward colonization and "without regard to the expense it might cause the royal treasury." [24] The order was delayed by shipwreck, and by the time it arrived, the galleon for 1607 had departed and Vizcaíno was en route to Spain seeking royal favor for the projects deflected by Montesclaros.

The viceroy persisted in his views and cast doubt upon the practicality of a settlement at Monterey, asserting that it would be ineffective in protecting towns on the west coast of New Spain from pirate attacks. Ships from Manila entering the belt of favorable winds came on to Acapulco with little

22. "Relación o diario muy circunstanciado del viaje que hizo el General Sebastián Vizcaíno," in *Colección de diarios y relaciones para la historia de los viajes y descubrimientos* (Madrid, 1944), 4 : 67–68. AT.

23. Charles E. Chapman, *A History of California: The Spanish Period* (New York, 1921), p. 138; Holmes, *From New Spain*, p. 214.

24. Felipe III to Marqués de Montesclaros, San Lorenzo [del Escorial], August 19, 1606, SpAGI (V, Aud. Guad. 418); Schurz, *Manila Galleon*, pp. 332–34.

difficulty. He shared with others the conviction that disastrous consequences would ensue if explorations revealed a northwest passage. Monterey was too close to Acapulco, and he preferred to search for rumored islands in mid-Pacific. Being closer to Asia, they would provide a site for a settlement of greater utility to stricken galleons. The viceroy's plan eventually secured royal approval.[25]

There is some evidence, however, that shortly after Montesclaros's letter was sent off, he was obliged to provide otherwise and make dispositions for a new survey of the port at Monterey Bay. A royal command for a renewed effort there may have compelled him to take action upon the project he had opposed. The endeavor seems to have involved settlers, foodstuffs, arms, and munitions, with the expectation that within several months two more supply ships would be sent to Monterey with additional men and supplies. Confusion accompanying Montesclaros's replacement in 1607 by Luís de Velasco, marqués de Salinas (for a second, nonconsecutive term as viceroy of Mexico), is offered as the reason why an expedition with reinforcements for Monterey failed to get underway in 1608. In addition, a mutiny and deaths among the settlers allegedly hastened abandonment of the effort.[26] Whether or not the abortive colonization attempt of 1607 actually took place, the certainty is that Spanish explorations in the North Pacific soon became channelled in the direction of searching for the islands called "Rica de Oro" and "Rica de Plata," with the immediate effect of inhibiting further inspection beyond Cape Mendocino.

Legends of an archipelago in the North Pacific populated by natives of advanced culture with quantities of silver and gold had been current for many years. In 1584 Fray Andrés de Aguirre wrote the archbishop of Mexico, then acting viceroy, to suggest exploring the northwest coast, and he repeated an account given him by Fray Andrés de Urdaneta, discoverer of the return route from Manila. A Portuguese vessel driven off course had encountered two large islands between 35° and 40° north latitude, well to the east of Japan. Their name derived from an Armenian trader said to have won the friendship of the rulers of the islands, possessors of a fabulously rich culture. The archbishop dutifully transmitted Aguirre's report to the king.[27]

25. Montesclaros to Felipe III, May 24, 1607, royal approval, Sept. 27, 1608; cited by Erik W. Dahlgren, *Were the Hawaiian Islands Visited by the Spaniards Before Their Discovery by Captain Cook in 1778?* (Stockholm, 1916 [1917]), pp. 70–71.

26. Felipe III to Marqués de Montesclaros. San Lorenzo, October 5, 1606, SpAGI (V, Aud. Guad. 133). Holmes, *From New Spain,* p. 182n, is the first modern author to mention this episode; he derives his evidence from SpMN, "California, historia y viajes," vol. 1, doc. 1, sec. 4, fol. 1.

27. Aguirre to Pedro Moya de Contreras, archbishop of Mexico, 1584, in Carrasco, *Documentos Referentes,* pp. 9–12; Moya de Contreras to Felipe II, January 22, 1585, SpAGI (Aud. Mex. 336), partly trans. in Wagner, *Spanish Voyages,* p. 132.

Pedro de Unamuno, captain of the *Nuestra Señora de la Buena Esperanza*, sought these islands during his return from the Philippines in 1587. Some historians assume that the "Islas del Armenio" and "Rica de Oro" and "Rica de Plata" all derived from the same legend. Unamuno's log made a distinction, and he sought them in different areas, finding nothing but insignificant islands with no inhabitants, harbors, or signs of fresh water. Despite his negative results, the legendary isles continued to appeal to the imagination of mapmakers. The possibility of discovering rich archipelagos in mid-Pacific held great fascination for Felipe III. A letter from Fernando de los Ríos Coronel, in the Philippines, prompted a royal order in 1602 to assemble more information about the Strait of Anián and another passageway nearer New Mexico, rumored to traverse North America, and to investigate the expediency of taking possession of the "Isla del Armiño" (*sic*) as a way station for the Manila galleon.[28]

Vizcaíno departed from Acapulco for Manila in 1611 in obedience to royal orders, his plans for Alta California set aside indefinitely. After visiting Manila and Japan, he searched the Pacific fruitlessly for months without finding islands with civilization of consequence, encountering only volcanic peaks and atolls similar to those already known. Upon reaching Acapulco he continued on to Madrid to request leadership of another expedition to Alta California. His petitions were never approved.

It has been asserted that Vizcaíno's diversion from colonization of Monterey to the search for fanciful islands delayed settlement of Alta California for over a century and a half.[29] Pilots of Manila galleons continued to seek such isles but never located anything to fit the legend. The advanced native culture of Hawaii eluded discovery. The route from Acapulco led westward along the tenth to twelfth parallels, utilizing the North Equatorial Current. On the eastward journey the Japan Current carried the voyagers as far as 40° north. Hawaii, at 20° north, lay midway between the two routes—never approached in the normal course of navigation. Hundreds of galleons crossed the Pacific during more than two centuries and are never known to have sighted the garden isles—a discovery reserved for Captain Cook, who in 1778 set a course from Tahiti to the northwest coast that chanced to coincide with Hawaii. Some scientists thought the archipelago to be the "Islas de la Mesa," supposedly seen by Juan Gaitán in 1542. This theory, widely accepted, even led Spanish authorities to assume a claim to Hawaii by right of prior discovery, but modern research has shown that Gaitán's narrative (of Ruy López de Villalobos's expedition from Acapulco to Manila in 1542) does not provide sufficient evidence for such a conclusion.[30]

---

28. Felipe III to Pedro de Acuña, governor of Manila, February 16, 1602, in *Colección de documentos inéditos para la historia de España* (1849), 15 : 234–35.

29. Schurz, *Manila Galleon*, p. 232.

30. Dahlgren, *Hawaiian Islands*, pp. 28, 213.

### THE OFFICIAL POLICY OF DISCOURAGING EXPLORATION

After Vizcaíno's time, those wishing to undertake explorations northward could not obtain official backing or even permission. An influential segment of opinion thought Spain's interests would be damaged by discovery of Anián. If such a waterway were found, word could not be kept from rival nations, and it would be difficult for Spain to police the strait to keep foreigners from the Pacific.

In attempting to rally support for his projects, Vizcaíno led others to dream of exploiting the pearl beds of California. In his wake came a succession of men trying to secure permission for explorations in return for rights to pearl fisheries. Carmelite friar Antonio de la Ascensión, a veteran of Vizcaíno's expedition of 1602, persisted sedulously in urging additional exploration. His "Brief Account" (1620) described Alta California and asserted that in 1603 Vizcaíno had reached 43° of latitude, "head and limits of the realm and mainland of California and beginning and entrance for the Strait of Anián, and if it had not been for the fact that on this occasion on the flagship there were not even fourteen men still sound of health, without doubt we would have risked reconnoitering and passing through the Strait of Anián."[31] In 1627 he composed a new account for the same purpose, and directed to Felipe IV. This time his views were noticed, and the Audiencia in Mexico City was ordered by the king to open an investigation into the advisability of permitting private exploration of the Pacific coast.

> And because Captain Pedro Bastán has come to this realm to petition for said conquest, having discussed it in my Council of Indies, and taking into consideration that since said discovery has always been held to be of slight esteem, for nothing substantial has ever been obtained there the many times it has been attempted, with such bad results; because in order to resolve upon it I need to know what can be learned about the matter, I order you: that having first heard Antonio de la Ascensión, barefoot friar of the Order of Our Lady of Carmen, and other persons who may have information about that land, you advise very particularly the form and manner in which said discovery could be accomplished in case it is convenient to put it in execution.[32]

In 1629 the Audiencia commenced the inquiry. Fray Antonio's three declarations repeated previous predictions of the political importance, economic benefits, and Christian duty of exploring and pacifying the western coast of the continent beyond the point of earlier discoveries. Others

---

31. Antonio de la Ascensión, "Relación breve en que se dá noticia del descubrimiento que se hizo en la Nueva-España, en la mar del Sur, desde el puerto de Acapulco hasta más adelante del cabo Mendocino," 1620, in Portillo, *Descubrimientos,* pp. 427–28. AT.

32. Royal Order, Madrid, August 2, 1628, SpMN (Col. Navarrete, vol. 19, no. 11, fol. 191–92), pub. in Portillo, *Descubrimientos,* pp. 437–38. AT.

consulted were Gonzalo de Francia (boatswain on the *San Diego* in 1602),
Vizcaíno's nephew, and Enrico Martínez, cartographer of the expedition.
The latter cast cold water upon speculations that auriferous wealth might
be found in Alta California, for the natives had never been observed to
possess gold ornaments. He doubted any benefits from settlement of Monterey. Ships coming from Manila, although desperately in need of water,
firewood, and repairs, had a steady stern wind that enabled them to reach
Acapulco in a few more days. Spain need not fear rivals colonizing any of
the bays in California because settlers would arrive too exhausted after
3,500 leagues of journey to sustain their enclave or resist eviction by concerted Spanish effort.[33]

Fray Antonio's speculations about the importance of searching for Anián
were outweighed. The inquiry marks the last official Spanish effort for
more than a century that might have led to further explorations northward
subsidized by the royal treasury. Henceforth, such documents as refer to
the Californias relate to private pearl fishing enterprises. Viceroys preferred
to contract with individual entrepreneurs, authorized to make explorations
at the same time as they searched for pearls, and pay the Crown a fifth of
their harvest. Evidence that Frenchmen using false documentation as to
nationality were engaged in such activities led to revocation of all previous
licenses in 1636. Viceroy Marqués de Cadereyta, commenting upon cancellation of Pedro Porter y Casanate's license to search for Anián, asserted
that more damage than good might result from its discovery. If such a passage did exist, which he was inclined to doubt, its revelation would provide
a door whereby enemies might more readily enter and infest the northern
Pacific.[34]

Despite these objections, Felipe IV took an interest in Porter's projects,
naming him head and admiral of the South Sea (*Cabo y Almirante del Mar
del Sur*). Porter was about to dispatch an expedition in 1644 when his
ships, supplies, and armaments were destroyed in a fire supposedly set by
rivals. Four years later, two of his vessels explored the east coast of Baja
California, and in 1649 he sent still another expedition to the same area,
but his radius of exploration was so limited that his final voyage, in 1650,
still did not reach the Gulf of California's northern terminus, and he was
able to write with entire confidence: "What until now was distrusted has
finally been assured—that there is a navigable strait to the North Sea."[35]
Royal concessions granted to Porter and others show that throughout the
seventeenth century Madrid sustained some interest in extending her

33. Henrico Martínez, "Parecer," Gueguetoca, July 30, 1629, in Portillo, *Descubrimientos*, pp.
447–51.

34. Cadereyta to the king, Mexico City, July 12, 1638, SpMN (1509, fol. 33–34v).

35. Porter to Viceroy Conde de Alva, August 18, 1651, trans. by Holmes, *From New Spain*,
p. 224.

dominion northward but chose to do so by depending entirely upon private capital for exploratory expeditions. The significance of the pearling ventures is that they absorbed the efforts of individual adventurers that otherwise might have been directed to further exploration of the northwest coast. Madrid perceived no serious threat in that quarter from foreign rivals, so long as a northwest passage remained unfound. Spanish concern with Mexico's northwestern frontier did not die, but official policy put a damper upon explorations by sea and failed to provide knowledge of the coastline beyond Cape Mendocino. Beyond, to Anián, the coast would avoid becoming a source of trouble and expense by remaining *terra incógnita*. Exploration of Alta California came to a halt before even the major features of the region were ascertained. Previous expeditions had revealed no trace of the precious metals or large, sedentary Indian populations that made Spanish colonization in other parts of the hemisphere advantageous. Failure to obtain tangible economic benefits from explorations beyond Monterey discouraged those who might have invested further time, effort, and fortune —before much had been disclosed about the hinterland behind the precipitous and unpromising coastline. Fertile inland basins remained unknown, and the dominant impression from the sea was of steep, forested slopes plunging abruptly into the surf.

During the seventeenth century, missionaries and explorers planted settlements in Baja California and extended a chain of outposts northward into New Mexico. In 1701 Padre Kino's treks northward eliminated the myth of California as an island. At the urging of Julio de Oliban, judge in the Audiencia of Guadalajara, Felipe V suggested in 1719 that a settlement be established at either San Diego or Monterey Bay, to colonize the area "before the enemies of my crown occupy it." His fears had their origin in occasional depredations of English, Dutch, and French freebooters along the west coast of New Spain. The settlement could be reinforced by colonists forcibly recruited from among the excessive number of idlers, vagrants, and beggars who infested Mexico City and constituted a perennial problem. The order was never implemented. In 1748 a prominent judge of the Audiencia of Manila, Pedro Calderón y Henríquez, warned Fernando VI that it was urgent to occupy Monterey Bay, but his recommendation was not translated into action.[36]

Successive viceroys allowed the immense cartographic blank to persist on New Spain's northwestern perimeter, a titillation for geographers' imagination, to be filled in with features suggested by legends of Fu Sang, Anián, and Quivira, and details gleaned from apocryphal narratives of daring voyages. Madrid's interest in the northwest coast was stirred from time to time by some loyal subject conceiving a promise or threat to Spanish

36. Schurz, *Manila Galleon,* pp. 243–44.

dominions in North America, but until another nation actually penetrated the region, official policy was to neglect further reconnaissance northward and stifle with restrictions any enterprise that ran the risk of opening what proved, in its historical consequences, a veritable Pandora's box for the Spanish Empire—international competition for discovery and control of a northwest passage.

## 2 Myth, Legend, and Fraud in the History of the Northwest Coast

IN ADDITION to authenticated Spanish explorations, there are several voyages often mentioned in the literature about the northwest coast that are probably apocryphal. They play an important part in the early history of that area, however, because of their effect upon eighteenth-century explorers, both as a stimulant and an obstacle to authentic discoveries. Knowledge of some aspects of these tales is essential to an adequate understanding of the concepts and objectives of subsequent Spanish activities in that area.

### FERRER MALDONADO'S CURIOUS ACCOUNT

In the 1770s, at a time when Madrid was newly concerned about a northwest passage being discovered by mariners of other nationalities, a manuscript that caused quite a stir came to light in the archive of a noble Castillian family.[1] Written about 1609 by one Lorenzo Ferrer Maldonado, it described his alleged voyage in 1588 from the Atlantic around the top of North America to the Strait of Anián, then into the North Pacific and back. Initially many geographers accepted its veracity. But when careful search during the 1790s failed to reveal a northwest passage in the specified latitude, Spanish explorers were the first to brand the tale false. Geographer Martín Fernández de Navarrete subsequently found evidence that Ferrer Maldonado had enjoyed a certain notoriety in his day and labeled him "a deceiving promoter, faker pursued by justice, swindling alchemist and inventive charlatan."[2] That Ferrer Maldonado was well informed about navigation, cartography, and explorations of his time is evidenced by his memorial to the king offering a new kind of compass and a method of finding longitude at sea. One of his geographical treatises was published a year after his death, evincing a certain authority among contemporaries.[3]

The route that Ferrer Maldonado described coincides amazingly with the actual location of the true Northwest Passage charted in modern times from the Atlantic through Davis and Hudson Straits, Foxe Basin, Fury and

1. Lorenzo Ferrer Maldonado, "Relación del descubrimiento del estrecho de Anian," Ms. in Archivo Duque del Infantado, Madrid; first pub. by the Abbé G. T. F. Raynal, *Histoire philosophique* (Amsterdam, 1770); most accessible edition: *Colección de documentos relativos al descubrimiento . . . del Real Archivo de India*, 42 vols. (Madrid, 1864–84), 5 : 420–47.

2. Fernández de Navarrete, "Introducción," p. lii.

3. Lorenzo Ferrer Maldonado, *Imagen del Mundo sobre la esfera, cosmografía, geografía y arte de navegar* (Alcalá de Henares, 1626).

Hecla Straits, Gulf of Boothia, Bellot Strait, Franklin Strait, Queen Maud Gulf, Dease Strait, Coronation Gulf, Dolphin and Union Straits, to the Beaufort Sea and Bering Strait. The match between Ferrer Maldonado's account and known waterways led Arctic specialist and explorer Vilhjalmur Stefansson to speculate that certain climatic variations might have permitted a voyage across the top of North America during unusually warm years. Stefansson concluded that Ferrer Maldonado had authentic information about the Gulf-of-Boothia-to-Coronation-Gulf area of northern Canada, farther west than any known expedition up to that time is thought to have penetrated.[4]

His account may have been based on information from the explorations of John Davis and others. Where legitimate sources left off, Ferrer Maldonado may have inserted fantasy. If some of his guesses coincided with reality, others erred enormously. Describing what would correspond to the Bering Strait, he depicted scenery and inhabitants of such exotic detail as to suggest the falsehood of his entire tale. His account was of sufficient persuasiveness, however, to influence the writings of renowned French geographers Joseph Nicholas Delisle and Philippe Buache de Neuville, and his strait was long sought and distorted the efforts of Spanish, British, French, and American explorers.

JUAN DE FUCA'S TALE OF A GREAT STRAIT

Publication in 1625 of the widely read *Purchas, His Pilgrims* placed in circulation the curious account of an alleged discovery of a northwest passage in 1592 by one Juan de Fuca, born Apóstolos Valerianos.[5] Ever since, Fuca's tale has been subject to controversy. The elderly Greek pilot claimed to have made an otherwise undocumented voyage of discovery far to the north of any other navigator on the Pacific coast in that century. His name was placed for all time on maps of the Pacific Northwest in 1787, upon discovery of the broad strait separating Vancouver Island from the Olympic Peninsula in approximately the same latitude as Fuca's alleged passageway. Every historian of Spanish voyages on the Pacific coast, from Martin Fernández de Navarrete down to the most recent authors, has withheld from this voyage the seal of authenticity. Yet the tale had considerable effect upon early cartography of western North America and led Spanish and

4. V. Stefansson to H. R. Wagner, August 27 and Sept. 9, 1931, Mss in CtY (Memorabilia, Yz. 884. Wlap).

5. Michael Lok, "A Note Made by Me Michael Lok the Elder, Touching the Strait of Sea, Commonly Called Fretum Anian, in the South Sea, Through the North-west Passage of Meta Incognita," in Samuel Purchas, *Hakluytus Posthumus, or Purchas His Pilgrimes: Contayning a History of the World in Sea Voyages and Lande Travells by Englishmen and Others*, 4 vols. (London, 1625), 3 : 849–52; reprinted in Hakluyt Society, *Works*, ex. ser. 14 (Glasgow, 1906) : 415–21.

English explorers to an enormous expenditure of effort searching for a canal leading eastward from the complex interior waterways opening off the strait bearing Fuca's name.

The only known contemporary assertion that such a voyage was undertaken in 1592 is the account itself, written by Michael Lok from what Fuca told him in Venice in 1596. It was among papers left to Samuel Purchas by Richard Hakluyt, the famous geographer and editor of narratives of explorations, who was Lok's associate. A prominent English merchant-adventurer, sometime director of the Muscovy Company and governor of the Cathay Company, Lok was a perennial promoter of expeditions in search of a northwest passage, expending in such efforts the greater part of his once considerable means. He was instrumental in backing the renowned expeditions of Martin Frobisher in 1576, 1577, and 1578. They were spurred on by a manuscript provided by Sir Humphrey Gilbert and said to have been obtained in Ireland from a Spaniard name Salvaterra, who claimed that about 1560 Friar "Andro Urdaneta" had shown him a sea chart of his journey through a passageway from the Pacific to the Atlantic. According to Salvaterra, Fray "Andro" had shown the chart to the king of Portugal, whose reaction was to suggest that it not be made public so that it would not aid the English.[6] In 1560–61 Fray Andrés de Urdaneta is known to have been engaged in persuading Felipe II that a passage through North America had been discovered by some Frenchmen, and in 1580 Felipe placed himself on Portugal's throne. No other mention of Urdaneta's having traversed a northwest passage is known, and Salvaterra may have had his data confused, but the tale was sufficient to persuade Lok and Frobisher of the existence of such a waterway.

While Frobisher's expeditions made important contributions to geographical knowledge of North America, they were a financial disaster for Lok. A cargo of ore brought from Labrador in 1577 proved worthless, and before the expedition of 1578 returned Lok had been clapped into debtor's prison. At the time he met Fuca in Venice, the Englishman was still in difficult economic straits, and his projects had been somewhat discounted in England. Yet his penchant for speculative ventures made Lok as willing as ever to promote another search for the conjectured waterway to the Pacific. Fuca no doubt couched his story in terms calculated to excite his listener, and its details have enticed and annoyed explorers and scholars ever since. Lok's account is not well known today, and its extensive historical consequences and the difficulty of determining either its falsehood or its veracity warrant considering the document in full (see Appendix A).

Geographic realities prove that Fuca did not discover a northwest passage.

---

6. Dodge, *Northwest by Sea*, pp. 66–67; D. B. Quinn, *The Voyages and Colonizing Enterprises of Sir Humphrey Gilbert*, 2 vols. (London, 1940), 1 : 154–55.

Although Wagner asserts that this fact alone would "deprive the subject of all practical interest," [7] Fuca's significance does not lie in his claim to discovery of an interoceanic waterway, an anachronism that has led to the discounting of his entire tale. Our concern is whether he actually visited the northwest coast in 1592 and penetrated the strait bearing his name, concluding from its broad dimensions and its length that he had discovered the fabled passage. Some facets of his account correspond to known events. The galleon on which he claims to have been captured and had 60,000 ducats in goods stolen may have been the *Santa Ana,* seized by Cavendish in 1587. The expedition that aborted after a mutinous crew rose in arms against their sodomitical captain coincides with an obscure incident not mentioned in print until modern times: the revolt against Sebastián Pérez del Castillo, captain of the *San José.* Charged with an "unnatural offense," he was brought back for trial before the Audiencia, but succumbed in prison before the case was resolved.[8] Pérez del Castillo, Sebastián Vizcaíno, and Hernando de Sanctotis were associates in an enterprise directed toward exploring and exploiting the Californias. Sanctotis, a royal accountant in New Spain, obtained license in 1583 to construct vessels for use in exploring California. In 1584 the viceroy gave him an extension of ten years. A year later the archbishop, as acting viceroy, conceded to the Sanctotis enterprise a license for pearl fishing in the Californias. In 1586 the new viceroy informed Felipe II that a vessel was about to sail on a mission of discovery along the coast of the "Mar del Sur"; this is thought to be a reference to Sanctotis's efforts.[9]

When Cavendish raided La Navidad in 1587, several 200-ton vessels being constructed there were put to the torch. One of them belonged to Antonio del Castillo, an associate of Sanctotis. Wagner is of the opinion that, despite this setback, "the company seems to have sent one or more expeditions to California either before or after this, as it was subsequently alleged that they found some pearls which they had not registered." In a later publication he remarks that the Sanctotis company "managed to send out by 1592 one ship, or possibly more, of which no account remains." [10] Wagner confesses that many aspects of this subject remain obscure because of the lack of documentation. He found that the Sanctotis-Vizcaíno enterprise

7. Wagner, "Apocryphal Voyages," p. 217.

8. Antonio de Morga, "Relación," Manila, June 8, 1598, SpAGI (V, Filipinas 8); Wagner, *Spanish Voyages,* p. 170.

9. Pedro Moya de Contreras, License to Sanctotis and associates, August 7, 1685, pub. in H. R. Wagner, "Pearl Fishing Enterprises in the Gulf of California: The Expedition of Sebastián Vizcaíno," *HAHR* 10 (1930) : 188–220; Viceroy Álvaro Manrique de Zúñiga, marqués de Villamanrique, to Felipe II, May 10, 1586, SpAGI (Aud. Mex. 20), in Carrasco, *Documentos referentes,* pp. 12–14 (erroneously dated May 10, 1585); Wagner, *Spanish Voyages,* pp. 168, 374.

10. Wagner, *Spanish Voyages,* p. 169; Wagner, "Pearl Fishing Enterprises," p. 194; Wagner, "Apocryphal Voyages," p. 189.

eventually broke up in bitter rivalry between the partners. In 1592 Vizcaíno and several others petitioned for exclusive rights to pearling activities in California, precipitating a lawsuit with Sanctotis. The Audiencia resolved that, if Sanctotis turned over his ships and supplies, Vizcaíno should pay for them at their appraised price.[11] As mentioned in chapter 1, in 1593 Viceroy Velasco informed Felipe II that his treasury lacked funds to conduct explorations northward along the Pacific coast but that certain persons were interested in sending out expeditions at their own expense. Velasco suggested that they be allowed to continue and be given advantageous concessions as added incentive.[12] The reference was to Vizcaíno and associates. Fuca's alleged voyage in 1592 is compatible with what we know of Velasco's policy of encouraging private efforts and depending upon them to carry out explorations. The Greek's account was accepted as valid until the 1790s, when its authenticity was cast in doubt by explorers who could not find a transcontinental passage within the strait bearing Fuca's name. To allow ourselves to be influenced by opinions of eighteenth-century navigators about Fuca's veracity would be a mistake; instead, his tale should be evaluated in the light of other documents of the 1590s concerning exploratory activities and attitudes toward that coast.

The most persuasive factor against Fuca's story is that no contemporary, other than Lok, mentions an expedition under Fuca's command to the northwest coast in 1592. Yet the archives of Mexico and Spain are well-nigh inexhaustible sources of unstudied documents. Destruction by fire of much of the early viceregal archives in Mexico City makes it hazardous to assert that documentation for Fuca's tale never existed. Several significant voyages to California were unknown to subsequent viceroys or to eighteenth-century explorers. The expedition in 1542 led by João Rodrigues Cabrilho, in which Bartolomé Ferrelo reached the high water mark of sixteenth-century expeditions northward, was never mentioned in subsequent reports of California explorations. Similarly, Pedro de Unamuno's voyage and excursion ashore at Morro Bay in 1587 were unknown until publication of his journal in 1923.[13]

If Fuca made his alleged voyage, a powerful motive existed for sequestering all trace of the orders sending him northward and any record of the results, that is, the concern for keeping knowledge of such a strait from rival nations. Fuca's mission is made plausible by the orders, at this juncture, from Felipe II to stop marauders from entering the Pacific through straits that it was feared had been discovered in the north. To assist in locating

---

11. Wagner, *Spanish Voyages*, pp. 152, 363; Wagner, "Pearl Fishing Enterprises," p. 200.

12. Velasco to Felipe II, October 8, 1593, in Carrasco, *Documentos referentes*, pp. 15–16.

13. Wagner, *Spanish Voyages*, pp. 152, 363n; idem, "The Voyage of Pedro de Unamuno to California in 1587," *CHSQ*, 2 (1923–24) : 140–60.

and fortifying the entrance to such a passage was the purpose of Vizcaíno's expeditions to Baja California in 1596 and Monterey Bay in 1602. If Fuca truly lobbied in Madrid to persuade Spanish officials that the waterways he found were the Northwest Passage, it is hardly surprising if he received the treatment described to Lok. The decade from 1592 to 1602 saw an unusual spurt of exploratory activity. The viceroys backed the ill-fated effort begun by Rodrigues Cermenho in 1594 and continued by Vizcaíno. Their principal objective was to secure adequate knowledge of the bays of Alta California to counter foreign penetration of the North Pacific.

Wagner expressed the opinion in 1926 that, "while on the whole Lok probably concocted the story of the expedition to the Strait of Anián to support his well-known views about the existence of a northwest passage, it is not beyond the realm of probability that there may have been some foundation to it after all." [14] In another publication that same year, Wagner remarked:

> There is no record of any expedition to the northwest coast between the abortive one of 1589 or 1590, financed by Hernando de Sanctotis, in which Fuca perhaps took part (he certainly knew of it), and the time that he appeared in Italy, but it does not follow that none was made. There are cartographical indications, beginning in 1592, that there had been some expedition on the northwest coast of which no other record exists. There might have been one, therefore, in 1590 or 1591, and if so, while it is not probable that it ever sailed as far north as the entrance to the Strait of Juan de Fuca in 48°, some river might have been found large enough to give some color to the idea that it was the mouth of a strait.[15]

A search of Wagner's writings reveals no specifics as to these "cartographical indications" of an unknown voyage in 1592. In a subsequent publication he assigned a date of late 1593 or early 1594 for the voyage of the *San José,* aborted because of Pérez del Castillo's aberrant behavior.[16] Wagner offers no explanation, but it would appear that he decided upon that date because in the litigation between partners, the court rendered judgment in November 1594.[17] Very little is known about that voyage, but taking into account the languor of legal action and the fact that the imprisoned captain succumbed before being brought to trial, Wagner's previous assignment of 1589 or 1590 for the thwarted voyage seems more likely than 1593–94. By

14. Wagner, *Drake's Voyage,* pp. 477–78.
15. H. R. Wagner, "Some Imaginary California Geography," *PAAS,* n.s. 36 1926) : 101.
16. Wagner, *Spanish Voyages,* p. 170.
17. Wagner, "Pearl Fishing Enterprises," p. 200, citing Mss in SpAGI (1–1–1/30).

1931 Wagner had come to reject the possibility that Fuca ever visited the northwest coast, and although he acknowledged that the Levantine pilot was in New Spain between 1588 and 1594, he stated categorically:

> All that Fuca knew was something about a voyage up the Gulf of California. I think that Michael Lok did the rest, as when we come to compare Fuca's story with Lok's map published by Richard Hakluyt in his *Divers Voyages* in 1582, we find that Fuca's voyage must have been made through Lok's strait located between about 47° and 50°. Only a part of the northern coast extending from west to east for about twelve degrees of longitude is laid down on this and the strait then opens into the Polar Ocean. We may do Lok an injustice in thinking that he fabricated this part of the narrative; he was looking for information to verify his theory of a Northwest Passage and possibly the Greek was quite willing to supply it and thus gain employment.[18]

Wagner's opinion seems based on absence of confirmation of a voyage in 1592 to a high latitude, yet his writings concede that Sanctotis may have sent out an expedition in 1592 for which documentation has not come to light. Wagner conjectured that Fuca may be the pilot called "Juan Griego," who was taken prisoner by Drake at Valparaíso in 1578, upon capture of the *Capitana,* and who acted as the latter's pilot until released at Callao, in Peru. Coincidentally, in 1587 Cavendish seized a vessel coming from Valparaíso from which he took a pilot called "George," a Greek, who served as guide to the Chilean coast. Wagner suggests that "Juan Griego" and "George" may have been the same experienced pilot, and that Cavendish put him ashore at Cape San Lucas with the survivors of the *Santa Ana.*[19]

One charge made against Fuca's story is that after the passengers of the *Santa Ana* reached Acapulco, an account compiled of their losses makes no mention of Fuca and his alleged 60,000 ducats. But the list is not necessarily complete, and in view of the link among Fuca, Pérez del Castillo, Sanctotis, and associates, it is significant that Vizcaíno was aboard the *Santa Ana* at its capture.[20] His losses may have led to Fuca's claim. Nor can the 60,000 ducats be discounted on grounds of exaggeration. Officers and passengers aboard the galleons made enormous profits from selling silks and other exotic items crammed into small packages. With great care as to value in proportion to size, contents of a single *fardo* were worth a great sum in Mexico. Fuca's

---

18. Wagner, "Apocryphal Voyages," pp. 187, 189–90.

19. Wagner, *Drake's Voyage,* pp. 101, 477; Wagner, "Apocryphal Voyages," pp. 187–88.

20. Manuel Fernández de Navarrete and Eustaquio Fernández de Navarrete, "Examen histórico-crítico de los viajes y descubrimientos apócrifos del Capitán Lorenzo Ferrer Maldonado, de Juan de Fuca y del Almirante Bartolomé de Fonte," *Coleccion de documentos inéditos para la historia de España* (Madrid, 1849), 15 : 104; Wagner, *Spanish Voyages,* p. 169.

claim would have been based on what he expected the goods would bring in Acapulco.

Fuca's reference to the Pérez del Castillo affair does not authenticate the rest of his tale, but it shows his acquaintance with little-known exploratory efforts of the time. His claim of a connection with that abortive voyage is quite persuasive. That a foreigner should be placed in command of an expedition is not unusual. Pilots and captains of Portuguese, Italian, and Levantine origin appear frequently in the records, as witness Ferrelo, Rodrigues Cabrilho, and Rodrigues Cermenho. Upon notifying Felipe II of his selection of a foreigner to command the expedition of 1594, Viceroy Velasco offered as excuse that Rodrigues Cermenho was "a man of experience in his calling, one who can be depended upon and who has means of his own—although he is a Portuguese, there being no Spaniards of his profession whose services are available." [21]

### FUCA'S "STRAIT" AND FUCA'S "PINNACLE"

While geographical realities prove that Fuca did not traverse a northwest passage, they do not preclude the possibility that he penetrated the waterway separating Vancouver Island from the mainland and gained the impression that it communicated with the polar sea. In many ways, the strait described in Fuca's account corresponds to the waterway that bears his name, together with the Straits of Georgia and the Inland Passage to Alaska. A reasonable hypothesis is that Fuca followed those channels until he emerged into Queen Charlotte Sound and the Pacific at Dixon Entrance. Then, conceiving that he had reached the "Sea of the North," he retraced his course to Mexico. Fuca located his passage between 47° and 48°, whereas the strait bearing his name is between 48° 25′ and 48° 38′—fairly accurate for 1592. The opening is fifteen miles wide at the entrance and from a small vessel seems much wider unless the humidity is very low—an uncommon occurrence there. At its inner extremity it is much broader, and if a vessel follows the main channel, it must at various times sail southeast, northeast, north, and northwest among a myriad of islands, precisely as described by Fuca to Lok.

F. W. Howay regards as "a little thin" the possibility that an experienced pilot could follow such a route and believe that he had reached the "Sea of the North," and remarks: "In that whole distance the navigator is never out of sight of land; nowhere is the strait 30 to 40 leagues wide—it is not that many miles wide—but before the twenty days or one-half of them were sailed out the strait instead of widening would narrow to less than half a mile." [22] Howay's objection loses its force when we make allowances for

21. Velasco to Felipe II, April 6, 1594. In Carrasco, *Documentos Referentes*, p. 18.
22. F. W. Howay, "Presidential Address," *BCHA Annual Report* 3 (1924) : 22–23.

Lok's rehashing of details and note that if Fuca emerged into Queen Charlotte Sound, there was justification for estimating that waterway to be thirty to forty leagues wide.

The "exceeding high Pinacle, or spired Rocke" described in the account is not to be seen on the north side of the strait, but in 1788 Captain Charles Duncan of the *Princess Royal* drew a profile and map of the entrance to the famous waterway, on the south side of which is depicted a pinnacle that he assumed was Fuca's landmark. It is still there today, between Cape Flattery and Tatoosh Island, clearly visible from both ocean and strait as one approaches from the south. Lok places the pinnacle on the north side of the strait, but it must be noted that the old Greek communicated with him in a garbled tongue, as evinced by Fuca's letter, and the pilot's verbal account may have been somewhat distorted by faulty translation, misunderstanding, and forgetfulness on Lok's part. Still another explanation was suggested by Rear Admiral Thomas Stowell Phelps, a mariner familiar with the Inland Passage, who points to a landmark such as Fuca described at the northwest terminus of the passage, where it opens into Queen Charlotte Sound.[23]

Fuca's report of finding gold, silver, and pearls is manifestly a fabrication, but in this the story differs little from prevarications in many authentic accounts of sixteenth-century exploits—calculated exaggerations of the slightest signs or rumors whereby explorers sought support for further expeditions by offering tantalizing prospects of fabulous wealth. Most authors defer to the judgment of Fernández de Navarrete, Howay, and Wagner in pronouncing Fuca's voyage apocryphal, but the old pilot's tale still arouses controversy. While it is probable that Fuca was an experienced pilot in Pacific waters, there is no corroboration that he led an expedition to a high latitude in 1592. Yet the absence of confirmation of such a voyage does not remove it from the realm of the possible, since it coincides so closely with the known information about an endeavor directed toward California, Anián, and fantasies of gold, silver, and pearls. The archives of Spain and Spanish America are far from plumbed and may yet provide evidence to confirm or disprove Fuca's claims. Until such a time, the old Greek's curious tale cannot be left out of any account of early voyages to the northwest coast.

## THE FONTE VERSION OF A NORTHWEST PASSAGE

Another controverted voyage through a northwest passage is alleged to have been made in 1640 by one Bartholomew de Fonte, an account of which appeared in 1708 in the April and June issues of a London magazine, *Monthly Miscellany or Memoirs for the Curious.* The story persuaded some

23. Phelps, as cited by William W. Woollen, *The Inside Passage to Alaska 1792–1920,* 2 vols. (Cleveland, 1924), 2 : 36–37.

cartographers to add imaginary features to their maps. Internal anachronisms, such as references to nonexistent titles of Spanish officials and the unlikelihood of an expedition's being sent from Callao to search for a northwest passage lead modern historians to conclude that it is spurious. Wagner, upon republishing the account in 1931, examined the question at length, concluding that its "slender array of facts" may have been taken from *New Voyage Round the World* (London, 1697), William Dampier's description of his buccaneer exploits and explorations in the Pacific. No evidence has been found that such a person as Fonte ever lived, and the account is generally held to be the invention of James Petiver, publisher of the journal in which it appeared.[24]

There is little likelihood that an early voyage across the top of North America ever took place, but the possibility fascinated explorers, geographers, and governments for centuries. Roald Amundsen's expedition of 1903–06 actually traversed a chain of straits and gulfs across the top of the continent, but his group took more than one season. Recently, the topic has taken on renewed interest with the cruise of ships of the Canadian Navy from one ocean to the other in a single season during a brief period in summer when the ice pack recedes, and with the opening of a potential commercial route by an ice-breaking oil tanker in 1969.

The controversial tales of Ferrer Maldonado, Fuca, and Fonte, although generally held to be fictitious, have a permanent place in the history and cartography of the New World for their important role in stimulating generations of explorers to undertake hazardous voyages and overland explorations in search of an easy means of traversing the North American continent. Arthur Dobbs's efforts to encourage discovery of a northwest passage led Parliament in 1744 to approve a bill offering £20,000 to captain and crew of the first British vessel to pass through such a waterway. Later, as governor of North Carolina, Dobbs communicated his enthusiasm to Major Robert Rogers, who sought to translate it into action by overland explorations.

English voyages in search of a northwest passage did not go unnoticed in Spain and Spanish America and caused considerable preoccupation in some quarters. Andrés Marcos Burriel's edition of Jesuit Miguel Venegas's *Noticia de la California* (Madrid, 1757) had an appendix describing British attempts at finding a passage into the South Sea; this was intended to underscore the threat to Baja California.

The propensity of early geographers to accept any and all accounts in order to fill in vacant areas on their maps and globes created a considerable problem for those interested in obtaining authentic cartographic information. The misinterpretation of genuine accounts also gave rise to difficulties, as in the case of Torquemada's transferral of Vizcaíno's "Río de Martín

24. Wagner, "Apocryphal Voyages," pp. 197–202; Dodge, *Northwest by Sea*, p. 183.

Aguilar" to 43° north latitude. The maps of Guillaume Delisle (1675–1726), often called the "father of modern cartography," showed the "Río de Martín Aguilar" and Fuca's strait as outlets for a vast "Mer de l'Ouest." When Spanish explorations northward along the Pacific coast were renewed in the eighteenth century, such concepts would be obstacles to effective exploration—worse than total ignorance—for wholly imaginary features would become the objects of diligent search and influence Spanish strategy, motives, and activities until all possibility that they existed was eliminated. The "Río de Martín Aguilar" and "Sea of the West" were conceived to be avenues for foreign approach to New Mexico and New Spain itself, threatening productive silver mines that were pillars of the colonial economy.

In the seventeenth century, however, there was as yet no evidence of foreign penetration in western North America. Viceroys could afford to let the hinterland go unexplored, at all appearances safe behind a curtain of silence, secrecy, and ignorance. In the absence of an official Spanish policy encouraging further exploration northward, the area invited cartographic speculation and stimulated the novelist's imagination. There, in 1726, Swift would locate his Brobdingnag, with its grotesque inhabitants, and even in the nineteenth century it could accommodate Verne's *500 Millions of the Begum*.

### THE NEHALEM BEESWAX SHIP

Manila galleons never tarried long on the California coast, for an opinion prevailed that scurvy was lessened on long voyages by reducing the time spent in higher latitudes. On at least one occasion, however, one of them followed a more northerly route, was blown off course, or was chased toward the north coast by a pursuer. Carrying, among other things, a large cargo of beeswax, it was wrecked on the Oregon coast far to the north of any known explorations up to that time. Clues to this episode began to accumulate when Lewis and Clark reached the mouth of the Columbia. Clark's journal for December 31, 1805, relates:

> With the party of Clatsops who visited us last was a man of much lighter colour than the natives are generally. He was freckled with long duskey red hair, about 25 years of age, and certainly must be half white at least. This man appeared to understand more of the English language than the others of his party but did not speak a word of English. He possesses all the habits of Indians.[25]

Soon after the founding of Astoria in 1811, one of Astor's men ascended the Columbia to the limit of navigation where, in a native village, he en-

25. Reuben Gold Thwaites, ed., *Original Journals of the Lewis and Clark Expedition*, 8 vols. (New York, 1904–05), 3 : 301.

countered an old man, nearly blind, who said that his name was "Soto." Through an interpreter it was learned that

> he was the son of a Spaniard who had been wrecked at the mouth of the river; that a part of the crew on this occasion had got safely ashore, but were all massacred by the Clatsops, with the exception of four, who were spared and who married native women; that these four Spaniards, of whom his father was one, disgusted with the savage life, attempted to reach a settlement of their own nation overland, but had never been heard of since; and that when his father, with his companions, left the country, he himself was yet quite young.[26]

Alexander Henry, who arrived at the Columbia's mouth in 1813 with explorer David Thompson, told of an old Clatsop chief who visited them and added:

> There came with him a man about thirty years of age, who had extraordinarily dark red hair, and is the supposed offspring of a ship that was wrecked within a few miles of the entrance of this river many years ago. Great quantities of beeswax continue to be dug out of the sand near this spit, and the Indians bring it to trade with us.[27]

Several months later Henry reported: "They bring us frequently lumps of beeswax fresh out of the sand which they collect on the coast to the S. where the Spanish ship was cast away some years ago and the crew was all murdered by the Indians." [28] Rox Cox, another early visitor to Astoria, wrote that in 1814 an Indian who belonged to a small tribe to the south of the Clatsop came to them occasionally.

> He was a perfect *lusus naturae;* and his history was rather curious. His skin was fair, his face partially freckled, and his hair quite red. He was about five feet ten inches high, was slender and remarkably well made; his head had not undergone the flattening process; and he was called Jack Ramsay, in consequence of that name having been punctured on his left arm. The Indians allege that his father was an English sailor, who had deserted from a trading vessel, and had lived many years among the tribe, one of whom he married; that when Jack was born he insisted on preserving the child's head in its natural state, and while young had punctured the arm in the above manner. Old Ramsay had

26. Gabriel de la Franchère, *Narrative of a Voyage to the Northwest Coast of America in the Years 1811, 1812, 1813 and 1814 or the First American Settlement on the Pacific* (New York, 1854), p. 113.

27. Alexander Henry, *The Manuscript Journals of Alexander Henry and of David Thompson, 1799–1814: New Light on the Early History of the Greater North-west,* ed. Elliott Coues, 3 vols. (New York, 1897), 2 : 768, entry for December 8, 1813.

28. Ibid., 2 : 841, entry for February 28, 1814.

died about twenty years before this period; he had several more children, but Jack was the only red-headed one among them.[29]

These reports are not mutually exclusive; dark hair genes being dominant over light, the fellow must have inherited red hair from both parents, a possibility if his mother descended from a survivor of the beeswax vessel reported by Franchère and Henry. As physician Olaf Larsell has suggested, red-haired Nehalem natives boasted of their castaway ancestry, and women of that lineage may have been predisposed toward receiving subsequent whites as kin.[30]

Missionaries, pioneers, and early historians mention the wreckage of this vessel at Nehalem Beach, thirty-five miles south of the Columbia's mouth. The cargo consisted in great part of beeswax, as testified by the quantity found there in historical times. When the natives learned that the Hudson's Bay Company would pay a good price for the strange substance, digging it from the sand became a prosperous enterprise. Six tons were carried to Hawaii about 1847, and by 1908 an estimated twelve tons had been found.[31] The chunks range in size from about seventy-five pounds to small, round sections with holes down the center from which a wick has rotted away. Some specimens have large serif letters, numerals, and symbols stamped into them. One such, preserved in the Tillamook County Pioneer Museum, bears the numerals "67," and portions of broken digits on either side seem to read "1679." In 1961 it was carbon-14 dated at 280 years old, plus or minus 110 years, with a 95 percent confidence-level of accuracy. Microscopic examination revealed bee stingers and pollen from a plant indigenous to Southeast Asia.[32]

The hull of the beeswax vessel is presently covered by the ever-shifting sand of a windswept spit at the mouth of Nehalem Bay, at what once may have been its outlet but is now dry land, several miles from the base of towering Neah-kah-nie Mountain.[33]

Beeswax in bulk frequently made up a part of the cargo of Manila galleons. Of Cambodian and Siamese origin, it was shipped to Acapulco by Philippine exporters in response to a demand in Spanish for millions of candles for homes, public buildings, and church altars. By custom, cargo was divided into bales (*fardos*) of uniform size, which in turn were composed of smaller units (*piezas*). A *pieza* averaged thirty inches by twenty-four inches

29. Ross Cox, *Adventures on the Columbia River*, 2 vols. (London, 1831), 1 : 151.

30. Olaf Larsell, *The Doctor in Oregon* (Portland, Ore., 1947), pp. 59–60.

31. Orin Fletcher Strafford, "Wax of Nehalem Beach," *OHQ* 9 (1908) : 26, 29–32.

32. "The Oregon Beeswax Mystery," *Shell News* 29, no. 12 (New York, 1961) : 20–21.

33. Attempts to probe its secrets have always been thwarted because the hull is buried too deep for excavation without extensive cofferdams to prevent seepage; the efforts are chronicled by Ruby El Hult, *Lost Mines and Treasures of the Pacific Northwest* (Portland, Ore., 1960), pp. 1–42.

by ten inches, and the largest chunks of beeswax found at Nehalem have approximately these dimensions. Schurz sees similarities between the marks stamped into the Nehalem beeswax and symbols on galleon cargo manifests identifying ownership of individual *piezas*.[34]

The Horner Museum at Oregon State University in Corvallis displays a pulley recovered from the beeswax vessel in 1896 and identified as teakwood. In 1898 an excavation with the hull yielded a sterling silver jar that authoritative opinion pronounced the work of Dutch silversmiths, with a hallmark similar to that used in several European cities, but particularly in Utrecht.[35] Possibly a container for holy water, spices, or sugar, it is not necessarily an indication that the vessel was Dutch, for objects manufactured in the Low Countries had wide circulation in the Spanish Empire, which still traded with that area for some articles long after the northern provinces broke away from the Hapsburgs in the 1580s. It would not have been at all unusual to find such a receptacle aboard a Manila galleon.

There is no record of a Spanish vessel being cast away on the Oregon coast, but at least six galleons left the Philippines for Acapulco and never reached their destination, aside from the one Cavendish waylaid off Cape San Lucas. Of these, the *San Juanillo* (1578) and *San Juan* (1586) disappeared too early to correspond to the carbon-14-dated beeswax. In the case of the *San Antonio* (1604), a quantity of goods found soon afterward on the northeast coast of Luzon suggests that it met its doom there. The *Santo Cristo de Burgos* (1693) is thought traceable to burned ship timbers encountered not long after in the Marianas. The *Nuestra Señora del Pilar* (1750) is also believed to have been wrecked off Luzon.[36]

The *San Francisco Xavier* departed from Manila in January 1707 and failed to reach Acapulco. Nothing ever came to light about the fate of the 1,000-ton vessel captained by Santiago Zabalburú. On a previous trip, in 1697, it had been so overloaded that royal inspectors insisted that a portion of its beeswax cargo and passengers be left behind. Upon sale in Acapulco, the cargo brought a grand total of 2,070,000 pesos.[37] On his final voyage from Manila, Zabalburú embarked 500 cakes of beeswax of from 10 to 14 arrobas (250 to 350 lbs. apiece, somewhere between 62 and 87 tons) valued at 150,000 piasters (pieces of eight, or dollars). Two thousand packages of silks, an equal number of bundles of diverse merchandise, gold ingots to the sum of 2,500 piasters, and a quantity of porcelain, pepper, cloves, nutmeg,

34. Ibid., pp. 36–37.

35. E. W. Giesecke to the author, Olympia, Wash., March 2, 1966; Alexander Walker, curator of the Tillamook County Pioneer Museum, to the author, Tillamook, Ore., March 23, 1962.

36. Dahlgren, *Hawaiian Islands*, p. 139.

37. Ibid., p. 111; Erik W. Dahlgren, *Les Relations commerciales et maritimes entre la France et les côtes de l'Océan Pacifique* (Paris, 1909), 41n, 69n; Schurz, *Manila Galleon*, pp. 189, 260; Hult, *Lost Mines*, p. 36.

and aromatic drugs composed the rest of the cargo, for an estimated total value of 4,000,000.[38]

SPANISH CASTAWAYS AT NEHALEM

Indian legends shed some light upon the fate of castaways from the stricken galleon. John Hobson visited Nehalem in 1848 and saw remnants of the beeswax vessel, which he assumed to be a Chinese junk.

> All they could tell us was that long before they were born, the wax vessel was lost on the spit, and another anchored near the shore, and some people brought a chest up on Necanny Mountain and carried sacks of money and put them in the chest and killed a man, and put him also in the chest. Afterward they marked a stone, or very large rock, rolled it on the chest, and went back to the ship and sailed away.[39]

When Warren Vaughn visited Nehalem in 1852–53, not an Indian was living who remembered the beeswax vessel episode, the story having been passed down from ancestors, and he calculated its occurrence as sometime between 1690 and 1740. The massacre's sole survivor had been a Negro, a "chickamin" (blacksmith) whose skill at making knives and other metal tools from remains of the vessel resulted in his life's being spared. He married an Indian woman, raised children, and Nehalem chief Kilchis claimed to be his descendant. "Kilchis had two brothers here," Vaughn noted, "but they did not look as much like a negro as Kilchis." He made a distinction between the beeswax vessel and a subsequent event, described by a blind couple reputed to be the oldest Indians in the area. The squaw said that when she was a girl, picking berries with her mother on Neah-kah-nie Mountain, a ship had sent a boat ashore with five or six men to bury a small chest. A large rock was rolled on top, marks carved upon it, and a Negro slain and placed atop the rock, with two long knives crossed upon his chest. Fear of the black man left on watch kept the Indians from meddling with the coffer, and a landslide later covered the site.[40]

Another early source of such legends was Silas W. Smith, son of a frontiersman who came to Oregon with Nathaniel Wyeth in 1832 and married Celiast, daughter of Cob-a-way, chief of all the Clatsop. His mother's people

---

38. "Compte du produit de la cargaison du Galion appelle le St. francois Xavier du port de 1000. Thonneaux venu de Manille a Acapulco au Commencement du mois De Janvier 1707," in Jean de Monségur, "Nouveau Mémoires touchant le Mexique ou la Nouvelle Espagne," 1707–08, FrBN (Ms. Fr. 24228), pp. 339–41. Writing shortly after the galleon's departure, Monségur assumed that it would arrive in Acapulco safely.

39. John Hobson, Letter, *Portland Oregonian*, June 20, 1894, p. 6, cited by Hult, *Lost Mines*, pp. 11, 16–17.

40. Warren N. Vaughn, "Diary" [actually memoirs] covering the years 1851–63. Ms quoted by Arthur H. Winters, "History of Tillamook County" (Master's thesis, Willamette University, 1941), pp. 265–66, excerpts provided by E. W. Giesecke.

told of a vessel's being driven ashore just north of the Nehalem River, but all or most of those aboard survived and lived among the natives for several months, until disregard for Indian marital relations provoked a massacre of the entire lot. Since they defended themselves with slingshots, Smith concluded that they had lost their arms and ammunition. He knew of the legend concerning a buried chest but believed it had no connection with the beeswax vessel; he felt the former event had occurred later, and those responsible for it had put to sea again.[41]

It should be noted that Hobson (accompanied to Nehalem in 1848 by Silas Smith's father) did not specifically make the beeswax vessel and the ship bringing a chest for burial contemporary with one another. Hobson, Vaughn, and Smith agree upon the existence of more than one ship. The two episodes are linked, however, in a version told by Mrs. Edward Gervais, Cob-a-way's daughter and Smith's aunt. According to her understanding of the matter, the Indians were much surprised to see so many objects new to them floating ashore from the giant wrecked "canoe." There were some thirty survivors of the disaster, which occurred during the night, and she believed it was these who buried the legendary chest.[42] Hobson, Vaughn, and Smith all mention a marked rock atop the buried coffer. A stone with carvings was uncovered at the base of Neah-kah-nie about 1890, and others were excavated later at the same site. Letters, numerals, crosses, and arrows can be recognized on them but defy all efforts at interpretation or identification of the nationality of the inscribers.

The castaways lived at peace with the natives long enough to leave behind some descendants, as one of the Indian families of Nehalem in the nineteenth century cherished a tradition about feats of an ancestor said to have been one of the bearded survivors of the beeswax vessel. Their story was confirmed by a legacy of red hair and freckles.[43]

A detailed but relatively recent version of this episode, gathered from the Nehalem Indians by an old-timer in the area when he was a boy, tells of two ships appearing at dawn on the horizon, one in pursuit of the other, "thundering" at each other until one headed for shore under full sail and stuck in the sand. The combat continued until nightfall, when the second vessel departed. Little boats from the wreck came ashore and the sixty survivors built cabins for refuge. The Indians saw a huge chest carried up the side of the mountain, buried, and large stones rolled into the hole. After several years, violations of Indian women led the chief to summon his allies from up and down the coast, gathering fifteen hundred warriors. In a pre-

41. Silas B. Smith, "Address to the Oregon Historical Society, December 16, 1899," *Oregon Native Son* 1 (1899–1900) : 443–44.

42. Hult, *Lost Mines*, p. 8.

43. Samuel A. Clarke, *Pioneer Days of Oregon History* (Portland, Ore., 1905), pp. 153, 173.

dawn assault, flaming pitch brands were put under the cabins, and the occupants burned up or slain as they fled.[44] Since the "thundering" is not mentioned by early sources, the validity of this version has been questioned on grounds that, "if such a dramatic naval battle had occurred off Neahkahnie, obviously it would have been much talked of by the Clatsop Indians."[45]

Although many of its aspects remain obscure, this episode has considerable significance in the history of the Pacific Northwest, for the castaways at Nehalem were the first Europeans to set foot upon the northwest coast. Their vessel, most likely the *San Francisco Xavier,* strayed off course or, as some versions suggest, was pursued to the Oregon coast by an assailant. A corsair off Oregon is not an impossibility. Between 1575 and 1742 there were at least twenty-five different pirates or privateers preying upon shipping on the west coast of the Americas.[46] Dutch Admiral Joris van Spielbergen raided Mexico's west coast with six vessels in 1615. Hugo Schapenham's fleet, which started out with ten ships and over 1,600 men, attacked the same area in 1624. English, Dutch, and French corsairs sought to waylay the Manila galleon time and time again. The itinerary of the marauders is for the most part shrouded in mystery, and there are references in Spanish sources to pirate vessels along the west coast of Mexico whose identities have never been established.

After Cavendish seized the *Santa Ana* in 1587, one of his vessels, the *Content,* set sail northward along the west coast of Baja California and was never heard from again.[47] Englishmen Thomas Peche (1675) and Woodes Rogers (1709) prowled the same area.[48] The latter seized a Manila galleon (*Nuestra Señora de la Encarnación*) as it passed Cape San Lucas, but another (*Begonia*) fended off his assault. Rogers's squadron had been augmented with vessels captured off the west coasts of South and Central America, and the chronicle of his exploits does not cover all their movements.[49] Less is known about Nicholas de Frondat and the heavily armed *Saint-Antoine-de-Pade,* which sailed from China in February of 1709 and is said to have reached a maximum of 44° 52′ north latitude (Nehalem is at 45° 30′ north). By the following July, Frondat was off Mexico's Banderas Bay, seeking to trade some of his cargo for jerked beef. His merchandise was eventually smuggled to eager purchasers in out-of-the-way ports in Peru and Chile, and he returned to France with a profit of almost two million pounds sterling.[50]

44. Charles Pike, died 1955, as quoted by Winters, "History of Tillamook County, p. 20.
45. Hult, *Lost Mines,* p. 18.
46. Gerhard, *Pirates on the West Coast,* p. 239.
47. Ibid., pp. 93–94.
48. James Burney, *A Chronological History of the Discoveries in the South Sea or Pacific Ocean,* 5 vols. (London, 1803–17), 3 : 393–94.
49. Gerhard, *Pirates on the West Coast,* pp. 209–15.
50. Burney, *Chronological History,* 4 : 487–88; Gerhard, *Pirates on the West Coast,* pp. 208–9.

Frondat was just one of many Frenchmen frequenting the Pacific at this time, many of whom were not above resorting to piracy when opportunity knocked. Madrid's naval power was at an ebb during the War of Spanish Succession, and Spanish protests to Paris against such depredations were ignored. A recent study asserts that "in the ten-year period between 1695 and 1705 a total of twenty-two French ships had sailed either openly or secretly for the Pacific, but thirteen sailed in 1705, eleven in 1706, and thirteen in 1707."[51] Such activities underscore the increasing bankruptcy of Spain's traditional policy of depending upon secrecy and remoteness to protect her long-standing claim to western North America. They also suggest that the Indian legend of an early naval encounter off Nehalem is not an impossibility.

CASTAWAYS AT THE MOUTH OF THE COLUMBIA

Another cycle of legends about a shipwreck and castaways existed among the Indians at the Columbia's mouth. In 1894 Franz Boas published one version in the original Chinook, telling of a masted vessel that went aground near today's Seaside, Oregon, was set afire by the Clatsop to obtain the metal in it, and from which two survivors were enslaved.[52] From his mother's people, Silas Smith learned essentially the same legend, with additional details about the fate of the castaways. One named "Konapee" proved his skill at fashioning tools of metal salvaged from their wrecked vessel, and eventually his talents won both men their freedom. They said their homeland was toward the rising sun, and after a year or two departed up the Columbia. Upon reaching the Cascades they stopped and married native women. Although some details coincide with references by Gabriel de la Franchère and Alexander Henry to survivors of the beeswax vessel, Smith was persuaded that they derived from different events. His mother said that at Fort Vancouver in the 1820s "she met a Cascades woman who was represented to be a descendant of Konapee; that she was already past mid-life, and was much fairer in complexion than the other natives." Smith knew of the historical references to "Soto" and believed this woman to be his daughter. The Clatsop term for all whites was *Tlon-hon-nipts* ("of those who drift ashore"), which Smith judged to be "a name of first impression suggested by the conditions under which they first met that race of people."[53]

Smith inherited some Chinese coins with square holes in the center, strung

51. John Dunmore, *French Explorers in the Pacific*, vol. 1, *The Eighteenth Century* (London and New York, 1965), p. 16.

52. Franz Boas, *Chinook Texts* (Washington, D.C., 1894), pp. 275–78, collected in 1890–91 at Bay Center, Washington, from Charles Cultee, descendent of the Clatsop, Katlamat, and Tinneh tribes, one of the last remaining speakers of Chinook.

53. Smith, "Address," pp. 443–44.

together with wampum, which the Clatsop called "Konapee's money." A similar coin and shell ornament was acquired about 1900 from "Cheesht," an aged Clatsop woman living at Shoalwater Bay, north of the mouth of the Columbia, who said that when her great-great-grandmother was a child, five white men were marooned along the coast, from whom the coins derived. The castaways remained with the Clatsop a long time but eventually went up the Columbia and never returned. Cheesht knew about the legends of Nehalem and insisted that there was no connection between the two traditions. The coins were identified as minted during the reign of K'ienlung (1735–95).[54]

What to make of all this? The gradual intertwining of the Nehalem and Clatsop is a historically and linguistically documented process.[55] If "Soto" were descended on his maternal line from a Spanish castaway at Nehalem and his father were from a European fur-trading vessel wrecked near Seaside, all the evidence would fit neatly together. Whether this hypothesis is correct we may never know.

As to the ultimate destiny of the castaways who ascended the Columbia, the trail does not end there. Bancroft relates: "Long ago the natives of the upper Columbia had their Spanish guest, who came they knew not where, and went they knew not whither." [56] Unfortunately, his source for this information is today unknown. Major R. D. Gwydir, an Indian agent to the Spokan (*sic*) tribe beginning in 1886, learned of a visit by white men "very many years" before the coming of Lewis and Clark.[57]

A connection has been suggested between traditions of castaways departing inland seeking settlements of their own kind and information reaching the western perimeter of civilization. Major Robert Rogers's conviction that a route existed from the upper Missouri to a "River of the West" is suspected by J. M. Barry to have derived from testimony of an overland traveler from the Columbia; Barry believes that Rogers possibly learned of this in 1760 upon visiting Fort Michilimackinac. The historian sees this as an explanation for the name "Oregon." The term first appeared in Jonathan Carver's journal, 1766–68, referring to the "Great River of the West." Carver was sent out by Rogers, who no doubt shared with him all his knowledge of the region.[58] A Spanish origin for "Oregon" is not warranted on the basis of "Konapee," since it seems likely that the castaways

---

54. Judge James Wickersham of Tacoma, Washington, as cited by Hult, *Lost Mines*, p. 10.

55. Boas, *Chinook Texts*, p. 5.

56. Hubert H. Bancroft, *History of the Northwest Coast*, 2 vols. San Francisco, 1886–88, 2 : 532n.

57. J. Neilson Barry, "Spaniards in Early Oregon," *WHQ* 23 (1932) : 30.

58. Ibid., pp. 32–33. "Oregón" is an archaic spelling of *orejón* ("big ear"), meaning artificially enlarged ear lobe. For various opinions upon this topic, see the articles by Elliott, Galvani, Lewis, Meyers, and Rees listed in the bibliography under "Other Works Utilized."

among the Clatsop who disappeared up the Columbia were not from the beeswax vessel.

If the first Europeans to set foot on the northwest coast were Spanish castaways, there were no consequences of the event other than the minor cultural and genetic effect noted upon the Indians of the immediate area. The Spaniards did not suceed in communicating word of it to their distant homeland. The terror, deprivations, and despair that Captain Zabalburú and his unknown companions experienced on lonesome Nehalem spit and their violent end are scenes that probably can never be documented at greater length, but may be imagined with little difficulty. When the *San Francisco Xavier* failed to arrive in Acapulco, it was fruitless to search the vast Pacific for it. The Spanish had no recourse but to accept its disappearance as a tribute exacted by the merciless sea. Centuries later, a few fragments give some idea of the ship's fate, a chilling drama that predates the known history of the Pacific Northwest. That corsairs may have been implicated in this episode reaffirms an important point: Spain's rivals had access to that coastline—scantily documented as this fact may seem. Madrid's conviction that, by a policy of secrecy and neglect, she could retain hegemony over the vast Pacific, and with it the west coast of North America beyond Cape Mendocino, was illusory. The illusion could endure only so long as Spain's European rivals did not rise to their opportunity.

# 3 The Iberian Thrust to Alta California and Alaska, 1769–1775

MADRID did not shake off her lethargy about exploring the northwest coast of America, to which she so long assumed and asserted a claim of ownership, until rivals posed a tangible threat of encroaching upon the territory and endangering more valued regions in New Spain. Evidence of foreign activities on the northwestern frontier stirred Spanish authorities into action where the possibility of discovering fabled wealth, christianizing pagan nations, and satisfying geographical curiosity had failed. The blow that shook Spain's confidence at being able to conserve to itself the North Pacific and the western portions of North America came from a totally unanticipated quarter—Siberia.

In the 1680s, under Peter the Great, Russian sovereignty expanded rapidly across northern Asia, with its economic basis exploitation of that area's immense wealth in furs. Intensive hunting and depletion in successive regions of fur-bearing animals led fur traders to extend their range ever eastward. Soon after the wave of conquest reached the Pacific, Vitus Bering, a Dane in the tsar's service, explored the Asian shoreline northward, discovering in 1728 the strait that came to bear his name. To ascertain its relationship to North America, Bering organized an expedition out of Petropavlovsk in 1741 with himself on the *St. Peter* and Aleksei Chirikov commanding the *St. Paul*. The two captains lost contact, but both traversed the North Pacific far enough south to bypass the Aleutian Islands. At its southernmost point, the *St. Paul* reached 47° north latitude (approximately opposite the mouth of the Columbia, but far at sea), and Chirikov first sighted land at 56° 15′ north. On July 15, he logged a position of 55° 21′ north, within sight of land, the farthest documented point of Russian advance toward California until after 1800. At Chatham Strait, sixty miles south of Sitka, Chirikov sent pilot Abraham Dementiev ashore with ten men to reconnoiter and fill water barrels. They disappeared around a headland and were never heard from again. Six days later, the boatswain and three men with the remaining boat went in search of the first, and likewise failed to return. Chirikov had no alternative but to forgo landing or taking possession. On his homeward voyage he discovered Adak, one of the southernmost Aleutians, the great arc of which dips to the same latitude as northern Vancouver Island and London.

Bering's first landfall, considerably north of Chirikov's, was near the majestic peak he named Mount St. Elias. He made no attempt to go ashore or take possession. On the return voyage he discovered portions of the Aleutian chain. The *St. Peter* ran aground on an island off Siberia, and Bering and many companions died during the winter from scurvy and exposure. Some of the castaways were able to survive, however, thanks to the abundance of sea otters on the island; they found the animals so unacquainted with humans that they could be approached and slain with clubs. In spring the survivors from the *St. Peter* built a rude craft and returned to civilization with a cargo of 900 pelts. The elevated price these brought in Chinese markets set off the search for more, and soon Russian vessels were frequenting the westernmost Aleutians.

*Enhydra lutris* was the lodestone which, virtually overnight, drew the civilized world to the northwest coast. Now an endangered species, in Bering's time the sea otter ranged from Kamchatka to Baja California. A relative of land otters, minks, and other mustelines, rather than seals or sea lions, it is adapted to an oceanic life by webbed feet, insulating folds of fat, and long-hafted fur. A swift swimmer, able to submerge minutes at a stretch, the sea otter forages in the shallows upon sea urchins, molluscs, crabs, and seaweed. It spends much time floating on its back, paws closed over its face, or employing small stones brought from the bottom as anvils to crack open mussels and clams, one of the rare instances of tool use in a nonhuman species. Having an ungainly gait, it remains at sea most of the time, mating and giving birth the year around atop thick kelp beds in areas of ten to twenty-five fathoms. The pup is carried under its mother's arm until able to swim, and is left on the kelp while she dives. The entangled stalks keep away marauding sharks and killer whales. Always wary of danger, the otters come ashore on rare occasions in isolated spots to sun or take refuge during storms. The coldness of the Japan Current obviates shedding in the summer, and their fur is of prime quality year around. The loose folds of skin result in a pelt several feet longer than the donor; most pelts average five feet in length, excluding tail, with a rich, brownish-black surface and silvery roots showing when the fur is blown open. They were highly prized by the aborigines for their warmth and beauty.

A lone hunter had little chance of harpooning a sea otter, unless he approached from downwind as it slept. Once alerted, it could be speared only by groups pursuing until it could no longer submerge but must swim helplessly upon the surface. Pods of sea otters were vulnerable to fleets of Aleuts in their skin-covered *bidarkas,* but the hunt was so arduous that in prehistoric times the moderate numbers taken constituted no threat to the species. After the coming of the white man, pelts of all sizes had trading value, and the female's unwillingness to abandon her young proved the species' undoing. When alarmed she would seize her pup by the scruff and dive. Its squeal when they surfaced guided the hunter to his prey, and when the mother tired both were slain.[1]

The species first entered international trade when introduced to China by the Spanish. In 1733 Father Sigismundo Taraval described great numbers at Cedros Island on the west coast of Baja California—so docile that seamen clubbed them to death with sticks. Several skins were cured and remitted to Mexico City.[2] Pelts from Baja California were soon being sent to China by way of Manila, but the trade never became very important because, once the creature learned to distrust humans, the natives were not able to provide much of a supply. When the Russians reached the Pacific, they soon built up a thriving commerce in pelts with China. Sea otter became the imperial fur, prized in the extreme by the royal family, mandarins, and wealthy classes for its warmth and glossy beauty. Even tails were fashioned into mittens, caps, and trim for gowns. For a century the sea otter trade would dominate commerce in the North Pacific. However, Europeans had to rely on the skill and endurance of natives possessing the weapons and vessels adapted for such prey, and the symbiosis between trader and native hunter imposed a pattern deeply influencing the earliest chapter of the history of the Pacific Northwest.

The first Russians coming to the Aleutians were a ragged, poorly outfitted lot, sailing in clumsy, makeshift vessels of planks sewn together with thongs. The natives, who hunted sparingly because their needs were limited, had few pelts for trading. In any case, the *promyshleniki,* or "free-lance exploiters of natural resources," carried few trade goods, and they devised a more direct way of securing skins, descending upon villages by surprise and compelling the men to hunt by holding their women as hostages. The "traders" passed their time consuming quantities of fiery drink and propagating a hybrid generation afflicted with tuberculosis and venereal disease, while Aleut males scoured surrounding waters knowing that until they returned with sufficient catch they could not rejoin their women. Fleets of five to fifteen *bidarkas* would approach the prey from downwind. The man in the stern paddled noiselessly while his companion poised to hurl a lance with a detachable, barbed point connected by cord to a bladder that prevented the prey from diving deep or fleeing too far.

Within a decade, cargoes from the Aleutians grossed millions of dollars, and the trade became important to the Siberian economy, providing a stimulus for Russian expansion into America, with seal, walrus, fox, mink, and ermine adding to the take. Soon several independent companies were flourishing. In 1748 an imperial decree imposed upon the Aleut the *yasak,* a

1. Victor B. Scheffer, "The Sea Otter on the Washington Coast," *PNQ* 31 (1940) : 377–80.

2. Adele Ogden, *The California Sea Otter Trade, 1784–1848* (Berkeley and Los Angeles, 1941), p. 2.

system of taxation dating from Genghis Khan's code of laws, exacting tribute equal to one-tenth the annual yield in peltry. Henceforth, a tribute collector accompanied every trading vessel. Natives not producing the tribute, for which they were given small paper vouchers, or not able to show such receipts upon demand, could expect reprisals or even death. Revolts were frequent but in the end unsuccessful and discouraged by swift and cruel retaliation. Despite this extortion, the Aleut benefited from the symbiosis in that he gained an advantage over neighboring peoples. The massacres and oppression of the early decades gave way to cooperation in exploiting furry resources in others regions. With Aleuts as warriors, the Muscovites extended operations to other areas where native hostility posed an obstacle. Every decade their range would extend farther eastward, as described later, in sequence with rival Spanish, British, and American activities. What must be underscored is that Russian subjects would not revisit the area seen by Chirikov near Sitka or touch the coastline southeast of there until 1799, when Muscovite activities entered a new and—from their rivals' viewpoint —ominous phase of expansion.

### SPANISH ALARM OVER RUSSIAN DISCOVERIES

French astronomer Louis Delisle de la Croyère accompanied Chirikov in 1741 and perished on the return from hardships endured. His papers fell to a brother, Joseph Delisle, astronomer of the Imperial Academy of St. Petersburg, who returned to Paris, assumed a professorship at the Collège Royal, and commenced publicizing the importance of Russian discoveries in the North Pacific. A member of the royal academies of science of Paris, London, Berlin, and Stockholm, he enjoyed international renown and in 1750 delivered a paper defending the legitimacy of Fonte's account of a voyage through a northwest passage. Delisle and his brother-in-law published several maps combining authentic Russian data with their interpretation of Fonte's strait.[3] They included the legendary concepts of Fu Sang, Quivira, Cíbola, a Sea of the West, Martín Aguilar's river, and Juan de Fuca's strait, resulting in a revival of interest in a northwest passage.

Russian activities and the persistent search by English mariners for a passage through North America did not go unnoticed in Spain and Spanish America. A work published in Madrid in 1757 demonstrated detailed knowledge of these subjects and revealed an acute preoccupation with the threat posed by foreign encroachments on Spanish territory, endeavoring to show why missionary activity should be extended into Alta California and urging settlements at San Diego, Monterey Bay, or near Cape Mendocino

3. For the publications of Delisle and Buache on the subject, see the bibliography under "Other Nationalities on the Northwest Coast."

to counter foreign colonization.[4] Another warning was sounded by a prominent Spanish Franciscan in *I Moscoviti Nella California* (Rome, 1759; republished in Venice a year later). Fray José Torrubia had lived in Mexico and the Philippines, was worried about maintaining Spanish claims in the Pacific, and was intent upon alerting Madrid to the danger of Russian expansion toward California.

At mid-eighteenth century the Spanish Empire had emerged from the lassitude characterizing the last Hapsburgs, largely as a consequence of a salutary infusion of elements of the French Enlightenment. Shortly before his demise in 1700, Carlos II had designated as successor a grandson of his sister María Teresa, wife of France's "Sun King."[5] The coronation of Philippe, duc d'Anjou, as Felipe V was challenged by Austrian Hapsburgs in the War of Spanish Succession (1701–14), a struggle involving most Western powers. Louis XIV and the house of Bourbon emerged triumphant, invigorating Spain with a current of new ideas and practices, and the dynastic connection—the Family Compact—would be the foundation of Spanish foreign policy during much of the eighteenth century. Felipe V's second spouse was Isabel Farnesio (Elizabetta Farnese), a princess of Parma, one of the strongest-willed and most influential women of her time. Since Felipe had sons by a deceased first wife, it became the queen's dominant passion to seek crowns in Italy for her children. Her oldest son, Carlos, was placed on the throne of Naples and Sicily, and his younger brother, Felipe, inherited the Duchy of Parma. (Generations later, Spain's continued concern for Parma would influence western North America.) At Felipe V's death in 1746, his oldest son ascended the throne as Fernando VI but died in 1759 without male issue, whereupon the crown passed to his half-brother, the king of Naples and Sicily, who became Carlos III of Spain. Governing the smaller kingdom had served as a useful apprenticeship for larger responsibilities, and Carlos III proved one of the most capable men ever to govern the Spanish Empire—surely the most outstanding Bourbon. The reforms, improvements, augmented revenues, the strengthened defenses with which he and his able ministers are credited brought the empire to an apex of power, organization, and relative efficiency (considering handicaps of distance and the unwieldiness of tradition) rivaled only by the Golden Age in the time of Carlos V and Felipe II, two centuries earlier.

Russian fur trade in the Aleutians and its by-product, greater geographical knowledge of the North Pacific as reflected in Russian cartography,

---

4. Andres Marcos Burriel, ed., *Noticia de la California, y de su conquista temporal, y espiritual hasta el tiempo presente. Sacada de la historia manuscrita . . . por el Padre Miguel Venegas* (Madrid, 1757), passim.

5. For a genealogy of the Spanish Bourbons, see appendix F.

eventually drew official Spanish attention. Diplomatic relations between Madrid and St. Petersburg, suspended for two decades, were reestablished in 1760 when Carlos III named the marqués de Almodóvar ambassador to the court of Peter III. In 1761 Almodóvar first reported on the subject of Russian activities in the North Pacific, in response to a direct query from Madrid. His account of the 1741 activities of Bering and Chirikov is so detailed he must have had access to excellent sources, committing what surely would have been considered espionage, had the tsar known of it, to obtain the data. Almodóvar minimized the menace to Spanish America from Russian maritime expeditions, a danger he considered "today so remote as hardly to merit consideration," and he sent a map of the North Pacific published by the Royal Academy of Sciences of St. Petersburg, 1758, showing the extent of discoveries in Alaska.[6]

A conspiracy in 1762 eliminated Peter and elevated to power his German-born empress, Catherine II, who took a more active interest in expanding Russian activities in North America. Almodóvar's successor in St. Petersburg, the vizconde de la Herrería, sent disturbing reports of new discoveries in the Aleutians and organization of Russian stock companies for the exploitation of North America. He warned of a new expedition, to be led by a Colonel Blensner, and remitted another copy of the 1758 map as proof of the danger to territory claimed by His Catholic Majesty.[7]

For centuries, Madrid had been complacent about its claim to all lands in America bordering on the Pacific. The original division of the New World by papal bull in 1493 and the Spanish-Portuguese Treaty of Tordesillas (1494), followed by discoveries of hosts of conquistadores and navigators carrying the banner of His Catholic Majesty had led the Spaniards to assume that the Mar del Sur could be preserved as a Spanish lake, proscribed to mariners of other nations. Depredations by foreign corsairs did little to dispel Madrid's convictions. Elsewhere, bits and pieces of empire had been whittled away by Dutch, British, and French interlopers, particularly in the Caribbean. Such encroachments usually commenced with little more than pirate lairs or camps of logwood cutters. Spain consistently refused to recognize such establishments as legitimate, and, indeed, until Cromwell's forces seized Jamaica in 1655, these inroads were usually confined to islets or coasts that Spanish settlers disdained as undesirable or insignificant. Moreover, the pressures of European rivalry, diplomacy, and warfare made Madrid acquiesce to such losses. The Treaty of Westphalia (1648), ending

6. Almodóvar to Ricardo Wall, St. Petersburg, October 7, 1761, SpAGI (Estado, Amer. Gen. 1, 83), T in DLC.

7. Vizconde de la Herrería to marqués de Grimaldi, St. Petersburg, March 30, 1764, and Sept. 18, 1764, SpAGI (Amer. Gen. 1–83).

the Thirty Years' War, forced Madrid to accept the presence of tiny Dutch outposts in the Caribbean. The Treaty of Madrid, by which England and Spain agreed to each other's territory on the basis of *uti possidetis* in 1670, legitimized British claims to a number of Caribbean islands. The War of the League of Augsburg and Treaty of Ryswick (1697) cost Spain the western half of Santo Domingo, today's Haiti, wrested from Spanish control by buccaneers. Despite such setbacks, Madrid endeavored to prevent other nations from making settlements in unoccupied areas it claimed by right of prior discovery. By mid-eighteenth century, erstwhile Spanish hegemony over sea routes in the Pacific had diminished considerably, and the threats were no longer confined to pinpricks by occasional pirates. British and French discoveries in Oceania foretold the futility of Spanish hopes to exclude other nations from the Pacific.

Dynastic conflict and imperial rivalry in North America led to the Seven Years' War (1756–63), the "French and Indian War" of American history books. Although it was a worldwide struggle, its major consequence was to determine who would gain the upper hand in North America, and the Treaty of Paris altered extensively the political boundaries upon that vast prize. The English had captured Havana and Manila, and to redeem those places Spain had to cede all claims to territory east of the Mississippi, with the exception of the title to the "island" of New Orleans, between the Mississippi and Lake Pontchartrain. The cession involved ancient and cherished pretensions to Florida, which Spain considered vital to control of the Caribbean. Carlos III had wished to continue the war in hope of recovering Gibraltar, but France persuaded him to make the forfeiture by ceding to Spain the immense colony of Louisiana. Since in mercantilist theory extensive colonies constituted the principal source of wealth, Madrid's expectations from control of all North America west of the Mississippi were running high when word arrived portending a challenge from the Muscovites.

Active Spanish expansion toward the northwest coast resumed when a renewed report from Herrería reached Madrid early in 1768 indicating that the empress persisted in extending Russian dominion in the New World and had ordered additional explorations—the more significant, Herrería felt, because preparations were enveloped in the greatest secrecy.[8] The Muscovites were said to have reached the mainland, "making a landing in

---

8. Herrería to Grimaldi, Moscow, November 31, 1767, SpAGI (Estado, Amer. Gen. 1–83), original in cipher, with translation interlined, T in DLC. The rumors probably concerned preparations for the official expedition of the *St. Catherine* and the *St. Paul* (Krenitzin and Levashev) to the Aleutians in 1768, chronicled by William Coxe, *Account of the Russian Discoveries Between Asia and America* (London, 1780).

a spot seemingly populated by Savages, with whom they fought, with the death of 300 Russians." [9]

Prior to this message, an effort was already underway in Mexico to counter Russian activities, fruit of the vigorous planning of Visitador José de Gálvez and Viceroy Carlos Francisco de Croix, marqués de Croix. Gálvez would emerge as the person most responsible for Spanish colonization of Alta California and extension of Spanish activities to Alaska. Born in 1720 of provincial gentry in Mancharavialla, near Málaga, the intense Andalusian's energy and capability elevated him rapidly. As inspector general, he arrived in New Spain in 1765 with almost unlimited powers to examine and reform administration, tribunals of justice, and collection of revenues. At once he commenced visiting the provinces, giving much attention to Sonora, where an Indian revolt menaced frontier settlements and figured heavily in his deliberations about the larger issue of defending the entire perimeter from Louisiana to the Californias. His alarm over Russian activities came from Lieutenant General Antonio Ricardos, who provided details on the subject. Before Ricardos left for Madrid in 1767, Gálvez agreed that the general should urge the ministry to extend Spanish dominion northward to protect the exposed coast of New Galicia, as the region northwest of New Spain was then called.[10] Alarm over the status of the northwestern frontier led to the formation of a junta in January 1768. Its members—the viceroy, archbishop, judges of the Audiencia, and other leading officials—entrusted Gálvez with countering the danger from foreign encroachments.

Viceroy and visitador drafted a *"plan"* expressing, better than any other document, the theory behind the effort that would colonize Alta California, explore to the Aleutians, and occupy Nootka, to reach the high water mark of Spanish territorial extension in America. If Cortés's successors had continued with the same perseverance, they declared, the light of the Gospel and the dominion of the kings of Spain would have reached the ultimate and still unknown edges of the immense American continent. To revitalize the process of expansion, they proposed establishment of a General Command of the Interior Provinces, comprising Sonora, Sinaloa, New Vizcaya (Durango), and the Californias. This reorganization would eventually allow for the repayment of a portion of the vast sums that the area had cost the royal treasury since its discovery; and the new governmental structure would be less expensive than another viceregency in Guadalajara. The commandant of the Interior Provinces should have complete authority, indispensable

9. Grimaldi to Viceroy Carlos Francisco de Croix, marqués de Croix. January 23, 1768, MxAGN (Reales Cédulas y Ordenes, vol. 92), fol. 58, AT.

10. "Providencias de Gálvez en su visita," August, 1773, SpAGI (Estado 34–9) The author, probably Gálvez's secretary Viniegra, thought Ricardo's warning led to the royal order of January 23, 1768; Herbert Ingram Priestly, *José de Gálvez, Visitor-General of New Spain (1765–1771)* (Berkeley, 1916), pp. 245–46.

at such a remote distance, to seize opportunities heretofore lost for want of effective action. Local government would give "spirit and movement to territories so extensive, abundant and rich by nature, that they may in a few years constitute a new Empire equal to, or better than this one of Mexico," provinces "without a doubt the most abundant and rich in minerals of any discovered so far in North America." An active and able commandant could forestall foreigners establishing a colony in Monterey or another of the good ports in the west coast.

British efforts to find the Northwest Passage were notorious.

> England, owner now, as a result of the late war, of Canada and a great part of Louisiana, will spare no expense, diligence or effort to advance discoveries of the French toward Lake Boyes, from which flows the River of the West, directing its course toward the sea of the same name, and if it disembogues there or in the South Sea, or is—perhaps—the famous Colorado River that forms the Gulf of Californias, there is no doubt that in any case we have the English very close to our towns of New Mexico, and not very far from the west coast of this continent.[11]

The report also underscored the danger from Russia, as manifested by published accounts from which it appeared that the Muscovites were engaged in traffic on a continent or island only 800 leagues from the Californias. English and Dutch corsairs raiding west coast ports doubtless acquired knowledge of bays in Baja California, and "it could not be deemed impossible, or even very difficult, that one of the two nations, or the Russians, when least expected, might establish a colony in the Port of Monterey, and possessing in it such proportions and commodities as might be desired, we would see our North America invaded and disputed from the South Sea as it is from the North." Spain must take the precaution of planting settlements at Monterey and other appropriate ports. The Interior Provinces should be administered temporarily from Chihuahua until a capital could be established in the heart of the new territory, near the Gila River. "Certain it is," the *plan* concluded, "that in no part of America are there such beautiful proportions or such abundance to be harvested as in the confines of Sonora and the California missions, because the nations of Indians are numerous and their natural inclinations the most apt for persuasion of the infallible truth of the Catholic Faith." [12] Gálvez and de Croix envisioned a new realm someday surpassing Mexico itself, centered on the rivers flowing into the Gulf of California and embracing all the American Southwest

11. Viceroy Marqués de Croix and José de Gálvez, "Plan para la erección de gobierno y comandancia general que comprenda la península de California y las provincias de Sinaloa, Sonora y Nueva Vizcaya," Mexico City, January 23, 1768, SpAGI (V, Guad, 252, 39 and Indif. Gen. 1713), fol. 2v, AT.

12. Ibid., fol. 3, AT.

and northwestern Mexico. The project led to settlement of Alta California and Arizona, whose wealth exceeded the Spaniards' wildest expectations. But its larger goals were much too advanced for the eighteenth century, and in its prematurity the effort would fall short of establishing a locus of power in the Far West of sufficient strength to keep the area within the Spanish Empire.

### THE CHOICE OF SAN BLAS AS A BASE OF OPERATIONS

As early as 1767 Gálvez conceived the utility of equipping a port on the Gulf of California as a base for naval operations, ship construction, and the embarkation of troops and supplies for the Sonora campaigns. He sent Manuel Rivero Cordero to examine the extant ports, and San Blas, a small town on an inlet some 140 miles due west of Guadalajara, was chosen as the most promising site.[13] Its selection would have a far-reaching effect on events to follow. The visitador was en route there when, a day beyond Guadalajara, a special courier overtook him bearing the royal order of January 23, 1768, for an expedition to occupy Monterey Bay and take measures against the danger that the Russians "might make landfalls on the coast of Northern California." [14] It took Gálvez eight more days to reach the edge of the Mexican plateau and the dank, mosquito-infested mangrove swamp paralleling the sea and enclosing San Blas. He must have perceived the town's handicaps. The definitive study of San Blas concludes that it "should never have been selected as the prime naval station for Spanish forces on the Pacific coast." [15]

San Blas, due east of Cape San Lucas, is mentioned in early accounts of the west coast. Nicolás de Cardona and Pedro Porter y Casanate had bases of operations in that area. Three miles southwest lies Santiago de Matanchel (now Matanchén), the port sustaining Baja California missions during the early eighteenth century, but its roadstead is an open bay offering no protection as anchorage or shipyard, and after 1768 it virtually ceased to be used. The harbor at San Blas is no more than an *estero,* or tidewater channel. Less than a mile from the sea, the anchorage is excessively shallow at low tide and subject to constant silting. Every storm alters the characteristics of the bay-mouth bar—a hazard for vessels entering or leaving. Half a mile inland from the town lies "El Basilio," a flat-topped bluff, steep-sided on the seaward face where, by 1773, a noble complex of buildings took shape. Still

13. Marqués de Croix, "Ynstrucción que ha de observar el Comandante Comisionado Don Manuel Rivero para la población de San Blas y havilitación del puerto de este nombre en la costa del Mar del Sur," Mexico City, January 11, 1768, MxAGN (Marina 44).

14. Gálvez, "Ynforme," Dec. 31, 1771, cited by Michael Thurman, "The Establishment of the Department of San Blas and its Initial Naval Fleet: 1767–1770," *HAHR* 43 (1963) : 66.

15. Michael Thurman, *The Naval Department of San Blas, New Spain's Bastion for Alta California and Nootka, 1767 to 1798* (Glendale, Calif., 1967), p. 31.

to be seen are the ruins of a church and an arched customs house, fronting on an esplanade overlooking the port. At the apex of naval activities on the northwest coast, San Blas had a population of 20,000, and in 1791 official personnel numbered 772.[16]

Four factors determined the choice of San Blas as a naval base: (1) it was convenient for expeditions to both Sonora and Alta California; (2) it had a sheltered harbor; (3) it enjoyed access to fresh water streams of year-around flow; and (4) it was surrounded by an abundance of hardwoods promising an ample supply of timbers for ship construction. An unfortunate concomitant was that San Blas owed its timber to its climate: from November to May the humidity is relatively low, but from June to October the rainy season can make life exceedingly difficult. Swamps separating it from high ground choke with water, and transit was almost impossible, except by canoe.[17] With the approach of summer, always oppressive on the Tropic of Cancer at sea level, hordes of mosquitoes invade from the surrounding jungle. Early accounts of San Blas are full of complaints about this plague, and about the high incidences of fever, and of tropical ailments endangering the lives of everyone frequenting the port. Expeditions had to be equipped and sent out between November and May, when there was access from the interior and life in San Blas was tolerable. One cannot fail to be impressed with the obstacle to efficiency constituted by this single factor for the Department of San Blas, which included the Californias and Nootka. Naval officers adopted the practice of residing in nearby Tepic and descending to the base only during winter months; expeditions northward were scheduled for departure and arrival at that time of year. Some forty miles away, Tepic lies in a verdant valley at the foot of the volcano Sangarguey. The altitude insures a moderate climate year around. The inadequacies of San Blas as a naval base were obvious to Spanish officials; and in 1773 a great storm made the entrance more shallow and dangerous. For several years there were plans to build a port elsewhere, but the other sites considered had similar or worse defects. The transfer controversy raged anew from 1792 to 1794, but advocates of relocation were outvoted by those opposed to abandoning improvements at San Blas.[18]

### THE COLONIZATION OF ALTA CALIFORNIA

Shortly after his arrival in San Blas, the visitador summoned a council to decide how to implement instructions for establishing the Naval Department of San Blas and occupying Alta California. The department had been

16. Edward L. Inskeep, "San Blas, Nayarit: An Historical and Geographic Study," *JW* 2 (1963) : 140; Thurman, *San Blas,* p. 349n.

17. For life under such conditions in nearby Mexcaltitán, see W. E. Garrett, "Mexico's Little Venice," *National Geographic Magazine* 133 (1968) : 876–88.

18. Thurman, *San Blas,* pp. 108, 112, 223, 227, 305, 356.

designated as an independent administrative unit, not subject to the Audiencia of Guadalajara, and the commandant would be responsible directly
to the viceroy and the Ministry of the Marine. Present were Gálvez, officials
of his retinue, an engineer and cosmographer, and several pilots with experience on the west coast of Mexico, including Juan Pérez, who would play a
primary role in exploring the northwest coast. Plans were drafted for a
series of voyages with the double objective of supporting the Sonora campaign and expanding into Alta California. Supplies, soldiers, missionaries,
and settlers would be transferred to towns in Baja California. From there,
a column would march overland to meet an expedition by sea to San Diego
Bay.

Gálvez submitted to Fray Junípero Serra, president of the Franciscan
missions of Baja California, a plan for a chain of missions at intervals of
one day's ride along the route to Monterey, predicting that Christianizing
the Indians would lead to settlements thwarting any Russian colonies
along that coast. The visitador personally attended to all details and embarked for Baja California on May 24, making La Paz his headquarters
while waiting for the vessels to come there for final outfitting. The *San
Carlos,* under Vicente Vila, sailed from La Paz in January, and the following month Juan Pérez and the *Príncipe* set out from San Bernabé, at Cape
San Lucas, to carry out the historic feat of planting the first permanent
settlements in Alta California. The overland expedition left in March, commanded by Fernando Rivera y Moncada and accompanied by Franciscan
Juan Crespi and a party of soldiers; a second group followed in May, led
by Gaspar de Portolá and Padre Serra. Land and sea expeditions met at
San Diego Bay, and proceeded separately to Monterey. Portolá, designated
first governor of Alta California, led a party northward in search of Rodrigues Cermenho's "Bahía de San Francisco" and discovered what had
eluded previous explorers by sea: the broad estuary of San Francisco Bay.

Charles Chapman asserts that the Russian threat was but one of several
reasons impelling colonization of Alta California. Reports from St. Petersburg may have accelerated such plans, but Chapman thinks it probable
that as early as 1767 Gálvez had decided to occupy Monterey, "before the
occurrence of the events usually alleged as causing the expeditions of 1769,"
and he traces the desire for expansion into Alta California in a series of royal
decrees throughout the early eighteenth century.[19] But until Gálvez, a man
of exceptional zeal and energy, arrived upon the scene simultaneously with
the Russian threat, such aspirations were not translated into action.

Coinciding with Gálvez's efforts, warning arrived from another source
pointing to the need for occupying not only Monterey but the coastline

19. Charles E. Chapman, *The Founding of Spanish California: The Northwestward Expansion
of New Spain, 1687–1773* (New York, 1916), p. 81; see also pp. 68, 84.

far to the north. Pedro Calderón y Henríquez, a judge in the Audiencia of Manila for the preceding twenty-five years, sent a memorial to the ministry in 1768 asserting that if Russian explorers sailed southward along the coast as far as 44°, as seemed imminent, they were likely to encounter a large river (the legendary Río de Martín Aguilar) giving access to the interior, New Mexico, and the Great Lakes of the St. Lawrence. He emphasized that settlement and garrisoning of Monterey were essential to discovery and control of the coastline beyond.[20]

Having set in motion his most important project, Gálvez returned to the mainland to inspect progress of the campaign against the rebellious Seris, Pimas, and Apaches. Their hit-and-run tactics, laying waste outlying settlements, defied resistance by conventional methods and posed a serious obstacle to plans for extending effective dominion beyond the Gila and Colorado rivers and into Alta California. Frustrations of the Sonora campaign undermined the visitador's health and in July he took ill, complaining of fever, his state being described as "profound melancholy." In Baja California his secretary, Juan Manuel de Viniegra, had noted signs of impending trouble. Intent upon countering the Muscovite threat, for a time Gálvez insisted upon going to Monterey himself. Viniegra would later report: "So stuck in the head did he carry this goblin that several days after disembarking in California he wrote the Archbishop that he had seen Russians."[21] His condition had so deteriorated by late August that, dictating a letter from his sickbed at Los Álamos, the visitador predicted it would be his last, commending to the viceroy those dependent upon him and urging aid and protection for the new establishments in California.[22] After a brief rally, he lost touch with reality, claimed to have received a message direct from St. Francis of Assisi, and threatened some of his officers with death, giving his retinue cause for grave concern and embarrassment. Confinement and bleeding only made him rant uncontrollably, imagine he was king of Prussia, Sweden, and even the "Eternal Father," scandalizing everyone within earshot. Subordinates endeavored to conceal his derangement, hoping it would pass, but word spread and disheartened everyone in the campaign. In March, when his condition had not improved, aides took

20. Pedro Calderón y Henríquez to Manuel de Rada y Arrieta, Madrid, April 14, 1768; English trans. by H. R. Wagner, "Memorial of Pedro Calderón y Henríquez Recommending Monterey as a Port for the Philippine Galleons with a View to Preventing Russian Encroachment in California," *CHSQ* 23 (1944) : 219–25.

21. [Juan Manuel de Viniegra] "Providencias," fol. 9v, AT. The mania that led Gálvez "to see Russians behind every rock" had no foundation in reality, but it seems to have given rise to a historical weed found in a number of respected textbooks in Latin American and American history, crediting the Muscovites with frequenting the California-Oregon coast in the 1760's, an assertion not corroborated by Russian or Spanish documentation.

22. Gálvez to the Marqués de Croix, Real de los Álamos, August 22, 1769, SpAGI (V, Aud. Guad. 417).

him to Chihuahua. Once away from Sonora, he recovered completely and in April 1770 undertook the return to Mexico City.

Although reports of Gálvez's malady had reached de Croix, the episode was hushed up, and the visitador's secretaries were ordered to refrain from writing about the expedition.[23] The effort was successful in Gálvez's lifetime, for his political star continued to rise. He returned to Spain in 1772 and three years later married a third time. That same year, at fifty-nine years of age, he succeeded Julián de Arriaga as minister of Indies, the maximum position of authority over Spain's colonial empire and a post he would occupy for eleven years, giving him an opportunity to continue promoting the effort he had set in motion—expansion of Spanish dominion northward in the Far West.

The visitador's mental crisis is indicative of the depth of his obsession with the territorial impulse and his vulnerability to real or imagined threats to his expansionist dreams. Confronted in the field by problems that were virtually insoluble by available means, his intense, driving personality not surprisingly withdrew from contact with reality—nor is it surprising that his sanity returned once he was bodily removed from the scene of his frustrations.

### PÉREZ REACHES BRITISH COLUMBIA, 1774

Insistent letters from the conde de Lacy, Herrería's successor in St. Petersburg, communicated details of important new discoveries in America, obtained from someone who had "read and handled" (*leído y manejado*) the tsarina's most secret archives. Chirikov was said to have made further explorations in 1769–71 and to have reported that the navigation in the Far North was not as difficult as believed. After a visit to the capital, Chirikov had set forth again on an expedition to North America, the details of which were so secret that Lacy was unable to learn much of them. In a subsequent letter he warned that the tsarina planned to pursue her conquests in the New World and that a project was underway to send a fleet to Kamchatka by way of the Cape of Good Hope.[24] Such messages raised fears in Madrid that the new establishments in Alta California would be insufficient to ward off Muscovite encroachments. Lacy's letters were remitted to Antonio María de Bucareli y Ursua, the viceroy of Mexico, and he was ordered to learn

23. Juan Manuel de Viniegra, "Expedición de Gálvez a California, Sonora y Nueva Vizcaya relatada por su secretario," Madrid, October 10, 1771, SpBN (Ms 4494), fol. 411–530; Priestly, *José de Galvez*, pp. 278–83; Mario Hernández y Sánchez-Barba, *La Ultima Expansión Española en América* (Madrid, 1957), pp. 247–49. The visitador's mental crisis would have gone unrecorded had the secretaries not been jailed for a time, and Viniegra defended his actions with an account of the details.

24. Lacy to Marqués de Grimaldi, St. Petersburg, October 22, 1772, February 7, 1773, and May 11, 1773, SpAGI (Estado 20–1).

whether the purported explorations were going ahead (*si pasan adelante*).[25]

Spanish worries were not confined to the Russians, but included the British as well. Reports reaching Madrid of a projected voyage from England to California across the top of North America alarmed Carlos III, and Bucareli was ordered to take preventive measures against all nationalities, strengthen Alta California outposts, and send expeditions northward to explore the continental coastline. Mere occupation of Alta California could not be expected to check foreign intrusion into the rest of the western portion of the continent, to which Madrid's claims aspired. It would be necessary to scout the coast for foreign activities and determine likely places to establish Spanish settlements and fortifications before foreigners occupied the places of greatest advantage.[26] In response, Bucareli ventured the opinion that "any establishment by Russia, or any other foreign power, on the continent ought to be prevented, not because the king needs to enlarge his realms, as he has within his known dominions more than it will be possible to populate in centuries, but in order to avoid consequences brought by having any other neighbors [there] than the Indians."[27] He discounted reports of Russian trade along the northwest coast, on the assumption that such scantily clad, small, isolated bands as he understood lived in California would be unlikely customers.[28] Nonetheless, he commenced preparing an expedition to push discoveries farther northward, locate Russian settlements if such existed, and determine the extent of their activities. Juan José Pérez Hernández, who was, in the viceroy's opinion, the pilot of greatest experience and ability in the Department of San Blas, was selected to command the effort.

Pérez belonged to the *Cuerpo de Pilotos,* a corps of graduates from a school preparing petty officers for lower ranks in the navy. San Blas had the reputation of being one of the least desirable posts in America, and in 1774 there was no one there above Pérez's rank of frigate ensign.[29] (The ministry had just assigned six lieutenants of the royal navy to New Spain for the express purpose of carrying out operations in the north, but they would not arrive

25. Julián de Arriaga to Viceroy Bucareli, April 11, 1773, SpAGI (Estado 20–1).

26. Narrated in retrospect by Bucareli, June 26, 1776, MxAGN (Corr. Virreyes, ser. 1, vol. 12, no. 2296).

27. Bucareli to Arriaga, July 27, 1773, SpAGI (Estado 20–1), AT; Thurman, *San Blas,* pp. 97, 123.

28. Bucareli to Grimaldi, Mexico City, August 27, 1773, SpAGI (Indif. Gen., Mex. 1630), T in DLC.

29. *Piloto* is roughly equivalent to "pilot"; from second pilot (*piloto de segunda clase*), first pilot (*piloto de primera clase*), frigate ensign (*alférez de fragata*), and ship's ensign (*alférez de navío*), a mariner aspired to frigate lieutenant (*teniente de fragata*), a rank achieved by very few former pilots. Commissioned officers graduated from marine academies as frigate lieutenants and aspired to ship's lieutenant (*teniente de navío*), frigate captain (*capitán de fragata*), and ship's captain (*capitán de navío*). The chief officer of a Spanish ship of this time was the *comandante,* regardless of rank; the *piloto* was a mate; the *pilotín,* a pilot's mate; *contramaestre,* the boat-

until the expedition was well on its way.) The Mallorcan mariner had considerable experience in Pacific waters, having been a pilot on the Manila galleon route, and since participating in the 1769 expedition he had revisited Alta California several times in command of supply vessels. As Pérez's second officer, the viceroy appointed thirty-nine-year-old second pilot Estéban José Martínez, whose role in subsequent events makes him the most controversial figure in chapters to come.

Pérez learned of his selection for the mission through the fiscal commissioner in San Blas, whom the viceroy cautioned to keep preparations "in greatest secret so that nothing gets out about the project." [30] Bucareli remarked directly to Pérez, "By various means I have learned of your eager wishes to carry forward discoveries following the coastline from Monterey, and since these are laudable and proper of one who would perform with honor, they are in my estimation that much more appreciable, because I am animated by the same ideas, because of the advantages that may be derived." [31] The viceroy requested that Pérez explain as soon as possible exactly what he conceived could be accomplished, how high in latitude he intended to go, and how many men would be needed. Somewhat taken aback by the suddenness and dimensions of the responsibility thrust upon him, Pérez replied that he was honored, "but since I had not thought about such an undertaking, I have absolutely nothing ready on that score," to which the viceroy responded that complete instructions would be sent as soon as possible. The frigate ensign's self-confidence soon rallied and he said he intended to reach 45° to 50° of latitude, where he had heard there was a Russian fort, see if it were certain, and return southward, reconnoitering the coastline.[32]

Bucareli's secret instructions are dated December 24, 1773, but Pérez was ordered to keep them sealed and not even read them himself until he had departed from Monterey, last port of call on the northward journey. The voyage would be made in the frigate *Santiago*, alias the *Nueva Galicia*. The 225-ton craft, largest ever built at San Blas and pride of the department for many years, measured only eighty-two feet from prow to stern, with twenty-six feet of beam. Besides Pérez and Martínez, the vessel's complement included a chaplain (the venerable Fray Junípero Serra, returning to his flock at Monterey), a surgeon, boatswain, first and second mate, two carpenters, two caulkers, two stewards, one sergeant of marine artillery, a coxswain,

---

swain; and the *condestable,* the sergeant of marine artillery. Francisco de las Barras de Aragón, *D. Estéban José Martínez, el alumno del Colegio de San Telmo de Sevilla* (Madrid, 1953), p. 4.

30. Bucareli to José del Campo Viergol, commissioner for San Blas, Mexico City, July 18, 1773, MxAGN (Hist. 61–1), AT.

31. Bucareli to Pérez, Mexico City, July 18, 1773, MxAGN (Hist. 61–4), AT.

32. Pérez to Bucareli, San Blas, Aug. 4, 1773, Bucareli to Pérez, Sept. 1, 1773, Pérez to Bucareli, San Blas, Sept. 1, 1773, all in MxAGN (Hist. 61–4).

fourteen gunners, forty-nine seamen, four cooks, and two pages, a total of eighty-four. As armament it carried six bronze cannons and thirty-six muskets with bayonet, five hundred cannon balls, six boxes of cartridges, two boxes of powder, one hundred pounds of musket balls, three hundred flints and thirty-six machetes.[33] The provisions included five and a half tons of jerked beef, thirty-four hundred pounds of dried fish, seventeen tons of hardtack, and half a ton of lard. A sizable portion of the supplies was to be left in Alta California, as the *Santiago* carried provisions which ordinarily would have been taken there by the regular supply ship, then undergoing repairs. Vast quantities of beans, rice, lentils, chickpeas, onions, cheese, and chili peppers provided staples for basic dishes in the Spanish and Mexican menu. In proportionate but smaller quantities the inventory lists such necessities as salt, vinegar, sugar, ham, pork, fine crackers, cinnamon, cloves, saffron, six pounds of pepper, three big boxes of powdered chocolate, twelve barrels of brandy and four of white table wine, plus a barrel of sweet wine for the chaplain's use in the Mass. Two jars of lemon syrup and two of *toquixtle* were included as antiscorbutic measures. On deck, matching the crowding of armament, supplies, and men below, were twelve young bulls, twenty-four sheep, fifteen goats, and seventy-nine chickens. Supplies included enough hay, corn, and chicken feed to husband this menagerie for a good many weeks. An ample store of firewood and sufficient barrels of drinking water to sustain the lot for several months completed the list of stores.[34]

The *Santiago* sailed with the high tide at midnight on January 25, 1774, her objective a closely guarded secret. They lingered twenty-five days at San Diego, and it was May 8 before they reached Monterey, where Fray Junípero disembarked, appointing Franciscans Juan Crespi and Tomás de la Peña Saravia to accompany the expedition northward. Another twenty-six days elapsed at Monterey. The anchor was hoisted finally on June 6, but adverse winds kept Pérez from leaving the bay for eight more days. Until out of sight of the last port of call, he had been constrained from opening the sealed instructions; now his curiosity could be satisfied. "The benevolence of the king," Bucareli declared,

> who put in my care this government of New Spain, not only imposes on me the obligation of conserving these vast domains, but also of

33. Francisco Hijosa, comisario de San Blas, "Nota del estado en que se hallan las embarcaciones de este puerto," MxAGN (Hist. 61, fol. 212–14); idem, "Lista de los oficiales, artilleros, marineros, grumetes, cosineros y pages, que tripulan la fragata de Su Magestad nombrada Santiago, alias la Nueva Galicia," January 22, 1774, MxAGN (Hist. 61), fol. 226–28; Juan Pérez, "Inventario de la fragata Santiago, alias la Nueva Galicia," San Blas, January 23, 1774, MxAGN (Hist. 61), fol. 229–41.

34. Pérez, "Estado y reglamento de rancho, para doce meses," January 23, 1774, MxAGN (Hist. 61), fol. 242–47v.

trying to augment them insofar as possible, by means of new discoveries in unknown areas, so that numerous Indian inhabitants drawn into the sweet, soft, desirable vassalage of His Majesty may be bathed in the light of the Gospel by means of spiritual conquest, to separate them from the utter darkness of the idolatry in which they live and show them the road to eternal salvation, which are the true intentions of these undertakings which animate the pious heart of His Majesty.[35]

Pérez was to sail as far north as he wished, so long as on his return, from at least 60° north latitude, he navigated as close to shore as possible, trying never to lose it from sight and going ashore at such spots as feasible without undue risk. He was prohibited from making any sort of settlement, no matter how easy or advantageous it might seem, but was to take note of likely sites so that they could be found with ease in case colonization plans resulted from his explorations. In places adequate for settlement, he should take possession, using the standard form attached to his instructions, and erect a large wooden cross supported by a cairn of stones hiding a glass bottle, stoppered with pitch, containing a copy of the act of possession signed by the commander, chaplain, and two pilots, "so that in future times this document will be kept and will serve as an authentic testimony." If he found some foreign establishment, he should proceed to a higher latitude to perform the ceremony of possession, "and since it is so important to the service that it be done thus, I charge you especially to treat this matter with all consideration and care which it requires, so as not to spoil the effort by lack of attention." If a foreign settlement were sighted he was to avoid direct contact but observe from a distance, noting location, landmarks, and especially the size and number of vessels there. If another ship were encountered he was to do everything in his power to avoid contact. If this proved impossible, "which must be justified upon return," he should try to hide his objectives. If confronted with superior force and obliged to answer, he should merely say he was taking supplies to California but unfavorable winds had carried him far beyond.

If Pérez found Indians where he went ashore, he was to give them presents from the four boxes of articles carried for that purpose. He should inquire as to their customs, qualities, life, numbers, and neighbors, whether they lived in peace or at war, their religion, idols, sacrifices, and ritual. Likewise, he should seek to know if they had any kind of learning, how they were led and governed, whether they had kings, a republic, or clans, the tributes they paid, and the things they most esteemed. Subsequent articles amounted to a questionnaire about such metals, crops, spices, drugs,

35. Bucareli, Instructions to Juan Pérez, Mexico City, Dec. 24, 1773, MxAGN (Hist. 61–4). AT.

woods, plants, and animals as might be found among the natives. He was to inquire "whether the Indians had seen other ships before, if they know of other people different from themselves, and when; what were their pretensions, if they penetrated inland or followed the coast, if they gave gifts or dealt with them; if some of their belongings were left behind, or signs, and whether they offered to return." It was naïve to expect that all this could be accomplished without knowing the Indian languages, but Bucareli's scientific curiosity paid off when the resulting journals attempted to rise to the challenge, providing treasured ethnological sources.

Pérez and his men were forbidden to take anything from the natives against their will and unless it were in trade or given in friendship. The Indians should be treated with amiability and kindness, the two most powerful means of gaining their friendship and estimation, so they would welcome those who might return to settle, if that were determined necessary. He was to distribute gifts with diplomacy, taking care to give more to chiefs than to their inferiors. He was cautioned to keep good discipline among his crew and be vigilant to see they treated the Indians well, "against whom force should never be used, unless it is necessary to defend yourselves." Under no pretext were the aborigines to be given any cause for hostility or their land to be taken by force. If there were difficulties in taking possession of a certain likely place, the same purpose could be accomplished in another spot nearby. "The recompense for your efforts and of those who accompany you," Bucareli promised, "can be expected from the charity of the king in proportion to your zeal, and the good results that you produce, since I will give account of everything to His Majesty in due time." [36]

Pérez set a northwest course, reaching 50° before veering straight north, which presumably would bring the *Santiago* toward the coast. He knew that Bering and Chirikov had sighted land at that longitude, far to the north, but all concepts of the intervening area were mere speculation. The frigate continued onward day and night, in all weather, and the diaries of Pérez, Martínez, and the two friars reflect the tension, fear, and awareness that if constant vigilance were not observed in the fog and darkness they might find themselves swept onto shoals or against some rocky, wave-tossed coast in the trackless expanse ahead.

They first sighted land on July 18, near the present Alaska-Canada boundary. The following day, off the northernmost of the Queen Charlotte Islands, three canoes came out to greet them, the largest some forty-four feet long and seven feet wide, more than half as long as the frigate. The rowers stroked in cadence to a chant and halted a musket-shot away, singing and dancing to the rhythm of drums and rattles. A brave standing in the prow of the largest canoe sprinkled feathers upon the water, extending his

36. Ibid., AT.

arms wide and then bending them, hands clasped against his chest, in what Pérez interpreted as a gesture of welcome. Shouting and gesticulating, the natives at first ignored all signs to come closer. Martínez finally went to the balcony at the frigate's stern and tossed toward them a cracker wrapped in an attractive handkerchief. At this they came right up to the side and soon were trading with the crew—seal, bear, and sea otter skins for knives, old clothes, and other things from civilization. They seemed very accustomed to haggling, demanded Spanish objects first and then, having made a selection and "caressed it with eyes and hands," insisted upon receiving more than the original bargain or keeping their own merchandise. Pérez concluded that they must already practice barter with their neighbors.[37] He acquired four beautifully decorated woven blankets of snowy white wool—the handsome "Chilkat" blankets of mountain goat fleece portraying monstrous mythical creatures and adorned with long fringe. The Indians refused all enticements to come aboard and followed along as the vessel drifted southward until they were several leagues away from home. Other canoes approached during the afternoon and after dark, eager to acquire trinkets and pieces of metal. Pérez gave them strings of beads and they responded with gifts of dried fish, indicating that the Spanish would be welcome on shore, where they could obtain food and water. The commander's diary indicates that fear of treachery made him hesitate to accept, although the Indians carried no weapons. He stalled with promises of a visit another day. These were the Haida, one of the most advanced cultures of the northwest coast, but their subsequent record of attempting to overpower trading vessels without provocation suggests that Pérez's caution was well advised. The wind and the pronounced current prevented remaining overnight.

The following day Pérez turned northward and revisited the same area. This time more than twenty canoes came out, and some two hundred men, women, and children clamored to trade. The fleet dugouts were elaborately decorated, even the paddles ornamented with elegant carving. Two had twenty rowers apiece. Another pair were loaded with women, as dexterous at maneuvering as the men, although some had babies at the breast. Now they crowded around the frigate without fear, setting up a chant to the beat of many drums. For cloth, beads, and pieces of copper they proffered soft, tanned skins, sea otter pelts, admirably sewn buckskin garments, and more Chilkat blankets. In the canoes the Spanish observed intricately carved wooden boxes with tight-fitting lids, inlaid with mother-of-pearl and adorned with figures of birds, animals, and men, in which the Indians guarded their possessions and newly acquired treasures. At first the natives rejected small knives and pieces of iron, indicating with disdain that they

37. Pérez, "Diario," MxAGN (Hist. 61–12), entry for July 19, 1774.

were too little and that only swords or large chunks of metal would be accepted. When none were forthcoming, they took what was available, seeking in particular pieces with a cutting edge. They already had a few little plaques of metal, half a bayonet, and a piece of sword beaten into a spoon, which Martínez assumed came from spoils of the landing party that Chirikov had lost near there some thirty-three years earlier.[38] The most sought-after objects were the abalone shells that some foresighted sailors had brought from Monterey—giant discs of iridescent blue, green, and pink unknown to colder shores. Shell inlay was a favorite technique among the Haida, but local mollusks offered nothing comparable. In the largest canoe, estimated at fifty-five feet long and eighteen wide, came an old chieftain accompanied by a retinue of some thirty persons, including dancers and drummers rattling and shouting. He took a fancy to the second officer's red cap, and when Martínez made him a present of it, the courtesy was returned with an exquisite cape from his own shoulders. Sent as a present to the viceroy, it was handsomely decorated on one side in black and white, checkerboard fashion, with squares of sea otter fur.[39]

During these sessions both officers took pains to inquire about the topics detailed in Bucareli's instructions, but they could not make themselves sufficiently understood. Although their accounts were limited to what could be gleaned by observation, they are rich in ethnological detail. The journals remark upon what was regarded as native innocence; braves would trade for some cheap trinket the sole garment covering their nakedness, an ample sea otter robe draped across the shoulders. The luxurious pelts excited no unusual interest, and the new owners used them as bedding that evening. But Father Crespi's journal notes, "Some of the sailors who bought cloaks passed a bad night, for having put them on, they found themselves obliged to take to scratching, on account of the bites they suffered from the little animals these pagans breed in their clothing."[40] The men wore their hair long and unkempt, while the women usually had braided tresses; the latter also had perforated lower lips stretched with thin shell discs, increasing in diameter with the age of the wearer. Pérez notes that their chattering made the discs flip up and hit their noses and that they were inordinately fond of metal rings on arms and fingers.

Two braves mustered the courage to come aboard. Escorted around the frigate, expressing great wonder at everything, they halted in the friars' cabin before an image of the Virgin, rapt with admiration; suddenly one

38. Pérez, "Diario," entry for July 21, 1774; Martínez, "Diario," MxAGN (Hist. 61–13), entry for July 20, 1774; "Primera exploración de la costa septentrional de California," SpMN (331), fol. 35–35v.

39. "Ynventario de las prendas cambalachadas con los Yndios," Dec. 27, 1774, MxAGN (Hist. 61–14).

40. Fray Juan Crespi, "Diario," *PHSSC* 2 (1891): 194.

reached out and stroked it, to the priests' considerable dismay. Two sailors jumped down into the canoes and were received with jubilation, daubed with paint, and encouraged to participate in a boisterous dance. At an invitation to go ashore to eat and sleep, however, they hastily declined and clambered back aboard, for the current had carried the becalmed frigate some distance from land and they were reluctant to be taken to the native village unless accompanied by an armed party. Martínez thought this tribe very amiable in appearance and behavior, but they warned him not to go onward, that other tribes would shoot them with arrows and try to kill them. Pérez says he was generous in distributing gifts of bread, cheese, and beads, hoping to ingratiate himself sufficiently to go ashore if the weather permitted. "It was a very pleasant afternoon for everyone but me," he remarks, "for the desire to anchor and the inability to do so for want of a wind had me disquieted, and all the more so seeing that without wind the furious current was taking me away from the coast." "I had thought," he continues, "to anchor in a bay formed by the coast which is protected from the winds on all sides, but since the current and calm deprived me of it, I had to conform myself with the will of God." [41] The *Santiago* remained in the neighborhood four days but was never able to enter this bay. To the north, in what Pérez estimated at 55° north latitude, he observed a promontory which he named "Punta Santa Magdalena" (Cape Muzón, Dall Island, southern tip of the Alaskan panhandle). The logs give a latitude of 55° 30' on July 30. Strong currents and adverse winds kept him from ascending farther, and on July 22 he decided to forgo his attempt to follow the viceroy's instructions to reach 60° north latitude.

Pérez seems to have lacked in full measure the intrepid qualities requisite for meeting the challenges of his mission. He wasted much time at San Diego and Monterey that could have been utilized to better purpose in the Far North. Unable to find a means of reaching a higher latitude and timorous about making a landing, although he needed fresh water and it was important to take formal possession, Pérez did little more than ascertain that in the area surveyed there were a number of offshore islands. He presumed correctly that the continent had not been sighted. The archipelago seemed well populated with diverse tribes eager to trade. The journals describe the scenery as forbidding and too thickly forested to be of apparent value—steep-sided mountains that in most places came down abruptly to the water's edge, an environment of little attraction for those accustomed to the temperate climes of Spain and Mexico. Each day brought the *Santiago* farther southward, sometimes within sight of shore, but more often far at sea, groping in the fog or plowing into giant seas. Fear of being caught by an unfavorable wind and carried into dangerous breakers or reefs deterred

41. Pérez, "Diario," entry for July 21, 1774, AT; Martínez, "Diario,' fol. 2.

Pérez from obeying the viceroy's specific orders to examine the coast carefully, even in the clearest weather, for the heavy vessel had difficulty tacking back and forth in confined channels. The situation became much more hazardous when thick fog crept in to hang about the ship for days, creating a constant threat of wrecking on an uncharted shore.

### THE SANTIAGO AT NOOTKA

Continuing southwest, Pérez sighted what is now called Vancouver Island, but to him and many subsequent explorers it seemed a portion of the continent. Its insular character was not demonstrated until 1792. On August 8 the captain dropped anchor off an opening penetrating into the interior, which he named "Roadstead of St. Lawrence" (*Surgidero de San Lorenzo*). Some fifteen canoes soon encircled the *Santiago* but hesitated to approach. Pérez decided to remain at anchor and enter the waterway the next morning. This was the first documented sighting of Nootka Sound, destined in the next two decades to become the prime focus of international rivalry, for it was held to be the port of greatest strategic importance north of San Francisco Bay.

Near the entrance to the sound the mountains are relatively low and rounded, with occasional flat areas and beaches, but in the interior the maze of narrowing channels is steep-sided and walled in by lofty peaks whose spurs and sides were bevelled by Pleistocene glaciers. At the end of each fjord, a brief beach and flat-bottomed valley leads to a cirque basin on the side of a mountain peak, at the head of the vanished glacier. During earlier millennia the natives evolved a way of life adapted to this habitat, customarily spending spring and summer at small villages near the mouth of the sound and retreating in winter to larger towns at the heads of the fjords, whose lofty walls offered some protection from the gales of the inclement months.

At the very mouth of the sound, inside its northern lip, is a convenient cove separated from the sea by a low neck of land and buttressed by rocky outcrops that curve around and protect against destructive wave action. The natives referred to it as "Uquot," or "Yucuatl," meaning "village exposed to the winds." [42] From time immemorial this was the summer village of a band that in winter lived at the head of Tahsis Canal, deep within the sound. Although Pérez is assumed to have been just outside, the first European to enter the cove would be Captain James Cook, in 1778; he called it "Friendly Harbor," from the cordial reception accorded by its

---

42. [José Cardero], *Relación del viaje hecho por las goletas Sútil y Mexicana en el año de 1792*, 1 vol. and atlas (Madrid, 1802), p. 117 (hereafter cited as *Sútil y Mexicana*). Long attributed to others, its authorship has been established by Donald Cutter, "Early Spanish Artists on the Northwest Coast," *PNQ* 54 (1963) : 153.

dwellers. The native name is assumed to be his source for "Nootka." In subsequent usage, "Friendly Harbor" became "Friendly Cove." Pérez's name for the waterway, "San Lorenzo," was later grafted to "Nootka," becoming "San Lorenzo de Nuca," and the cove itself was distinguished as "Santa Cruz de Nuca," or "Cala de los Amigos." The cove is on an island some twenty-two miles long and fourteen miles wide, separated from Vancouver Island proper by a narrow arm of the sound communicating to the sea by a fjord emerging at Esperanza Inlet, northwest of Nootka. Years would elapse, however, before careful examination revealed such intricacies and disproved the widespread initial assumption that Friendly Cove was on the mainland of North America.

The *Santiago* rode out the night in perfect tranquility at anchor off San Lorenzo; the journals remark that August 9, 1774, proved bright and clear. On just such a morning in August 1960, the author landed off Friendly Cove in a chartered seaplane, the only ready means of reaching what has proven inaccessible to those previously writing about Nootka—except the British Columbia historian F. W. Howay. The sound's azure arms, velvet brown and green headlands, and blue, forest-covered ranges ascending ever higher inland were an unforgettable sight. The view that Pérez and Martí-nez obtained in 1774 would have differed very little from that of today. At dawn on that morning two centuries ago, a number of dugouts came out to observe the *Santiago*. The commander ordered his launch put over the side and rigged with mast and sails, preparatory to entering the sound to look for a good anchorage, fresh water, and a site for the act of possession. When the natives saw these activities, they hastily retreated to a safe dis-tance and gathered to palaver. No sooner had the launch hit the water than the wind shifted and increased in intensity. The frigate swung on its anchor, drifting perilously close to a dangerous shoal, and Pérez found it necessary to cut the chain, losing his anchor, to keep from running aground. The launch and the men it contained were in considerable peril for a few minutes, until they could be brought back aboard the mother ship. As soon as the natives saw the vessel pulling away from shore, their attitude changed and they came to the frigate's side, signaling a desire to trade.

During the exchange that followed, evidence was established that the Spaniards would cite in 1789 when the English were challenging them about which nation had a better right to sovereignty over Nootka. The natives eagerly bartered their sea otter robes for abalone shells, and years later Nootka's chief Ma-kwee-na still treasured the shells he had acquired that day. Moreover, he confirmed the story that Estéban José Martínez had accidently struck a brave on the head with one of the heavy shells as he was dropping it into a canoe. Another occurrence provided further evidence of the *Santiago*'s visit: several warriors came aboard, and one managed to pilfer several spoons belonging to Martínez. When Cook visited Nootka four years later he purchased those spoons, recognized their manufacture, and mentioned in his journal that he regarded them as proof that the Spanish had been at or near the place.[43]

### NOOTKA CULTURAL PROCLIVITIES AND THE SPANISH ARRIVAL

Peculiar facets of northwest coast Indian culture would lead to certain consequences from the Spanish advent, with considerable influence upon the historical outcome. In the ensuing two decades the Nootka Indians would enter into closer contact with whites than did any other culture of that area in the eighteenth century, excepting the Aleut-Russian meld. Nootka customs and proclivities were closely involved in the outcome of subsequent events at San Lorenzo de Nuca; thus an understanding of those customs is essential at this point.

There were twenty-two native villages around Nootka Sound, some with great lodges described as up to twenty-five yards in length and housing as many as 400 individuals apiece. Rather than being nomadic like most other hunter-gatherers lacking any domesticated plants or animals but the dog, the northwest coast cultures enjoyed an environment permitting considerable population density, giving rise to elaboration in social and political structure, artifacts, and art forms. Lacking ceramics, they nonetheless practiced some metallurgical techniques with rare chunks of native copper, pounded into thin, highly prized sheets. When the first Spanish vessel appeared off Nootka, its men offering to barter pieces of the prized metal, iridescent shells, beads, and other trinkets, the natives welcomed into their world the purveyors of such entrancing novelties. This eagerness was primed by the potlatch system—famed in anthropological literature and common from Alaska to Oregon—wherein social and political prestige hinged upon feasts at which the host enhanced his status by outdoing rival chiefs in the abundance and quality of gifts distributed.

A chief's power to amass the requisite possessions depended upon his sway over a band of followers—hunters, gatherers, fishermen, weavers—whose allegiance stemmed from his fame as a slayer of whales, the largest creatures in their environment. Three or four braves in a dugout would attempt to get within striking distance of a basking whale without alerting it. Standing in the prow, his harpoon ready, the chief had to know the precise spot for a thrust into its vitals. A seal skin float, connected by a long rope to the detachable point, served to tire the great mammal and indicate its location upon resurfacing. The prey was harpooned again and again until it expired and its enormous carcass could be towed home—often a considerable dis-

---

43. Estéban José Martínez, "Diario" [1789], SpMN (732), pp. 46–47; James Cook, *A Voyage to the Pacific Ocean* (3 vols. and atlas, London, 1784), 2 : 282.

tance. A single kill would provide more food than could be consumed by one village before it spoiled. Consequently, an invitation to a great banquet was issued to surrounding bands; this offered occasion for elaborate masked dances retelling the legendary feats of the host chief's ancestors, which made for his upward mobility in the acknowledged hierarchy of chiefs. A conical hat, reserved to nobles, contained a design alluding to the host's prowess at hunting the ferocious killer whale, a pursuit requiring exceptional skill and bravery. A chief gave much attention to the fasting and rites intended to insure good fortune in slaying the great beasts. His sway over his subjects derived from their concept that the general welfare depended upon his ritual intercession with the Creator. Close kinship to him conferred noble status, but since he often had multiple wives and abundant offspring, this class was sizable. Nobles and commoners alike were conceived as receiving their sustenance from the chief, who was seen as the proprietor of all resources within tribal territory and the controller of the products of all labor.[44] The toil of prisoners taken in war added substantially to a chief's power. In such a competitive hierarchy, conflict was common, and the most powerful chieftains often had a reputation for surprise attacks, treachery, and guile.

Nootka dugouts were not so fleet as Aleut skin *bidarkas,* and, unless a sea otter was impaled before it awakened, it could outswim any canoe. "The outcome was otherwise," a Spanish source relates, "when they are burdened by their young; male and female defend them on those occasions with the greatest effort, splintering the arrows and harpoon with their teeth and sometimes even attacking the canoe; but finally they are seized by their pursuers and die covering and guarding their little ones." [45] Since the luxuriously soft sea otter pelts were difficult to obtain, they constituted a symbol of hunting skill and enhanced the prestige of the possessor. Several large skins, sewn together, and a conical hat were the sole garments worn year around by a Nootka man of rank. Draped loosely over the shoulders, the skin garment (which came to be called a *cutsark* among the fur traders) was sufficiently ample to cover the upper portion and rear of the body, but it left the torso exposed from the front. Nootka women were more modest, wrapping themselves from shoulders to knees in a sheath of pliable, finely woven cedar bark cloth, trimmed with sea otter fur to soften harsh edges and tied at the waist with a belt. The properly attired male wore a variety of ornaments suspended from three or four punctures in his earlobes, and a hole in the septum permitted him to suspend additional decorations from

44. Fray Francisco Miguel Sánchez, "Historia compuesta de todo lo acaesido en la expediccion [*sic*] hecha al Puerto de Nuca. año de 1789," CtY-BWA (415), fol. 76v, 8ov; Martínez, "Diario" [1789], p. 112; *Sútil y Mexicana,* pp. 135–36, 141.

45. *Sútil y Mexicana,* p. 135, AT.

his nose on special occasions. Habitually covered head to toe with whale oil and colored powder, for some events men and women also adorned themselves with bird down, which adhered to the grease of their coiffures. The foreheads of both sexes had been artificially flattened by boards bound across the skull in early infancy.[46]

The vigorous life style of these hunters of the sea, integrated around a pattern of subsistence that put a premium upon audacity and rivalry for prestige, which was based upon possessions, made the Indians of the northwest coast peculiarly vulnerable to blandishments afforded by the white man. California abalone shells and Mexican copper had a tremendous impact upon northwest coast art forms. When the sea otter trade put an abundance of prestige-conferring novelties in native hands, potlatch competition swelled accordingly, with gifts distributed in ever more spectacular quantities and with the resultant sociopolitical fluidity. Native acquisitiveness would be a catalyst propelling remote Nootka Sound, within a decade and a half, onto the international scene as the most sought-after mecca of its time.

### PEREZ AND FUCA'S STRAIT

Gratified by his success in trading with the friendly natives of San Lorenzo, Pérez was impressed with the potential strategic value of the roadstead; but thwarted in his initial attempt to send a party ashore, he made no second try. This fateful omission would have profound diplomatic consequences and be much lamented by Spanish officialdom.

Resuming a southward heading, Pérez bestowed the name "Punta San Estéban" upon a promontory jutting into the sea south of Nootka, thus honoring the second officer's personal saint, an irony considering Martínez's future role at Nootka. The spot still bears the name Estéban Point. Moving southward, Pérez sighted the shore only occasionally, and then at a distance. He sailed right by the Strait of Juan de Fuca, but none of the diaries report that he sighted it. In 1789 Martínez would assert that on this occasion he had spied a large opening and had urged Pérez to investigate, but he had had to obey his superior, who was reluctant to approach any closer.[47] Since Fuca's alleged strait appeared on many maps at that approximate latitude, Pérez's refusal is surprising. Martínez's word on this score is uncorroborated, but if he truly sighted the strait, the incident is a serious reflection upon Pérez's qualities as an explorer. Some historians have preferred to question Martínez's truthfulness; they consider the assertion motivated by a desire to bolster Spanish claims vis-à-vis the British. In July 1789, when Martínez made this claim, his actions indicate he was confident of the justification for

46. Sánchez, "Historia," fol. 75.
47. Martínez, "Diario" [1789], entry for June 14, 1789.

Spanish claims to the northwest coast. It seems unlikely he would adulterate with a lie the legitimate claim to Nootka, to which he had been witness. While personal vanity may have motivated his assertion, there is no evidence that Martínez ever sought to blow his own horn by repeating it. His claim could be spurious, because by the time he entered it in his journal, he may have learned of the strait's existence from Captain Robert Gray. One author charges him with "inventing an attractive rationalization for his 'failure' to record observing the strait in 1774," and then uses this as a fulcrum for an argument that Martínez, a catalytic figure in subsequent events, was an unprincipled liar.[48] No proof in Martinez's defense is known; however, an opinion about his truthfulness is important and must rest upon a judgment of the man's character and credibility in other episodes. Such a conclusion is not easy to reach, but evidence will accrue.

During the four days that the *Santiago* was in the neighborhood of the Strait of Juan de Fuca, the weather was sufficiently clear for the explorers to see a great snow-covered peak, which Pérez named "Sierra Nevada de Santa Rosalía," today Mount Olympus. Columns of smoke in many places testified to the presence of numerous Indian villages. The good weather did not last; fog, debilitating scurvy, and the dangers of uncharted seas unnerved the crew and reduced the expedition's effectiveness. The peasants commonly recruited as sailors were little accustomed to the cold of higher latitudes, and after several months at sea, more and more of the crew fell ill, giving Pérez added reason for hurrying southward. The diaries written at this time are permeated with fear; Fray Tomás de la Peña Saravia noted on August 19:

> During the whole day the fog did not lift, nor could the sun be seen. It was quite cold and a heavy mist fell. I think the dampness is the cause of the *mal de Loanda,* or scurvy; for although during the whole voyage there have been some persons affected with this sickness, these cases have not been as aggravated as they are now, when there are more than twenty men unfit for duty, in addition to which many others, though able to go about, have sores in their mouths and on their legs; and I believe that if God does not send better weather soon the greater part of the crew will perish from this disease, judging from the rate at which they are falling sick of it during these days of wet and cold fog.[49]

As soon as the frigate reached San Blas, the expeditionaries' diaries were speeded to the viceroy, but the recorded results fell short of satisfying him.

48. Charles L. Stewart, "Martínez and López de Haro on the Northwest Coast, 1788–1789," (Ph.D. diss. University of California, 1936), pp. 172–75.

49. Fray Tomás de la Peña Saravia, "Diario," *PHSSC* 2 (1891) : p. 138.

There had been no landings or acts of possession, which he considered essential. Only the most general trend of the coastline had been ascertained. Reporting to Madrid he lamented:

> The darkness of the weather, the cold to which they were not accustomed, the fear of a shortage of water and of an unknown coast seem to have been the causes that the instructions with which I dispatched the expedition were not entirely complied with; but, nevertheless, I consider what has been accomplished very useful, as I didn't count on much success in the first exploration; but it will facilitate the success of later ones, and it is persuasive of the fact that in the 19° higher which we have advanced, there is no danger of foreign establishments.[50]

Two Indian robes were remitted to Carlos III so he might observe the handiwork of the newly discovered peoples, recognized as far advanced over the aborigines of California. Despite Perez's meager accomplishments, the viceroy recommended him as worthy of reward, although the very letter acknowledging receipt of the *Santiago*'s logs ordered Pérez to prepare for another voyage northward in 1775.[51]

Bucareli was more charitable than a veteran of subsequent expeditions over the same route, who considered the expeditionaries' description of the coastline day after day to be in such vague terms "that it characterizes the insufficiency of Commander Pérez and his pilot Martínez." Instead of maps they brought back only generalized notes, so that despite considerable expense to the royal treasury, "we are left almost in the same ignorance."[52] Had they been more capable and persistent, their discoveries and acts of possession could have placed a stamp of ownership upon the northwest coast so indelibly that subsequent international rivalry for that region might have been discouraged, just as Spain's claims to analogous fjords and islands in southern Chile were never successfully challenged.

### THE HEZETA-BODEGA EXPEDITION, 1775

Although it seemed unlikely that the tsarina's subjects had settlements within hundreds of leagues of Monterey, Bucareli thought it urgent to send a second expedition northward the following season to accomplish what Pérez had failed to do—for renewed warning had arrived from St. Petersburg about Russian discoveries and establishments in America. Com-

50. Bucareli to Arriaga, Mexico City, Nov. 26, 1774, in *Publicaciones del Archivo General de la Nación* 30 (1936) : 225–28, AT.

51. Bucareli to Grimaldi, Mexico City, Nov. 26, 1774, SpAGI (V, Indif. Gen., Mex. 1630); Bucareli to Pérez, Nov. 14, 1774, MxAGN (Hist. 61–14).

52. Francisco Antonio Mourelle, "Compendio de noticias" [1791], SpMN (331), fol. 39v–40.

mand would be given to one of the navy lieutenants recently transferred to New Spain for just such purposes.[53]

Coinciding with Bucareli's report to Madrid of plans for the upcoming expedition, the ministry sent him full instructions for the effort, enunciating a vigorous and aggressive new policy toward the northwest coast, in case subjects of another nation were found ensconced in what was deemed Spanish domain. If such establishments were encountered to the north of California, the commander should attempt to secure eviction, first by making a formal demand, then, if he met resistance, by using force. These orders would not reach the Mexican capital, however, until the expedition had already sailed northward.[54] At this juncture the ministry far exceeded Bucareli in zeal for extending Madrid's control over the western portion of North America. José de Gálvez's militant attitudes were being shared at the highest level. His selection as minister of Indies, replacing Julián de Arriaga, who died on January 28, 1775, suggests that his views appealed to Carlos III as reflecting the sovereign's own intentions.

The six officers designated for transfer to San Blas were chosen to make up for the previous lack of trained men in the department, build up naval capabilities there, strengthen control over Alta California, and assure sovereignty over the northwest coast. Their orders were to proceed to Mexico to participate in "discoveries of the northern coast of California" (*Costa Septentrional de California*). Each of the young men—Bruno de Hezeta, Miguel Manrique, Fernando Quirós, Juan de Ayala, Diego Choquet, and Juan Francisco de la Bodega y Quadra—received a bonus of 500 pesos prior to embarking. Traveling as a group, they arrived at the Mexican capital in October 1774. None had proven himself as yet, and seniority alone determined who would lead the expedition for 1775. Command fell to Bruno de Hezeta, a twenty-four-year-old Basque from Bilbao. As captain of the *Santiago,* he would have Juan Pérez as second officer, with such crew of the previous year as were well enough to embark again. As escort, Juan de Ayala would command the schooner *Sonora.* The two would accompany Miguel Manrique and the supply ship *San Carlos* to Monterey with the annual provisions for California. They took aboard sufficient provisions for a year's voyage. Ostensibly because of seniority—but more likely because he was a creole, born in Peru, and thus entitled to less preference—thirty-two-year-old Bodega was passed over in favor of the other,

53. Grimaldi to Arriaga, Aranjuez, April 30, 1774, and [Arriaga] to Bucareli, Aranjuez, June 15, 1774, SpAGI (Estado 20–10); Bucareli to Grimaldi, Mexico City, Nov. 26, 1774, SpAGI (V, Indif. Gen., Mex. 1630), T in DLC; Bucareli to Pérez, Nov. 14, 1774, MxAGN (Hist. 61–14).

54. Bucareli to Arriaga, Mexico City, Dec. 27, 1774, SpAGI (Estado 20–13); minute of a royal order to Bucareli, Madrid, Dec. 23, 1774, SpAGI (Estado 20–4); Juan Francisco de la Bodega y Quadra, "Diario" [1775], SpMN (662), fol. 3v; Chapman, *Founding of Spanish California*, p. 242.

younger lieutenants when Bucareli designated their assignments. Reluctant to remain inactive in Tepic until the following year's expeditions, he volunteered as second in command aboard the *Sonora*. His diary remarks:

> Recognizing that the schooner's smallness and inadequacy for such a long and exposed voyage might occasion a delay if it carried only one officer, I decided in the best interests of such an important commission that I should request embarcation as its second officer, disregarding the obstacle of having to serve under the orders of another of my same rank.[55]

Volunteering for service aboard the *Sonora* was truly a self-effacing gesture; scarcely thirty-six feet long, shallow of draft and narrow in beam, it was constructed with no more ambitious purpose in mind than short trips to Baja California. As the schooner's pilot noted:

> The deck and tiny cabin were all it had to offer for security or living quarters, with no chests or other baggage than a bed and what could be contained underneath in a box; the height and width of the sleeping space necessitated remaining in a sitting position; the small deck did not offer the possibility of a walk, and in this inaction one lived for the space of ten months.[56]

Its close quarters would have to suffice for the captain, second officer, a pilot, and fourteen sailors, ten of whom had never before been to sea, being ranch hands (*vaqueros*) newly recruited in Jalisco and Nayarit. Only a compulsion to serve could have persuaded Bodega to voluntarily undergo the rigors ahead. Such unself--seeking willingness characterized the man destined to have the most important role in Spanish activities on the northwest coast, next to the controversial Martínez. But Bodega and Martínez were cut from entirely different cloth; Bodega's personality traits would significantly influence the course of Spain's relationships with its rivals, but in an opposite direction from those of the unpredictable mariner from Seville. Born in Lima in 1743, son of a Spanish-born official in the colonial bureaucracy and descended through his mother from one of Peru's most prominent families, the young Limeño entered the marine guard at nineteen years of age and became a second lieutenant in 1774, shortly before his assignment to San Blas.

The expedition departed northward on March 16, but three days out of port the *San Carlos* hoisted a distress signal. A boat sent from the *Sonora*

55. Bodega, "Diario," fol. 3v, AT; he was the son of Tomás de la Bodega y de las Llanas, a Basque deputy of the *Consulado* in Cuzco, and of Peruvian-born Doña Francisca de Mollinedo y Losada. Javier de Ybarra y Bergé, *De California á Alaska: Historia de un descubrimiento* (Madrid, 1945), pp. 14–17.
56. Mourelle, "Compendio," fol. 81v–82v, AT.

found Captain Manrique exhibiting signs of insanity. Calmed somewhat by his fellow officers, he was taken aboard the *Santiago*, but medicines and bloodletting only augmented his apprehension and manic symptoms. Throughout the ensuing night his rage and tears continued unabated. It being obvious that he could not continue, Hezeta named Ayala to command the *San Carlos* and Bodega replaced Ayala as captain of the *Sonora*, Manrique being sent back to San Blas in the supply ship's launch. A quirk of fate had placed Bodega in his first command; his bravery, fortitude, and zeal would have decisive bearing on the expedition's results. One of his biggest assets would be unstinting support from his twenty-year-old Galician pilot, Francisco Antonio Mourelle de la Rúa, from San Adrián de Corme, near La Coruña. Already a veteran of service in the Guianas, Trinidad, and the Antilles, the young Gallego had been transferred at Bucareli's request from a warship at Veracruz to San Blas. He would figure importantly in subsequent activities related to the northwest coast and, through exploits in the European theater in later life, attain even greater fame in his own time than Bodega.

Hezeta carried instructions to reach 65° north latitude before turning southward. He was to avoid foreign settlements, take possession where able to go ashore in safety, find out what the Indians offered in trade, and take pains to demonstrate that the Spanish would treat them well. On the cruise northward they spent nine days in a bay on the north California coast, near the present Little River, which Hezeta named "Santísima Trinidad." As testimony of formal possession they erected a large cross bearing the inscription: "Carlos III, King of Spain by the Grace of God" (*Carlos III Dei G. Hyspaniarum Rex*).

The two vessels approached the coast on July 13 at a cove in the lee of what Wagner identifies as Point Grenville, several miles south of Washington's Quinault River. Bodega sent Mourelle in the ship's canoe to advise Hezeta to stand off, as there was insufficient depth alongside the *Sonora* for a vessel of greater draft; he requested Hezeta to remain at anchor overnight so that on the morrow a party could go ashore to gather firewood, secure fresh water, and cut a pole to replace a topmast cracked in a storm. The *Santiago* stayed where it cast anchor initially, about a league away.[57] Bodega could see a village not far from the beach. Soon nine canoe-loads of stalwart

57. Francisco Antonio Mourelle, *Voyage of the Sonora in the Second Bucareli Expedition to Explore the Northwest Coast . . . 1775* (San Francisco, 1920), pp. 35–36. His log for July 13 and 14 gives latitudes of 47° 28′ N. and 47° 20′ N.; this information is the basis for Wagner's identification of "Rada de Bucareli" and "Punta de los Mártires" with Point Grenville (47° 21′ N.). H. R. Wagner, "Creation of Rights of Sovereignty Through Symbolic Acts," *PHR* 7 (1938): 312. The expedition's maps suggest that "Isla Dolores" (Isle of Sorrows) corresponds to Destruction Island, twenty-five miles north, near the Hoh River. A historical marker on Route 101 opposite Destruction Island erroneously places the massacre nearby.

men came out to circle the schooner, gesturing as if inviting them ashore. Bodega gave those who came on board some food and beads. The braves were naked, except for beaver or deerskin capes, copper rings in their noses, and varicolored shells dangling from punctures around the entire circumference of their ears. All carried bows, arrows, and long lances. By twilight the tribe's friendliness seemed well established, but about nine that night the canoes reappeared, their occupants making a dreadful noise. Bodega remarks, "Although I had no motive to doubt their sincerity, the visit at such a late hour made me suspect that they intended some mischief, and I positioned my men well armed, ready for any betrayal; but it was just the opposite from what I had thought." Obliged by Bodega's presents, they had returned with whale meat, salmon, sardines, "sweet onions," and other foodstuffs. Bodega thanked them profusely and handed out a few handkerchiefs, beads, and some rings and earrings for the women, at which the natives departed in apparent contentment.

At midnight Mourelle returned from the frigate with a message for Bodega to attend a conference the next morning as to whether he should attempt a higher latitude, as at times during the previous week Hezeta had feared the *Sonora* unequal to the high seas and winds. The entire crew of the *Santiago,* including the commander, had been sick for several days and Hezeta did not contemplate remaining along the coast much longer. The conference concluded, he intended sailing at once. "This news was no novelty to me," Bodega states, "for since the first days after the departure from San Blas they have tried to dissuade me from such a mission and urge my return to port, attempting to make me believe that it was impossible to reach a higher latitude than Monterey; and I judge it to be of great merit that I have not paid any more attention to such pessimistic predictions than to the inconveniences and labors I have had and await me in such a lengthy voyage." [58]

During the night the tide went out; dawn revealed dangerous shoals not far from the *Sonora*'s bow, separating it from open water, and the anchorage was a scant fathom in depth. Waves crashing upon the rocks belabored the schooner, but there was no chance of getting out until the tide rose. Hezeta was too far away to observe Bodega's predicament. At 6:00 A.M. a canoe containing nine warriors approached the *Santiago* making signs inviting them ashore. The commander motioned for them to come aboard, but the Indians were unwilling to seize any lines. They carried no bows or other visible weapons, except a large-bladed, new-looking knife that one warrior held. They offered Hezeta a present of fish, and the sailors exchanged a few trinkets for sea otter skins. In a short while he went ashore to perform the formal act of possession, accompanied by a group including the

58. Bodega, "Diario," fol. 19v–20, AT.

chaplain (Fray Benito Sierra), second officer Pérez, the surgeon, and twenty armed sailors. They erected a large cross, but Fray Benito did not say Mass because of bad weather and their poor anchorage. A cluster of Indian boys squatted on the sand nearby, eating roasted fish, and made gestures of offering to share their repast, with a show of affability and no sign of fear. The site, now known as Grenville Harbor, was named Bucareli Anchorage (*Rada de Bucareli*) in homage to the viceroy, but the name soon fell into disuse because of the cove's unimportance and the episode about to occur, which made it a place of macabre memory, thereafter called Martyr's Point (*Punta de los Mártires*).[59] By 7:00 A.M. Hezeta and his party were back aboard the frigate.

To the north, just barely in sight, the *Sonora* continued in serious straits, confined within the ring of dangerous shoals. At sunrise the visitors of the previous evening returned, demonstrating the same amiability as before, exchanging furs, bows, and arrows with the crew. In what was interpreted as a sign of confidence, the chief brought his wife aboard, accompanied by two other women. The captain gave them some beads and other presents, believing a firm bond of friendship had been established, and received an invitation to visit their village. During this exchange the ship's boat was moored to the stern of the *Sonora*. Some of the braves insisted on trading their furs for a linchpin holding its rudder in place. Assuaged with no little difficulty by an additional gift of strips of metal ripped off some old chests, they eventually departed in apparent content.

Since it appeared Hezeta would sail that same day, Bodega judged that additional months of navigation under unknown circumstances necessitated refilling the depleted water casks. He had been liberal in rationing water to avoid illnesses thought to be aggravated by excessive thirst and his supply was now short. There were several springs visible on the beach, and while awaiting the tide there was a golden opportunity to obtain water, cut a topmast, and gather firewood. The six most capable men for these tasks were sent to shore with boatswain Pedro Santana, a man "outstanding among those of his class for his good conduct and valor." [60] Given the Indians' ami-

59. "Viage que por orden del Exmo. Señor Virrey, el Bailio, Frei Don Antonio Maria Bucareli, hizo la fragata de S. M. nombrada Santiago, la Nueva Galicia . . . ," MxAGN (Hist. 24–8), fol. 276–76v; Acta de posesión, July 14, 1775, MxAGN (Hist. 324).

60. Sources for reconstructing this disaster are "Viage," fol. 271–77v; Bodega, "Diario," fol. 19v–22v; Juan Francisco de la Bodega y Quadra, "Comento de la navegación y descubrimientos hechos en dos viajes de orden de S. M. en la costa septentrional de California," SpMN (618), fol. 8v–11v; Mourelle, *Voyage of the Sonora*, pp. 36–40; Francisco Antonio Mourelle, "Relación de los descubrimientos hechos en el viaje que D. Francisco Antonio Mourelle emprendió en la goleta 'Sonora' a las órdenes de D. Bruno Hezeta para las costas N. de California en 1775," SpMN (575), fol. 140–40v; and Francisco Antonio Mourelle, "Segunda exploración de la costa septentrional de la California en 1775 con la fragata Santiago y goleta Sonora," SpMN (331), fol. 61–63v, 82v–83. The latter are variant versions, often richer in detail, of Mourelle's *Voyage of the Sonora*.

able behavior, Bodega had little reason to suspect treachery, but each man carried a musket and cutlass, and some had a pair of pistols apiece. Bodega ordered them not to leave the beach until he and Mourelle reached shore. They should avoid offending the natives and only make use of weapons if necessary for their own defense. Due to the small size of the boat, one of the sailors would have to return with it and bring the captain, pilot, and empty barrels ashore in a second trip. "If the canoe had been bigger," Bodega later recalled, "we would have gone with the first group." Fortunately this was not the case, as the surf was rough, resulting in some confusion as the men clambered out; backwash pulled the stern down, and the succeeding wave swamped it. The *Sonora* was anchored only about thirty yards from shore, but thick underbrush came right down to the beach and kept the Spaniards from perceiving that it hid an ambush. The seamen no sooner reached dry land than about 300 shrieking warriors sprang from the bushes in full attack, seized the water-filled boat, pulled it ashore, cut off the seamen's escape, and commenced hacking them to pieces, in full view of their stunned companions watching in anguish from the *Sonora*. Bodega ordered his remaining men to fire at the assailants with the swivel gun and muskets, but the missiles fell short, and the braves paid no attention whatsoever. The *Santiago* was too far away to notice the sound or see the signal of distress quickly hoisted.

The victims were caught completely by surprise and did not have a chance to use their firearms—or else in their obedience to orders hesitated to use them until too late. Bodga had the rueful experience of watching the whole episode through a spyglass, and he relates, "during the period of two hours, in the midst of the tumult, I saw no more than one flash, but without the noise of an explosion, from which I concluded that it misfired." From this Mourelle concluded that perhaps the powder in their guns had been ruined in the calamitous landing. Bodega saw two of the men break away, brandishing swords, plunge fully clothed into the bay, and swim frantically toward the schooner. Since their sole landing craft was in savage hands, a barrel was put over the side and a seaman paddled toward those struggling in the waves, to no avail. "The coldness of the water, I suspect, if they were wounded and bleeding profusely, would have kept them from making it," Bodega conjectured, "so that I remain in doubt as to whether they drowned or died at the hands of the traitors." When last sighted they were swimming landward, but no one saw them emerge on shore. The attackers carried the bloody cadavers off into the woods and then turned to smashing the boat to pieces, searching for such metal as it might contain. After several hours the whole tribe went away, leaving the beach deserted. Those watching through the spyglass for some sign of the swimmers saw scarcely a vestige of the canoe.

At noon the tide ran high and Bodega endeavored to escape the cul-de-sac threatening to become a deathtrap for them all. Five seamen lay bedridden with scurvy. The remaining hands hastened to hoist sail. When the Indians spied their preparations to depart, nine or ten canoes with upwards of thirty warriors apiece came out to surround the schooner. Bodega relates:

> One of them with nine of the most robust youths (who the day before had each commanded one of the other canoes) coasted up to our side, bows at the ready, and shielded by some beautiful hides of great thickness, but trying at first to persuade us with their past lies; but we, although few, already under sail, and among shoals, were disposed in the best order: it had cost me a lot to understand those twisted intentions and to save myself on this occasion from the assault they intended to make, persuaded certainly by the few remaining to us: unworthy payment with which they responded to the noble treatment that had been given them.[61]

For a long time the lead canoe stayed near the prow, its occupants holding up handsome garments and food. The crew held out some beads, hoping to entice them closer. The braves soon tired of subterfuge and other canoes approached the schooner's stern. "I didn't want to fire on them," Bodega relates, "until I knew what their intentions were and so as to make our first shots count, as the only ones able to fire were the mate, myself, and my cabin boy, because I had one of the seamen at the wheel, one taking soundings, one at the topmast scouting shoals, another making cartridges, a boy to bring them to us, and five who lay ill." They got underway with very little wind, the canoes keeping pace at about the same distance, until it appeared the *Sonora* might reach deep water and escape. Observing no one in the prow, the warriors in the lead canoe started to clamber aboard there. At that instant Bodega and his men opened fire with swivel gun and muskets, peppering them with shot. Six or seven died in the first salvo and the thin-walled canoe was riddled. Two or three survivors were badly injured but managed to paddle out of range. The effect of the schooner's defenses stunned the rest, who perceived for the first time the potency of the white man's weapons. They retrieved the swamped canoe, retreated to a safe distance, and covered dead and wounded with skin armor. Then all of the canoes backed off to hold council. Bodega turned his attention to threading a way through to deeper water. The natives finally retreated to their village, as Bodega remarks, "reflecting upon the difference in outcome of their first assault and the second."

On the *Santiago*, a league away, a single salvo had been audible. Hezeta surmised it was a signal for anchor and cable to pull the *Sonora* into deep water, but before a launch got underway the schooner was approaching. A

---

61. Bodega, "Diario," fol. 21–21v, AT.

boat went to bring Bodega and Mourelle aboard the flagship. The Limeño says he implored Hezeta to provide thirty armed men for "the objective of taking the most vigorous satisfaction for such execrable evil," and to search for the two sailors last seen swimming away, who might be hiding in the underbrush. Hezeta held a hurried council. His own opinion was that they were anchored in a dangerous position, exposed from every direction to winds that might come up at any instant; it seemed unlikely any of the seamen could have survived, and the distance to the village made it unsafe to undertake a punitive mission away from protection of the frigate's cannons. Nevertheless, he asked for the other officers' views. Bodega and Mourelle favored punishing the tribe, which otherwise might treat future explorers in the same treacherous manner. Pilots Juan Pérez and Cristóbal Revilla were opposed, on grounds that safety of the vessels came first, and Hezeta tended to agree. It was resolved to follow the opinion of the majority and forgo sending an armed party ashore. They also discussed the *Sonora's* future usefulness. Revilla was for sending it homeward; Bodega and Mourelle thought it should continue. Pérez was of the opinion that, "although one could not deny that the weather was rough and the schooner of slight resistance, it seemed that if they had reached that latitude with success, without doubt they could take it farther." Again Hezeta bowed to the majority and consented for it to continue. Its crew had to be reinforced with five seamen and a mate from the frigate, itself short-handed, for many were already laid up with scurvy. The luckless participants in the previous year's expedition had been quick victims of the debilitating disease, and many paid with their lives for the folly of being sent northward two years in a row. The sick from the *Sonora* were transferred to the flagship, and Hezeta provided another boat and a cannon. Later that day the two vessels started tacking against an adverse wind. On July 29 Hezeta again summoned Bodega and Mourelle. In the ensuing discussion their suspicion was confirmed that he would seek approval to head toward San Blas within a short time, forgoing an attempt to reach a higher latitude. That night the vessels lost contact, and by morning they were far apart. In successive days no trace of the schooner was seen, and Hezeta could only hope it would arrive safely at the appointed rendezvous in Monterey.

### DISCOVERY OF THE COLUMBIA

Aboard the flagship there were few not bedridden with scurvy. A storm, Hezeta asserts, would have found him without sufficient hands to manage the frigate; there were scarcely enough with strength to reef the topsails, and all the able-bodied together were unable to lay hold of the point of the foresail or brace the mainsail. Despite petitions to turn homeward, Hezeta says he persisted in sailing northward until August 11, in 49° of latitude, when a renewed memorial from some of the officers and crew persuaded him to head toward Monterey. The commander declared his resolve to follow the coast carefully on the way south, in obedience to the viceroy's instructions, but the pledge did not keep them from missing the wide entrance to the Strait of Juan de Fuca a day or so later.[62] The third day after turning back they were again in the neighborhood of the Point of Martyrs. A canoe came out and made signs inviting them ashore. The seamen recognized some of the braves as having come aboard on the former occasion, and Hezeta decided to capture two as hostages and send the others ashore with an offer to trade for the sailors that had jumped into the bay, in case they were still alive and in captivity. Luring the dugout to the frigate's side, they dropped the 300-pound anchor into it to hold them fast. A journal relates that "it fell on the bare back of one of the heathens, who bent down and was almost squashed; but then, almost as if nothing had happened, with great dexterity he lifted it up and tossed it into the water." [63] The Indians fled upwind and eluded capture.

As he proceeded southward, at six in the afternoon on August 17 Hezeta sighted a large bay between two capes, penetrating so far inland that it reached the horizon. He named it "Bay of the Assumption of Our Lady" (*Bahía de la Asunción de Nuestra Señora*), honoring a holiday celebrated that week. From a position midway between the capes, Hezeta made every effort to enter, but the current was so strong that, although under full press of sails, he had to desist, leading him to conclude it to be "the mouth of some great river, or of some passage to another sea." [64] He decided it corresponded to the strait discovered by Juan de Fuca, and that the Levantine mariner had misjudged the latitude. After consulting his fellow officers, he gave up investigating further, as night was about to fall. The *Santiago* was short of hands to handle both frigate and longboat, which must necessarily guide them over the bar, and if the anchor were dropped inside the bay, he feared the crew would be too ill to weigh it again. By dawn they had been blown far to the southwest. This is the earliest recorded sighting of the Columbia River by a European. Hezeta prepared a chart of the estuary on the basis of what could be seen from outside the bar, and the feature appeared on subsequent maps as "Hezeta's Entryway" (*Entrada de Hezeta*) and "St. Roc's River" (*Río de San Roque*). Even so, for many years its existence was ignored, overlooked, or discounted by other nationalities. Had Hezeta explored it further, his discovery would have stood a better chance of redounding to Spain's credit; as it turned out, his hesitancy and the policy of

62. Cristóbal de Revilla, Antonio Ramírez, Juan Millán Pérez, and three others to Bruno de Hezeta, aboard the *Santiago*, August 11, 1775, SpAGI (Estado 20–20); Fray Benito de la Sierra, "Diario," English trans. in *CHSQ* 9 (1930) : 232–33.

63. "Viage," fol. 280–80v, AT.

64. Bruno de Hezeta, "Diario," MxAGN (Hist. 324), extract in Mourelle, *Voyage of the Sonora,* pp. 86–88.

secrecy deprived Madrid of the feat's political value. Seventeen years later, Robert Gray sighted the river and named it after his ship, *Columbia Rediviva.* Unlike the Spanish, he made no attempt to keep his "discovery" a secret, and the name supplanted Hezeta's name even on Spanish maps, leading to an American claim to Oregon based in part on Gray's deed.

The remainder of Hezeta's journey southward was uneventful, and within twelve days he anchored at Monterey. The sick—that is, most of the crew— were transferred ashore to await the *Sonora* amidst the mission settlement's comforts.

### THE SONORA REACHES ALASKA

The course on July 29 which made the *Sonora* lose all contact with its consort has been interpreted as evidence that Bodega, irritated at Hezeta's timidity and reluctance to fulfill Bucareli's instructions concerning their objectives in latitude, clearly intended to leave the *Santiago* behind.[65] This conjecture is proven by one of the variant accounts Mourelle subsequently composed. Their drastic action was a consequence of the junta on the day they separated. Bodega and Mourelle were disgusted to find Hezeta and his subordinates ready to head back. That evening in their cramped quarters the two men deliberated for more than three hours as to their course of action. Despite the lamentable state of the *Sonora,* Mourelle says they "formulated the temerarious project of separating, and dying in their craft rather than return without enlightenment." They were well aware of the risks involved,

> that they would navigate unmapped seas; perhaps find themselves in an archipelago where it would not be easy for a small, lone boat to emerge felicitously; that any illness would put them in the ultimate risk at such an advanced season; that from the moment of separation they would have to stretch their rations to last the rest of the trip; and finally, that if they returned to port without progress worthy of consideration, at once there would be leveled against them accusations of insubordination and others natural in such a prolonged voyage. But none of this could overcome the shameful feeling which they could imagine if two young men turned back toward San Blas from that latitude; and hoisting all their sails at ten that evening, by navigating toward the west they found themselves in control of their own destiny by the following day." [66]

Although short of water, their rations reduced to a smaller daily allowance, and the hardtack near spoilage from leaking sea water, the crew agreed to continue onward and decided among themselves to contribute

65. Stewart, "Martínez and López de Haro," p. 32.
66. Mourelle, "Segunda exporación," fol. 82v–83.

jointly to a solemn Mass to Our Lady of Bethlehem, whom they entreated for help in reaching 65° of latitude and making a safe return to San Blas. The captain declared himself highly gratified by their ardor and devotion. "We continued unanimously of the opinion to execute our orders," Mourelle states, "as if we did otherwise, His Majesty must have incurred the expenses of another expedition." [67]

After taking a westward course, and then heading straight north, they made landfall again on August 15, at 57° north. An impressive, snow-capped peak dominating the coastline was named "San Jacinto," today's Mount Edgecumbe. Three days later Bodega encountered a sheltered bay with a small river where the *Sonora* could get water, although he observed an Indian lodge, surrounded by a parapet of stakes, not far from the stream. About ten men and a number of women and children were visible, but the lack of cover for an ambush made the river's mouth a safe landing spot. Bodega named it "Port of Our Lady of the Remedies" (*Puerto de Nuestra Señora de los Remedios*). Having dropped anchor within pistol shot of the beach, he sent a five-man landing party, alert against any attack, to unfurl the Spanish flag, erect a large cross, and cut a cross-shaped design into a nearby rock. After they returned aboard, a few Indians came out of hiding and uprooted the cross, carrying it off to erect in prominent view before their lodge. "They made us signs with their arms," Bodega relates, "giving us to understand that they would keep it there." [68]

The following day a party went ashore at a more isolated spot to secure much-needed water, firewood, and a likely tree for a topmast. The men were heavily armed and stayed within range of the schooner's swivel gun. While they were on the beach, a chieftain approached them cautiously. They offered him some trifles in exchange for a fish. Soon more warriors appeared and, growing bolder, made it understood payment was expected for the water, grimacing angrily and brandishing long, flint-tipped lances as if about to attack. The sailors kept up their guard, went on filling the casks, and were able to return safely to the schooner without a clash. In their absence, companions had found the fishing excellent, making a catch that provided welcome relief from the scanty diet of days past. A decade later there was an opinion current among the fur traders that this sole Spanish contact in 1775 was responsible for a smallpox epidemic that subsequently ravaged the coast, killing a substantial proportion of the population.[69] There is no reference to smallpox aboard the *Sonora*, and a more

67. Mourelle, *Voyage of the Sonora*, p. 41.

68. Bodega, "Diario," fol. 27, AT; acta de posesión, August 18, 1775, MxAGN (Hist. 324). This is today's Sea Lion Bay, near Salisbury Sound, north of Sitka.

69. Nathaniel Portlock, *A Voyage Round the World; but More Particularly to the North West Coast of America; Performed in 1785, 1786, 1787, and 1788 in the King George and Queen Charlotte, Captains Portlock and Dixon* (London, 1789), pp. 271–73.

likely explanation is that the report referred to contagion spread by the
Spanish expedition of 1779, which was hit by an epidemic of unspecified
nature while at Bucareli Sound—an expedition of which the fur traders
had no knowledge.

Bodega examined every bay and inlet, expecting to find at that approximate latitude the Strait of Bartholomew de Fonte. Each night the schooner
rode at anchor to avoid passing any entrance in the darkness. After taking
such pains and discovering nothing, they concluded that no such waterway
existed.[70] The *Sonora* entered a placid bay where the temperature was so
mild they ascribed its warmth to nearby volcanoes, whose glow was perceived by night. Bodega was ill that day, so Mourelle went ashore and
took possession for Carlos III, calling the place "Puerto de Bucareli," in
the viceroy's honor. Located on the western side of Prince of Wales Island,
at 55° 14′ north latitude, it still bears the name Bucareli Sound today. Subsequent references to it in official papers suggest that if the threat of Nootka's
being occupied by foreigners had not drawn the Spanish there in 1789,
Bucareli Sound would have been the site of the first Iberian settlement on
the northwest coast, so excellent were its qualities for a settlement and naval
base.

Upon leaving Bucareli, Bodega tacked northward again, and on August
27 he reached a maximum of 58° 30′ north latitude before being turned
back by dangerous inshore winds. With regret, he started homeward, since
five of the crew were suffering intensely from scurvy. When violent weather
struck a few days later, there were insufficient hands to manage both sails
and rudder. Great seas breaking over the prow threatened to swamp the
little vessel. Several of the seamen still on their feet were injured and in-
capacitated when the schooner was rolled on its beam by a giant wave,
"most of which ended up in the hold." Captain and second officer were
obliged to take turns at the bilge pump to keep the hold from filling with
water seeping through seams sprung by blows of the prow against the waves.
As Mourelle tells it, "they resolved to undertake this labor which in no
ways conformed to their past exercise, and which could only have been
withstood by two youths who sought heroism." [71]

One of the *Sonora's* greatest sources of trouble was the defective diet.
The restricted space beneath deck had prevented taking aboard all 1,900
pounds of jerky corresponding to their share of the supplies; the balance
had been put aboard the flagship. Thus, when the two ships parted company,
Bodega's crew were reduced to a fare of beans, soggy hardtack, lard, and
such fish as could be caught. Soon everyone began to experience the excru-
ciating pains of scurvy; only four men were fit for duty, and even these

70. Mourelle, *Voyage of the Sonora*, p. 48.
71. Mourelle, "Segunda exploración," fol. 81v–82v, AT.

were much affected by the little-understood affliction. Remedial measures at the time consisted of burning sulphur between decks as fumigation, extinguishing the cooking fire from time to time by pouring vinegar on the coals, and adding lemon juice or vinegar in small quantities to the casks of drinking water. Their vitamin C deficiency was too great, however, for such negligible amounts as this method provided to have any effect.

During the *Sonora*'s return to Monterey, an accomplishment worth noting was the discovery on October 3 of strategically located Tomales Bay, pointing dagger-like at San Francisco Bay. The Captain bestowed upon it his patrilineal surname, but in later years "Puerto de la Bodega" became confused with a smaller inlet just to the north, which persists today as Bodega Bay.[72] In the early hours before dawn the next morning, the *Sonora* had its closest call yet when the receding tide from within long, narrow Tomales Bay changed direction, and a tidal bore suddenly enveloped the schooner. The ship's canoe, tied alongside, was smashed to splinters, and the crew considered themselves fortunate to have escaped drowning.

By the time the *Sonora* cast anchor in Monterey Bay on October 7, Hezeta had been waiting for over five weeks. There is no evidence of strained relations; Hezeta may have been too relieved at having them return alive and with the schooner intact to complain of insubordination. Or perhaps he felt apologetic at failing to match their exploits and was grateful that they had done better justice to the viceroy's instructions. Everyone aboard the schooner was ill with scurvy, but Bodega and Mourelle were the sickest of the lot and had to be carried ashore. The mission fathers outdid themselves at nursing the enfeebled explorers. "In truth," Mourelle notes, "we could not possibly have so soon recovered from our distressed situation, but by their unparalleled attentions to our infirmities, which they removed by reducing themselves to a most pitiful allowance."[73] To nurture their guests back to health the friars had to deprive themselves, for the Alta California settlements were still critically short of anything that had to be brought from Mexico, but of fresh food they were soon able to produce more than needed. In time San Francisco and Monterey would take on an important function in sustaining Spanish activities on the northwest coast, as "R and R" liberty ports, in every sense of the phrase.

The two vessels resumed voyage on November 1, and two days later Juan Pérez succumbed after a lingering illness, broken in health by two consecutive expeditions and the rigors they entailed. The much-respected pilot was buried at sea with a Mass, a salvo of muskets, and a cannonade.

72. That the *Sonora* entered and examined Tomales Bay is evident from Bodega's harbor chart in SpAGI (Estado 38, Mex. 19). See Clinton R. Edwards, "Wandering Toponyms: El Puerto de la Bodega and Bodega Bay," *PHR* 33 (1964) : 253–72.

73. Mourelle, *Voyage of the Sonora*, pp. 58–59.

Upon arrival in San Blas on November 20, Hezeta rushed their journals and reports to the viceroy, who remitted them to the Ministry, recommending promotions for the officers involved. The effort had not disclosed a trace of foreign encroachment, and Bucareli was of the opinion that Spanish claims over the area had been secured by the four official acts of possession performed at Port of the Remedies, Bucareli Sound, Bucareli Anchorage (Martyrs' Point), and Trinidad Bay. Copies of these formalities were remitted to Minister Gálvez.[74]

The expeditions sent northward in 1774 and 1775 had cost 15,455 and 36,740 pesos, respectively, without any really tangible benefit to the royal treasury; keeping the new settlements in Alta California supplied with essentials took priority over additional explorations on the northwestern frontier. The settlers' requirements increased sharply after the Anza expedition of 1775 brought a host of men and cattle overland from Mexico to strengthen the mission outposts. The increment buttressed Spanish control, but for at least a few seasons the settlements became increasingly dependent for much of their sustenance upon supplies brought by the few available ships in the Department of San Blas.[75] In the absence of an evident challenge, the last thing in Bucareli's mind would be to waste another peso on what, to all appearances, was safe within Spain's sphere of domain "on the coast to the north of California."

Nor did policy for the northwest coast rank as the ministry's chief concern at the moment. In 1775 Madrid's attention was being demanded by its establishments in Morocco, as a consequence of the Moorish siege of Melilla. The ministry assumed that Britain had inspired the sultan of Morocco to attack Spanish holdings in North Africa. Simultaneously, Carlos III was engaged in counteracting the aggressive designs of Portugal's Marqués de Pombal in South America; in 1776 a Spanish expedition retook Colonia de Sacramento, on the eastern bank of the Río de la Plata. Of greater consequence, Spain had followed France's lead in a strategy designed to weaken British strength in North America through sending money and munitions by secret channels to American revolutionaries. Not that His Catholic Majesty felt any enthusiasm for a republic in North America, conceiving it a dangerous encouragement to malcontents in his own colonies, but he was persuaded to participate in the struggle in expectation of shifting the balance of power away from what seemed to be Madrid's most dangerous rival. Great Britain had sent a formidable body of troops to North America to keep the lid on her rebellious subjects, and if she succeeded, in the flush of triumph these forces might be turned with devastating effect to the conquest of Spanish possessions. Madrid could hardly expect to get involved

74. Bucareli to Arriaga, Mexico City, Dec. 27, 1775, SpAGI (Estado 20–23).
75. Chapman, *Founding of Spanish California*, pp. 242–43.

in such a maneuver without being attacked in America, and fear of assaults upon its territories in the Caribbean led to orders early in 1776 instructing Bucareli to give preference to precautions in that area over further explorations northward in the Pacific.[76]

Simultaneously, however, José de Gálvez was becoming uneasy over rumors reaching Madrid about a scientific effort being prepared in England and directed toward the northwest coast, in the guise of an expedition around the world, to be commanded by a mariner whose discoveries in the South Pacific had given him a reputation of world renown—an ominous portent for Spanish claims over the newly discovered shores to the north of California.

76. Referred to in Bucareli to Grimaldi, Mexico City, March 27, 1776, SpAGI (V, Indif. Gen., Mex. 1630), T in DLC.

# 4 *Spanish Claims to the Northwest Coast Challenged,*
# *1778–1788*

THE VEIL OF SECRECY that Spain hoped to extend over its activities in the North Pacific could not be sustained effectively. Pérez's voyage in 1774 had not gone unnoticed by Russia. As early as April 1775, Ambassador Lacy advised that the court was uneasy about reports of Spanish explorations on the northwest coast of America. Although alarmed letters continued to arrive concerning intensified Muscovite activities in America, there is no evidence that Lacy's warnings were forwarded to Bucareli or that the viceroy continued to worry about a threat from that quarter.[1] Despite official barriers, reports of Spanish activities on the northwest coast filtered through to other nationalities. News of the first two expeditions soon reached England, for example, for in 1776 a short account of them appeared as an appendix to a pamphlet discussing the practicability of finding a northwest passage.[2]

Somehow Mourelle's journal of the 1775 expedition reached London—by clandestine means, as Spanish officials would never have released it willingly. Cook's journal mentions his own utilization of Mourelle's account, so he must have received it before sailing from Plymouth in July 1776 on his third and last voyage. It was regarded as sufficiently important for translation and publication in 1781 by the Honorable Daines Barrington, an eminent London barrister and prominent figure in a circle of lords, merchants, explorers, and promoters with a common interest in discovering a northwest passage and a shorter route to Chinese ports.[3] For years Barrington had been assembling and publishing accounts of voyages at high latitudes in the Atlantic in an endeavor to encourage such a discovery. He

1. Lacy to Grimaldi, Moscow, April 31 [*sic*], May 1, and June 26, 1775, SpAGI (Estado 38–10).
2. "Short Account of Some Voyages Made by Order of the King of Spain, to Discover the State of the West American Coast From California Upward. Dated Madrid, 24 March, 1776," in *Summary Observations and Facts Collected From Late and Authentic Accounts of Russian and Other Navigators, to Show the Practicability and Good Prospect of Success in Enterprises to Discover a Northern Passage for Vessels by Sea, Between the Atlantic and Pacific Oceans* (London, 1776), pp. 28–29.
3. Francisco Antonio Mourelle, "Journal of a Voyage in 1775," in Daines Barrington, *Miscellanies* (London, 1781), pp. 469–534; 2d ed., *Voyage of the Sonora in the Second Bucareli Expedition to Explore the Northwest Coast . . . 1775* (San Francisco, 1920). Barrington's important naval connections may have put him in possession of this journal. His older brother, William Wildman, 2nd Viscount Barrington, was chancellor of the exchequer (1761–62) and secretary of war (1755–61 and 1765–78). A younger brother was a rear admiral in the royal navy.

was a member of the council of the Royal Society, which is credited with intellectual authorship of the project that brought Cook to the North Pacific. The council's plan, as submitted to the admiralty, suggested that, rather than repeat attempts to discover a northwest passage from the Atlantic it would be easier to determine whether such a waterway existed by exploring the northwest coast of America in the high latitudes.[4] Bering's and Chirikov's discoveries had been known for years without prompting such a project, so one suspects that reports of Spanish discoveries triggered British interest. Word of a promising area of coastline known only to Russian and Spanish mariners aroused considerable concern among those privy to such knowledge in British commercial and naval circles, especially since Drake's claim to "New Albion" made many Englishmen feel the northwest coast of America belonged to His Britannic Majesty.

Parliament's bill of 1744 offering a reward of £20,000 to the first British merchant ship to traverse a northwest passage was broadened in 1776 to make vessels of the British navy eligible. Captain James Cook's two highly successful expeditions to the South Pacific (1768–71 and 1772–75) made him the logical choice to be commander of an official effort to reap Parliament's reward. Although he had just returned from circumnavigating the globe, it proved relatively easy for John Montagu, fourth earl of Sandwich and first lord of the admiralty, to induce him to lead the new venture. He was given instructions to approach the coast at 45° north latitude and proceed from there northward without delaying to make extensive surveys, in order to reach 65°, the latitude to which knowledge of central Canada had relegated any such strait. Although search for a northwest passage loomed large among his objectives, Cook's chief purpose was to visit and explore the northwest coast of America with a view to determining its future economic and strategic relevance to Britain's imperial interests. From Mourelle's journal he was aware of many details of Spanish activities in 1774 and 1775, and he had the impression that the *Sonora* had reached 58° 20′ north latitude.[5] His orders were to take possession of any spot not already discovered by another European nation. His warships, the *Discovery* and the *Resolution,* sailed from Plymouth in July 1776, despite the outbreak of hostilities in the colonies. Sailing master of the *Resolution* was William Bligh, of *Bounty* fame, and the roster reveals a number of seamen, as yet obscure, whose experience with Cook enabled them to play larger roles in subsequent Pacific Northwest history: George Vancouver, Joseph Billings, Nathaniel Portlock, George Dixon, and John Ledyard. They came by way of the Indian Ocean and consumed two years visiting Tasmania, New Zealand, and the Friendly Islands. An inscription left on a rock in Tahiti

4. Dodge, *Northwest by Sea,* p. 227.
5. Cook, *Voyage,* 2 : 332.

by a Spanish expedition in 1774 was defaced by Cook's orders before departing. Upon publication in 1784 of his journal mentioning the obliteration, Madrid would order an expedition outfitted at San Blas to restore it and occupy Tahiti.[6] Cook's instructions were to seek landfall on the Pacific coast at 45° north, as Mourelle's journal told of Hezeta's *Entrada* and Cook wanted to find it. The course he followed from Tahiti to North America traversed an area midway between the westward and eastward routes of the Manila galleons, where no Spanish vessel is known to have crossed, and he was rewarded with discovery of the Sandwich, or Hawaiian, Islands, which had eluded Spanish navigators for two centuries.

On March 7, 1778, Cook sighted the Oregon coast at 44° 31' north, near the cape he named "Foul Weather." Excitement ran high among the crew, for by now they knew of Cook's secret objective—the fabled Northwest Passage, whose discovery would yield to each a portion of the handsome reward. Driven by offshore winds, Cook could not spy the Columbia's mouth, and thus he assumed Hezeta mistaken in placing a great river at that latitude. Coasting onward, he named a prominent headland "Cape Flattery" because it "flattered them" with the expectation that beyond lay the Strait of Juan de Fuca; but he was deprived of that discovery too because contrary weather forced his vessels out to sea. Upon approaching land once more, they were off the entrance to a promising estuary. As a gesture to his sovereign, Cook called it "King George's Sound," but the name that prevailed would be his understanding of the native term for Friendly Cove. While at Nootka he purchased the two silver spoons mentioned earlier that persuaded him the Spaniards had already visited the place.[7] The lustrous cutsarks of Nootka inevitably drew attention and could be obtained in barter for trifles catching the braves' fancy. With little effort some 1,500 sea otter pelts were acquired by the crew, who were not aware of their actual worth in China.

Continuing northward, Cook bestowed names upon prominent islands, straits, and mountains—nomenclature displacing the Bodega-Mourelle toponymy. At a large sound which he named Cook Inlet, the commander performed his first act of possession for Great Britain, at 61° 30' north. His avoidance of such a ritual any place short of that latitude has been interpreted as deference to Spanish acts of possession in 1775, which Mourelle's journal placed at 58° north.[8] The two warships followed the coastline past Kodiak to the Aleutians, traversed Bering Strait, and entered the Arctic

6. Upon stepping down as commandant general of the interior provinces, Teodoro de Croix, in a memorial to his successor, noted that circumstances had prevented complying and he commended the unfinished task, but nothing ever came of the project. Stewart, "Martínez and López de Haro," pp. 55–56.

7. Cook, *Voyage*, 2 : 282.

8. Wagner, "Creation of Rights of Sovereignty," p. 314.

Ocean. Cook continued northward within sight of the American coast until the ice pack made further advance impossible, and he concluded that no passageway to the Atlantic existed across the top of the continent. On the return, Cook was visited at Unalaska by the local Russian factor, one Ismailov, who proved quite ready to exchange geographic information. The Englishman spoke freely of his discoveries and mentioned the abundance of sea otters at Nootka. Their numbers in Aleutian waters were diminishing, and Muscovites were ranging ever eastward in search of untapped areas to deploy fleets of *bidarkas*. News of Nootka's promise would have interested Ismailov. Unalaska was the only settlement Cook found, and the Russian assured him there were no more outposts to the east.

From the Aleutians the expedition proceeded to Hawaii to pass the winter; there the great navigator was slain at Kealakekua Bay. Captain Charles Clerke was gravely ill with consumption when command fell to him, but he took the vessels northward again in 1779. Having explored the Asian coast as far as the ice pack permitted, they headed for Kamchatka. Clerke died before they reached Petropavlovsk, and command devolved upon Captains John Gore and James King, who completed the mission and compiled volume three of the official journal. Upon visiting Macao, they found that the cutsarks obtained so cheaply at Nootka brought as much as 100 Spanish dollars a pelt. The crew wanted to return directly and reap the bonanza, and there was a near mutiny before the homeward voyage could be resumed.[9]

### SPANISH EFFORTS TO CHECK COOK'S EXPEDITION

Bucareli's complacency about the northwest coast contrasted dramatically with the attitude of the minister of Indies, the individual responsible for the Iberian surge northward. Standing now at the head of the administrative pyramid for Madrid's overseas dominions, Gálvez could be expected to persist in his endeavor to confirm Spain's control over western North America. Several months before Cook's vessels left Plymouth harbor for the Pacific, Spanish espionage had learned that one of the Englishman's principal objectives would be to visit the northwest coast in search of the Northwest Passage.[10]

Madrid's instinctive reaction to word of British interest in the North Pacific was suspicion, well nigh a conditioned reflex fostered by past experience. Spain was motivated not only by hostility to territorial encroachments but by fear that English activities in the North Pacific would lead to in-

9. Cook, *Voyage*, 3 : 437. Centuries of Manila galleon trade had made Hapsburg pesos (*thalers*, the etymological origin of our dollar) as popular in the Orient as in the United States, which did not coin its own dollars until 1794.

10. Royal order, March 23, 1776, summarized in Bucareli to Gálvez, Mexico City, June 26, 1776, in *Publicaciones del Archivo General de la Nación* (Mexico) 29 (1936) : 307–12.

creased contraband trade with Spanish subjects along the west coast of the Americas, which in mercantilist theory was tantamount to economic hemophilia. This had been the pattern elsewhere in the New World and Madrid was loath to see it repeated in an area that had been relatively free of such debilitation. As Britain's sea power developed, she became increasingly aggressive in expanding trade, a major portion of this effort being directed toward opening up markets in Spanish America, while Madrid's mercantilist policy sought to exclude other nations from commerce with Spanish colonies. For centuries England made a consistent effort—sometimes by warfare but more often when ostensibly at peace—to infiltrate, occupy, seize, revolutionize, or otherwise undermine weak or unoccupied areas in Spain's American colonies. Madrid had always been aware of the pattern, and under Carlos III vigorous efforts were expended to thwart such activities. When they learned of Cook's projected visit to the northwest coast, the Spanish felt compelled to take instant action to counter the challenge. Gálvez foresaw that such a visit would lead to British territorial claims and undermine his dreams for western North America. His reaction was characteristically energetic. Bucareli was instructed to take precautionary measures and advise Spanish commanders along the Pacific coast to do everything possible to neutralize the English explorer's efforts, without resorting to armed force. They should withhold aid and supplies, and employ "other means that a sage policy might require." If Cook's vessels were encountered, their instructions, orders, and intentions should be examined with all the formalities necessary to permit an investigation and formal protest against the encroachment, to be presented to London by representatives of His Catholic Majesty's government.[11]

Two months later, Gálvez received the first news of Bodega's explorations in Alaska and Hezeta's discovery of a great river in western North America, potential access to the continent's unexplored interior, just beyond the California and New Mexico settlements. His immediate response was to order a third expedition for 1777, using the same officers and vessels as before, to consolidate Spanish control over the newly explored coasts.[12] He specifically recommended that Bodega captain one of the vessels. The young man's bravery and determination to carry out his instructions had evidently caught the zealous minister's eye.

Gálvez's frustrations in the Sonora campaign had not upset his plan for a *Comandancia General de las Provincias Internas*. A royal order in 1776 set up the jurisdictional unit intended to create a new realm, autonomous from New Spain, centered in the American Southwest. Ultimately it would extend from Louisiana through Texas, Coahuila, New Mexico, New Vizcaya (Durango), Chihuahua, Sinaloa, and Sonora to the two Californias

11. Ibid.
12. [Gálvez] to Bucareli, Aranjuez, May 20, 1776, SpAGI (Estado 20–23).

and the northwest coast.[13] The capital, temporarily Chihuahua, was intended to be at Arizpe, a village on the Sonora River near the present Arizona border. The California supply system was left in the viceroy's hands, to be administered from San Blas. Before leaving office the Marqués de Croix had secured his nephew's nomination to head the new jurisdiction. Chapman blames Gálvez himself for the election of "so inefficient an instrument as Teodoro de Croix." [14] From the first the young commandant general had to give the Sonora revolts most of his attention, and he was unable to devote sufficient effort to securing Spanish claims over the northwest coast. The Yuma Massacre of 1781 severed overland connections between Mexico and Alta California. Chapman believes that if the inland route to California had not been interrupted, that province would have witnessed such an influx of settlers that gold would have been discovered many years earlier than was the case. What is significant for Pacific Northwest history is that Indian raids in northwestern Mexico hamstrung the effort to create an administrative unit in the Southwest of sufficient strength to exert dominion as far as Gálvez aspired—the entire western portion of the continent as far as the Arctic. The dream never overcame its initial artificiality, and its geographic unwieldiness seriously undermined coordination of Spanish efforts along the Pacific coast, foreordaining trouble.

The ministry's newly militant stance placed Bucareli in a dilemma. As mentioned, in March 1776 an order had arrived from Madrid giving preference to protection from British attack in the Caribbean over further exploration on the Pacific coast. In full agreement, the viceroy responded:

> Those discoveries could be very useful, but to follow them up opportunely, it would be necessary to enter into very great expenses—not needed when we know that, in almost 500 leagues of coast reconnoitered, there is no cause for worry, and since we have now occupied the famous port of San Francisco, we ought to limit ourselves to expanding those new settlements so that, by maintaining themselves, they will encourage more distant ones.[15]

Then in June came Gálvez's alarmed message about Captain Cook and the instructions to thwart the Englishman's efforts. Faced with such an abrupt reversal, Bucareli decided that the most he could do to counteract Cook would be to withhold supplies, where there was such a deficiency of

13. Carlos III to Bucareli, San Ildefonso, August 22, 1776, MH (Sparks Coll., 98–3). As originally defined, it did not include Texas and Coahuila, but little by little they came under that jurisdiction. Luís Navarro García, "El Norte de Nueva España como problema político en el siglo XVIII," *Revista estudios Americanos* 103 (Seville, 1960) : 26.

14. Chapman, *Founding of Spanish California*, pp. 386–87, 412, 416.

15. Bucareli to Grimaldi, Mexico City, March 27, 1776, SpAGI (V, Indif. Gen., Mex. 1630), T in DLC, AT.

them anyway, for in his opinion the Spanish navy on the Pacific coast would be unable to oppose Cook by force.[16] In August, Gálvez's plan for a third expedition to the northwest coast arrived, and Bucareli's response was something less than enthusiastic. The *Santiago* was in drydock being overhauled, the *San Carlos* and the *Príncipe* had gone to Monterey with the annual supplies, and the *Concepción* and the *Sonora* were on missions to Baja California. The acute shortage of vessels precluded carrying out the project in 1777. The *Santiago,* when repaired, would also be needed to take supplies to Alta California. Bucareli deemed it his "first and most urgent objective" to protect the area already settled in California. Perhaps the exploration could be undertaken by the *San Carlos* and the *Príncipe,* with captains Hezeta and Bodega, when they returned from Monterey. Construction of additional ships was hindered by the difficulty of securing iron parts. Providing newly built vessels with armament was a tremendous obstacle, for cannons had to be brought overland from Veracruz. Bucareli requested that the viceroy of Peru be instructed to have two frigates built at Guayaquil for use in further explorations on the northwest coast.[17]

Perceiving the trouble that would ensue if he completely disregarded Gálvez's instructions for an expedition to counter the British threat, Bucareli convoked a junta of officials having the greatest acquaintance with the Californias to determine what should be undertaken. Participating were Hezeta, Bodega, Mourelle, and two other officers who would later command Spanish vessels on the northwest coast: Ignacio de Arteaga and José de Cañizares. The five-day meeting at Tepic in November 1776 merely ratified Bucareli's letters to the ministry. His own views sustained, the viceroy cancelled Gálvez's plan.[18]

The minister of Indies had informed Bucareli of Cook's departure from Plymouth in July 1776, within a few days of the event. At the first indication that the viceroy was dragging his feet—the receipt of his letter of August 27—the testy minister shot back a strongly worded directive insisting that previous orders be carried out, emphasizing that they were given in full cognizance of handicaps in San Blas and the Californias. He now added that if sufficient force were at hand to detain Cook's vessels, the English explorer and his men should be arrested and prosecuted under the Laws of Indies. After the long voyage to the North Pacific, it was likely they would be unable to resist capture.[19] If Gálvez had his way, there would

16. Bucareli to Gálvez, Mexico City, June 26, 1776, in *Publicaciones del Archivo General de la Nación,* 29 (1936) : 307–12.

17. Bucareli to Gálvez, Mexico City, August 27, 1776, SpAGI (V, Aud. Guad. 516).

18. Bucareli to Gálvez, Mexico City, September 26, 1776, and Bucareli to Hezeta, Mexico City, December 7, 1776, SpAGI (V, Aud. Guad. 515).

19. Royal order, October 18, 1776, quoted in Bucareli to Gálvez, January 27, 1777, MxAGN (Corr. Virreyes I, 13), summarized in Chapman, *Founding of Spanish California,* pp. 379–80.

be a confrontation that—given the international situation—would become entangled with other aspects of the American Revolution.

Bucareli was left with no choice but to answer that he would obey. However, using the excuse that the Californias had been separated from his control and put under the jurisdiction of the commandant general of the Interior Provinces, the viceroy said he was sending the royal command to Chihuahua.[20] In effect he was shifting responsibility onto the lesser official in the newly created post—the minister's own brainchild. It would be a practical impossibility to dictate measures for defense of the Pacific coast from Chihuahua, as Bucareli well knew. Teodoro de Croix, his attention absorbed by the chronic Indian rebellions, would be unable to take any action to counteract Cook. Bucareli's letters evince no great alarm over the threat to Spanish interests from the famed explorer's visit, and he saw no feasible means of intercepting the English vessels. Bucareli frequently has been cited as the prime activist and promoter of the northward expansion of Spanish dominion, but the viceroy's biographer, Bernard Bobb, deprives him of the credit, holding that at the most he was merely carrying out orders set in motion by Gálvez, first as visitador and then as minister of Indies. Bobb rejects the opinion of Chapman and others, who considered California Bucareli's first concern. Rather, the biographer believes, financial matters were his main preoccupation. "How much will it cost?" determined his choice of alternatives.[21]

When Gálvez received Bucareli's report of the reasons for not forestalling Cook's expedition at once, he replied acidly that he had "read to the king your letter of September 26 in which you describe the irresolution in which the explorations are found which were ordered to be repeated." Carlos III gave his approval to Bucareli's measures, and an order was sent to the viceroy of Peru, "charging him with the rapidity of construction and good quality" of the vessels to be built there for the next expedition to the northwest coast.[22] Bodega was sent to his homeland to bring the two vessels to San Blas, and Hezeta was appointed commandant of the department, replacing Ignacio de Arteaga, who would lead the next expedition, once readied.[23]

Concurrently, the San Blas "transfer controversy" was causing much concern in the department; some thought Acapulco so superior it should

20. Bucareli to Gálvez, January 27, 1777, MxAGN (corr. Virreyes I, 13); Chapman, *Founding of Spanish California*, pp. 388–89.

21. Bernard Bobb, *The Viceregency of Antonio María Bucareli in New Spain, 1771–1779* (Austin, 1962), pp. 160–62, 165, 171; Chapman, *History of California*, pp. 271, 275.

22. [Gálvez] to Bucareli, Madrid, December 24, 1776, SpAGI (V, Aud. Guad. 515).

23. Hezeta never returned to the northwest coast. Transferred to the Philippines and then to Cuba, from 1787 onward he commanded naval bases at Rosas and Algeciras; he died at Málaga in 1807 (*Enciclopedia Espasa*).

be headquarters for naval activities to Alta California and the northwest coast. Others opposed abandoning San Blas, on the grounds that the gigantic expenses incurred in making improvements there would have been wasted. At one point Bucareli contemplated creating a central base of operations at one of Alta California's excellent ports for sustaining activities of "high latitude." A royal order decided the matter: if evidence of Russian bases was discovered close to California, necessitating augmented military defenses along New Spain's west coast, then San Blas should be forgone in favor of a better harbor somewhere else. If such were not the case, the little port would continue as the main base, despite its defects.[24]

Faced with the sovereign's acquiescence to Bucareli's halfhearted measures, Gálvez was not the kind to take satisfaction from seeing his worst fears confirmed. As the very process that he sought to counteract set in, the impatient Andalusian doubtless experienced many a pang of disappointment at seeing his projects advance so haltingly as to be outrun by the pace of events. Nothing to impede Cook's effort could get underway until Bodega returned to San Blas in February 1778 with a seventy-two-foot frigate built in Peru, the *Nuestra Señora de los Remedios,* alias the *Favorita.*[25] He brought from Callao two young pilots who later commanded vessels sailing to the northwest coast: Juan Pantoja and José Tovar y Tamáriz. Pantoja was a graduate of Seville's famous Seminario de San Telmo, an academy offering a special course of study preparing young men for careers in the Spanish navy, and his skill as a cartographer is reflected in many excellent charts and maps of the northwest coast. Another frigate almost identical to the *Favorita,* the *Nuestra Señora del Rosario,* alias the *Princesa,* had just been completed at San Blas.

As Cook headed from Tahiti toward Oregon in the spring of 1778, Spanish officials had not the slightest idea of his whereabouts, and Bucareli was still far from prepared to dispatch the *Princesa* and the *Favorita* on their dangerous mission. A year elapsed and the British warships were about to lose their commander at Kealekekua Bay when, in February 1779, the Spanish expedition that Gálvez had ordered for 1777 started northward.

### THE ARTEAGA EXPEDITION TO ALASKA, 1779

When Cook's vessels left Hawaii in 1779 to resume examination of the North Pacific, the British had no inkling that they were the object of pursuit by Spanish warships. Leadership of this effort fell to ship's lieutenant Ignacio de Arteaga, ranking officer in the Department of San Blas; the

---

24. Bucareli to Gálvez, Mexico City, July 27, 1776, SpAGI (Guad. 104); Royal order to Bucareli, El Pardo, January 9, 1777, SpAGI (Guad. 497), cited by Thurman, *San Blas,* pp. 225–28.

25. Bodega, "Navegación y descubrimientos hechos de orden de S. M. en la Costa Septentrional de California . . . Año de 1779," SpMN (332), fol. 12v.

*Princesa* was his flagship. Ship's lieutenant Fernando Quirós would be second officer, José Camacho and Juan Pantoja the pilots, Franciscans Juan Antonio García Riobó and Matias Santa Catalina Noriega the chaplains, with a crew totaling ninety-eight. Second in command would be Bodega as captain of the *Favorita*. Its complement of 107 included second officer Francisco Antonio Mourelle, pilots José Cañizares and Juan Bautista Aguirre, with Don Cristóbal Díaz, a cleric, as chaplain. One hundred and seventeen men had sailed from England aboard the *Resolution,* with a comparable number on the *Discovery.* How Arteaga expected to prevail in any show of force with a total of only 205 men is nowhere discussed. The frigates carried fourteen cannons and fifteen swivel guns, evenly distributed between the two, with enough cannonballs, powder, grapeshot, muskets, pistols, and swords to provide what was judged to be a sufficiency for defense against any enemy. Thirty-nine of the crew were classed as marine artillerymen. Supplies were embarked for thirteen and fifteen months respectively, although the expedition was intended to return before winter. Arteaga carried various charts of the North Pacific: one published in Mexico and inspired by Delisle's fanciful map of 1752; Bellin's map of 1766; and the chart printed in St. Petersburg in 1758. Of greater utility was another that Bodega, Mourelle, and Arteaga had prepared from maps of the 1775 expedition, to which they added Delisle's coastline in black dots, Bellin's data in red, and the Russian information in yellow. Arteaga was instructed to reach 70° north latitude, if possible.[26]

The frigates left San Blas on February 11 and followed a course far from the continent, so that upon heading northward, landfall would occur at a high latitude. Early in May they arrived off Bucareli Sound, which Spanish officialdom assumed was the most promising site for a naval base. The natives gathered in a long line atop a point jutting out into the bay, chanting solemnly and performing the feather-sprinkling ritual, which Arteaga recognized as expressing a desire for peace. He gave presents of trinkets and beads to those bold enough to come near. In turn, the natives offered dried fish, small woven mats, sea otter pelts, and sea lion and deer skins. The warriors wore suits of wooden armor, ingeniously sewn, protecting torso and limbs, with helmets carved to resemble ferocious animals, the mouth-opening serving as visor. Beads, mirrors, and rings brought especially for trading had relatively little appeal compared to the eagerness displayed for

26. "Tercera exploración de la costa septentrional de Californias con las dos fragatas Princesa y Faborita, mandadas por el Teniente de Navío D. Ignacio Arteaga, y por el de la misma clase D. Juan de la Quadra en el año de 79," SpMN (331), fol. 92v–93; Francisco Antonio Mourelle, "Navegación hecha por el alférez de fragata D. Francisco Antonio Mourelle en la fragata 'Favorita' desde el puerto de San Blas a los descubrimientos de la costa de Californias en el año 1779," SpMN (332), fol. 95–96.

iron and copper and even short pieces of barrel hoop, which could be fashioned into sharp cutting tools.[27]

While the frigates remained at anchor, replenishing water casks, cutting wood, and loading ballast, Arteaga sent his longboats to explore interior channels. In their absence, an epidemic of unspecified nature broke out aboard the *Princesa* and many fell ill, including the commander. Several men died, and, at the advice of the *Favorita*'s surgeon, Don Mariano Núñez de Esquivel, a barracks was constructed on shore where the sick could be isolated and receive special care. This checked the malady's spread; only two more died, and the rest recovered rapidly. The ailing would scarcely have dared remain on shore had the Indians not given ample signs of friendliness, every day bringing fresh fish, pelts, woven mats, and other products for barter. But there was much petty thievery by those allowed to come aboard, and one foolhardy sailor who strayed away from his companions to bathe was seized by the aborigines, stripped, and robbed of everything he wore, although allowed to return unscathed. When the launches had been gone several weeks there was growing anxiety for their safety, for soon after they departed more than a hundred canoes of Indians took up residence not far from the frigates. The initial feeling of confidence dissipated after the cross erected on shore was smashed solely to get its nails, evincing the natives' increasing audacity.

The belated return of the launches, after almost a month, brought some hint of the complexity of the archipelago, and the many waterways separating sound from continent. They had found several different exits to the sea, and intriguing channels penetrating a long distance inland; lack of time prevented exploring these thoroughly, however. The day after their return, a group of sailors went ashore to wash clothes and bathe. When it was time to go back, two were missing. Arteaga immediately ordered a nearby canoe intercepted and its occupant held as hostage for the missing men. A white-haired chieftain came within shouting distance and promised to turn over the tars in exchange for the hostage the following morning. The robust captive managed a friendly countenance and was given several items of clothing and some beads. He ate at the crew's mess, was demonstrably pleased by music made for his entertainment, and spent the night in a bunk in the fo'c'sle. In the morning the canoes coming from shore showed no signs of yielding up the seamen, and the hostage pleaded with them, his visage becoming more and more contorted with rage. The braves derided

27. "Relación del viaje echo a la alaska p(o)r. las fragatas de su Mag(esta)d. la princesa y favorita," CtY-BWA (Coe 12), fol. 2–2v. The author, a priest, refers to "Fray Matías" as his companion; hence he must have been the other chaplain aboard the *Princesa*, Juan Antonio García Riobó. A variant Ms of his journal was published in *Catholic Historical Review* 4 (1918–19): 222–29.

him, paying little heed to his protestations as to the Iberian's friendly intentions. In a dugout at some distance, the seamen spotted one of the prisoners, hidden under a mat. His compatriots shouted at him, and he seized a stick and commenced stroking frantically toward the nearest ship. At this, his captors took away the makeshift paddle and, as his companions watched impotently, made off with great hubbub and war whoops, returning to their village.[28]

Arteaga tried to lure the chief, hoping to gain his men's release with a hostage of greater rank. The wary old fellow would not come aboard unless a Spaniard came down into a canoe to answer for his safety. The commander ordered a sailor to descend—but to be ready to clamber back when the chieftain came up. No sooner had he reached the canoe, however, than the warriors seized him and pulled away for shore. To frighten them into returning, Arteaga ordered one of his cannons fired without ball. When this occurred, the cry went up on the *Favorita* that an assault on the flagship had commenced, and Bodega's men opened fire. In the noise and confusion several canoes overturned, and boats raced to seize the men, women, and children floundering in the water before they could swim away or be rescued by other canoes. Twenty-one were picked up. One native perished in the single fusillade and another drowned. To convince the survivors that their capture was motivated solely by the hope of redeeming his seamen, Arteaga gave them all presents of cloth, blankets, and trinkets. With such a large group of hostages, he was sure the seamen could be rescued, and he put Mourelle and Pantoja in charge of a well-armed landing party, which set out in four launches for the beach in front of the village. They resumed bargaining and after lengthy negotiations the unhappy sailors were yielded up and the hostages set ashore.

Under duress the two confessed leaving their companions voluntarily and asking the occupants of a canoe passing nearby to take them to the village. Once inside the craft, the haste with which their request was granted made them realize the danger, but it was too late to escape. Upon seizing paddles and attempting to row toward safety, they had been overpowered. At the village the thoroughly frightened seamen had found themselves the center of attention, and in the wild and bloodcurdling orgy that ensued they were stripped and throughout a night of terror and discomfort not allowed a moment of repose. Dearly repenting their foolishness, they fully expected death at any moment. When ransom finally came, they were much relieved at being saved from the greater danger, but Arteaga sentenced

28. Juan Pantoja y Arriaga, "Extracto del diario del viaje de la exploración de las Costas Septentrionales de la California . . . ," 1788, CtY–BWA (Coe S–216), fol. 37v–40v. Although dated 1788, it narrates events of the 1779 expedition.

them to a hundred lashes apiece for jeopardizing the expedition's safety by obliging him to come to their rescue.

The Indian who spent the night aboard the *Princesa* soon revisited the frigate, showing no fear of his erstwhile captors. Arteaga gave him a number of presents for demonstrating such confidence in Spanish benevolence. During the stay at Bucareli the natives offered three boys and two girls in trade for pieces of iron, beads, and clothes. Out of pity and charity the friars and seamen felt constrained to purchase them, convinced that they were orphans or captives destined to be eaten or kept as slaves.[29]

Resuming his explorations northward, near the entrance to Prince William Sound Arteaga took a party ashore, performed formal possession, and erected a cross at a bay named for Spain's patron, "Saint James the Apostle," today Port Etches, Hinchinbrook Island.[30] The northernmost point at which possession was ever executed by Spanish subjects in America, it was the foundation for Madrid's subsequent claims to sovereignty as far as 61° north latitude. Cañizares and Pantoja were sent with a launch to explore the interior channels to determine whether they led to a northwest passage. At one spot the natives had a red, white, and blue flag which the pilots were unable to identify, but the find received no further notice. Arteaga observed that the continent formed a great bight, and a lofty chain of snow-clad mountains extended beyond the horizon to the southwest. Resuming their voyage, the Spaniards were driven, helpless, before a violent storm, and threading among numerous islands and reefs they eventually obtained shelter in the lee of a cape. When the wind abated, another possession was taken at a bay named "Our Lady of the Rule" (*Nuestra Señora de la Regla*), near the tip of Kenai Peninsula.[31] The expedition reached Afognak Island, near Kodiak, before heavy rains, seven deaths, and many grave cases of scurvy persuaded them that their mission had been fulfilled.

Arteaga's intinerary failed to reveal that Cook's vessels had ever reached the northwest coast, and he was led to believe that Russian activities were confined to the Aleutians. The sense of security his expedition induced would allow Carlos III and his ministers to assume that Madrid could rest on its laurels and still retain dominion over that coastline, by virtue of

29. "They succeeded in buying five little heathen, three boys and two girls, three of whom were baptized in this mission [San Francisco], while the two larger ones were taken to San Blas to be baptized there, for as they were now ten years old and did not know the language well, they needed instruction, which was not necessary for the three who were baptized in this mission as they were infants." Francisco Palóu, *Historical Memoirs of New California*, 4 vols. (Berkeley, 1926), 4: 178–80; Pantoja, "Extracto del diario," fol. 40–44v; "Relación," fol. 3–3v.

30. Acta de posesión, Puerto de Santiago de Apóstol, July 22, 1779, in *Boletín del Archivo General de la Nación* (Mexico) 14 (1943) : 411–14.

31. Acta de posesión, Ensenada de Nuestra Señora de la Regla, August 2, 1779, in ibid., pp. 414–17.

previous discovery and symbolic acts of possession. No one foresaw that the decade to follow would bring traders of half a dozen nationalities swarming into the very area visited by Arteaga and Bodega.

Although Viceroy Bucareli had more than a few doubts about the relevance of the northwest coast to Spanish interests, his death on April 9, 1779, acted as a further impediment to dominion over that area; a period of confusion in government ensued, in part as a consequence of José de Gálvez's penchant for nepotism. Martín de Mayorga succeeded Bucareli, but only in an interim capacity, since the minister of Indies had obtained the post for his older brother, Matías. For various reasons Mayorga continued in office until 1783, and Matías de Gálvez died after holding it less than a year, to be succeeded by his son, Bernardo, conde de Gálvez, formerly governor of Louisiana, who likewise succumbed after about a year as viceroy. From 1779 until Manuel Antonio Flores's appointment in 1787, the post was vacant a total of approximately twenty-four months. During such intervals authority passed to the Audiencia three times and to the archbishop once. Inevitably, administration and policy suffered from indirection because of the short period that any one authority held office. Madrid's involvement elsewhere also served to suspend her attention to the northwest coast. While Arteaga was in Alaskan waters, motives inducing Carlos III to provide secret aid to the American Revolution led to the Convention of Aranjuez (April 12, 1779), by which Spain joined openly in the war against Great Britain, stipulating that France could not make a separate peace until Carlos had regained Gibraltar. José de Gálvez confided to his nephew, then governor of Louisiana and soon to become viceroy of Mexico, that another objective for siding with the American insurgents was "to drive the English from the Gulf of Mexico and neighborhood of that province [of Louisiana], liberating ourselves by this means of the damage to our commerce and continual anxiety in which their ambitious designs keep us."[32] The Floridas, in English hands since 1763, soon fell before a Spanish invasion and reverted to Madrid in the treaty of 1783.

Spain's zeal to weaken her British rival was matched with plans in London to undermine the Spanish Empire and detach such portions as might be vulnerable. One such project was presented to the Shelburne ministry by Richard Oswald, an elderly Scottish merchant of considerable influence. To cripple the house of Bourbon for all time, Oswald endeavored to show that "it is in the power of Russia to make a compleat conquest of the Spanish settlements on the coast of the South Seas, in a short time, at a small expence, and with a certainty of maintaining them against Spain and every

32. José de Gálvez to Bernardo de Gálvez, August 29, 1779, SpAGI (Cuba 174, A), cited by Fernando de Armas Medina, "Luisiana y Florida en el reinado de Carlos III," *Estudios Americanos*, 19, no. 100 (Seville, 1960) : 69. AT.

other power in Europe." [33] The tsarina should be encouraged to seize California, attack the Pacific coast of Mexico and South America, and push through to the Gulf of Mexico. Oswald had lived in Virginia and the West Indies, and he had built a fortune trading in slaves to America. He and Benjamin Franklin were old friends, so in 1782 Shelburne sent him to Paris to negotiate the terms of a peace treaty. When the Scot disclosed to him the plan for a concerted attack upon California and Mexico, Franklin noted, "This appear'd to me a little visionary at present, but I did not dispute it." [34] In subsequent months Oswald renewed, modified, and elaborated upon the utility of seizing Spanish possessions on the Pacific coast, suggesting that rumors of such seizures might persuade Madrid to agree to a treaty more favorable to Great Britain.[35] Probably that is why Oswald mentioned it to the American, in the expectation that Franklin would reveal it to his allies. There is no evidence that Shelburne gave the plan serious attention or that word of it reached Madrid.

The American Revolution weakened Spain's policy for the northwest coast by diverting her energies to protecting more valued territory in the Caribbean, the Philippine Islands, and the Río de la Plata, and to the unsuccessful effort to retake Gibraltar. Upon the Department of San Blas would now fall responsibility for building up the military defenses of Manila, to prevent a repeat of its capture in 1762 by the British. Since the 1779 expedition revealed no serious threat of foreign encroachments on the northwest coast, the ministry saw no immediate economic or strategic advantage from military occupation or settlement there. It figured that British forces and vessels would be engaged elsewhere, against France and the United States. The three wholly unremunerative expeditions to the Far North had been an enormous financial drain on the Department of San Blas, to the extent that by 1779 it was financially unsound largely for that reason, and a royal order in 1780 suspended further expeditions northward in the Pacific.[36] All available vessels, talent, and monetary resources were channeled into the war effort. Bodega and other commissioned officers with experience on the northwest coast were transferred to Havana or Manila, and a concerted effort was made to reduce expenses in the department to

33. Richard Oswald, "Plan for an Alliance with Russia, in Order to Carry on the American War," April 12, 1781, Shelburne Papers, vol. 72 (Clements Library, U. of Michigan), pub. by R. A. Humphreys, "Richard Oswald's Plan for an English and Russian Attack on Spanish America, 1781–1782," *HAHR* 18 (1938) : 95–101.

34. Benjamin Franklin, *Writings*, ed. Albert H. Smyth 10 vols. (New York and London, 1905–07), 8 : 486, cited by Humphreys, "Richard Oswald's Plan," p. 98.

35. Richard Oswald, "Minutes Relative to the Situation of England in the Present War," June 26–July 1, 1782; supplements July 3–July 5, 1782, Shelburne Papers, vol. 72, cited by Humphreys, "Richard Oswald's Plan," p. 96.

36. José de Gálvez to Viceroy Martín de Mayorga, Aranjuez, May 10, 1780, SpAGI (V, Aud. Guad. 497); Thurman, *San Blas*, pp. 193, 241–42.

an absolute minimum. Salary reductions were decreed, and men transferred out were not replaced. Within five years official personnel in the
department fell off by 50 percent.[37]

The decision to curtail further explorations northward, while it achieved
economy, had a baneful effect upon the long-term political objectives, for
it weakened Spain's hand on the newly discovered coastline precisely when
Cook's explorations were magnifying the challenge. Failure to publicize
accomplishments of 1774, 1775, and 1779 undermined claims of ownership
by virtue of prior discovery. Save for Mourelle's journal, published without
Madrid's consent, no detailed accounts of Spanish deeds had penetrated the
barrier of secrecy which, by official design, had been the chief strategy for
protecting Spain's claims to western North America. In the end that policy
was counterproductive. Carlos III and his ministers did not perceive the
fact as yet, but the vast stretch of coastline would no longer be ignored by
Spain's rivals. Forces were being generated which would open it to those
more appreciative of its natural resources—a direct consequence of the
casual gathering of pelts by Cook at Nootka.

### THE RISE OF THE SEA OTTER TRADE

At a time when external factors brought Spanish activities on the northwest coast to a standstill, other nationalities learned of the potential re-
source which, while Madrid had failed to foresee it, would give the area
great economic importance and make it a focus of international rivalry.
Cook's vessels reached England in October 1780. Elaborate precautions
were taken to prevent the crew from smuggling ashore any diaries or journals that might get into print. Despite admiralty efforts to keep a lid on news
of the sea otter wealth until peacetime, when British traders could get a
head start in exploiting it, word leaked out long before the official journal
was published in 1784. Two anonymous accounts that came off the press
in 1781 told of the bartering at Nootka. Another clandestine journal appeared the following year.[38]

There is probably a connection between the return of Cook's vessels and
the publication in 1781 of Mourelle's 1775 journal in English translation.
Encouraged by the economic promise of Nootka, Barrington was endeavoring to stimulate British interest in the northwest coast. In one of the footnotes he remarked: "It should seem from this journal, that the Spaniards
deem all the N. W. coast of America beyond California to be a part of that

37. From a high of 372 in 1782, the number was reduced to almost half by 1787. Viceroy
Flores to Antonio Valdés, Mexico City, October 27, 1787, SpAGI (Mexico 1514); Thurman, *San
Blas*, pp. 189–91, 245–50, 335.

38. *A Journal of a Voyage Around the World* (London, 1781); [John Rickman], *Journal of
Captain Cook's Last Voyage to the Pacific Ocean* (London, 1781); William Ellis, *An Authentic
Narrative of a Voyage Performed by Captain Cook*, 2 vols. (London, 1782).

province." In another, Barrington denied that Spanish acts of possession established valid territorial claims, because the land had been peopled previously by Indians sufficiently civilized to build houses and fishing stages, whereas the Spanish had asserted claims without making a settlement or even intending to do so.[39] His disdain for Spanish pretensions would be echoed by other Englishmen.

Word of the prices brought by sea otter pelts in China sparked expectations in British commercial circles of a bonanza, and with the peace treaty (September 1783), the merchant marine was unleashed. First comers stood to reap the largest harvest, and, as news spread, each year the number of vessels setting out for that remote shore increased. First to arrive was the *Harmon,* an English merchantman brought from China in 1785 by Captain James Hanna. While at Nootka it was attacked by Indians in broad daylight, but the assault was repulsed "with considerable slaughter." The skirmish occurred after Hanna opened fire upon the Indians in retaliation for the theft of a chisel.[40] The native side of the story was related to the Spanish several years later. Upon visiting the *Harmon,* Chief Ma-kwee-na was invited to sit in a chair on deck. A sailor sprinkled a small pile of gunpowder under the seat, with a thin trail of the substance leading out from it as a fuse. Ma-kwee-na was given to understand they were rendering him a salute reserved to honored personages, and he assumed the powder to be black sand until it was lit. Before he could get up, a blinding flash and roar elevated him from the deck. His robe offered scant protection from the searing blast, wounding both person and chiefly dignity; as proof he showed the Spanish the scars still visible on his rump.[41] Salvaging slighted prestige was an important consideration in that culture area, but the attempt at vengeance failed. Hanna offered to treat the wounded, reestablished trade relations, and was able to sail for China with a cargo that sold for over 20,000 Spanish dollars.

In 1786 he returned to Nootka with another vessel, appropriately named *Sea Otter,* eager to repeat the feat. Six other vessels arrived from England and Bengal that year, operating under licenses from the East India Company, which London had given a monopoly over British trade eastward from the Cape of Good Hope. The South Sea Company held similar privileges over the west coast of America, from the mainland to three hundred leagues at sea. To operate legally on the northwest coast and sell furs in China, British vessels had to have licenses from both companies. The East India

39. Mourelle, *Voyage of the Sonora,* pp. 13n, 45n.

40. F. W. Howay, "An Early Account of the Loss of the Boston in 1803," *WHQ* 17 (1926): 284n; idem, ed., *The Dixon-Meares Controversy* (Toronto and New York, [ca.1929], p. 30.

41. Martínez, "Diario" [1789], SpMN (732), p. 118; "New Fur Trade," *London World,* October 6 and 13, 1788; 2d ed., *'New Fur Trade,' An Article From the World . . . Describing the Earliest Voyages to the Northwest Coast of America* (San Francisco, 1941).

Company sought to monopolize the sea otter trade and exclude all others. Two of its vessels, the *Captain Cook* and the *Experiment,* were outfitted in Bengal by James Strange, son-in-law of Henry Dundas, president of its board of control.[42] Hoping to further Britain's claims, Strange performed acts of possession for His Britannic Majesty at several places on Vancouver Island in 1786. He left his surgeon at Nootka in July, to remain all winter and insure that the furs gathered would not be traded to others. Dr. John Mackay went ashore confident of the protection of Ma-kwee-na, whose daughter he had cured of a scabby disease, and took up residence in the chief's great lodge at Friendly Cove. Mackay carried ashore with him a musket, pistols, and ammunition. Strange endeavored to persuade the Indians that firearms were only fatal in the hands of a white man and had dangerous results if otherwise used. To make his point, a musket was loaded with excessive powder and offered to the assembled braves. From among the many volunteers stepping forward, Strange selected Ma-kwee-na, who "very composedly received the piece, took his aim & fired; and had not some of his attendants been standing near him, he could not have failed measuring his length on the ground." "The terror and dread of all present," Strange continues, "was now strongly painted in each countenance, and my Hero in particular, when he recovered from his fright, could not help condemning his imprudence in having thus inconsiderately brought a mischief on himself, and complained most bitterly of the pain which the shock occasioned." When Strange offered the reloaded gun to the others, they all declined, swearing never to touch firearms again.[43]

Long-lived Ma-kwee-na's education in the ways of the European was only beginning; he was acquainted with every captain from Pérez to John Salter, of the *Boston,* massacred at Nootka in 1803. From an initial position as one of several rival chiefs, Ma-kwee-na employed his familiarity with European captains to enhance his own political stature, receiving deferential treatment as sovereign over other bands in the immediate area of the sound during the period of Spanish dominion over Nootka. Ma-kwee-na, of subtle intellect and considerable diplomatic talents, quickly learned to pit one nationality against another. His acculturation proceeded rapidly, and he adopted such elements as proved useful or enjoyable, but the experience would be acquired at considerable injury to himself and his people, victims of the guile and vices of visitors of every nationality.

42. Henry Dundas (1741–1811), member of Parliament from 1774 onward, of Lord North's party, belonged to a circle of influential men whose lobbying led to the Nootka Crisis. Appointed to the cabinet in 1791 as home secretary, from 1794 to 1801 he was secretary of war. Elevated to the peerage in 1802 as Viscount Melville, he became first lord of the admiralty in 1804. Wagner, "Creation of Rights of Sovereignty," p. 315.

43. James Strange, *James Strange's Journal and Narrative of the Commercial Expedition From Bombay to the North-west Coast of America* (Madras, 1928), pp. 22, 33–34.

In 1787 four British fur trading vessels were operating on the northwest coast. That same year, Captain Charles William Barkley came with the *Imperial Eagle,* ostensibly representing a nonexistent Austrian East India Company. Actually, the ship was originally the British *Loudoun,* some of whose owners were directors of the East India Company, and others employees of the company serving in China. The *Loudoun's* registry had been transferred to Ostend, in Flanders, and its name officially changed so as to sail under the Austrian flag, but so superficial was the disguise that Barkley's log never used the new name. While his ship was being outfitted, the twenty-seven-year-old captain courted and won the hand of Frances Hornby Trevor, daughter of a clergyman residing in Ostend. Unlike most masters, Barkley took his seventeen-year-old bride with him. Frances Barkley was the first white woman to visit the Pacific Northwest; and for almost ten years, during a series of cruises to the northwest coast, China, and Japan, she would have no other home than her husband's cabin.[44]

The *Imperial Eagle* was the first to enter Nootka in 1787. No sooner had it cast anchor than a dirty and emaciated white man, clad solely in a cut-sark, clambered aboard. Announcing he was John Mackay, erstwhile surgeon of the *Captain Cook,* he begged to serve Barkley as medical officer to escape his wilderness prison. Even for the Indians winter was a lean season; reduced to their diet of dried fish heads and similar viands, by spring Mackay had been close to starvation. On several occasions he had accompanied hunting parties, and his observations had led Mackay to believe that Nootka might be located on a large island, and not on the mainland, as generally assumed. Barkley then sailed southward searching for a waterway that might confirm Mackay's suspicions, discovering the large indentation still bearing his name: Barkley Sound. They continued southward, and as Mrs. Barkley's journal relates: "to our great astonishment, we arrived off a large opening extending to the eastward, the entrance of which appeared to be about four leagues wide, and remained about that width as far as the eye could see, with a clear easterly horizon, which my husband immediately recognized as the long lost strait of Juan de Fuca, and to which he gave the name of the original discoverer."[45] The *Imperial Eagle* did not enter the strait, but continued south along the coast. Today Barkley is usually credited with its discovery, despite Martínez's assertion that he spied it in 1774. Near Destruction Island, close to the mouth of Washington's Hoh River, the mate, purser, and four of Barkley's seamen went ashore in a small

44. Frances Barkley's diary, cited by F. W. Howay, "Early Navigation of the Straits of Fuca," *OHQ* 12 (1911) : 6, 9; F. W. Howay, "Letters Concerning Voyages of British Vessels to the Northwest Coast of America, 1787–1809," *OHQ* 39 (1938) : 307.

45. Her journal, in actuality reminiscences, was written several decades later. Before it was accidentally destroyed by fire, this portion was copied by John T. Walbran, whose personal communication of May 5, 1910, is cited by Howay, *"Early Navigation,"* pp. 8–9.

boat but were cut off by the natives and slain. The incident occurred not far from the ambush of 1775, giving rise to the belief that south of Cape Flattery the Indians were unusually treacherous. The *Imperial Eagle* did not return to trade in 1788, for the dodge of changing registry became too well known, and to avoid losing their posts with the East India Company her owners were forced to sell out.

The most important fur trading enterprise, from the standpoint of advancing British claims to the northwest coast, was King George's Sound Company, sometimes called London Company, of which Richard Cadman Etches was guiding spirit, but in which many prominent London merchants had an interest. The firm secured licenses to operate on the northwest coast and in Canton, and its first expedition was led by Captains Nathaniel Portlock and George Dixon, veterans of Cook's last voyage. The semiofficial blanket covering the enterprise is illustrated by the names borne by the two vessels, *King George* and *Queen Charlotte,* which reached Alaska in July 1786, wintered at Hawaii, and revisited Alaskan waters in 1787. The company contemplated erecting a number of trading posts, but despite instructions to this effect, Portlock and Dixon expended no efforts ashore.[46] The firm sent a third and a fourth vessel to the North Pacific in 1786, again named in a fashion calculated to invoke respect: *Prince of Wales* and *Princess Royal.* In command was James Colnett, a principal protagonist in chapters to come. Born in Plymouth about 1755, he served aboard several warships before accompanying Cook to the South Pacific in 1772–75, but he left the great explorer's service before the latter's last voyage. As master of the *Adventure,* Colnett took part in campaigns against the American revolutionaries, became a lieutenant in the royal navy in 1779, and was still on half-pay while commanding the London Company's effort. Calling at Nootka and the Queen Charlotte Islands in 1787, he wintered in Hawaii, traded at Prince William Sound in 1788, and that autumn returned to Canton, where his activities merged with those of John Meares—a matter examined below. What must be underscored is that, at this point, Portlock, Dixon, and Colnett had not attempted to carry out the London Company's instructions for planting settlements on the northwest coast to further British claims to the area. Had they done so, an entirely different cast might have been given to events which, in 1789, comprised the Nootka incident.

New England merchants learned of opportunities to be pursued in the sea otter trade from John Ledyard. In 1773, the twenty-one-year-old native of Groton, Connecticut, had abandoned studies at Dartmouth to go to sea on a ship engaged in the triangular trade from New England to the West Indies and North Africa. Happening to be in London three years later and

---

46. F. W. Howay, "The Fur Trade in Northwestern Development," in *The Pacific Ocean in History: Papers and Addresses Presented at the Panama-Pacific Historical Congress, 1915* (New York, 1917), p. 277.

eager for adventure, he enlisted in a group of marines accompanying Cook's third expedition, just before news arrived of the Declaration of Independence. Upon the *Resolution*'s return, in 1780, the young American resisted transfer to a warship headed for combat against the United States, and for two years he languished in an English barracks until forcibly impressed upon a vessel destined for North America. Upon reaching Long Island, Ledyard managed to desert and fled to safe hiding with an uncle in Hartford, where he composed an account of Cook's voyage, published as soon as the war ended. In describing Nootka Sound he told how "it afterwards happened that skins which did not cost the purchaser sixpence sterling sold in China for 100 dollars." Ledyard's interest in Nootka gave him an ambition —to return to the northwest coast and traverse North America west to east, mapping and opening up the Far West to his countrymen. Through his widely read book and his personal efforts to promote a trading voyage to the northwest coast, he was instrumental in propagating to American commercial circles a knowledge of the furry resources of that region. Unsuccessful, however, in securing immediate financial backing to reach Nootka from the United States, in 1784 he sailed for Spain and from there went to Paris, where Commodore John Paul Jones contributed to his support for a time. Ledyard impressed Thomas Jefferson, then American minister to France, with the potential value to the United States of the northwest coast, and when Jones backed out of the venture as too risky and Ledyard could not find a vessel in London on which to reach the North Pacific, it was Jefferson who proposed Ledyard's crossing Siberia and accompanying a Russian expedition to Alaska, then proceeding alone toward the western frontier of the United States.[47] Penniless and dependent upon the hospitality of strangers, the robust young American journeyed by way of Denmark, Sweden, Lapland, Finland, and St. Petersburg, reaching Yakutsk before Russian officials set obstacles in his way. An order from the tsarina put him under arrest; he was transported back across Russia and released at the Polish border. Thwarted in his original plan but undaunted, he resumed correspondence with Jefferson, who in 1789 informed a friend:

> My last accounts from Ledyard . . . were from Grand Cairo. He was just then plunging into the unknown regions of Africa, probably never to emerge again. If he returns, he has promised me to go to America to penetrate from Kentucky to the western side of the Continent.[48]

47. John Ledyard, *A Journal of Captain Cook's Last Voyage to the Pacific Ocean* (Hartford, Conn., 1783), p. 70. For his peregrinations, see E. M. Halliday, "Captain Cook's American," *AH* 13, no. 1 (1961) : 60–72, 84–87. For his letters to Jefferson, see Thomas Jefferson, *Papers*, ed. Julian P. Boyd, 17 vols. to date (Princeton, N.J., 1950–65), 9 : 260–61; 10 : 97–98, 258–59, 548–49; 11 : 216–18, 637–39.

48. Jefferson, *Papers*, as cited by Halliday, "Captain Cook's American," p. 87. See also Jefferson to William Short, Paris, February 28, 1789, in Jefferson, *Papers 14* : 596–98.

Ledyard had become the agent of an "Association for Promoting the Discovery of the Interior Parts of Africa," and he envisioned traversing that continent in search of the Niger's source. Nothing was too great to undertake, except coping with reality. In January 1789 he succumbed in Cairo from the consequences of improper medication, but his enthusiasm had infected Jefferson, who continued to urge others to fulfill Ledyard's dream until, as president, he finally had an opportunity to send an expedition across the continent.

Ledyard's promotion of the idea that Americans should take an interest in the northwest coast had its most immediate effect upon Joseph Barrell, a Boston merchant who interested five other businessmen of Boston, Salem, and New York in setting up a venture to tap the sea otter wealth. The valuable pelts would be exchanged for luxury items in Canton that would bring fabulous prices in New York and Boston. At a cost of $50,000, they outfitted the 212-ton *Columbia Rediviva* and a 90-ton sloop, the *Lady Washington*. The two vessels set out in September 1787, under the leadership of Captain John Kendrick, former whaler and captain of a privateer in the Revolution. The sloop was captained by Robert Gray, a thirty-two-year-old bachelor from Newport County, Rhode Island, who had commanded a privateer in the revolutionary war.[49] They rounded Cape Horn safely, but off Chile Kendrick put in at the Island of Juan Fernández under plea of distress, where Blas Rodríguez, the Spanish commander, interrogated him and learned that the *Columbia* and the *Lady Washington* were headed for the northwest coast. Rodríguez received the mistaken impression from Kendrick's passport, perhaps purposely cultivated, that the Americans represented the personal interests of General Washington, and he gave his superiors a full report, only to be reprimanded and relieved of his post for aiding the visitors and not having arrested Kendrick forthwith. Consequently, the governor of California ordered the commandant at San Francisco's presidio and presumably officials at other California ports that if Kendrick appeared, "you will take measures to secure this vessel and all the people on board, with discretion, tact, cleverness, and caution, doing the same with a small craft which she has with her as tender, and with every other suspicious foreign vessel, giving me prompt notice in such case in order that I may take such action as shall be expedient."[50]

49. F. W. Howay, ed., *Voyages of the "Columbia" to the Northwest Coast, 1787–1790 and 1790–1793* (Boston, 1941), pp. vi, x. Kendrick retained command of the *Columbia* until July 1789, when he switched vessels with Gray.

50. Pedro Fagés to Lt. José Darío Argüello, Santa Barbara, May 13, 1789, CU–B (Prov. State Papers, 1 : 53–53); English trans. in *CHSQ* 11 (1932) : 29. The *Columbia* and the *Lady Washington* may not have been the first American vessels on the northwest coast; there is some evidence that they were preceded by the *Eleanora* (Capt. Simon Metcalfe) in 1787 or the summer of 1788. F. W. Howay, "Captain Simon Metcalfe and the Brig 'Eleanora,'" *WHQ* 16 (1925) : 114–21; Howay, *Voyages of the Columbia*, pp. x–xi.

However, Kendrick did not touch anywhere until arriving at Nootka in September 1788, and the *Columbia* and the *Lady Washington* rode out the winter inside the sound. He and Gray were thus in a position to intervene importantly in the events soon to follow.

### SPANISH ENGAGEMENT IN THE SEA OTTER TRADE

Iberians had long known of the value of sea otter pelts, from those taken in Baja California and sold in China, but the trade stagnated for want of native hunters of sufficient prowess. Six years before the first British fur traders came to the northwest coast, officials in the Philippines learned of Cook's crew selling pelts from Nootka Sound at fabulous prices in Canton, information garnered from deserters during Britain's attack on Manila in 1779.[51] *Enhydra lutris* abounded near Monterey, and especially within San Francisco Bay. The California Indians were unaccustomed to fur garments, had little interest in pursuing the elusive creatures, and possessed no well-developed techniques for killing them. Sometimes a sleeping sea otter floating on its back could be approached from downwind by an Indian astride a reed raft and dispatched before it dived. Another method was to catch a pup on the kelp beds where it had been left while the mother dived to the bottom for food. Tying a long cord to its paw, the hunter waited until whimpers brought the parent, heedless of danger, to defend its offspring, when both could be slain with ease.

The padres were eager to develop resources that could provide exportable products, and they encouraged their converts to bring in sea otter pelts, which commenced flowing to the Orient in growing quantities. When the *Princesa* left Acapulco for Manila in 1783 on the regularly scheduled annual voyage, its cargo included over 700 sea otter skins from the missions. This was two years before the first British trader came to Nootka. As early as 1782 a project was formulated in Manila for building ships to gather sea otter pelts on the Pacific coast of North America. In 1785 the *Hercules* arrived in San Blas for this purpose, having come from Manila by way of Canton.[52] What happened to the venture is not known, but evidently it failed. 1784 Vicente Vasadre y Vega, a Mexico City *comerciante,* suggested official participation in sea otter trading and sent a plan to both ministry and viceroy. Carlos III ordered Vasadre's project examined to determine its practicality. The pelts were to be used to purchase quicksilver, available in China but very much in demand in New Spain, for refining gold ore. Vasadre warned of signs that the English were being attracted to the sea otter trade, which would threaten areas claimed by Spain. The California

51. Vicente Vasadre y Vega to Viceroy Matías de Gálvez, Mexico City, September 26, 1784, summarized in Ogden, *California Sea Otter Trade,* pp. 2–13.

52. Holden Furber, "An Abortive Attempt at Anglo-Spanish Commercial Cooperation in the Far East in 1793," *HAHR* 15 (1935): 452n.

supply ships returned empty, and could well transport pelts for transshipment to China.[53] Viceroy Gálvez put the plan into effect, and Vasadre sailed
for Monterey in 1786 with 8,000 Spanish dollars in cash and a monopoly of
the trade. Furs from beyond San Francisco Bay did not figure in his scheme,
at least for the time being, as there was a seemingly inexhaustible supply
from the central California coast, if the natives could be encouraged to do
their part. A fixed sum was paid for each skin according to grade, size, color,
and whether cured or not. In three months Vasadre collected over 1,000
pelts. The variety from California was not as dark a brown, and hence was
less prized in China than that of more northern waters, but it still commanded a handsome price. In 1787 Vasadre sailed for Manila with his furs,
but collection of pelts continued under Franciscan supervision. A letter
from José de Gálvez ordered Manila officials to give Vasadre their cooperation, but he nevertheless ran into grave problems arising from a clash of
interests with the Royal Philippine Company, previously granted the privilege of bringing quicksilver from China.

The first British traders to negotiate sea otter pelts in China caught the
attention of Ciriaco González Carvajal, Spanish intendente in Manila, who
informed José de Gálvez that a ship outfitted by the English but sailing
under the Portuguese flag had departed from Macao in April 1785, spreading word that it was going to Kamchatka. Instead it went "to the north of
the Californias" to a bay called "Nuutka." Pelts it brought back were worth
forty-five pesos each, and in 1786 the same company planned sending another
and possibly two more ships to the northwest coast. Pelts from Alta California were selling in Canton for forty pesos (i.e. dollars) or more, and
González Carvajal suggested that the profit ought to be pursued for the
benefit of the Philippines, by establishing a commerce directly between
California, the northwest coast, and Manila. Cloth and other articles needed
for trading were cheaper in the Philippines, as were armament and crew's
salaries. Such a commerce would serve various purposes: maintaining
Spanish sovereignty over the northwest coast, transporting mail to the
various ports, and carrying supplies to California.[54] That year Mourelle
arrived from San Blas, commanding the schooner *Felicidad,* and presented
González Carvajal with a map of Bucareli Sound. Mourelle's data prompted
the intendente to write Gálvez anew, recommending the California fur
trade be extended to embrace all the coast to the Sound and be expanded to
include beaver and sea lion skins as well. Fortified posts should be established at appropriate spots as nuclei for settlements colonized by married

53. Vasadre to Gálvez, Sept. 26, 1784; the project submitted to the ministry is referred to in
[Vasadre], "Plan propuesto para el establecimiento y acopio de nutrias en la costa occidental de
la antigua y nueva California," n.d., SpMN (335), fol. 49.

54. Ciriaco González Carvajal to José de Gálvez, Manila, February 3, 1786, confidential, SpAGI
(V, Aud. Guad. 492), T in DLC.

couples transported there at government expense, extending Christian religion and civilized customs among the Indians as a bulwark against foreign encroachment. He thought it undeniable that,

> by treating those miserable natives with gentleness and affability, and having them know the advantages of clothing themselves and of living under a pious chief who will direct and govern them, enjoying all the rights of humanity, we shall be able, through their assistance, to secure control of a rich and powerful commerce to which other strong nations now aspire and to which, if we are negligent, they may perhaps gain sole rights while we are still making plans.[55]

He suggested instituting the practice, used successfully by England, Portugal, and other nations, of exiling convicts and undesirables to sparsely populated colonies to foster their growth. Each ship engaged in the fur trade could take northward a number of exiles, ridding Manila and Mexico City of the prostitutes and vagrants "infesting those capitals."

In July 1786, the Philippine Company petitioned successfully for permission to conduct the sea otter pelt–quicksilver exchange, and this was the shoal upon which Vasadre's project ran aground when he reached the Orient in 1787. The solicitor representing the viceregency of Mexico would not consent to the Philippine Company's plan unless the company assumed the costs of what had already been invested in Vasadre's venture.[56] This the Philippine Company was loath to do, and after eleven months of deliberations, its directors concluded that the traffic involved too many imponderables, risks, and difficulties to warrant the sizable investment necessary to establish a string of outposts and employ the number of vessels that González Carvajal's plan envisioned. After inquiries in Mexico they declared that "sending vessels from San Blas to run along the coast in order to purchase skins in exchange for money or goods is expensive, risky, and of very doubtful result because of the great scarcity of skins, the lack of inclination in the natives, and of subjects established in those places capable of directing the business of hunting, buying, and shipment."[57] Gonzáles Carvajal, in his endeavor to debilitate Vasadre's influence, actually thwarted his own designs by arousing anxiety in Madrid among the conservative directors of the Philippine Company as to the risks of participation in the sea otter trade. They spiked Vasadre's enterprise and also rejected that proposed by the

55. Ibid., June 20, 1786, AT.

56. Audiencia de México to José de Gálvez, Mexico City, March 26, 1787, MxAGN (Corr. Virreyes 141).

57. Directors of the Philippine Company to Antonio Valdés, Madrid, August 13, 1788, SpAGI (V, Aud. Guad. 492), partially trans. in Adele Ogden, "The Californias in Spain's Pacific Otter Trade, 1775–1795," *PHR* 1 (1932): 461.

intendente, even though the threat against which both were directed continued to grow in momentum.

To carry out his own project, Vasadre had ignored the demands of Manila officialdom. In Canton he feted influential officials, distributed expensive presents in appropriate places, and cemented a bond of friendship with the famed Kingqua, before whom everyone had to kowtow. After considerable delay the exchange for quicksilver was arranged. Using as an excuse the procrastination encountered in Canton and the lavish bribes handed out, Philippine Governor Félix Berenguer de Marquina took the next consignment of pelts out of Vasadre's hands, demanding he turn over the quicksilver thus far acquired. Vasadre's efforts to disprove González Carvajal's exaggeration and protest intervention by Philippine officials were held out as evidence of his being "one of those proud men foolishly pleased with their own judgment and who aspire to independence." [58] He found it impossible to overcome such handicaps, gave up in disgust, turned everything over to the Royal Philippine factors, and sailed for Spain to present his grievances to the ministry. In his absence from California, the elaborate pricing system for pelts lacked the flexibility to cope with changing conditions, unforeseen circumstances, and human greed. If its author had been on the spot, perhaps imperfections in the system could have been remedied. As it was, the commerce gave rise to abuses that clamored for justice brought on additional governmental control, and dampened enthusiasm in many quarters for the growing trade.

In 1790 the government decreed a new schedule of prices for each class of pelts and regulations to prevent abuses, theft, and graft. To insure a profit upon sale in Canton, lower prices were assigned, despite Franciscan advice they be increased to encourage hunting. A first class pelt in California thereafter brought only five to seven pesos, depending upon its color, as opposed to the previous rate of seven to ten pesos. The new schedule had hardly arrived in Monterey when word came that Vasadre's project was suspended as a result of his differences with Philippine officials.[59] The Council of Indies took Vasadre's protest under consideration, but the Royal Philippine Company's influence was too great. The schemes of Vasadre and González Carvajal went down the drain—not because of economic obstacles

58. Juan Gutiérrez de Piñeres to Pedro Aparici, Madrid, December 5, 1790, T in DLC; Vasadre, "Informe sobre prejuicios en la comisión que se le dió de conducir á la China pieles de nutria," Madrid, April 11, 1791, T in CU–B; both cited by Ogden, "The Californias," pp. 446n, 457–58, who discusses Vasadre's difficulties at considerable length.

59. "Tarifa por donde se han de satisfacer las pieles de nutria que se recibiesen de cuenta de S. M. en las misiones de ambas Californias, y nuebos establecimientos de altura," Mexico City, May 18, 1790, SpMN (335), fol. 51–52; Viceroy Revillagigedo to Minister Pedro [López] de Lerena, Mexico City, July 27, 1790, and August 27, 1790, MxAGN (Corr. Virreyes 158); Council of Indies, "Consulta sobre proyecto de Vicente Basadre para comerciar pieles de nutria," Madrid, June 22, 1791, MxAGN (Corr. Virreyes 141). See Ogden, "The Californias," pp. 446, 456n, 461.

or scanty profits but because of bureaucratic snarls, selfish rivalry among vested interests, and the unadaptability of timid conservatism. Hampered by a rigid framework of monopolies, Spanish fur traders did not enjoy the freedom and resiliency that enabled traders of other nationalities to achieve great success in the sea otter trade. Spanish interest in the traffic north of San Francisco was inhibited by difficulties experienced in exploiting the wealth of pelts available in the very area of the California missions. If there were more of the sleek creatures in San Francisco Bay than the natives could possibly catch, it seemed illogical to undertake hazardous voyages to the northwest coast to tap another supply. The promoters of this view took no cognizance of the superiority of the northwest coast Indians as hunters, or of the fact that the natives of California were not culturally predisposed by the potlatch system to be acquisitive. Values are not universal, but culturally conditioned. California aborigines evinced little enthusiasm for the demands and rigors of sea otter hunting, whereas Nootka, Haida, and Kwakiutl braves would go to great lengths for pelts exchangeable for attractive and useful trade articles. The passion of the northwest coast tribes for such items was insatiable, as they could be bestowed upon others in the escalating competition for status.

In 1802 Martín Fernández de Navarrete concluded that Vasadre's failure "was the reason that, once this first attempt was ruined, the favor and enthusiasm declined among those who should have continued it by themselves and at their own risk with better plans and bases." [60] As Donald Cutter remarks, "Vasadre was doubtless too far ahead of his times, an era in which Spain was not yet convinced that inter-colonial trade was beneficial." [61] The significance of Vasadre's efforts to the history of the northwest coast is that his failure dissuaded mercantile elements in Mexico City and Manila who otherwise might have invested in ventures directed toward exploiting the furry wealth of the northwest coast as soon as Spanish dominion extended to embrace that area. Vasadre's undoing blighted the one economic activity that stood a chance of making Spanish settlements there self-supporting and even lucrative.

### FRANCE PUTS IN ITS BID

In 1786 Madrid received warning of an infringement from still another quarter. In emulation of Cook, and to insure that France would not be excluded from exploiting the newly revealed area in the North Pacific, the French ministry organized an elaborate expedition commanded by Jean François Galaup, Comte de la Pérouse, an officer renowned for exploits in the American Revolution. Enthusiastic over the promise of Pacific explora-

---

60. Fernández de Navarrete, "Introducción," pp. cl–cli, AT.
61. Donald C. Cutter, *Malaspina in California* (San Francisco, 1960), pp. 76–77.

tions, Louis XVI took personal interest in the endeavor. La Pérouse and
an able corps of scientists set sail from Brest in August 1785 with the frigates
*Astrolabe* and *Boussole,* intending to circumnavigate the globe. Soon after
entering the Pacific they called at Talcahuano, port for Concepción, Chile,
where one José Miguel Urezberoeta, through his knowledge of French,
gained the confidence of several scientists in the party, who showed him
their maps and told what they knew of the North Pacific. At once Urezberoeta wrote the intendente of Santiago and president of the Audiencia,
warning of the danger to Spanish interests from Russia, which reportedly
had settlements in four places: "Nooka", Prince William Sound, the Trin-
ity Islands (west of Kodiak), and Unalaska.[62] Several months later, the intendente of Concepción wrote directly to José de Gálvez expounding at
length his concern over the peril from foreign activities—as gleaned from
La Pérouse's maps, warning against Russian expansion toward California
from Kamchatka, and predicting British attempts to secure control over
the west coast of North America by means of the sea otter trade, in order to
offset the loss of the recent war. He recommended that Spain occupy Tahiti
and Hawaii and that an expedition probe Russian expansion on the northwest coast and establish a Spanish outpost at Cook Inlet, in Alaska.[63]

La Pérouse had instructions to take possession at some spot north of
Bucareli Sound, which Paris considered the northernmost point of Spanish
territory, and he was to examine the possibilities of the fur trade. On July 3,
1786, the illustrious commander performed such formalities in the name
of Louis XVI at Alaska's Lituya Bay, which he named "Port des Français."
Ten days later twenty-one of his officers and men perished when two of the
ships' boats, while taking soundings, were swamped by a sudden squall as
they attempted to cross a line of breakers at the bay's entrance. Although
initially optimistic about finding a northwest passage, or a river leading
to the interior of the continent, La Pérouse soon was convinced by the
coastline's complexity that searching its many indentations would be a slow
process and beyond his means. From Port des Français he followed the
coast to Monterey and was piloted into the harbor by Estéban José Martínez,
there on a routine mission as commander of the *Princesa* and the *Favorita*
with that year's supplies. Vicente Vasadre y Vega was there as well, actively engaged is setting in motion his peltry enterprise, and the La Pérouse
journal describes him as "a young man of great spirit and worth." [64]

62. José Miguel Urezberoeta to Ambrosio Benavides, Concepción, March 24, 1786, SpAHN
(Estado 4289).

63. Ambrosio Higgins (father of Chile's national hero) to the Marqués de Sonora, Concepción, July 20, 1786, SpAHN (Estado 4289); [Francisco Antonio Mourelle], "Cuarta exploración
de la costa septentrional de Californias . . . en el año 1788," SpMN (331), fol. 120–120v.

64. "Jeune homme plein d'esprit et de mérite," in Jean François Galaup de La Pérouse, *Voyage
de La Pérouse Autour du Monde,* 4 vols. and atlas (Paris, 1797), entry for September 24, 1786.

Despite Martínez's humble rank, he enjoyed by default a position of relative importance and authority in the Californias. Eager to protect Spain's interest, he queried La Pérouse extensively about the northwest coast, reporting to Viceroy Bernardo de Gálvez that he was assured that Russians operating out of Unalaska frequented the coast to the eastward, obliging the Indians to pay tribute with sea otter skins, "and those who didn't pay, they took their lives." La Pérouse claimed to have had in his hands vouchers of tribute payment which the Muscovites gave out in exchange for furs. Two middle-sized Russian vessels reconnoitered the province of Alaska annually, gathering tributes. Martínez tried to find out more but reported that, "although I solicited to know in detail the discoveries made by both frigates, they excused themselves giving as reason that until their court knew of their operations nothing could be revealed." [65] Martínez also sent substantially the same account directly to the minister of Indies.

La Pérouse's supplies had diminished to the point where the diet of his crew was limited to dried foodstuffs. In compassion Governor Fagés provided fresh food, including forty head of beef, fifty-one sheep, 200 chickens, wheat, barley, peas, and green vegetables. During the ten days at Monterey, they were supplied with a barrel of milk a day, a much-appreciated gesture that, accompanied by the exercise ashore, went far toward restoring the ailing to health.[66] Resuming voyage, after visiting several ports in Asia and searching for the legendary isles Rica de Oro and Rica de Plata, La Pérouse headed for the South Seas, and, after visiting Australia's Botany Bay, he was never heard from again.[67]

The journals of La Pérouse's visit to the northwest coast were spared the expedition's fate by having been remitted overland from Kamchatka. He had hard words for Spain's policy of secrecy about its domains in America, which kept the rest of Europe ignorant of the extent of Spanish claims on the northwest coast. He remarked that he would not even have known of Monterey but for the English edition of Mourelle's journal. After discussions with Martínez, La Pérouse advised his government that Madrid would regard any French claim to territory on the northwest coast as a violation of Spanish sovereignty. The advantages that France might ob-

65. Martínez to Viceroy Conde de Gálvez, San Blas, December 18, 1786, MxAGN (Hist. 396); also SpAHN (Estado 4289), AT; Martínez to the Marqués de Sonora, San Blas, December, 1786, SpAHN (Estado 4289).

66. Fagés to Jacobo Ugarte y Loyola, comandante general of the Interior Provinces, Monterey, September, 1786, SpAHN (Estado 4289).

67. Years passed without further word; several French expeditions made fruitless searches. In 1827 on Vanikoro in the New Hebrides, Peter Dillon learned of two vessels driven aground in a storm, most of whose crews drowned; others died in hostilities with the natives. After about a year, the survivors departed in a makeshift vessel. A tradition on Ponape in the Carolines told of a boatload of whites slain at about this time. Dunmore, *French Explorers in the Pacific,* 1 : 332–41.

tain from the sea otter trade were insufficient to justify the slightest altercation between Versailles and Madrid. He suggested encouraging individual
French businessmen to engage in the fur trade, but he advised against
authorizing monopolies for any single company or trying to establish a
permanent factory or other outposts in the North Pacific.[68]

RUSSIAN RESPONSE TO RIVALRY FOR ALASKAN FURS

La Pérouse left Martínez with the impression that the Muscovites already had an establishment at Nootka. This was erroneous, but such a move
would not be long in abeyance, as indicated by developments in the Far
North. Profits in the Aleutian sea otter trade led to the formation of
the Shelikhov-Golikov Company, which in 1783 sent out the *Three Saints,*
the *Saint Michael Archangel,* and the *Saint Simeon the Friend of God and
Anna His Prophetess.* In 1784 the company made the first permanent settlement on Kodiak Island (Three Saints Bay), and in 1786 it planted another
on the continent nearby (Fort Alexander, named to honor the tsarevitch). A
Russian subject named Potap Zaikov built a hut of woods and reeds at a
harbor on the east side of Montague Island in Prince William Sound and
is alleged to have wintered there in 1783–84, but the site was then abandoned.[69] In 1786 Gregori Shelikhov told the company's factor at Kodiak
that, "for rapidly extending the power of the Russian people it is possible
to step farther and farther along the shore of the American Continent, at
the farthest extension to California." He ordered the distribution of copper
medals bearing the Russian imperial arms to the chiefs in each place visited,
trying "to extend the land of Alyaska to California from 50 degrees north
latitude . . . generally to put settlements of Russians for accommodation
of the Americans [i.e. aborigines] and glorification of the Russian government in the profitable land of America and California to 40 degrees." [70] In
obedience to this order, in 1788 the Kodiak settlers sent the *Three Saints*
and pilots Gerasim Ismailov and Dimitri Botsharov with forty men to
found a settlement at Yakutat Bay. In their formal act of possession, they
declared a protectorate over the Kolosh, or Tlingit, in the name of "His
Imperial Highness Paul Petrovich," heir apparent.[71]

The goad to Russian disquiet about its edge in America at this point

68. La Pérouse, "Mémoire sur le commerce des peaux de loutre de mer," in *Voyage de La
Pérouse,* 4 : 140–49.

69. Martin Sauer, *An Account of a Geographical and Astronomical Expedition to the Northern Parts of Russia* (London, 1802), p. 197n; Michel Poniatowski, *Histoire de la Russie d'Amérique et d'Alaska* (Paris, 1958), p. 46.

70. Shelikhov to Samoilov, Kadiak, May 4, 1786, in C. L. Andrews, "Russian Plans for American Dominion," *WHQ* 18 (1927) : 83–84, trans. from Petr Aleksandrovich Tikhmenev, *Istori-
chesko Obozrenie Obrazovaniia Rossiisko-Amerikanskoi Kompanii* [Historical Survey of the
Establishment of the Russian-American Company], 2 vols. (St. Petersburg, 1861–62).

71. Poniatowski, *Histoire,* p. 50.

stemmed not from Spanish activities but from the undisclosed objectives of La Pérouse. Russian officials were correct in suspecting one of his purposes to be the establishment of French claims to a port for use in the fur trade. The Muscovites planned a counter effort, to anticipate La Pérouse's arrival. The Russian expedition would sail from Archangel by way of the Arctic Ocean; this route was judged speedier than other ways. Command of the effort was given to an Englishman in the tsarina's service, Joseph Billings, astronomer's assistant on Cook's last expedition. Less than three months after La Pérouse sailed from Brest, Spain's ambassador in St. Petersburg sent Madrid a detailed report of what the tsarina's ministers hoped to accomplish by the Billings expedition. It would have a duration of five to six years, in order to chart islands and territories tributary to Russia, particularly areas frequented by fur trading vessels along the Pacific coast of North America. A month later, the ambassador advised that Billings had departed on his supposedly secret mission.[72] Catherine's ukase for the effort is dated August 8, 1785. The attempt to reach Alaska by way of the Arctic Ocean soon had to be abandoned because of practical difficulties, and the expeditionaries crossed Siberia by land. At Yakutsk, Billings and his geographer, Martin Sauer, encountered John Ledyard, who had been Billings's companion on the Cook voyage. Ledyard asked to accompany them to Alaska; but Russian officials were suspicious of the penniless American's intentions and sent him back to Irkutsk, where at the tsarina's order he was arrested and deported. La Pérouse was long gone from the North Pacific before Billings arrived on the scene. (See chapter 8 for an account of the Russian expedition's encounter with the forces of His Catholic Majesty.)

The details transmitted to Madrid by Chilean officials concerning what they had learned from La Pérouse actually added nothing (except some distortion) to those given in accounts of Cook's last voyage. What is significant is that they triggered the next phase of Spanish activity on the northwest coast.[73] The warnings from Ambassador Normande in St. Petersburg, Intendente Higgins in Concepción, and Martínez in San Blas all prognosticated danger to Spanish interests from expanding Russian activities. Intense and incisive as ever, the newly ennobled minister of Indies (henceforth known as the Marqués de Sonora) took emphatic action against the renewed threat on the northern frontier, probably before the report from Martínez

72. Pedro Normande to the Conde de Floridablanca, October 29 and November 29, 1785, extract in SpAHN (Estado 4289).

73. A point stressed by José Espinosa y Tello, "Noticia de las principales expediciones hechas por nuestros pilotos del Departamento de San Blas al reconocimiento de la costa noroeste de América, desde el año de 1774 hasta el 1791, extractada de los diarios originales de aquellos navegantes," in Alejandro Malaspina, *Viaje político-científico alrededor del Mundo por las corbetas Descubierta y Atrevida,* ed. Pedro Novo y Colson (Madrid, 1885), p. 428.

had time to reach Madrid. A royal order to Viceroy Conde de Gálvez set in march a fourth expedition to the Pacific Northwest to probe the Russian danger and reconnoiter "the coast toward the North and ascertain if there are, in effect, such establishments." [74] Normande was directed to investigate whether the rumors from Chile were accurate. He replied that news had been received in Russia about English trading vessels bringing sea otter skins to China at immense profit, "from the coasts of America facing Kamchatka, which are a continuation of those of California." This had reawakened the tsarina's attention, but great care was being taken to hide all signs of official concern. Captain Moloski, natural son of Count Ivan Chernychev, minister of the marine, had been chosen to command a squadron of four men-of-war being sent to Kamchatka to protect Russian interests. Secret meetings in the admiralty with a secretary of the tsarina's cabinet had resulted in some sort of official manifest, plans, and maps for Moloski. Despite the wraps under which these talks were conducted, Normande's espionage revealed that Catherine and her ministers were contemplating a ukase declaring Russian sovereignty over all the continent from Mount St. Elias eastward to the neighborhood of Hudson's Bay. Announcement of this sovereignty would be communicated to other powers of Europe, declaring that Moloski's expedition was to secure those possessions and defend them against other nations seeking to make settlements there. The two frigates and two transports would sail by way of the Cape of Good Hope and join the Billings expedition at Okhotsk.[75] Normande's warning cannot be dismissed as what some have regarded as Spanish paranoia about the Russian threat. The tsarina hoped to stake a claim to much of North America, unless she was deterred by vigorous and immediate action. Pursuit of the sea otter would take Russian vessels closer and closer each year to California and New Spain. The certainty of Normande's prophecy would be borne out by events.

The ominous reports from America and St. Petersburg touched a matter close to the aged minister of Indies' heart—his dream for Spanish control over western North America. In 1769 it had been excessive preoccupation about Russians in California that had pushed him temporarily beyond the edge of sanity, to the nadir of his distinguished career. In April 1787, Prime Minister Floridablanca remitted to Gálvez the alarming report from St. Petersburg, requesting an investigation of everything pertaining to the threat of Russian expansion in North America, the alleged settlements, and the rumored expedition led by Captain Moloski.[76] As of that date, the marqués was in full possession of his faculties, but within two months, at Aranjuez on the night of June 17, 1787, he suddenly died of an *accidente*,

74. Royal order, El Pardo, January 25, 1787, SpaHN (Estado 4289), AT.

75. Normande to the Conde de Floridablanca, St. Petersburg, February 16, 1787, SpAHN (Estado 4289), AT.

76. Floridablanca to Marqués de Sonora, Aranjuez, April 24, 1787, SpAHN (Estado 4289).

a term that Priestly considers is "usually taken to mean an attack of insanity—perhaps a return of the malady from which he suffered during his
campaign in Sonora in 1769–70." [77] For two decades, first as visitador and
then as minister, Gálvez had been engaged in creating a ring of defensive
establishments around the perimeter of Spain's colonial empire. There is
no evidence that the Russian bugaboo precipitated his death, but it is
ironic that his last days were embittered by the recurrence of the worry
that had troubled him most—Russian threats to the great realm in the Far
West that he envisioned for Spain.

No individual was more important to the Spanish in the Pacific Northwest than José de Gálvez, even though he never came closer to the area
than Baja California, for it was his enthusiasm that propelled Spain to the
high water mark of its territorial claims in the New World. The zealous
Andalusian had conceived it to be within Madrid's grasp—indeed he saw
it as Spain's "manifest destiny"—to dominate western North America to its
Arctic extremities, a feat he thought could be achieved by establishing another administrative unit in the heart of the Southwest, flanked on one side
by a vigorous colony in California and on the other by a strengthened
Louisiana. From today's perspective his dream was not so estranged from
reality, but at the time it flew in the face of immense difficulties posed by
hostile Indians and trackless wilds. Gálvez is identified today as one of the
exemplary figures of the period of Bourbon reforms distinguishing Carlos
III's reign. In imagination and enthusiasm for advancing his nation's interest, he ranks among the outstanding figures of the Enlightenment in
Spain. The achievements of the Spanish in the Far Northwest were to a
great extent the consequence of his irrepressible but erratic zeal.

### SPAIN'S MOST AMBITIOUS EXPEDITION TO THE NORTH PACIFIC

After Gálvez's demise Carlos III placed the ministry of Indies in the able
hands of Antonio Valdés y Bazán, since 1783 minister of the marine. Born
in Burgos in 1744, Valdés was a veteran of the defense of Havana against the
British in 1762. Rising rapidly through posts of growing importance, he
had been only thirty-eight when named minister of the marine. He retained
the Indies portfolio until 1790 and that of marine through 1795, and he
was influential in formulating and executing policy toward the northwest
coast.

In 1788 Valdés was recipient of a plan for the most elaborate scientific
expedition ever attempted in Spanish history.[78] Accounts of the official expeditions sent out by Britain and France under Cook and La Pérouse fas-

---

77. Priestly, *José de Gálvez*, pp. 10–12, discusses the sources that suggest such an interpretation.

78. "Plan de un viaje científico y político alrededor del Mundo," Isla de León, September 10,
1788, in Malaspina, *Viaje*, pp. 1–2.

cinated European scientific circles and public alike, and the tragic fate
suffered by both commanders served to enhance their fame. The political
importance of such undertakings was obvious. The acclaim hailing Cook's
accomplishments upon posthumous publication of his journal, in 1784,
made Madrid realize belatedly the importance of publicizing geographical
discoveries. Spain's place in the first rank of European powers demanded
that such feats be matched or surpassed. A carefully planned expedition
with navigators and scientists of the highest caliber could do much to explore, examine, and knit together Madrid's far-flung empire, report on
problems and possible reforms, and counter the efforts of rivals to obtain
colonial possessions at Spain's expense. It was hoped that the projected
effort would result in new discoveries, careful cartographic surveys, important geodesic experiments in gravity and magnetism, botanical collections, and descriptions of each region's geography, mineral resources, commercial possibilities, political status, native peoples, and customs. The
plan typified the encyclopedic impulse that was the very quintessence of
the Enlightenment. The Malaspina expedition, as it would be called, would
coincide with the apogee in territorial expansion of the Spanish Empire.

Commander Alejandro Malaspina was born of noble lineage on November 5, 1754, in Mulazzo, a town in the Duchy of Parma, which was ruled
by Carlos III's younger brother and subject to Spanish suzerainty. At twenty
he embarked upon a naval career as a member of the marine guard at
Cádiz,[79] and throughout his life he gave undivided allegiance to Spain. But
he retained enough of his Parmesan upbringing (as evidenced in his prose
style) to make him a foreigner in the eyes of most Spaniards—an important
factor when he later became one of the empire's most outspoken proponents
of institutional reforms. As an ensign Malaspina served in the Mediterranean
and the Atlantic, and in the Philippines. In the American Revolution he
participated in naval encounters against the British and was taken prisoner.
He sailed to the Philippines again in 1782, visited India, and in 1784 departed from Cádiz in command of the frigate *Astrea*, circumnavigated the
globe, and acquired a reputation as one of Spain's most competent navigators. Scarcely thirty-four when his ambitious plan for a survey of Spain's
overseas dominions obtained ministerial approval, Malaspina was five years
the senior of his co-captain, José Bustamante y Guerra, from Ontaneda,
Santander. In common with Malaspina, Bustamante had seen naval combat
and had suffered a period of British captivity during Spain's alliance with
the American revolutionaries.

A brilliant constellation of accomplished naturalists, astronomers, and

---

79. The often repeated assertion that he was Sicilian is contradicted by his service record
in SpMN, cited by Humberto F. Burzio in Bonifacio del Carril, *La Expedición Malaspina en los
mares Americanos del sur: La Colección Bauzá, 1789–1794* (Buenos Aires, 1961), p. 13.

artists were selected to accompany the Malaspina expedition. Twin corvettes, the *Santa Justa,* alias *Descubierta,* and the *Santa Rufina,* alias *Atrevida,* were especially constructed with a view to the demands of the tasks ahead. Weighing 306 tons apiece and measuring 120 feet in length, they had a draft of fourteen feet when loaded. Eighty-six men and sixteen officers, individually selected for physical vigor, intelligence, and moral reputation, made up the complement of each vessel. No expense was spared to provide every item judged necessary. To combat scurvy, the scourge of long voyages, a special diet would include ample quantities of sauerkraut, bacon, vinegar, wine, and grog. Malaspina had confidence in the salubrious effect of hot meals, exercise, fermented drinks, and frequent bathing. Officers and crew would be held to a regimen to keep them as free of illness as possible. The vessels were outfitted in grand fashion; the *Descubierta* even had a harpsichord in its main cabin. A journal mentions that Tadeo Hanke, a well-known Bohemian naturalist accompanying them, often played the instrument "with his accustomed skill" for the officers' entertainment.[80] A calculated effort to surpass Cook's achievements motivated the careful planning and expense invested in the Malaspina expedition. The ministry hoped to accomplish a number of purposes by the effort, not the least of which was a proportionate measure of recognition for the Spanish navy.

Construction and preparations occupied many months, and the corvettes did not leave Cádiz until July 30, 1789. Extended visits to Trinidad, the Río de la Plata, Chile, Peru, and Mexico consumed two full years, and Malaspina and his companions did not reach the northwest coast until the summer of 1791. The expedition had departed for America at a time when peace reigned between Spain and its neighbors, and the spirit with which it had set out was one of friendly but intense scientific rivalry. Iberian pride and confidence in the strength and glory of its empire was at full surge. Before the party reached the North Pacific, however, a series of events had totally altered the situation in that area and in Europe. An account of what befell this most elaborate of Spanish expeditions to the northwest coast must await a narration of the turbulent episodes that preceded its arrival at the scene of action.

### THE SPANISH REACH THE ALEUTIANS, 1788

When Carlos III ordered a fourth expedition to the northwest coast on January 25, 1787, word had not yet reached Madrid of the sudden death of Viceroy Bernardo conde de Gálvez. The urgent command arrived in Mexico City at a time of disruption in administration. Judges of the Audiencia made all decisions of importance until May, when Archbishop Alfonso

---

80. Tomás de Suría, "Quaderno q. contiene el ramo de historia natural . . . 1791," CtY-BWA (Coe 464), English trans. in *PHR* 5 (1936) : 242.

Núñez de Haro y Peralta was designated to fill the viceregal office until a new appointee arrived. At once the archbishop commenced preparations for the new sally northward, so that when Viceroy Manuel Antonio de Flores arrived three months later, he found the effort well underway.[81] The ministry was advised that the expedition would set out from San Blas in January 1788, although Flores was of the opinion that La Pérouse's information added nothing to what Cook found, "according to what I see from the copy I have." He felt that the French explorer had acted somewhat less than honorably in withholding his own observations on the northwest coast—especially after the hospitality accorded him by Governor Fagés, which was given with such punctuality for that reason." There had been great difficulty "finding pilots who wanted to serve in the Department of San Blas, because of the unhealthiness of that climate and the small salary of twenty pesos with which they are paid." In that department only two persons held the rank of officer, although Flores managed to get two more from Veracruz. He requested that additional naval officers be sent especially for service there, so that he would be prepared should it be necessary to continue sending such expeditions northward, or to evict the Russians or other nationalities from outposts planted within Spanish territory. The new officers, he felt, should be selected from among the most capable candidates—he wanted not just pilots but men with other special skills as well.[82]

Originally it was intended that the new expedition be led by José Camacho, commandant of San Blas, with Francisco Antonio Mourelle as captain of a companion vessel, but Camacho proved too aged and infirm, and Mourelle was on a voyage to Manila. Hezeta and Bodega were serving in Europe and were not immediately available either. Of vessels usually operating out of San Blas, the *Concepción* was away and the *Favorita* out of commission. There was still the *Princesa*, employed by Arteaga in 1779 and in subsequent years commanded by Estéban José Martínez in the supplying of Alta California. As consort, Flores chose the *San Carlos*, alias *Filipino*, so called because it had been constructed in Manila. Martínez would command the mission, with the *San Carlos* captained by Gonzalo López de Haro, a young pilot recently arrived from Havana in response to an emergency appeal for additional officers.[83] The selection of leadership

81. [Mourelle], "Cuarta exploración," fol. 121–121v. Bernardo, conde de Gálvez, died November 30, 1786.

82. Viceroy Flores to Antonio Valdés, Mexico City, October 27, 1787, SpAHN (Estado 4289), AT. In addition to the twenty pesos monthly, pilots received food, uniforms, servants, and other incidentals provided all other Spanish naval officers (Stewart, "Martínez and López de Haro," p. 60, the fundamental study to date of the 1788 expedition).

83. [Mourelle], "Cuarta exploración," fol. 136v. López de Haro sailed from Spain for the Philippines in 1777, two years after entering the corps of naval pilots. Between 1783 and 1785 he made successive voyages from Cádiz to Montevideo, Cartagena, Algiers, and Havana, and while in Cuba he was transferred to San Blas. Stewart, "Martínez and López de Haro," pp. 62–63.

for the 1788 expedition had more than incidental importance, since it would result in the same men being sent northward again in 1789 and hence determine who would be the two Spanish principals at Nootka during the year of the great confrontation. Both men ranked low in officialdom, but deficiencies of the department propelled them into responsibilities beyond their experience, with a decided impact upon history.

Estéban José Martínez Fernández y Martínez de la Sierra was born in Seville, capital of Andalusia, an ancient and proud city located many miles from the Atlantic but which, by virtue of the navigable Guadalquivir, served as a door to Spain's overseas empire. A portrait still in possession of his descendants gives Martínez's birth date as December 9, 1742. At thirteen he matriculated in Seville's renowned Seminario de San Telmo to study for a naval career. The scant documentation of his early life reveals only that within three years he had put to sea, married Doña Gertrudis González in Seville's Parroquia del Sagrario on September 10, 1770, and by 1773 was serving as second pilot in the Department of San Blas, far from home and wife. His chief adversary at Nootka in 1789, James Colnett, says Martínez told him he was a nephew of Viceroy Manuel Antonio Flores Maldonado Martínez de Angulo y Bodquín.[84] While Colnett is the sole source of this assertion, it seems unlikely the Sevillano's sworn enemy would invent such a claim. Martínez was one of the viceroy's family names, both men were Sevillanos, and a naval career had been the vehicle for Flores's rise to prominence. Of one thing we may be certain: Martínez did not owe his command to nepotism. No one outranked him in the department, and he enjoyed a certain reputation as an authority on the subject of the North Pacific coast.

He had been just a second pilot upon accompanying Pérez in 1774, and he was excluded from the expedition northward in 1775. The dossier resulting from his petition for promotion to first pilot reveals the reason: to a routine inquiry from José de Gálvez, Bucareli replied that first reports of Martínez's performance had been entirely favorable, but when named to accompany Hezeta in 1775, "Juan Pérez had hardly learned of my selection when by confidential letter of December seventeenth of said year of 1774 he informed me that it was not in the service's best interest, because of some qualities noted in Pilot Martínez, the most special being his backwardness in the art, and his limited practice in handling the maneuvers."

84. James Colnett to the ambassador of Great Britain in Madrid, Mexico City, [May 1], 1790, SpAHN (Estado 4291), in Colnett, *The Journal of Captain James Colnett Aboard the Argonaut from April 26, 1789 to Nov. 3, 1791*, ed. F. W. Howay (Toronto, 1940), pp. 319–21; Colnett to [Richard] Cadman Etches, Mexico City, May 1, 1790, SpAHN (Estado 4291); "Nomina de los Pilotos que actualmente sirven en el Departamento de San Blas," SpAGI (V, Aud. Guad. 520); Roberto Barreiro-Meiro, "Estéban José Martínez," in *Colección de diarios y relaciones para la historia de los viajes y descubrimientos* (Madrid, 1964), 6 : 17.

Instead, Bucareli sent Martínez as second officer to Fernando Quirós aboard the *Príncipe,* which was conducting supplies to San Diego. "The most recent information I have at hand of the conduct and skill of the petitioner," Bucareli continued, "is diametrically opposite to that Don Juan Pérez had given me." When queried, Quirós had responded in terms of complete content and said that Martínez had fulfilled the mission without any fault being noted in his "behavior, conduct or ability." [85] As a consequence of Bucareli's favorable report, the promotion was granted. Pérez's charges of professional incompetence could be dismissed as little more than an aversion if similar accusations had not come from other sources following the 1788 expedition. However, the friction with Pérez takes on greater significance when events of 1789 make us seek insight into the personality of this pivotal character.

Between 1776 and 1788 Martínez conducted a succession of supply trips from San Blas to the Californias, giving him a reputation as the most experienced commander on that route. He was engaged in such a mission when the expedition of 1779 was outfitted, and thus missed participating in it. Promoted to frigate ensign in 1781, he became interim commandant of the department in 1785. While in that post he applied for promotion to ship's ensign, and although his petition received a satisfactory recommendation from the viceroy, it was denied by the ministry without a specified reason.[86]

Viceregal instructions for the 1788 expedition northward had been made out to José Camacho, but this made them no less binding upon Martínez. He was ordered to ascend to a latitude of at least 61°, reconnoiter and investigate any Russian settlements, endeavor to discover their number, nature, and location, and learn the strength of their land and sea forces, ascertain whether the settlements were permanent or seasonal, and discover what kinds of commerce were practiced. He was to take official possession for Carlos III wherever convenient. His charts should indicate places with good harbors, fresh water, readily available firewood and lumber, and signs of fertility, "in order that there may be no difficulty in finding them again in case of a decision to colonize." He must avoid any occasion for quarrel with vessels or subjects of Russia or any other nation, and should bring back one Indian of each different idiom, if they would come voluntarily, to prepare good interpreters for future expeditions.[87]

85. Bucareli to José de Gálvez, Mexico City, June 26, 1777, SpAGI (V, Aud. Guad. 516), AT.

86. José María de Monterde, certificate of merit for Estéban José Martínez, San Blas, December 1, 1784; Martínez to the king, San Blas, April 6, 1786; Martinez to José de Gálvez, San Blas, April 6, 1786; Conde de Gálvez to Marqués de Sonora, Mexico City, May 26, 1786; Marqués de Sonora to Viceroy of New Spain, San Lorenzo [del Escorial], October 23, 1786. All in SpAGI (V, Aud. Guad. 520).

87. Flores to José Camacho, Mexico City, November 27, 1787, MxBN (30), a volume titled "Reconocimiento de los quatro establecimientos que el Imperio Ruso ha formado al Norte de la California," containing the essential documents of the 1788 expedition, Ph in DLC.

Accompanying Martínez were pilots Estéban Mondofía (an Italian with some knowledge of Russian) and Antonio Serantes, a pilot's apprentice, a surgeon, two chaplains, and a crew totaling eighty-nine. Serving under López de Haro were pilots José María Narváez and Juan Martínez y Zayas, a pilot's apprentice, a chaplain, and crew of eighty-three in all. They sailed on March 8, the earliest that they could get underway. In mid-May, at the mouth of Prince William Sound, there began a series of episodes that reflected seriously upon Martínez's character, if we take at face value the testimony against him, upon the expedition's return, by López de Haro and Serantes, corroborated by Narváez and pilot's apprentice José Verdía. As events turned out, Martínez had no chance to present his version of the incidents, and the historian is limited to details supplied by his detractors.

The trouble erupted with a dispute about an island encountered on May 17. The commander insisted it was "Isla del Carmen" from 1779 charts, whereas Serantes sought to prove it was Cook's "Montague Island," farther west. Serantes testified that Martínez thereafter treated him with contempt and demanded his journal altered to conform to the captain's log. Fearful of "condescending to such a crass equivocation," he tried, "with all submission and greatest professional decorum possible," to make Martínez see his point, to no avail.[88] Among all the officers only Mondofía concurred with Martínez. The commander refused to yield to the majority viewpoint and, according to his detractors, procrastinated and delayed, resisting the will of the others to enter Prince William Sound. López de Haro later testified that Martínez,

> with his loud language and bad behavior, had reduced everything to so much foolishness, without taking any resolute action from one day to the next, and in this manner from the seventeenth to the twenty-third of May we navigated in such a disjointed fashion as Your Excellency will see in the logs, and will know that due to this defect a good many days were wasted and we lost the opportunity of entering where Captain Cook did in Prince William.[89]

He asserts that Martínez ordered the logging of false courses and winds to cover up such deficiencies. At first López de Haro agreed to do as commanded, but later he had misgivings and, out of an overriding sense of duty to the Crown, decided not to obey. Martínez sent a party ashore to take possession, and the next day the dispute broke out anew over their position. At the height of the argument, in full view of everyone on the quarterdeck, Martínez slapped Serantes in the face with the palm of his hand, spat on him, and knocked the pilot flat on the deck. A day later he ordered Serantes

---

88. Serantes to the viceroy, n.d., SpAHN (Estado 4289), AT. This dossier, in archives of the Council of State, shows that the dissonant episode was pondered at the highest level.

89. López de Haro to the viceroy, October 28, 1788, SpAGI (Estado 20–34), AT.

arrested, transferred to the *San Carlos,* prohibited from holding further responsibility, and replaced on the flagship by Juan Martínez y Zayas. López de Haro did not deprive Serantes of any authority but would not let him leave the *San Carlos* thereafter, to avoid further friction, "for having oriented myself about what incident resulted in such a criminal imprisonment, I have established that there was no such crime." [90] Serantes testified that following his removal to the *San Carlos,* on several occasions Martínez came aboard, "with the object of excusing himself for the referred incident: saying that shortly [I] would be returned to the frigate and everything would be rectified, and seeming to him that thus he could manage to keep Your Excellency from knowing about these things, he sent this petitioner the logbook in order that it be adjusted to fit his concepts." In Serantes's opinion there was no other reason for the commander's conduct "than a total insanity due to drunkenness, in such a degree that only a man full of liquor could have committed such excess." On various occasions Serantes had suffered other indignities—"every time the said Don Estéban Martínez got intoxicated, for frequently he had more than one drink, particularly when in sight of Prince William Sound." [91] López de Haro was in accord that all of the commander's actions at this point were designed "to conceal his disinclination to enter Prince William Sound." [92]

In a cove on Montague Island, they found a house of wood and reed construction—probably Potap Zaikov's winter quarters 1783–84. Although they described it in their journals, there is no indication that it was recognized as evidence of Russian presence.

Eventually López de Haro became so disgusted with the commander's erratic courses that he headed westward toward Unalaska Island, their appointed rendezvous, ceased attempting to maintain visual contact with the flagship, and instead followed the coastline seeking signs of the Muscovites. On the south shore of Kenai Peninsula he encountered natives bearing small scraps of paper with Russian writing; he was given to understand they were vouchers for payment of tribute. He bartered for five of the little bills, and was handed a letter in English, which no one could read. Bills and letters were later remitted to the viceroy and ministry for examination. [93] At Three Saints Bay, Kodiak Island, a launch came out to greet the *San Carlos.* The leader of the Russian outpost there, Evstrat (Eustrate) Delarov, would be named the following year to head the Shelikhov-Golikov Company in America. [94] Welcoming the Spaniards cordially, Delarov informed them

90. Ibid, SpAHN (Estado 4289), AT.

91. Serantes to the viceroy, n.d., SpAHN (Estado 4289), AT.

92. López de Haro to the viceroy, October 28, 1788, SpAGI (Estado 20–34), AT.

93. SpAHN (Estado 4289) contains the tattered, yellowed, and soiled little documents, as well as the letter, from William Douglas to "Horeman Sycoff," "Cook's River," June 25, 1788

94. Poniatowski, *Histoire,* p. 50.

he was of Greek ancestry, born in Constantinople. To their ears his name sounded very similar to "de Haro," and this engendered a hearty familiarity between the two leaders. López de Haro was invited to lunch ashore, and in their conversation he pointed to Nootka on a map and asked whether the Tsarina's subjects had an outpost there. Delarov denied it, but admitted anticipating an expedition from Siberia in 1789, composed of two frigates, whose mission would be to occupy Nootka Sound, since the sea otter were known to be abundant in that region. Delarov pointed out the location of seven Muscovite establishments in Alaska, all between Unalaska and Prince William Sound, with a total of more than 460 inhabitants. At the latter spot he claimed there were forty Russians and a sloop, which frequently followed the coast as far as Nootka seeking to trade for furs.[95] The wily Delarov probably was trying to deceive the Spanish, for claims of Russian voyages beyond Yakutat at this time are not supported by any other known source. At Unalaska, López de Haro would see for himself how Delarov exaggerated, although he may have been counting as "inhabitants" the somewhat acculturated Aleut hunters. It served Muscovite interests to bluff the Spanish out of any designs their government had upon Nootka. Our knowledge of Russian activities at this time is so incomplete, however, as to render any certainty on this score impossible.

After losing touch with the *San Carlos*, Martínez continued along the coast and on July 19 traversed Unalga Pass, between Unalaska and Akutan, naming it Canal de Camacho, honoring the commandant of San Blas. Two days later he anchored at today's Dutch Harbor, Unalaska. Heading the Russian establishment was Potap Zaikov, "Sycoff Potap Cusmich" or "Cosmichi" in Spanish accounts, the trader wintering on Montague Island in 1783–84. The lonely Russian was delighted to have company and received his visitors warmly, marveling at their dark complexions. Martínez explained that most of his crew were either Negroes, Indians, or mulattoes, and that very few were actually Spanish-born. Zaikov told him that "after Bering and Chirikov, none of his nation had passed beyond Cape St. Elias, but the next year he awaited two frigates from Kamchatka which, together with a schooner, would go to settle the Port of Nootka to block English commerce." [96] His government intended taking this action because a British trading vessel had come to Canton from Nootka in 1785 loaded with a variety of furs, and its captain had claimed that the English had a right to trade and possess land along that coast by reason of the discoveries of Captain Cook. Obviously Delarov and Zaikov knew of plans for the Billings expedition. It is amazing that Zaikov was so candid with his interrogator, but he may have hoped to forestall any move Madrid might be contemplating

95. López de Haro to Flores, San Blas, December 5, 1788, SpAHN (Estado 4289).
96. Extract of Martínez's journal, in Mourelle, "Cuarta exploración," fol. 153, AT.

with regard to Nootka. Martínez was convinced from what he heard that Russia intended to occupy Nootka Sound in 1789 and establish a settlement to counteract British fur trading activities in that area. He became aware for the first time, it would seem, of the extent of foreign interest in Nootka, the "roadstead of San Lorenzo" of the 1774 voyage.[97]

For several weeks Zaikov and Martínez regaled each other in reciprocal "banquets." The fresh meat, black bread, and vodka of the Russian's table were as welcome an addition to the Spanish commander's diet as the *Princesa*'s larder of ham, cheese, chocolate, wine, and brandy was to the Muscovite factor. When López de Haro arrived on August 1, he was disgusted to find Martínez residing ashore with Zaikov, carousing with the greatest familiarity. Martínez came aboard the *San Carlos*, accompanied by Zaikov, and at once began to revile López de Haro for having collected a lot of worthless information, since he had been able to learn everything from Zaikov. The least of his insults, López de Haro asserts,

> was to say that all naval pilots were a bunch of rascally cabin boys [*unos picaros grumetes*], and that if he were on land he would give them thirty whacks; and leaving the cabin he went back aboard his own vessel declaring, in the presence of the seamen, that they were lousy [*unos piojosos*]. In view of such a scene even the sailors were astonished, and those of us who were in the cabin would have been more surprised if we had not noted that all that happened was the effect of the excess of liquor he had in his body, as actually had been observed on different occasions, particularly in all the time he was in Prince William.[98]

Zaikov did not comprehend the cause of the argument, but he became quite grave and went ashore at once. Upon reaching the *Princesa*, Martínez dictated a letter summoning López de Haro with his logs and putting the *San Carlos* under Narváez's command until the captain's "case has been decided." Juan Martínez y Zayas and pilot's apprentice Antonio Palacios threw themselves at the Sevillano's feet,

> and on their knees begged him, *for God's sake*, not to send the order, and in this fashion with great effort they were able to restrain him, although at each moment he became more and more inflamed, saying that if I did not yield he would remove the men from the packetboat and would sink it; he added that upon arrival at San Blas all the king's pilots could lodge a protest, but declared that neither money, gifts, nor laws could beat him.[99]

97. Fernández de Navarrete "Introducción," pp. ciii–cvi.
98. López de Haro to Flores, December 5, 1788. AT.
99. Ibid.

Ashore, López de Haro realized how untrustworthy Delarov's information was, as he had described Unalaska as having 120 "Russians," whereas Zaikov was the lone Muscovite, his subordinates all being Aleut. The settlement consisted of one large barracks, to which Zaikov's quarters formed a small annex, several storehouses, and about twenty Indian huts. The contrast may explain Martínez's ridicule of the data gleaned from Delarov. On August 5 Martínez, his officers, the chaplain, and a group of crewmen went ashore as unobtrusively as possible, gathered at a spot at the center of the waterfront, and surreptitiously performed a brief ceremony of possession, despite Russia's prior discovery and presence. The sailors buried a copy of the official document of possession, sealed within a bottle. To honor the wife of the heir apparent, it was named "Puerto de Doña María Luisa Teresa de Parma, Princesa de Asturias." The litany, mass, and customary cross were omitted, the official act admits, "so that those of this Nation would not comprehend anything about our designs." [100] Martínez must have conceived that the incongruous performance would have some future diplomatic utility, or he would not have risked alienating his drinking buddy by being discovered at such deception. The action was not discovered, however, for the Spanish remained there ten more days without incident.

López de Haro testified that from time to time during this interval Martínez dropped hints that "upon arriving at Monterey he intended requesting everyone's logs, and if he found any account of the trouble that had occurred, he would destroy it, and if he encountered in mine the slightest hint he would take the packetboat away and carry me under arrest to San Blas, and would deal rigorously with anyone found writing to Your Excellency even the slightest account." [101] Before weighing anchor, Martínez instructed López de Haro to make every effort to keep in visual contact, but if they became separated, to rendezvous at Monterey. He returned southward through Unimak Pass, but contrary winds and fog obliged López de Haro to spend four days more at the same maneuver. By that time the *Princesa* was nowhere to be seen. Off Oregon, López de Haro held a junta, which decided that, since the season made examination of the coastline excessively difficult and dangerous, they should forgo following it to Monterey, and instead head directly toward San Blas. There was a powerful motive for disobeying Martínez's instructions to rejoin him at Monterey. By reaching San Blas ahead of the *Princesa*, there would be an opportunity to lodge a protest with the viceroy before Martínez could make it difficult for them. Although this entailed ignoring express orders, laying themselves open to charges of insubordination, López de Haro and his mates chose

100. All of the acts of possession from 1788 are in SpAHN (Estado 4289).
101. López de Haro to Flores, December 5, 1788. AT.

that alternative. Martínez arrived in Monterey on September 17 and waited nearly a month. At length it became apparent the packetboat would never arrive, so the urgency of communicating his findings to the viceroy obliged him to hoist anchor on October 14, and the *Princesa* reached San Blas on December 5.

The San Carlos had anchored there on October 22, but it was six more days before López de Haro and Serantes affixed dates to the testimony remitted to Viceroy Flores from which the dispute with Martínez has been reconstructed. Narváez and pilot's apprentice José Verdía also sent a short, joint protest in which they made known "to Your Excellency that they had experienced from the commander of the expedition, don Estéban Josef Martínez, a treatment very contrary to what was proper to them," and implored that he take steps to keep them from suffering "outrages similar to those endured by second pilot don Antonio Serantes." [102] The reports were remitted to the ministry with an accompanying letter in which the viceroy remarked: "If the accusations against Commander Martínez were correct, I would be immediately distrustful of the reports and results of this expedition and would be compelled to take measures against the accused." [103] He intended to suspend judgment until hearing what Martínez had to say in his own defense. Although López de Haro sought to justify avoiding Monterey because of the threat to confiscate his journals, Flores was more impressed by his failure to follow orders than by the charges levelled at Martínez. Because López de Haro had disregarded instructions to reconnoiter Nootka Sound and explore the coastline to Monterey, Flores dismissed the accusations as pretexts designed to exculpate himself.

The viceroy's inclination to give Martínez the benefit of the doubt tends to corroborate Colnett's assertion that Flores was the commander's uncle. But Flores informed the ministry of having sent José Camacho, commandant of San Blas, an order to investigate fully and arrest the guilty persons, "Martínez, López de Haro or any other." [104] In his own absolution, Flores stated that Camacho's age and infirmities had left him with no other recourse but to have Martínez lead the expedition of 1788, as "the only person available, on whom I was obliged to depend," despite a royal order, given at the request of Martínez's wife, commanding his return to Spain. The rest of the officers in San Blas were just pilots or pilot's apprentices, unqualified for such a grave mission. Flores reiterated the necessity for reforms in the department's, as detailed in his past letters—stating that naval officers with higher rank, more skills, and better salaries should be sent from Spain for more effective conduct of expeditions northward.

102. Narváez and Verdía to the viceroy, n.d., SpAHN (Estado 4289), AT.
103. Flores to Antonio Valdés, Mexico City, November 26, 1788, SpAGI (Estado 20–34), AT.
104. Ibid.

The very day he arrived in San Blas, Martínez dispatched a report of his expedition, making no mention of the disagreements with his fellow officers. Zaikov had told him "that as a result of his having notified his sovereign of the commerce that the English are carrying on from Canton to Nootka, he expected four frigates from Siberia with persons ready to depart the following year to settle and establish themselves in the port of Nootka." [105] That Martínez made this four frigates, not two, suggests that Zaikov had word of Moloski's four men-of-war coming by way of the Cape of Good Hope to join Billings. Since Zaikov admitted that the Russians knew the coastline only to Cape St. Elias, but had learned from English traders of the wealth to be obtained in the Nootka Sound area, Martínez recommended that Spain occupy Nootka by May 1789, at the latest. From what he had seen in 1774 and from Cook's journal, it had all the requisites for a naval base. "By carrying this out, we would gain possession of the land between the port of Nootka and San Francisco, 317 leagues distant, and dominion over a multitude of Indians." "I offer to carry out this commission," he declared, "sacrificing my last breath in the service of God and king if Your Excellency so desires." [106] Martínez may not have been the first Spaniard to entertain the idea of occupying Nootka, but his report from Unalaska and his offer to carry out the mission so impressed the viceroy that the latter "conceived" the bold step that, duly gestated, gave birth to San Lorenzo de Nuca. Small wonder that in 1789 Martínez would behave in so paternally defensive a manner!

Whether through coincidence or guile, Martínez had taken the only tack that could have spared him an onerous legal confrontation with his fellow officers, which probably would have landed them all in some calaboose. His assertions were not just a pose; every statement is corroborated independently, and the danger he portrayed seemed very real in the perspective of 1788. If quick action were not taken, every indication was that Nootka Sound and the long coastline that Spain claimed by right of prior discovery would be lost by default.

### THE DECISION TO OCCUPY NOOTKA

Martínez's report triggered a reaction in Mexico City and Madrid that had wide repercussions for years to come. As soon as it arrived in his hands, Flores warned the ministry that Russia intended to seize Nootka "this next year of '89, and not in '90, as I stated erroneously in a previous letter." He perceived the threat as coming from multiple directions and read an ominous portent into the arrival of the *Columbia* and the *Lady Washington*,

---

105. Martínez to Flores, aboard the *Princesa*, San Blas, December 5, 1788, SpAHN (Estado 4289), AT.
106. Ibid.

suspected of "carrying the objective of discovering a port and appropriate land on our north coasts of the Californias to form and sustain some new colony of their nation." Although this was obviously a business venture, he warned:

> We should not be surprised if the English colonies of America, republican and independent, put into practice the design of discovering a safe port on the South Sea, and try to sustain it by crossing the immense land of this continent above our possessions of Texas, New Mexico, and the Californias. Much more might be expected of an active nation that bases all its hopes and resources on navigation and commerce; and, in truth, it would obtain the richest trade of Great China and India if it were to succeed in establishing a colony on the west coasts of America. Obviously, this is a feat that would take many years, but I truly believe that as of now we ought to try to elude its effects, all the more when we see that now we are threatened by the probes of Russia, and those that can be made by the English from Botany Bay, which they are populating.[107]

Until now Flores had seen no reason for grave concern about Muscovite designs, "but if the free intrusion of these four frigates into the port of Nootka should be carried out, we would have them very close to our California establishments, and they would then pretend to dispute with us the legitimate right we have to the port of Nootka and all of the country, which runs beyond 61°, of which our expeditions of 1774, 1775, and 1779 took possession." The essential objective of another expedition in 1789, he declared, "is none other, as I have already insinuated, than that we beat the Russians in taking possession of the Port of San Lorenzo, or Nootka, pretending, if these or other foreigners arrive, that we already formally occupy it, and in order to assure our permanence a commandant and respectable body of troops go about on shore, with missionaries, settlers, cattle, and other auxiliaries proper to such enterprises." [108] He was sending four Franciscans with the expedition to carry Christianity to the Indians. A supply ship would take additional provisions later in the season. The coast would be explored from San Francisco Bay to Nootka, and from there to Cook Inlet. To do all this he requested more ships for expanded operations out of San Blas.

Despite the trouble between Martínez and his fellow officers on the ex-

---

107. Flores to Valdés, December 23, 1788, "Carta reservada," SpAHN (Estado 4289), AT.

108. "El objeto esencial de esta nueva Expedicion no es otra, como yá he insinuado, que el de anticiparnos á los Rusos en tomar posesión del Puerto de S. Lorenzo, ó Nootka, fingiendo, siempre que lleguen estos ú otros Extrangeros, que yá le ocupamos formalmente, y que para asegurar nuestra radicación, transitan por tierra Gefe, y Partida de tropa respetables, Religiosos Misioneros, Pobladores, Ganados, y demás auxilios propios de estas empresas." Ibid.

pedition just concluded, Flores had no recourse but to send them all northward again, as they were the only available men of sufficient rank and experience young enough to withstand the physical demands. "For these reasons," he declared,

> I have been compelled to order a cessation of investigations or legal proceedings which I ordered formed concerning complaints brought forward by pilots of the packetboat *Filipino* against commander Don Estéban José Martínez, requiring of all that, having forgotten and put aside whatever causes might lead to discord, they should seek to carry out their obligations in the desire to please and serve the King, with the expectation of just reward and in the firm belief that whoever in the future should revive past disagreements would suffer the most severe penalties." [109]

For Martínez, it meant a chance to redeem himself and to postpone, perhaps indefinitely, charges that could ruin his career. For López de Haro and the others, it meant another season of service under a commandant who knew they had gone over his head seeking redress. On the voyage ahead, the Sevillano's will would be law. Nothing short of a miracle could sweep past conflicts under the rug, despite Flores's warning of the consequences if trouble erupted anew.

The urgency of occupying Nootka made it inadvisable to await Madrid's approval. The very day that Flores reprimanded Martínez and his accusers, he drafted instructions for the attempt to beat the Russians and the British to Nootka. "The intentions of both countries are as pernicious to our own as they are baseless," he asserted, "because neither the Russian commanders Bering and Chirikov knew of the ports our expedition discovered in the year 1779, and of which formal possession was taken, nor the English Captain Cook saw Nuca before the Spanish, for in the year '78 he arrived at the spot where in '74 the frigate *Santiago* was anchored, commanded by graduate ensign Don Juan Pérez, and on which you served as second pilot." Flores was convinced that "for these, and many other powerful reasons, it is clear we have a preeminent and strong right to occupy coasts discovered to the north of the Californias, defending them from other foreign colonies." After the standard injunctions for such expeditions, he stipulated: "In any case, you ought to pretend you are trying to plant a formal establishment, making dispositions for the cutting of lumber and the construction of a shed to serve as barracks and shelter from the inclemencies of weather, an assembly place to meet with the Indians, and a trench to defend yourselves from their invasions in case they attempt such." These facilities were for use by day; at night the men were to retire "to the ships

109. Ibid.

for greater security, but if you observe that Indian behavior offers the opportunity, proceed on this point as you see fit, and in obedience to the
concept that my injunctions relative to construction of that humble edifice
are directed essentially to manifest ownership of the the domain of our
sovereign in the Port of Nuca and on the coast to each side." [110] Flores's
reference to the "pretended" occupation of Nootka is significant in view of
subsequent events. He did not regard the settlement as permanent. This
would put Martínez in a difficult spot once the ensuing summer's events
made control of the sound more urgent than ever.

If Russian or English vessels arrived, Martínez was instructed to receive
them "with the civility and good manners required by the peace and friendship we maintain with both nations, but manifesting the just reason for
our establishment in Nuca, the preeminent right we have to continue
making others on all the coastline, and measures that our superior government is taking to carry them out, directing the respective expeditions by
land of troops, priests, and colonists, in order to attract and convert the
Indians to the religion and mild dominion of our august sovereign." All this
Martínez was to explain with "prudent firmness, but without being prodded
into the harsh expressions that cause great displeasure and might bring
about a clash; and if, in spite of these maxims, the foreigners should try to
use force, you will repel it as far as your own strength permits, trying also
to keep them, insofar as possible, from dealing or trafficking with the Indians." With the Muscovites he was to stress the reasons for preserving
friendship with Spain, who admitted Russian vessels to her Mediterranean
ports,

> without which they could not subsist in those seas, and therefore it
> would be a grave injury to the vassals of His Catholic Majesty if on
> the part of the Russians they experienced hostilities in America, giving
> motive to a just break between two friendly powers. In this case Spain
> could count on the powerful aid of its ally France, without there re-
> maining to Russia any other alternative to sustain herself in the Medi-
> terranean when she is so engaged in the war with the Turks.[111]

If the English came to Nootka, Martínez was instructed to "demonstrate
with clarity and sound reasons how our discoveries anticipated those of
Captain Cook, because he arrived in Nuca, as it is said, in March of 1778,
where he bartered, as is referred in chapter one, book four, page forty-five
of his work, for the two silver spoons that in 1774 were stolen from you by
the Indians."

110. Flores, instructions to Martínez, Mexico City, December 23, 1788, in Martínez, "Diario"
[1789], pp. 23–25, AT.
111. Ibid.

The viceroy told Martínez of the warning about the American frigate calling at Juan Fernández, "said to belong to General Washington," and headed for the northwest coast. To the Americans, he said, "you can make more powerful arguments," and he gave Martínez permission "to take such measures as you can and seem convenient to you." He was to send the *San Carlos* northward to explore from 55° southward to Nootka, taking formal possession in those areas not previously examined. Bucareli Bay should also be reconnoitered and he was to take such measures as necessary to investigate all of the coastline from Nootka to San Francisco Bay. A large order, indeed! Three times as many men and vessels as Martínez had would not have sufficed. That he accomplished so much of his mission is seldom recognized in the dust raised by the acrimony of the following season. It is significant that efforts set in march for 1789, while triggered specifically by the Russian threat to Nootka, were not limited to countering the menace from that quarter alone. These instructions show that, anxious as Flores was to head off the Muscovites, he was equally determined to prevent British and American settlements on the northwest coast.

A month and a half of the new year elapsed before the two vessels could be repaired and readied for departure. On February 17, 1789, Martínez and his fellow officers finally embarked, but adverse winds kept them inside the inlet for two more days—a loss of time sorely begrudged, as it was crucial to win the race to Nootka. Aboard the *Princesa,* accompanying Martínez, were pilots Estéban Mondofía and José Tobar y Tamáriz, pilot's apprentice Juan Carrasco, a chaplain, lesser officers, fifteen soldiers, and seamen totaling one hundred and six. On the *San Carlos,* López de Haro had as assistants his companions of 1788, Narváez and Verdía. Including a chaplain, lesser officers, and sixteen soldiers, his crew numbered eighty-nine. Each vessel carried two of the four Franciscans sent to Christianize the natives. Martínez could count upon a total strength of 195 men, including officers and men of the cloth.[112] Neither vessel carried a surgeon; the sole medical treatment available would be such ministrations as the priests were able to give, or the simple remedies known to the bloodletter (*sangrador*) found in every crew. The twenty-eight soldiers—hardly more than a token force—were led by a sergeant and two corporals. The frigate *Aranzazú* would follow later with additional supplies.

Two months after Martínez departed on his fateful endeavor, the viceroy's alarming report about the foreign threat to Nootka Sound arrived in Madrid. Word of the new challenge could not have come at a worse time,

---

112. Fray Francisco Miguel Sánchez who was born in Castilla la Vieja, Fray Severo Patero from Extremadura Baja, Fray José Espi a Valenciano, and Fray Lorenzo Socies from Mallorca, all members of St. Ferdinand's Royal School for the Propagation of the Faith (*Real Colegio de Propaganda Fide de San Fernando*), in Mexico City. Sánchez, *"Historia,"* fol. 3; Martínez, "Diario," p. 27.

for the court was in mourning and a new and inexperienced sovereign wore the crown. Carlos III, four years senior to the Marqués de Sonora, survived his ardent minister by not quite six months, succumbing on December 14, 1788. Felipe, the first-born son, had died in idiocy before reaching adulthood, and so the seventy-two-year-old monarch's second son, Carlos, became fourth and last of that name to rule the Spanish Empire. A period of irresolution was to be expected, but it was somewhat ameliorated by Carlos IV's decision to retain the Conde de Floridablanca at the head of his cabinet, and Antonio Valdés in charge of both marine and Indies. Hence it is not surprise that Flores's energetic measures to occupy Nootka received immediate and full approval. Valdés replied that His Majesty gave permission to make any expenditures necessary to maintain Spanish sovereignty over the northwest coast of America. As the ranking naval officer with experience on the northwest coast, Juan Francisco de la Bodega y Quadra was transferred from the European theater to be the new commandant of San Blas, and six other naval officers were named to accompany him to the department. All would embark with the Conde de Revillagigedo, named to succeed Flores as viceroy. Orders were sent for construction of additional vessels at Realejo, in Nicaragua, for use in operations out of San Blas. In addition, four surgeons had been contracted for service there. Madrid would inform the Tsarina's government of having learned "that some Russian navigators and explorers have situated themselves in lands and spots discovered and reconnoitered with much anticipation by the Spanish, and of which formal possession had been taken in the King's name; and it was hoped that if other Russian explorers were to go to those seas and coasts they would not abuse the good harmony and sincere friendship existing between the two courts by trying to establish themselves in the said regions, that belong to Spain." [113] If all went well, a show of force at Nootka coupled with a resolute diplomatic stance ought to dissuade Russia from greater ambitions in North America and deflect the British and Americans as well.

### A PLAN TO DISLODGE THE MUSCOVITES FROM AMERICA

Concern with counteracting Russian expansion toward California was not confined solely to official circles. A long memorial on the subject, designed to capture the government's attention, was composed by Antonio de San José Muro, a Bethlehemite friar from Navarre, of some prominence in Medico and Guatemala. He underscored the danger to Spanish dominions if, as learned by the most recent Spanish visitors to the northwest coast, a

113. Minutes of the Junta Suprema de Estado, Madrid, April 7, 1789, SpAHN (Estado 4289); [Valdés] to the viceroy, Madrid, April 14, 1799, SpAHN (Estado 4289). The appointees, all of whom would serve on the northwest coast, were Jacinto Caamaño, Francisco de Eliza, Salvador Fidalgo, Salvador Meléndez, Manuel Quimper, and Ramón Saavedra.

Russian expedition was anticipated with 300 families of colonists, and he warned:

> It is a very natural supposition that they will not cease endeavoring to expand as far as the Port of San Francisco. I base this assertion on the character that nation has revealed up to the present century in Europe and Asiatic Turkey. It keeps its neighbors restless and on the alert; but to perfect its system it has caused rivers of blood to run, even of its own vassals. If it doesn't meet any opposition from the Indians, it is very proper to fear the worst, if the Castilian lions do not contain the rapid ambition that gives it impulse.[114]

In Fray Antonio's opinion, if the religion dominant in Russia were looked upon as in error, the spread of that belief among the Indians in places colonized by the tsarina would only lead them to eternal fire. How could a pious monarch look with indifference upon souls of so many pagans being bound by new chains? The danger in matters of religion was matched by the baneful political effect of having Russian colonies close at hand, in a position to disturb Spanish commerce in the Pacific, endanger exposed towns and haciendas to surprise assault, and cost the royal treasury vast sums for adequate protection. If Russia remained in her Alaskan settlements, she could cause contraband trade with Spanish territories to be much greater than in past years. Rather than await a time when the tsarina's settlements might be stronger and more numerous, Muro proposed evicting them while they were still weak and isolated. He advocated marshaling a force to "throw the Russians out of all their establishments on the Gulf of Alaska." Four to six frigates would suffice to reduce their outposts one by one. The task could be accomplished with additional officers from Cuba and ships, crews, cannons, powder, and ball from Peru. Instead of being punished, the vanquished should be well treated, as they had no choice but to obey their sovereign's precepts. It would be well to bring the prisoners to Mexico, so as to diminish Muscovite strength in Alaska and avoid the reproach other nations would heap upon Spain if they were treated oppressively. The outposts would then have to be colonized by the Spanish to keep the sea otter trade from drawing foreign vessels, as would occur if the coast were left deserted. If the good anchorages and likely sites for settlements were occupied, alien traders would find it difficult to come into contact with the Indians. Far from their homelands, they would have difficulty subsisting without food, water, and firewood, and they could not come ashore without risking imprisonment.

114. Fray Antonio de San José Muro, "Al Plan de conquista, y población de lo reconocido en el sur el año de 1779 se añade algunas reflexiones, por la noticia cierta de los establecimientos Rusos; y de haber subido n(uest)ros descubridores asta los 68 g(rados) de lat(i)t(ud). norte," Mexico City, February 22, 1789, CtY-BWA (Coe 355), AT.

The advantages of the sea otter trade beckoned to Spain, Muro suggested, as revealed by the efforts of Vasadre in California. If the Muscovites were drawn to California waters by the abundance of sea otters there, it would be only a matter of time until the tsarina cast covetous eyes upon the California settlements, whose products would be useful in sustaining Alaskan outposts. "This dire moment I see as not so distant as some others imagine," he warned, and it should be forestalled by expelling the Russians and colonizing Alaska's likely sites. "The number of vagrants of both sexes in Mexico City alone would give us useful families for the greater part of this." The people transplanted to Alaska ideally should come from those areas of Mexico by nature cool in climate, so as to adapt with greater ease to the cold of higher latitudes. The initial cost of planting the settlements would soon be repaid to the royal treasury by revenues from the growth in commerce. Making a fervent plea for free trade by Spanish merchant ships, Muro assured that profits from supplying the Indians of the northwest coast with products from New Spain would subsidize Spanish settlements there, once the government gave the initial support necessary to get them started. If such a commerce once got underway, there would even be a lucrative market along the Asian coast for such products as flour, beans, sugar, wine, brandy, tobacco, raisins, almonds, figs, and coffee. An active commerce would develop resources such as silver, mercury, and other raw materials that might be found in those areas. Spanish manufactures would also be drawn into the traffic, which might eventually extend to Tartary and eastern China.[115]

A note at the end of the manuscript states that Fray Antonio remitted it to Madrid in February 1789; whether it was ever considered by the ministry is not known. It was the sort of thing to send Gálvez's imagination soaring, and Carlos III might have seen merit in some of its ideas, or been talked into them by the ardent marqués, but both men were in their tombs. On the throne sat a man by predisposition placid and conservative, and before 1789 was over, events occurred and currents were set in motion that would destroy any dreams of bringing pressure to bear on Russian establishments in Alaska.

### MEARES'S PLAN TO COLONIZE NOOTKA

When Martínez set out for Nootka Sound in February 1789, he knew that Englishmen had been frequenting the spot, but none of the details were known in Mexico. A number of English trading vessels had visited Nootka, but no attempt was made to establish any sort of camp along the coast until that made at Friendly Cove in 1788 by John Meares. Upon Meares's controversial exertions would depend the claims later asserted

115. Ibid.

by Great Britain to Nootka Sound; hence the precise details assume considerable importance. Although he held the rank of lieutenant in the British navy, it was as a merchant captain that Meares came to the North Pacific in 1786. His vessel, the *Nootka,* was outfitted in Bengal by a group of business associates who, as with Barkley's *Imperial Eagle,* were employees of the East India Company seeking to profit on the side by evading their own firm's monopoly. Making landfall on the Alaskan coast late in the season, Meares wintered at Prince William Sound. Scurvy killed twenty-three of his crew before spring arrived. Shortly afterward he encountered the *King George,* which carried proper licenses. Out of charity, the *Nootka* was provided with sufficient supplies for Meares to complete his cruise safely, but Captain Nathaniel Portlock's journal remarks that the *Nootka* could have been seized for operating under the British flag without the required licenses.

Portlock's threat had its effect; prior to undertaking another cruise in 1788, Meares and his associates contrived to fly another flag. João Carvalho, a merchant of Macao, was given one share in the venture for his services, and Meares used Carvalho's firm as a front for the true owners. He would reap a double advantage: circumvent the monopoly companies and partake of privileges that the Portuguese enjoyed with Chinese officials, who exacted higher port charges from other nationalities.[116] When Meares returned to the northwest coast in 1788 with the *Feliz Aventureira* and the *Ifigenia Nubiana,* the latter commanded by William Douglas, he brought papers from the governor of Macao and carried a Portuguese "captain" to sustain the disguise. Each ship carried instructions in Portuguese, but a secret set of orders in English outlined their real objectives. Meares and Douglas were listed in the Portuguese papers as supercargoes, whereas the English instructions showed them in complete authority. That the two men knew they were coming to an area claimed by Spain is shown from a note in Douglas's journal that he possessed a chart of Spanish discoveries in 1775, doubtless a reference to the map in the London edition of Mourelle's journal, where Barrington discusses Spanish pretensions to the northwest coast.[117]

116. The details of this legal dodge became public in 1791 when George Dixon, a properly licensed captain, published a pamphlet in London revealing the shady nature of Meares's enterprise and challenged the veracity of Meares's publications in 1790 claiming for himself discoveries that Dixon attributed to other men. George Dixon, *Further Remarks on the Voyages of John Meares, Esq. in Which Several Important Facts, Misrepresented in the Said Voyages, Relative to Geography and Commerce, are Fully Substantiated. To Which is Added, a Letter From Captain Duncan, Containing a Decisive Refutation of Several Unfounded Assertions of Mr. Meares, and a Final Reply to His Answer* (London, 1791); 2d ed., Howay, *Dixon-Meares Controversy,* p. 116.

117. João Carvalho, instructions to Francisco José Viana, Macao, December 23, 1787, MxAGN (Hist. 65), fol. 98–102; "Instructions to John Meares, 24 December 1787," in Vincent Todd Harlow, ed., *British Colonial Developments, 1774–1834: Select Documents* (Oxford, 1953), pp. 30–32;

Meares and his associates came to Nootka for the first time in May 1788. Two years later, in a memorial to Parliament, he asserted that on this occasion "Maquilla" (Ma-kwee-na) sold him "a spot of ground" at Friendly Cove, payment consisting of a pair of pistols. The chief's brother "Callicum" (Ke-le-kum) took a particular liking to the English, and Ma-kwee-na designated him as their protector. This account is contradicted by Robert Duffin, who testified in 1792 that he, Meares, and fellow officers went ashore and bought "the whole of the Land which forms Friendly Cove" from Ma-kwee-na and Ke-le-kum "for 8 or 10 Sheets of Copper and several other trifling articles and the Natives were fully satisfied with their agreement and their chiefs and likewise their subjects did homage to Mr. Mears as their Sovereign using those formalities that are peculiar to themselves and which Mr Mears has made mention of in his publication." When Duffin's testimony was translated to him, Ma-kwee-na angrily denounced it as false, declaring he "had only sold Meares sea otter skins, in exchange for sheets of copper." The chief habitually referred to the captain of the *Feliz Aventureira* as "Liar Meares" (*Aita-Aita Meares*).[118] At the same inquiry the Americans Robert Gray and Joseph Ingraham, who wintered at Friendly Cove in 1788–89 aboard the *Lady Washington,* would testify:

> As to land, which Mr. Mears says he purchased of Maquinna, or any other Chief, we never heard of any, although we remained among these people nine months, and could converse with them perfectly well. Besides we have asked Maquinna and other Chiefs, since our late arrival, if Captain Mears ever purchased any land in Nootka Sound? They answered, No: that Capt. Kendrick was the only man to whom they had ever sold any land.[119]

Meares and Duffin may be suspected of enlarging upon the facts to build a better case for British claims to Nootka. By 1792 it appeared that the

---

William Douglas, "Extract of the Journal of the Iphigenia [April 20–June 2, 1789], in John Meares, *Authentic Copy of the Memorial to the Right Honourable William Wyndham Grenville, One of His Majesty's Principal Secretaries of State, by Lieutenant John Mears, of the Royal Navy; dated 30th April, 1790, and presented to the House of Commons, May 13, 1790. Containing Every Particular Respecting the Capture of the Vessels in Nootka Sound* (London, 1760 [i.e., 1790]); 2d ed., *The Memorial of John Mears to the House of Commons Respecting the Capture of Vessels in Nootka Sound,* introduction and notes by Nellie B. Pipes (Portland, Ore., 1933), pp. 68–69.

118. Meares, *Memorial,* p. 2; John Meares, *Voyages Made in the Years 1788 and 1789, From China to the North West Coast of America* (London, 1790), p. 182; Duffin to Capt. George Vancouver, [Nootka, September, 1792], in [Edward Bell], *A New Vancouver Journal on the Discovery of Puget Sound, by a member of the Chatham's Crew,* ed. E. S. Meany (Seattle, 1915), pp. 27–29; José Mariano Moziño Suárez de Figueroa, *Noticias de Nutka. An Account of Nootka Sound in 1792,* trans. and ed. Iris Higbie Wilson (Seattle, 1970), p. 88.

119. Gray and Ingraham to Juan Francisco de la Bodega y Quadra, Nootka, August 5, 1792, MxAGN (Hist. 70), in *BCPAD Report, 1913* (1914): 15–17 (from the copy presented to Captain Vancouver).

Spanish might soon be dislodged from Friendly Cove, and the chief stood to gain favor with the British by supporting their case, yet he refuted Duffin vehemently. As veterans of the Revolution, Gray and Ingraham may have harbored anti-British prejudice, but there is no evidence of other than friendly relations between them and British traders during successive visits to the northwest coast. Since the Americans were responding to a questionnaire from the Spanish commandant, they may have supported Spanish interests expecting rewards in the form of concessions for continuing trading activities. If the British gained exclusive control of Nootka, Americans would be excluded from traffic that, under Spain, they had been permitted to enjoy; hence their testimony can only be accepted at face value where confirmed by other sources and fitting the overall pattern of information without anachronisms. Over the years one observes that Gray was limited by few scruples in his ruthless pursuit of peltry, whereas Ingraham emerges as a man of intellect, interested in the history, geography, and indigenous peoples of the northwest coast. He was friendly to Spanish and British alike, and it seems unlikely that he would falsify history for the sake of ingratiating himself further with the Spanish, with whom he always enjoyed excellent relations. We may never be sure who told the truth about the controversial land purchase. When Meares made his alleged acquisition, there was a considerable linguistic barrier. Despite Ma-kwee-na's emphatic denial of having sold land to Meares, it is evident that in May of 1788 enough gift-giving or trading took place to insure his friendliness and acquiescence to Meares's activities at Friendly Cove. The chief may not have thought of it as a 'sale," but it is evident that his consent was acquired.

Much debate has centered upon the size of the house Meares built at Friendly Cove. His publications describe it as two-storied, but to anyone who has visited Nootka it is evident that the illustration accompanying his journal was done by an artist who never saw Friendly Cove. The site of the camp was close to Ma-kwee-na's village, in a corner of the cove where a rocky promontory almost reaches the water's edge, providing isolation for a small stretch of beach. In this snug and sheltered area the carpenters from Macao built a small vessel for trading along the coast, and Meares had them erect a structure for their own shelter and protection. It was finished in a week, at the most. A breastwork was set up, and a small cannon provided for defense.[120] Duffin represents it as more elaborate, saying that it

> consisted of 3 Bedchambers for the Officers and men, and a Mess room. The above apartments were about 5 feet above the ground and under them were apartments allotted for putting our stores in. Exclusive of this house were several sheds and outhouses for the convenience of

120. Meares, *Voyages,* pp. 182–83.

the Artificers to work in, and on Mr Mears' departure the house &c was left in good condition, and he enjoin'd Maquinna to take care of them until his (Mr Mears's) return or else some of his associates on the coast again.[121]

Francisco José Viana, Portuguese captain *de ruse* of the *Ifigenia Nubiana,* testified that the only construction on shore in 1788 "was very small and made from a few boards got from the Indians, and when we sailed it was pulled to pieces." [122] Gray and Ingraham concurred.

On the arrival of the Columbia in the year 1788, there was a house, or rather a hut, consisting of rough posts, covered with boards made by the Indians; but this Capt. Douglas pulled to pieces, prior to his sailing for the Sandwich Islands, the same year. The boards he took on board the *Iphigenia,* the roof he gave to Capt. Kendrick which was cut up and burnt as fire wood on board the *Columbia:* so that on the arrival of Dn. E. J. Martínez there was no vestige of any house remaining.[123]

Haswell's log of the *Lady Washington,* by contrast, describes Meares's breastwork ashore as a "tolerable strong garrison or place of defence." [124] Meares and Duffin had an axe to grind by exaggerating the house's size, and the latter's penchant for reshaping the facts to fit British interests makes him untrustworthy as a source. The Americans may have discounted the size of the house too readily. As a Portuguese, Viana had no reason for partiality to the Spanish, and he was financially involved with the British fur traders. Meares knew of Ma-kwee-na's attempt to overpower Hanna in 1785. It is reasonable to assume he would not leave Funter and the Chinese artisans at Friendly Cove without seeing to their adequate protection and shelter. Their defenses were sufficient to discourage any assault while he was away, and there were enough carpenters to construct the little vessel in a remarkably short time.

While it was being built, Meares visited the Strait of Juan de Fuca and traded along the coast as far as Tillamook Bay. At a latitude corresponding to the "Entrada de Hezeta" or "Río de San Roque" on Mourelle's map, Meares searched diligently but concluded: "We can now with safety assert that . . . no such river as that of St. Roc exists, as laid down in the Spanish charts." [125] Returning to Barkley Sound, he sent Duffin with a

---

121. Duffin to Vancouver, in [Bell], *New Vancouver Journal,* p. 29.

122. Viana to Bodega, [Nooka, August], 1792, in *BCPAD Report, 1913* (1914) : 13–14. Viana returned to Nootka in 1792 as captain of the *Feliz Aventureira.*

123. Gray and Ingraham to Bodega, in *BCPAD Report, 1913* (1914) : 15–17.

124. Robert Haswell, "Log of the First Voyage of the *Columbia,*" in Howay, *Voyages of the "Columbia,"* p. 48. At the time, Gray and Kendrick had not yet exchanged vessels, and Haswell served aboard the *Lady Washington.*

125. Meares, *Voyages,* pp. 167–68.

longboat and thirteen men to investigate the Strait of Juan de Fuca. In China, Meares had acquired Barkley's valuable maps and journals, but this did not prevent him from claiming that strait's discovery as his own. Duffin penetrated as far as Port San Juan, an inlet on the north shore, at its very entrance. Two war canoes with forty to fifty Indian warriors came out to meet them. In the fierce combat that ensued, three Englishmen were badly wounded. Duffin narrowly escaped death when his thick hat deflected an arrow.[126]

The schooner was well advanced when Meares returned in late July. A month later the *Ifigenia* rejoined them, having been equally successful in trading north of Nootka. The *Lady Washington*, newly arrived from Boston, warped into Friendly Cove several days before the *Northwest America* was ready for launching. The Indians gathered in great numbers to watch the bulky little hull slide down greased logs into the water. In the excitement preceding the launching, no one thought to have a rope or anchor aboard, and its momentum almost carried it out of the cove. Meares's text and engraving depict it as launched under the British flag. Duffin asserts that on important occasions Meares flew the British banner at Nootka, "and not the Portuguese flag as has been intimated by several people who were not present at the time and consequently advanced these assertions without foundation." [127] Haswell's log, written on the spot, says the *Ifigenia Nubiana* and the *Feliz Aventureira* flew Portuguese colors at Friendly Cove. In his memorial to Parliament, Meares claimed to have flown the British flag at Nootka, but he was challenged by Captain Charles Duncan of the *Princess Royal*, who encountered Meares off Nootka on August 7, 1788, and exchanged certain supplies to alleviate their respective shortages. When Duncan asked whence he came, the answer was "from Lisbon, and that she was commanded by Don Antonio Pedro Mannella, or some such stuff, which I knew to be false." Meares told Duncan that he had "a small vessel on the stocks at Nootka; where he had a fort, guns mounted, and *Portuguese colors* flying." Before departing for Macao, Meares left instructions for Robert Funter, placed in command of the *Northwest America,* specifying: "You are on no account to hoist any colours until such time as your employers give you orders for this purpose, except on taking possession of any new discovered land; you will then do it, with the usual formality, for the Crown of Great Britain." [128]

A few conclusions are tenable. The *Ifigenia Nubiana* and the *Feliz Aventureira* both carried papers identifying them as Portuguese; the dis-

126. Robert Duffin, "Journal," [July 13–18, 1788], in Meares, *Voyages,* appendix IV.

127. Meares, *Voyages,* frontispiece and p. 355; Duffin, ibid.

128. Haswell, "Log"; Duncan to Dixon, Iflington, January 17, 1791, in Dixon, *Further Remarks,* 2d ed., p. 107. The italics are Dixon's. Meares to Funter, Friendly Cove, September 10, 1788, in Meares, *Memorial,* pp. 33–34.

guise was for use with any strange vessel, whether at sea or within Friendly Cove. If the Portuguese flag was flown in the presence of strangers, is it likely that a British flag would be hoisted very often at Meares's camp, with the risk that a properly licensed British trader might see the British flag, yet be told Meares's vessels were of Portuguese registry? It is equally evident that Meares, Duffin, Douglas, and Funter never considered themselves Portuguese subjects. Hence it is probable they would unfurl their true colors on the festive occasion of the launching, despite the *Lady Washington*'s presence, as it would have been naïve to expect that after several days' contact the Americans would fail to recognize the enterprise as British, not Portuguese.

With the approach of winter the *Feliz Aventureira* prepared to depart with all the furs gathered thus far. After explaining to the chiefs that he would return the following year, Meares relates:

> Maquilla thought proper, on the instant, to do obedience to us as his lords and sovereigns. He took off his tiara of feathers, and placed it on my head; he then dressed me in his robe of otter-skins; and, thus arrayed, made me sit down on one of his chests filled with human bones, and then placed himself on the ground. His example was followed by all the natives present, when they sung one of those plaintive songs, which we have already mentioned as producing such a solemn and pleasing effect upon our minds.—Such were the forms by which he intended to acknowledge, in the presence of his people, our superiority over him.[129]

Nothing made Ma-kwee-na angrier in 1792 upon testifying before a mixed group of Europeans about the inaccuracies in "Liar"-Meares's story than this alleged obeisance to the Englishman as sovereign. Perhaps that is what Meares read into a Nootka ceremony in his honor. Before leaving, Meares gave Douglas instructions for the following year, ordering the *Ifigenia Nubiana* and the *Northwest America* to winter in the Sandwich Islands and rendezvous with him at Friendly Cove in the spring. He was confident of monopolizing the season's trade. Douglas was exhorted to leave Hawaii for the northwest coast as early as possible. Since Spanish vessels were bringing a great many sea otter pelts to Canton, Meares suggested that he seek out the rich source they must be tapping, suspecting they must come from south of 46° latitude, as he had never seen Spanish trading articles in areas he had visited north of that latitude.[130] As the furs did not occupy much space,

---

129. Meares, *Voyages*, p. 349; Ma-kwee-na's deposition, September, 1792, in Juan Francisco de la Bodega y Quadra, "Viaje a la Costa N. O. de la America," 1792, CSmH (HM 141), fol. 60v–62, quoted in chapter 9, p. 380.

130. Meares to Douglas, Friendly Cove, September 20, 1788, in Meares, *Voyages*, appendix V.

a great many tall trees had been felled, trimmed, and loaded aboard the *Feliz Aventureira,* to be sold as ships' masts for an added profit.

Duffin's claim that the house was left intact in Ma-kwee-na's care is belied, as we have seen, by the testimony of Viana, Gray, and Ingraham. The day after Meares departed, the *Columbia* joined the *Lady Washington* in Friendly Cove, and the Americans prepared to spend the winter there. Before the *Ifigenia* sailed on October 26, Douglas ordered the house on shore dismantled, took the useful boards with him, and gave the remainder to Kendrick, who used them as firewood during the ensuing winter.[131] When the Spanish arrived, there was no trace of the building. After their competitors departed, the Americans pulled the *Columbia*'s longboat up on shore, turning it upside down as a shed for water casks moved ashore to make more room aboard ship. The barrel hoops proved so tempting to the natives that a constant guard had to be posted over them. On the *Columbia*'s deck Kendrick built a forge, with a chimney at the mizzen mast, and around it he constructed a house large enough to shelter all hands. The seamen prepared charcoal for the blacksmith, who worked all winter shaping "toes"— small blades the width and thickness of heavy hoop iron, sharpened on one end into a chisel—as well as other metal articles calculated to command a high price in sea otter pelts. Kendrick also set about systematically courting the friendship of Ma-kwee-na and his people—long since removed to winter residence in a sheltered location at the head of Tahsis Canal.[132]

Shortly after Meares arrived in China with his valuable cargo, his firm was absorbed through purchase by the King George's Sound Company, alias the London Company, representing the Etches interests, which had operated four trading vessels on the northwest coast between 1786 and 1788 but had not yet carried out its directors' aim of planting a number of trading posts or factories on shore. Following the merger, the new company was known as the "Associated Merchants Trading to the Northwest Coast." The *Feliz Aventureira* was sold, and Meares cooperated in preparations to send two other vessels back to the northwest coast in 1789—the *Argonaut* and the *Princess Royal.* Merger with the London Company brought proper licenses from the East India and South Sea companies. The effort would be commanded by James Colnett, captain of the *Argonaut,* who would also have subject to him the *Ifigenia Nubiana* and the *Northwest America,* which could drop the ruse of Portuguese disguise and fly their true colors. That Meares and his associates knew full well that Spain asserted a claim over the northwest coast, whatever they subsequently pretended to Parlia-

131. Gray and Ingraham to Bodega, in *BCPAD Report, 1913* (1914): 15–17. Meares gives October 27th as Douglas's sailing date, but he did not adjust for the difference on opposite sides of the Pacific, across what is now the International Date Line.

132. Haswell, "Log," pp. 54–55.

ment and the British public, is acknowledged in the very wording of the license from the South Sea Company to Richard Cadman Etches and Company, under which the Associated Merchants operated. That license gave them permission to trade in the lands on the Pacific coast, "to the most northerly part of America in all the territories, islands and places that are looked upon as belonging to the Crown of Spain." [133]

For his purposes at Nootka, Colnett took aboard the *Argonaut* twenty-nine Chinese artisans, including carpenters, blacksmiths, bricklayers, tailors, shoemakers, and a cook. Subsequently they would charge having been lured aboard ship by trickery, under the impression they were emigrating to Bengal and not to the wilds of North America. The cargo included everything essential to building ships and planting a permanent settlement. Among the provisions crammed into every available space, above and below decks, were most of the pieces for building a sloop, intended to be ninety-two feet long at the keel. A name for it had already been chosen— the *Jason*—perhaps in expectation of the fleece that they hoped would be collected and that was virtually worth its weight in gold.[134] Colnett's instructions commented that, "in planning a factory on the coast of America, we look to a solid establishment, and not one that is to be abandoned at pleasure." He should choose the most appropriate site, taking care that it was "fully protected from the fear of the smallest sinister accident." It was to be called "Fort Pitt," in honor of the prime minister. Once securely entrenched, he was to turn his attention to constructing other trading houses up and down the coast at advantageous points.[135]

These busy preparations on the China coast occurred simultaneously with the activity at San Blas, equally zealous, designed to occupy and fortify the same small spot of land. As Martínez and his compatriots set out with their two warships to protect Nootka Sound against the threat of foreign encroachments, in far off Macao a comparable force was about to depart on a collision course. The Sevillano had no knowledge of his British adversaries, but he probably lost a lot of sleep wondering just where the four Russian warships rumored coming to Nootka were at that moment. If he had a tippling problem, as López de Haro and Serantes charged, the stress

133. South Sea Company, license to Richard Cadman Etches and Company, London, August 4, 1785, Spanish translation in SpAGI (V, Aud. Mex. 1529); retrans. in Colnett, *Journal*, pp. 306–07; Howay, *Dixon-Meares Controversy*, p. 21.

134. According to protests lodged by the Chinese against Colnett, subsequent to the *Argonaut's* detention. Revillagigedo to Valdés, Mexico City, December 27, 1789, SpAHN (Estado 4289); Colnett, *Journal*, pp. 15, 40.

135. Meares to Colnett, Macao, April 17, 1789, in Meares, *Memorial*, pp. 19–27. Nellie B. Pipes, the *Memorial's* modern editor, points out that in publishing this letter as his own, Meares misrepresented the circumstances, exaggerating his position within the enterprise. A copy in SpAGI taken from Colnett is signed "Daniel Beale, for himself and for Messrs. Etches, Cox & Co."

was greater now than it had ever been off Prince William Sound. The stage was set for a clash at Friendly Cove between mutually exclusive colonial designs. The actors, self-appointed representatives of their respective national ambitions, would hardly have been the choice—had there been a choice—of Carlos IV and George III, or of Floridablanca and Pitt, for so delicate a matter. The outcome of their encounter would resound throughout the Western world, push Spain and Britain to the very edge of war, and profoundly influence the fate of the Spanish Empire in America.

# 5 The Clash at Nootka, 1789

As THE WINTER of 1788–89 abated, the only whites on the northwest coast, aside from those at the aforementioned Russian outposts, were the Americans who had wintered at Friendly Cove. In March, Gray took the *Lady Washington* on a trading cruise, while Kendrick moved the *Columbia* seven miles up the sound to Mawina, a cove that he favored. He remained there for many weeks, making extensive alterations in his vessel and erecting on shore a house and battery that he named "Fort Washington." [1] Kendrick would occupy the spot only a few months at a time, but he liked it so much that in 1791 he formally purchased a deed to it from chief Ma-kwee-na.

Martínez's cruise northward was for the most part uneventful; however, an outbreak of venereal disease aboard the *Princesa* boded ill for the natives of the northwest coast. [2] The *Princesa* and the *San Carlos* were still far from their destination when Colnett and Hudson sailed from Macao with the *Argonaut* and the *Princess Royal*, likewise intending to occupy Nootka Sound, but for His Britannic Majesty. First to arrive at the scene of contention, however, were the *Ifigenia* and the *Northwest America;* Meares had ordered them to winter in Hawaii so that they could get the jump on traders of other nationalities in the coming season. When the *Ifigenia* dropped anchor in Friendly Cove (April 19) there were no signs of any competitors, as the *Columbia* was still at Mawina. Captain Viana and supercargo were still prepared to employ the *Ifigenia*'s Portuguese disguise, as they had yet to learn of their firm's absorption by the London Company.

Gray took the *Lady Washington* twenty or more miles within the Strait of Juan de Fuca. Upon returning to Nootka (April 22) he greeted Douglas and Viana, then took his launch up to see Kendrick. The next morning the *Northwest America* hove into sight. The American captains came to Friendly Cove, and after meeting the new arrivals they decided to remove the *Lady Washington* to Mawina. Haswell remarks that, upon arriving alongside the *Columbia,*

> we were greatly surprised to find the ship not reddy for sea. She was now mearly a Hulk, had not been graved or scarce aney prepairation been made for sea. They had indeed landed their Guns, built a Good

---

1. Alpheus Felch, "Explorations of the Northwest Coast of the United States. Report on the Claims of the Heirs of Captains Kendrick and Gray," *HM,* 2d ser., 8 (1870) : 156.
2. Martínez, "Diario," 1789, p. 53.

house, built a good battery, landed most of their provision and Stoars, and had their blacksmith forge erected in the House, and when we arrived in the cove they were casting their balles prepairing to grave her bottom.[3]

Gray was annoyed to find that Kendrick preferred to abandon cruising in favor of erecting an outpost ashore where the blacksmith could forge trade articles.

The *Northwest America,* under Captain Robert Funter, remained at Friendly Cove just a week. Since the Americans had drained Nootka of the season's yield in pelts, Funter went northward in search of untapped areas. Two days later Gray followed suit; the *Columbia* and the *Ifigenia* stayed at their respective anchorages. A day out of Nootka (May 3), the *Columbia* met the *Princesa.* Martínez saw that the unknown vessel was armed and flew the American flag. Coming within range, he ordered a shot fired across her bow, hoisted Spanish colors, and hauled within speaking distance to ask that a boat bring her captain aboard. Gray was reluctant to obey and instead sent two officers. Through interpreter Gabriel del Castillo, Martínez asked about the *Columbia*'s home port and destination, and he sent pilot Tobar and the interpreter to see if the captain's answers matched. Gray said he was bound northward seeking lumber for barrel staves, as the natives had stolen most of his barrels to get the hoops. Martínez inquired about the vessels then at Nootka and was told of the *Ifigenia,* which had a Portuguese captain but carried a Scot as supercargo and an English crew. Haswell remarks: "When he was informed Captain Douglas lay there he said it would make him a good prize." [4] Gray's men made it clear that the *Ifigenia* and her crew were not Americans. A smoke screen of misinformation hid Martínez's intentions. He told them that

his ship was fitted out in companey with two others from Cadaz [*sic*] to make discoveries on this Coast; that he had put in on the Coast of new Spain and loss't most of his European seamen. The defishancy he was obliged to supply with the Naturelized natives of California. That he had been to the northward and we noticed he had a Northern skin canoe lashed on his quarter. He said he had been in Berings straits and that he had found much snow. And that he had parted with his consort a fue days ago in a gale of wind and he expected them to Joine him at Nootka sound.[5]

Gratified at the Americans' deference, Martínez inquired whether they needed supplies, made them a handsome present of Spanish brandy, wine,

3. Haswell, "Log," p. 82, somewhat emended for clarity.
4. Ibid., pp. 84–85; Martínez, "Diario," p. 61.
5. Haswell, "Log," pp. 84–85, somewhat emended, for clarity.

hams, sugar, and other delicacies, and said he was ready to supply anything else within his power. Gray reciprocated with two carmine feather robes, a woven hat, three attractive bird skins from Hawaii, and harpoons, bows, and arrows from the northwest coast. Upon parting, Gray acknowledged the commander's courtesy with a seven-gun salute, which was returned by the *Princesa*.[6]

Martínez arrived off Nootka in the early hours of May 5. When the strange sail appeared, Douglas sent a message to Kendrick by Ke-le-kum, and the American came down in his longboat. A dory from the *Ifigenia* reached the *Princesa* at 8:00 A.M. and offered to pilot it into the harbor; this was accomplished by 11.00 A.M. After the *Princesa* had cast anchor, the Spanish colors were unfurled and the friars led officers and crew in a prayer of thanksgiving to Our Lady of the Rosary, the vessel's patroness, followed by a fifteen-gun salute and three resounding cheers of "Viva el Rey." Douglas assumed that the salvo was in the *Ifigenia*'s honor, so Portuguese colors were hoisted and the salute corresponded. The Spanish commodore sent his compliments, inviting the *Ifigenia*'s captain to dine. Captain Viana and Douglas, in his capacity as supercargo, went to Martínez with a present of a Hawaiian feather cloak and cap. The Sevillano identified Douglas as the trader who had passed out medallions at Unalaska in 1788 and showed him a copy of a letter from Douglas to a Russian, picked up at Cook Inlet the previous summer (see chapter 4, p. 124). Martínez repeated the story of having just come from Unalaska, encountering the *Lady Washington* north of Nootka, and said two more Spanish warships were expected momentarily. Douglas responded with an account of the *Ifigenia*'s almost foundering before reaching Friendly Cove, said that he was in dire need of pitch and tar for repairs, and added that if his consort did not arrive from Macao, he would be obliged to request assistance. With a great show of courtesy, Martínez offered to grant aid if necessary. While they were still at lunch, Kendrick arrived and was invited to join the repast.

That afternoon Martínez, some of his officers, and the British and American guests went ashore to visit Ma-kwee-na with three of the Franciscans who had come to Christianize the Indians. Douglas comments that in this he "thought they had taken a hard task in hand." [7] The natives received them at water's edge with greetings of friendship but raised a ruckus about the armed escort, so Martínez ordered his guard back to the frigate. At the great lodge Ma-kwee-na staged an elaborate welcoming ceremony. His braves covered their heads and faces with a sticky substance that was then

6. Ibid. Since neither Gray nor Kendrick had as yet been to Hawaii, Howay suggests that these objects had been obtained from the *Ifigenia*. F. W. Howay, "Captains Gray and Kendrick; The Barrell Letters," *WHQ* 12 (1921) : 243–71.

7. William Douglas, *Journal of the* Ifigenia, pp. 59–61; Martínez, "Diario," p. 62.

sprinkled with fine white feathers. The chief and his brothers wore large plumes in their hair, a badge denied those of lesser rank. Grotesquely painted dancers chanted interminably, repeating over and over "Martínez, Martínez," to whom, in his daughter's name, Ma-kwee-na presented a fine sea otter pelt. The commandant responded with gifts of cloth, beads, scissors, and other items. "While I was in his house," Martínez notes,

> he showed me the shells I gave him in '74, when I came to his port with the frigate *Santiago,* commanded by first pilot and graduate frigate ensign Don Juan Pérez. Thus all the Englishmen verified what I had told them over the lunch table. Macuina agreed and said that the Indian who stole the two silver spoons (which Captain Cook cites in his work) had been dead for some time now.
>
> Likewise I verified in presence of the aforementioned Englishmen that the Indian whom I hurt upon tossing the shells from on board was a brother of said Macuina. Both recognized me and said that when I was here on that other occasion, the aforementioned year of '74, they were then boys.[8]

At sunset Martínez went back aboard the *Princesa* and posted a competent guard, not only to protect the frigate from assault but also to observe whether the nearby village was restless. All was silent, however, and none were seen to leave their lodges during the night.

At dawn the following day the *Princesa* was surrounded by canoes, whose occupants clamored to exchange fish, plants, and skins of all kinds for pieces of copper and abalone shells, but they turned down cloth, beads, scissors, and other trifles. Martínez, some of his officers, the friars, and Douglas went to Mawina to accept an invitation from Kendrick. Thrice during the meal toasts were offered to Carlos III, and the American responded each time with a salute of thirteen cannons, representing the thirteen states of his young republic. Kendrick told Martínez that his reason for being there was that the *Columbia* had entered in distress, mainmast cracked, stern damaged, hull leaking badly, and had spent the winter making repairs. Later, the magazine had caught fire, and, in peril of losing the entire vessel, they had had to chop through a considerable portion of the foredeck and cabin to get at the storage space for auxiliary sails, which was ruined by the conflagration.

After lunch they all visited a village nearby, where, Martínez relates, Kendrick told the natives in their own language, "that I [Martínez] was their brother, that I had come to live with them for some time, that not only did I not come to do them harm, but that in case some foreign nation tried to molest them, I would defend them, and that therefore it was

8. Martínez, "Diario," p. 63, AT.

necessary that they be very friendly, without doing me any harm." With amicable visages, the chiefs all clasped Martínez by the hand saying, "Wacass, Wacass," which he understood to mean, "Friend, friend." [9] At sundown Martínez returned to the *Princesa* and invited officers of the other ships for a late evening meal.

Viana and Douglas came to the flagship the next morning and were asked for the *Ifigenia*'s passport. In Portuguese and too long to be copied at once, it was left with Martínez for transcription and translation. For the time being he seemed satisfied with their answers; there was no indication of impending trouble. Kendrick sent a letter explaining the circumstances that had obliged him to enter Nootka and declaring that he was preparing to leave "with all possible dispatch." His innocence was somewhat compromised that day, however, when Martínez acquired from the Indians two pewter medallions, excellently coined, picturing the *Columbia* and the *Lady Washington*, with a legend commemorating their visit. The commandant's diary records his reaction: he planned to send these medallions to the viceroy, for he believed them to be not merely trinkets, but intended indications of American presence—a "sign of possession." [10]

To return the hospitality received, the officers of the American and Spanish ships and the Franciscans were invited to as excellent a banquet as the *Ifigenia*'s nearly exhausted provisions would permit. As Douglas relates, "Having one Sandwich Island hog left, and a few yams, I sent the hog on board the Spanish ship and had it dressed after their own fashion; they added two or three other dishes; so that we made it out pretty well." [11]

Sunday dawned miserably and rough weather continued all day, the cloud ceiling scarcely mast-high and a steady drizzle falling. By now the villagers had become accustomed to the Spanish and were particularly solicitous of the commandant, whose diary remarks, "Whenever they come alongside in their canoes they keep shouting 'Martínez, Martínez,' and since I treat them with kindness and give them wool, flannel cloth, and other things, even though it is not what they most prefer, that being copper and shells, nevertheless my name has spread throughout all the neighboring villages, from which they come to visit me." [12] After dinner he, his fellow officers, and the friars were invited to witness the ceremonial naming of one of Ma-kwee-na's sons. Prominent chiefs had come from surrounding tribes, and there were many dancers covered with feathers, as before, chanting to the rhythm of beating sticks. The celebrants circled around the boy, who was dressed in a sea otter robe. Ma-kwee-na and Ke-le-kum participated

9. Ibid., p. 64. "Guacáss, Guacáss," in the original.
10. Kendrick to Martínez, Nootka Sound, May 8, 1789, MHi (Barrell Letters), in Howay, "Captains Gray and Kendrick," pp. 247–48; Martínez, "Diario," p. 65.
11. Douglas, *Journal*, p. 61. Saturday evening, May 9.
12. Martínez, "Diario," p. 66, AT.

in the dance, then removed their bearskins and donned sea otter robes. All the guests then offered the child gifts. Kendrick told Father Sánchez this signified that the boy should be treated as a noble and as his father's successor. The Sevillano's diary remarks that long after he retired the chanting kept him awake.[13]

Early the next morning the commandant went to visit Kendrick, taking cot and bedding so as to remain as long as he desired. Douglas charges that during this sojourn Martínez made the American privy to plans for seizing the *Ifigenia*.[14] Very likely he wanted to determine whether Kendrick would support, or at least not hinder, the moves he was contemplating. Later that day word came that a two-masted ship had been sighted during a break in the mist. Douglas, ill and confined to his bunk, assumed it must be bringing Meares and ordered an officer to go out and assist them into the cove. His disappointment was great when he was told that the ship had stopped a mile short of the entrance and hoisted Spanish colors. The *San Carlos* had lost contact with its consort and taken several days longer to reached Nootka. The fog kept López de Haro from entering for still another day. The morning of May 12 he dropped anchor, and the Spanish vessels saluted one another with a five-cannon salvo; the *Ifigenia* responded similarly. The officers of the other ships were invited to lunch aboard the *San Carlos*. That afternoon Martínez returned with Kendrick and was relieved to find that his second warship had arrived safely.

### THE FIRST ARREST

Martínez had devoted considerable study to the *Ifigenia*'s papers. With the additional strength conferred by the *San Carlos*, he was ready to act upon what he had learned. The *Ifigenia*'s Portuguese disguise was paper-thin. Although he makes no mention of it, Martínez may already have been put wise to Douglas's use of Portuguese papers, as the ruse was described to Gálvez in 1786 by the intendant of the Philippines. In any case, the Sevillano had learned as much from Gray before reaching Friendly Cove. The papers bore the governor of Macao's signature, but most of the officers were obviously English. It is often stated that the Nootka incident occurred because of a linguistic misunderstanding. But from the Portuguese text of the vessel's instructions one readily perceives the terminology that Martínez found offensive and that led him to conclude that Spanish claims to sovereignty over the northwest coast were being violated. The most objectionable clause ordered the *Ifigenia* to resist any Russian, Spanish, or English vessel attempting to seize her or divert her voyage, specifying: "Supposing that in such a case you have superiority, then you should take pos-

13. Ibid., pp. 66–67; Sánchez, "Historia," fol. 12v–13v.
14. Douglas, *Journal,* pp. 62–63.

session of the vessel which attacks you, and of its cargo, bringing the ship and its officers to Macao, to be condemned as a legal prize, and officers and crew punished as pirates." [15] This was an offense in that it gave license to capture Spanish vessels which, in the performance of their duty, were obliged to detain foreign ships entering Spanish ports illegally. The instructions also asserted a right to frequent the northwest coast that derived from the purported discoveries of Bartholomew de Fonte, presumed Portuguese. There is no indication that Martínez ever saw the English instructions setting forth the *Ifigenia*'s true objectives—exploiting the fur trade.

Martínez made out a notarized affidavit (May 13) charging Viana and Douglas with having anchored in Spanish domain without a license from the king and with possessing instructions violating Spanish sovereignty. When they were unable to offer a satisfactory defense, he gave them to understand that they were under arrest. His position was based on the Treaty of Madrid (1670), by which England and Spain recognized each other's rights in territory already occupied in the New World, and confirmed by the Treaty of Paris (1763), which prohibited British vessels from visiting or trafficking in Spanish domains in the New World.[16] Even if he had a legal basis for arresting the *Ifigenia*, however, it is evident that in doing so Martínez violated article eleven of the viceroy's instructions: to explain Spanish claims with "prudent firmness," but to avoid "harsh expressions which cause great displeasure and might bring about a clash," unless the foreigners attempt to use force to carry out their designs. No source asserts that the *Ifigenia* endeavored to use force, or was about to do so. According to Douglas,

> As soon as I was on board he took out a paper, and told me, that was the king of Spain's orders to take all the vessels he met with on the coast of America; that I was now his prisoner. I urged the distress we were in before we reached the harbour; the vessel without cables; no pitch nor tar on board to stop her leaks; no bread on board, nor any thing to live on but salt pork; that if I had steered for any port in South America, the Spaniards would not have seized my vessel, but supplied me with the necessaries I was in want of, agreeable to the laws of nations; to take me a prisoner, in a foreign port that the king of Spain never laid claim to, was a piece of injustice that no nation had ever attempted before: but that, sooner than be detained as a prisoner

15. "Suposto qᵉ em sem. caso Vᵐ tenha a superioridad então deve Vᵐ tomar posessão do Navio qᵉ o ataca e da sua carga trazendo tanto o Navio como offˢ a Macao pa q. sejão comdenados p. preza legal e aos offˢ e equipagem punidos como Piratas." João Carvalho, instructions to Francisco José Viana, Macao, December 23, 1787, MxAGN (Hist. 65), fol. 98–102, Ph in DLC.

16. Revillagigedo to Valdés, Mexico City, May 27, 1790, CU-B (Robbins Collection), Revillagigedo Papers, vol. 21, fol. 249v–54. The viceroy cited a royal order of November 25, 1692, to support his opinion that they were legitimate prizes.

(although the vessel had like to have foundered before we got into the harbour) if he would give me permission, I would instantly leave the port. This was denied.[17]

Douglas's account was the only version of this first episode to reach England in 1790, and it provided the tinder by which Parliament and public became inflamed. Douglas said he knew nothing about Spanish claims to the northwest coast, a claim belied by his use of the Mourelle journal chart of 1775, whose English editor had underscored that wherever the Spanish landed, they took formal possession, and remarked, "It should seem from this journal, that the Spaniards deem all the N. W. Coast of America beyond California to be a part of that province." [18]

Despite Douglas's remonstrances, Martínez sent pilot Tobar and forty to fifty men to board the *Ifigenia,* whose crew offered no resistance. After the Portuguese flag had been replaced by the Spanish banner and saluted by a cannonade from the flagship, the *Ifigenia* was disarmed; its guns, ammunition, and crew were taken aboard the Spanish warships to be kept under guard. Douglas relates:

> The keys to my chest was demanded; my charts, journals, papers, and in short, every thing that was in the vessel, they took possession of. I was not so much as allowed to go on board. I enquired the cause of his not taking the *Washington* sloop, as he had orders from the king of Spain to take every vessel he met with on the coast. He gave me no satisfactory answer; but told me, my Portuguese papers were bad; that they mentioned, I was to take all English, Russian, and Spanish vessels that were of inferior force to the *Iphigenia Nubiana,* and send or carry their Crews to Macao, there to be tried for their lives as pirates. I told him, they had not interpreted the papers right; that though I did not understand Portuguese, I had seen a copy of them in English at Macao, which mentioned, if I was attacked by any of those three nations, to defend myself, and if I had the superiority, to send the captain and crew to Macao to answer for the insult they offered the Portuguese flag. The padries [sic] and the clerk read the papers over, and said they had interpreted the papers right. The Portuguese captain, Viana, was silent, although he must have known to the contrary.[19]

The Indians perceived the friction at once, and the next morning they dismantled their lodges alongside Friendly Cove and set them up several miles north along the seacoast. Father Sánchez's diary attributed the move to a shortage of fish nearby, but Douglas says it was from fear of an Anglo-

17. Douglas, *Journal,* p. 62.
18. Mourelle, *Voyage of the Sonora,* p. 13n.
19. Douglas, *Journal,* pp. 62–63.

Spanish clash.[20] That same day Martínez had his men begin constructing a schooner at Mawina. He purchased from Kendrick the necessary iron parts, nails, caulking, and canvas, as well as several two-handed saws. Since there was scant reason for not constructing it at Friendly Cove, handy to the Spanish establishment, it is probable that Martínez had an ulterior motive—gaining sway over Kendrick's favorite anchorage. Besides rumors about Meares's impending arrival, Martínez had to anticipate the Russian expedition, heard about in Unalaska, which might attempt to challenge Spanish occupation of Nootka. To counter such an eventuality, the men were put to work felling trees and preparing lumber for a shed on shore and constructing, on an island at the entrance to the cove, a fort named for the patron of Spanish armed forces, San Miguel. Laborers terraced the island's rocky crest to make emplacements for a battery of cannons, protected by earthen battlements. A tent, and later a house of planks, sheltered the constable and troops on constant duty within. A second fortification, distinct from the first, and called "Baluarte de San Rafael," was constructed to defend the settlement. Martínez says a canal separated San Rafael from the "Isla de los Cerdos" (Hog Island, where the lighthouse now stands), and since both are distinguished from San Miguel (Observatory Island) at the cove's mouth, San Rafael must have been atop a hill south of the cove and adjacent to the settlement, a spot that commands a superior view of the ocean. Its guns would have been in a better position than those on San Miguel to repel any assault from the seaward side. In a level clearing near the beach, three buildings were erected to house the men working ashore, store supplies, and shelter a forge and bake-oven. Nearby, ground was tilled and seeded for gardens which, toward the end of summer, furnished a welcome dietary supplement of cabbages, turnips, radishes, lettuce, onions, and potatoes.[21]

According to Douglas, Martínez had Kendrick's blacksmith make some leg irons with which to secure the English prisoners. "Having been informed captain Kendrick was privy to my being taken prisoner," Douglas remarks,

> and that it was settled when the Spanish commodore was last at Moweena, when he came on board the *Iphigenia* I refused to see him. This being reported to the Spanish commodore, I was ordered at ten o'clock at night (although I was very unwell) to turn out, and carry my bed on board the Spanish snow [a ship resembling a brig], it both raining and blowing at the time. Here I remained for some time without a soul to speak to. My servant, that was a Manilla man, and spoke the language very well, was not permitted to come near me, for fear of

20. Sánchez, "Historia," fol. 16; Douglas, *Journal*, pp. 63–64.
21. Martínez, "Diario," pp. 69, 103, 108; Sánchez, "Historia," fol. 16–16v, 74v.

his discovering some of their proceedings that was carrying on. In short, they stole a number of things, and afterwards laid the blame on my servant.[22]

Douglas accuses Martínez of having extorted "in as gentle a manner as he possibly could," his sextant, charts, stove, gold watch, feather capes and other souvenirs of Hawaii, shoes, boots, and even his bed clothes. By his own admission, his confinement was not so strict that it kept the Scotsman from arranging with Ma-kwee-na to send out a canoe to try to intercept the *Northwest America,* if sighted in the offing, and warn it away. The Indians asked if he was to be a Spanish slave, as in their warfare. They told Douglas that if he would slip away with them, they would provide him with a canoe to use when his captors were off guard, to help him get back to his countrymen. The offer was declined. The Scot's journal relates that several days later his Philippine servant was bartering for fish when the Spanish got suspicious and put the man into stocks aboard the *Princesa,*

> where he was strictly examined, and threatened severely, if he did not tell whether he had mentioned to the natives for them to go and acquaint captains Mears and Funter not to come in to Nootka. When they found he had not mentioned any thing about the other vessels, they wanted to know if the natives had not told him they had seen a vessel in the offing. He told them they had not. He was after this set at liberty, but ordered never to converse with the Indians, nor speak to them in future.[23]

Having been more than a year out of Macao, the *Ifigenia* was in considerable disrepair, and Martínez had it beached, caulked, and the sails mended. Anchors, hawsers, naval stores, and other things needed to make it sea-worthy were supplied from Spanish stores. He pressed Douglas to choose half the crew to accompany it to San Blas, the rest to go aboard another vessel. The strong-willed Scot declined, however, and his men resisted all blandishments to enter Spanish service. Unable to spare the hands necessary to send it to San Blas, Martínez was obliged to reconsider his alternatives. If the captives were retained, they would have to be fed from stores needed for his own forces. So Martínez changed his mind and on May 17 presented an inventory of everything found aboard the *Ifigenia* when seized, requiring as a condition for sailing that Viana and Douglas sign the inventory in triplicate. By doing so, Martínez states, "they would oblige themselves henceforth to be responsible for the value of the prize, in case the Viceroy

22. Douglas, *Journal,* p. 63. By "snow" he meant the *San Carlos,* with a fore and mainmast resembling a brig (i.e., square-rigged, but carrying a fore–and-aft sail, with gaff and boom, attached to the mainmast), but having a small trysail mast aft of the mainmast.

23. Ibid., pp. 63–64.

of New Spain should declare it to be justified, so that they would not be kept from returning to Macao, in view of my shortage of men to send it to San Blas and attend to the diverse labors there are to be done on land, and aboard ship, and since they don't have supplies enough to stay any longer in this port." [24] Douglas refused to sign unless provided with witnesses and a translator other than Castillo. Kendrick and Ingraham were summoned from Mawina, but the disgruntled Scot relates that he still refused because,

> the Spaniards could lay no claim to a port they had never before seen, nor had any of the King of Spain's vessels ever entered. The commodore said, in the year 1775 he was second officer on board a king's frigate that was on discovery, that saw the port, and named it the Bay of St. Lawrence. I told him, having the chart of that voyage by me, I begged leave to differ in opinion from him.[25]

At best Martínez's temper was short-fused; when Douglas in effect called him a liar, the dispute grew heated and the Americans left. They continued arguing, with the Scot reproaching Martínez for giving the Americans such favored treatment. "The same evening," Douglas notes, "he told me his orders were to take captain Kendrick, if he should fall in with him any where in those seas; and mentioned it as a great secret that he would take both him and the sloop *Washington* as soon as she arrived in port." [26] If we accept this face value, Martínez was astoundingly loose-tongued and foolhardy in revealing to a prisoner his intentions regarding the Americans, who until then had been useful accomplices. That a decree for their arrest existed has been noted in the governor of California's order of May 13, 1789, to commanders of California ports. Except for Douglas's remark, however, there is no evidence that it reached San Blas before the *Princesa*'s departure for Nootka in February. Martínez's journal states that he did not possess instructions to arrest the two American vessels; since in the normal course of events the journal would be sent to the viceroy and the ministry, he would not dare have written this had he received such orders.[27]

On May 25, a gale came up which raged for two days. The Spanish warships had to put out anchors in all four directions to prevent being swept aground. Martínez asked Douglas to take some of his men and make the *Ifigenia* fast, but the Scot refused to have anything to do with saving the ship, and the Spaniard had to employ his own men and hawsers to prevent its destruction. By now Martínez was eager to rid himself of the vessel, sub-

24. Martínez, "Diario," p. 69, AT, entry for May 17th.
25. Douglas, *Journal,* p. 68.
26. Ibid., pp. 68–69.
27. "Yo a esta Balandra y a la Fragata Comandanta pudiera haver apresado, pero no tenía orden para ello y mi situación no me lo permitía." Martínez, "Diario," p. 133.

ject to several conditions. His journal remarks that, "having reflected thoroughly on the instructions written in Portuguese" motivating the arrest, he decided "it might be possible to give them a different interpretation to that we had given," since none on the Spanish ships had a perfect command of the Lusitanian tongue. The original instructions would be sent to the viceroy; and if he so decided, the value of ship and cargo could be demanded of Carvalho in Macao.[28] One suspects Martínez of grasping at Douglas's contention of a linguistic misunderstanding as the easiest way out of his dilemma, for the Portuguese instructions offer no difficulties of translation; their legal rather than their linguistic interpretation was probably giving him pause.

"My people were after me every hour of the day," Douglas relates, "requesting I would sign the papers, that they might get on board their own vessel." [29] When Martínez presented the affidavits anew, Viana gave in, and the Scot felt constrained to do the same. Kendrick and Ingraham acted as witnesses. Upon returning the *Ifigenia,* Martínez admonished Douglas to depart at once for Macao, not to attempt to sail northward in search of furs, and to "abstain in the future from coming to trade with the natives of these coasts." [30] The crew went aboard, raised the Portuguese flag, and saluted it with a cannonade. A half-hour later, Douglas says he was summoned once more to Martínez's cabin, to be told,

> he would not permit me to sail till the arrival of the schooner *N. W. America,* and that I must sell her to him for the price that captain Kendrick and officers should set on her. I told him the schooner did not belong to me; that I had no power to sell her; that he might act as he thought proper on the occasion. In the afternoon the Spaniards left the ship, each carrying off what he could lay his hands on.[31]

Spanish and American sources insist that the *Ifigenia*'s own supplies were insufficient to allow the ship to reach the Hawaiian Islands but that Martínez provided from his own stores enough for a margin of safety. As a condition for sailing, Viana and Douglas had to sign a list of the provisions supplied, so that the owners could be held liable. Douglas later accused Martínez of billing him for five times as much as the jerky, rice, beans, brandy, and other provisions cost, but he had no other recourse than to acquiesce.[32]

28. Ibid., p. 70, AT; Douglas, *Journal,* p. 69.
29. Douglas, *Journal,* p. 70.
30. Martínez, "Diario," p. 71, AT.
31. Douglas, *Journal,* p. 70.
32. "I was going to return most of them, but I found if I returned any I must return the whole. As I had no charge against him of my pork, iron, copper, watch, stove, sectant, my cloaks, caps, and charts, which he had deprived me of; on this account I granted him the bills he requested." Douglas, *Journal,* pp. 71–72.

When he was prepared to sail, Douglas asked for the return of the *Ifigenia's* small arms and ammunition, a request immediately granted. Martínez invited Douglas and Viana to a farewell dinner aboard the *Princesa,* in company with Kendrick and Ingraham, who were to sail the next day. Douglas says, "Every method was made use of by captain Kendrick and others, to find out if I intended to touch to the northward." He answered that for want of supplies he would have to go directly to Hawaii and China. "On this day," he relates, "they drank my health, wishing me a good voyage to Macao, and accompanied it with thirteen guns." [33] The dinner concluded, Martínez and several Americans went to the *Ifigenia* and remained aboard as it maneuvered out of the sound of a five-gun salute from the fort. Douglas begged off from returning the gesture, claiming a shortage of ammunition. All the while, he says, Martínez tried to persuade him to sell the *Northwest America.* The Scot steadfastly denied authority to do so but consented to leave a letter behind for Funter, if the schooner returned to Nookta. The Americans got the impression that by signing bills for supplies provided, Douglas had acquiesced to the commandant's demand.[34] In mid-afternoon the launch returned to shore and the *Ifigenia* set sail for Point Estéban, thus ostensibly headed away from the continent. Once out of sight, however, it shifted to a northwesterly course, despite Martínez's admonition. Douglas remarks:

> Having got out of the hands of my enemies, I was now at liberty to judge for myself, knowing it would be a length of time before the Spaniards could have their snow ready which they intended to send to the northward, and being of the opinion they would not permit captain Kendrick to sail before she was ready, the interval was therefore mine. I had no idea of running for Macao, with only between sixty and seventy sea otter skins which I had on board. My people had been accustomed to short allowance; I therefore gave orders at midnight to put the ship on the other tack, and stand away to the northward. I was in great hopes I should fall in with captain Funter, and I am fully resolved if I do, to take the people and cargo out of her, and set her on fire, if I find I cannot carry her along with me.[35]

During a month of successful trading that followed, Douglas failed to sight the schooner. He brought his log up to date, describing at length his arrest and release, and gave the narrative to Meares in Macao. It was published the following spring in London, becoming the most widely disseminated version of this portion of the events at Nookta. Douglas com-

33. Ibid., pp. 73–74, May 31, 1789.
34. Haswell, "Log," p. 101.
35. Douglas, *Journal,* pp. 75–76, entry for June 2.

plained of being robbed, but the inventory of effects confiscated and returned and the list of supplies with which he was provided testify to the meticulous, legalistic way in which Martínez proceeded to insure that his prisoners would have no excuse for claiming ill treatment. Gray and Ingraham stated that the *Ifigenia*'s officers and crew, upon being made prisoners, "were divided: some on board the *Princessa,* and others on board the *Sn. Carlos,* where they were treated with all imaginable kindness, and every attention paid to them," and the vessel, "while in possession of the Spaniard, from being a wreck was put in complete order for Sea; being caulked, rigging and sails repaired, Anchors, Cables, &ca. sent from the *Princessa.*" "Upon the whole," they affirmed, "we both believe the *Iphigenia* being detained was of infinite service to those who were concerned in her." Having arrived in distress, it would have had to wait several months until compatriots arrived, whereas with Spanish aid it got underway sooner, sailed northward, "and there being no Vessels there, they collected upwards of seven hundred sea Otter skins: which has often been represented to us by Captain Douglas and his Officers, after our arrival in China." [36] That there were sufficient trade articles on board to allow successful bartering belies Douglas's contention that his ship was stripped of most of what it contained.

With the departure of the *Ifigenia,* life at Friendly Cove settled into a regime of laborious clearing of the nearby forest, preparing lumber, and putting the final touches to fort "San Miguel" preparatory to installing cannons in their emplacements. Initially little more than a jagged pile of rocks, the island had to be filled in with stones and gravel, terraces leveled for gun platforms, and earthenwork walls constructed as protection for artillery, oriented in three directions: toward the sea, the sound, and the cove's entrance. Behind the bastions, in the center, was a low building to shelter the gunners, powder, and ball. Strengthening the defenses was Martínez's chief concern, his diary declares, "in order to fortify ourselves in the best and briefest manner possible for the arrival this spring or summer of the ships we are expecting." [37] On shore, the barrel shed was converted to an infirmary, so the sick might be housed there, walk around, and get exercise on serene days. Father Sánchez's diary for May 30 confides, however, that since his arrival it was a rare day on which there had been no rain.

One morning they received a visit from chief Wee-ka-na-nish, of neighboring Clayoquot Sound, accompanied by four giant canoes crowded with warriors in full regalia. Returning from war and loaded with spoils and a few prisoners, they came right to the side of the *Princesa* with cries of "Martínez, Martínez, Wacass, Wacass!" In contrast to Ma-kwee-na, who

---

36. Gray and Ingraham to Bodega, August 5, 1792, in *BCPAD Report, 1913* (1914): 15.
37. Martínez, "Diario," p. 71, AT, entry for May 27.

endeavored to profit from trade with the Europeans by serving them in every way, Wee-ka-na-nish followed a policy of negotiating from a position of force. He had obtained a good many guns from Kendrick and Gray, and word soon spread that traders entering Clayoquot did so at considerable risk. On occasion he visited the Spanish at Nootka, but he greatly resented their steadfast refusal to sell him guns or gunpowder.[38] On this first call his spoils included a number of sea otter pelts, which he hoped to barter with Martínez, whose diary remarks that he "wanted me to give the only things they appreciate, which are copper and shells; they paid no attention to the wool, flannel and beads which I offered them, for they only want these when they are gifts." He invited the chief and two subordinates to the main cabin, gave them a few presents, and they departed with every appearance of friendliness, went ashore to eat their fish, and disappeared at sundown. Late that night an alarm spread throughout the cove that the warriors from Clayoquot were about to make a surprise attack to pillage the stores of food and ammunition. A few hours of tense vigilance followed, but the assault never took place.[39]

### CONFISCATION OF THE NORTHWEST AMERICA

The second act in the confrontation at Nootka began on June 8 when the lookout reported sighting a sail which was recognized as the schooner belonging to the owners of the *Ifigenia*. Robert Funter had not seen a sign of his consort and was returning to Friendly Cove, knowing nothing of the altered situation. Martínez sent two launches to tow the unsuspecting craft in, and, with a show of cordiality, invited Funter and fellow officer Thomas Barnett to dinner that evening. The next morning he went aboard to examine the cargo and papers, and since the ship belonged to the same firm as the *Ifigenia,* it was arrested on identical charges. He subsequently maintained that it had been detained, in any case, as security for payment of the supplies provided to Douglas. The crew were confined aboard the Spanish warships. Tobar was delegated to ascertain the schooner's condition and make an inventory of its contents. Funter had been lucky to get back to Nootka. His supplies had run out some twenty days earlier and his men were subsisting solely on fish. Shipworms had so damaged the ship's bottom that the planking would have to be almost entirely replaced to make it seaworthy again. Despite the deprivations, the crew had collected 207 sea otter pelts. The schooner could be handled by a small crew, so there was no obstacle to manning it with Spanish sailors, and Martínez had need of just such a craft for carrying out his instructions for further explorations. It was careened and carpenters set to work readying it for use.[40]

38. *Sútil y Mexicana,* pp. 19–20.
39. Martínez, "Diario," p. 73, AT, entry for June 6; Sánchez, "Historia," fol. 21–21v.
40. Martínez, "Diario," p. 74; Sánchez, "Historia," fol. 21v–22v.

On the feast of Corpus Christi, June 11, all labor was suspended, and a fifteen-gun salute was fired at dawn and again at noon. The day was saddened by the first Spanish death at Nootka: a cabin boy succumbed to pneumonia. Attended by the padres at the last, he was shrouded in a Franciscan habit and buried that same afternoon in a plot of ground chosen as a cemetery and hastily consecrated for the purpose. Many more would be laid to rest there in years to come. At dusk two canoes came to the *Princesa* clamoring for attention. A lad whose head had been split open by a rock lay inert in one of the craft. The braves made it understood that they wished him cured by Spanish medicine. Martínez ordered the *sangrador* to do what he could, which was much appreciated.[41] Requests for such ministrations entailed potential disaster, yet they could hardly be refused. The boy must have recovered, for trouble would have ensued had he succumbed, and the sources contained no further reference to him.

The evening of June 15 the sentinel perceived a sloop approaching the sound. Anticipating that it would be the *Lady Washington,* Martínez took two of his launches to escort Gray in, and Kendrick and Funter went along. It was, however, the *Princess Royal,* one of the vessels with which the "Associated Merchants" hoped to colonize Nootka. Captain Thomas Hudson later testified he was "not a little surprised" to see two strange launches rowing swiftly toward him, and he gave orders putting his vessel "in the best state of defense that the circumstances permitted." By the time they neared he had two cannons loaded, and the crew were ready for any eventuality. A voice asked in English whether Captain Duncan was in command. When told that Hudson was now master, having succeeded Duncan, the same voice requested permission to come alongside. Still cautious, someone aboard the sloop asked if they were armed. To the response "Just with a bottle of brandy!" Hudson replied, "Come aboard, and about time!" Darkness closed in just as Martínez and his companions climbed over the gunnel.[42]

Hudson was astounded to find that his visitors, who at first seemed to be Americans and Englishmen, were actually led by a Spanish commandant who, unknown to him, now held sway over Nootka Sound. He obtained from Funter a full account of what had befallen the *Ifigenia* and the *Northwest America.* Martínez set a boat ashore to have a beacon lit atop San Miguel, to guide them in at once. The boat returned at midnight and the beacon was plainly visible, but absolute calm reigned and the launches were insufficient to tow them into the cove, so Hudson dropped anchor. Martínez and companions stayed aboard all night, and his diary confides that this circumstance gave him an opportunity "to inform myself about

41. Martínez, "Diario," p. 75.
42. Thomas Hudson, "Relación de su apresamiento," San Blas, September 18, 1789, SpAHN (Estado 4289). There is no known version of this account in English.

his voyage and some other news that was useful to me, and were I to come
back inside he might weigh anchor and put to sea without my having inquired of all that seemed relevant to my government." [43] At midmorning
the sloop rounded San Miguel Island and came into full view of the Spanish
warships, giving the Castilian banner a five-gun salute, answered by cannons
from the fort and the *Princesa.* Hudson went aboard the commandant's
flagship to pay his formal respects, and he and Kendrick were invited for
lunch.

Two days later Martínez sent Hudson an inquiry as to the motive of his
visit, stating that if there were any doubt about the coast's belonging to
Spain, Hudson should consult with Joseph Ingraham, mate of the *Columbia,*
who had taken care to inquire into such matters, and would set him
straight. Hudson answered that 116 days out of Macao, after several storms,
his sloop leaked badly and needed repairs, fresh water, and firewood. After
obtaining these he would continue his journey, with the commandant's
permission.[44] Since he had made no use of Portuguese papers and the plea
of distress could not be refused, Martínez consented to these requests. Hudson brought word of the business failure of Carvalho and Company in
Macao, or so he led Martínez and the Americans to believe; this fact was
thereafter cited by the Sevillano as justification for his retention of the
*Northwest America* as security for payment of the supplies provided the
*Ifigenia.* Hudson kept under his bonnet the information that Meares's
interests had merged with the "Associated Merchants."

The first of several incidents that would blacken the reputation of Martínez among the Indians occurred the next day. Needing materials to construct barracks for troops on guard duty at San Miguel, Martínez had his
men take some long, flat planks from the abandoned Indian encampment
alongside the cove. Laboriously fashioned with crude tools and regarded
by their owners as possessions of great value, they were too heavy for easy
removal to the new village. The next morning Ma-kwee-na, Ke-le-kum,
and eight canoeloads of relatives came to deplore the loss and clamor for
justice. The gifts that Martínez distributed did little to assuage their resentment, which long afterward Ma-kwee-na took satisfaction in airing to
other nationalities.[45]

Martínez's relations with Kendrick, Gray, and Ingraham contrast notably
with his behavior toward the English. The Americans persuaded him that
their stay was temporary, that they had no intention of encroaching upon
Spanish rights. Faced with a potential clash with the English and the

43. Martínez, "Diario," p. 77, AT; Hudson to Colnett, Nootka Sound, June 30, 1789, in
Colnett, *Journal,* pp. 56–67.

44. Hudson to Martínez, Nootka Sound, June 19, 1789, in Colnett, *Journal,* p. 63.

45. Sánchez, "Historia," fol. 24, June 16–17.

Russians, Martínez avoided antagonizing the Americans, who would only have augmented the forces opposing him. Their freedom to frequent Nootka, one suspects, was due solely to the Sevillano's apprehension about the arrival of further adversaries.

Gray had not witnessed the opening episodes of the Nootka incident, but he returned in time to observe its climactic scenes at close range. Cruising near Bucareli Sound, the *Lady Washington* had narrowly escaped disaster when swept onto a shoal. The longboat took an anchor to deep water, and at high tide each wave permitted easing a few inches backward until the vessel slid from its jagged perch. Leaking badly, the sloop limped back to Nootka in search of a safe beach to careen. Gray was surprised to find a fort at the entrance to Friendly Cove. A cannon shot from the *Princesa* signaled him to stop. Not knowing what the temper of events there might be, he paid no heed, and taking advantage of a favorable wind continued on to Mawina, where the *Columbia* still lay at anchor. Martínez chose to disregard this snub to Spanish authority, and his attitude toward the Americans remained amicable.[46]

On June 20 Fray Severo Patero went aboard the confiscated *Northwest America,* newly caulked, repaired, rigged with new sails, and refloated, to christen it the *Santa Gertrudis la Magna,* honoring the patroness of navigators. Shallow in draft and apt for certain exploratory tasks, the schooner gave Martínez the means to investigate a matter of particular concern. His diary remarks:

> Having remembered that in '74 when I was at this port, on my return to the Department [of San Blas], sailing close to land I had sighted on the coast at about 48° 20′ quite a large passageway entering inland, which was not reconnoitered at that time because I was under the orders of the first pilot and frigate ensign, Don Juan Pérez, who did not want to approach the coast; cautious that my sight might be misleading me, I decided not to put it in my log book, since I couldn't swear to it, and thus I was unable to prove it to myself.[47]

Martínez now had means of fulfilling the viceroy's instructions for additional explorations south of Nootka, and satisfying his own curiosity about the mysterious waterway, which he and his contemporaries identified with Fuca's strait. Little was known of its extent, for Barkley, Meares, Gray, and other traders had scarcely penetrated its entrance. From the Indians, Martínez learned of extensive interior channels leading north and south from

46. Haswell, "Log," pp. 93–94, 100, entry for June 17.

47. Martínez, "Diario," p. 76, AT, entry for June 14. The erstwhile *Northwest America* underwent several metamorphoses. Lengthened later in 1789, in 1790 it was taken apart, reassembled, and rechristened the *Santa Saturnina.* In 1792 a different *Santa Gertrudis,* a frigate, visited Nootka.

its inner reaches; these he thought might connect with the inland sea
featured on many early maps and possibly link with, or at least lie near,
the headwaters of the Mississippi.[48] To investigate these possibilities, José
María Narváez was put in command of the little schooner, and David
Coolidge, second mate of the *Lady Washington,* went along as Indian interpreter, a measure of Spanish-American cooperation at that moment. Although Narváez did not penetrate much farther than Port San Juan, an
area already visited by Gray and other traders, he returned enthusiastic
about the passage's width and extent and brought seventy-five sea otter
pelts obtained by barter. Martínez was convinced that the straits of Fuca
and Fonte and a northwest passage would soon be disclosed, and he wrote
in his journal: "If Captain Cook had lived to the present time, there is no
doubt that he would have become undeceived about the existence of these
straits, as all Europe will be made to see within a short time." [49] With such
a prospect at hand, it was crucial that Spain defend its claim to sovereignty
over both sides of the strategic passage.

On Sunday, June 21, Kendrick, Gray, Hudson, and all the officers of the
foreign and Spanish vessels were invited aboard the flagship for a banquet,
which the commandant's diary describes as *espléndida.* The Sevillano seems
to have been seeking to win over with victuals and spirits what he would
rather not have to extract by force. Three days later, calling a halt to all
other activities, he took formal possession of Nootka for Carlos III, an
observance previously neglected for the more urgent tasks of protecting the
base. With his men drawn up in military order, and the British and
Americans as spectators, Martínez physically demonstrated Spain's effective
control and possession by taking sword in hand and, asking those present to
witness that he did so without contradiction from any quarter, proceeding
to slash at tree trunks, cut off branches, and move stones from one spot to
another. In solemn procession the Franciscan and seamen carried a giant
cross to a prominent spot for erection; on one side it was lettered "INRI
Jesus Christus Carolus Tertius Hispaniarum, et Indianum Rex," and on
the other "1774, 1789. P. EJM." [50] A document of possession was signed by
the highest ranking Spanish and foreign witnesses, inserted in a bottle,
stoppered with tar, and buried nearby. To show his English guests that
Cook was not the first to visit Nootka, Ma-kwee-na was summoned and
asked to describe the flag flown by the first European vessel ever seen there
—a description recognized as corresponding to a banner carried by Spanish

48. Martínez to Flores, Nootka, July 13, 1789, MxAGN (Hist. 65), fol. 388–91, Ph in DLC.

49. Martínez, "Diario," pp. 79, 90, AT. Narváez departed June 21 and returned July 5.

50. "I[esus] N[azarenus] R[ex] I[udaeorum] (Jesus of Nazareth, King of the Jews) Jesus
Christ, Carlos the Third, King of Spain and the Indies," and "1774, 1789 P[or] (By) E[stéban]
J[osé] M[artínez]." Sánchez, "Historia," fol. 26–31v; act of possession, Nootka Sound, June 24,
1789, SpAGI (V, Aud. Mex. 1529).

naval vessels in 1774 and no longer in use. A volley by the assembled troops was answered by fifteen-gun cannonades from the *Princesa,* the *San Carlos,* and San Miguel fort. After Martínez and his officers went on board the flagship, another salute echoed across the sound, while the crew, arrayed in the rigging "as the ordinance prescribes" shouted "Viva el Rey" seven times, at each instance echoed from on shore (the commandant's diary would have us believe) by a similar shout from the Bostoners and Englishmen.

At noon Martínez again invited the American and British officers to as sumptuous a feast as could be mustered. At its conclusion there were successive rounds of toasts by host and guests "to the health of our August and Catholic Monarch," [51] followed by a third series of fifteen-gun salutes from the warships and the fort, and three more rounds of "Viva el Rey" from all hands. Such conspicuous consumption of gunpowder conformed to a tradition that at first glance might seem bizarre, but that had a function comparable to today's ostentatious military parades, at which foreign military attachés are the most interested spectators. The ability to blast away with disregard for expense demonstrated power—at the same time showing a willingness to remove the lethal contents of one's weapons in a rival's presence, a gesture of both good faith and self-assurance. The effect that all this noise, belching flames, and smoke had upon the natives is not on record, but it no doubt increased their awe of the white man's weaponry. The sources are in accord that this day's ceremonies testified to the acquiescence of all non-Spanish witnesses to the legitimacy and effectiveness of His Catholic Majesty's dominion over Nootka.

The American captains were most careful in paying deference to Iberian protocol. Far from flaunting any opposition to the monarchical principle, they participated enthusiastically in salutes and libations in homage to the Spanish sovereign. Martínez's attentive treatment, in reciprocation, convinced Kendrick and Gray of his benign intentions toward them to the point that on June 28 the *Columbia* and the *Lady Washington* cast anchor under the very brow of the cannons of San Miguel. Kendrick said he would sail soon for Macao, and Martínez requested he take along the seamen from the confiscated schooner. Funter's cargo was loaded aboard the *Princess Royal,* for delivery to the owners in Macao, as Hudson ostensibly was sailing directly to the Orient. In conversing with Hudson, Martínez learned of several other English, American, and Portuguese vessels allegedly trading on the coast that season. Hudson mentioned that his company owned a brigantine operating in the trade, and the Sevillano tried to pry from him every possible detail about his associates and the size of the effort he represented. When Hudson requested permission to sail, Martínez admonished him

---

51. Martínez, "Diario," pp. 80–81; José Tobar y Tamáriz, Informe, September 18, 1789, in Fray Luís de Sales, *Noticias de la Provincia de California* (Valencia, 1794), pp. 75–76.

never again to approach the coast, unless he was "beyond the entrance to Prince William Sound, because His Catholic Majesty's domains extend to there." The Sevillano says he warned Hudson that "if I or any of the ships under my command cruising there to impede commerce with the Indians should find him in a spot where they should be persuaded that he was trafficking with said natives, they would make him a prisoner, for they had been given this order respecting all foreigners encountered." [52]

The *Princess Royal* left Nootka with a smaller crew than when it arrived. Seaman Robert Cant approached Martínez on the eve of departure requesting sanctuary and asking to serve under the Spanish banner. He wanted to leave the sloop because the crew had not been paid in twenty months, nor had loans been extended to buy basic necessities; in addition, Cant claimed he had been ill treated by Hudson. His buddy, George Eaton, made the same request, and Martínez granted them both permission to remain, but Eaton went back to get some personal effects and failed to return. It was assumed he had changed his mind, but the sloop subsequently returned to Nootka and Eaton came once more to Martínez, who notes:

> He now informed me of his reason for not having come when his companion, Robert Cant, had done so. Captain Hudson had found out that he desired to transship and had bound him to the rigging, where he was kept until the ship cleared the coast. When I found his story was true, I admitted him under the banner of my sovereign and assigned him a place as an artilleryman. [53]

At dawn on July 2 the Spanish launches were put at Hudson's disposal to tow the *Princess Royal* out to catch an adequate wind to speed the ship to the Orient—or so Martínez was led to believe.

### COLNETT'S DETENTION

All day long the sentinels could see the *Princess Royal* trying to make headway toward Estéban Point. The breeze fell off about seven in the morning and Hudson dropped anchor to avoid drifting backward. In the afternoon a zephyr stirred briefly, but then a profound calm returned and an anchor had to be put out to keep the ship from drifting onto a shoal. (Hudson's maneuvers are important because of charges later made against him by his associates.) The sloop remained there until ten that evening, when a breeze enabled it to get underway. "In this maneuver," Hudson relates, "when we were anchored we saw two cannonades, which made me conjecture that some ship was entering [Nootka], and supposed that it was

52. Martínez, "Diario," pp. 81–82, AT.
53. Ibid., pp. 82, 94–95, entries for July 1 and 13.

that of Captain Colnett from Macao." [54] The *Princess Royal* proceeded around Estéban Point and south to Clayoquot, disregarding the warning from Martínez, and engaged in very profitable trading with Wee-ka-na-nish. Hudson implies he did not actually see the vessel approaching Nootka, but he was correct in assuming it to be the *Argonaut*. As Colnett neared the sound that morning, several canoes came out to meet him, one of them bringing an Indian who had visited Macao on an early trading vessel and had returned to Nootka with Meares in 1788. He spoke some English and told Colnett of the *Northwest America*'s arrest; he added that a number of vessels were inside the cove, but he was unable to specify their nationalities. Colnett supposed that representatives of the South Sea Company had seized the schooner for lack of proper licenses. From time to time, during breaks in the  fog that came up in midafternoon, he sighted a ship sailing away but could not tell whether it was the *Princess Royal* or an American sloop said to be on the coast.

At eight in the evening the San Miguel lookout sighted the new sail in the offing. Martínez hoped it was the *Aranzazú,* with supplies. Taking an escort of troops, "to inspire more respect" in case of meeting war canoes, he personally went out to meet it, and Gray sent along his own launch. Night fell before they reached the *Argonaut*. There was considerable surprise on the English vessel when, out of the darkness, a voice in Spanish requested permission to come aboard. Martínez's attire in no way distinguished him from his men, and at first Colnett was disinclined to accept him as the commandant of Nootka, until assured of the fact by the Americans. Upon being invited to Colnett's cabin, Martínez presented a letter from Hudson telling of civilities received from the Spanish and commenced inquiring as to the Englishman's objectives on the northwest coast. Colnett said he came on behalf of the "Company of Free Commerce of London" and bore the title of governor of the port that the king of England ordered established at Nootka Sound. He readily admitted hoping to fortify the establishment, construct additional vessels there, and exclude other nations from the fur trade.[55]

Martínez responded that he commanded the garrison at Nootka in the name of the king of Spain, to which Colnett replied that the northwest coast belonged to Britain, by virtue of the discoveries of Captain Cook. The London Company now owned the *Ifigenia Nubiana* and the *Northwest America,* transferred in payment of debts, and the Portuguese firm had

54. Hudson, "Relación," pp. 3–3v, AT.

55. Hudson to Colnett, *Princess Royal,* Nootka Sound, "Maquella Bay," June 30, 1789, in Colnett, *Journal,* pp. 56–57; Martínez, "Diario," p. 83; Duffin to Meares, Nootka Sound, July 12, 1789, in Meares, *Memorial,* pp. 76–78; Martínez to Flores, Nootka, July 13, 1789, MxAGN (Hist. 65), fol. 561–61v.

ceded its claims to Friendly Cove by virtue of activities there in 1788. The Sevillano countered with an account of Spanish discoveries in 1774–75, three years and eight months prior to Cook's arrival, and he cited as proof the silver spoons, originally his own, mentioned in Cook's journal. Ma-kwee-na would confirm his gift of the abalone shells still kept in the chief's lodge. As to claims inherited from the Portuguese, "They had proceeded very badly in selling land which was not theirs, for the possessions and dominions of His Catholic Majesty extend and ought to extend beyond the entrance to Prince William Sound."[56] His journal confides that by this time he had concluded that Colnett's objectives "could in no way be favourable to the interests of the Spanish Crown," and the British company's designs had to be checkmated in some fashion. Without attracting attention he had the launches take the becalmed vessel under tow. "When he had recognized that the reasons which I had given him were well founded," Martínez relates,

> he asked me in a friendly manner to permit him to construct a strong building for the security of his own person and of those who accompanied him, so that they could take some precautions and be protected from irruptions, raids, and thievery of the Indians. However, I divined his intentions and answered him that I could under no consideration permit it, since it was contrary to the orders which I carried. When Colnett saw that it was useless to try to put his plans into effect, and seeing that we were near the anchorage, he expressed his desire to anchor in the place where Captain Cook had cast anchor. I saw, however, that this was merely a pretext to get away from us, so that, secure from harm, he could leave with less risk to continue his way, or proceed to some place where he could act to better advantage.[57]

"After many compliments had passed," Colnett relates, in an account that he sent to the British Ambassador in Madrid,

> the Commodore informed me he was in want of every kind of provisions and stores, his store ship not having arrived. I offered to supply all his wants out of my vessel having plenty of every kind. he politely thank'd me & at the same time by his Interpreter offered me all assistance in his power and entreated me to anchor in Friendly Cove where his vessels lay. Humanity pleaded for me to go in but from his un officer like appearance and behaviour raised some doubts in my mind. The commodore perceiving that I hesitated to give my confidence, he informed me that he was a man of honour, Nephew to the Vice king and Grandee of Spain, and if I would go in on those declarations of his honour I

56. Martínez to Flores, July 13, 1789, MxAGN (Hist. 65), fol. 561v–62, AT.
57. Martínez, "Diario," p. 84, trans. by Schurz, in Colnett, *Journal*, pp. 309–10.

should depart when I pleased. It was late and thick weather; I took his word and honour.[58]

Colnett let his vessel be towed into the cove despite learning from those in the American launch about the Sevillano's detention of the *Ifigenia* and the *Northwest America,* and despite a warning from Thomas Barnett, erstwhile mate on the latter (and now a passenger on the *Columbia,* awaiting Kendrick's departure for Macao).[59] Perhaps he assumed that time would afford an opportunity to evade the strictures placed by the humbly dressed and seemingly affable commandant. When he finally came out on deck, Colnett was mortified to see that the *Argonaut* would be unable to leave without passing beneath the cannons at the harbor's entrance. Martínez forbade him to drop anchor and ordered the prow made fast by a hawser to the *Princesa* and the stern moored to the *Columbia.* Martínez stayed aboard the *Argonaut* until 2:00 A.M., conversing amicably and drinking "freely," but he would not consent to a British post on shore or to the construction of new ships. Permission was granted solely to erect a tent, replenish water casks, and barter for food. Before retiring, he posted a guard to observe whatever movement occurred aboard the *Argonaut.*[60]

As dawn broke on July 3, the waters of Friendly Cove were already rippling with activity foreshadowing the turbulence soon to erupt. The sentinel awoke Martínez to report that Colnett and some of his men had been out in a longboat since before sunrise. They had rowed out of the cove and around San Miguel, into the ocean, and then back, scouting the location and strength of the fortification; then they had coasted along the beach, examining the installations on shore before returning to the *Argonaut.* Soon after sunrise Spanish flags rose over the *Princesa,* the *San Carlos,* and the fortified island. The two American vessels acknowledged by hoisting their own emblem, as custom dictated, but aboard the *Argonaut* no similar gesture occurred. "This failure to raise the flag of his nation," Martínez remarks, "though I thought it might be due to an oversight on the part of

58. Colnett to the ambassador of Great Britain in Madrid, Mexico City, [May 1], 1790, SpAHN (Estado 4291), in Colnett, *Journal,* pp. 319–21. The assertion about Martínez being the viceroy's nephew is repeated in Colnett to [Richard] Cadman Etches, Mexico City, May 1, 1790, SpAHN (Estado 4291).

59. "I must add, that Mr. Barnett, with others of our well-wishers, advised us to anchor without side the Cove, that we might take a view of the surrounding objects in the morning." immediately (Martínez to Flores, July 13, 1789, MxAGN (Hist. 65), p. 562). From his journal Robert Duffin (1st mate of the *Argonaut*) to Meares, Nootka Sound, July 12, 1789, in Meares, *Memorial,* appendix 13, pp. 76–77.

60. Colnett, *Journal,* pp. 55–56. Duffin insists that Colnett was informed about the fort on San Miguel Island *before* being towed into the cove. Duffin in Meares, *Memorial.* Martínez told the viceroy that he ordered the *Argonaut* towed into the cove about midnight and went ashore it is evident that he remained aboard until inside the harbor and secured to the *Princesa* and the *Columbia* (Martínez, "Diario," p. 84).

the English captain, in spite of his being so near, seemed as much an evidence of his little regard for our country as a result of oversight or preoccupation." "Nevertheless," he declares, "I sent him by my interpreter of
English the order to raise his colours immediately, in order that it might be
known who he was." Colnett then hoisted flags at bow and stern, and at
the main masthead, instead of a streamer, flew a broad blue pennant with a
white square in the center. "He thus gave us to understand by this standard
that he was an officer of high rank." [61]

Martínez invited Colnett to breakfast aboard the *Princesa* and requested
he bring with him passport, instructions, and cargo manifest. By Colnett's
own account, Martínez received him amiably and they agreed to dine that
evening aboard the *Argonaut,* an engagement that would never take place,
for it soon developed that Colnett had not brought his papers, offering as
excuse that his chests were in disorder and he could not lay hands on them
readily, but stating that they would be brought as soon as found. "Since I
understood that this was actually the case," Martínez reports, "I replied
that he should not worry about the matter, but that there was time to do it."
He gave Colnett permission to drop anchor and take time to look for them.[62]
The Englishman returned to his own vessel, inviting Martínez to accompany
him, but the commandant preferred to go in his own launch. Colnett's
account says that in an endeavor to play the genial host, he presented
Martínez "with everything he took a fancy to." Noting the stores crowded
into Colnett's cabin, the Sevillano says he began to suspect that their
project was more ambitious than he had been given to understand. The
bulk of the cargo consisted of canvas and sailcloth which, he concluded,
"were intended for the refitting of the ships which he counted on receiving
and the equipment of those which he was to build." Pressed for details,
Colnett repeated his assertion of bearing the commission of governor of
Nootka. Of the officials accompanying him, "some were to take command of
the company's vessels, and others were to have charge of the books of the
factory, with which purpose they had left London." Martínez's response was
"that he should consider his commission as discharged, since there was no
place for the company's pretensions, and I could in no wise allow him to
carry out the instructions he had outlined to me." [63] Declining the invitation
to supper, Martínez took leave and returned to the *Princesa.*

In midafternoon Martínez received what he describes as a "friendly
letter" in which Colnett made no mention of papers but requested the loan
of a launch to raise anchor, since his own boat was stored away, and asked
to be towed out of the sound so as to set sail before dawn with the offshore

61. Martínez, "Diario," p. 85, trans. by Schurz, in Colnett, *Journal,* pp. 310–11
62. Martínez, "Diario," p. 85; Colnett, *Journal,* p. 58.
63. Martínez, "Diario," p. 85, trans. by Schurz, in Colnett, *Journal,* p. 311

breeze. At this Martínez decided that Colnett had not presented his documents in order to avoid disclosing the company's full plans, and he replied:

> My friend, in the present circumstances it is necessary that you put into my hands at once your passport, instructions, and other papers that I have asked of you. Such are the orders of the King of Spain, my sovereign. When this affair is settled, I shall serve you as far as lies in my power, but I cannot fail to carry out the King's orders.—your humble servant, E. J. M.[64]

Colnett went aboard the *Princesa* at once, a guard escorted him below, and he found Martínez accompanied by some Americans, another Spanish officer, and one of the padres. He was received, Colnett says, with distant politeness. Holding up his passport, written on parchment, which he stated bore the signature of George III, Colnett declared that "the instructions which he carried were directed to him alone, and that he was not authorized to show them to anyone." Martínez responded "that it was imperative that he show me these papers, as well as the invoice of his cargo, so I could obtain complete information and comply with my sovereign's orders." As the Sevillano describes it:

> When Colnet saw that I was determined and able to force him to produce these documents, he ceased his evasions and answered me in a most arrogant tone that he had no other instructions than the passport (even though he had just finished saying he could not show them because they were directed to himself alone). He would not let go of the paper or even allow me to make a copy so I could become aware of its contents. To this he added haughtily that I should tell him at once whether I would lend my launch to help him raise anchor and make ready to set sail immediately. I gave him to understand that I had no thought of doing so unless he should first disclose the contents of his passport and of the other documents requested of him.[65]

The argument grew in intensity, prompting the Americans to leave. Martínez produced a copy of the Laws of Indies, pointing to articles requiring seizure of foreign vessels visiting Spanish shores illegally. Colnett flourished his license from the South Sea Company, claiming it was a grant and license from the king of England for a project on the northwest coast. This did nothing to dispel his opponent's conviction that the enterprise was entirely of a private nature. Martínez took affront at Colnett's assertion that he was an ambassador of the king of England, when it was obvious that he was merely the employee of a commercial firm. He reminded the Englishman

---

64. Martínez, "Diario," p. 86, trans. by Schurz, in Colnett, *Journal*, pp. 311–12.
65. Martínez, "Diario," p. 86, AT; Colnett, *Journal*, pp. 59–60.

that he was talking to the ranking representative of His Catholic Majesty on the northwest coast, whereas Colnett, being on half salary from the British navy and not truly in an official capacity, was not entitled to style himself governor or representative of the English monarch.[66] "At last I told him," Colnett relates,

> I was thoroughly acquainted with the Law of Nations in Maritime Cases, and that he would too late find he was wrong to detain me, at the same time to recollect if there was anything in his favour to give him the most distant hopes of making a prize of me, he should remember as a representative of the King of Spain his promise of word and honour that if I went into port I might depart when I pleased, and, as an old King's Officer myself, never knew an instance of an Officer in his situation ever violating his word and honour, much more pleading distresses of every kind to get a Vessel in his possession, to detain and make a Prisoner of a Man, who by an Act of humanity had put himself in his power; I also put him in mind how un-officer-like he came on board me, in his outward appearance not having the smallest distinction of an Officer, and how much he had put himself in my power and what would have been his situation had I taken the same advantage of him. He told me he did not capture me, only detained me and that I should not sail till he pleas'd. I answered that was unprecedented, that I must sail when I went on board without he fired at me. In that case as my intentions were not hostile, I must strike my colours, for I was not prepared for war having only two swivels mounted.[67]

Spanish sources say Colnett stamped on the floor, swore, slapped the table in front of the commandant with the palm of his hand, and declared in a loud and insolent manner that he intended to leave the cove with or without Spanish permission; if they did not like it, they could open fire, as he was not afraid of them. Martínez says he took offense because of such "slight regard for His Catholic Majesty's flag, and for myself, who as the king's commander represented his royal person." Colnett ranted and raged, "accompanying this talk by placing his hand two or three times on his sword, which he wore at his back, as if to threaten me in my own cabin," and shouted "the evil-sounding and denigrating words 'Gardem España.' "[68] Rubbed the wrong way on a score of points and certain that his nation had been insulted, the commandant lost his patience. According to Colnett, Martínez "flew" out of the cabin and sent in three or four armed sailors to take him by force.

66. Martínez to Flores, July 13, 1789, MxAGN (Hist. 65), pp. 566–67.

67. Colnett, *Journal*, p. 60.

68. Sánchez, "Historia," fol. 33–33v; Martínez, "Diario," p. 86, AT; Martínez to Flores, July 13, 1789, MxAGN (Hist. 65), pp. 567–68.

One pointed a cocked musket at his breast; another collared him, tearing shirt and coat; a third snatched his sword away. "Stocks were ordered," he says, "to put both legs in; but an Officer that had been in the British navy, but at this time belong'd to the American ship, Advis'd them not to." [69] As the Americans recounted it, "Captain Colnett insulted the Commodore, by threatening him, and drew his sword in the *Princesa*'s Cabin; on which the Commodore ordered his Vessel to be seized." "We did not see him draw his sword," they admitted, "but were informed of the circumstance by those whose veracity we have no reason to doubt." [70]

The Sevillano's diary says that if he had suffered the king to be dishonored, many "would think I had failed to act, through fear, though I had no reason to be afraid, since I was superior in force to Colnett." What compelled action was

> that he had said to me in my own cabin that he was going to set sail at once for London, where he would report these happenings to the government. If he should do so as soon as he was on board his packet, I should have to fire on him, as he had said, to prevent his sailing. If I should proceed on this extreme course, it would be at the cost of the lives of some of those on his ship. In order to avoid the shedding of blood, I decided to arrest him in my own cabin." [71]

Martínez reported to the viceroy that, considering Colnett's actions, "if he were permitted to leave, it was likely that having come with orders to take possession to this port and not accomplishing it here, he would execute it at some more convenient place on the coast, and once he was established and fortified, it would subsequently require a lot of effort to evict him, which would have to be done by force of arms." Hence, "in accord with treatise 6, title 5, article 11 of the first part of the ordinances of the royal navy," he had decided to arrest Colnett and send him to San Blas, rather than allow him to sail directly to England and inform that court of the matter before Spain could take precautionary measures.[72]

The commandant asked Kendrick to load the *Columbia*'s guns and train them on the *Argonaut*. He armed the Spanish launches and sent them to board the British vessel as unobtrusively as possible and overpower the crew. This was accomplished without resistance, for only two swivel guns were

69. Colnett, *Journal*, p. 60.

70. Gray and Ingraham, in *BCPAD Report, 1913* (1914): p. 16. José Mariano Moziño gathered testimony at Nootka in 1792 about this episode; he concluded that it was Martínez who laid hand on his sword at the climax of the argument, and remarks: "It is likely that the churlish nature of each one precipitated things up to this point, since those who sailed with both complained of them equally and condemned their uncultivated boorishness." José Mariano Moziño, *Noticias de Nutka*, p. 74.

71. Martínez, "Diario," pp. 86–87, AT.

72. Martínez to Flores, in *ibid.*, pp. 569–70, AT. July 13, 1789.

ready for defense. Colnett had not anticipated trouble and his twelve cannon were stowed away in the hold. The English officers were required to haul down their flag in token of yielding themselves as prisoners, the crew were confined aboard the Spanish warships, and the *Argonaut* was put under strict guard, as Martínez says, "in order to protect it against the thefts which ordinarily occur on such occasions." The enraged captain remained under close vigilance, confined in the *Princesa*'s main cabin, and was not allowed to speak to his officers. "As evening drew near," Colnett relates, "I requested to have my bed on board which was refused; but an apology for one was found me, to which I preferred a Plank." [73]

Examination of the *Argonaut* disclosed powder, sulphur, bullets, pistols, bayonets, and naval stores in abundance. The presence of Chinese artisans and of the component parts of the *Jason* confirmed the ambitious shipbuilding project. Colnett said that in 1790 two English frigates of forty to fifty guns apiece were expected to come to the northwest coast, and Martínez advised the viceroy to counter this prospect immediately by sending warships from Spain or Peru. He justified the drastic measures taken with the rationale that, if the *Argonaut* had been allowed to leave Nootka, Colnett would have found it "entirely practicable to carry out his designs at some point up or down the coast, and we would have had a bad neighbor, and in time of war an enemy at hand, to whose attacks Old and New California would be exposed on account of their weak defenses." [74]

This confrontation between representatives of the world's two greatest colonial powers was considerably exacerbated by the circumstance that both men were unusually stubborn and hotheaded. We have already had occasion to note the Sevillano's impetuosity; and Colnett's caustic temperament is testified to by subsequent episodes. The objectives of the opposing sides were mutually exclusive; moreover, each principal carried instructions convincing him of the rectitude of his position, and each had been on the northwest coast in previous years without having heard of his adversary, whom he considered a johnny-come-lately and an interloper. Still, two wiser and more conciliatory leaders might have avoided such an acrimonious and dangerous dispute.

Wagner and Howay conjecture, without any direct testimony as a basis, that the clash grew out of a drunken quarrel, an opinion evidently derived from the Sevillano's intemperance during the summer of 1788.[75] One need not invoke an undocumented hypothesis, however, to explain how matters

73. Colnett, *Journal,* p. 60; Martínez, "Diario," p. 87, AT; George Vancouver, *A Voyage of Discovery to the North Pacific Ocean and Round the World,* 3 vols. and atlas (London, 1798), 3 : 492, as told to Vancouver by Colnett.

74. Martínez to Flores, July 13, 1789, in Martínez, "Diario," pp. 87, 570–71, AT.

75. Wagner, *Cartography,* 1 : 216; F. W. Howay, Introduction to Colnett, *Journal,* pp. xxiv–xxv.

came to such a head. Martínez realized that Colnett was a dangerous threat to Spanish control over Nootka Sound, the Sevillano's principal and personal responsibility. Although Colnett asserts that on the prior evening Martínez drank "freely," there is no other evidence to suggest that his behavior the next day derived from intoxication. From charges against him in 1788, one suspects that a smell of the cork was sufficient to send Martínez off on a bender, but there is no such evidence from 1789. The sources depict him as unusually active and as taking his responsibility very seriously. His voluminous letters, reports, and journal composed during those months are not the work of a man handicapped by periodic stupor; they mirror the zeal of an individual driven by duty to protect the interests of king and country. Behind the commandant's polite but taut exterior one perceives a thinly veiled resentment and perhaps a sense of insecurity, for which there was ample cause in his personal predicament. Official policy held salaries and promotions in the Department of San Blas to a minimum. Denied higher rank, perennially in a financial pinch, long separated from home and family, currently the butt of wifely petitioning for his transfer back to Seville on grounds of prolonged absence and nonsupport, Martínez nonetheless had to keep up a front becoming his command.[76] His career had been hindered by an inability to get along with others—first Juan Pérez, then his subordinates in 1788. Great responsibilities had been placed on his shoulders without an improvement in rank or salary. When Colnett ridiculed Martínez's mode of dress and behavior and reminded him that he was outranked, the Andalusian was unable to constrain himself. Colnett's arrival provided the missing link in understanding an ambitious project whose full scope could not be perceived from the successive appearances of the previous three vessels. Now Martínez realized that the plan would have to be cut off at the root.

An inventory was taken of the *Argonaut*'s cargo, and such articles and supplies as might be used for the Spanish settlement were appropriated. Despite Martínez's precautions against thievery, Colnett complained sorely about losses incurred during the confusion attending the seizure and before an inventory could be taken. Between decks, carpenters constructed two locked compartments, one for storage and the other to confine the English sailors by night. A large cabin near the captain's quarters was allotted for the officers. By day they were allowed to walk about or be in their original cabins, and Colnett's first mate credits Martínez with great civility for "obliging us in every liberty that can be expected as prisoners." [77]

---

76. Strings pulled by Doña Gertrudis González de Martínez resulted in a royal order for her husband's transfer home, before the Nootka fiasco became known in Madrid. Valdés to Flores, San Lorenzo del Escorial, October 13, 1789, MxAGN (Reales Cédulas 144), pp. 180–81.

77. "Relación de los víveres y demás pertrechos que se han tomado de cuenta de la Real Hacienda del paquebot Inglés apresado nombrado el *Arguenat*," Nootka Sound, July 5, 1789, SpAGN (Hist. 65); Colnett, *Journal*, pp. 60–61; Duffin, "Journal," pp. 81–82.

At sunrise on the day after the *Argonaut*'s seizure, a cannonade unexpectedly shattered the tranquility of Friendly Cove. Many a nervous tar probably tumbled from his hammock certain that an Anglo-Spanish battle had commenced, but it was the Fourth of July and Kendrick chose to salute the dawn with a salvo of thirteen guns, commemorating thirteen years of independence. The British doubtless did not appreciate it, but the American vessels repeated the salute several times that day. Martínez was not one to let his own potency be overshadowed, and by sunset a total of 161 cannon shots had reverberated across the waters from San Miguel. Kendrick gave a banquet aboard the *Columbia,* to which he invited the commandant, Spanish officers, padres, and officers of the *Argonaut,* as well as his compatriots from Gray's vessel. During the repast, described as splendid, the diners proposed three toasts to the young nation and to the Spanish king. Cannonades from the *Columbia,* the *San Carlos,* and the fort accompanied each toast. Martínez begged off joining in with the *Princesa*'s guns; these were loaded with ball and grape, prepared for any eventuality.[78]

Several days after his arrest, Colnett was transferred to his own cabin. Sulky and despondent, he particularly resented Martínez's seizing the *Argonaut* but allowing the Americans to operate unmolested. Vigilance was sufficiently lax to permit Robert Duffin, the second officer, to compose a series of letters relating each day's events. These notes were kept from Spanish eyes, sent to China, and published in 1790 as appendices to Meares's memorial to Parliament. "Since our being captured," Duffin relates,

> Captain Colnett has been in a high state of insanity; sometimes he starts, at other times he asks how long he has to live, who is to be his executioner, what death he is to be put to, with all such delirious expressions, accompanied by a number of simple actions, which induces me, and every other person who sees him, to believe his brain is turned, owing to the great charge that was under his care; and I am sorry to add, that he has not fortitude enough in this critical and disagreeable situation, to support this unexpected stroke.[79]

Colnett had blundered into a predicament for which there was no excuse. How could he justify having allowed the *Argonaut* to be towed into a position where Spanish guns could force him to submit to Martínez's will? His misjudgment had ruined the entire enterprise and placed his crew in jeopardy. After several days of reflecting upon his imprudence, he approached the side of the ship on the pretext of relieving himself. Before anyone noticed, he climbed upon the gunnel, poised to plunge overboard, but hesitated long enough to be seized by some of the Spanish seamen and his own

78. Martínez, "Diario," p. 87; Sánchez, "Historia," fol. 33v.
79. Duffin to Meares, Nootka, July 12 [11], 1789, in Meares, *Memorial*, pp. 81–82.

officers. Several days later he crawled out his cabin window. The splash attracted attention, and a nearby Spanish launch set out of retrieve him. He made no effort to swim and was saved only because someone grasped his ample shock of hair.[80] Half drowned, he was stretched out face down on the deck and resuscitated only after considerable water had been expelled from him. Confined thereafter in a cabin without a porthole large enough for escape, he was watched around the clock. Duffin agrees with Spanish sources that Colnett was saved against his will, and adds:

> His constant cry is that he is condemned to be hanged. I sincerely hope for his speedy recovery, but am apprehensive he never will recover his former senses again. I understand from the boy Russel, that it is a family disorder, and that they all have symptoms of madness, more or less. I have written the whole transaction concerning our being captured, &c. previously to this, as minutely as at present circumstances will permit, for I am apprehensive, if I am seen writing, they will take my book, paper, pens, ink, &c. from me, so that whatever I have written is by stealth; but Mr. Barnett has been so obliging as to assist me as much as lay in his power to do it. Gibson was seen writing one day, and they immediately took the paper and ink from him, and told him prisoners had no business to write.[81]

Duffin was confident that he and his compatriots would be released upon reaching San Blas. Martínez promised that "every thing that he has taken to himself shall be replaced at that port; but there has been a number of things taken out of the vessel by theft, that he knows nothing of." Colnett soon became rational again. "I have endeavoured," Duffin reported, "to persuade him to draw out every particular concerning our being captured, to send to his employers, which he refuses: his objection is, that he has involved himself and every one else in difficulties that he is not able to extricate himself from, and therefore declares to me that he will have no more concern with the charge of the vessel, but leaves every thing entirely to me." [82]

### CAPTURE OF THE PRINCESS ROYAL

Tobar would conduct the *Argonaut* to San Blas with a prize crew, and on Sunday, July 12, when he was ready to sail, the English officers were invited to a farewell dinner with Martínez. Late that afternoon another vessel was sighted, anchored at a considerable distance, its boat approaching the cove. Martínez sent two launches to meet it. After a short but profitable cruise,

---

80. José Tobar y Tamáriz, [Informe], September 18, 1789, in Fray Luís de Sales, *Noticias de la Provincia de California* (Valencia, 1794), pp. 70–71.
81. Duffin to Meares, July 13 [12], 1789, in Meares, *Memorial*, pp. 83–85.
82. Duffin to Meares, July 14, 1789, in ibid., pp. 85–87.

the *Princess Royal* had headed back toward Nootka, disregarding the warning that Hudson would be arrested if he came to the coast again without a Spanish license. He subsequently justified putting himself within Martínez's grasp again with the excuse of meeting Colnett to receive further orders. Recounting this to Meares, Duffin remarked, "Captain Hudson seems very much hurt from his misfortune, and candidly declares that it is entirely from his own simplicity, and being too credulous of the Spaniard's honour, that has brought him into this disagreeable dilemma." [83] Hudson's account of his capture reveals that he proceeded with more duplicity than credulity —and that he never intended to bring his vessel back into the cove. Instead, while still some distance away, he fired two cannons, hoping to attract some native canoes or launches from the American vessels, so as to inquire whether Colnett was there, as he suspected that the *Argonaut* had arrived the night he left. The wind dropped off completely and a tide sucked his vessel toward the sound, forcing him to cast anchor. Being this near, he decided to verify for himself what had transpired within. "Having parted with Don Estéban José Martínez on good terms," he continues, "I had no reason to fear he would put up any objection to my plan." [84] Nonetheless, he was sufficiently wary to take the precaution of disguising himself as a sailor, and he gave his second in command orders to fire on any Spanish launch or vessel that might approach.

They had not rowed more than a mile and a half when they were accosted by the Spanish launches. By now Martínez had full knowledge of Hudson's role in Colnett's plans. Mondofía and Narváez recognized Hudson among the seamen, despite the disguise. According to Hudson, Mondofía spoke a little English and said he had been sent to ask whether help was needed: in any case, he added, Martínez wished him to bring the sloop into port. Mondofía also reputedly said that Colnett was there and had sent the same message, and if he (Colnett) had not been very ill and in bed, he would have sent a letter to this effect. Hudson replied that he had no intention of bringing his vessel in, since there was no reason to do so other than to ask Colnett for a few things. He could find out what he wanted to know by going into the cove in his own boat just as well as if the sloop were brought in. Hudson relates that, "finding me firm in my resolve he invited me to accompany him in his launch, to which I couldn't think of any motive for refusing, and so as a consequence I transferred over into it." [85] It was almost dark, but once inside the Spanish launch, Hudson saw its occupants were armed to the teeth, with two swivel guns in the prow and two astern. When asked why they were so heavily armed, Mondofía replied

83. Ibid.
84. Hudson, "Relación," fol. 4v.
85. Ibid., fol. 5–5v.

that danger from the Indians necessitated it. The Englishman was hardly seated when they started rowing vigorously toward the cove. As Hudson stood up and shouted to his men to go directly to the *Argonaut,* Mondofía spied a pistol in his pocket, and before the captain could make a move, it was seized, discharged into the air, and tossed to the center of the boat. Asked if he had any other weapons, Hudson answered that anywhere there were Indians his boat never went unarmed. He was told to order it alongside, but by that time his sailors were too far away. Hearing the pistol shot, they made off to obey Hudson's last order. Since their boat was much lighter, they gained headway. Hoping to beat the launches to Colnett, they passed through the narrow channel between Hog Island and the settlement, only to be taken captive at the *Argonaut's* side.

Conducted to the *Princesa,* Hudson scorned a demand that he write a letter ordering his crew to surrender. Then, in Hudson's presence Martínez instructed Mondofía to put the English seamen to the sword without quarter if resistance were offered, in which case Colnett and Hudson would also be hanged. Martínez later claimed he had been bluffing, but his dire tone extracted the needed missive. The boarding party was told to proceed so that no one on either side would be injured, and their mission was accomplished before dawn on July 13, without a single shot being fired. A Spanish crew brought the sloop in, and the Sevillano could take satisfaction in one more bloodless round. Yet the perspective was not rosy for the relatively small force of Spaniards, now quite outnumbered by a motley crowd of Englishmen and assorted Asiatics, not to mention aborigines. A message remitted to Mexico aboard the *Argonaut* by one of the friars deplores: "We expect the Russians from one day to the next, and some other English vessels, so that if Spain does not take strong resolves on the particular, these coasts and our establishments are in imminent danger." [86] After such increasing turbulence, no one could foresee what new challenges to the Iberian presence might occur.

### KE-LE-KUM'S MURDER

Though Colnett, Hudson, and the crew of the *Princess Royal* were kept under close guard, the seamen of the *Argonaut,* whose departure was postponed for yet another day, were allowed to go ashore. Some went to Makwee-na and Ke-le-kum, criticizing Martínez's seizures, asserting that the Spanish had no right to keep them from trading at Nootka. They condemned the Sevillano's motives as avaricious and charged him with wanting to possess the precious cargo of furs aboard the seized vessels and keep the English from purchasing more. Although unsophisticated as to the crosscurrents of European rivalry, the chiefs had quickly discerned differences

---

86. Fray Severo Patero, "San Lorenzo de Noca," July 13, 1789, CtY-BWA, fol. 1v, AT.

between the various nationalities visiting Nootka. Given a choice, they opposed any nation having exclusive sway over their ancestral territory, preferring to play one nationality off against the other. The visible strength of Spanish forces led Ma-kwee-na to avoid coming near after the initial arrest. Ke-le-kum was less discreet, and not at all hesitant about defending the English, to whom he was particularly attached. The afternoon of July 13 he went aboard the *San Carlos* to denounce the commandant's actions to López de Haro, who tried to calm him with a few gifts. Martínez happened to be aboard the *Princess Royal* and seeing Ke-le-kum start for shore in a canoe with his wife and child, he signalled for him to come aboard, intending to give him some presents in an attempt to win him away from his allegiance to the British. The brave refused, and approaching the sloop, he began to revile Martínez for having captured Hudson, calling him "Martínez Pisec, Martínez Capsil!" Asking some of the prisoners to interpret, the Sevillano was told the words meant "rogue" and "thief." Ke-le-kum continued the harangue, complaining that Martínez was not content to seize English vessels within the cove, but even took them at sea. He and his brother would no longer be safe from the commandant's avarice and cruelty. The tirade evoked great mirth among the English spectators.

Funter, author of the version divulged by Meares to the British public, says the incident started when "Callicum" came to the *Princesa* with a gift of fish, which was taken from him in a "rough and unwelcome manner, before he could present it to the commander." At first Martínez paid little heed to the chief's diatribe, but the Indian kept it up, and after a time the commandant could contain his irritation no longer. Seizing a musket from a nearby guardsman, he took quick aim at the heckler and pulled the trigger. The weapon misfired. Another seaman, perceiving the intent, raised his gun and shot. The bullet passed completely through the hapless chief, and he plummeted forward into the water as his wife and child looked on in horror. Stupefied with shock, the woman had to be carried ashore amidst the wails of the dead man's relatives.[87]

The commandant, in his diary, attributes Ke-le-kum's audacity to Colnett's assurances, the morning after his arrival, that he had come to be "master" of the land and to expel the Spanish. The Sevillano's authority had been challenged in front of many bystanders, and while he justified the execution to himself as a necessary example of his intention to maintain effective dominion over Nootka, it is evident that the incident resulted from his ungovernable temper. The sight of Ke-le-kum's corpse tinting the waters of Friendly Cove shocked spectators of every nationality, and this episode, more than any other, gave shape to the cloud that came to surround Mar-

87. Meares, *Voyages*, pp. 183–84; Martínez, "Diario," p. 94; Sánchez, "Historia," fol. 36v–37; Tobar, Informe, October 7, 1789, MxAGN (Hist. 65), fol. 274.

tínez's name on the northwest coast. Among the Spanish as well, Ke-le-kum's death was held to be an assassination and an abomination.[88] Meares adds a macabre detail gleaned from Funter, whose animosity toward the Sevillano makes his veracity suspect, as shown by other portions of his testimony. According to Funter, the evil was compounded when the victim's relatives wanted to dive for the cadaver but were refused permission until they brought five sea otter skins to purchase the privilege. Other sources say that Ma-kwee-na immediately fled with family and belongings to Clayoquot, taking up temporary residence with Wee-ka-na-nish, Ke-le-kum's brother-in-law, and for several weeks the natives gave the opposing factions of whites at Friendly Cove a wide berth.[89]

The *Argonaut*'s departure for San Blas provided Martínez with an opportunity to send the viceroy an account of occurrences since his arrival, and in particular of his motives for the four arrests. A series of letters, all of the same date, presented his observations about conditions at Nootka, the advantages of maintaining a permanent establishment there, and the measures taken to repulse further attempts by foreigners to settle at that strategic site. Considering the tension-charged episodes of the previous twenty-four hours, it is unlikely that these missives were all composed on July 13. Rather, they were the product of weeks of thought and dictation, but were all given the last possible date prior to being sealed in a package for delivery by Tobar to Mexico. Martínez was careful to provide Flores with documents proving the legality of his seizures—originals and translations of the instructions taken from the captured vessels, inventories, and sworn testimonies. The voluminous documentation evinces the commandant's recognition that he must supply everything necessary to resolve questions regarding measures for the strengthening of Spain's position on the northwest coast, the defense of Nootka, and the handling of situations arising from the arrests. To bolster Spanish power on the northwest coast, he stressed the need to occupy "Owyhee, [*sic*]," or the Sandwich Islands, asserting that Spain's claim was superior to that of any other nation, because of the discovery of the islands in 1542 by "Juan Gaetano," a Spanish subject. Since most trading vessels on the northwest coast depended upon obtaining vital foodstuffs there, control of the archipelago would not only provide a source of supplies for Spanish settlements, but it would also exclude foreigners

88. Moziño, *Noticias*, p. 76.
89. Ibid.; Meares, *Voyages*, p. 184. Colnett says that upon his visit to Clayoquot a year later, Ke-le-kum's widow made a similar accusation. His journal was completed at a later date, with access to Meares's book, and echoing Funter's charge, Colnett accused the Spanish of "robbing, plundering, and murdering the Indians that oppos'd them in the smallest degree." Colnett, *Journal*, p. 193. An unbiased examination of Spanish relations with the Indians reveals, however, the degree to which Colnett's rancor and hatred for everything Spanish warped his testimony.

and deny them their favorite wintering spot.[90] Gaitán's feat is cast in doubt by modern scholars, but in 1789 it was accepted as fact and was more than sufficient to encourage Madrid's claim.

Martínez was confident that Spain could sustain before the courts of Europe its sovereign right to make legal prizes of foreign ships arriving at Spanish ports without proper licenses, unless in distress. Although with hindsight his conduct may seem imprudent, he correctly perceived British intentions, and his measures put an immediate end to the London Company's ambitious venture. He could not foresee that the very next day, on the other side of the globe, a Parisian mob would initiate a chain of events outweighing on the geopolitical scales all Madrid's legalistic arguments or internationally witnessed symbolic gestures of effective Spanish dominion over Nootka. Diplomatic astuteness, alliances, military potential, commercial interests, domestic politics, revolutionary spirit, and backstairs palace intrigue would all exercise greater influence upon the outcome of competition for the northwest coast than the laws, treaties, and details of British duplicity at Nootka by which Martínez endeavored to justify his actions.

The *Argonaut* sailed for San Blas at 2:00 A.M. on July 14, taking advantage of the offshore breeze. Colnett and his crew were locked in their quarters each night but allowed freedom of the ship by day. Martínez kept the Chinese artisans with him, to utilize their services in lumbering and construction. The next day, after what Gray and his officers considered unwarranted procrastination, Kendrick finally sailed, ostensibly to proceed directly to Macao. Aboard the *Columbia* were the crew of the *Northwest America* and the furs they had collected prior to arrest. Martínez asked Kendrick to sell the pelts, deduct the cost of transporting the crew, and divide the balance of the money among the English seamen to make up for salary lost because of their capture.[91]

The Sevillano not only gave the *Columbia* and the *Lady Washington* permission to depart but personally escorted them out of the harbor with his launch; he was accompanied by the four Franciscans, who went along to bid a final goodbye. A fraternal cordiality had reigned between the Americans and the Spanish during otherwise turbulent weeks. Martínez allowed Kendrick and Gray to go about their ways unmolested, for the possibility of Russian or additional English vessels arriving at any moment was a far greater preoccupation than the illegal presence of the Americans. The British were habitual interlopers in Spanish America, whereas the Americans and Spanish had been cobelligerents in the recent war. Although the viceroy's instructions alerted Martínez to the danger from Americans as well,

90. Martínez to Flores, July 13, 1789, MxAGN (Hist. 65), fol. 209–10v. Twenty-three of Martínez's letters to Flores, all with this date, are in the same legajo, Ph in DLC.

91. Martínez, "Diario," p. 96; Martínez, Certificate of ninety-six skins being shipped aboard the *Columbia*, St. Lawrence of Nootka, July 14, 1789, in Meares, *Memorial*, pp. 42–43.

the Sevillano preferred keeping Kendrick and Gray as allies, or at least neutrals, while seeking supremacy over those more overtly challenging Spanish pretensions. Contrary to what he allegedly confided to Douglas, Martínez never used force against Kendrick and Gray. The American vessels sailed in and out of Nootka Sound with impunity, anchoring at Mawina and Friendly Cove pretty much at will. "I could have seized this sloop," Martínez remarked apropos Kendrick's departure, "but I had no order to do so, and my situation did not permit it; out of an enemy I made a faithful follower, turning over to him 137 skins to be sold for my account in Canton," a reference to pelts acquired by barter or given to Martínez on various occasions. Kendrick had pleaded that, since for various reasons he had been unable to fulfill his commision on the northwest coast, he be permitted to return the following season. "I responded in the affirmative," Martínez relates, "as long as he carried a Spanish passport, which he said he was planning to do, and in this case I told him that he should buy for my account, in Macao, two ornaments for saying mass and seven pairs of boots for the officers of the *San Carlos* and my own [vessel], but I doubt any of this will be carried out." [92]

This pact leads Stewart to accuse Martínez of using his position for his own profit, and on such a basis is erected a framework of additional hypotheses: (1) that Martínez seized the *Northwest America* to have a convenient vessel for competing in the fur trade; (2) that he arrested Colnett to give the upper hand to a Spanish company which he hoped to promote. Stewart sees Martínez as motivated primarily by economic rather than political factors—very personal economic interests—in most of his actions at Nootka in 1789.[93] From recommendations that he forwarded to the viceroy upon returning to San Blas, it is evident that Martínez was greatly impressed by the economic importance of Spanish engagement in the fur trade. From those suggestions it emerges, however, that he perceived such a traffic not as an end in itself but as the principal means to make Spanish political dominion over the northwest coast economically self-supporting, while reducing the profits of foreign nations. It would be doing the zealous commandant less than justice to judge his actions as motivated more by personal considerations than dedication to Spain's interests. There was nothing underhanded about Martínez's consignment of furs to the *Columbia*. The action was reported in his journal, which practice decreed would be remitted in various copies to the viceroy and the ministry. Moreover, he entertained considerable doubt as to whether Kendrick would fulfill the deal and any benefit would be realized, which suggests that his motives were other than pecuniary.

Much of the cooperation that the Americans received was probably due

92. Martínez, "Diario," p. 133, AT, entry for October 30, 1789.
93. Stewart, "Martínez and López de Haro," pp. 172–75, 208.

to the deference they studiedly paid to Spanish sovereignty and the respect they showed to Martínez personally. In a letter to his backers, dispatched aboard the *Argonaut,* Gray told of his friendship with the commandant and referred to Spain as having, "I think, . . . the best right of any Nation" to sovereignty over the northwest coast.[94] The Sevillano's energetic measures gave an appearance that Madrid intended to make its claim prevail. By their shrewd conduct the American captains reached a modus vivendi enabling them to continue exploiting the furry resources of the area. The symbiotic relationship is borne out by a lengthy and informative composition in English, presented to Martínez by the mate of the *Lady Washington* on the eve of the ship's departure, which much ingratiated the mariner with the commandant.[95] Ingraham gave a full account of his inquiries among the Indians about prior visitors to Nootka. His detailed geographical description of the sound and the lengthy Nootka vocabulary demonstrate the extensive knowledge the Americans already had acquired; indeed, this account was superior to any other produced until the well-known Spanish investigations of 1791. Martínez was delighted with Ingraham's manuscript and remitted it to the viceroy with a glowing commendation.

Before the *Columbia* departed, Kendrick's oldest son, John Jr., made known his desire to embrace the Catholic religion and enter Spanish service. Several British mariners had expressed a similar wish, and Martínez was somewhat skeptical of their sincerity, but young Kendrick gained his consent. A Spanish witness says the old captain "embraced his son, crying, and told him that he had never considered there to be any greater fortune in life than to be a man of good will, and his advice was to follow that example, and many others words which I omit, leaving all of us very touched, and therefore he was given the best treatment that was possible, and since he was second pilot of the mentioned frigate *Columbia,* we treated him accordingly." [96] There is no evidence that Juan Kendrick (as he is referred to hereafter) made his decision with insincerity. His name appears repeatedly in roles of secondary importance, as pilot and later as captain in the Spanish service on the northwest coast. The immediate use to which Martínez applied the youth's talents was to interpret the Nootka tongue.

Martínez was under the impression that the American captains, once out of Nootka, would proceed directly to Hawaii and Macao, but once beyond

94. Gray to Joseph Barrell, Nootka Sound, July 13, 1789, in Howay, *Voyages of the "Columbia,"* pp. 122–23.

95. Joseph Ingraham, "[A Description of Nootka Sound and an Indian Vocabulary, addressed to] Don Estephen Joseph Martinez Commander of His Most Catholic Majesties Ship Princessa," [1789], MxAGN (Hist. 65), fol. 80–105, Ph in DLC.

96. Tobar, Informe, September 18, 1789, p. 86. See F. W. Howay, "John Kendrick and His Sons," *OHQ* 23 (1922) : 296–97.

Estéban Point they set a course for Clayoquot and resumed trading. While there, Kendrick exchanged vessels with Gray, sent the *Columbia* to China with the furs thus far acquired, and went himself to the Queen Charlotte Islands to continue trading as long as the weather permitted. Gray arrived in China by November, and in Canton the crew of the *Northwest America* made a group deposition telling of their schooner's confiscation. They gave Meares the Duffin letters smuggled out from under Martínez's nose, and soon the inflammatory deposition and accounts were on their way to London. Gray exchanged his cargo for oriental products prized in the United States, rounded the Cape of Good Hope, and became the first American captain to circumnavigate the globe.

With such a swollen labor force at his disposal, Martínez suffered no shortage of hands to prepare for the months ahead. The swift passage of summer and the inexorable approach of autumn could not be ignored. The *Princesa* was unrigged and its sails, ropes, and other equipment stored below deck in preparation for wintering in the cove. Cannons, powder, and other armament were removed from the *Princess Royal,* whereafter Hudson and his men were allowed aboard, the commandant remarks, "because they are men of confidence, and so they wouldn't be uncomfortable." Far from being confined, Hudson went anywhere he pleased and took great delight whiling away the time salmon fishing, for which the sound had already acquired due fame.[97]

The Spanish seamen and Chinese laborers cut trees and sawed lumber for a house for the commandant, the officers, and the friars during the winter months. The summer's chaotic events had not been anticipated when the Spanish ships had been outfitted at San Blas, and past months had placed an unexpected drain on supplies. Lavish invitations resulted in an unusual rate of consumption, but this was negligible compared to the amount consumed by all those under arrest from the four English vessels, with their crews of assorted Europeans, Hindus, Filipinos, Malays, Hawaiians, and Chinese. The need to maintain a strong garrison during the coming winter compelled Martínez to find emergency supplies, even if the long-anticipated supply vessel arrived from San Blas. His only choice was to send the *San Carlos* to Monterey with a request for live cattle, sheep, and other comestibles. López de Haro would commend the Spanish vessel and escort the disarmed *Princess Royal* as far as Monterey, for added security against British assault. Narváez was put in command of the prize sloop, whose cannons, arms, and powder were retained at Nootka to strengthen the garrison. The two vessels warped out on the cove on July 27, but contrary winds forced them to anchor nearby until the following day. They had scarcely disappeared from sight when the *Nuestra Señora del Aranzazú*

97. Martínez, "Diario," p. 97, AT; Sánchez, "Historia," fol. 39.

appeared on the horizon. If they had delayed several hours more, or the supply ship had arrived a bit earlier, subsequent events might have taken a somewhat different course, for the *Aranzazú* brought news that altered Martínez's plans entirely, a chance occurrence that thwarted the commandant's efforts to utilize his vessels and men with maximum effectiveness.

### THE ORDER TO ABANDON NOOTKA

As the *Aranzazú* arrived off Nootka, Captain José de Cañizares signaled his approach by firing a cannon, acknowledged from the fort. Martínez went out to meet him with a launch, but the wind fell off and they had to cast anchor until morning. Cañizares brought two shocking pieces of news: word of Carlos III's death, and, more importantly, since it stood to reverse the commandant's plans, an order from Viceroy Flores that Nootka was to be abandoned before winter set in. That evening word of the king's demise spread throughout the settlement. The Franciscans and the chaplain of the *Princesa* gathered in the flagship's main cabin to observe a solemn, all-night vigil for the deceased's eternal rest, and at long intervals a series of salvos thundered out across the otherwise still reaches of the sound. The following Sunday Martínez ordered another vigil for the soul of the departed monarch, followed by a mass attended by the entire community. During the exequies, tradition prescribed that all flags and streamers be lowered. At intervals throughout the morning there were cannonades. At midday banners were raised, frigates and fort fired three salvos honoring the accession of Carlos IV and Queen María Luisa, and the officers were invited to a banquet aboard the *Princesa*.

Contrary to expectations, the *Aranzazú*'s arrival brought Martínez more problems than ever. Preparations for winter had been futile. Cañizares was supposed to have called first at Alta California ports, but the supplies for Nootka were spoiling so he had headed straight for the northwest coast. Even so, most of the staples were useless because of the poor condition in which they had been embarked. What little remained was transferred to the *Princesa*, but the hardtack was fit only for the pigs. Half of the cheese went the same way.[98] The garrison's situation would have been perilous had the picture not soon changed. A scant six days after Martínez left San Blas for Nootka, Flores had ordered abandoning the establishment at Nootka and returning southward before winter set in. He referred to what Martínez himself had pointed out: a shortage of vessels in the department, which would prevent supplying both the California settlements and Nootka. Added to such an invincible difficulty was the basic consideration that it had been Flores's intention to "pretend" making a settlement but not to

---

98. Martínez, "Diario," pp. 101–02; Sánchez, "Historia," fol. 39v; Martínez to Flores, August 7, 1789, MxAGN (Hist. 65), fol. 385–86, Ph in DLC.

actually establish an expensive garrison there. Thus, the viceroy now wanted Martínez to send the *San Carlos* to explore the coast to the north, but not beyond Bucareli Sound; "the time spent in this and the pretended establishment of Nootka will doubtless take till winter, and since ordinarily in that season neither Russians nor vassals of other foreign powers will attempt any undertaking in those seas, you can then consider concluded your commission." Hence the expeditionaries would only need food for eight or nine months and for the return voyage.[99]

The new orders were far from adequate to meet the altered circumstances. If Martínez was sincere in his ardent declarations to defend Spain's claim to Nootka, his reaction must have been utter dismay. Were he essentially a coward, as Stewart suggests, he would have heaved a sigh of relief at being able to extricate himself from a situation that had turned all too dangerous. Here we have a touchstone for ascertaining the commandant's true mettle, by observing his reaction. Did he possess the requisite courage and determination to continue in a position increasingly encumbered with unforeseen responsibilities, or would he seize the first opportunity to retreat from the scene of action? His character is reflected in his next letters to Flores. As for the abandonment of Nootka, Martínez lamented, "I can't help telling Your Excellency that I'm very sorry, especially since this coast is so frequently visited by the English, Portuguese, Bostoners, and Russians."[100] Nootka should not be evacuated, even for a short time, although he would obey the order blindly, unless the prize ship's arrival at San Blas made Flores change his mind and send word for the Spaniards to remain at Nootka. If such a command did not arrive by the end of October, he would be obliged to depart for San Blas. Martínez's zeal to remain at Friendly Cove, if an affirmative order and sufficient supplies were forthcoming, acquits him of the charge of cowardice. The ensuing year might bring even greater challenges, but he did not shrink from the demands that would be made upon him if he stayed.

In the beginning the viceroy sought merely a "pretended" occupation of Nootka, and Martínez knew this from his instructions. The object was to deflect the Muscovite effort—a response to the intelligence gathered in Alaska. But the clash at Nootka in 1789 erased all expectations that Madrid could maintain its claims over the northwest coast with occasional expeditions and "pretended" settlements and without retaining and reinforcing a naval base at Nootka or Bucareli Sound. Martínez was painfully aware of this, and he could assume the same conclusion would be evident to Flores

99. ". . . la fundada consideración de que siempre ha sido mi animo fingir no radicar por termino alguno Establecimientos en Nooka . . ." Flores to Martínez, February 25, 1789, MxAGN (Hst. 65), fol. 374–77, Ph in DLC.

100. Martínez to Flores, August 7, 1789, MxAGN (Hist. 65), fol. 372–73, 380–83.

once the latter received the reports remitted aboard the *Argonaut*. Prior to then, he had no means of communicating the grave turn of events. If his letters reached Mexico in time for an expedition to be sent to their succor, it would be advantageous to stay at Nootka. If no such supplies arrived, he would be forced to remove all his men and equipment, at least for the ensuing winter.

Since the *Aranzazú* carried provisions essential for Alta California, it had to depart at once. However, by the viceroy's special order the vessel's surgeon, Don Carlos Álvarez del Castillo, was transferred to the *Princesa*, filling one of Martínez's most crucial needs. On August 10 the supply ship weighed anchor, only to be driven aground as it attempted to clear the harbor entrance, and although the hull was not damaged, several days were lost before it got underway again. Should an order arrive for him to remain all winter, Martínez had to insure that his garrison would be as strong and well-supplied as possible, so the *Aranzazú* took a letter to López de Haro, requesting his immediate return from California with much-needed supplies and advising that he would be awaited until the end of October.[101]

Despite the commandant's optimism about receiving an order to remain at Friendly Cove, the likelihood that it would not arrive had to be faced. Thus, Martinez took measures that would permit carrying out either possibility. The cannon of San Rafael were dismantled and brought to the beach preparatory to storage aboard the *Princesa*. The boxes of lime and the bricks brought from San Blas, as well as some 300 more received from Kendrick, were buried near the forge so that an oven for a bakery could be built the following spring; then the pit was filled and leveled off to hide the cache. The sloop under construction at Mawina was far from complete, so the unfinished pieces were floated to the cove and, together with the unassembled parts of the *Jason* (from aboard the *Argonaut*), were used to elongate and raise the sides of the *Santa Gertrudis la Magna*, to construct a vessel "capable of undertaking whatever navigation might be offered, so that we could take it to the Department [of San Blas] and present it for the benefit of the king." [102]

Saturday, August 15, dawned clear and windless; the sun beat down with unaccustomed strength, and the commandant's journal notes it was the hottest day yet experienced at Nootka. All labors were suspended, as it was the feast of the Assumption. The chaplain held solemn mass ashore

101. The letter to López de Haro is not known and may not have survived, but it is referred to in Martínez to Flores, December 6, 1789, MxAGN (Hist. 65), fol. 522–24), Ph in DLC.

102. Martínez, "Diario," pp. 100, 103, 105. If this interpretation of the sources is correct, it clarifies a matter perplexing previous authors: the fate of the *Northwest America*, the *Jason*, and the vessel built at Mawina. All contributed parts to the *Santa Gertrudis la Magna*, relaunched October 20. See Wagner, *Spanish Explorations*, p. 141; Howay, *Voyages of the "Columbia,"* p. 227n.

for the happy reign of the new sovereign, and the assembled troops fired several volleys in salute. Afterward, because of the extreme heat, the men were given permission to swim off the side of the vessels or go ashore to bathe. That day, for the first time since Ke-le-kum's death, native canoes returned to the cove and approached the *Princesa*, bringing some fish. Martínez gave them several machetes, pieces of iron and copper, beads, and other trifles in order to disabuse them, he says, "of the erroneous information that the English prisoners had given them to put us in a bad light." One canoe stayed all day, and late in the afternoon its two occupants went ashore and told the Spanish that, out of fear that Ma-kwee-na would kill them, they intended to spend the night in the nearby forest. Father Espi invited them to the flagship, but they refused and taking the canoe, disappeared into the woods. That evening several Spaniards on shore saw ominous shadows approaching in the darkness. Suspecting thieves sneaking into camp, the seamen fired a shot into the air to frighten them away. Upon hearing the report, Martínez sent his boat ashore, but in the blackness nothing was found.[103]

The next day Chief Na-tsa-pā, Ma-kwee-na's father-in-law and rival, came to visit Martínez and was cordially received. Never one to let other chieftains have the inside track with the Spanish, Ma-kwee-na himself came to the *Princesa* within the week. His band had been residing northwest of the sound on the open seacoast since the first Anglo-Spanish altercations. Now, as fall approached, they were moving to habitual quarters at the head of Tahsis Inlet. The long planks with which their lodges were constructed had to be floated directly past Friendly Cove, which may help explain the chief's desire to mend fences. Martínez invited him aboard, produced an assortment of gifts, and gave his companions some crackers, "which they eat very readily, and every time they come they ask for them." Through interpreter Juan Kendrick, the commandant said that the Spaniards were about to leave, to seek copper and abalone shells to give him, and declared that in their absence Ma-kwee-na should not permit his subjects, or any strangers who might arrive, to remove the cross or lumber cut for construction, "because I was to come and live with him and defend him from anyone who wished to harm him." They would leave him some goats, pigs, and cattle, which it was hoped would continue to multiply. Seemingly delighted, Ma-kwee-na declared that upon returning they would find everything in its place. Going to the rail, he spied some Indians not of his own group, commenced berating them in no uncertain terms, and told them to stay away from the cove, "that it was his [Martinez's] territory and he had given it to me to live there." He said that the strangers were from the other side of the sound and should not be permitted to visit the settlement since they came

103. Martínez, "Diario," pp. 105–06, AT.

solely to steal, as they had stolen from him on some occasions. He then asked to be served tea. Somewhat surprised at the chief's tastes, the commandant ordered the drink prepared, and his hospitality was rewarded by a present of four prime sea otter pelts and some fresh salmon.[104] The chief came again on September 1, renewing the pledge to care for everything at the cove, "just as if it were his," and the commandant promised to bring him some prized *chipoks,* pieces of beaten copper.

Prior to this exchange, relations between Martínez and the chief had been strained ever since the commandant had been told that Ma-kwee-na and Ke-le-kum had been accustomed to eating boys chosen from among prisoners taken by war parties and retained as slaves. The Sevillano had assumed this had ceased, but Captain Kendrick mentioned having been offered a human hand, as well as a chunk of meat from a four-year-old child. Such reports persuaded Martínez to purchase several slave children, hoping to save them from a similar fate. The Indians asked him if he wanted them to eat, confirming Martinez's worst fears. The first child, a five- or six-year-old boy, was acquired in June and turned over to the missionaries for instruction and baptism. In September Na-tsa-pā bartered a girl of eight for a pot and a frying pan. The boy was christened "Estéban," after the commandant, and the girl "María de los Dolores."[105] An anonymous Franciscan account relates:

> Macuina ate the little boys among his enemies who had the misfortune to fall prisoner. For this purpose he tried to fatten them up first, and then when they were ready, got them all together in a circle (he did this some eight days before our people left that waterway), put himself in the middle with an instrument in hand and, looking at all the miserables with furious visage, decided which one was to serve as dish for his inhumane meal. Then, advancing upon the unhappy victim of his voracious appetite, he opened its abdomen at one blow, cut off the arms, and commenced devouring that innocent's raw flesh, bloodying himself as he satiated his barbarous appetite.[106]

The topic is the touchiest in northwest coast ethnography. By 1789 Ma-kwee-na was aware that Europeans of every nationality abhorred cannibalism, and he steadfastly denied such practices. From time to time, reports of continuing anthropophagy elicited such intense responses from the Spanish that the natives denied it had ever existed among them. This is the orthodox opinion today.[107]

104. Ibid., pp. 108–09, AT, entry for August 25; see also pp. 106, 111, 128.

105. Ibid., pp. 81–82, 111, 113, 124.

106. "Noticias de Nutka," (by an anonymous Franciscan) MxAGN (Hist. 31), fol. 314v, AT.

107. Howay, *Voyages of the "Columbia,"* p. 66, and many in his wake, accept the opinion of the revered Franz Boas who, in the late nineteenth century, found no cannibalism on the

### THE SEIZURE OF AN AMERICAN VESSEL

September passed uneventfully, with no sign of more foreign vessels or of the *San Carlos* with supplies from Alta California. The fort on San Miguel Island was dismantled, the trenches and gun emplacements mutilated to make them useless if another nation tried to ensconce itself at Nootka during the Spanish absence. Martínez had need of red ochre and whale oil to paint his vessels, and sent a launch to Tahsis, where no white men had as yet penetrated, to see if these supplies could be purchased from Ma-kwee-na. To head this mission he chose Juan Kendrick, accompanied by Gabriel del Castillo and a party of husky seamen to row when sails were useless. They sighted a canal leading off Tahsis Inlet toward the northwest, a steep-sided cleft in the fjord, and on their return decided to investigate. The twisting passage eventually led to the sea northwest of Nootka, at Esperanza Inlet. On what they assumed to be mainland they erected a cross and took possession for Carlos IV before returning to Nootka by the ocean route, thus proving that Friendly Cove was on an *island* of considerable size. It was subsequently named Mazarredo, after José de Mazarredo, a famous admiral of the time. Not until 1792 would it be disclosed that the interior of the sound was an indentation in a much larger island.

With October's arrival the weather became progressively more distasteful, and there was still no sign of the supplies that would enable Martínez to remain all winter. The commandant had advised López de Haro that he would wait out the month, so there was no alternative but to endure. At times the drizzle let up. On October 13, and again four days later, an unidentified schooner was sighted tacking back and forth off Nootka, attempting to round Estéban Point against contrary winds. On October 20 it entered the sound, anchoring in the lee of a small island. Martínez sent two armed launches to summon the captain to Friendly Cove. When the *Fair*

northwest coast, and as a matter of principle rejected earlier sources. For a discussion of Boasian disregard for the historical dimension, see E. Adamson Hoebel, *Anthropology: The Study of Man,* 3d ed. (New York, 1966), pp. 88–89, 516–21. So deeply rooted was anthropophagy in northwest coast religious concepts and warfare that the practice could not be abandoned easily. Chronologically, the most specific references to it are: Ledyard, *Journal,* pp. 73–76; Strange, *Journal,* p. 27; W. Hunter, *Letter From W. Hunter Regarding the Voyage of the Vessels "Captain Cook" and "Experiment" to the Northwest Coast in the Fur Trade* (San Francisco, 1940), p. 3; Meares, *Voyages,* pp. 46–50; Haswell, "Log," p. 66; Hoskins, *Narrative,* pp. 288–89; Boit, "Log," p. 387; Martínez, "Diario," p. 124; "Noticias de Nutka," fol. 314v; Jacinto Caamaño, "Diario," MxAGN (Hist. 69), fol. 84–85; Juan Pantoja y Arriaga, "Extracto de la navegación . . . 1791," trans. in Wagner, *Spanish Explorations,* pp. 160–61; Malaspina, *Viaje,* p. 355; Suría, "Quaderno," trans. in *PHR* 5 (1936): 274–75; Moziño, *Noticias,* pp. 22–23; [Bell], *New Vancouver Journal,* pp. 39–40. Even in Boas's time, masked initiates to secret "cannibal" societies ran berserk, biting furiously at fleeing spectators, but without hurting them. F. Boas, "Social Organization and Secret Societies of the Kwakiutl Indians," *United States National Museum Report 1895* (Washington, D.C., 1897): 311–78.

*American* anchored alongside the flagship, Martínez was surprised to find its master a lad of eighteen. Thomas Humphrey Metcalfe had sailed from Macao with a crew of four on June 5, accompanying his father, Simon Metcalfe, and the brig *Eleanora* out of New York. They lost contact in a storm, reached Unalaska after forty-two days, and followed the coastline to Nootka, the agreed-upon rendezvous.[108] Their food supply was exhausted, masts cracked, and sails rent. Young Metcalfe said he hoped for assistance from his father, who was expected momentarily. From the *Lady Washington,* encountered at 54° 20′ north latitude, he learned that the *Eleanora* had been at Dixon Strait. This was unwelcome news for Martínez, as it revealed the duplicity of his American friends, who had not sailed directly for the Orient as stipulated but had continued to trade along the coastline. As for the new arrivals, Martínez remarks, "On the one hand pitying the situation in which the captain and other individuals of the said schooner find themselves, and on the other stimulated to fulfill my obligation to stop trafficking along this coast as I have been ordered by my superiors, I could not do less than retain the said schooner and conduct it to San Blas, where the authorities will determine what shall be done." He thought Metcalfe and companions were "worthy of the greatest commiseration." [109]

The *Fair American* had managed to barter for sixty-five sea otter pelts of all sizes. Juan Kendrick and seven of the Spanish seamen were put in charge of the prize, while the vessel's crew joined other prisoners aboard the flagship. The schooner had to be provided with new rigging, mainmast, and sails before it dared start south.

The carpenters had finished altering the *Santa Gertrudis,* discarding worm-eaten planks, adding ribs, elongating it about a yard, and raising the gunnels. Now much more seaworthy, it was ready for relaunching.[110] As yet no Spanish vessel had remained on the northwest coast all winter. Dank, chill winds warned of worse rigors to come. Thus, since López de Haro had not appeared, Martínez was forced to depart. He ordered two wooden tablets affixed to a tree behind the main house, in the most visible spot. Inscriptions were chiseled upon them, the inscribers taking particular care to make them legible for future visitors. One read:

> Reynando en España el Mui Poderoso Señor Don Carlos III.
> se descubrió este Puerto de San Lorenzo de Nuca en 1774.
> y en 1789. se tomó formal a nombre de dho. Señor Rey.
> P. D. E. J. M.

108. Martínez, "Diario," p. 132. As mentioned previously, Simon Metcalfe may have been the first American captain on the northwest coast, in 1787 or 88.

109. Ibid, pp. 132–33, AT.

110. Ibid., pp. 100, 131, entries for July 29 and October 20.

y en la Costafirme a nombre de su Augusto Hijo el Sor.
Don Carlos IV (Q. D. G.) en 23 de Agosto de dho. año.[111]

Beneath it, the other was addressed to the captain of the *San Carlos,* should he arrive and find the cove deserted: "Haro: Me he retirado de Nuca a fines de Octubre de Orden superior a S. B. Martínez." [112] At that moment López de Haro was not far away. The *San Carlos* had left Monterey with it vital supplies on September 24 but had been delayed three more days within sight of port by prevailing winds. As he approached the northwest coast on October 26, a vicious storm had arisen that for a time placed the ship in jeopardy, totally obscuring the coastline. The vessel's latitude was estimated as 53° 16′ north, well beyond Nootka, but rain and fog dissuaded the captain from probing for his goal. Since Martínez had said he would wait only until the last day of October, on the 29th López de Haro decided it unwise to endanger vessel and crew by further efforts to reach the cove, and he headed for San Blas.[113] On the final day at Nootka, the commandant wrote in his journal:

> We saw the rice begin to produce, and this day wheat was planted to try the land, if anyone returns next year. I was now ready to begin navigation, one of my regrets being to abandon a port discovered by me, so many years ago, in which all the nations find shelter and traffic, but I cannot do less than obey the order of His Excellency the viceroy of New Spain.[114]

The Chinese and the remaining crews of the captured vessels were taken aboard the flagship. José Verdía was put in command of the *Santa Gertrudis,* and Kendrick continued in charge of the *Fair American.* If separated at sea, they were to meet at Isabela Island, off Sinaloa, and proceed together to San Blas. That afternoon and evening they warped out of the cove, preparatory to sailing before dawn.[115] Sunrise found the cove lapsed into tranquility, broken only by the wind's whine in the forest, a portent of winter's impending embrace. One more episode remained, however, in the international incident on the northwest coast in 1789. At midmorning a

111. "Reigning in Spain the Very Powerful Lord Don Carlos III. this Port of St. Lawrence of Nuca was discovered in 1774, and in 1789 was formally occupied B[y] D[on] E[stéban] J[osé] M[artínez] and on the coast of the mainland in name of his august son the Lord Don Carlos IV (W[hom] G[od] G[uard]) on August 23rd of said year." Martínez, "Diario," SpMN (732), fol 128. The 1964 edition (p. 133) alters the sign's lettering considerably.

112. "Haro: I have departed from Nuca at the end of October by superior order to S[an] B[las]. Martínez." Ibid., AT.

113. Sánchez, "Historia," fol. 45v–48, 55–55v, 65v.

114. Martínez, "Diario," p. 133, AT.

115. Ibid., p. 133; Martínez to Flores, San Blas, December 6, 1789, MxAGN (Hist. 65), fol. 329, Ph in DLC.

strange sail appeared off the *Princesa's* bow, headed for the coast. Martínez tried to come within speaking distance, and when barely in sight raised the Spanish flag and fired a canon as a signal to heave to. The brig immediately raised the American flag, in acknowledgment, but hauled even closer to the wind. Through a spyglass young Metcalfe identified the new ship as the *Eleanora.* Although he must have recognized his son's schooner, the father doubtless was aware of the seizures at Nootka from the *Lady Washington.* Seeing two strange warships bearing down on him, one a heavily armed Spanish frigate, he probably suspected the worst. Maneuver for maneuver, the *Eleanora* outsailed the heavier craft, gradually gaining headway and disappearing over the horizon. By sundown Martínez abandoned pursuit and signaled to resume course. Although passing within sight of the coast off Monterey, they did not stop. "I thought this advisable," Martínez remarks, "since on board I had some Englishmen, in order that they not be aware of the slight forces of said Presidio, and of its missions, and that later they will not communicate this news to the Court in London." [116]

The *San Carlos* arrived in San Blas on December 2, the *Princesa* and the *Santa Gertrudis* four days later, and the *Fair American* on the 12th. During the voyage southward Martínez composed a letter to Flores expressing the hope of being given command of an expedition to return at once to Nootka with the *Princesa,* the *Argonaut,* and the *Santa Gertrudis* to "cut off at the root the commerce of the English." [117]

The northwest coast's great distance from decision-making centers in Mexico City and Madrid foreordained trouble for Spain if she chose to sustain her claims in the disputed area. Aside from the extended voyage from San Blas, the long trek overland to Veracruz and the time-consuming Atlantic crossing made communications a constant obstacle to coordinated action. As a painful illustration, just as Martínez was seizing English vessels to preserve Spanish control over those shores and Flores's order commanding Nootka's abandonment was on its way to Martínez, a royal order (April 14, 1789) was en route to Flores not only approving occupation of Nootka but stipulating that the sound be defended against all challengers.[118]

First word in Mexico City of the incidents at Nootka came with the arrival of the *Argonaut* in San Blas on August 15, followed less than two weeks later by the appearance of the *Princess Royal.* One of the viceroy's first reactions was to transfer to Nootka the Volunteers of Cataluña, a company of

116. Martínez, "Diario," p. 138, AT, entry for November 16.

117. Martínez to Flores, San Blas, December 6, 1789, MxAGN (Hist. 65), fol. 522–24, Ph in DLC; Sánchez, "Historia," fol. 65v.

118. Royal order, April 14, 1789, cited in Revillagigedo to Manuel de Godoy, Mexico City, April 12, 1793, p. 129, in Andrés Cavo and Carlos María Bustamante, *Los Tres Siglos de México durante el gobierno Español, hasta la entrada del ejército trigarante,* 4 vols. (Mexico City, 1836–38), 3 : 112–64.

crack troops previously garrisoned at Guadalajara.[119] Reports of trouble at Friendly Cove reached the capital almost simultaneously with word of Flores's replacement and Revillagigedo's arrival in Veracruz, accompanied by Bodega and the other six officers sent to reinforce naval operations out of San Blas. Martínez's actions portended trouble on an international scale, and Flores would leave the crisis in his successor's lap.

Juan Vicente de Güemes Pacheco de Padilla Horcasitas y Aguayo, conde de Revillagigedo, who governed New Spain from 1789 to 1794, is regarded by many historians as the most able man ever to hold that office. Son of a previous viceroy of Mexico, he distinguished himself by energy, competence, and scrupulous honesty. The first Conde de Revillagigedo, who governed from 1746 to 1775, is portrayed as "the biggest trafficker and speculator that New Spain has had; it is said that there was no kind of business in which he didn't have a finger." The son "tried to erase the unfortunate memory of his father, and was a perfect model of disinterestedness, although so economical that by night he checked up on his majordomo down to the last onion bought for the kitchen." [120] This was the man on whose approval would hinge further expenditures on the northwest coast. The second Revillagigedo's many reforms and public works left a great imprint on Mexico, but by his own admission, his chief concern while in office was policy toward the northwest coast.[121] His decisions as to objectives and policies on that frontier would have a large part in determining the outcome of Spanish efforts in the Pacific Northwest.

Upon turning over the reins of government, Flores informed Revillagigedo of the ominous events at Nootka. From Veracruz the new viceroy gave full approval of all actions Flores had taken. Impressed with the seriousness of the clash, Revillagigedo gave the matter his immediate attention. He regarded the incidents at Friendly Cove with the greatest displeasure, and from the first he concluded that Martínez should not have arrested any of the English vessels.[122] Several years later, reviewing the whole subject for a new prime minister, the viceroy complained that Flores neglected to mention his order to abandon Nootka before the onslaught of winter. Revillagigedo also admitted that from the very first he lamented that the shortage of naval officers had prevented Flores from putting the delicate mission to Nootka in charge of someone of greater ability and rank

119. Order of August 29, 1789, cited in Antonio Villa Urrutia to Viceroy Flores, Guadalajara, September 4, 1789, CSmH (HM 327), which also contains the original draft of Flores's order.

120. Carlos María Bustamante, in Cavo and Bustamante, *Tres Siglos*, 2 : 170n, AT.

121. Revillagigedo to Godoy, April 12, 1793, in ibid., 3 : 112.

122. Flores to Revillagigedo, Mexico City, August 27, 1789, SpAGI (V, Aud. Mex. 1525) and MxAGN (Hist. 65), pp. 292–93, Ph in DLC; Revillagigedo to Flores, Veracruz, August 30, 1789, SpAHN (Estado 4289); Revillagigedo to Valdés, Mexico City, October 27, 1789, CU-B (Robbins Collection), Revillagigedo Papers, vol. 21, fol. 1–4v.

than Martínez.[123] The ardent Sevillano could not count on much patience, sympathy, or backing within the viceregal palace once Flores departed. If he was indeed Flores's nephew, perhaps part of Martinez's disfavor with Revillagigedo had its roots in the latter's abhorrence of his predecessor's nepotism.

Revillagigedo ordered the new commandant of San Blas to prepare an expedition to relieve Martínez as soon as possible; this expedition was to be composed of the frigate *Concepción,* the *Argonaut,* and the *Princess Royal.* The Volunteers of Cataluña would garrison the port of Nootka, and he declared:

> At present, circumstances require no other effort on our part than sustaining our possession and our new establishment in San Lorenzo or Nuca, in case foreign nations attempt to attack it. Dislodging the Russians from places where they are situated depends on the sovereign will of the king, so that treaties of friendship with that empire may not be disturbed. As for Great Britain, our court has always known how to cope with them unless other questions of its authority, or reason and justice oblige it to withdraw from a harmonious accord.[124]

He ordered the newly revealed Strait of Juan de Fuca explored in its entirety, as he felt that it possessed particular strategic importance. He had no inkling, as yet, of Nootka's evacuation, for the *Princesa* had dropped anchor in San Blas just two days before this order was given.

In Madrid there was no indication that a bitter diplomatic conflict over the northwest coast of America was impending. In July 1789 a reassuring report arrived from St. Petersburg indicating that Madrid's protest (April 7, 1789) regarding Russian expansion toward territory claimed by Spain had elicited a satisfactory response. "Long ago," the tsarina replied, "command had been given to expeditionaries from Kamchatka not to establish themselves at any point belonging to another power; that she supposed her orders had been obeyed exactly; but that if perhaps her subjects had entered or were found to be in some parts of our America, she supplicated the King that the matter be composed or remedied amicably." [125] The sound and fury of the Nootka Crisis soon alerted Russia that Madrid was belligerent about its claims on the northwest coast. This realization seems to have put a damper on the ambitious plans, hatched in 1785–86 and entrusted to Billings and Moloski, involving expansion toward Nootka. Billings had suffered many delays and did not arrive in Alaskan waters until 1790, after word of Spain's militant stance at Nootka had reached Unalaska.

123. Revillagigedo to Godoy, April 12, 1793, in Cavo and Bustamante, *Tres Siglos,* 3 : 115, 124.
124. Revillagigedo to Bodega, Mexico City, December 8, 1789, MxAGN (Hist. 68), AT.
125. Floridablanca to Valdés, Real Palacio, July 26, 1789, SpAHN (Estado 4289), AT.

## MARTINEZ AND THE PRISONERS IN SAN BLAS

While still at Nootka, the Sevillano had formulated a project for creation of a company in Mexico City to engage in the sea otter trade. From San Blas he forwarded his plan to the viceroy. Martínez believed that the Spanish enjoyed advantages enabling them to virtually eliminate foreigners from the fur trade along the Pacific Coast. If the British could make the traffic lucrative, certainly the Spanish should be able to do even better, since the voyage from Mexico and the Philippines was easier than that from England. The Spaniards had a readier source of foodstuffs for their trading vessels in Alta California, and since California also yielded many sea otter pelts, the total product could be sold at great benefit in Canton. New Spain and Alta California yielded the two commodities most popular in trade— sheets of beaten copper and abalone shells. Moreover, the Spanish could offer more for pelts than other nationalities, thus destroying the traffic of rival nations. By effective competition, the supply of furs would be so diminished that other traders could no longer turn a profit. When this happened, foreign activity on the coast to the north of California would cease. If a fur trading company could be organized in Mexico City, Martínez felt that it should be exempt from payment of duties for fifty years in order to encourage investors. In addition, he called for development of unoccupied areas by the establishment of sixteen missions and four presidios, with 100 soldiers apiece. Twelve sloops would be needed—half to guard the coast and the rest for trans-Pacific commerce. Vessels going to the northwest coast should carry cattle and supplies from Monterey and San Francisco. Furs and lumber could be shipped from Nootka to the Orient, and cloth and garments obtained in China and the Philippines should be shipped to the northwest coast for the Indian trade, the garrisons, and the crews operating there.[126]

Revillagigedo was greatly dismayed when he learned that Friendly Cove had been left unoccupied, for he was actively engaged in plans for strengthening the Spanish base against all challengers. As for the arrests, he thought Martínez had proceeded with imprudence, and no good could come from actions "which might lead to unverifiable complaints and padded damage claims." [127] He sent Madrid a summary of Martínez's suggestions for a string of presidios and missions and a concerted effort to drive foreigners from the fur trade through competition, commenting that it should be executed

---

126. The Sevillano's description of his project is not known, but it can be pieced together from three letters from Revillagigedo to Valdés, Mexico City, December 27, 1789, January 12, 1790, and January 31, 1793, all in MxAGN (Corr. Virreyes 154); also see Revillagigedo to Godoy, April 12, 1793, in Cavo and Bustamante, *Tres Siglos*, 3 : 150.

127. These sentiments were recalled in Revillagigedo's subsequent review of the whole affair to Godoy, April 12, 1793, in Cavo and Bustamante, *Tres Siglos*, 3 : 132, AT.

by a private company, not by the royal treasury. He urged that Mexico City retain control over the collection of pelts and the founding of outposts on the northwest coast—but that the Philippine Company handle trans-Pacific transport and negotiations in China. The letter embodying Martínez's project was acknowledged by the ministry at the height of the Nootka Crisis in Europe with word that, "when His Majesty resolves upon it, his decision will be communicated to Your Excellency," and it was referred to the Philippine Company, in which the wheels of bureaucratic machinery turned slowly, at best.[128]

Revillagigedo's initial response to the problem of the prize ships and detained seamen was to order the *Fair American* released at once, on grounds that it had not encroached upon Spanish territory. Metcalfe set sail for the Sandwich Islands as soon as freed.[129] The viceroy then advised Madrid that keeping the Chinese artisans at San Blas was too costly, so they would be brought to Mexico City and given a choice of remaining in the capital to follow their respective trades or taking up residence in the Alta California settlements.[130]

Following the arrival of the prize ships in mid-August, the English officers and seamen languished month after month in the hot, humid, and pestilential port while the decision as to their fate hung in suspense. They received salaries corresponding to equivalent ranks in the Spanish navy and were subject to only loose vigilance, with entire freedom of the town, although they were prohibited from leaving its vicinity. In his journal Colnett complains bitterly about the quality of his quarters and the food, but since he and his officers slept in a room adjoining that of José María Monterde, the commissary officer and second in command at the post, they enjoyed the best accommodations available. They ate their meals with Monterde, and Colnett's complaints led to his being permitted to share the comisario's own bedroom. Despite efforts to cater to him, Colnett found no end of things to begrudge: heat, mosquitoes, bells ringing at dawn, and being obliged to eat at the same table with Robert Duffin and James Hanson, mates of the *Argonaut,* with whom he had been at odds ever since detention. By any criterion, San Blas in August 1789 was Hell's very vestibule. Soon most of the prisoners showed signs of dysentery and fever. In all, eight would die there, most of them presumably from tropical ailments. Hanson withstood San Blas only

---

128. Revillagigedo to Valdés, Mexico City, January 12, 1790; [Valdés] to Revillagigedo, Madrid, July 29, 1790, SpAGI (V, Aud. Guad. 492), AT.

129. Unfortunately, young Metcalfe and his crew jumped from the frying pan into the fire. Early in 1790 the *Fair American* was overpowered near Kawaihae, on the west shore of Hawaii, and all aboard were killed except Isaac Davis, who was enslaved (Howay, in Colnett, *Journal,* p. 222n). Four years later Metcalfe's father and younger brother, together with the entire crew of the *Eleanora,* were slain by the Haida (Howay, "Captain Simon Metcalfe," pp. 120–21).

130. Revillagigedo to Valdés, Mexico City, December 27, 1789, SpAHN (Estado 4289).

six days; for unknown motives, while he was alone in a latrine he tied a razor to his wrist and slit his throat.[131]

To their great relief, the prisoners were moved to Tepic in mid-November. There the climate was temperate, pleasant, and healthy, and the Englishmen immediately became a focus of curiosity and social life. The local curate became Colnett's self-appointed adversary, and to counteract the influence of so many Protestants wandering about town, he organized an open air morality play, titled "Henry the Eighth," which was performed repeatedly in the central plaza by a group of actors for the edification of the local people. "This was done to induce the Populace to detest us," Colnett remarks, "but as we always attended ourselves and laugh'd at it, and explain'd the life of Henry, &c., which few of them knew, it had not the desired Effect; and even the Young Lady that acted Anna Bullen prefer'd acting the more amorous part of Henry's Character with some of my Officers in Private to that in Public, and latterly refus'd to play at all without better paid for it than an absolution of Sins from the Padre. When we left the Country she had grown very fat and was past playing." [132]

For many months the Englishmen were kept at Tepic, whiling away the time with such amusements as the place afforded. Colnett grew ever more impatient awaiting some response to his importuning letters to Revillagigedo. A Spanish crew took the *Argonaut* to pick up artillery at Acapulco for the new settlement contemplated at Nootka. Far to the north, winter locked the chilly waters of Nootka Sound in silence. Not a single vessel or white man spent those months on the northwest coast south of the Russian outposts. As tranquility returned to the North Pacific, the focus of controversy shifted to Europe, where the Nootka Crisis would reach its apex.

131. "Noticias de Nutka," fol. 299v; Colnett, *Journal,* p. 73.
132. Colnett, *Journal,* p. 126.

## 6   To the Brink of War, 1790

THE SEEDS of grievance and strife grow exuberantly if nurtured by a mulch of distrust. Spain and England had cultivated a mutual resentment ever since Henry VIII's differences with Rome, an enmity that erupted time and again in war. Madrid took pains to shroud her American realm from foreign eyes, and particularly from the English, in the frequently confirmed belief that His Britannic Majesty's subjects would seize upon any portions that could be pried from Spain's grip. That such suspicion of British motives was justified is borne out by the documentary record of a myriad of plans for attacks on Spanish possessions, some set in march and others merely contemplated, throughout the period of Iberian activities in the Pacific Northwest. The flare-up over Nootka could not have occurred without the existence of responses conditioned by centuries of rivalry—embers fanned in 1790 when the British ministry perceived an unusual opportunity. On the Spanish throne sat an inexperienced sovereign whose lack of mettle invited a power play at a time when, given recent developments in Paris, it would be hazardous for Madrid to rely upon the Family Compact—the Bourbon alliance as important to Spain in the eighteenth century as Anglo-American unity was to the British in the twentieth.

As Carlos III was carried to his ultimate resting place, few could have foreseen that the empire was entering a period of rapid decline. At first sight, intimate details of Carlos IV's household and the gossip surrounding his impetuous wife seem far removed from our subject. As we shall see, however, Spain's endeavor to retain the Pacific Northwest was influenced more by the erosion and temporary eclipse of the Spanish monarchy than by any other single factor. The very backbone of the empire, and an important element in its people's sense of identity, common purpose, and self-confidence, was pride in Spain's historic past, from which stemmed respect for a dynasty descended, however remotely, from the *Reyes Católicos*. As a consequence of salacious talk—possibly based on fact, but perhaps groundless—respect for the incumbent sovereign plummeted so disastrously that by 1808 a significant segment of the power structure had coalesced about his son Fernando, the heir presumptive, who was placed on the throne in Spain's first coup d'état. The political and social turmoil that ensued permitted Napoleon to install his own brother as king. The long and bloody struggle to expel the Bonapartists undercut Spanish efforts to preserve a claim to the Pacific Northwest. A full account of Bourbon tribulations as they affected western

North America has never been told in English. Salient aspects of this drama necessarily form a backdrop for events in chapters to come.

Carlos IV was born not in Spain but in Portici, a Napoleon suburb, in 1748, while his father was king of Naples and Sicily. Only after Carlos III's ascension to the Spanish throne in 1759 did the Prince of Asturias come to the country he was eventually to rule. To increase the likelihood of heirs and keep a maximum of Bourbon blood in the royal line, the prince was espoused at seventeen to his first cousin, fourteen-year-old María Luisa of Bourbon Parma.[1] A tall tree casts a long shadow; in most respects Carlos III was exceptionally able, but he made a grave mistake in not preparing his heir apparent for the throne. Felipe, the firstborn, had been feeble-minded, and the old king found it difficult to be close to his namesake. Young Carlos was kept apart from matters that would have provided valuable experience, and in adulthood he retained many boyish ways. A mere glance from his father is said to have made the young man tremble.

Nor did the Princess of Asturias find life completely to her taste, having to repress a naturally vigorous personality to conform to the austere environment cultivated by her revered father-in-law. She was born in Parma in 1751 to Felipe, duque de Parma (younger brother of Carlos III, and hence a Spanish Infante), and Marie Louise Elisabeth de Bourbon, oldest daughter of France's Louis XV. Through paternal and maternal lines María Luisa inherited many of the same genes as her spouse, and they looked remarkably alike. Although he enjoyed a slight advantage in age, she soon prevailed over his placid nature, in a relationship closely resembling that of their royal kin and contemporaries, Louis XVI and Marie Antoinette. Carlos IV and his cousin Louis, five years his junior, shared the burden of self-indulgent and headstrong wives desirous of gratifying every whim, with scant regard for the expense involved or the talk that ensued. Each would be mortified by his queen's efforts to influence government through connivance with ministers, and both would lose their thrones because of crises aggravated in some measure by controversy surrounding their consorts. Carlos III's declining years were embittered by the increasing signs of weakness of character and mediocre ability displayed by his heir apparent, and by the prince's obvious submission to his domineering spouse.

As had been the case with his father, Carlos IV found Madrid's ornate

---

1. Baptized Luisa María Teresa de Borbón y Borbón, she signed her private letters "Luisa," and was thus called by her husband. See Manuel Izquierdo Hernández, *Antecedentes y comienzos del reinado de Fernando VII* (Madrid, 1963), pp. 11–12. Godoy, most contemporaries, and subsequent historians refer to her as María Luisa. Manuel de Godoy, *Cuenta dada de su vida política por Don Manuel Godoy, Príncipe de la Paz, ó sean memorias críticas y apologéticas para la historia del reinado del Señor D. Carlos IV. de Borbón*, 3 vols. (Madrid, 1836–42); most recent edition: *Memorias: Edición y estudio preliminar de Carlos Seco Serrano*, 2 vols. (Madrid, 1956).

1200-room Palacio de Oriente too urban, and he much preferred the royal country residences, moving the entire court from one to another according to a fixed schedule. For the transaction of important matters, ministers and envoys from foreign powers were obliged to follow him in the spring to the Palacio de Aranjuez, thirty miles south of Madrid; during the summer heat to "La Granja," an emulation of Versailles at San Ildefonso, forty miles to the northwest; and in the fall to the Escorial, Felipe II's somber palace-monastery at San Lorenzo, twenty-five miles northwest. Even when in the capital, the king favored the "Pardo" Palace, on the city's outskirts, which provided the rural surroundings he so craved.

Carlos IV was accustomed to rising at dawn for early mass. He was fond to an extreme of wrestling, abstemious to the point of disdaining Spain's superb wines, and he endeavored—as did his father—to fend off the melancholy that had mortified his predecessors by keeping himself physically fit and spending much time out of doors every day, rain or shine, preferably hunting. He was inordinately fond of tinkering with guns or working with his hands in the cabinet shop; he preferred to leave matters of government to his ministers, seeing them for only thirty minutes or so each day. His wife seems to have suffered comparable neglect, although there is no doubt of his affection for her. Reared amid opulence, María Luisa grew accustomed to having her own way, and her husband's occupation with matters of his own interest encouraged her to find separate sources of amusement. No longer burdened by her father-in-law's restraint, she demonstrated a penchant for influencing affairs of state, filling the vacuum left by her spouse. Carlos IV retained his father's ministers, but friction soon developed between these older advisors and the imperious new mistress of the royal residences, a tension that was to have extensive historical consequences.

Whatever attractiveness the dark-eyed princess once possessed had vanished by the time she became queen. In 1789 the Russian ambassador reported that "repeated miscarriages, indispositions and—perhaps—a germ of hereditary illness had wilted [her appearance] completely: the yellow tint of her skin and the loss of her teeth were a mortal blow for her beauty." [2] The first tales of her infidelities seem to have been calumnies resulting from a jockeying for power between partisans of the francophile conde de Aranda and those of the conservative prime minister, conde de Floridablanca. These politically motivated stories were gathered eagerly by foreign diplomats. The tactic commenced before Carlos III's death, as the various factions endeavored to gain sway over the heir apparent. María Luisa lived in an ambiance permeated by rivalry and intrigue and was surrounded by informers who

2. Alexandre Tratchevsky, "L'Espagne à l'epoque de la Revolution Française," *Revue historique* 31 (1886) : 9, AT.

were prone to read into any situation the most scandalous interpretation.[3]

The queen's image among her contemporaries was damaged chiefly as a consequence of the part in her life played by Manuel de Godoy, an ambitious young guardsman who, through favors showered upon him by the royal couple, became the most powerful figure in the realm. Upon his appointment as prime minister, in 1794, Godoy will step directly into our story as the designer of innovations in Spanish policy toward the Pacific Northwest. The sway that he came to exercise over the throne generated salacious rumors that titillated every court in Europe. Because it had such significant consequences, the relationship between Godoy and the royal pair has been a subject for considerable comment by students of the period.[4] What is important is that talk of their behavior had a baneful effect upon public faith in Carlos IV and the government of his most enduring minister, with disastrous consequences for the empire.

Born in 1767 to parents of noble ancestry but modest circumstances, Godoy had come at seventeen from Castuera, in Badajoz, to join an older brother in the select royal bodyguard. His special place in the affections of the royal couple began four years later when he was thrown from a horse while escorting the Princess of Asturias from La Granja to nearby Segovia. She screamed as he fell, stopped her coach, and watched as he remounted and subdued the charger, unmindful of the accident. Her inquiry as to his condition led to an introduction at court. Within a month of Carlos III's death, Godoy received the first of many rapid promotions. As to the explanation for his elevation to the ministry, in the most perceptive and best documented study of this period Manuel Izquierdo Hernández comments that María Luisa

> undoubtedly had a passion to rule: she dominated her husband from the first days of her marriage, demonstrating this publicly upon accompanying him to the first council over which he presided as king, something long unseen in Spain. But Carlos IV was a man of phlegmatic temperament, tranquil, and insipid, incapable of exercising power, even as a mere orderly for his wife, with the boldness and energy that Luisa desired, and which she demonstrated in all her correspondence. For this reason, with the tacit compliance of her husband, Luisa sought someone who could rule according to her wishes, without forgetting for one single moment the respect owed the king. In her correspondence with

3. Izquierdo, *Antecedentes*, pp. 37–51.

4. For opposing views compare Wenceslao Ramírez de Villa-Urrutia, marqués de Villa-Urrutia, *La Reina María Luisa, esposa de Carlos IV* (Madrid, 1927), with the sympathetic treatment by Juan Pérez de Guzmán y Gallo, *Estudios de la vida, reinado, proscripción y muerte de Carlos IV y María Luisa de Borbón, Reyes de España*, 2d ed. (Madrid, 1909).

Godoy and in the orders she transmitted to him, she put Carlos's name before her own.[5]

Izquierdo is inclined to defend the queen against her detractors. Yet enough of her contemporaries were of the opinion that her youngest children bore in their physiognomy evidence of Godoy's paternity that the Cortes of Cádiz in 1812 removed the Infante Francisco de Paula from the list of succession.[6] What transpires in the privacy of royal bedrooms usually escapes credible documentation, but fiction sometimes has more influence upon politics than fact. Indisputably, the royal couple became so dependent upon Godoy that the relationship undermined Carlos IV's rule. Justified or not, the malicious talk made "Manuelito" hated by nobles and commoners alike, and it tarnished beyond remedy the king's popular image. Carlos cannot have ignored the fact that opposition to Godoy was rife. Some see the king's indifference to the situation as evidence of a dim wit, an unjustified opinion if one surveys his life as a whole. Rather, as Henry Adams remarked, those who knew Carlos IV best thought his "religion, honor, personal purity, and the self-respect of a king of Spain made it impossible for him to believe ill of one who stood toward him in such a relation." [7]

5. Izquierdo, *Antecedentes*, p. 60, AT.

6. Ibid., p. 111. Francisco de Paula Antonio (1794–1865). Fernando VII evidently gave no credence to this charge insofar as it included the youngest daughter, Infanta María de la O Isabela, since as his third wife he chose her daughter, María Cristina de Borbón, his niece. Fernando's concern at the time was to secure male issue, and it is unlikely he would marry a girl whom he believed to be a granddaughter of his arch enemy, Godoy.

7. Henry Adams, *History of the United States of America* [during the administrations of Jefferson and Madison], 9 vols. (New York, 1890–91), 1 : 345–46. Godoy's comment on why he was raised so rapidly to the apex of power illuminates Carlos IV's dilemma. It has never been published in English, and warrants examination:

> I myself for some time did not know it; here is the enigma's explanation: King Carlos and Queen María Luisa, as was natural would happen, had received and continued to receive the most vivid and profound impressions from France's perturbations, and of the frightful situation and troubles of good King Louis XVI and Queen Marie Antoinette and their unhappy family. Always attentive to those events, all that long series of afflictions and misfortunes through which their relatives passed, they attributed it in great part (and to be certain they were not deceiving themselves) to the various ministries of the prince so poorly served and in so many ways rough-handled by the contrary, selfish, and sinister influences of his court. The two kingdoms' proximity made them fear at any hour that conflagration's propagation to their realm. Casting their eyes about, they lacked confidence in themselves and found no place to deposit it; they desired enlightenment and feared deception; they hungered for virtues and feared the caprices of vanity and love of self; the dangers augmented, and they heard the threats that seeped from France over all of Europe. I will not attempt to apologize for, nor censure, these perplexities that oppressed their spirits; I can only relate a true fact. Afflicted and uncertain in resolution, they conceived the idea of procuring a man and making of him an incorruptible friend, work of their hands alone who, united intimately to their persons and their house, would be one and the same with them so as to take care of them and their kingdom in an indefectible manner. Once I was admitted to familiarity with the royal couple, if they heard me discoursing sometimes, if they believed I understood something about debates of that time, if they judged my loyalty favorably and were able to convince themselves—is it a disgrace that they found in me whom they desired? [Godoy, *Cuenta dada de su vida politica*, 1 : 14–15, AT.]

## PITT'S DIPLOMATIC SNARE

If, at the advent of the Nootka Crisis, Spain was unfortunate enough to have as monarch an individual so weak-willed as to merit disrespect for the handling of his own domestic affairs, Britain fared little better in 1790. George III had suffered a bout of mental derangement shortly after his marriage, in 1765, but the symptoms abated until 1788, when on one occasion he dismounted from the royal carriage in Windsor Park to greet a venerable oak, convinced it was his cousin, Frederick the Great. The crisis lasted well into 1789 and could not be kept from public notice; the Regency Act (1789) gave the Prince of Wales limited powers to govern in his father's behalf. Although the king recovered within the year, he was never quite the same, and William Pitt the Younger enjoyed greater power and freedom of policy than any English minister before his time, a factor of considerable import in the handling of the Nootka Crisis.

First accounts of the clash at Friendly Cove reached London garbled and piecemeal. Distrust for everything Spanish distorted the scanty and often erroneous details. The diplomatic imbroglio began with the reception in London of a letter from the chargé d'affaires in Madrid, telling of the seizure of an English vessel at Nootka Sound. It was not known whether more than one ship was involved, to whom it belonged, or what had happened to its cargo.[8] The Duke of Leeds, secretary of state for foreign affairs, immediately asked the number of Spanish vessels operating on the northwest coast, the guns and crew of each, "it being a Matter of equal Delicacy and Importance, in which he ought to be very cautious of giving even a Hint, which might be construed into a Dereliction of our Right to visit for the Purposes of Trade, or to make a Settlement in the District in Question, to which we undoubtedly had a compleat Right, to be asserted and maintained with a proper Degree of Vigour, should Circumstances make such an Exertion necessary." [9]

The Spanish ministry notified Revillagigedo that a protest concerning British encroachments at Nootka would be made in London; the viceroy was also told that if he had already restored the vessels to their owners, such action would be in line with His Catholic Majesty's wishes. Madrid's protest, requesting punishment for those responsible, contained a fairly accurate account of the incident. It cited Cook's remark about the spoons of Spanish manufacture and noted that they had once belonged to the same Martínez who had made the arrests at Nootka.[10]

8. Anthony Merry to the Duke of Leeds, Madrid, January 4, 1790, in [Sir James Bland Burges], *A Narrative of the Negotiations Occasioned by the Dispute Between England and Spain in the Year 1790* (London, [1791]), pp. 1–3.

9. Leeds to Merry, London, February 2, 1790, in ibid., pp. 8–9.

10. Valdés to Revillagigedo, Madrid, January 26, 1790, MxAGN (Hist. 65), fol. 328–29; Marqués del Campo de Alange to Leeds, London, February 10, 1790, résumé in Burges, *Narrative*, pp. 9–11.

London's harsh reply, a fortnight later, revealed the stance Pitt would take throughout the controversy; that seizures at Nootka Sound in time of peace were an insult to His Britannic Majesty and an offense "against the law of nations." Leeds stated that he "had His Majesty's Orders to declare, that the Act of Violence, mentioned in his Letter, must necessarily cause all Discussion on the Claims, therein also mentioned, to be suspended, until a Just and Suitable Satisfaction should be made for a Proceeding so injurious to Great Britain.[11] Of the demand for satisfaction before discussion, a Canadian historian has observed: "The peculiarity of this method of procedure was that Spain was compelled to give reparation for an insult which she denied having committed, without being allowed to discuss the grounds which, if her contentions were correct, justified her actions, viz.: the Spanish claims to sovereignty on the coast."[12] It was a pitfall into which no able diplomat would knowingly blunder, and Pitt knew from the outset Madrid would reject his demand and that the incident could be parlayed into a confrontation. He seized upon it as a pretext for coercing Spain at a moment when Carlos IV was unable to depend for support upon France, Spain's traditional ally, under the Family Compact. Pitt saw in the ambiguities of the Nootka question a chance to drive a wedge into Spain's colonial empire in America and provide an entry for British commerce and colonization. Analyzing London's strategy, Under Secretary for Foreign Affairs James Bland Burges remarked, "The whole Tenor of the Duke of Leeds' Correspondence upon this Subject plainly indicated, that His Majesty's Object in this Negotiation had been, throughout, no other than the procuring from the Court of Spain an Acknowledgement of the Rights of His Subjects to exercise their Navigation and Fisheries, as well as to land and form Establishment on all *unoccupied* Coasts of the American Continent and Islands."[13] The clash at Friendly Cove provided a fortuitous occasion from which Britain might reap a windfall. Construed as an insult to flag and nation and employed adroitly, it could extort assent to a principle never before conceded by Madrid: recognition of a British right to make settlements in any unpopulated area nominally claimed by Spain by right of prior discovery, but never colonized. Pitt would contend that unless an area were settled and effectively controlled, titles based on prior discovery were not binding. The principle of occupation, once recognized in a treaty, would not only provide unhindered access to the northwest coast, but it would legitimize beachheads anywhere that Madrid's territorial claims were not bolstered by settlement. The ploy, if successful, would facilitate the achievement of a long-sought British objective: economic and political penetration of Spanish America.

11. Leeds to Campo de Alange, Whitehall, February 26, 1790, SpAHN (Estado 4291), résumé in Burges, *Narrative*, pp. 12–13.

12. Lennox Mills, "The Real Significance of the Nootka Sound Incident," *CHR* 6 (1925) : 112.

13. Burges, *Narrative*, p. 302.

Many areas in the Spanish domains that were populated only by Indians had suffered encroachments by British subjects, Belize (later British Honduras), the Mosquito shore (eastern Nicaragua), and Guiana being notable examples. To check Spanish reprisals against such enclaves, Pitt sought to cloak them with respectability by means of a treaty recognizing the above-mentioned principle. Madrid maintained that the absence of colonists did not give other nationalities the right to encroach, if the region belonged to Spain by right of discovery. The British pretension was weakened by the fact that in 1786 London had agreed to a convention acknowledging Spanish sovereignty over the Mosquito Coast, where for decades British logwood cutters had been seeking a toehold. Within the British ministry it was suggested circumventing the broader implications of this pact by asserting that the Convention of 1786 referred solely to the Mosquito Coast and Honduras, and not to the continent in general.[14] Here was a perfect occasion to press for a precedent undoing the previous limitation and forcing open the door for British activities in every uncolonized area in Spanish America, from Alaska to Tierra del Fuego. "The extravagant pretension of Spain was now denied"; Burges declared, "her exclusive right was not admitted to extend beyond her actual possession; and the right of British subjects to visit and occupy the unsettled parts of the American Continent was asserted." Britain felt that its subjects had a right to settle on the northwest coast in places not previously occupied by another power, "and from that right was deduced the complaint of the injury, arising from the seizure and detention of British subjects and property." In giving satisfaction for injury done by Spanish officers, Madrid would necessarily be admitting the principle.[15] Pitt's strategy was hardly subtle, and Spain would make every effort to avoid swallowing such a bitter pill. Pitt seized upon the Nootka Incident despite the shady circumstances surrounding Meares's activities in 1788, when the trader had employed a Portuguese disguise. As an English historian has pointed out:

> With a questionable claim to the occupation of Nootka and a status which could best be described as that of an interloper, Meares appeared to be a most unpromising symbol of the British Government's determination to protect British traders in their lawful pursuits. Yet the Government could not afford to be particular in its choice of symbols. With an election imminent, the Opposition was ready to make the most of any of the Government's mistakes in negotiating. Pitt was acutely aware that the defence of the rights of a British trader, especially one who

14. Alejandro del Cantillo, ed., *Tratados, convenciones y declaraciones de paz y de comercio que han hecho con las potencias extranjeras los monarcas Españoles de la casa de Borbón* (Madrid, 1843), pp. 614–17; [Sir James Bland Burges], *Letters Lately Published in the Diary on the Subject of the Present Dispute With Spain Under the Signature of Verus* (London, 1790), pp. 60–61.

15. [Burges], *Letters*, pp. 52–53.

represented a challenge to the monopoly of the East India Company, had a powerful attraction for the whig mind.[16]

If Pitt did not grasp the sword by the hilt, he risked having it wielded against him.

As one of its first moves, the admiralty ordered Lord Cornwallis, veteran of the American campaign and now governor-general of Bengal, to send a frigate to Port Jackson, Australia, to pick up supplies and colonists and proceed to a rendezvous at Hawaii with the warships *Gorgon* and *Discovery*. The three vessels would go to the northwest coast "to prevent a repetition of this extraordinary Conduct by the Spaniards, and to maintain the undoubted Right of this Country to an undisturbed Possession of such Parts of the Northwest Coast of America, as had been originally settled or visited, for the Purposes of Trade, by the English." Cornwallis should enjoin his subordinates "to forbear from Hostilities; but, at the same Time, to maintain the British Rights by Force, should it be found necessary." [17] The governor of New South Wales was ordered to prepare an expedition to plant a colony on the northwest coast with the vessel sent by Cornwallis. There is no known acknowledgment of this order, so it probably was recalled, as was the order to Cornwallis on April 30, when Pitt's strategy turned toward making the full strength of British force felt in the European theater, rather than on the northwest coast. Such a course held the advantage that British intelligence could more readily ascertain the degree of Spanish naval strength there than in the North Pacific—and an encounter could not be risked without a known superiority of force.[18]

### GROWING ALARM IN MADRID

The crisis intruded upon deliberations of Spain's supreme council of state for the first time on March 2, when a communication from the ambassador in London about the acrimony at Friendly Cove was discussed. A fortnight later the council took up the British protest, deciding that London's attitude was sufficiently menacing to warrant orders to Trinidad, Puerto Rico, and Honduras for reinforcements against attack. Revillagigedo was notified that Carlos IV approved release of the prize ships, and if this had not already been carried out, it was "convenient to the royal service that he do so as an act of grace on his own, made in usage of his own powers." [19] Such a procedure

16. J. M. Norris, "The Policy of the British Cabinet in the Nootka Crisis," *EHR* 70 (1955): 571–72.

17. Burges, *Narrative*, pp. 14–15. The admiralty order was dated March 31, 1790.

18. W. Wyndham Grenville to Governor Philip, March 1790, in *Historical Records of Australia*, ser. 1, 1 (Sidney, 1914): 162; extract in Thomas Dunbabin, "How British Columbia Nearly Became a Colony of Australia," *BCHQ* 15 (1951): 37; Burges, *Narrative*, pp. 14–15.

19. Minutes of proceedings of the Council of State, Madrid, March 15, 1790 SpAHN (Estado 919), fol. 96–96v; Floridablanca to Revillagigedo, March 24, 1790, quoted in the above minutes, fol. 99–100v, AT.

would remove the cause of quarrel without assenting to disadvantageous principles or setting precedents. Five days later Floridablanca showed the council his projected answer to London. Spain was not disposed to make satisfaction for the vessels seized, other than releasing them. His Catholic Majesty had no intention of relinquishing claims to exclusive sovereignty over the northwest coast. The vessels and seamen had already been freed as an act of grace, in the assurance that ignorance of Spain's legitimate claim to Nootka had led to the incident, and it was hoped that the matter might be considered at an end. In due time a letter to this effect was delivered to London.[20]

London's bellicose protest quickened fears of war in Madrid. The Supreme Council decided that further precautions were necessary against surprise attacks upon ports on the peninsula and in America.[21] Despite Spain's endeavor to keep such measures secret, the British chargé informed London within a week: "The Alarm, which the Court of Spain has taken at our Answer about the Affair of Nootka, is so great, that they have given Orders for Reports to be Immediately sent from the Spanish Arsenals of the Quantity of Copper for sheathing ships, which there is in the Storehouses, and of the Number of Ships of the Line which can be got ready for Sea at a short Notice."[22] This warning arrived in London on April 18, and other letters followed with further details of naval preparations at Cádiz and Cartagena. Floridablanca had no success trying to pass off the armament as a defense against the trend of events in France.[23] Madrid made every effort to keep the crisis from mushrooming into war by assuring the British chargé of its intentions to reach a peaceful settlement of the issues involved. Such hopes were destined for disappointment from the outset. Floridablanca's position was that His Catholic Majesty had an unquestionable claim to the northwest coast as far north as the entrance of Prince William Sound, acts of possession having been performed there by Spanish explorers in 1779. Such symbolic acts had been the recognized practice among nations in the eighteenth century as a prerequisite to claims of territorial sovereignty. Madrid resisted the new principle upon which London now insisted—that sovereignty could not exist unless backed by settlement. Pitt would have been at a loss to explain why Cook, Strange, and other British captains performed such rituals on the northwest coast, knowing that no attempt at settlement would follow within the foreseeable future. London had asserted claims to many islands in

---

20. Campo de Alange to Leeds, London, April 20, 1790, SpAHN (Estado 4291), English trans. in William Ray Manning. "The Nootka Sound Controversy," *AHA Annual Report, 1904* (1905). 374–75, the fundamental monograph on the Nootka controversy.

21. Minutes of the Council of State, March 29, 1790, SpAHN (Estado 919), fol. 99–100v.

22. Merry to Leeds, Madrid, April 5, 1790, extract in Burges, *Narrative*, pp. 18–19; extracts of Merry's subsequent letters on pp. 37–38, 69–70.

23. Merry to Leeds, April 19, 1790, UKLPRO (For. Off. 72/15), fol. 271, cited by Norris, "Policy," pp. 577–78.

the Pacific by virtue of discoveries not followed up by settlements for many years. The weight placed upon claims derived from the explorations of Captain Cook shows that the principle of prior discovery still had validity in English eyes as a basis for claims of sovereignty; thus, there was much hypocrisy in Pitt's stance concerning the northwest coast. An English historian asserts that this position was not "a formulation of a broadly inclusive doctrine, applicable in all other instances of a similar nature, but rather an *ad hoc* attempt to make a predatory policy look respectable." [24] And if Spain acquiesced, the "new" principle would be susceptible to extension to other unoccupied areas in Spanish America, giving British traders, whalers, fishermen, and contraband runners access to isolated bays in California, Central America, Chile, the Caribbean, and other widely scattered places.

Floridablanca's stance was undermined by Madrid's earlier failure to parade before the eyes of Europe her discoveries in 1774 and 1775, when Spanish navigators visited the long stretch of *terra incognita* between Cape Mendocino and the southernmost spot seen by Chirikov. Nor had expeditions in 1779 and 1788 been sufficiently publicized. Learned circles in Britain had no means of knowing about Spanish achievements and activities on the northwest coast, save for Mourelle's journal. As seen from London, Spanish pretensions to the northwest coast seemed preposterous. The growing turmoil in France could be used to bring Madrid face to face with the fact that it could no longer dominate the Pacific as a private preserve, nor exclude the British from areas where Spain asserted a paper claim but possessed no effective control.

### THE MEARES MEMORIAL

The arrival in London of John Meares aggravated the situation to a marked degree, for in depicting events at Nootka in 1789 he set forth an inflamed tale of insults and cruelties in which facts, distortions, and manifest fabrications were inextricably interwoven. The audience that he secured among highly placed figures in the government came about through the merger of his interests with those of the powerful "King George's Sound Company," in which men of considerable fortune and influence were involved. At Pitt's request, Meares submitted an account of the Nootka Incident to the cabinet. When news of the crisis became public, this account was published in pamphlet form and circulated widely to justify the ministry's bellicose measures. It attained considerable success as a propaganda device. Meares conveniently neglected to mention, among other things, that when the *Ifigenia Nubiana* and the *Northwest America* ran into difficulties with Martínez they were operating under the Portuguese flag, not under that of Great Britain. As appendices, the memorial contained depositions and letters from officers of the seized vessels that lent an appearance of factuality to

24. Norris, "Policy," p. 577.

the specious narrative. William Graham, just arrived from Macao, deposed that Hudson and the crew of the *Princess Royal* were beaten by the Spanish, a charge not corroborated by other sources but impossible to disprove.[25] Manning believes it was Meares's misrepresentations that led Pitt to believe that British rights to Nootka were beyond question and that Martínez's procedure was tantamount to robbery.[26] The memorial's publication and diffusion was a calculated effort to provide the ministry with public support for the power play that Pitt envisioned.

Before the Nootka incident showed signs of becoming a major crisis, Pitt had been developing other schemes to subvert Spain's American domains. In February 1790, he began repeated conferences with Francisco de Miranda, the perennial revolutionary from Caracas, and drew up a plan whereby, in case of an Anglo-Spanish war, the people of Spanish America would be encouraged and aided to rise in revolution and obtain independence. The ambitious design contemplated an empire governed by a hereditary Inca and allied with Great Britain, and it was coordinated with the strategy of coercing Madrid into backing down on its claims to vast, unoccupied areas in the New World. Simultaneously, Pitt was considering a plan to occupy the Isthmus of Panama. Another scheme, set in march by an order to the governor general of Canada, called for secret negotiations with the "Men of the Western Waters," in the Trans-Appalachian region of the United States, for an invasion of Spanish Louisiana and Florida. Common denominators in these plans were secret agents in key places who would have British assistance for attacks on vulnerable and strategic spots. As Manning perceives it, Pitt's grand strategy was aimed at seizing control of the heart of North America, making it a British colony, and gaining sway over the rest of Spanish America as a client state.[27]

Events at Nootka gave Pitt an opportunity to fashion an important cog for a larger wheel. In 1790 Carlos IV's empire was the largest and richest in existence. "In her own eyes and in those of the world at the time," a Canadian historian has remarked, "Spain was numbered among the mighty and Britain among the fallen." [28] Loss of the thirteen colonies in North America had damaged British prestige, while Spain's empire seemed intact, save for a

25. William Graham, "Information," Middlesex, May 5, 1790, in Meares, *Memorial*, pp. 34–41.
26. Manning, "Nootka Sound," p. 314.
27. Ibid., p. 412; William Spence Robertson, "Francisco de Miranda and the Revolutionizing of Spanish America," *AHA Annual Report, 1907*, 1 (1908) : 272. See also Robertson's *Life of Miranda*, 2 vols. (Chapel Hill, N.C., 1929). James Creassy, "A Plan for getting a superior naval force into the South Seas, taking or distroying the City of Panama, seizing the Spanish treasure, ruining their commerce in South America, the West Indies, and the Philipian Islands: and for securing the important passage accross the Isthmus of Panama forever to Great Britain. And other matters of the greatest national utility at this crises." May 15, 1790, CU–B, pub. by Lucia Burk Kinnaird, "Creassy's Plan for Seizing Panama," *HAHR* 13 (1933) : 58–78.
28. Alfred L. Burt, *The United States, Great Britain and British North America from the Revolution to the Establishment of Peace After the War of 1812*, 2d ed. (New York, 1961), p. 106.

few islands in the Caribbean. Meares's tale offered an opportunity to force the hand of the new and unproven Spanish monarch. Properly exploited, the situation could redeem Britannia's position as a colonial power at Spain's expense by legitimizing takeover of such portions of the New World as might be seized from Carlos IV's hands while his attention was focused on cousin Louis's travail.

It was easy to promote anti-Spanish fervor in Britain, since the two nationalities had been on opposite sides in war so many times. Rancor persisted from Spain's having joined with France to aid insurgent Americans, contributing to the misfortunes of a long, expensive, and humiliating conflict. Nootka offered a chance for revenge. An Anglo-Spanish war in 1790 would have been completely in context—one more turn in the tragic cycle of conflicts by which the great European powers sought hegemony over one another by striving to enlarge their colonial domains. France had suffered bitter defeat in 1763, and then had joined with relish in giving Britain a setback by persuading Spain to join the French in backing the colonists in the American Revolution. Now Pitt could force Madrid to eat humble pie and reap rich rewards to boot.

### BRITISH PREPARATIONS FOR WAR

Secretary of State William Wyndham Grenville presented Meares's *Memorial* to the Cabinet on April 30. "Your Majesty's Servants," it decided, "have agreed humbly to submit to Your Majesty their opinion that Your Majesty's Minister at the Court of Madrid, should be instructed to present a Memorial demanding an immediate and adequate satisfaction for the outrages committed by M: de Martinez; and that it would be proper in order to support that demand, and to be prepared for such events as may arise, that Your Majesty should give orders for fitting out a Squadron of Ships of the line." [29]

In all probability the news from Madrid concerning Spain's vigorous naval preparations hastened cabinet action. The chargé was instructed to demand satisfaction for the insult, and he was notified that a special ambassador would go to Madrid to pursue the delicate business of arriving at a proper settlement.[30] An individual of great skill and experience was needed, and Pitt selected Alleyne Fitzherbert, whose talent at diplomacy and espionage

---

29. Minutes of the cabinet, Whitehall, April 30, 1790, in *BCPAD Report, 1913* (1914): pp. 13–14. Those present, in addition to Grenville, were the lord chancellor (Edward Thurlow, 1st Baron Thurlow), the lord privy seal (George Granville Leveson-Gower, 1st marquess of Stafford, Earl Gower), the foreign secretary (Francis Godolphin Osborne, 5th duke of Leeds), the master-general of the ordnance (Charles Lennox, 3rd duke of Richmond and Lennox), and the first lord of the admiralty (John Pitt, 2nd earl of Chatham, the prime minister's older brother), and of course Pitt himself.

30. Leeds, Instructions to Merry, resumé in Burges, *Narrative*, pp. 41–44.

had been demonstrated in negotiations ending the American Revolution. His instructions indicated that satisfaction could be rendered only by an admission from Madrid that Spain had no actual and known sovereignty over Nootka. If Floridablanca insisted on discussing Spain's claims to the northwest coast, Fitzherbert should assert that they would never be admitted by Britain, as the area had never been possessed or occupied by Spanish subjects, and such claims were contrary to the Law of Nations and extant treaties. He should demand a declaration that in the future Spain would not take action against British subjects in unoccupied areas on that coast.[31]

For several days mobilization was a closely guarded secret, but in the early hours of May 5 squads descended upon pubs, rooming houses, and brothels in major ports, gathering up able-bodied men and impressing them into service aboard warships being outfitted for battle against Spain, an unheralded measure alerting the entire nation to the crisis. At 11:00 P.M. on the eve of the general impressment, Pitt sent George III a draft of a proposed message to Parliament, "which has undergone the consideration of your Majesty's confidential servants, and which he trusts will appear to your Majesty to be adapted to the circumstances of the occasion."[32] The next morning a stiff note to the Spanish ambassador declared that the government intended to defend the rights of British subjects on the northwest coast, where they had "an unquestionable right to a free and undisturbed enjoyment of the benefits of commerce, navigation, and fishery, and also to the possession of such establishments as they may form, with the consent of the natives, in places unoccupied by other European nations."[33]

The reason for impressment was not generally known until later that day, when Pitt read to Parliament the royal address setting forth British grievances. One of Thomas Jefferson's correspondents wrote him of witnessing the tumult in a "very much crowded" House of Commons. "As soon as the house rose I went amongst the members I was acquainted with, afterwards dined in company with others, and in my life I do not remember to have been amongst such insolent bullies," he reported. "They were all for war, talked

31. Leeds, Instructions to Fitzherbert, London, May 16, 1790, résumé in ibid., pp. 72–83; S. F. Bemis, *The Diplomacy of the American Revolution*, 2d ed. (Bloomington, Ind., 1957), pp. 206, 211n, 221, 240.

32. Pitt to George III, Downing Street, May 4, 1790, 11 P.M., in Arthur Aspinall, ed., *The Later Correspondence of George III*, vol. 1, *December 1783 to January 1793* (Cambridge, 1962), p. 589; "His Britannic Majesty's Message to Both Houses of Parliament," London, May 5, 1790, in Burges, *Narrative*, pp. 46–49, 51–54. Several Americans were caught in the impressment, but Gouverneur Morris, Washington's informal representative in London, secured their release within several weeks; this was the first occasion of a practice that aggravated Anglo-American relations until it became one cause of the War of 1812. S. F. Bemis, *Jay's Treaty*, rev. ed. (New Haven, 1962), p. 76n.

33. Leeds to Campo de Alange, Whitehall, May 5, 1790, SpAHN (Estado 4291), T in DLC (Manning Transcripts, 276–77).

much of *Old England* and the *british Lion,* laughed at the Idea of drubbing the Dons', began to calculate the millions of dollars they would be obliged to pay for having insulted *the first power on Earth,* and seemed uneasy lest the Spaniards should be alarmed at the british strength, ask pardon for what they have done and come immediately to terms." [34]

Pitt also found time on that eventful day to closet himself again with Miranda to enlarge upon their jointly elaborated plans for undermining Spain's American empire; that evening the plans were presented to the cabinet. Pitt's own speech before Commons the next day was couched in terms well-calculated to appeal to the economic interests of merchants and industrialists. If Britain accepted Spain's claim to Nootka Sound, he declared, "it must deprive this country of the means of extending its navigation and fishery in the southern ocean, and would go towards excluding His Majesty's subjects from an infant trade, the future of which could not but be essentially to the commercial interest of Great Britain." [35] Not to be outdone, Charles James Fox, leader of the opposition, rose to reprobate Spain's pretension "to the exclusive right of navigation, commerce, and territory in the South American and South Seas." "In the present enlightened age," he decried, "the obsolete claim to territory by grant of a Pope was done away, as was the right of territory by discovery without absolute settlement." He hoped that "an adequate satisfaction for the ships, without a termination to future claims, might not be accepted." "The point with Spain was no longer the trivial one, of the value of the ships seized, but a decision on her rights in Spanish America—Spain has always advanced her obsolete rights when she has wished to quarrel with this country:—We now have the opportunity, and ought to embrace it, of putting an end to the assertion of those rights for ever." [36]

Within a few days the government began to distribute copies of Meares's *Memorial* throughout the nation to justify its actions. The lieutenant appeared before the Committee of Council for Trade, stressing the importance of the sea otter trade in opening up markets for British manufactures in both the northwest coast area and China. Norris's study of the British cabinet during the Nootka Crisis suggests that a campaign by a pressure group in English politics against the East India Company had an important influence in escalating debate in Parliament. To attract Whig support in the coming election, Pitt defended Meares's rights as a trader independent of

---

34. John Rutledge, Jr., to Thomas Jefferson, London, May 6, 1790, midnight, endorsed as rec'd. June 18, 1790, in Jefferson, *Papers,* 16 : 413–15.

35. Pitt, as cited by Norris, "Policy," pp. 572–73; Bemis, *Jay's Treaty,* pp. 71–72.

36. Fox, as quoted in *Scots Magazine,* Edinburgh, 1790, reprinted in James Stirrat Marshall and Carrie Marshall, comp., *Pacific Voyages: Selections from Scots Magazine 1771–1808* (Portland, 1960), p. 74.

great monopoly companies.[37] Patriotic fervor constituted a strong element in the electioneering, with the opposition trying to outdo the government in protesting against Spain's misdeeds. The Nootka issue became entangled with resentment of Spanish claims to Pacific islands and the sore question of fishing grounds off southern South America and the Antarctic. American and British whalers had frequented those waters for some years, and, with the excuse of being in distress or dire need of supplies, they often called at ports in Spanish America. Ensuing abuses had led Spanish officials to regard such voyages as mere pretexts for illegal contact with Spanish subjects and a cover for contraband traffic.

The keystone of the debate in Parliament was ridicule of Iberian claims based on the Papal Bull of 1493 that divided the Indies between Spain and Portugal. Orators held such disputable paper claims insufficient to justify Spanish monopoly over so vast a coastline, where British commercial circles had been the first to see great economic promise. British outrage derived from a very one-sided portrayal of the circumstances at Friendly Cove. At this point it is unlikely that any of the debaters knew (since Meares avoided disclosing it) that the *Ifigenia* and the *Northwest America* had endeavored to pass themselves off as Portuguese. Self-righteous harangues waxed hot on the inflammatory material with which Meares fed the fire. The national pride was goaded with references to the "immortal memory of Jenkins' Ear," a comparable episode half a century earlier that had led Parliament to declare war on Spain. Once again, honor would be the ostensible reason for a conflict rooted primarily in economic motivations.[38] In Pitt's deft hands, the Nootka incident could prove as effective a catalyst as Captain Jenkins' disembodied relic. Nor would it have been the first time that Britain waged war for control of fur trading areas—a prime motive for the French and Indian War of 1754–63. Pitt could count on the national sense of outrage to back him to the hilt in the confrontation with Madrid.

"Since writing to you last," Jefferson's London informant reported, "every preparation for war has been carrying on here with an activity of which it is scarcely possible to have an Idea; the people have most vigorously seconded the efforts of the minister; and owing to a strange infatuation, there is not a man in this nation who does not seem to think he will be enriched by a

37. The opposition accused Pitt of "great supineness in suffering the matter to go on so long, and of great deceit in having drawn so flattering a picture of the prospect of peace on the day of the Budget," as related in Henry Temple, 2nd Viscount Palmerston, to Benjamin Mee, London, May 12, 1790, in Aspinall, *Later Correspondence*, 589n.

38. Norris, "Policy," p. 572. While engaged in contraband off what is now Uruguay, Captain Robert Jenkins had his ear cut off, or so he claimed, in a scuffle with a search party from a Spanish *guardacostas*. Several years later he waved the scrap of flesh before Parliament, and although skeptics claimed there were two whole ears under his wig, the Walpole ministry was prodded into declaring the "War of Jenkins' Ear" (1739–41), with the objective of opening Spanish America to English wares.

Spanish war." [39] Fox and other Whig leaders perceived an opportunity to belabor the ministry with charges of executive tyranny in keeping the negotiations with Madrid too secret and claims that the government was being unnecessarily soft in its demands; but motions in the House of Lords that exchanges with Spain be laid before it were conveniently defeated by Pitt's supporters. Pamphlets published by persons within the government defended the prime minister's measures, sustaining that less cautious means might incite hostility among other European powers and thwart the securing of Britain's principal objectives.[40] Differences of opinion on how to extract maximum advantage produced a split in the cabinet. The foreign secretary refused to attend a June 2 meeting out of displeasure at Pitt's unwillingness to present Spain with a blunt ultimatum demanding unqualified satisfaction —without discussing claims of sovereignty. The rupture was smoothed over, however, and Leeds's intransigent path forsworn. The resulting instructions to Fitzherbert allowed discussion of claims once Britannia's demand for satisfaction had been granted.[41]

There is no evidence that Pitt wanted war over Nootka, and he seems to have been gambling that Carlos IV would yield rather than fight without the assurance of French support. But many in Britain's ruling circles were convinced that conflict with Spain was not only inevitable but convenient. Leeds continued to obstruct Pitt's more pacific maneuvers and pressed for a stand that would induce Madrid to declare war while Britain had its fleet at the ready. It is assumed that Undersecretary Burges was reflecting Leeds's views in stating that "before we know where we are, we shall have the Americans, and possibly the Russians on our backs, if we lose a week commencing the war with Spain by some vigorous and decisive stroke, which may crush their naval power, and incapacitate them from standing against us at sea." [42]

It was essential to the British to secure the support of such allies as might be enticed into a struggle against Spain before Madrid had an opportunity to obtain aid from Paris, New York, or St. Petersburg. Messages were sent to the Netherlands and Prussia, allies under the Triple Alliance, calling for assistance. The Dutch fleet soon joined the English at Portsmouth for joint operations. Prussia offered passive encouragement. A series of orders sent throughout the empire proves that London actually started to marshal her resources in preparation for a conflict. Sixty warships of the line put to sea.

39. Rutledge to Jefferson, London, May 12, 1790, endorsed as rec'd, October 25, 1790, in Jefferson, *Papers,* 16 : 426–28.

40. Burges, *Letters,* pp. 30 ff.

41. Leeds to Pitt, June 2, 1790, UKLPRO (Chatham Papers 151), cited by Norris, "Policy," p. 575.

42. Burges to Leeds, June 27, 1790, UKLBM (Add. Mss. 28,066), fol. 5–6, cited in ibid., pp. 575–76.

Spanish proposals for mutual disarmament were rejected. An encounter between opposing fleets maneuvering dangerously near one another off the Spanish coast seemed only hours away.[43]

The stances of London and Madrid were mutually exclusive, and to both sides the issues seemed of sufficient importance to go to war, should the opponent refuse to yield. To the victor would belong the spoils of hegemony in the continuing struggle for colonial possessions. If a conflict ensued, the network of extant alliances would pit Spain, France, Austria, Denmark, Russia, and the United States against a coalition of Great Britain, the Netherlands, Prussia, Sweden, Poland, and Turkey—assuming that every nation held faithful to its allies. The consequences would engulf all the Western world in conflict, with combat on every ocean—truly a world war.

### THE PROPAGANDA OFFENSIVE

The war fever was abetted by the lobbying of powerful elements with stock in trading companies and a vested interest in promoting and protecting the sea otter traffic by attracting public and governmental attention to resources of the northwest coast and spreading a conviction that national honor demanded defense of British claims to western North America. Allied in sentiment were mariners, explorers, geographers, merchants, and speculators concerned for so long with the fruitless search for a northwest passage. Immediately preceding the Nootka crisis a great many books and pamphlets had diffused among the reading public the objectives of this circle. That the effort had big money behind it is manifest in the lengthy and elegantly printed accounts, accompanied by costly engravings, of some of the British fur traders' voyages. Best known of the lobbyists was Alexander Dalrymple, whose *Plan for Promoting the Fur Trade, and Securing it to This Country* (London, 1789) proposed that Hudson's Bay Company agents bring furs to the west coast of North America, where ships of the East India Company, or vessels operating under its licenses, could transport them to Asia. Dalrymple wrote several pamphlets that attempted to sway public opinion toward supporting a bellicose insistence on concessions from Spain.[44] Another trade lobbyist was John Etches, a leading stockholder in the company owning the seized vessels; his *Authentic Statement of all the Facts Relative to Nootka Sound* (London, 1790) was the most scathing item put out during the pam-

43. Ibid., p. 578, Burges, *Narrative*, pp. 55–65; Manning, "Nootka Sound," p. 409.

44. A. Dalrymple, *The Spanish Memorial of 4th June Considered* (London, 1790); idem, *The Spanish Pretensions Fairly Discussed* (London, 1790). See the bibliography for the works by Coxe (1780), Dalrymple (1789), Dobbs (1744), Doylé (1770), Drage (1748–49, 1768), Henry Ellis (1748), Goldson (1793), and Pickersgill (1782), as well as the journals by Beresford (1789), Colnett (1798), Meares (1790), Mortimer (1791), Portlock (1789), and the anonymous journal signed "C. L." (1789).

phlet war. Etches's "facts" often were distorted almost beyond recognition. Spain's laxity in publicizing its activities on the northwest coast allowed him to declare:

> It is yet a profound mystery to every rational being, with what shadow of excuse the Spanish Court can attempt to colour this enormous outrage, this premeditated robbery, and improvoked hostility. They cannot have the effrontery to arrogate to themselves the fruits of the discoveries made by the late Capt. Cook, and other British adventurers, in a region so remote from their settlements.[45]

It particularly annoyed Etches that the *Columbia* and the *Lady Washington* had lain at anchor under Martínez's very nose, while the British vessels were seized, and "to aggravate the insult to the British nation, several days after the captivity of Capt. Colnet, the anniversary of the American Independence was commemorated with every demonstration of joy." If London had not protested spiritedly, he thought it likely they "would have been condemned to linger out a miserable existence, in the most dreadful of all dungeons, the *mines of Mexico*." In terms calculatedly exploiting the Black Legend surrounding the Spanish conquest, he invoked:

> the ghosts of murdered millions of the natives of that continent yet screaming for vengeance on their remorseless butchers. Ten millions more of their wretched descendants are, with broken hearts, incessantly supplicating Heaven to relieve them from their rigorous bondage—to send to their deliverance some generous and compassionate nation, to break their chains asunder, and to place them in the rank of human beings. It is well known they have the means amply to testify to their gratitude, and to repay their deliverers from the most flagitious of all human tyranny and oppression; from the shackles and scourges of unbridled despotism; from the fiery fiends of gloomy bigotry and priestly inquisition.[46]

Addressed to George III, Etches's tract clamored for redress of offenses suffered at Nootka, calling to memory the "late insidious and mercenary conspiracy in the assistance of our revolted American colonies and in the dismemberment of our empire," and Spanish repossession of Florida, the Mosquito Shore, and Minorca, characterized not as the "victorious blows of a generous and manly foe" but as "the stabs and rapine of a dastardly assassin."

Britain's case for demanding satisfaction over the Nootka incident de-

45. J. Etches, *An Authentic Statement of All the Facts Relative to Nootka Sound; its Discovery, History, Settlement, Trade, and the Probable Advantages to be Derived from it; in an Address to the King* (London, 1790), p. 16.

46. Ibid., pp. 24–25.

pended greatly upon the veracity of Meares's version of the discovery of the northwest coast and the events leading to the clash at Friendly Cove. Before long, however, rumors spread in informed circles that Meares's word was something less than trustworthy. The first to make such a charge, quite expectedly, was the Spanish ambassador. Endeavoring to learn more about British activities at Nootka and the circumstances surrounding the charges against Martínez, the Marqués del Campo de Alange consulted Captain Barkley, at that time in London. The discoverer of the Strait of Juan de Fuca provided a wealth of data about Meares's covert affairs, including the fact that João Carvalho had been no more than a front for Meares's English backers, who were East India Company factors in the Orient. The marqués informed Floridablanca that Meares, in whose name the protest was being made, "had no property or even a share in the outfitting" of the seized vessels, "because he doesn't have even a house or home." For a few guineas Meares had made the protest as dictated by the "Associated Merchants," whose names could not appear in it since they had no right, as employees of the monopoly company, to have engaged in such an enterprise. Moreover, the marqués had learned that aboard one of the English vessels had been two Germans knowledgeable in ores who had found veins of silver and gold somewhere along the coast. The exploratory cuts were covered up and hidden, however, in the expectation that the find could be exploited once a British settlement had been planted at Nootka Sound.[47]

Meares continued to jog Pitt with additional information. Kendrick's arrival in Macao brought news which, by the time it reached London, became considerably garbled: the ministry was informed that the *Lady Washington* "had gone up de Fuca's Straits and discovered a New Sea, extending to the Northward," leading to the supposition that Nootka "and all the places which have lately been visited, are situated in Islands, and not on the Continent." Also, Meares said that the Spanish were busily working a mine at Nootka and that samples of the ore had been smuggled out and brought to London.[48] Although such rumors were groundless, they lent weight to hopes for a northwest passage and valuable mines, whetting British interest in the northwest coast.

In a memorial to Home Secretary Baron Grenville, Meares stressed the economic advantages lost through the Spanish seizures and Madrid's assertion of exclusive sovereignty over the northwest coast, underlining the reasons why it behooved Britain to seek redress for the insults suffered, as a

47. Campo de Alange to [Floridablanca], London, May 28, 1790, SpAHN (Estado 4291 bis), AT.
48. "Information Obtained from Lt. Mears," July 3, 1790, and "Memorandum by Lieutenant Meares," July 4, 1790, UKLPRO (F. O. Msc. 5, app. 2, 3), in *BCPAD Report, 1913* 1914): pp. 30–31. These reports appear to have stemmed from Gray's cruise within the Strait of Juan de Fuca and Spanish excavations at San Miguel to make gun emplacements.

means of securing her own title to that coastline.[49] He had a vested interest in promoting the quarrel, for as long as he remained in the eye of the storm, his personal fortunes flourished in the glow of publicity, and he stood to gain from any monetary settlement exacted from Madrid. Meares had arrived from Macao with his personal finances in disarray, but he possessed some skill as a writer, and within a short time had finished a long and detailed account of his voyages. Published in 1790 in a deluxe edition on fine paper and accompanied by numerous elegant maps and engravings, this volume is tangible evidence of affluent sponsorship. As appendices he offered twenty-three documents, including Martínez's inventories, which lend the work an appearance of historical solidity that would be highly convincing if not challenged by other testimony. Read by itself and uncritically, it is an absorbing narrative of what purports to have been the first extensive exploration of the northwest coast. But Meares had little respect for the truth, and he appropriated for himself discoveries made by Cook, Barkley, Dixon, and Duncan, not to mention those made by Spanish explorers. Some of his misinformation was perhaps unintentional. For example, he credited the *Lady Washington* with circumnavigating the island on which Nootka Sound was located; this "fact" probably derived from garbled information that had young Kendrick and Castillo sailing around Mazarredo in a Spanish launch.

The lieutenant's self-glorifying falsifications of history did not go unchallenged for long. Several who could refute his most serious deviations from fact happened to be in London at the time, and he became embroiled in a pamphlet polemic with Captain Dixon, who charged that "To point out half your absurdities would fill a volume large as your own, and require much more time than I at present can spare; however, the duty I owe the public and myself, obliges me not to pass over them in silence."[50] Dixon

---

49. Meares to Grenville, July 30, 1790, UKLPRO (F. O. Miscel. 5, app. 5), in ibid., pp. 32–33. Meares's *Voyages* enjoyed several subsequent, cheaper editions in English within the next few months, and the work appeared in French, German, Italian, and Swedish translations within the next half dozen years.

50. George Dixon, *Remarks on the Voyages of John Meares, Esq. in a Letter to That Gentleman* (London, 1790), pp. 27, 49; John Meares, *An Answer to Mr. George Dixon, Late Commander of the Queen Charlotte in the Service of Messrs. Etches and Company . . . in Which the Remarks of Mr. Dixon on the Voyages to the North West Coast of America, & Lately Published, Are Fully Considered and Refuted* (London, 1791); Dixon, *Further Remarks on the Voyages of John Meares, Esq. in Which Several Important Facts, Misrepresented in the Said Voyages, Relative to Geography and Commerce, are Fully Substantiated. To Which is Added, a Letter from Captain Duncan, Containing a Decisive Refutation of Several Unfounded Assertions of Mr. Meares, and a Final Reply to His Answer* (London, 1791). All three pamphlets are published in facsimile edition by Howay, *Dixon-Meares Controversy*. Manning labeled Meares's account of the Nootka incident exaggerated and distorted. Howay demonstrated that Meares "omitted material factors, falsified documents, and made knowingly untrue statements." The able Canadian historian's conclusions "justify the student in doubting any important and uncorroborated statement in Meares's writings." Howay, *Dixon-Meares Controversy*, pp. 8, 12, 15–16, 22; Manning, "Nootka Sound," p. 376.

went into considerable detail to debunk a number of what he called "palpable falsehoods or studied misrepresentations." Meares tried to exonerate himself with a pamphlet *Answer,* but Dixon renewed his attack with *Further Remarks,* which, for a knowledgeable reader, left the lieutenant's reputation in tatters. However, Dixon's revelations about Meares's personal integrity had little or no effect on the chain reaction that Meares had set in motion. Details conflicting with his version of events at Friendly Cove were never brought out in the confrontation between London and Madrid. With Meares as dramatist, the episode proved more than sufficient for Pitt to stage a spectacular. And it is Meares's scenario that has been handed down in many otherwise respected texts as the purported history of the most important incident in the Pacific Northwest in the eighteenth century. The Pitt ministry initially built its case around wrongs inflicted upon Meares's enterprise, but as details of the shoddier aspects of his tale spread among those best informed, his misfortunes receded into the background and were replaced by the lofty issues of freedom to navigate the Pacific and frequent uncolonized spots on the shores of erstwhile Spanish America.

A partisan of the Spanish point of view—perhaps the Spanish ambassador —countered with an anonymous pamphlet, ostensibly authored by a British subject, ridiculing Pitt's retreat from championing Meares.

> The honour of the British flag is abandoned:—he discovers, at the very sound, that he has not wholly forgot to blush. The policy of fighting for the cat skins of Nootka, the justice of precipitating his taxed country into a war, the character of which throughout Europe would be a WAR OF PIRATES TO PROTECT SMUGGLERS, is wholly abandoned also. . . . the Southern whale-fishery, that source of inexhaustible prosperity to the commerce and navigation of Great Britain, is now affirmed to be the material point in the dispute, and the true justification for our immense and profitless exertions.[51]

The pamphleteer would not have found many sympathizers, for the quarrel appealed to emotions rooted deep in English experience. The crisis had become a political bonanza in a jingoistic election campaign, stirring up widespread anti-Spanish prejudices among the populace. The impressment of seamen, passionate oratory in Parliament, and inflammatory propaganda brought public sentiment to a high pitch, which rumors of an impending sea battle did nothing to lower. At the height of the "Nootka fever," a playbill for London's Theater Royal, Covent Garden, advertised that on June 9, sharing the evening with a "Grave Historical Romance Called the Crusade," there would be for the fourth time:

51. *The Errors of the British Minister in the Negotiations with the Courts of Spain* (London, 1790), p. 31.

A New Pantomimic, Operatic Farce, in One Act, Called,
Nootka Sound;
Or, Britain Prepared.
With New and Selected Music and Songs; Scenes and Decorations.[52]

The conviction grew in England that satisfaction should be exacted by arms. Naval forces were in readiness for the expected clash, and war seemed imminent.

### FLORIDABLANCA'S STRATEGY FOR DEFENSE

While parrying the British chargé's questions with assurances of Spain's peaceful intentions, Floridablanca drew up a "plan of what ought to be done in Spain's actual circumstances regarding England," submitted it to the ministers of war and marine, "to see if they had anything to add to the first draft, and informing them that the king is in agreement with it for now, and desires that everything which did not require His Majesty's particular knowledge be carried out as soon as possible." [53] Floridablanca proposed:

1. continuing the mobilization in Cádiz, gathering together all the maritime forces possible in order to bring them to bear wherever necessary in Europe or America;

2. moving as many infantrymen and dragoons as feasible to the Department of Cádiz, for the defense of that zone, in order to counteract an English attempt to get the new Moroccan king to attack Spanish territory and to make it look as if a blockade and siege of Gibraltar were being renewed (thus Britain would have to keep much of her land and sea forces in Europe, forestalling expeditions against Spanish America);

3. strengthening garrisons at La Coruña and Ferrol to protect against raids on arsenals there;

4. persuading the French to bring their naval forces from Toulon to Cádiz, to form a fleet superior to any the English might assemble;

5. proposing that the French mobilize troops in Brest and on the English Channel, "to give cause for apprehension in England and take advantage of any careless English move, in case the opponent had more than just a threat in mind and took its naval forces elsewhere, leaving its coast unguarded";

6. agreeing with the French upon an early rendezvous with the Span-

52. An original of the handbill, octavo size, belonged to J. J. Shalleross, of Victoria, B.C.; copy in CaBViPA (MM/N73).

53. Floridablanca, "Plan de lo que conviene hacer en las circunstancias actuales de España con Ynglaterra," Aranjuez, May 21, 1790, SpAHN (Estado 4291).

ish navy, so that neither group would be attacked by a superior fleet before joining forces;

7. "finishing the war quickly by a swift strike and landing in England —in accordance with the plan agreed upon in the last conflict but never carried out because of the timidity or poorly understood politics of Count Maurepas";

8. increasing the chances of French aid by sending a firm demand that Louis XVI "state what he can do and [then] carry it out by active measures; that otherwise he should not take offense if Spain sought other allies ready to come to her aid and satisfaction, without ruling out any other power" (By this means, if Louis should bow to the will of the French Assembly, "at least we will know what to expect from that Nation, and we can take other action, if we see that it [France] is entirely null.");

9. assembling on the south coast of Cuba as many troops as possible, together with a naval squadron, to make it appear that an expedition against Jamaica is contemplated;

10. renewing warnings and sending some frigates to America, particularly to Puerto Rico, Trinidad, and Honduras, to protect against any attack from Jamaica;

11. sending warnings to the Philippines by way of both Mexico and the Cape of Good Hope to insure their arrival;

12. continuing to solicit the support of Russia, and Denmark as well, while also persuading the Swedish to distrust England (Irish "patriots" should be encouraged to shake off the English yoke and ally with Spain; even the king of Prussia might be cultivated with some profit, as he showed signs of discontent with England);

13. continuing to reassure the king of Morocco by every means and at any expense, so he would not distract Spain's attention and energy at such a moment;

14. instructing the court at Lisbon of the justification for Spain's position, and demanding no more than what had been requested during the last war;

15. maintaining greater vigilance in the Canaries and Minorca than anywhere else, exposed as they were to English insults.

"In effect," Floridablanca closed, "we should make an offensive war, and examine means of accomplishing this with some success, for a defensive fight is impossible because of the many and distant points we have to guard." As for challenges in the Pacific, "it has already been agreed to send the ships and frigates which seem necessary."

This plan was submitted for perusal on a Friday and approved the following Monday (May 24) by the supreme council of state, which agreed to advise all viceroys and governors in the Indies of the possible rupture so they could take the necessary precautions. Two frigates were to leave at once for California, by way of Cape Horn, to aid in asserting Spanish dominion over the northwest coast. At its next meeting the council approved a proposal that Madrid base its position on the strongest diplomatic grounds available: Article VIII of the Treaty of Utrecht (1713), by which England had agreed that navigation and boundaries in America would remain the same as during the reign of Carlos II; this agreement had been specifically renewed by the Treaty of Paris (1763), which entitled Spain to prohibit British ships from operating along the Pacific coast of North America in areas claimed by Spain. The Spanish ambassador in London was advised accordingly.[54]

Floridablanca countered London's position that sovereignty depended upon effective occupation with a memorial in which he offered satisfaction for the Nootka incident but sustained Spanish claims to the northwest coast, reasoning that "Spain's not having fixed establishments on a coast, port, or bay does not prove that it is not hers; if this reasoning should prevail, any nation might establish herself on the very coasts of the dominions of another nation in America, Asia, Africa, and even Europe, where there might be no fixed establishment." [55] That same day Madrid sent a declaration of its views in the dispute to every major European court.

Alleyne Fitzherbert no sooner presented his credentials in Madrid than his discussions with Floridablanca reached an impasse. For an opener he presented a demand that Spain yield exclusive sovereignty to all the Pacific coast north of 31° north latitude, roughly the head of the Gulf of California. By such an exorbitant demand he probably hoped to reconcile his dismayed opponent to renouncing a substantial portion of the northwest coast. Floridablanca had already asserted that satisfaction for the seized vessels would not be granted unless Madrid's claim to sovereignty over Nootka was recognized. Fitzherbert rejected proposals that might have led to quick reparations, because indemnification was not Pitt's real objective. As Manning points out:

> The English Court had decided to force from Spain once and for all an
> acknowledgment of the British principle of colonization. Nothing less

---

54. Minutes, Council of State, May 24, 1790, SpAHN (Estado 919), fol. 108v–109, and May 31, 1790, fol. 111–11v.

55. Floridablanca to Merry, Aranjuez, June 4, 1790, SpAHN (Estado 4291), T in DLC (Manning Transcripts, p. 285), AT; "Declaration of His Catholic Majesty, June 4, transmitted to all the European Courts," in *Annual Register, 1790* 32 (1793) : 292–94. This was sent to France, Portugal, the Netherlands, Russia, Austria, Prussia, Denmark, and Sweden.

would be accepted. It was this, and not simply justice, that she demanded.[56]

Floridablanca assembled voluminous evidence from Spanish archives to prove Spain's rights to the northwest coast by prior discovery, but he found it impossible to shake Fitzherbert's insistence that Britain had a right to establish settlements there and elsewhere in America in unoccupied places.[57] Subsequent instructions allowed Fitzherbert to modify his demands to make them slightly more palatable: if satisfaction were given, the question of Spanish claims to the northwest coast would be discussed if Madrid could put forth any valid claims *other* than those previously enunciated: prior exploration and Martínez's occupation of Nootka in 1789![58] Spain's circular to the major European powers, stating the historical and legal bases for its claims to the northwest coast, merely prompted Fitzherbert to withdraw London's offer to discuss Madrid's pretensions in exchange for satisfaction. Negotiations could not resume, he asserted, until Spain met British demands for restoration, indemnity, and "satisfaction due to the sovereign for the injury done to his flag." He made no mention of discussing Spanish claims, the implication being that if the claims were not abandoned, Madrid should expect war. Floridablanca attempted to blunt such bellicosity by suggesting an alliance between Madrid and London if the revolutionary trend in France became more serious, a gambit that did not weaken Fitzherbert's stance.[59]

Madrid's predicament worsened when, on June 18 at the entrance to the Palace of Aranjuez, a fanatic French surgeon stepped forward as Floridablanca passed nearby and stabbed him twice in the left breast. The would-be assassin, Jean Paul Pairet, would have killed his victim had several lackeys not come to the rescue. It has never been shown that the attack was related to the Nootka crisis, and Pairet carried the secret of his political connections with him to the executioner. But Madrid took it for granted that he was a radical agent, because Floridablanca had endeavored to erect a *cordon sanitaire* between France and Spain to keep out revolutionary ideas and publi-

56. Manning, "Nootka Sound," p. 402.

57. One vestige of this effort is José García de León y Pizarro's "Compendio Histórico, y cronológico, que demuestra el descubrimiento del Mar del Sur, y de las Californias, hecho p(o)r los Españoles; y asimismo el fundamento, que asiste á España, para excluir á todas las naciones de la navegación de los mares de Yndias, y de establecerse, y comerciar en ellas," ICN (Ayer Collection). Compiled in response to a ministerial order (June 7, 1790), it extracted all royal orders relating to the northwest coast and was submitted on June 18, 1790. Subsequently augmented with additional data, it was presented to Godoy in 1796. The compiler would himself become prime minister in 1817.

58. Leeds to Pitt, June 2, 1790, UKLPRO (Chatham Papers 151), cited by Norris, "Policy," p. 577.

59. Fitzherbert to Leeds, June 16, 1790, UKLBM (Add. Mss. 28,066), fol. 32–34, cited in ibid., p. 578.

cations and the Jacobins saw in him an arch enemy.[60] The episode can be assumed to have left a lasting impression, but Floridablanca was already inclining away from the traditional French alliance and toward an understanding with Great Britain before the attempt on his life. The sixty-two-year-old diplomat made a remarkable recovery from his wounds, and negotiations with Fitzherbert soon resumed. There had not been time for an answer from Paris to the formal demand for support under the Family Compact. It would appear, however, that Floridablanca, uncertain about support from that quarter, had decided to compromise with Pitt's demands rather than continue on a course that almost certainly meant war. He proposed that, while Spain must retain Nootka Sound, she would share with Britain common rights from Nootka northward, and inland for twenty leagues. He also offered other concessions in the Pacific that Madrid had never before been willing to grant. Though rejected by Fitzherbert, these proposals disclosed the trend of subsequent adjustments. Floridablanca's indication of a willingness to compromise only served to reveal the uncertainty of Madrid's stance, and therefore strengthened Pitt's hand.

The crisis intensified after London scorned Madrid's request that the dispute be submitted to arbitration by a neutral sovereign, or that Britain prove its claims and offer guarantees for the protection of Spanish rights if satisfaction for the Nootka incident were granted. Sensing a deterioration in Madrid, Pitt pressed the opportunity and instructed Fitzherbert to insist that adequate satisfaction could be given only if Spain would give up her claims to exclusive sovereignty over the entire northwest coast, and he sent drafts of a declaration and counterdeclaration embodying such terms, to be pressed upon Carlos IV for quick action. The envoy presented them with the implication that they had to be accepted as the price of peace. Floridablanca eventually yielded almost completely, and the drafts were signed and exchanged on July 24.[61]

Word that Madrid had given in to these initial demands reached Whitehall on August 11. Spanish agreement to give compensation for the incident at Nootka did not erase the prospect of war, however, for now Pitt saw his way clear to insist upon the more important point toward which he had been maneuvering: the right of British subjects to settle and carry on commerce at places in America where Spain's claims had not been bolstered by actual settlements.

### DESTRUCTION OF THE FAMILY COMPACT

Pitt moved to head off French support for Madrid by sending Hugh Elliot and W. A. Miles, no strangers to diplomatic intrigue, on a supersecret mis-

60. Fernando Soldevila Zubiburu, *Historia de España*, 7 vols. (Barcelona, 1952–59), 6 : 99.

61. Leeds to Fitzherbert, July 5, 1790, UKLBM (Add. Mss. 34,431), fol. 33–36; "Declaration

sion to Paris. Elliot is most often recalled as British minister to Prussia, where in 1775 he supervised the pilfering of secret papers from American diplomat Arthur Lee's dispatch box. Elliot and Miles were provided with funds to bribe key figures in the French ministry and National Assembly, in the expectation of countering any tendency to rally behind Spain.[62] In effect, they sought nothing less than nullification of the Family Compact. Little is known of what they accomplished behind the scenes, but Pitt could take much encouragement from public developments.

At the first sign of British sabre-rattling over Nootka, Madrid turned out of habit to its traditional ally for a naval force sufficient to discourage conflict, but developments over the preceding months encouraged little optimism among the partisans of monarchy. The Bastille had fallen almost simultaneously with the incident at Friendly Cove. As political unrest intensified, Louis XVI and his family were summoned to Paris from Versailles at the people's demand and immobilized not by guards but by the populace, living in virtual confinement within the Tuileries. Yet Louis still exercised nominal power. Mirabeau and Lafayette, the leading figures of his court, headed a party of moderate reformers which enjoyed sufficient popularity to preserve an appearance close to normality.

Conferences had begun early in May between the Spanish ambassador, Conde de Fernán Núñez, and the French foreign minister, Comte de Montmorin, regarding the assistance Carlos IV might require from his royal cousin in the event of war over Nootka. Word of the Anglo-Spanish crisis precipitated a famous debate in the National Assembly, May 16 through 23, which is recognized as an important factor in the growth of revolutionary spirit and self-assurance.[63] On the political left the attack was led by Antoine-Joseph Barnave, reputedly the most powerful orator of his time, and by Robespierre, the two Lameths, and Adrien Duport. The moderate viewpoint was advocated by Mirabeau, Lafayette, Pierre Samuel Dupont de Nemours, Jacques Cazalès, and the Abbé Jean-Siffrein Maury. At issue was the monarch's prerogative to handle foreign policy and, in a case such as that arising from the Nootka Crisis, whether he had a right to elect a course that might entail war.

---

and Counter Declaration, exchanged at Madrid, the 24th July, 1790," *Annual Register, 1790* 32 (1793) : 300–01; Manning, "Nootka Sound," pp. 405–6; Norris, "Policy," p. 579.

62. Bemis, *Diplomacy*, pp. 115, 115n. Son of a baronet and brother of a member of Parliament, Elliot had also been minister to Denmark (1783–89), and was later governor of the Leeward Islands (1809–13) and Madras (1814–20). Aspinall, *Later Correspondence*, p. 223; Ricardo Caillet-Bois, "La Controversia del 'Nootka Sound' y el Río de la Plata," *Humanidades*, 20 (Buenos Aires, 1930) : 347; George Verne Blue, "Anglo-French Diplomacy During the Critical Period of the Nootka Controversy," *OHQ* 39 (1938) : 178.

63. Fernán Núñez to Floridablanca, Paris, May 11, 1790, SpAHN (Estado 4038); James M. Thompson, *The French Revolution*, 2d ed. (Oxford, 1962), p. 199.

The enemies of monarchy perceived that a war would tend to rally the people behind Louis and imperil the revolutionary trend. Orators of the left insisted that the crisis was no more than a counterrevolutionary intrigue between conniving monarchists, designed to whip up artificial enthusiasm for the throne by threat of a foreign war. They decried the Family Compact, dynastic wars, and secret diplomacy held in the king's hands, and they demanded revision of existing alliances to make them conform to the spirit of the times. In assailing the Family Compact and the Austrian Alliance, they recalled the part that such entanglements had played in the Seven Years' War and its deleterious effect upon France's fortunes. The Anglo-Spanish conflict over Nootka appeared to be a similar trap. The people, they asserted, should have the sole right to declare war, make treaties, and control major issues of diplomacy. If these things were left to the king, one orator exclaimed, "the whims of a mistress, the ambition of a minister, would decide the fate of a nation." The king was no more than an official of a nation, and he was obliged to implement its will. He should obey the decisions of the representatives of the people, who "would always have a direct and even a personal interest in preventing war." [64]

Orators of the right pointed to the Nootka Crisis as an example of excessive British ambition that France should oppose; they argued that diplomacy would best be left in the king's hands. Too many cooks spoil the broth, they said, and they deemed the National Assembly too numerous, unwieldy, and impressionable to handle diplomatic matters requiring great secrecy and speed. They warned against depriving the monarch of so much power that he would become merely a symbol, shorn of prestige.

When the crucial vote came, on May 23, the radicals carried the day, amending Montmorin's request for a decree in ways that changed its sense. The king retained a right to propose peace or war, but the Assembly would have the power of veto. When hostilities threatened, the king would be obliged to make the causes and motives known to the Assembly. Treaties of peace, alliance, or commerce henceforth would not be valid until ratified by the Assembly. A diplomatic committee was appointed to examine existing treaties and set them in accord with the Constitution. In short, the king's prerogatives in foreign policy and diplomacy were reduced to the conduct of diplomatic negotiations, subject always to the Assembly's ratification. As a special article of the decree, the Assembly declared piously that "the French nation renounced entering upon any war with a view to conquest, and would never use its forces against the liberty of any people." [65] Partisans of the revo-

64. Albert Mathiez, *The French Revolution* (New York, 1962), pp. 71–72. For a firsthand account of the debate, see William Short to John Jay, Paris, May 16 and May 23, 1790, in Jefferson, *Papers*, 16 : 430–32, 436–40.

65. "Decree of the National Assembly of France on the Family Compact," in *Annual Register, 1790* 32 (1793) : 303.

lution hailed its passage as a triumph. The Nootka crisis had contributed substantially to Louis XVI's predicament, and the resounding debate in the National Assembly had yielded a decree so modified and weakened as to offer little assurance in Madrid that it would be honored should war occur.

When a formal request for assistance under the Family Compact, dated June 16, reached the Conde de Fernán Núñez, he presented it at once to Montmorin, but it was not made known to the National Assembly for more than six weeks, a circumstance attributed to Louis's hesitancy, the consequence of his steady decline in power.[66] Records of Spain's supreme council of state shed additional light on the matter, revealing that Madrid's demand caused fear and dismay within the Tuileries, and that Louis's delay in confronting the National Assembly had the consent and sympathy of Carlos IV. The degree of alarm in the French royal household is testified by a dispatch from Fernán Núñez in Paris describing efforts made to get the Spanish demand withdrawn. He had been summoned to a secret meeting with Marie Antoinette in the quarters of her daughter's governess. The queen disclosed her feelings of uncertainty for monarchy's fate, which was very likely to be revealed at the upcoming "Fête de la Fédération," commemorating the first anniversary of the Bastille's fall. She was perturbed "that to try to negotiate the matter of our memorial before that day had passed would be to give rise to excitation, whose results could not be favorable to us and would be truly damaging to the king's party, and even perhaps to his own existence and that of his family—to this state her fears have progressed." She hoped that Carlos IV would be satisfied with a reply from the king, without demanding that the matter be put before the National Assembly.[67]

The ambassador had responded that "the Spanish memorial made no mention of the National Assembly, although its role was implicitly understood, because without its consent the sovereign's best intentions now are null: for which reason it is impossible for him to be content with anything casting the slightest shadow of uncertainty, impossibility, and even inactivity in execution of what has been stipulated, according to the clear and positive orders that he has received." Although Lafayette (no longer marquis, but commander in chief of the national guard) had met Fernán Núñez on only one previous occasion, he sought out the ambassador to make substantially the same plea as the queen. Montmorin also approached the conde with a similar remonstrance, to receive the identical answer. The very night that Carlos IV received Fernán Núñez's message, he dispatched by extraordinary post a reply, which Floridablanca presented to the supreme council for their confidential inspection. Carlos wrote:

66. Mathiez, *French Revolution*, pp. 72–73; Fernán Núñez to Comte de Montmorin, Paris, June 16, 1790, in ibid., pp. 301–03.

67. Minutes, Council of State, July 5, 1790, SpAHN (Estado 919), fol. 125v–26, AT.

That His Majesty, after reflecting maturely upon all the events and reasons set forth by the ambassador, has resolved to suspend presentation of said memorial as long as there is the slightest risk of it producing agitation and movements prejudicial to the sovereign or nation. That in case there are no such risks, he will limit the memorial to references to or copies of papers and official letters that on our part have been extended and communicated in the matter of the dispute with London, and conclude with liberal expressions of the letter-order of June 4. And finally, of course you will declare secretly to the Christian king and his ministry, that in view of the impossibility of that court's currently fulfilling usefully what is stipulated in the Family Pact, His Majesty considers himself honestly and reciprocally free to take other resolves, if necessity obliges him to do so; although in this he would never lose sight of the consideration due a sovereign relative and friend, and a nation with which we have had, until now, so many motives for good correspondence. This secret declaration should be in the precise terms in which it is expressed.[68]

This heretofore unpublished exchange provides a rare glimpse of the anguish Carlos IV was undergoing because of the plight of his French cousin. Marie Antoinette's forebodings about the anniversary of the Bastille's fall were allayed when Lafayette staged an elaborate spectacle for the occasion. Possessing immense personal popularity, the hero of the American Revolution was acclaimed deliriously by the crowds. Accompanying him at the *fête,* Louis and his queen basked in the general applause, "which seemed to mark the harmonious unity of all Frenchmen." [69]

Late in August, when Montmorin finally presented Carlos IV's request to the French Assembly, the heated debate that ensued resulted in the substitution of a national agreement between France and Spain for the old Family Compact; only the old defensive and commercial articles were preserved. Although a Franco-Spanish alliance was nominally sustained, the weakened arrangement served warning on Madrid that it could no longer count upon France as a makeweight in the confrontation with Britain. Nonetheless, the National Assembly voted to arm forty-five ships of the line, hoping that such step would influence a peaceful settlement of the controversy. The English ambassador asked for an explanation, and was assured by Mont-

68. Ibid., fol. 126v–27, AT.

69. Leo Gershoy, *The French Revolution and Napoleon* (New York, 1933), p. 175; Mathiez, *French Revolution*, p. 73. Fernán Núñez had gained the queen's lasting confidence, and upon seeking means of escape to the protection of a friendly monarch, she again made him privy to her most secret thoughts. He held out no hope, so she found assistance elsewhere for the attempt of June 20, 1791, when the royal family set out in disguise for the northeast border but was recognized and arrested at Varennes, just short of safety. James Thompson, *French Revolution,* pp. 198–203.

morin that armament would be carried out with "the greatest slowness." Two days later, Louis XVI wrote Carlos IV that mobilization would proceed with "all possible activity." [70]

Ambassador Miguel de Gálvez had been instructed to seek support in St. Petersburg, but he replied that although there had been no negotiations for an alliance with London, Russia would not back Spain because of the tsarina's fear of alienating Britain.[71]

The last week in August 1790 witnessed the highpoint of tension and anxiety in Madrid, London, and Paris over the possibility of a war because of the Nootka incident. At that moment few could foresee whether either side would back away from the brink of the abyss.

PITT'S ULTIMATUM

London's most ambitious demand, recognition of the right of British subjects to settle in spots claimed by Spain but not actually settled, met with the stiffest resistance in Madrid. Throughout August and September, Floridablanca and Fitzherbert strived to find a basis for agreement while preparations for war continued on each side. The Spanish and British citizenry had no means of reassurance that hostilities could be avoided. The British cabinet agreed that if Richard Earl Howe, admiral of the fleet cruising in the Bay of Biscay:

> should find that the Spanish fleet are approaching to the latitude of Brest, he should signify to the Spanish Admiral that he expects the Spanish fleet should return to their own coasts; apprising the Spanish Admiral if necessary that he is ordered to consider a refusal, under the existing circumstances, as evidence of hostile intentions, and to act accordingly. And that if the Spanish Admiral should not comply with this intimation Lord Howe should proceed in consequence thereof to treat the Spanish ships as vessels belonging to an enemy.[72]

By the time word reached Madrid of the uncertain measures taken by the French Assembly, Floridablanca and Fitzherbert had reached the approximate terms of a convention. Pitt's instructions permitted an adjustment of wording so as to avoid offending Madrid by requiring a complete and humiliating renunciation of rights, but the British leader cautioned that the convention must not contain an admission of Spanish claims to Nootka.

During those turbid weeks, the Spanish court followed the royal couple to the Escorial and then to La Granja, away from Madrid's heat. The unhappy

70. George Granville Leveson, dispatch of August 27, 1790; Louis XVI to Carlos IV, August 28, 1790, cited by Blue, "Anglo-French Diplomacy," p. 170.

71. Miguel de Gálvez to Floridablanca, St. Petersburg, August 4, 1790, SpAHN (Estado 4631).

72. Cabinet minute, [Whitehall, August 31, 1790], Fortescue Archive (Grenville Papers), Dropmore, Eng., cited by Aspinall, *Later Correspondence*, p. 494.

monarch could elude the oppressive temperature but not the diplomatic pressure to which he was being subjected. Louis XVI's assurances no longer carried much weight with his royal cousin, who by now was cognizant that he must go it alone, shorn of the defunct Family Compact. In a conversation with Fitzherbert on September 13, Floridablanca let slip an admission that proved a tactical error: he confided that Carlos IV abhorred the national compact offered by the French Assembly and actually preferred an alliance with George III, if Britain would cease badgering Spain over Nootka. There was good reason to fear recent developments in Paris, where monarchy was being inexorably undermined. Prospects of the French example's influence within Spanish borders made king and prime minister ponder the consequences of embarking upon war while such a danger loomed. The very day that he broached the possibility of an Anglo-Spanish alliance, Floridablanca presented the supreme council of state with a draft of a treaty tentatively agreed upon with Fitzherbert and asked the members to state their opinions at the next session. As the wording stood, the treaty represented a substantial compromise on Madrid's part, into which Floridablanca had been maneuvered by adroit diplomacy and the exigencies of Spain's perilous position.[73]

Floridablanca's concessions were futile and only served to reveal the debility of Madrid's hand, encouraging Pitt to press his advantage and squeeze a more bounteous vintage from the Nootka affair while Carlos IV's embarrassment lasted. As Floridablanca's stance faltered, Pitt stiffened his bellicosity. The crisis could not be prolonged indefinitely, for public criticism was beginning to mount in England over the expense of sustaining the martial display without obtaining notable satisfaction. Perceiving that Carlos IV no longer entertained hope of help from Paris, Pitt pushed aside the draft upon which Floridablanca and Fitzherbert had labored for months and dispatched to Madrid two alternate drafts of a new convention much more favorable to British interests. He instructed Fitzherbert to tender an ultimatum to the effect that he would break off negotiations and leave if Floridablanca did not agree to one or the other draft within ten days.[74] Increased preparations for war intensified the effect of the ultimatum. Floridablanca advised the supreme council of state that London had gone back to insisting upon its earlier pretensions. "And since this matter is one of the most grave

73. "Proyecto de convención con Inglaterra," September 8, 1790, SpAHN (Estado 4291), T in DLC (Manning Transcripts, 294–301); "Plan que fue á Londres acordado con el embaxador," [September 8] 1790, SpAHN (Estado 4291), T in DLC (Manning Transcripts, 323–25); minutes, Council of State, September 13, 1790, SpAHN (Estado 919), fol. 140.

74. "Nuevo proyecto Inglés propuesto por el Señor Embaxador de Inglaterra," October 14, 1790, SpAHN (Estado 4291), T in DLC (Manning Transcripts, 325–27). As of November 11, 1790, expenses were calculated at £3,072,114 9s. 8d. "Accounts, as far as can be made up, of the expences of the armament on account of the Dispute with Spain, up to Nov. 11, 1790, presented to the House of Commons," in *Scots Magazine*, 1791, Reprinted in Marshall, *Pacific Voyages*, pp. 92–93.

that could occur, because of its consequences," the prime minister "was of the opinion that, before making a decision, the king should listen to a junta which he had ordered to be formed, composed of the councillors of state, governors of the councils, and other ministers, to whom all the facts would be sent, informing it likewise of our present interior and exterior situation, so that it can form its opinions with complete knowledge of everything." [75]

The junta began its deliberations three days later in Floridablanca's offices in Madrid's Palacio de Oriente, meeting in secret and without ceremony, etiquette, or rules of precedence. It reached a verdict on October 25, declaring that "since Great Britain has augmented her unjust pretensions as our conduct has moderated, this demonstrates that the Nootka matter was a mask which chance provided for British ambition in order to cover her hostile designs, which most likely had been conceived as soon as the internal revolutions of France offered her a favorable occasion to take on, successively, the divided members of the house of Bourbon." [76] The junta predicted that the concessions sought by Pitt would permit English settlements at many places in Spanish America, and it declared that the conditions and articles of the drafts newly arrived from London were "in no way admissible, being firmly convinced that such sacrifices, if made now, would produce so rapid and unfortunate an effect as soon to oblige His Majesty to undertake the very war which we desire to avoid, but one which would be made more costly, ruinous, and ineffective, in recovering domains ceded or usurped as a result of the very concessions made to elude the present evil and postpone the hard necessity and last extreme of a recourse to arms." [77] They were of the opinion that a clash was preferable to yielding to Pitt's demands. Allies should be sought and precautions taken against enemy attack. To make concessions would only bring other disputes and eventually war, and England would then have the convention with which to support its stance. The junta's advice amounted to a recommendation for a declaration of war.

Carlos IV, María Luisa, and Floridablanca had been followed to La Granja by the British ambassador several days before the junta commenced its deliberations, and while the councillors were arriving at their militant decision, Fitzherbert was pressing upon Floridablanca, and through him upon the king, the advisability of accepting Pitt's terms. Initially the shrewdly worded drafts were rejected, but, by dint of slight modifications, Fiztherbert slowly got

75. Minutes, Council of State, October 18, 1790, SpAHN (Estado 919), fol. 146v, AT. Members of the junta were the duque de Almodóvar and Don Manuel Flores of the Council of State, conde de Campomanes and Don Miguel de Mendinueta of the royal council, Don Juan Joseph de Vertiz and Don Francisco Saavedra of the council of war, and the conde de Tepa and Don Bernardo Yriarte of the council of Indies. Yriarte acted as secretary.

76. "Dictamen de la Junta sobre lo que conviene hacer referente a la disputa con Inglaterra," October 25, 1790, SpAHN (Estado 4291 bis), fol. 4–4v, AT.

77. Ibid., fol. 12v–13, AT.

them accepted. He was skilled at playing his cards for maximum effect. Subsequently the opponents transferred their dickering to the Escorial, following the royal couple, until Floridablanca yielded almost word for word to
one of the drafts dictated by Pitt.[78] At word of this, the supreme council of
state decided that, although the junta had recommended resistance rather
than an unfavorable convention, "it seemed that under the circumstances it
is as favorable as can be expected, and that gratitude is merited by the zeal,
ability, and prudence with which the Count [of Floridablanca] has labored
to avoid a ruinous war, without any objective that would justify it." [79] The
junta's deliberations notwithstanding, the final decision in favor of peace
was made within the walls of the Escorial. There, on October 28, 1790, in a
regal salon of the palace epitomizing Spain's majestic past, Floridablanca
and Fitzherbert put their signatures to the Nootka Convention, a pact that
in hindsight marks a watershed in Iberian history, the perceptible inception
of an ebb tide in empire.

Some Spanish historians attribute to the imperious and self-indulgent
queen the responsibility for following the course of appeasement to avoid
war, with the dangers, diminished revenues, and expenses it would entail.
This opinion regards the episode as part of her effort to destroy Floridablanca's ascendancy over Carlos IV. But when the convention is examined
against the background of events in Paris, secret communications with Marie
Antoinette, and Spain's perilous position, one need not invoke María Luisa's
influence to explain her husband's backing down. The terms of the convention gave London every objective that government had been pursuing, so
the specter of war vanished as quickly as it had appeared. Ratifications were
exchanged within a month's time. As Bemis remarks, "Pitt won the fruits
of a war without firing a gun." [80]

### THE NOOTKA CONVENTION OF 1790

As are many treaties, the Anglo-Spanish Convention of 1790 is sufficiently
complicated in wording to be ambiguous, hence palatable to even the less
satisfied of the parties. Several articles are susceptible to widely varying inter-
pretations, especially when translated from the original French to English
or Spanish. Article one stated: "It is agreed that the buildings and tracts of
land situated on the Northwest Coast of the continent of North America, or
on islands adjacent to that continent, of which the subjects of His Britannic

---

78. Fitzherbert to Floridablanca, San Ildefonso, October 23, 1790, SpAHN (Estado 4291);
Floridablanca to Yriarte, San Ildefonso, October 23, 1790, SpAHN (Estado 2848); Fitzherbert to
Floridablanca, San Lorenzo [del Escorial], October 26, 1790, SpAHN (Estado 4291); Floridablanca
to Yriarte, San Lorenzo, October 26, 1790, SpAHN (Estado 2848); T of all four in DLC (Manning
Transcripts, 302, 366, 381).

79. Minutes, Council of State, October 27, 1790, SpAHN (Estado 919), fol. 148, AT.

80. Bemis, *Diplomatic History*, p. 88.

Majesty were dispossessed about the month of April, 1789, by a Spanish officer, shall be restored to the said British subjects." [81] In agreeing to this, Madrid inexorably conceded exclusive dominion over Nootka Sound. At the least, a part of Friendly Cove would be restored to Meares and his associates. The convention places the initial clash as "about the month of April 1789," an error of fact. The first seizure occurred on the May 13. Why this inaccuracy, when Floridablanca had ample time to be aware of the proper date? If Floridablanca did not yet know the true date and Fitzherbert possessed more accurate knowledge, the Briton may have been seeking to outwit his opposite number by specifying "about" April, knowing that Madrid would find it impossible to prove a Spanish establishment at Nootka by April 1789, thus destroying Spain's claim to Nootka and fatally weakening any pretension to exclusive sovereignty north of San Francisco Bay. Or was Floridablanca knowingly compelled to accept such wording as the price of peace? As we shall see, several weeks after the convention he submitted a memorial defending the diplomatic accord, asserting that it did not give Britain any claim to the coastline from Nootka southward. If we take his statement at face value, his agreement to the seizure's approximate date was made in good faith and he was unaware of the inaccuracy. If this be the case, it highlights the ignorance under which he labored regarding details of the clash.

The convention's second article obliged Spain to make reparation for all seizures and dispossessions committed since April 1789. In article three, each party agreed not to obstruct the other's subjects from navigating, fishing, trading with the natives, or making settlements on the shores of the Pacific Ocean "in places not already occupied," subject to restrictions in the next three articles. In article four, Britain assumed responsibility for taking measures to keep its subjects from using the right to navigate and fish in the Pacific as a pretext for illicit trade with Spanish settlements. To this end, they should not approach within ten leagues of any coast already occupied by Spain. Article five, the most significant part for Pacific Northwest history, stipulated: "It is agreed that in the places which are to be restored to British subjects by virtue of the first article as well as in all other parts of the Northwest Coast of North America or of the islands adjacent, situated to the north of the parts of the said coast already occupied by Spain, wherever the subjects of either of the two powers shall have made settlements since the month

81. *Convención entre el Rey Nuestro Señor y el Rey de la Gran Bretaña, transigiendo varios puntos sobre pesca, navegación y comercio en el Océano Pacífico y los Mares del Sur, firmada en San Lorenzo el Real á 28 de octubre de 1790, cuyas ratificaciones se canjearon en el mismo sitio á 22 de noviembre siguiente* (Madrid, [1790]); first British edition in Burges, *Narrative* (1791, in French), pp. 292–97; first edition in English in *Annual Register, 1790* 32 (1793): 303–05; modern edition in English in Manning, "Nootka Sound," pp. 454–56, from which portions quoted here are taken. See appendix B for the Spanish version.

of April 1789, or shall hereafter make any, the subjects of the other shall have free access and shall carry on their commerce without disturbance or molestation." [82]

The French original reads *depuis* the month of April 1789, which translates into Spanish as either *desde* (since) or *después de* (after). When published in Spanish and English translations, *depuis* was rendered as *desde* and *since*. Floridablanca interpreted the pact as entitling Britain to coastal access solely from Nootka northward. The British consistently construed article five as giving subjects of both nations free access to the coast north of the northernmost Spanish settlement extant in April 1789. (Martínez had arrived at Nootka on May 5.) The latter interpretation permitted the British to make settlements anywhere north of San Francisco Bay, to which the Spanish would also have free access. However, from 1790 onward, British cartographers were wont to depict His Britannic Majesty's domains as extending to just short of San Francisco. Was Floridablanca aware of the linguistic ambiguity, and did he let the equivocal word stand, so as to provide a loophole while yielding to Pitt the concession that his ultimatum demanded? Did Fitzherbert employ a semantic snare to secure a point not otherwise accessible? Floridablanca's answers to these questions will be examined shortly. As a consequence of the ambiguity in article five, Spanish and British statesmen subsequently felt legally and morally justified in their respective and mutually exclusive positions regarding the coastline between Nootka and San Francisco.

Article six prohibited any future settlements by either party in South America to the south of existing Spanish settlements. Article seven committed both nations to report any infractions of the convention, rather than to commit violence or assault upon the other. In eight it was agreed to exchange ratifications within six weeks. A final, secret article agreed that article six would cease to be binding should a third nation make a settlement on the coast in question, that of Patagonia.

Pitt's carefully tailored draft, forced down Madrid's throat by ultimatum, was designed to extract recognition that Spain had no sovereignty over areas in North and South America beyond its northern and southernmost settlements made prior to the Nootka incident. Relinquishment of exclusive sovereignty over Nootka Sound was a blow to national pride, but the area had not yet yielded any appreciable benefit to Spain. And by making concessions concerning the northwest coast, Floridablanca secured Britain's agreement to stipulations that he hoped would check British territorial and commercial encroachments elsewhere in the New World. Britain had promised to employ effective measures to prevent her subjects from using fishing and whaling in the South Atlantic and Pacific as a pretext for illicit

82. "Convention," in Manning, "Nootka Sound," pp. 455–56.

commerce with Spanish colonies, a major source of grievance to Madrid. Moreover, British subjects could not approach Spanish American shores closer than ten maritime leagues, a stipulation that Madrid found very attractive.

When the respective ratifications were ready for exchange, Floridablanca submitted to the Supreme Council an explanation for overruling the junta's advice. "I was ordered to tell you to manifest to the junta and to each individual in it," he declared, "the royal gratitude for the punctiliousness with which they set forth their opinions, assuring them that His Majesty would not have delayed an instant in conforming entirely to their advice if motives absolutely secret to his person had not obliged him to order the signing of the convention, a copy of which I enclose, improved in some points relative to the plans or projects that the junta has seen." He also remitted "the accompanying 'reflections' which His Majesty took into consideration in addition to the enunciated secret motives, so that the junta, with all secrecy, can understand in great part the concept and sense of the convention." [83] So sensitive were these papers considered that Floridablanca advised returning them without making a copy. The prime consideration had been to avert war, especially in view of the unfavorable circumstances in which Spain found herself, that is, without useful allies, money, or credit to carry on a foreign war. The accord had merely consented to what was actually being practiced by the English in fishing, navigation, and commerce. It did not mean absolute renouncement of Spanish rights on the northwest coast, but Britain would lose her rights there unless she adhered to the pact's stipulations. No other country would have any rights there unless it made a similar agreement, which could be granted or denied, as chosen. Article five, he stressed, did not speak of places that had been "populated, inhabited, or actually occupied." Since it referred to places "already occupied" by Spain as of April 1789, it could be construed to justify Spain's title to areas acquired prior to that date by formal acts of possession.[84]

Floridablanca's inaccurate knowledge of events at Friendly Cove in 1789 is again demonstrated by his assertion that, "when the Spanish Commander Martínez arrived in Nootka, employees of the English expedition who were there before him and had come over in Portuguese ships, had made or had begun work on a house or shed, and as a result of what Martínez did, those works were taken down or suspended." He was mistaken; there is no

83. Floridablanca to Yriarte, San Lorenzo, November 21, 1790, SpAHN (Estado 919), fol. 148, AT.

84. "Porque no se habla de los *poblados, ó ó no,* ni de los *habitados, desamparados, desiertos,* ú de los *ocupados actualmente;* sino de los *no ocupados ó ocupados ya* y adquerido su dominio, aunque sea en otro tiempo." Floridablanca, "Reflexiones sobre la convención hecha con Ynglaterra en 28 de Octubre de 1790," SpAHN (Estado 4291), fol. 1–1v, AT.

evidence of such activity ashore in 1789 by anyone but the Americans, prior to Martínez's arrival. From such a misunderstanding Floridablanca could conclude: "therefore, in a sense it is certain that British subjects were dispossessed of some land and buildings," so Spain would be obliged to return the land and make a just reparation.[85] Had he possessed more accurate information, his negotiations with Fitzherbert could have proceeded from a stronger initial position.

He reasoned that "since we are established in Nootka and the concurrence and settlements of the English are permissible only *to the north* of those ports of the coast *already occupied* by Spain, according to article five of this convention, we have managed to restrict these dangerous neighbors to more than 200 leagues from the northernmost settlement in our California, while we retain liberty to frequent, traffic in skins, and establish ourselves on the more northern and Asiatic coast and adjacent islands, the same as the English, Russians, and other nationalities." The risk of British settlements on that coast of sufficient size to threaten Spanish domain was negligible, since there were Russian competitors, well established at eight different spots, who looked with jealousy upon the English traffic and would do everything possible to limit and obstruct it. "We have approached the Russian court to see if it could join in a boundary settlement with us in that area, and thus combine Russian ideas with ours," he confided, "but while we were not refused the matter has been postponed and avoided, since that court doesn't wish to become embroiled with England." The northwest coast's enormous distance from England had obliged British ships operating there to depend on Macao. Floridablanca suggested that negotiation with Lisbon might put a check upon such operations. He acknowledged the reality of London's position, for the Pacific Ocean bathed innumerable islands and shores, and "there is no power or navy in all the world capable of monopolizing and preventing entry and settlement in those seas." London had proposed negotiating a specific boundary, which might be desirable "to cover not only our coasts, but also our interior possessions, and avoid, even from 55° and above, the penetration by English subjects." Madrid's most important objective had been to get London's agreement to article six, promising not to make permanent establishments in southernmost South America. For this reason the convention consented to what was already taking place—landings and the construction of temporary sheds for use by fishermen. Fitzherbert had resisted specifying "adjacent islands" as well, but eventually "it was managed to get them included, and this makes us presume that the English had designs of establishing themselves there, and even on the coasts of the continent." [86]

85. Ibid., fol. 2, AT.
86. Ibid., fol. 2–4v, AT.

Floridablanca's "Reflections" offer no clues as to Carlos IV's "motives absolutely secret to his person" for yielding to drastic and humiliating concessions rather than risking a war. Doubtless the fear of fighting without allies, while having revolutionary turmoil next door, loomed large in the monarch's mind, but this had been admitted to the council, as had Marie Antoinette's pleas. Carlos would be inviting contempt if he hinted at yielding to pressure from within his own household. Was the phrase a device, comparable to a top secret classification, employed to disguise pusillanimity at the highest level of decision making? The known documentation gives no further clue.

The convention was the most satisfactory accord possible, Floridablanca asserted, given Spain's precarious situation. He nursed the conviction that it did not weaken Madrid's claim to the coast from Nootka southward, and to the interior of the continent even beyond 55° north latitude. How unrealistic! No matter how many loopholes Floridablanca thought he saw in the accord, Pitt contrived to have it worded so that ever afterward it bound Madrid in semantic coils that weakened her claims to everything north of San Francisco. This is what London sought and, justifiably or not, this is the way most historians have since interpreted the convention.

Not long afterward, Under Secretary Burges stated the official British view of the accord's significance: that by agreeing to restitution at Nootka, Spain had conceded the principle that "her exclusive right was not admitted to extend beyond her actual possession." [87] As translated and published in London, the convention gave British subjects the right to frequent and settle on the Pacific Coast of North America beyond the northernmost spot actually occupied by the Spanish prior to April 1789. Since this version differed greatly from Madrid's interpretation, the impression that a settlement had been reached was illusory. Trouble would ensue as long as the two nationalities held mutually exclusive viewpoints regarding the territory between Nootka and California.

Canadian historian Lennox Mills has asserted that in essence the Nootka controversy reflected an inevitable conflict between mutually exclusive principles of sovereignty, but J. M. Norris, an Englishman, points to inconsistencies in British practice which reveal Pitt's stance of 1790 as dictated by something less than noble defense of principle.[88] In previous decades in Georgia, Honduras, and on the Mosquito Coast, it had been in Britain's interest to subscribe to the theory that sovereignty derived from occupation rather than discovery. However, English claims to Newfoundland had rested for centuries upon claims of discovery without actual occupation. Before 1790 London had recognized as Spanish territory certain areas in the New

87. Burges, *Letters,* pp. 52–53.
88. Mills, "Nootka Sound Incident," pp. 110 ff.

World that had no civilized inhabitants. The "occupation principle" was invoked during the Nootka Crisis, Norris asserts, to justify British activities in areas known to be claimed by Spain, "to give a gloss of respectability to a ruthless act of expropriation; and the decision to commit that act was not occasioned primarily by a desire to correct injustice, still less by a coherent theory of imperial domain." Norris believes that "Domestic political considerations in an election year, the ambitions of certain trading interests, and the desire to secure Britain's position in Europe determined British policy in the crisis of 1790." [89]

Despite the promise in article four that Britain would "employ the most effective measures" to guard against abuses by its subjects, the convention opened the floodgates for British contraband runners all along the Pacific coast of the Americas. The consequences of this bear comparison to the notorious *asiento* in the Treaty of Utrecht (1713), one of the spoils of the War of Spanish Succession (Queen Anne's War), whereby London wrested from Madrid the privilege of sending one slave ship a year to the trade fair in Puerto Bello, Panama; this article served as an umbrella for British smugglers encountered thereafter by Spanish warships in the Caribbean. Until the 1790 convention, British vessels in Spanish waters along the Pacific coast were exposed to capture on sight; henceforth they could cruise the coast at will, as long as they avoided being caught trafficking at spots controlled by Spain. The Nootka convention eased the way for smuggling British merchandise into areas along the west coast of the Americas, where there was considerable demand for such articles as were heavily taxed, more expensive, or not available through regular Spanish channels. At once British ships became more frequent visitors to the coastal waters of Chile, Peru, and Argentina. Spanish archives contain a wealth of documentation, which increased rapidly in volume soon after 1790, of instances in which English vessels called at minor ports on one pretext or another and engaged in illicit commerce.[90] Petty smuggling was no mere annoyance to Spanish authorities; mercantilist doctrine held that such activities, by draining off an incalculable volume of specie, sapped the vitality of the empire.

Had Spain refused to knuckle under to Pitt's ultimatum, there is little doubt that war would have ensued. George III told the French ambassador that, at the climax of the crisis, pressure being put upon Madrid had him greatly preoccupied:

> For two days I did not sleep, and I ate very little; I was in a state of
> mortal disquiet at the news I was receiving from Spain, and I confess

89. Norris, "Policy," p. 580.

90. For a number of *expedientes* concerning such violations at the Peruvian ports of Supe, Chancay, Quilca, Pisco, Huarmey, Sechura, and Tumbes, see SpAHN (Estado 4285 bis).

that I was convinced that there would be war. I reproached myself for nothing; I had asked only what my conscience told me I owed to the honor of my crown. But although I did not go a step beyond what strict justice prescribed, I could not envisage without shuddering the woes that were, perhaps, going to overwhelm my subjects and those of my neighbors.[91]

Had George III been aware of the seamier aspects of the incident upon which Pitt chose to stake British honor, the crown would have rested even heavier upon his brow. As for his inexperienced counterpart in the Escorial, Martínez's zeal to protect Spain's interest at remote Nootka and the frightening trend in Paris had combined to place Carlos IV in a position fraught with peril. Spain was ill prepared to fight single-handed against the one nation powerful enough on the seas to sever Madrid's vital connection with its sources of wealth in America. Shorn of his traditional protection— the Family Compact—Carlos was unwilling to be swept into a dangerous war over a far-off, uncolonized coastline of debatable relevance to Spain's vital interests, where lines of supply and defense were too extenuated to insure success. To back away from hostilities, Carlos IV bowed to concessions that eventually brought about the liquidation of Spanish sovereignty over the northwest coast. The Nootka Convention of 1790 has been called "the first decisive step in a series of events by which the English-speaking people in America extended their territory and their sphere of influence at the expense of Spain." [92] The Nootka crisis signals the beginning of the end of the Spanish Empire in America. Madrid's territorial claims in 1789 stretched from Tierra del Fuego to Alaska's Prince William Sound, and from outposts in Africa to the Marianas and the Philippines—indeed, the high tide of Spanish imperial ambition. But with the crisis an ebb became apparent that within a very few years would tear apart that proud domain, a tide sweeping away in its relentless undertow the finest jewels in the vast crown of colonies bequeathed by Isabel la Católica, Carlos V, and Felipe II. The thirty-four-year period from 1790 to 1824 saw Spain removed from the first rank of world powers by the combined effects of diplomatic blackmail, forced territorial cessions, political chaos, internal revolution, invasion, and conquest. By the 1830s mere vestiges of an empire that had stretched around the world still remained in Madrid's hands—an ignominious decline from eminence—and the initial setback over Nootka's "cat skins" had long since faded from memory.

91. Conversation with the Comte de la Luzerne, at the king's levée on November 4, 1790, as reported by La Luzerne to Montmorin, November 5, 1790, no. 62, France, Archives des Affaires Étrangères, Paris (Cor. Pol. Angl. vol. 575), fol. 151–59, cited by Blue, "Anglo-French Diplomacy," pp. 170–74.

92. W. S. Robertson, *AHA Annual Report, 1907*, p. 284.

Reflecting upon this process, one cannot help wondering about the consequences had Floridablanca been as willing as the junta to go to war. Could
he have swayed Carlos IV in that direction? Throughout his reign the mild-
mannered sovereign was led by either his chief ministers or his wife. If
hostilities rather than appeasement had resulted from Nootka, Madrid was
prepared to move with vigor to assert her claim over western North America.
Despite handicaps at San Blas, Spain enjoyed the advantage of bases around
the Pacific's rim from Chile to the Philippines. Thus, the northwest coast
would have witnessed a much greater expenditure of Spanish efforts, with
such political, ethnic, and toponymic consequences as resulted where Spanish
dominion was of longer duration. On the other hand, an Anglo-Spanish war
in 1790, without French assistance, might have been disastrous for Madrid,
depriving her of the areas most vulnerable to British attack, such as Louisiana or California. The standoff in 1790, aside from preserving the peace,
made it impossible for either contender to assert exclusive pretensions to
Nootka and the adjacent coast, and with the passage of time both Madrid
and London became reconciled to having their sovereignty on that far-off
shore be something less than exclusive.

### NOOTKA AND FLORIDABLANCA'S DOWNFALL

The diplomatic defeat suffered at Pitt's hands over Nootka was bitterly
criticized in Spain for years to come. Floridablanca's failure to devise a more
favorable solution than the humiliating treaty, signed virtually at gun point,
served as the ostensible, if not the real, reason for his removal after fifteen
years at the helm of government. Developments in Paris undermined Floridablanca's position in Madrid. His efforts to keep revolutionary ideas and
institutional changes expounded by the French National Assembly out of
Spain earned him implacable enemies in France, and these men brought
pressure to bear upon Carlos IV for the prime minister's removal. But it
was the faithful official's stance regarding intimate affairs within the royal
household that led to his actual removal from office on February 28, 1792,
following an angry scene in which he denounced the conduct of María
Luisa and Godoy. The mortified sovereign is reported to have flown into a
terrible rage, heaping insults and reproach on his wife. Subsequently, however, something transpired to change his mind, for at dawn the next day an
official came to Floridablanca's bedchamber to warn of a royal order of
banishment from the monarch's residence.[93] Again the queen triumphed
over her husband's will, and "Manuelito" remained within the royal bosom,
more entrenched than ever. From his home in the little Murcian town of
Hellín, Floridablanca sent a series of thirteen memorials to the ministry in

93. Soldevila, *Historia*, 6 : 99–100.

the following weeks. A recent editor has aptly labeled them his "political testament." Looking back over the Nootka Sound controversy, he remarked:

> When the French Revolution put France in the condition of being a useless ally for Spain and the latter was judged to be alone in any war effort, England seized upon the pretext of the occurrence at Nootka and in the Pacific Ocean to arm herself, and threaten and meditate the ruin of our commerce in Indies and our navy. This was the *true motive* of all the armaments and formidable preparations . . . with no less a thought than to open indiscriminately the commerce and navigation of the Pacific Ocean and even the freedom to make establishments in any deserted part of the Peruvian or California coast, pretending and asserting that this privilege ought to belong to all nations, doubtless to attract and flatter them.[94]

He suggested that the best policy regarding Britain would be "to maintain with her the best possible harmony without placing any faith in her words or conduct, despite the promises and wishes for our closer union and friendship that they have frequently expressed to us." He warned his successor against British designs to expand southward along the Pacific Coast, underscoring what he considered Spain's vital interests. He deemed it necessary to check at any cost British attempts at planting settlements on unoccupied spots on the coasts of California, Peru, Chile, and the Straits of Magellan.

The advice counted for little, as Floridablanca's political star continued to decline, and Carlos IV was persuaded to sign an order for his arrest (July 11, 1792). Conveyed to the fortress of Pamplona, he was held incommunicado for many months and might have starved but for a brother's intercession. His successor was his enemy and political antithesis, Pedro Pablo Abarca de Bolea, tenth conde de Aranda. Onetime master of the Freemasons in Spain and friend of Voltaire and other prominent Encyclopedists, Aranda had been ambassador to France during the American Revolution. Because of personal connections with the new leaders in France and identification with the most applauded ideas of the Enlightenment, the aged Aranda had some chance of maintaining better relations with the tumultuous government in Paris. When Austria and Prussia went to war in April 1792 to suppress the French Revolution, Aranda put Spain in a pose almost friendly to France. Aranda's premiership was a screen for the growing power of Godoy. To continue in office Aranda had to curry the queen's support, which meant rendering increasing obeisance to "Manuelito." In 1792 the latter was promoted to lieutenant general, elevated to the nobility as duque de

---

94. José Moñino y Redondo, conde de Floridablanca, *El Testamento político del Conde de Floridablanca*, ed. Antonio Rumeu de Armas (Madrid, 1962), p. 34, AT.

Alcudia, and named to the Council of State, all because of his hold upon the royal affections. In August of that year, French military defeats and an insurrection in Paris created the Commune, under the effective control of Danton and Robespierre, and the growing violence drove Spain and France apart. Aranda's francophile background was no longer an asset when the excesses of the new leaders and the increasingly precarious situation of Louis XVI made all things French anathema for Carlos IV. Aranda's neutral position became unpopular and finally untenable, and the seventy-three-year-old minister was advised (November 15, 1792) that due to his years he had been replaced by a younger man. The twenty-four-year-old duque de Alcudia displaced Floridablanca and Aranda through no noteworthy achievements other than an acknowledged ability to garner and retain royal favor. His biographer, Carlos Seco Serrano, asserts:

> To explain the fall of Floridablanca and Aranda as maneuvers of the queen to open the way for Godoy is too simple. Rather, one must consider that the paths of the revolution in France discarded as rejects—for one motive or another—the old ministers inherited from Carlos III. The vacuum gave the favorite room, but it had not been made for him. This is not to say, either, that Godoy was necessarily the most appropriate to fill it.[95]

Though his tenure had elapsed, Aranda continued to attack Floridablanca, and eight days after notification of being put out to pasture, he presented a memorial to the council of state criticizing his predecessor's handling of the Nootka Crisis. In Aranda's opinion, Floridablanca had bowed too readily to Pitt's coercion, and if greater pressure had been brought to bear upon France to back Spain in its hour of need, the British would have been obliged to desist from demanding acceptance of such a disadvantageous convention. The censorious document exhibits little sympathy for the Murcian's difficult situation. About to depart from the precincts of power, Aranda also dared assign part of the blame for the unfortunate pact to the king's want of interest and his preference for spending his time hunting.[96]

Floridablanca's honesty and competence gave his enemies a scant toehold for criticism, but he was nevertheless tried on charges of misuse of public funds and abuse of authority, and the prosecutor asked for the death penalty. Despite the enmity of Godoy and Aranda, there was insufficient evidence to dispose of him, and after he had spent three years in prison,

---

95. C. Seco Serrano, "Estudio Preliminar," in Godoy, *Memorias* (Madrid, 1956), p. xi.

96. Aranda, "Extracto de lo mediado para la combención con Ynglaterra firmada en 28 de Octubre 1790," and "Observaciones á la convención de 28 Octubre 1790," San Lorenzo, November 23, 1792, SpAHN (Estado 4291 bis).

Carlos IV ordered the accusations dropped and his confiscated property restored. Floridablanca's release was granted under condition that he never again return to Madrid or set foot within one of the royal *sitios*.[97]

### BRITISH RECEPTION OF PITT'S TRIUMPH

In the first week of November 1790, before word arrived from Madrid of the Anglo-Spanish convention, passions were running high in London. A day before news of the settlement came, Alexander Hamilton's brother-in-law, a member of Parliament, wrote him that, "a mad Credulity prevails here, just as it did at the Commencement of the American War, we despise our Enemy, and dream of nought but Victory, and the capture of Spanish Wealth, the Mines of Mexico and Peru are already ideally in our Possession."[98] Word that the crisis had evaporated with the mere signing of a paper took seven days to reach London, dashing cold water on such feverish aspirations. If there was disappointment in some sectors, the ministry was jubilant that by its bold gamble it had exploited the Nootka incident without actually provoking a war. Voicing the opinion of the foreign office, Burges hailed the settlement as a great coup. "Such was the Progress, and such the Termination of this momentous Negotiation," he crowed, "by which, without Bloodshed, and by an Expenditure trifling, in comparison of the Object in View, inconsiderable indeed, when compared to the Benefits resulting from it, the most essential Advantages were obtained for this Country; Advantages probably much greater than could have been procured by the most successful War."[99] For his skill in obtaining the signal diplomatic victory, Fitzherbert was elevated to the peerage as Baron St. Helens. Spain's ambassador in London reported the British reception of the news:

> There are three dominant opinions. The ministry, the court, and their party consider it the most advantageous negotiation England has ever made, and that it could well have been the fruit of a war of several years duration, happy and glorious. The opposition paints it to be a triumph for the Spanish ministry, which in reality concedes nothing to the English that they do not already enjoy, or from which they were able to benefit without possible contradiction from Spain. The third sector looks at the convention as an accommodation full of ambiguity, doubts, and confusion that decides nothing; without affirming whether this derives from the astuteness of the Spanish or the British cabinet,

97. Floridablanca returned to Murcia until Godoy's downfall in 1808, when he was summoned to head the ministry, but he died within the year. Soldevila, *Historia*, 6 : 99.

98. John Barker Church to Alexander Hamilton, November 3, 1790, in Alexander Hamilton, *Papers* ed. Harold C. Syrett, 7 vols. to date (New York, 1961–63), 7 : 136–37.

99. Burges, *Narrative*, pp. 306–07. In 1792 Vancouver paid homage to Fitzherbert in naming Mount St. Helens, a majestic snowcapped volcano towering high above the Cascades in southwestern Washington.

this group is sure that the pact was conceived on purpose in those terms so that in its execution there will be a thousand difficulties, and that in the future the two nations will have new and frequent motives for a falling out, instead of the plan that was proposed to eliminate them forever.[100]

Although ratified in Parliament by a huge majority, the convention was criticized by the opposition on grounds that Britain should have insisted on exclusive sovereignty over the northwest coast, rather than allow equal rights to Spain to trade and settle there. Since Spain had delayed giving full satisfaction, she should pay the cost of the armament that Britannia had been compelled to undertake to vindicate her honor and right.[101] Pitt was berated in the House of Lords by his predecessor, the Marquis of Lansdowne (Earl of Shelburne before 1784), who particularly censured the choice of cases upon which to rest British honor, commenting: "the whole falls under the command of a young gentleman of the name of Mears; who is instructed and instructs his followers, in terms becoming the form and pomp of office, to violate a system regarding Spanish America, which it has been the policy of Europe, and in particular this country, to adhere to for ages. Occurrences, arising out of this enterprise of a few individuals, begun without any due warrant for it, or any proper subordination to the public at large," Landsdowne further deplored,

> form the ostensible ground of a dissension with Spain. We arm in a manner regardless of expence, and summon Spain to submit in a manner alike unprecedented and insulting. The convention then follows, which Parliament, with pretty much the same peremptoriness, is called upon to approve.[102]

Many in Britain regretted that such a convenient incident had not been utilized to reap the spoils of conflict. Miranda had nothing but disgust for the settlement. "It would never," he declared, "compensate England for her expenses and for the immense advantages she might have drawn from war." [103] He had hoped that British military effort would be directed toward severing Spain from some or all of her American colonies—and that the inhabitants of Spanish America would seize the opportunity to revolt and

100. Campo de Alange to Floridablanca, London, November 26, 1790, SpAHN (Estado 4291), AT.

101. *Comments on the Convention with Spain* (London, 1790), pp. 11–15; Great Britain, *Cobbett's Parliamentary History of England*, ed. William Cobbett, 36 vols. (London, 1806–20), 28 : 977–78, 990–97.

102. William Petty, 1st marquis of Lansdowne, *The Substance of the Speech of the Marquis of Lansdown, in the House of Lords, on the 14th of December, 1790: on the Subject of the Convention with Spain, Which Was Signed on the 28th of October, 1790. By One Present* (London, [1790]), pp. 12, 14.

103. Miranda, in an unpublished manuscript cited by Robertson, "Francisco de Miranda," p. 284.

establish their independence. It is by no means certain that Miranda's plans would have turned out the way he envisioned, as British military campaigns in Spanish America stood to create additional English colonies. Such was the case, for example, in Jamaica, Trinidad, and other former Spanish territories in the Caribbean that the British seized.

THE CONVENTION OF 1790 AND SPANISH CLAIMS TO THE PACIFIC NORTHWEST

Events at Friendly Cove in 1789 generated a crisis that took Madrid within a hair's breadth of war, but Carlos IV and Floridablanca eventually backed away from a conflict in which there was no likelihood of assistance from any useful ally. Distressing circumstances in Europe, rather than particular assets and liabilities of Spain's position on the northwest coast, determined the outcome. Madrid's yielding had little to do with the validity of Spanish claims to the area in question; the consequence was a matter of which contender could marshal the most coercive power in Europe.

As borne out by historical comparisons with other such confrontations, once Madrid's position with regard to its claims in the Pacific Northwest yielded ever so slightly, the trend would prove irreversible, bringing about a succession of modifications in Spanish claims in that area, always in the direction of retreat. The Nootka Convention of 1790 gave Britain her first internationally recognized title of access to a portion of the Pacific coast of North America. Its terms made an irreparable breach in Spain's claim to exclusive sovereignty along that coast. Henceforth the dispute would center on how far south the British could push their claims toward more valuable objectives in Alta California and Mexico. As of 1790, however, the direction of the continuing contest was scarcely apparent in Madrid, Mexico City, or Nootka.

The first of the series of retreats in Spanish territorial claims on the northwest coast occurred with a royal order (August 25, 1790) that was issued a month before the convention, specifying that force should not be used to hinder English settlements at Nootka, as long as they were north of the Spanish settlement. No hostilities should be permitted against English settlements or peaceful fishing activities, as long as they refrained from selling contraband to Spanish settlements.[104] Following the convention, a royal order to Revillagigedo set forth a new policy for the northwest coast.

> As of now you should not disturb the English when they repossess the land that they began to occupy at Nootka or whatever construction they might have made there, nor should they hinder the Spanish in use and possession of the establishment we have formed in the same port

104. Royal order, August 29, 1790, acknowleged as transmitted to the commandants of San Blas and Nootka in Revillagigedo to Floridablanca, Mexico City, November 26, 1790, CU–B (Robbins Collection), Revillagigedo Papers, vol. 21, fol. 475–78v; copied at greater length in Revillagigedo to Bodega, October 29, 1791, MxAGN (Hist. 67), fol. 238–42v.

of Nootka or other parts of the continent or islands, nor [our] commerce in pelts. Your excellency should follow the rule that the English stay on the north side and the Spanish on the south. If the English try to come toward our side, they should be warned, a protest made against it, as contravening the recent adjustment with England, and a complaint made to their court so that they may be punished, for which Your Excellency will send an exact account of everything.[105]

A message sent directly to the Spanish commandant at Nootka informed him that an official would come there and, together with his English counterpart, would "designate a point to the north of the coast now occupied by Spain below which English navigators and traders should not come, thus avoiding suspicion of contraband in Spanish establishments: thereafter from said point northward shall be where the two nations establish reciprocity, use, and common traffic without controversy." [106] Athough Madrid accepted that she no longer had exclusive sovereignty over the coast beyond Nootka, Spanish officials at the highest level still entertained hopes of sustaining claims to the interior beyond Nootka's latitude. Victims of an enduring belief in mythical straits and imaginary rivers, they were concerned about preventing foreigners from penetrating from the west and approaching Spanish settlements and mines in the Interior Provinces by as yet undisclosed routes. Such illusions pervade a document at this juncture titled "Copy of what has been insinuated to the Court of London." "The last establishment of Spain in that direction," it declares,

> is the port of San Francisco, at about 38° latitude, and its dependencies and missions ascend in the interior to more than 45°; and going even farther inland are near 55°; thus it would be advisable to fix the point of division on the coast at 48°, for that would take into account all districts purchased by the English, leaving in common the trade, navigation, and establishments of both nations from the said 48° northward. Thus there will be a neutral area between the Spanish port of San Francisco and the new establishments that will aid all parties in avoiding transgressions and discords.
>
> It would also be advisable to establish a boundary to the interior of these lands so that English traders do not penetrate to the missions; and it should run as far north as Prince William and Bucareli, at 55° and 60°, to avoid the turbulence, jealousies, and suspicions that those traders might introduce into New Mexico and its missions.[107]

105. Royal order to Revillagigedo, San Lorenzo, November 27, 1790, SpAHN (Estado 4285 bis), AT.

106. Floridablanca to the "Gobernador o Comandante de San Lorenzo de Nootka," Madrid, December 25, 1790, SpAHN (Estado 4285).

107. "Copia de lo que se ha insinuado a la Corte de Londres," December 25, 1790, SpAHN (Estado 4285 bis), AT.

Spanish subjects had visited localities on the upper Missouri only as far north as 47° north latitude, but Madrid justified claims to the interior by acts of possession along the Alaskan coast in 1775 and 1779. That the boundary aspirations in this memorandum were transmitted to Revillagigedo on that same date is proven by his reference to such an order, which itself has not yet come to light.[108]

Some historians give the impression that, after her diplomatic defeat in 1790, Spain backed out of the Pacific Northwest without a further nod. Quite the contrary, the period of most intense Spanish activity there occurred during 1790–92, as Madrid strived to reinforce what Pitt and Fitzherbert had undermined. But the principle that Britain secured in the convention spelled the doom of Iberian claims there, whether Madrid recognized it or not. Henceforth, claims resting solely on discovery and exploration would be insufficient to warrant respect. Sovereignty over the Pacific Northwest would go to nations able to exert influence there, by one means or another—trading posts, garrisons, or loyal colonists. Madrid would be obliged to compete by means of similar measures. If Spanish officials would not, could not, or did not accept this new state of affairs, Madrid's aspirations in western North America were fated for attrition.

Britain was not the only nation to profit from the Nootka crisis at Spain's expense. Thereafter sovereignty, according to a historian of the Pacific Northwest, "became a matter of occupancy—the hinge on which, before another half century was out, the whole Oregon question between the United States and Great Britain would swing." [109] Pitt loosened His Catholic Majesty's grip there, which had been grounded on prior discovery, a heretofore legitimate and internationally respected basis for claims of sovereignty. By challenging and destroying the effectiveness of such claims, Pitt's brazen strategy opened the way for other challengers soon to push into the Pacific Northwest, with even less respect for hoary papal bulls, archaic rites, wooden crosses, and interred bottles testifying to possession. The United States would be the chief beneficiary of Pitt's accomplishment. The Nootka controversy played an important and often unappreciated part in the process whereby the English-speaking people, Americans and Canadians, extended their territory from sea to sea. For Madrid, it was the first in a series of mounting disasters that would eventually bring about a collapse of the Spanish colonial system.

108. Revillagigedo to Godoy, April 12, 1793, in Cavo and Bustamante, *Tres Siglos*, 3 : p. 134.
109. David S. Lavender, *Land of Giants: The Drive to the Pacfic Northwest, 1750–1950* (New York, 1958), p. 39.

## 7  The Nootka Crisis and Eastern North America

UNTIL 1790 Nootka Sound was unknown outside fur trading circles, but as Spain and Great Britain teetered on the brink of war, the Nootka crisis set up reverberations that swelled rapidly in ever-widening circles. Overnight the impending struggle so disturbed the balance of power—because of the accompanying situation in France—that significant consequences were felt elsewhere in North America, and especially in international rivalry along the American frontier.

Long after the American Revolution, Britain continued to deny her former colonies diplomatic recognition and would not negotiate formally with the United States in any way. To circumvent outright rejection of his overtures, in 1789 newly installed President Washington designated Gouverneur Morris as an informal representative to seek a rapprochement by sounding out solutions to existing issues between the two nations, particularly the sore question of continued British occupation of forts on American territory in the old Northwest, which had not been evacuated as stipulated in the peace treaty. The threat of Anglo-Spanish conflict over Nootka played into American hands, by forcing upon Pitt the necessity of securing American friendship, or at least neutrality. Where Morris had previously been snubbed, he suddenly found himself received cordially by high officials, who showed a willingness to discuss outstanding problems. By the third week in May 1790, Morris thought he perceived signs of London's giving up the forts in question to avoid provoking American support for Spain. He recognized in the crisis an opportunity to exact a price for American neutrality from Madrid as well as London, and advised Washington that the moment was favorable to press Spain for concessions that would open the Mississippi's mouth to Americans.[1]

Hopes of attaining these much desired objectives in return for neutrality were undermined by the maneuvers of a member of Washington's cabinet who was seeking to sway American foreign policy behind the back of Secretary of State Thomas Jefferson, in whose hands such delicate negotiations belonged. In 1923 Bemis underscored the significance of Treasury Secretary Alexander Hamilton's intimate discussions during the Nootka Crisis with Major George Beckwith, "a diplomatic *liaison* which became the controlling

---

1. Morris to Washington, May 21, 1790, U.S. Congress, *American State Papers*, Class I, *Foreign Relations*, 1 : 123–25; Morris to Washington, May 29, 1790, DLC (Washington Papers), cited by Julian P. Boyd, *Number 7: Alexander Hamilton's Secret Attempt to Control American Foreign Policy* (Princeton, N.J., 1964), p. 34.

personal factor in Anglo-American relations for at least the next seven years." [2] More recently, Boyd pursued the subject, showing that Morris's efforts in London failed because a more direct means of contact with the workings of Washington's cabinet had been established, through which it was in Pitt's interest to operate because of the nature of the connection. That channel led through Lord Dorchester, governor-general of British North America, via Beckwith, to Hamilton. Beckwith's secret effort in the United States to exploit the Nootka Controversy is one of the most fascinating repercussions of that crisis.

Major Beckwith had won his spurs in secret service during the American Revolution, as aide-de-camp to General Wilhelm von Knyphausen. In Sir Henry Clinton's absence, he had conducted the correspondence culminating in Benedict Arnold's defection from the American cause, and after Sir Guy Carleton had succeeded Clinton as commander of British forces, Beckwith continued in charge of intelligence activity. When Carleton, now raised to the peerage as Lord Dorchester, returned to Canada in 1786 as governor-general, he brought Beckwith along, and in 1787 he sent him to New York to renew contact with "those of the British interest" and gather intelligence, keeping Whitehall informed of whatever might be of importance as the United States made the crucial change from a confederation to government under the new Constitution. Beckwith's secret reports told of growing favor toward Britain and the possibility of detaching disaffected frontier areas in Vermont and the Ohio valley, and he covertly commenced establishing a network of connections among such elements. His reports referred to key personages and informants by code numbers (no. 7 designating Hamilton). His initial contact with the secretary of the treasury had been through Senator Philip Schuyler (no. 2), Hamilton's father-in-law and one of Beckwith's informants "in the British party." At their first meeting, in October 1789, Washington's nominee for secretary of state had not yet returned from his former post as ambassador to France. "When Jefferson some months later arrived at his desk," Bemis remarks, "the relation thus established in an informal way between Hamilton and this unaccredited agent of the British Government had grown so intimate and at the same time so subtle that the real Secretary of State was never able to conduct his office with thorough independence." [3]

"I have requested to see you," Hamilton announced upon his first interview with Beckwith, ". . . from a wish to explain certain points relative to our situation, and from a desire to suggest a measure, which I conceive to be both for the interest of Great Britain and of this Country to adopt," and he went on to propose a commercial treaty advantageous to both

2. Bemis, *Jay's Treaty*, pp. 57–58; Boyd, *Number 7*, pp. 8–9.
3. Bemis, *Jay's Treaty*, p. 62. Jefferson assumed the duties of office in February 1790.

countries. "I have always preferred a connexion with you, to that of any
other country, *we think in English,* and have a similarity of prejudices and
of predilections," Hamilton admitted, and went on to make disclosures,
offers, and pledges for which there had been no authorization from the
president, an indiscretion apparently motivated by his fervent desire to improve relations with Britain. Although he told Beckwith that theirs was
"merely a private conversation," he said that the ideas expressed "may be
depended upon as the sentiments of the most enlightened men in this
country," and that "they are those of General Washington, I can confidently
assure you, as well as of a majority in the Senate." [4] Perhaps surprised by
the implications, Beckwith inquired: "Pray what use do you intend me to
make of it? Is it with a view to my mentioning it to Lord Dorchester?"
"Yes," Hamilton responded, "and by Lord Dorchester to your Ministry, in
whatever manner His Lordship shall judge proper; but I should not chuse
to have this go any further in America." The significance of this interview,
as Boyd points out, is that without Washington's knowledge, "so far as the
records and plausibilities indicate," Hamilton represented the administration
as dedicated to a policy of rapprochement with Britain.[5] The report of this
conversation reached London shortly after Morris began dickering with
Whitehall and just as the Nootka crisis came to a head. Hamilton's assurances permitted Pitt to bring full pressure to bear upon Madrid without
worrying too much about a Spanish-American alliance. The ministry was
able to counter Morris's complaints about British-occupied forts with what
Leeds called "a language of firmness." The American position had been
weakened, Boyd suggests, "by those most anxious to make it secure," and
those favoring the British interest "had damaged their cause by placing
themselves and their nation not in the posture of negotiators but in that of
petitioners." [6] Thereafter, Morris found his efforts frustrated, for it behooved Pitt to employ the Hamilton channel, through which he might learn
and even influence the American position in regard to the Nootka Crisis.
Any attempt to insure American neutrality through Morris, Boyd comments, "would have brought on all the risks of negotiation—offers, counter
offers, perhaps pledges—and it would not have enabled the ministry to
pursue its growing interest in Vermont and Kentucky." [7]

Morris never learned that his cool treatment, following initially cordial
interviews, had its explanation in the Beckwith-Hamilton connection. Following the Nootka Convention, he was denied access to the foreign minister

4. Beckwith, "Conversations with different persons," enclosed in Dorchester to Grenville,
October 25, 1789, UKLPRO (C. O. 42/66), fol. 278, in Douglas Brymner, *Report on Canadian
Archives . . . 1890* (Ottawa, 1891), pp. 121–29.

5. Boyd, *Number 7,* p. 25.

6. Ibid., pp. 31, 35.

7. Ibid., p. 35.

and received what amounted to a "brush-off" by lesser officials. Nevertheless, although Morris's mission had little effect, the Nootka crisis broke the diplomatic ice between London and Washington's administration, impressing upon Pitt the importance of retaining American neutrality in case of war and American friendliness toward British commerce in time of peace.

### NOOTKA AND THE CANADIAN FRONTIER

The day after a general impressment order had revealed the Nootka Crisis to the British public, three secret dispatches were sent to Lord Dorchester relating to (1) the Canadian-American frontier, (2) Vermont, and (3) an effort to sway the United States to the British side in the Nootka dispute. The first warned that, in the event of war over Nootka, the United States might seize the opportunity to demand evacuation of forts between the Ohio River and Canada. Madrid would support the American position to gain an ally. Dorchester was to take precautions against such a possibility.[8]

A possibility of American alignment with Madrid, in the event of war over Nootka, made it important for Pitt to cultivate the Republic of Vermont. Rival claims by New York and New Hampshire over the Green Mountain state had blocked its admission to the Continental Congress, with the result that in 1777 Vermont framed a constitution and went its independent way. Led by the five Allen brothers, it steered a hazardous course of uncertain destiny. In 1788 Ethan Allen assured Dorchester that Vermont did not choose to subject itself to the new American Constitution, and he boasted of being able to muster 15,000 armed men who, allied with anti-Federalists elsewhere, "might form so strong a junction as to crush the promised federal government." The relationship which the Allens proposed to the governor-general was not a "formal and public alliance," but it would answer all the purposes, allowing the Vermonters to maintain their independence, at least "till they can on principles of mutual interest and advantage, return to the British government without war or annoyance from the United States." [9] When the Nootka crisis erupted, Levi Allen was in London dickering for a separate commercial treaty with Britain that would grant Vermont products free entry into Quebec, as well as passage from Lake Champlain to the St. Lawrence and the sea. The treaty would provide international recognition of Vermont's independence, a sought-after objective of the separatists.

The encouragement of "buffer communities" under British protection

8. Grenville to Dorchester, May 6, 1790, no. 22, UKLPRO (C. O. 42/67), fol. 93, in Brymner, *Report,* pp. 131–32; Henry Motz (sec. to Dorchester) to Sir John Johnson, head of the Dept. of Indian Affairs, September 27, 1790, CaOOA (Series Q, vol. 46, pt. 2), cited by Bemis, *Jay's Treaty,* pp. 91–92.

9. Ethan Allen to Dorchester, July 16, 1788, UKLPRO (C. O. 42/60), fol. 231–39, cited by Boyd, *Number 7,* pp. 142–43n.

along the American frontier fitted well into Pitt's strategy for guarding against surprise American assaults upon Canada. Commercial concessions to the Vermonters would attach them to the British interest. The ministry was confident that Dorchester would "give this subject the attention it deserves, and that you will neglect no proper steps for ensuring so considerable an accession of strength as that which we should derive from the friendship of Vermont." [10] The privy council took Allen's request under consideration, deciding "it would be well for the benefits of this country commercially to prevent Vermont and Kentucky and all the other settlements now forming in the interior part of the great continent of North America, from being dependent upon the Government of the United States or on that of any other foreign country," but they recommended that, "all circumstances considered," it would not be politically prudent to make a separate treaty with Vermont, for fear of offending the United States government and inclining it toward Spain in the present controversy.[11] Allen did not return home empty-handed, however; to satisfy his request, yet avoid alienating the United States, Parliament granted all American imports into Quebec equal treatment with that accorded British colonial products brought to England.

### THE MISSISSIPPI LOOMS AS AN ARENA OF ANGLO-SPANISH CONFLICT

The third order to Dorchester on May 6, 1790, concerned means of counteracting within the United States any inducements that Spain might offer to gain allies in the impending struggle. The ministry stressed that "it will certainly be our object to establish, if possible, a greater degree of interest than we have hitherto had in that country." To establish contact with those favoring Britain, the governor-general was instructed "to find the means of sending the proper persons who may, though not authorized by any public commission, forward this object, and at the same time be able to give your Lordship the earliest information of hostile designs, if any such should be meditated against the forts or against Canada itself." London even set forth the line of argument to be used with those of the British interest.

> The right which Spain has asserted is exclusive against all the world, against the United States as well as against any European powers: And the Fur trade from the North West Coast of America may become a valuable accessary and assistant to the China trade in which the Americans have already embarked extensively. The object which we might

10. Grenville to Dorchester, May 6, 1790, no. 23, in Brymner, *Report,* p. 132.

11. Stephen Cottrell to W. W. Grenville, Office of the committee of the privy council for trade, Whitehall, April 17, 1790, in Frederick Jackson Turner, "English Policy Toward America in 1790–1791," AHR 7 (1902–03) : 78–86; Burt, *The United States . . . ,* p. 70.

hold out to them particularly to the Kentucke and other Settlers at the back of the old colonies, of opening the Navigation of the Mississippi to them, is one at least as important as the possession of the Forts, and perhaps it would not be difficult to shew, that the former is much more easily attainable with the assistance of Great Britain against Spain, than the latter is by their joining Spain in offensive operations against this Country.[12]

Spanish mercantilist restrictions threatened economic expansion beyond the Appalachians. Resentment among "Men of the Western Waters," as they called themselves, toward the Atlantic seaboard for neglecting the Mississippi question had led to secessionist intrigues in Kentucky and elsewhere in the West. Frontier animosity toward both the Spanish and the easterners provided a toehold for British diplomacy. Madrid had been obliged by the treaty of 1763 to allow British subjects free passage to the Gulf of Mexico by way of the lower Mississippi, but after the American Revolution, Carlos III had no longer considered himself bound by that commitment. In 1784, pursuing mercantilist policies intended to strengthen the sinews of empire, José de Gálvez closed the lower Mississippi to all but those paying allegiance to His Catholic Majesty.[13] The American confederation's efforts to negotiate with Madrid for privileges of Mississippi navigation got nowhere. Floridablanca preferred a policy of containment, courting disaffected elements on the American frontier and strengthening alliances with Indian tribes of the Old Southwest. The frontier intrigues, some of whose details reached New York and London as well as Madrid, demonstrated that if the United States could not or would not press for Mississippi navigation, influential men beyond the Appalachians were disposed to forgo American allegiance and negotiate with other powers to achieve that goal. Such troubled waters were an invitation to British as well as to Spanish intrigue. Whitehall received encouraging reports about the growth of separatist inclinations in Kentucky. In 1789 Dorchester had been instructed to cultivate leaders of such efforts, to prevent their moving closer toward Spain, but he was cautioned against making promises of immediate or eventual assistance against states of the Atlantic seaboard.[14]

Peter Allaire, a respected New York merchant and secret British agent, reported in the summer of 1790 that 5,000 to 7,000 men in the United States were willing to assist any nation in dislodging Spain from the banks of the

12. Grenville to Dorchester, May 6, 1790, no. 24, in Brymner, *Report*, p. 132.

13. José de Gálvez to the governor ad interim of New Orleans, Aranjuez, June 26, 1784, in Louis Houck, *Spanish Régime in Missouri* 2 vols. (Chicago, 1908), 1 : 237.

14. Grenville to Dorchester, October 21, 1789, CaOOA (series Q, vol. 42), fol. 153, cited by Bemis, *Jay's Treaty*, pp. 60–61; S. F. Bemis, *Pinckney's Treaty; A Study of America's Advantage From Europe's Distress, 1783–1800*, rev. ed. (New Haven, 1960), pp. 74–92.

Mississippi in return for free navigation. The Nootka Crisis made the time ripe "to bind us in Adamantine Chains of Friendship and Alliance with you," he asserted. "Take the Floridas, Open a free Navigation of the Mississippi for the Western Inhabitants, and you bind that Country and its inhabitants for Ever in spite of Congress and all the world." [15] In his next dispatch, Allaire remarked that many in the west would join in a descent upon the Spanish settlements, "not by Order consent or Approbation of the United States, but by those who Acknowledge Allegiance to None." Hardy and inured to fatigue and danger, they were expert woodsmen who "want Employ being most of them destitute of Clothes and Money." [16]

Word of the Nootka crisis reached the American government late in June 1790. Washington's diary indicates that Vice-President John Adams was of the opinion that, "as a rupture betwn. England and Spain was almost inevitable . . . it would be our policy and interest to take part with the latter as he was very apprehensive that New Orleans was an object with the former; their possessing which could be very injurious to us; but he observed, at the same time, that the situation of our affairs would not justify the measure unless the People themselves (of the United States) should take the lead in the business." [17] Because the Franco-American alliance continued in effect, it would be difficult to escape obligations to France, Carlos IV's ally under the Family Compact. Three days later, the president's diary notes:

> I was informed this day by General Irvine (who recd. the acct. from Pittsburgh,) that the Traitor Arnold was at Detroit and had viewed the Militia in the Neighborhood of it twice. This had occasioned much Speculation in those parts—and with many other circumstances— though trifling in themselves led strongly to a conjecture that the British had some design on the Spanish settlements in the Mississippi and of course to surround these United States.[18]

The propect of Benedict Arnold's leading an overland campaign against San Luís de Ilinueces (St. Louis) and other Spanish settlements in Louisiana posed a grave threat. The victor would turn against the United States for miscalculating the outcome of the contest. In the event of conflict in that

---

15. "Occurrences" from July 5 to August 3, 1790, UKLPRO (F. O. 4/8), fol. 284, cited by Boyd, *Number 7*, p. 60. Allaire served for many years as a secret informant, receiving £200 a year in return. He took in members of Congress as boarders, submitted regular reports to Whitehall, and was not revealed as part of Britain's intelligence network until recent times. See Boyd, pp. 60–61n.

16. "Occurrences" from August 6 to September 1, 1790, UKLPRO (F. O. 4/8), fol. 307, cited by Boyd, *Number 7*, p. 61.

17. George Washington, *Diaries . . . 1748–1799*, ed. J. C. Fitzpatrick, 4 vols. (Boston and New York, 1925), 4 : 132, entry for July 1, 1790.

18. Ibid., p. 136. The report was conveyed to him by General William Irvine on July 4.

arena, American neutrality could only be preserved with the greatest difficulty. News of the crisis widened the existing division between francophiles and francophobes. The secretary of the treasury perceived that Jefferson, Madison, and other southerners would be inclined toward utilizing the situation to bargain with Madrid for concessions at the Mississippi's mouth —which would upset Hamilton's plans for a rapprochement with London. The possibility of a Spanish-American entente had to be countered, and Hamilton's opportunity appeared when Beckwith returned from Quebec.

The major carried two sets of instructions for this new mission to New York City, one for his own eyes alone and another "of a less secret nature," as Dorchester put it, to be shown to such as discretion indicated. On July 8 he showed this innocuous set to Hamilton, who later that day acquainted the president and secretary of state with the conversation, set down in a memorandum that Washington recorded in full in his diary.[19] The treasury secretary toned down nuances in Dorchester's phraseology that might have seemed unfriendly, magnified the appearance of amiability, and made it look as though *Britain* were seeking an alliance, whereas the alliance idea stemmed from Hamilton's overtures to Beckwith in October 1789. Boyd emphasizes that the ministry "had expressly forbade Dorchester to clothe his agent with authority to speak under a public commission." If Hamilton had quoted Dorchester's instructions exactly, questions would have arisen as to when, where, and how the United States had shown a "good disposition" toward establishing an alliance with Britain. This would have led to disclosure of Hamilton's previous interviews with Beckwith and exposed him "as having committed the administration on his own authority to a position it had not assumed and of having done this in secret negotiations, pledging in support of the commitment his own honor and character." [20]

Hamilton's misrepresentation of the British posture, Boyd suggests, was motivated by his desire to weaken the hand of those in the cabinet and Senate who might incline toward Spain and use the war scare as leverage to secure Mississippi navigation. He needed every makeweight available to counter negotiations with Madrid, which would ruin his efforts to promote an accord with London. The deception was, in Boyd's view, "a desperate act to salvage the policy at a critical moment." [21]

Reflecting upon Hamilton's conversation with Beckwith, Washington concluded that London had no intention of answering protests about the western posts until she ascertained whether the United States would back away from an alliance with Spain. In that case, the president noted with irony,

19. Both sets are in UKLPRO (C. O. 42/68), fol. 255–60, and are pub. in Boyd, *Number 7*, pp. 143–46; see also pp. 137–38.
20. Boyd, *Number 7*, pp. 41–42.
21. Ibid., p. 46.

the British "promise perhaps" to fulfill what they were already treaty-bound to perform.[22] In view of the ominous news from Europe, the president turned to his cabinet for advice—the new government's first foreign policy crisis.

Within four days Jefferson submitted an outline of a policy upon which he and Madison concurred. Spain could not hope to win, he said, unless France went to her aid. If Britain invaded the Floridas and Louisiana, and Spain was unable to retake them, the United States would be obliged to enter the war to seize those territories for herself. Caution was advised until the trend of events could be determined. "Delay enables us to be better prepared: to obtain from the allies a price for our assistance." As to hints of an Anglo-American alliance, Jefferson opined, "we can say nothing till it's object be shewn, and that it is not to be inconsistent with existing engagements," an allusion to the Franco-American alliance. He suggested that Beckwith be told:

> We should view with extreme uneasiness any attempts of either power to seize the possessions of the other on our frontier, as we consider our own safety interested in a due balance between our neighbors. It might be advantageous to express this latter sentiment, because if there be any difference of opinion in their councils, whether to bend their force against North or South America, or the islands, (and certainly there is room for difference) and if these opinions be nearly balanced, that balance might be determined by the prospect of having an enemy the more the less, according to the object they should select.[23]

Hamilton and John Jay, the chief justice, presented their recommendations verbally on July 14. Since Beckwith did not bring proper accreditation, the government could not negotiate with him formally. Therefore, it was decided that Hamilton should continue conversations with the major, extracting as much information as possible while avoiding commitment in any fashion, and providing the president with a written account of each interview.[24] In the talks that followed, as Boyd so masterfully shows, Hamilton would say one thing to Beckwith while reporting a subtly different version of what was said to the president, creating an illusion of rapprochement where none existed.

While Hamilton tugged and strained to bend American foreign policy toward favoring London, the secretary of state was formulating a strategy in a quite different direction. By holding to a position of strict neutrality, Jefferson hoped to attain two objectives: to keep Britain from surrounding the

22. Washington, *Diaries*, 4 : 139.

23. Jefferson to Washington, July 12, 1790; enclosure: Jefferson's "Outline of a Policy Contingent on War Between England and Spain," in Jefferson, *Papers*, 17 : 108–10. This and other documents in Jefferson's *Papers* which emanate from the Nootka Crisis are also published in Boyd, *Number 7*.

24. Washington, *Diaries*, 4 : 143, entry for July 14, 1790.

United States, and to secure from Spain navigation rights on the Mississippi. If the Floridas and Louisiana could be pried from Spain's grip, so much the better. Disruption of the balance of power in Europe offered Jefferson an opportunity that he had been anticipating for some time. Realizing that Mississippi navigation was a requisite for retaining the loyalty of the "Men of the Western Waters," in 1788 he wrote a Kentuckian known to have been involved in the so-called Spanish Conspiracy:

> I should think it proper for the Western country to defer pushing their right to that navigation to extremity as long as they can do without it tolerably; but that the moment it becomes absolutely necessary for them, it will become the duty of the maritime states to push it to every extremity to which they would their own right of navigating the Chesapeak, the Delaware, the Hudson or any other water. A time of peace will not be the surest for obtaining this object. Those therefore who have influence in the new country would act wisely to endeavor to keep things quiet till the Western parts of Europe shall be engaged in war.[25]

Jefferson's policy emerges in a letter to the American chargé in Madrid, William Carmichael. The Nootka crisis provided an opportunity to approach Floridablanca regarding American use of the Mississippi, "and though it must be done delicately, yet he must be made to understand unequivocally that a resumption of the negotiation is not desired on our part, unless he can determine, in the first opening of it, to yield the immediate and full enjoyment of that navigation." Madrid should be pressed not only for free navigation but also for port facilities near the outlet. "You know that the navigation cannot be practiced without a port where the sea and river vessels may meet and exchange loads, and where those employed about them may be safe and unmolested," he pointed out. "The right to use a thing comprehends a right to the means necessary to it's use, and without which it would be useless." As a persuader, Carmichael should stress the American government's inability to control its rambunctious frontiersmen.

> There is a danger indeed that even the unavoidable delay of sending a negociator here, may render the mission too late for the preservation of peace: it is impossible to answer for the forbearance of our western citizens. We endeavor to quiet them with the expectation of an attainment of their rights by peaceable means, but should they, in a moment of impatience, hazard others, there is no saying how far we may be led: for neither themselves nor their rights will ever be abandoned by us.[26]

25. Jefferson to John Brown, Paris, May 28, 1788, in Jefferson, *Papers*, 13 : 211–13.
26. Jefferson to Carmichael, New York, August 2, 1790; enclosure: "Heads of consideration on the Navigation of the Mississipi for Mr. Carmichael," in ibid., 17 : 111–16.

Jefferson predicted that war would have begun before Carmichael received his missive, but added that, should the Nootka controversy be settled without a conflict, "we retain indeed the same object, and the same resolutions unalterably; but your discretion will suggest that, in that event, they must be pressed more softly; and that patience and persuasion must temper your conferences, till either these may prevail, or some other circumstance turn up which may enable us to use other means for the attainment of an object, which we are determined in the end to obtain at every risk." [27] Spain's conduct had shown that "occlusion of the Mississippi is system with her," and a treaty would be no guarantee against Madrid's using irregularities, real or pretended, as a pretext for revoking American navigation privileges once the present crisis passed. "Prudence, and even necessity," Jefferson declared, "imposes on us the law of settling the matter now *finally,* and not by *halves.*" [28] Madrid should be pressed to cede all its territory east of the Mississippi, on condition "that we guarantee all her possessions on the western waters of that river." If Britain were to seize the Floridas and Louisiana, they would serve as bases by which she could "proceed successively from colony to colony," engulfing other areas of Spanish America, hence it would be

> "safer for Spain that we should be her neighbor, than England. . . Conquest [is] not in our principles: inconsistent with our government," he declared, and it was "not our interest to cross the Mississippi for ages. . . . If we preserve our neutrality, it will be a very partial one to her. . . . If we are forced into the war, it will be, as we wish, on the side of the H[ouse] of Bourbon. . . . In fine, for a narrow slip of barren, detached, and expensive country, Spain secures the rest of her territory, and makes an Ally, where she might have a dangerous enemy." [29]

To augment the pressure upon Madrid for such important concessions, a copy of these instructions was sent to William Short, the American chargé in Paris, so that in the event of an Anglo-Spanish war, they could be shown to Lafayette. "He and you will consider," Jefferson wrote,

> how far the contents of these papers may be communicated to the Count de Montmorin, and his influence be asked with the court of Madrid. France will be called into the war, as an ally, and not on any pretence of the quarrel being in any degree her own. She may reasonably require then that Spain should do every thing which depends on her to lessen the number of her enemies. She cannot doubt that we shall be of that

27. Ibid., p. 112.
28. Ibid., pp. 113–16.
29. Ibid.

number, if she does not yield our right to the common use of the Missisipi [*sic*], and the means of using and securing it.[30]

In the American view, no one in Europe seemed in a better position than Lafayette to press the American case for privileges on the lower Mississippi. The next day Washington sent his friend a letter obviously designed to back Jefferson's ploy with Madrid, in the course of which he remarked on the state of the nation.

> Gradually recovering from the distresses in which the war left us, patiently advancing in our task of civil government, unentangled in the crooked politics of Europe, wanting scarcely any thing but the free navigation of the Mississipi (which we must have and as certainly shall have as we remain a Nation) I have supposed, that, with the undeviating exercise of a just, steady, and prudent national policy, we shall be the gainers, whether the powers of the old world may be in peace or war, but more especially in the latter case. In that case our importance will certainly increase, and our friendship be courted. Our dispositions would not be indifferent to Britain or Spain. Why will not Spain be wise and liberal at once? It would be easy to annihilate all causes of quarrels between that Nation and the United States at this time. At a future period that may be far from being a fact. Should a war take place between Great Britain and Spain, I conceive from a great variety of concurring circumstances there is the highest probability that the Floridas will soon be in the possession of the former.[31]

### WASHINGTON CALLS FOR COUNSEL

Increasingly alarming news from Europe, Arnold's activities in Detroit, and Beckwith's efforts, as portrayed by Hamilton, to promote an alliance, had the cumulative effect of convincing Washington that war over Nootka was imminent, and that the Mississippi basin would be a principal arena of combat. On August 27 he queried each cabinet member, requesting individual answers:

> Provided the dispute between Great Britain and Spain should come to decision of Arms, from a variety of circumstances (individually unimportant and inconclusive, but very much the reverse when compared and combined) there is no doubt in my mind, that New Orleans and the Spanish Posts above it on the Mississippi will be among the first attempts of the former, and that the reduction of them will be undertaken by a combined operation from Detroit.

30. Jefferson to William Short, New York, August 10, 1790, in ibid., 17 : 121–23.
31. Washington to Lafayette, August 11, 1790, in George Washington, *Writings*, ed. J. C. Fitzpatrick, 39 vols. (Washington, D.C., 1931–44), 31 : 85–88, cited by Boyd, *Number 7*, p. 56.

The *Consequences* of having so formidable and enterprizing a people as the British on both our flanks and rear, with their navy in front, as they respect our Western Settlements which may be seduced thereby, as they regard the Security of the Union and its commerce with the West Indies, are too obvious to need enumeration.

What then should be the Answer of the Executive of the United States to Lord Dorchester, in case he should apply for permission to march Troops through the Territory of the said States from Detroit to the Mississippi?

What notice ought to be taken of the measure, if it should be undertaken without leave, which is the most probable proceeding of the two? [32]

The secretary of state responded that British seizure of Louisiana and the Floridas would be a calamity; it would be preferable to join the war on Spain's side than to have that happen. But he advised preserving a position of neutrality as long as possible, "because war is full of chances which may relieve us from the necessity of interfering." If permission to send troops across American territory were requested and an answer could not be avoided, the passage would have to be permitted. If they were to pass without asking leave, he was for "expressing our dissatisfaction to the British court, and keeping alive an altercation on the subject, till events should decide whether it is most expedient to accept their apologies, or profit of the aggression as a cause of war." [33]

Chief Justice John Jay thought that if Dorchester requested permission for troop passage, he could not be refused without risk of its being attempted anyway, resulting either in war or in the humiliation of seeing them proceed with impunity. If they attempted to cross without asking permission, circumstances made it advisable to avoid opposition. Jay thought it more prudent, "*at present* to permit Britain to conquer and hold the Floridas, than engage in a War to prevent it." [34]

Vice-President Adams, initially inclined to join the Spanish side, changed his mind and now recommended remaining neutral as long as possible, because "the People of these States would not willingly Support a War, and the present government has not Strength to command, nor enough of the general Confidence of the nation to draw the men or money necessary, untill the

32. Washington to [members of the cabinet] August 27, 1790, in Jefferson, *Papers*, 17 : 128–29. This query and the responses it elicited were the substance of Worthington Chauncey Ford, *The United States and Spain in 1790: An Episode in Diplomacy Described from Hitherto Unpublished Sources* (Brooklyn, N.Y., 1890). Boyd's masterful reevaluation underlines the catalytic effect of the Nootka Crisis upon Hamilton-Jefferson rivalry, of such consequence to subsequent American history.

33. Jefferson to Washington, August 28, 1790, in Jefferson, *Papers*, 17 : 129–30.

34. Jay to Washington, August 28, 1790, in ibid., pp. 134–37.

Grounds, causes and Necessity of it Should become generally known, and universally approved." An honest neutrality could be preserved only by refusing passage to British troops, for to do otherwise "would not only have an appearance offensive to the Spaniards, of partiality to the English, but would be a real Injury to Spain." Adams was of the opinion that "a tacit Acquiescence under Such an Outrage, would be misinterpreted on all hands; by Spain as inimical to her and by Britain, as the effect of Weakness, Disunion and Pusillanimity." The only alternative was to present a vigorous protest to London and negotiate some satisfaction for the insult.[35]

Secretary of War Henry Knox counseled against concurring in any "arrangements" leading to British possession of the Mississippi and West Florida. The United States had the right to refuse passage to British troops, since their objective would tend to injure American welfare. Permission should be denied, but no measures should be taken that might lead to war. The act would be just cause for war, when and if the United States wished to seize the opportunity, but commercial motives made it in the American interest to remain neutral. Knox advised replying that "the real causes of dispute between England and Spain were too little understood at present by the United States for the President to consent to a measure which would seem to be inconsistent with that strict neutrality the United States would desire to observe." If the troop movement took place, Congress should be convened, since it was vested with the powers to provide for the common defense and to declare war.[36]

The rest of the cabinet answered Washington's query within several days, but Hamilton took more than two weeks to compose a treatise three times as extensive as all the other replies combined, a masterful analysis of great interest. He counseled against siding with France out of a "spirit of romantic gratitude calling for sacrifices of our substantial interests." As for Spain, the aid received from her during the war was inconsiderable, he opined,

> compared with her faculty of aiding us. She refrained from acknowleging our independence, has never acceded to the Treaty of Commerce made with France, though a right of doing it was reserved to her, nor made any other Treaty with us. She has maintained possessions within our acknowledged limits without our consent. She perseveringly obstructs our sharing in the navigation of the Mississippi; though it is a privilege essential to us, and to which we consider ourselves as having an indisputable title. And perhaps it might be added upon good ground that she has not scrupled to intrigue with leading individuals in the Western Country to seduce them from our interests and to attach them to her own.

35. Adams to Washington, August 29, 1790, in ibid., pp. 137–40.
36. Knox to Washington, August 29, 1790, in ibid., pp. 140–42.

Spain therefore must be regarded, upon the whole, as having slender claims to peculiar good will from us. There is certainly nothing that authorises her to expect we should expose ourselves to any extraordinary jeopardy for her sake. And to conceive that any considerations relative to France ought to be extended to her would be to set up a doctrine altogether new in politics. The ally of our ally has no claim, as such, to our friendship. We may have substantial grounds of dissatisfaction against him, and act in consequence of them, even to open hostility, without derogating in any degree from what we owe to our ally.

This is so true, that if a war should really ensue between Great Britain and Spain, and if the latter should persist in excluding us from the Mississippi (taking it for granted our claim to share in its navigation is well founded) there can be no reasonable ground of doubt that we should be at liberty, if we thought it our interest, consistently with our present engagements with France, to join Britain against Spain.[37]

The tenor of Hamilton's presentation, as a whole, was to suggest the advisability of an Anglo-American combination, although the statement did not emerge in plainer terms than in the foregoing. He admitted a danger to the United States if Britain should possess Louisiana and the Floridas, thereby securing greater influence over Indian tribes within our boundaries and obtaining areas whose products would in time rival staples exported from southern states, causing not only material injury but a removal of motives for treaties with the United States containing liberal terms for commercial intercourse. If the British acquired the Missisippi's mouth and opened it to inhabitants of the western country, "by conciliating their good will on the one hand, and making them sensible on the other of their dependence on them for the continuance of so essential an advantage they might hold out to them the most powerful temptation to a desertion of their connection with the rest of the United States."[38]

To refuse the British permission to cross American territory and be unable to stop them in the event they did so would bring disgrace.

Britain would then think herself under less obligation to keep measures with us, and would feel herself more at liberty to employ every engine in her power to make her acquisition as prejudicial to us as possible; whereas, if no impediment should be thrown in the way by us, more good humour may beget greater moderation, and in the progress of things, concessions securing us, may be made, as the price of our future neutrality. An explicit recognition of our right to navigate the Missis-

37. Hamilton to Washington, September 15, 1790, in ibid., pp. 149–50.
38. Ibid., p. 151.

sippi to and from the Ocean, with the possession of New Orleans, would greatly mitigate the causes of apprehension from the conquest of the Floridas by the British.[39]

He catalogued the many reasons for avoiding a war, citing the large proportion of Americans who, although advocates of the Revolution, retained "prepossessions in favour of Englishmen, and prejudices against Spaniards," a factor not to be overlooked in political calculations. He saw no justice in Madrid's stance over Nootka, "and certainly the monopoly, at which those pretensions aim, is intitled to no partiality from any maritime or trading people." He advised against entering a war on the weaker side, for without French support, Spain could not hope to counter Britain's challenge, and his augury of the trend in Paris was pessimistic. Every sign counseled against becoming embroiled with Britain. Evacuation of western posts and Mississippi navigation were our key objectives.

> It is not impossible if war takes place, that by a judicious attention to favourable moments we may accomplish both, by negotiation. The moment however we become committed on either side the advantages of our position for negotiation would be gone. They would even be gone in respect to the party, with whom we were in cooperation; for being once in the war we could not make terms as the condition of entering into it.[40]

If Madrid continued to deny navigation to those in the western part of the country, there would undoubtedly be war with Spain or separation of that area from the United States. War would be preferable to the latter alternative; aid could be sought from Britain; France probably would be on Spain's side, bringing about a total revolution of existing alliances. Britain's retention of the western posts was of less consequence than Mississippi navigation, hence the United States had greater reason to differ with Madrid than with London. Even if Britain succeeded in capturing the Mississippi's mouth, "the acquisition, if made, may in the progress of things be wrested from its possessors." If pressed, London "may deem it evident to purchase our neutrality by a cession to us of that part of the territory in question, which borders on the Mississippi accompanied with a guarantee of the navigation of that river." [41]

If a request came for permission to march overland against Spanish territory, Hamilton favored consent rather than silence. The American commander on the Wabash, the direct route, would be obliged to resist the maneuver, unless he had orders to the contrary. Possessing the inferior force,

39. Ibid., p. 153.
40. Ibid., p. 156.
41. Ibid., p. 158.

his outpost would probably be captured, constituting an act of war, "and thus silence, with less dignity, would produce the same ill consequence, as refusal." "If to avoid this," he warned, "private orders were to be sent to the commanding officer of that post not to interrupt the passage, his not being punished for his delinquency would betray the fact and afford proof of connivance." If the maneuver took place without asking permission, the troops would pass through almost uninhabited country. If any violence to American citizens or posts occurred, "it would seem sufficient to be content with remonstrating against it, but in a tone that would not commit us to the necessity of going to war." [42]

Hamilton's careful reasoning added up to a persuasive conclusion: that the national interest necessitated granting permission to cross American territory, while intimating to London that our neutrality could be secured by conceding the eastern bank of the lower Mississippi and guaranteeing American navigation on that waterway. On paper Hamilton's logic seemed inescapable. But Britain was not yet disposed to treat the United States as a sovereign power, much less enter into an alliance. Hamilton knew this, and he had been hiding the fact from Washington. Jefferson's messages to Carmichael, Short, and Morris, and the president's letter to Lafayette all indicated that the current was running against Hamilton's design. Unless he could secure some important concession from Britain, the tide would be irreversible. While finishing his memorial about how to confront the Nootka crisis, Hamilton pressed Beckwith for some assurance, pledge, or sign that Britain would grant the United States the right to Mississippi navigation in the event of war. Boyd demonstrates that Hamilton's efforts to influence American policy postponed rather than hastened his objectives, and made British behavior seem more equivocal than it was. His distortion of the Pitt ministry's feeler, through Beckwith, merely augmented suspicions of British intentions held by Jefferson and others of a similar persuasion, driving them even farther from those of the "British interest." More seriously, Hamilton's covert maneuvers were at cross purposes with those of the secretary of state, in whose hands foreign policy should have remained, subject to the president's approval. Hamilton may have justified usurping Jefferson's prerogatives by the conviction that a misguided policy deserved counteracting. In hindsight, Hamilton's assessment of the situation seems more accurate and realistic than that of the francophiles. He predicted correctly that developments in Paris would undermine Spanish foreign policy by hamstringing its defensive posture. It would be doing the secretary of the treasury less than justice to highlight his stratagems to thwart Jefferson's conduct of foreign policy without recalling the perspective of events apparent to Americans in the summer of 1790, when to some it looked as if a war over Nootka might entangle them on the losing side.

42. Ibid., pp. 159–60.

The president was very reluctant to see the United States drawn into war via the Franco-American alliance, and he found highly distasteful the pressures to which he was subjected by the Anglo-Spanish controversy. As he had remarked to Lafayette, it was vital to keep the nation "unentangled in the crooked politics of Europe." The Nootka crisis has been credited with clarifying the doctrine eventually embodied in Washington's Farewell Address.[43] The experience underscored the benefits to be extracted from remaining neutral in future wars between colonial powers. The first formal articulation of the American principle of opposing the transfer of New World territories between colonial powers also was a result of cabinet deliberations during this episode.[44]

Fortunately for the young republic, an Anglo-Spanish struggle for possession of the Mississippi basin did not develop in 1790. It has yet to be shown that Arnold's activities in Detroit had anything to do with a potential descent upon Spanish Louisiana. Such designs as the British entertained upon New Orleans seem to have involved naval operations, rather than an overland attack. Pitt was prepared to wage war in 1790 had Carlos IV not yielded to his ultimatum. Bemis believes Pitt's strategy would have been to stultify American opposition by "fanning a backfire of western separatism or by voluntarily relinquishing the posts if the United States appeared to be ready and able to take them by force." [45] Had a campaign to seize control of Louisiana and the Floridas succeeded, Britain would have obtained an area commercially reciprocal with the West Indies and secured a staging area for pushing on toward the silver mines of Chihuahua and Sonora.

### NOOTKA AND THE OLD SOUTHWEST

The Nootka controversy also had a perceptible effect on another American frontier. Word of the war scare led Alexander McGillivray, half-breed chief of the Creeks, to put less store upon his previous alliance with Spain and to recognize a need to mend fences with the United States. The anticipated con-

---

43. Thomas A. Bailey, *A Diplomatic History of the American People,* 7th ed. (New York, 1964), p. 68; S. F. Bemis, *A Short History of American Foreign Policy and Diplomacy* (New York, 1959), p. 42.

44. "So long as there were European possessions on its borders, the United States could not be indifferent to shifting combinations of power across the Atlantic which might directly affect its security, but as the Nootka crisis revealed, alliances were considered with extreme reluctance, and only to ward off dire calamity. The long-range aim of American diplomacy was the displacement of European sovereignty in North America entirely—continental expansion always had strategic overtones—and later on in South America as well, but meanwhile policy was directed toward preserving the colonial *status quo* or improving upon it. This meant if possible maintaining a balance of rival powers on our borders, preventing the displacement of a weak power by a stronger one, and remaining free of any engagements that would worsen our bargaining position when and if European conditions offered opportunities for the New World to 'fatten on the follies of the old.'" John Logan, Jr., *No Transfer: An American Security Principle* (New Haven, 1961), p. 47.

45. Bemis, Jay's Treaty, pp. 85, 98.

flict would cut off his Spanish source of arms and increase the difficulties of fending off American encroachments from Georgia and South Carolina. Journeying to the American capital with other Creek leaders, he signed the important Treaty of New York (August 7, 1790), making the Creek nation an American protectorate. A secret article provided that if an Anglo-Spanish war obstructed the normal trade route from Spanish ports, goods worth up to $50,000 annually might be imported duty free through American territory. A large area in what is now Georgia and Alabama was ceded to the United States in return for a guarantee of perpetual Creek ownership of their remaining lands. Washington made McGillivray a brigadier general in the United States army, with an annual salary of $1,200. "These satisfactory arrangements," Billington says, "and the acknowledged bribe to the chief, brought peace to the southern frontier for the first time in a decade." [46] McGillivray did not let the treaty keep him from accepting subsequent blandishments and a pension from the Spanish governor of Louisiana, but the episode served notice upon Madrid of the unreliability of alliances with Indian tribes, regardless of the funds involved.

In the area claimed by both the United States and Spain, land speculators from South Carolina, Virginia, and Tennessee had persuaded the Georgia legislature to sell them a vast tract along the eastern bank of the Mississippi, the so-called Yazoo purchase. It was an operation of questionable validity, since other seaboard states had ceded their lands in the west to the federal government. Upon learning of the Nootka crisis, a leader in the Yazoo speculation, Dr. James O'Fallon, sent the Spanish governor of Louisiana a bellicose message declaring that unless settlers whom O'Fallon was assembling in Kentucky were allowed to settle peacefully on the Yazoo claims, a filibustering expedition enjoying British assistance would descend upon New Orleans and evict the Spanish from Louisiana. O'Fallon's plans were proceeding apace, with George Rogers Clark recruited as the expedition's leader, when word arrived of the Nootka Convention, erasing the prospect of a conflict. The president looked upon the Yazoo speculation as threatening to provoke both the Creeks and the Spanish. The project had gone too far to be ignored, and federal action put a stop to it. By bringing to a head and destroying the plans of the speculators, the Nootka crisis assisted Washington in eliminating a serious danger to the peace on the southwestern frontier.[47]

The Treaty of New York and the threat of an American descent upon New Orleans emphasized in Madrid a need for closer attention to Spanish policy for the Mississippi basin, policy hitherto based on three measures:

46. Ray Allen Billington, *Westward Expansion: A History of the American Frontier*, 2d ed. (New York, 1960), p. 236; Arthur P. Whitaker, *The Spanish-American Frontier, 1783–1795: The Westward Movement and the Spanish Retreat in the Mississippi Valley*, 2d ed. (Gloucester, Mass., 1962), pp. 137–38.

47. Whitaker, *Spanish-American Frontier*, chap. 11: "Yazoo."

making alliances with Indian nations; wooing the allegiance of "Men of the Western Waters," and attracting Anglo-American immigrants to colonize underpopulated Spanish territories and become loyal subjects of His Catholic Majesty. In 1791 the ministry named the Baron de Carondelet to replace Estéban Miró as governor of Louisiana. Zealous to distinguish himself, Carondelet instituted a vigorous frontier policy, leading to a period of expansion of the northern perimeter of Spanish territory. His plans involved strengthening Spanish-Indian alliances by providing increasing supplies of arms to fend off white Americans and improving the defenses of Spanish outposts at Fort San Estéban (Washington Co., Ala.), Fort Confederación (Gainesville, Ala.), Natchez, Nogales (Vicksburg, Miss.), Fort San Fernando (Memphis, Tenn.), and San Luís de Ilinueces (St. Louis, Mo.). At the same time Carondelet intensified efforts, through agents among the "Men of the Western Waters," to sway white settlers' loyalty toward Spain.[48] His measures also included strengthening Spanish control over the upper Missouri, and attempting to discover an overland route to the Pacific in order to erect a chain of outposts linking St. Louis with Nootka Sound—activities examined at length in chapter 11. The consequences of the Nootka crisis in the old Southwest impressed upon Spain her essential weakness in the Mississippi basin and triggered a new and more vigorous resistance to foreign encroachments there, whether British or American. But pressures on that perimeter and Spain's plight in Europe would soon put Madrid in a mood to seek American agreement on a fixed boundary. The objective upon which Jefferson set his sights in 1790 would ultimately be attained in 1795 in the Treaty of San Lorenzo, better known as Pinckney's Treaty, one of the signal achievements in the history of American diplomacy. At the time when Jefferson initiated this demand, Bemis remarks,

> there seemed not the slightest reason why one of the greatest and oldest monarchies in the world should grant to the feeblest sovereign state in existence demands which were supported by nothing more formidable than reliance on highly disputable interpretations of treaties, mooted principles of ill-defined international law, and very vulnerable deductions from vaguely described natural rights. Still less to a government strained by sectional interests and containing conspiracy within its own household.[49]

Five years earlier the challenge on the northwest coast doubtless would have elicited from Carlos III and José de Gálvez the same bellicose response as that shown toward Captain Cook. But Carlos IV faced a dangerous new environment, shorn of his principal defensive alliance and personally im-

---

48. Billington, *Westward Expansion,* pp. 237–39.
49. Bemis, *Pinckney's Treaty,* p. 149.

periled by potent doctrines mushrooming ominously beyond the Pyrenees. After the diplomatic defeat over Nootka, it became urgent for Madrid to construct a new network of allies and pledged neutrals. To protect her colonies, Spain was obliged to cultivate American friendship.

Learning of the Anglo-American understanding formalized in Jay's Treaty (November 19, 1794), Prime Minister Godoy felt compelled to purchase American neutrality in the event of an Anglo-Spanish conflict. To placate American demands for Mississippi navigation, erase motives for an attack upon Louisiana, and forestall a possibility of joint Anglo-American action against more valuable portions of Spanish America, Madrid gave in to most of the demands that Jefferson had set forth in 1790. In San Lorenzo del Escorial on October 27, 1795, Godoy and Thomas Pinckney affixed their names to the momentous treaty setting a boundary at the 31st parallel, securing for the first time an undisputed American claim to all of Tennessee and Georgia and most of Alabama and Mississippi, guaranteeing navigation on the lower Mississippi, and giving American subjects the right of deposit and transshipment at a location on the New Orleans waterfront.

The destruction of the Family Compact in 1790 so upset the balance of power as to initiate a deterioration of Spain's stance vis-à-vis her territorial competitors that proved irreversible. Given the French situation, the National Assembly's reaction to a Spanish request for assistance anywhere would have been the same. But since the crisis occurred over the northwest coast, it was Nootka's name that echoed through diplomatic corridors and that, through the centuries, became the wedge that produced the fatal crack in Spain's defenses.

## 8 *The Apogee of Spanish Exploration, 1790–1791*

THE MONTHS of greatest turbulence for Madrid and London during the Nootka crisis were ones of great placidity for the northwest coast. The diplomatic imbroglio temporarily halted British fur trading, doubtless because the Britons feared capture by Spanish warships. Until Colnett and his companions were released, late in the season, Captain Metcalfe's *Eleanora* and one or perhaps two other Americans and a trader of Swedish registry were the only non-Spanish vessels on the northwest coast south of the Russian outposts in 1790. All of these stayed away from Nootka. The sound and fury of the Nootka controversy scotched Muscovite plans for the occupation of Nootka, but Russian traders continued as active as ever from Prince William Sound westward. In 1791 with the crisis past, trading renewed; one English, one French, and five American ships came to exploit the renowned wealth. In 1792 six American and ten or more English vessels were there, and in subsequent years they came in even greater numbers. The diplomatic showdown opened the door for all nationalities on the northwest coast by undercutting the legalisms with which Spain had hoped to prevent foreigners from trafficking there. Despite increasing signs of the impossibility of excluding other nations from the area, Spanish activity in the Pacific Northwest grew more intense during the ensuing years. Carlos IV and his ministers clung to the conviction that justice confirmed Madrid's claims to the western portion of North America, and Spanish authorities were disposed to make every effort necessary, short of war, to insure continued sovereignty there. Paradoxically, Iberian activities at Friendly Cove reached an apex *after* the Convention of 1790 had deprived the Spanish commandant of absolute authority over the port. From 1790 to 1792 Nootka throbbed with activity as never before or since.

With the seven naval officers and four surgeons designated for San Blas who had accompanied him to Mexico, Revillagigedo was in a much better position than his predecessor to take energetic action to defend Spain's claims on the northwest coast. He had not known of Flores's order to abandon Nootka, and two days after the *Princesa* returned to San Blas, but before any hint of this unexpected turn of events reached the viceroy's ears, he informed Bodega, the new commandant of San Blas, that paramount among Spanish preoccupations should be maintenance of the new establishment at Nootka. However, unless the king decided to the contrary, he was of the opinion that nothing could be done to dislodge the Russians from their settlements in Alaska, lest treaties of friendship with that empire be disturbed.[1] Nine days later, Revillagigedo received Martínez's message urging prompt reoccupation of Nootka, the heading off of British fur trading companies, and the minimization of the expense by trading copper for pelts. "I concur of course in this project," the viceroy replied,

> and in all accessory points about which you consult with me, as a consequence of which I now direct the commandant of that department to see to the prompt departure of ships to be employed in this new expedition. It would have been better if they could have gone to meet you in Nootka, but now there is no other remedy than that you return to that destination, as you laudably propose in your letters . . . commanding the packetboat *Argonaut* and exercising functions of second-in-command of the expedition, so that in this manner you can instruct perfectly the first [in command] in all that you have learned to assure occupation of Nootka, conclude examination of the coastline, and achieve felicitous progress in successive enterprises. All this is very important to the king's service, and since you have manifested zeal in your efforts and praiseworthy spirit to continue them, I request that you execute the foregoing until the new commander of Nootka advises me that he is completely instructed in all matters relative to their punctual discharge, when I shall order your return, recommending your services to His Majesty so they may have their just reward.[2]

The viceroy's letter discloses no trace of censure of the Sevillano's ability, personality, or actions. That same day Revillagigedo advised Bodega of Martínez's orders and told him to make no change in previous instructions (from December 8), other than to place Martínez as second in command and to send along five or six thousand pounds of copper plates to trade for sea otter skins, which would be sold by the Philippine Company in China for the benefit of the royal treasury.[3]

These suggestions did not fit the plans that Bodega had already set in motion. The *Argonaut* had yet to return from Acapulco with the cannons for the three warships that he hoped to send in February 1790 to reoccupy Nootka. In March he intended to dispatch a second expedition to reconnoiter the Hawaiian Islands and then proceed to the latitude of Bucareli Bay, whence the coast would be inspected southward to Nootka. Supplies would be left to reinforce that garrison before the expedition returned to Alta California for the purpose of putting those settlements in a state of readiness

1. Revillagigedo to Bodega, December 8, 1789, see chapter 5, n. 124.

2. Revillagigedo to Martínez, Mexico City, December 17, 1789, MxAGN (Hist. 65), fol. 525–27, AT.

3. Revillagigedo to Bodega, Mexico City, December 17, 1789, cited by Wagner, *Spanish Explorations*, p. 13.

to repulse possible British attacks. Bodega expected to command the second effort himself, if the *Argonaut* arrived from Acapulco with the hoped-for heavy artillery. If the cannons could not be obtained, he would be limited to supplying Alta California, fortifying Nootka, and examining the Strait of Juan de Fuca.[4] As for the Sevillano, Bodega commented,

> Martínez is a graduate pilot; if I name him second in command of the expedition, I will not be able to send on it any other officer or even pilots of earlier graduation; thus, those who ought to command because of their character and circumstances will remain ashore without obtaining a knowledge of the coastline. These reflections and the consideration that Your Excellency was not motivated by any other cause in giving this order than a desire for better service, judging perhaps that there was no one who had Martínez's knowledge, oblige me to entreat that you kindly order him sent as route pilot, since his selection as such does him ample honor and favor, and he knows that there are in the department men whose conduct, ability, practice, and solid principles would enable them to fulfill this office without leaving the commandant anything to desire.[5]

Bodega said he was setting Martínez's nomination aside, unless the viceroy made a further disposition, "for I am appointed to have regard for the opinion of those who serve under my orders, and avoid all motives for offense." From this moment onward, the Sevillano was subordinated to a number of officers of higher rank on the expedition to Nootka in 1790. His chief responsibility would be overseeing the acquisition of peltry for benefit of the royal treasury, and he was provided with 508 copper sheets and ten rolls of common cloth for such purposes.

Revillagigedo informed the ministry of Martínez's recommendation to occupy Hawaii, but he felt that Captain Cook's murder had demonstrated that a single establishment would be insufficient to dominate all of the archipelago. Spanish ships could obtain supplies there without maintaining a settlement, so he "had ordered that for now no thought be given to Hawaii or to any other location because it was a grave matter, and very proper to to the sovereign decision of His Majesty." [6] Martínez's plan for a string of presidios and missions and a fleet of twelve swift vessels was discounted as too visionary. Revillagigedo was unwilling to use royal funds to set in motion the commercial enterprise suggested as a means of eliminating foreign competitors from the fur trade. Instead he proposed that a private

4. Bodega to Revillagigedo, December 23, 1789, partly trans. in ibid., p. 12.

5. Bodega to Revillagigedo, Tepic, December 26, 1789, MxAGN (Hist. 68), T in CaBViPA, AT; Bodega to Eliza, April 13, 1790. MxAGN (Hist. 68), T in CaBViPA.

6. Revillagigedo to Valdés, Mexico City, December 27, 1789, SpAHN (Estado 4289), AT.

company be formed in Mexico City to initiate Spanish trade in furs, bringing pelts from the northwest coast to Monterey, where galleons returning from Manila could pick them up. The viceroy thought it unlikely that clothing of the type Martínez envisioned for trade on the northwest coast could be found in China, and he recommended that the furs be traded for quicksilver, perennially needed in New Spain. Wanting to keep the fur trade under control from Mexico City, Revillagigedo opposed the Philippine Company's sending ships directly to engage in the northwest coast traffic.[7]

Even this modified plan was destined to be shredded by the bureaucratic gears. Six months after its referral to the Philippine Company, the firm's governing council adopted a proposal for provisional settlements on the northwest coast, "constructing for the time being some barracks in order to take possession of the best ports before the English arrive there and to observe them when they establish themselves." If this gained the king's approval, the company asked that Revillagigedo be sent an order to give all necessary aid to those commissioned to execute the plan. The very day he received these recommendations, Floridablanca remitted them to the minister of marine and Indies, "so that Your Excellency may make the proposals he deems most convenient." [8] Instead of deciding for himself about the plan's merits, however, Valdés remitted it for Revillagigedo's opinion. Fully two years elapsed before the viceroy replied that he considered it "inopportune, difficult, costly, badly conceived, and worse assembled." He objected to the excessive cost and practical difficulties of supplying the projected settlements. Instead, he suggested that individual Spanish entrepreneurs be allowed to compete in the trade, but he expressed doubts that any would do so, because men with capital to invest had an opportunity for greater return from the unexploited mines and placer fields in New Spain.[9]

Martínez's ambitious plan for a string of missions and presidios to maintain Spanish sovereignty over the northwest coast would have warmed the hearts of José de Gálvez and his royal mentor, but they were no more. Their successors were cut from different cloth; they were less venturesome, by nature cautious and reluctant to embark on anything involving "unnecessary" expense to the royal treasury, however promising. Revillagigedo, in particular, was predisposed to take a dim view of projects for the extension of empire. Defense and improvement of exiting sources of revenue were his cardinal objectives. Given the dangerous international situation following

7. Revillagigedo to Valdés, Mexico City, January 12, 1790, MxAGN (Corr. Virreyes 154).

8. Minutes of the junta de gobierno of the Philippine Company, Madrid, December 17, 1790; [Pedro López de Lerena] to Floridablanca, Palacio, January 2, 1791; Floridablanca to [Valdés], Palacio, January 2, 1791. AT; all in SpAGI (V, Aud. Guad. 492).

9. Revillagigedo to Valdés, Mexico City, January 31, 1793, CU-B (Robbins Collection), Revillagigedo Papers, vol. 24, fol. 181–88.

the destruction of the Family Compact, it became difficult to dispute the wisdom of such a stance.

### THE REOCCUPATION OF NOOTKA

Martínez's abandonment of Friendly Cove in the fall of 1789 accelerated plans already underway for an expedition northward in 1790. Spanish officials were unanimous in believing that the strategic harbor should be reoccupied and fortified as quickly as possible. The force designated for this purpose was composed of three warships, captained by the newly arrived officers. Francisco de Eliza, with the frigate *Concepción,* would be the new commandant at Nootka. Salvador Fidalgo and Manuel Quimper would command the packetboat *San Carlos* and the sloop *Princesa Real* (the erstwhile *Princess Royal*). Eliza was a veteran of many campaigns, including that which led to the recapture of Pensacola from the British during the American Revolution. Fidalgo had participated in the most ambitious Spanish effort, to that time, at mapping the Mediterranean, and his cartographic experience would prove exceedingly valuable on the northwest coast.[10] Eliza carried instructions for a vigorous assertion of force against any foreign challenge to Spanish claims, from whatever direction that might come. His primary task was to seize and fortify "Santa Cruz de Nuca" before any other power did so. He should reach it as soon as possible, and "if during this brief interval someone has taken advantage of the absence of our arms, you will make known the right and preference we have and that you carry orders to evict anyone attempting to oppose you, and only in this case, or an insult to the flag, may you use force to contain and punish the offense; for our sovereign wishes to maintain peace and harmony, and under this concept you will deal with the greatest prudence, friendliness, and discretion with foreign ships encountered; you will not insist on examining them scrupulously, nor will you arrest them, but aid their departure, without permitting any traffic with the natives." [11]

To avoid foreign assault and make himself respected, Eliza should erect a fort with twenty cannons sent for the purpose; this fort should be run by the captain and the company of Volunteers of Cataluña. Once the establishment had been made capable of withstanding an attack, the other two vessels should explore the coast. Beginning at Regla anchorage (Cook Inlet), they were to determine whether Russia had a fortification there, as Colnett said, and examine the coastline to the Strait of Juan de Fuca. Using copper sheets

10. Luís de Córdoba, "Informe reservado de la oficialidad de la Armada, dados por el capitan general de la misma, D. Luís de Córdoba," Cartagena, n.d., SpMN (1533), fol. 48, 58v.

11. Juan Francisco de la Bodega y Quadra, "Instrucciones secretas para el Teniente de Navío Don Francisco Eliza," San Blas, January 28, 1790, SpMN (575bis), fol. 73–77, AT.

to exchange for all furs found, they should keep an exact account of the trade and remit the pelts to San Blas at the first chance.

The three vessels set sail from San Blas on February 3. Later in the spring the frigates *Princesa* and *Aranzazú* were scheduled to follow. A north-easterly storm caught the *Concepción* and the *San Carlos* as they prepared to enter Nootka on April 1. A boat from the *San Carlos* capsized, two men drowned, and several anchors were lost before the vessels made it into Friendly Cove four days later. To Eliza's relief, the area was empty, with no sign that anyone had been there since Martínez's departure.

Although lumbering and shallow of draft, the *Concepción* was the largest warship in the Department of San Blas. When fully armed, it carried thirty cannons and afforded the settlement considerable protection against attack. Following Nootka's reoccupation, one or more warships were maintained there in a constant state of readiness to insure Spain's dominion over the strategic site. Captain Pedro Alberni and his seventy-five Catalonian volunteers would remain permanently stationed at Nootka. Convinced that the best means of forestalling illness and discontent was an abundance of exercise in fresh air, Eliza and Alberni put sailors and soldiers alike to rebuilding a fort at the cove's entrance, cutting trees and underbrush bordering the beach, and making additional clearings in places suitable for cultivation. Carpenters were set to work constructing barracks, sheds, storehouses, and a main administration building that would serve as living and working quarters for the commandant and his fellow officers. Deep wells had to be dug, for the nearest year-around fresh water stream was two miles away. Pieces of a schooner had been brought from San Blas; the keel was laid in May and on November 1 it was christened the *Santa Saturnina*, alias *Orcasitas*.[12]

Alberni is credited with making the base at Friendly Cove a haven of comfort and succor for all nationalities in years to come. To determine the best seeding time for different vegetables and grains, he took care to sow a row of each variety each week for a certain period of time. Barley, potatoes, and beans grew readily, but wheat, corn, chickpeas, and tomatoes failed to ripen sufficiently. Cabbages, onions, garlic, turnips, beets, carrots, spinach,

---

12. Pantoja, "Extracto," 1791, in *Colección de documentos inéditos para la historia de España,* 15 : 115 (a variant text from both Pantoja's "Extracto," SpMN (331) and the version in CU-B trans. by Wagner, *Spanish Explorations,* pp. 155–198); Malaspina, *Viaje,* p. 362; Menzies, *Journal,* p. 125; Pedro Alberni, "Relación pequeña de la fuerza armada en el puerto de San Lorenzo en el año 90," SpMN (330), fol. 87; Jacinto Caamaño, "Diario," 1790–91, MxAGN (Hist. 69), fol. 76. The *Concepción,* alias *Princesa,* built at Realejo (Nicaragua), is not to be confused with the *Princesa,* alias *Nuestra Señora del Rosario,* of previous expeditions, constructed in San Blas. Both frigates went to Nootka in 1790 and spent the ensuing winter at Friendly Cove. That the *Santa Saturnina* was assembled from prefabricated pieces leads Wagner to suggest that it was a further reincarnation of the *Santa Gertrudis la Magna,* built at Friendly Cove in 1789 from parts of the *Northwest America,* the *Jason,* and the schooner commenced at Mawina. Wagner, *Spanish Explorations,* p. 141.

squash, artichokes, and parsley flourished. Radishes and lettuce grew to extraordinary size. However, a plague of rats developed toward the end of the season and, together with other rodents, menaced the gardens and broods of baby chicks, destroying everything not shut up tight. Successful husbandry of plants and animals faced many difficulties. One night the flock of chickens was almost wiped out when a weasel got into the coop and killed sixty at one fell swoop. Thereafter greater precautions were taken for their protection, and the flock grew very satisfactorily, each hen producing up to two broods a year. The settlement also had the first cows, goats, sheep, pigs, and turkeys introduced in the Pacific Northwest. Cattle fared well off the land, and by the following year a visiting scientist reported that animal husbandry was practical at Nootka, as long as enough dry feed was stored to suffice for three to four months of rugged winter.[13]

### THE FIDALGO EXPEDITION TO ALASKA, 1790

Effectively garrisoning Nootka Sound would not be sufficient to maintain Spanish dominion over the furthermost point claimed by Madrid. The rumored Muscovite attempt to colonize Friendly Cove had not materialized, but specific information was needed about the extent and strength of Russian activities farther north and about whether they had made additional outposts east of Kodiak. To achieve such objectives Fidalgo and the *San Carlos* left Nootka on May 4 and headed for Alaskan waters. With Fidalgo were interpreters of Russian and English, in case of foreign contacts. Inside Prince William Sound he took possession of a bay that he called Córdova, from which today's Alaskan city derives its name. Nearby Valdez is on a bay that Fidalgo named to honor the minister of marine and Indies. Although formal possession within the sound had already been taken for Spain in 1779 and 1788, for good measure the prescribed ceremonies were performed again in the three most propitious sites for ports and settlements. At one point the Spaniards heard an ominous thundering at the mouth of a cleft in the mountains, and they maneuvered up a fjord until they encountered a great ice field, lower terminus of a glacier, where masses of ice were breaking off with a roar, plunging into the bay, and raising dangerous waves—all of which kept them from examining the area at any length.[14]

Inside Cook Inlet they found a Russian fort with the tsarina's arms over

13. "Noticias de las semillas de Nooka," SpMN (330), fol. 51; Pantoja, "Extracto," p. 162; Malaspina, *Viaje*, p. 363.

14. *Compendio histórico de las navegaciones practicadas por oficiales y pilotos en buques de la Real Armada sobre las costas septe[n]trionales de California, con el objeto de descubrir y determinar la extensión y posición de sus distritos e islas adyacentes. Ordenados por un oficial de la Marina Real Española. Mexico: Año de 1799* (Mexico City, 1948), chapter III, passim. The acts of possession at Bahía de Córdova (June 3, 1790), Ensenada de Méndez (June 8), and Puerto de Gravina (June 10) are detailed in MxAGN (Hist. 68).

the gate, two blockhouses at opposite corners, and a catwalk along the top of the palisade, where sentries kept watch. The packetboat sailed on by, without stopping, to the inlet's inner reaches, sighting another Russian post near today's town of Kenai. Backtracking to just south of the first Russian establishment, Fidalgo performed an act of possession at a port named after Revillagigedo.[15] The *San Carlos* did not pass unnoticed. Nearby were the two warships commanded by Captain Joseph Billings; this was the expedition sent by the empress to counteract non-Russian activities in Alaskan waters and facilitate Muscovite expansion eastward. By native canoe Billings sent Fidalgo a letter, in English, with an invitation to join him at Prince William Sound, if that was not out of the Spaniard's way. The message reached Fidalgo, but since his course lay toward Kodiak, there was no reason to court trouble by seeking such an encounter. Billings remained at the rendezvous point from July 19 to July 30 and then sailed eastward to within sight of Mount St. Elias, where his vessels turned back toward Unalaska and Kamchatka without sighting the Spanish warship.[16]

Fidalgo reached Kodiak on August 15, ascertained the location of the Russian post, and headed toward Nootka. In two weeks he was at the corresponding latitude, but adverse winds discouraged his trying to reach the Spanish base, so a course was set for Monterey and San Blas. Although Fidalgo's explorations did much to complete Spanish cartographical knowledge of the Gulf of Alaska, and some of his place names are still on modern maps, the voyage had no political consequences because of events taking place simultaneously in Europe, which undermined all claims that Spain had asserted to the coastline.

### QUIMPER EXPLORES THE STRAIT OF JUAN DE FUCA, 1790

Martínez had emphasized the potential importance of unexplored waterways deep within the Strait of Juan de Fuca, and ship's ensign Manuel Quimper and the *Princesa Real* were elected to investigate. As pilot, Quimper was assigned the experienced Gonzalo López de Haro, whose valuable maps would be the first ever made of the interior of that important waterway. During these explorations Quimper was instructed to trade for such sea otter pelts as were available, for which purpose he carried a large supply of beaten copper sheets. They left Friendly Cove on May 31, put into Clayoquot Sound, and at Opitsat—largest Indian settlement on the northwest coast—Quimper and some of his men went ashore to visit Weeka-na-nish. His diary describes the chief's lodge as housing over 100 persons, with giant carved figures supporting three ninety-foot tree trunks that

15. Act of possession at Puerto de Revillagigedo, July 15, 1790, MxAGN (Hist. 68).

16. Joseph Billings to the commander of the Spanish ship, aboard the *Slava Rusa*, July 13, 1790, MxAGN (Hist. 68).

served as roof girders. The principal entrance, in the center of the façade, was through the mouth of a carved figure.[17]

Quimper was surprised to find Ma-kwee-na living there with the kinsmen of his late brother's wife. Asked why he was not at his own home, the Nootka chief answered that "it was because Martínez was in his port." Recognizing López de Haro, Ma-kwee-na inquired whether it was true Martínez had returned; he was told that "he need have no fear, as, although Martínez was in his port, he was not the chief in command of the frigate, but another named Don Francisco de Eliza was, and he should go to his port, as Eliza as well as Martínez desired to see him and entertain him." Hearing this, the chief appeared content and satisfied. That afternoon he and Wee-ka-na-nish came aboard in response to an invitation, to be presented with sheets of copper, some bracelets, and beads. "Still it was observed," Quimper relates, "that this chief had no confidence in Martínez's friendship or in our words, because he asked the seamen if Martínez or Eliza was captain of the frigate in Nuca." "When they gave him the same answer as he had previously received he embraced us with much joy, saying 'Amigo amar a Dios,' words he had learned in Nuca." The following day he returned to request a sail for his canoe, so as to proceed home, and it was furnished at once. Although sails were unknown on the northwest coast before the white man came, Ma-kwee-na was never backward about adopting such elements of European culture as he deemed useful. Wee-ka-na-nish immediately insisted upon a gift of the same kind. Quimper remarks that, "although I had already presented to him two large sheets of copper and three yards of scarlet cloth, I decided not to refuse him, as the friendship of this Indian is very advantageous in view of the fact that the foreign vessels which come to this coast have their greatest trade here." [18] On their fourth day there, Wee-ka-na-nish sent a large, exotically decorated war canoe with an invitation to a ceremony in Quimper's honor, but the commander declined and instead sent a small gift. Shortly, the war canoe returned with the chief's brother, who said that Wee-ka-na-nish "did not want gifts but instead would give me sea otter skins, and only wished me to come to the dance, and that Macuina and all the other chiefs were expecting me." "This obliged me to embark in the canoe with only two men from my ship," Quimper relates,

> making them see by this proof of confidence that I had no distrust of their friendship. When we landed the men, women, and children dis-

17. Manuel Quimper, "Diario . . . 1790," MxAGN (Hist. 68), SpAHN (Estado 4286). Partly trans. in Wagner, *Spanish Explorations*, pp. 85–86. Similar entrances seen in recent times often have as their door the mouth or womb of the lowest beast on a totem pole.

18. Quimper, "Diario," p. 87 (author's adaptation of Wagner's translation).

played great joy, Huiquinanichi and his brothers receiving me on the beach and accompanying me to the house where Macuina was. The latter rose joyfully and made a very natural bow with the words "amigo, amigo." He made me sit down close by him and told me repeatedly, as did Huiquinanichi, that I should not go to the strait with such a small vessel, as the chief who lived there was very bad, as were also the other Indians, who had killed two captains, but that I should return to my country and come back with copper and shells to trade in Nuca and Cayucla. They were all our friends while those in the strait and the neighborhood of it were very bad and treacherous.[19]

Afterward Quimper gave the two chiefs and their relatives gifts of copper and abalone shells and exchanged sheets of copper for some more pelts. He remained within Clayoquot Sound for a total of ten days, examining its many interior waterways. Upon continuing southward, he gave particular attention to searching for strategic harbors, ascertaining in each case the situation with regard to fresh water, firewood, fertility, climate, prevailing winds, and Indian behavior. Every likely port was the object of careful soundings and an act of possession. In this fashion he charted Puerto de San Juan (which still bears that name), Puerto de Revillagigedo (Sooke Inlet), Rada de Valdés y Bazán (Royal Roads), and Puerto de Córdova (Esquimalt Harbor, near Victoria), all on the northern shore of the strait.[20]

From the natives Quimper learned that along the south shore "there was a large inlet in the basin whose spacious channel carried its waters until they passed into the ocean," and so he set a course southward in search of this opening, discovering a commodious bay that he named after himself, Bahía de Quimper (New Dungeness Bay). He sent a longboat, under ensign Juan Carrasco, eastward along the coast. Carrasco found another large bay and named it Puerto de Bodega y Quadra (Port Discovery). Just beyond the farthest point reached on July 5, Carrasco sighted an opening judged to be a shallow bay, which he named Ensenada de Caamaño, after Jacinto Caamaño, one of the new naval officers serving out of San Blas. Carrasco did not go far enough east to perceive that this was a channel leading into the maze of waterways comprising Puget Sound. Quimper concluded that native information about an important channel in that vicinity was false. Two years later the British explorer Vancouver would follow this route, name it Admiralty Inlet, and acquire one of his major claims to fame.[21]

Cruising about in the broad strait, the Spaniards had noted a promising opening leading northward; this they named Estrecho de López de Haro

19. Ibid., pp. 88–89. The only known incidents prior to this date were assaults on boats sent ashore from the *Sonora* (1775) and the *Imperial Eagle* (1787).

20. The acts of possession are in SpMN (332) and AGI (Estado 43–12).

21. Quimper, "Diario," pp. 110–11.

(today's Haro Strait) after the first pilot. There was a discussion as to whether to follow the enticing passageway northward, but since their orders were to be back in Nootka by August 15, the consensus was that, with only two months of provisions left, they must defer exploration of the channel. Attempting to return seaward, they were carried on an irregular track by strong tides and adverse winds, and they crossed the strait from side to side several times. Quimper's haphazard course explains why the San Juan archipelago, revealed by Spanish explorers two years later, appeared to him to be one solid coastline, and why he failed to sight a prominent spit and harbor on the south shore, at Port Angeles, a discovery reserved for Spanish explorers in 1792.

On the south side of the strait, just inside the entrance, Quimper found a bay which he named Núñez Gaona, after Commodore Manuel Núñez Gaona, one of the highest ranking officials in the Spanish navy. It had been known for some years to British and American traders, who called it "Poverty Cove." The natives of a nearby village told Robert Gray in 1789 that it was called "Nee'ah," and today it is still known as Neah Bay, a fishing resort and the largest community on the Makah Indian reservation. Because of its strategic location, Quimper took extensive soundings. Núñez Gaona was to play an important role, two years later, as the second site on the northwest coast where the Spanish established a naval base; it thus became the first white settlement in what is now Washington State. Although it had abundant fresh water and timber, it was its location at the Strait of Juan de Fuca's entrance that gave Núñez Gaona such importance in Spanish eyes.

Several miles to the west, on diminutive Tatoosh Island, off Cape Flattery, lived one of the most prominent chiefs of the northwest coast. Ta-toosh, whom the Spanish called Tutusí, owed his prestige to the great potlatches for which his lineage was renowned. Until the American government eventually prohibited them, the gatherings periodically held on Tatoosh Island were reportedly attended by guests from as far away as Alaska.[22] The Makah were great hunters, and Quimper found them eager to trade an "infinite number" of sea otter pelts for copper sheets. Many of their canoes surrounded the sloop, the braves offering skins, fruit, and what Quimper describes as "delicious fish, among which were salmon of 100 pounds or more in weight." Today the area is justly renowned among sport fishermen for its giant salmon. The Spanish captain heard the natives boast of having killed "captains" of two European vessels in previous years. Before their audaciousness dawned on him, one of his men had been ambushed. "I sent the armed canoes ashore with half the soldiers and

22. Winifred Elyea, "The History of Tatoosh Island," *WHQ* 20 (1929) : 227. "Tu-tutsh" in Makah meant the "thunderbird."

sailors to wash their clothing and that of those who remained on board,"
his diary relates.

> At 8 a canoe of Indians came close to where the men were washing; at
> 9:30 we noted that my men were yelling and running after two small
> canoes which had come up after the others. I immediately sent the other
> canoe, armed, to the assistance of those on land. A little later it came
> back carrying a soldier who had been wounded in the head as a re-
> sult of his having strayed from the other men and gone into the woods
> to eat salmon berries and other fruits. The Indians, aware of the fact
> that the rest could not give him prompt help, came up to him, pre-
> tending friendship and giving him the fruit that he craved so much.
> When they saw that he was off his guard they advanced on him, took
> away his cutlass, and gave him several blows on the head with it. As
> he sought to defend himself, they fired arrows at him until he fled, one
> of them striking him in the face. Fearful of the support sent him,
> they went away leaving two small canoes on the beach. These I had
> brought alongside to see if they would come for them. At 10, not-
> withstanding the fact that the Indians who were alongside the sloop in
> numerous canoes were aware of the anger I felt at the daring of their
> comrades, three Indians in a small canoe decided to come alongside
> and carry off one of the captured canoes, which was tied to the ship.
> They paid no attention to our warning to let go of it until I fired a
> swivel gun. At this, they let loose of the canoe and fled.[23]

The next day Ta-toosh sent a message that he had punished the offend-
ers. Quimper returned the canoes and sent him an amiable reply. Friendly
relations soon resumed, but the difficulties of remaining on good terms with
the Makah are seen in an episode several days later.

> At 5 in the afternoon, notwithstanding the rough weather, two canoes
> came with Captain Tutusí, his brother, and his son. The second sold to
> the first pilot an Indian girl of eight or nine years of age, his daughter,
> for a little copper and a small cutlass. At 7 they returned to their
> settlement, having meanwhile exchanged twenty large and small sea-
> otter skins for the king's copper.[24]

Two nights later, Quimper's diary relates:

> At 11 a canoe with three Indians was seen approaching very silently.
> As they came alongside, and then approached the poop, the sentinel
> fired a shot, and at this they promptly fled to their settlement. We

---

23. Quimper, "Diario," pp. 123–24, entry for July 26, 1790 (author's adaptation of Wagner's
translation).
24. Ibid., p. 125, entry for July 29.

inferred that the father of the Indian girl whom the pilot bought was in this canoe for the purpose of stealing her, having some agreement with her, because all during the night she did not wish to go below to the place assigned to her in which to sleep, and when it was necessary to force her to do so, her grief was manifested by copious tears.[25]

On Sunday Quimper, his pilots, and most of the crew went ashore with a large cross. In a loud voice the commander announced that, by virtue of the donation and bull of Pope Alexander VI to the Crown of Castile and León, he was taking possession of those lands in the name of Carlos IV. As a sign of dominion, he cut grass and branches, moved stones, and walked about, asking those present to witness that he did so without contradiction. Taking the cross on his back and followed by his officers and men, chanting a litany, he marched with formality to a prominent spot near a creek flowing into the bay. There the cross was erected, the base surrounded by a pile of stones, and all knelt for a prayer. Pertinent lettering was carved upon the cross, and a bottle containing a copy of the act of possession was buried at the foot, to the accompaniment of the customary three volleys of musketry and a cannonade.[26] Quimper's scrupulous attention to such formalities every time he took possession absorbed much of his time during this expedition. By and large it was wasted effort, for Spain's rivals paid little heed to such practices. His care would have been more profitably lavished upon following and charting every channel in the strait's interior and making the results known to the world, to strengthen Madrid's claim to the area. This, however, would have gone against the grain of Spain's traditional policy of secrecy about her domains.

After eleven days at Núñez Gaona, Quimper sailed for Nootka, and in a week he was off the sound, but six more days of probing amid dense fog and adverse currents discouraged further attempts to find the entrance. Dwindling supplies obliged him to head for Monterey. The *San Carlos* arrived there from Kodiak, and in mid-October the two vessels proceeded to San Blas. Quimper's explorations were the first to confirm the extent of the Strait of Juan de Fuca's interior. The readjustment of Spanish objectives after the Convention of 1790 gave added significance to the area he mapped. Although he failed to reap the credit that fell to Vancouver for discovering Puget Sound, Quimper sighted Haro Strait, a potential northwest passage, which loomed as both a promise and a threat until it could be fully explored. On many occasions Indians came to the *Princesa Real* with sea otter pelts, and bartering took place in the same fashion as aboard

25. Ibid., p. 126, entry for July 31.
26. Act of possession, Bahía Núñez Gaona, August 1, 1790, SpMN (332), fol. 126–29.

British and American traders. The total gathered was 208, despite the fact that much of the time the Spanish were deep within the strait, where *Enhydra lutris* was seldom found, and Quimper's attention was focused on surveying port sites, not trading. But the captain demonstrated the feasibility of Spanish participation in the sea otter traffic by using trade articles readily available in Mexico and California. From this modest beginning, the Spaniards felt it would be possible to compete successfully against rival nationalities, driving them from the commerce while simultaneously charting and patroling the coast.

### ELIZA AND THE INDIANS OF NOOTKA

The natives largely avoided Friendly Cove following its reoccupation. Although Eliza showered with presents those few who appeared, they continued suspicious of Spanish motives. Before Ma-kwee-na's return from exile in Clayoquot, several incidents occurred that led to extremely strained relations. On one occasion, the Indians' apparent docility having habituated some of the seamen to come and go from ship to shore in any craft that happened along, a lone soldier climbed into a canoe at water's edge, expecting to be taken to the *Concepción.* Instead, once away from shore, his taxi sped off toward a native village. Martínez, who relates this episode, was of the opinion that the fellow would have been doomed had Eliza not secured his return through an appeal to Wee-ka-na-nish, with whom Ma-kwee-na was still residing.

One day a warrior came to the cove and boasted to several Spaniards that he intended to kill the Sevillano, whom he held responsible for the death of Ke-le-kum, his "king." Evading attempts at capture, the anonymous brave climaxed his harangue with the declaration that he and others would set fire to the *Concepción* that very night. Eliza was skeptical of the assault threat, but took every precaution that evening. About midnight the quiet was broken by war whoops on the beach, followed by shouting aboard the frigate. Shots blazed in the darkness and a number of warriors plunged into the bay and swam to their canoes, while others retreated into the forest. Eliza had his men follow those fleeing on foot, and five braves were slain.[27]

This incident is illuminated by Philip Drucker's analysis of northwest coast practices whose function was to shield a tribe against outside aggression.

> Protection of the group took the form of prompt and drastic action to
> punish offenses committed against its personnel, the threat of this ac-

27. Juan Bautista Matute to Bodega, Tepic, December 2, 1790, MxAGN (Calif. 79), fol. 151–52v; [Martínez] to Bodega, December 3, 1790.

tion serving as a deterrent just as punishment meted out by modern law is intended to deter crime. An Indian group that failed to act decisively in response to an injury to one of its members would be regarded as impotent; consequently, others would commit aggressions against it, convinced they could do so with impunity. While the Indians did not draw the nice modern distinction that we do when we say that our society does not revenge itself on criminals when it punishes them for their misdeeds, their legal actions were inspired by an attempt at social control rather than by a "savage thirst for vengeance." [28]

The brave's announcement of his intentions suggests that he wanted the attack recognized as an act of retribution. By killing Martínez or some of his compatriots, the warrior would restore his own group's reputation and be able to challenge Ma-kwee-na's vacillating leadership, because the latter had not avenged his brother's murder. The code underlying this episode seems to clarify the motives for most of the attacks upon trading vessels about which sufficient details are extant, an exception being the 1775 ambush of the *Sonora*.

A third incident was touched off by Eliza's urgent need of lumber for sheds, barracks, and an administration building. Several boats were sent to a village deep within the sound to procure some of the planks with which the natives roofed their lodges. It is not clear whether the villagers rebuffed offers to purchase or—more likely—had temporarily decamped, but when the Spaniards started to remove some of the boards, they were attacked and driven back to the launches. One brave was killed. The next day the seamen returned with two four-pounders, drove the inhabitants off into the forest, and carried away the desired timbers. Colnett, the source for this incident, relates that, before fleeing, the villagers "left at the Landing Place the Indian they had murdered hanging on a Cross, that their Pretended religion, and wanton Cruelly might stare them in the Face." [29] From his inquiries in 1792 Moziño identified the village as that of Tlu-pa-na-nootl, and he deplored the expropriation, since the chief "had no other lumber than that used in his lodges, and it is an injustice as great as that of robbery to compel any man by force of arms to sell what he needs for himself and does not wish to give up for any price." Moziño contends that "Eliza's mistake in this episode was in not sending with the soldiers and sailors who carried out this attack some of his pilots, whose innate good nature would have served as a brake on those men who ordinarily become brutal and fierce when they are given a little authority." [30]

28. Philip Drucker, *Cultures of the North Pacific Coast* (San Francisco, 1965), p. 72.
29. Colnett, *Journal*, p. 209.
30. Moziño, *Noticias*, p. 79.

Such incidents caused Ma-kwee-na to shun the Spanish even after the friendly encounter with Quimper and López de Haro at Clayoquot had persuaded him to return home. Moziño tells of the calculated method of breaking down his suspicions:

> With his rare insight, Alberni realized Maquinna's tendency to listen with appreciation to flattery, and, in order to induce him to visit the Spanish, with whom he had broken all familiar communications since the tragic passing of Quelequem, he composed a verse, with a few words he then knew of the language, celebrating the greatness of Maquinna and the friendship which Spain professed for this chief and all his nation.

> Macuina, Macuina, Macuina
> Asco Tais hua-cás;
> España, España, España
> Hua-cás Macuina Nutka.[31]

Roughly translated it meant: "Ma-kwee-na, Ma-kwee-na, Ma-kwee-na is a great prince and our friend; Spain, Spain, Spain is the friend of Ma-kwee-na and Nootka." Alberni taught his troops to chant the verse to the tune of a popular Andalusian song. The natives heard it and carried word to their chief who, compelled by curiosity, soon appeared and requested that it be sung for him. Gratified in the extreme, he insisted that it be repeated again and again until he memorized the tune. Two years later the chant could still be heard among the natives.

Ma-kwee-na evidently still entertained the hope of regaining his traditional village site. A Spanish pilot at Nootka in 1790 comments that the Indians were "continually asking when we are going to leave, the eagerness with which they solicit this being noteworthy." [32]

### MARTÍNEZ BOWS OUT

Where a year earlier his will at Nootka had been supreme, in 1790 Estéban José Martínez suffered the indignity of holding a more or less hollow title, with little or no authority. Even so, the commandant of San Blas had sent the volatile Sevillano back to the northwest coast against his better judgment. "I cannot fail to say to Your Excellency," Bodega informed the viceroy, "that I have never considered that his knowledge would have been in any way useful to the commandant of Nootka, nor should I have embarked him had not Your Excellency thus commanded me." [33] The erstwhile commander resented the inferior position that was henceforth his

31. Ibid., p. 78.
32. Pantoja, "Extracto," pp. 159–62, AT.
33. Bodega to Revillagigedo, Tepic, February 12, 1790, MxAGN (Marina 70), AT.

lot, and his bitterness is reflected in a letter to Revillagigedo, written the day before going northward, requesting transfer to Spain at the earliest opportunity. The royal order sending him home, as a consequence of his wife's protests, reached San Blas after he had left on the *Concepción* for Nootka, and it was carried northward by Juan Bautista Matute, captain of the supply ship *Aranzazú,* which remained at Nootka only briefly.[34] In July the Sevillano embarked with Matute and left for the last time the scene of his fateful role in history. The day he arrived in San Blas, Martínez informed the viceroy that he would leave for Spain as soon as his personal affairs were settled. Difficulties in disposing of his cattle ranch near Tepic led to an extension of his permit to remain until September 1791.[35]

That Martínez regretted returning to Spain and wanted to come again to the northwest coast and refurbish his reputation is shown by a petition he sent to Revillagigedo a month before the permission to remain in New Spain expired. He requested command of "an expedition to make a renewed search" of the Strait of Juan de Fuca, to reveal whether it contained a northwest passage. This was long his pet theory, and Martínez aspired to the mantle of glory that would fall upon the discoverer of such a waterway. The petition was remitted to Dionisio de Alcalá Galiano, one of Malaspina's officers then in Mexico City, who counseled against Martínez's proposal.[36] Just such an effort was then in preparation, however, in compliance with a royal order issued in response to one of Martínez's reports from Nootka in 1789. Two weeks after the Sevillano was turned down, the viceroy gave orders for an expedition such as Martínez had originally suggested, putting Francisco Antonio Mourelle in charge of it. As we shall see, circumstances prevented Mourelle from leading the effort, and the famous expedition of the *Sútil* and the *Mexicana* would be commanded by Alcalá Galiano and Cayetano Valdés. It was Revillagigedo's preference for those in whom he had greater confidence, rather than the inadvisability of Martínez's project, that denied Martínez an opportunity to return to the northwest coast.

Upon arriving in Spain, Martínez requested an interview with Minister Valdés. There is no evidence that it took place, but his request to return to the Department of San Blas was granted, on condition that his wife consent to follow him, "otherwise not, because of the long time in which he had

---

34. Martínez to Revillagigedo, San Blas, February 2, 1790, MxAGN (Marina 70); Revillagigedo to Bodega, Mexico City, February 18, 1790, MxAGN (Marina 70).

35. Martínez to Revillagigedo, San Blas, October 23, 1790, and Mexico City, June 11, 1791; Revillagigedo to Martínez, Mexico City, June 19, 1791; all in MxAGN (Marina 70).

36. Martínez to Revillagigedo, Mexico City, August 22, 1791; Revillagigedo to Alcalá Galiano, Mexico City, August 24, 1791; Alcalá Galiano to Revillagigedo, Mexico City, August 24, 1791; Revillagigedo to Martínez, Mexico City, August 26, 1791; all in MxAGN (Marina 70).

been separated from her, since he went to those realms." [37] Petitioning the king (June 26, 1793), Martínez offered to make himself personally responsible for placing the entire coast between the Strait of Juan de Fuca and Cape Mendocino under Spanish control within two years. For this he would need three hundred soldiers, nine officers, and forty friars from Mexico City's School for the Propagation of the Faith. He predicted that in this manner overland contact could be established between Fuca and Mexico, just as it had been between Monterey and Mexico. Asked for his opinion, Revillagigedo responded that "it was one of many projects that had kept Martínez's lightweight imagination working overtime, without a necessary understanding of the difficulties, expenses, and rules." [38]

After several years' service out of Cádiz as officer aboard a convoy escort, Martínez was promoted in February 1795 to frigate lieutenant and, since his wife had agreed to follow him, was transferred back to San Blas. A year later he was in Mexico City, soliciting attention for one of his perennial projects for the northwest coast.[39] As the ensuing chapters will reveal, by the time he returned to San Blas there had been a tremendous alteration in Spanish policy toward the northwest coast, and the Sevillano's aspirations were now out of the question. Little is known of these last years of his life; he is presumed to have captained vessels engaged in traffic between San Blas and Baja California, and he apparently fell ill while on one such voyage. His last testament was given on October 25, 1798, in the presence of the commandant at Loreto, on the western shore of the Gulf of California, and he died three days later, at the age of fifty-six.[40]

There is little of the heroic in Martínez's role in history, but if his intemperateness made the expedition of 1788 a series of fiascoes, the same cannot be said of his part in events of 1789. Chastened by Flores's warning, he seems to have subdued a penchant for tippling and quarreling with his fellow officers to the need for a united front against Spain's rivals. His rashest act, leading to Ke-le-kum's death, has no excuse, but in view of the mutually exclusive designs of Spain and Britain upon the northwest coast, a confrontation with the men from Macao was almost inevitable. Nor can the Sevillano be blamed for the magnification of the incident by Meares and Pitt. But a wiser man than Martínez might have extracted a triumph for Spain from the encounter by temperately but forcefully asserting

37. Valdés to Don Luís de Córdoba, October 30, 1792, as quoted in a letter from Córdoba to Estéban José Martínez, cited by Roberto Barreiro-Meiro, "Estéban José Martínez," *Colección de diarios y relaciones para la historia de los viajes y descubrimientos* 6 (1964) : 14–15.

38. Revillagigedo to Valdés, January 31, 1793, cited by Barreiro-Meiro, *Colección*, 6 : 15, AT. A portion of this letter is trans. in Thurman, *San Blas*, p. 321n, from a copy in CU-B (Robbins Collection), Revillagigedo Papers, vol. 13.

39. Martínez to Viceroy Branciforte, Mexico City, January 27, 1796, MxAGN (Marina 70).

40. Barreiro-Meiro, *Colección*, p. 17.

Spain's claims by dint of superior firepower. At the same time, while ingratiating himself with his rivals through largesse, he might have assembled various kinds of testimony to convince the British and Americans of Spain's rights by virtue of prior discovery, and obliged their tacit acceptance of Iberian dominion over Nootka. If Martínez had shirked his responsibility to halt Colnett's project before it got a good start, within the year a strong British enclave would have been planted on the northwest coast, north or south of Nootka, which Spain could not have uprooted without using considerable force. Colnett's obduracy compelled Martínez to use force.

Wisdom was not one of Martínez's strong points, and he is a classic example of the individual of mediocre talents occupying, through chance, a key position at one of the unforeseen crossroads of history. Nootka Sound in 1789 was one such intersection, where rival imperial designs met head-on. In the scramble for that heretofore obscure spot, only one of the contenders could obtain hegemony. The manner in which Martínez rose to the challenge, however unsatisfactory his decisions and actions may have been, had a profound influence upon the outcome of Spain's effort to retain control of the Pacific Northwest and, because of the consequences for the Family Compact, upon the larger history of his time. A Spanish naval historian calls Martínez "a victim of the failure of the Family Compact." [41] It would be more appropriate, however, to say that the Sevillano's conduct during the confrontation at Nootka gave the crisis a tone apt for Pitt's use in splitting asunder the Family Compact. One cannot call Martínez a victim of a process to which he contributed—as a little-known but nonetheless significant shaper of history.

### THE BRITISH PRISONERS RELEASED

From the time they arrived in San Blas, there is no evidence that Martínez and Colnett had any further contact with one another. The rectitude of Spanish officialdom is called into question by the English captain's subsequent complaints about the treatment accorded him and his associates during their sojourn in Mexico and upon their release. An examination of the evidence is warranted, since the charges reflect upon the judgment of Bodega and Viceroy Revillagigedo.

Months of impatient waiting, first in San Blas and then in Tepic, weighed heavily upon Colnett's spirit, to the detriment of his already irascible temper. Revillagigedo eventually let him come to Mexico City for the personal interview he requested. Colnett left Tepic for the capital in March 1790, accompanied by an interpreter and a Portuguese manservant. The long overland journey on horseback through Jalisco and Michoacán did little to improve his disposition. "Before I got half way to Mexico [City],"

41. Ibid., pp. 16–17.

his journal remarks, "I was seiz'd violently with the Blind Piles, the Skin two thirds off my Posterior, and the Sun had entirely strip'd my face."[42] He was unimpressed by the magnificent scenery, and his account is chiefly a record of his many displeasures. Between whirlwinds of dust, want of someone of his own station for company, and lack of meat (it being Lent), he was thoroughly miserable. Arriving in the capital after about a month, he importuned the viceroy relentlessly, finally exhausting Revillagigedo's patience, without shaking his position that seizure of the British vessels had been lawful. Pursuant to orders from Madrid, however, Colnett was informed that his ships would be released. He would be given the equivalent of the confiscated supplies and paid a sum sufficient to cover salaries and rations of the crew during their arrest, equal to that of Spanish sailors on the Pacific coast. If, above and beyond that, he needed more money, a moderate sum would be advanced.[43]

At long last he was allowed to write to his mother, admiralty officials, and the British ambassador in Madrid. To the latter he gave a brief account of the Nootka incident and of occurrences since his detention. "The Viceking does not let me be in want of anything to make me comfortable and happy in my present situation," Colnett wrote the head of his company. "No restraint [is] laid on any of my inclinations; every attention and respect paid me; not a request but is immediately granted me."[44] Upon departing for San Blas, he received a passport from Revillagigedo permitting him to call at Nootka to repossess the *Princess Royal,* but "with an Express prohibition of going, without very urgent necessity, into any Port or Bay belonging to our South Sea Coast of this America, or forming any Settlement, or trade on them, with the Indians: but this they may do in other places, Islands, or Coasts, which do not belong to the Dominions of his Catholic Majesty."[45]

Prior to permitting the *Argonaut* to sail, the commandant of San Blas presented Colnett with a reckoning of the expenses involved in feeding his crews during their detention, putting the English vessels in good repair, and providing supplies for the voyage back to Macao, deducted from salaries and rations paid him to cover the period of their detention. "There were few articles but I found fault with," Colnett notes.[46] His own account

42. Colnett, *Journal,* pp. 90–94.

43. Revillagigedo to Colnett, Mexico City, April 27, 1790, SpAHN (Estado 4291), in Colnett, *Journal,* pp. 101–02.

44. Colnett to Richard Cadman Etches, Mexico City, May 1, 1790, SpAHN (Estado 4291); Colnett to the ambassador of Great Britain in Madrid, [May 1, 1790], SpAHN (Estado 4291). The letters to his mother and the admiralty are in CaBVIPA (A.A./40/C71).

45. Revillagigedo, passport to James Colnett and Thomas Hudson, Mexico City, May 11, 1790, in Colnett, *Journal,* pp. 119–21.

46. Colnett, *Journal,* pp. 126–27.

of the haggling reveals him, however, as argumentative beyond measure and impossible to satisfy. No one dealing with Colnett ever succeeded in getting acceptance of a single point without his finding some reservation or complaint, as evidenced by his journal, in which he took private revenge upon everyone who incurred his rancor, whether Spanish, English, or Indian, venting his spleen with remarks ranging from manifest contradictions to proven untruths and coarse vulgarities. Howay, the journal's editor, opines that Colnett may have been justified in complaining that everything aboard the *Argonaut* not bolted down was appropriated for use, either officially or unofficially.[47] But an inquiry instituted by Revillagigedo showed some of Colnett's charges to have been false, casting doubt upon the veracity of the rest. The Englishman asserted that upon his arrest Martínez offered to set him free if some presents of value were forthcoming, and that his watch, a telescope, and a sextant had been sent to the Spanish flagship. When questioned, Martínez said that he was given the sextant and telescope and that he had intended to reciprocate with objects of equal value, before Colnett went out of his mind. As for the watch, the Sevillano insisted that John Kendrick, Sr., had purchased it from Colnett for 140 pesos and then had made him a present of it. Summoned to tell what he knew, Juan Kendrick testified that all he could bear witness to was that he had seen the watch in his father's possession.[48] Detailed inventories of the prize ships testify to the effort Martínez made to give a strict account of what was confiscated, but it was inevitable that some things would be stolen. The 218 pesos that Colnett received in remuneration, before leaving San Blas, was obviously insufficient compensation for a multitude of things, large and small, which it may be presumed he had aboard ship, and for the trade objects he had planned to parlay into a value many times larger in sea otter pelts. If he wanted to depart, Colnett had to accept Bodega's definition of his losses, the alternative being additional months of detention while the problem was referred to the viceroy. Deciding to relent, Colnett wrote Revillagigedo for the last time to report he had been cleared for departure and was leaving satisfied with the behavior of the commandant and *Comisario* of San Blas.[49]

The prize ships were released on July 9, 1790. Loading all the Englishmen and those of the Chinese who chose to return with him aboard the *Argonaut*, Colnett set sail for the northwest coast, seeking the *Princess Royal*. He had to proceed up the coast at a slow pace, due to the contrary pattern of winds, and the endeavor failed, for as luck would have it,

---

47. Howay, Introduction to Colnett, *Journal*, p. xxvi.

48. Revillagigedo to Floridablanca, Mexico City, March 31, 1792, CU-B (Robbins Collection), Revillagigedo Papers, vol. 23, fol. 209–10.

49. Colnett to Revillagigedo, San Blas, July 8, 1790, SpAGI (Estado 20–51).

Quimper put in at Monterey on September 1, before the *Argonaut* reached that latitude, and on September 11 Colnett anchored in uninhabited Bodega Bay, forty-eight miles north of San Francisco. There the ship's longboat, fitted out with a deck at San Blas, was unloaded and rigged as a schooner. Colnett placed Robert Gibson in command, ordering him and his seven companions to trade for sea otter skins along the coast and rendezvous at Barkley Sound, southeast of Nootka. Instead of proceeding there or to Nootka, however, Colnett anchored in Clayoquot Sound on October 8, to commence trading at what had been the most copious source of pelts anywhere along the coast, thus violating the terms of Revillagigedo's passport, which specifically forbade trafficking in areas claimed by Spain. Gibson and his companions bartered at several spots along the present Oregon-Washington coast, and made a specific search for Hezeta's *Entrada*, somehow missing the Columbia River, to the good fortune of subsequent American claims derived from Gray's sighting it two years later.[50]

From Clayoquot, Colnett sent one of his men to Barkley Sound in a native canoe, to inform Gibson of his whereabouts. Rather than proceed to the Spanish base, he chose to remain at Clayoquot and prolong the profitable trade with Wee-ka-na-nish. To Thomas Hudson, erstwhile captain of the *Princess Royal,* he delegated the unwelcome mission of going to Nootka in the *Argonaut's* jolly-boat to see whether Quimper and the other prize vessel were there. Hudson and five companions departed on October 17 for what amounted to a suicidal effort in such a small craft at that time of year—in an area noted for treacherous Indian behavior. Soon after they started, a violent storm arose, driving the boat onto a half-submerged ledge, where breakers soon dashed it to pieces and all of its occupants perished. An American trader visiting Clayoquot the following season learned the details. The natives of Hesquiat Harbor saw the little craft in distress and claimed to have gone to its rescue, but by the time they reached the site, all the whites had drowned. Some of the bodies were retrieved, brought to the beach, stripped of their garments, and thrown to the crows.[51]

Miraculously, the longboat accomplished its hazardous voyage from Bodega Bay without meeting a similar fate. Since no word had arrived from Hudson, on October 24 Gibson and the longboat were sent to Nootka in search of him. For more than a month Colnett cooled his heels in Clayoquot, without a hint as to the fate of either boat and crew. Gibson reached the Spanish settlement on October 28, and the following evening Ma-kwee-na brought word that the villagers of Yzcoat (Hesquiat) had seen a boat breaking apart on the rocks, with three bodies washed upon the beach. The

50. Colnett, *Journal,* pp. 174, 186–87.

51. Ibid., pp. 181–85, 189; John Hoskins, "Narrative of the Second Voyage of the *Columbia,*" in Howay, *Voyages of the "Columbia,"* pp. 187–88.

viceroy had entrusted Colnett with dispatches for Eliza, which Hudson was bringing to Friendly Cove. A Spanish officer present when Ma-kwee-na arrived relates that, "we promised to reward him if he brought a box, which was expected with our orders; he offered to search for it with the greatest diligence." [52]

Impatient at the lack of news from either Hudson or Gibson, Colnett feared they had been detained by the Spanish. He persuaded Ke-le-kum's widow, who now resided with her brother, Wee-ka-na-nish, to go in search of them. She eventually returned with two sailors from the longboat, a friendly letter from Eliza, and a message from Gibson urging Colnett to join them at Friendly Cove. "You have nothing to fear on the Spaniard's side, it is not Martínez," Gibson exulted. "They curse the day that he ever saw Nootka." [53]

Upon learning of the jolly-boat's fate, Colnett distrusted the native version, suspecting that some of his men had made it to shore, only to be slain. He seized Ta-toosh-ka-setl, the chief's brother, and another brave with him, threatening Wee-ka-na-nish that if the bodies were not brought within a week he would kill them and "every native he could find." Klee-shee-nah, a subordinate chief, later told some Americans that he went to Hesquiat, "where the dead bodies were, but being putrified and much eaten by the crows, he did not bring them; but brought all their cloaths: these not being bloody, Captain Colinet was satisfied, released the Chiefs, and made them a present of several sheets of copper, cloathing, etca. etc." [54] On December 16, Gibson and the longboat rejoined the *Argonaut* at Clayoquot, where Colnett intended to spend the balance of the winter. Wee-ka-na-nish was not one to forgive an affront. His brother's detention as a hostage was probably the excuse, if he needed one, for an attempt to overpower the *Argonaut* by frontal assault on December 31. The attack failed, but it was a close enough call to persuade Colnett to weigh anchor on New Year's Day and risk a perilous midwinter voyage to the safety of Friendly Cove, where he dropped anchor three days later. Eliza received the captain of the *Argonaut* and his men with unanticipated cordiality. Colnett was shocked to find the Spanish base in disastrous straits, with "great numbers" of those who had remained there all winter suffering from scurvy. His journal acknowledges that nonetheless he enjoyed a standing invitation to share Eliza's table, limited as the Spanish resources were, which he gratefully accepted as a means of escaping the diet of little else than hardtack and fish prevailing aboard the *Argonaut*. Colnett's account of the Nootka settlement's privations during the winter of 1790–91 is confirmed by other sources. In mid-October

52. Caamaño, "Diario," entry for October 29, 1790, AT.

53. Eliza to Colnett, October 29, 1790, and Gibson to Colnett, November 23, 1790, both pub. in Colnett, *Journal*, pp. 195–97.

54. Hoskins, "Narrative," p. 188.

excessive rain and cold destroyed the gardens. Strained relations with the Indians deprived Eliza of their services in supplying the settlement with fresh game and fish. The most generous offers of barter could not entice the natives out of their winter camps once the cold blasts commenced.[55] The 250 persons accompanying Eliza were the first of their nationality to spend an entire winter on the northwest coast, an unusual hardship for men accustomed to a milder climate.

The *Concepción*, the *Princesa*, and the *Santa Saturnina* rode out the long months unrigged, their stores suffering considerable damage from the excessive humidity as well as from rats, which infested them in epidemic proportions, making it necessary to construct tight, secure, and dry storage facilities on shore for all supplies. The construction of adequate storehouses took so long that winter arrived before they had built more than just enough barracks to house the soldiers and sheds where on rainy days the sailors might be kept busy at sawing and carpentry. The confined quarters, months of inclemency, and lack of fresh food other than fish were all factors in the calamitous state of health by winter's end. Caamaño lists catarrh, rheumatic pains, flatulent colic, diarrhea, dysentery, bloody stools, and scurvy as the most common complaints among the ailing. The most serious was scurvy, which the surgeons combatted by mixing their customary antiscorbutics (small amounts of lemon syrup and vinegar) with a tea made from boiled pine sprouts which, he says, had "marvelous effects." If any of the men fell ill with bloody dysentery, they were assumed to be doomed unless they could be taken to a more favorable clime.[56]

After their respective cruises in the fall of 1790, the *San Carlos* and the *Princesa Real* were to have left their surplus stores for the Nootka garrison and to have transmitted word to California of the settlement's dire need of supplies. This had not occurred, however, and in Eliza's desperate situation he was obliged to permit the slaughter and consumption of all the domestic animals intended for breeding stock. Arrival of the *Argonaut* compounded the strain upon Eliza's resources, but he presented Colnett with two of his remaining hogs, some chickens, and four hams. Colnett responded with a barrel of sugar and cask of wine, much valued as remedies for the scurvy-ridden.[57]

The English captain's cordiality was not without an element of self-interest. His journal confides that he told Eliza that the viceroy's passport had been lost with Hudson. Thus he avoided disclosing that Revillagigedo

55. Colnett, *Journal*, pp. 201–02, 205; Malaspina, *Viaje*, p. 362; Pantoja, "Extracto," SpMN (331), fol. 230v.

56. Malaspina, *Viaje*, p. 363; Caamaño, "Diario," fol. 80; Pantoja also asserts that at Nootka dysentery was virtually incurable. See his "Extracto," SpMN (331), fol. 231.

57. Eliza, "Extracto de la navegación . . . 1791," English trans. in Wagner, *Spanish Explorations*, p. 142; Colnett, *Journal*, p. 206.

specifically forbade trading along the coast. As soon as weather permitted, he talked Eliza into towing the *Argonaut* to Mawina Cove, ostensibly for careening and repairing with the aid of Spanish caulkers and carpenters. The greater freedom at Mawina permitted sweeping the sound of its yield in sea otter pelts. Since Eliza was specifically instructed to prohibit trading, Colnett presumably led him to believe that the viceroy's passport licensed such activities, and Eliza judged it advisable not to offend him. Gibson had obtained 100 pelts on the way from Bodega Bay. Colnett secured another 300 at Clayoquot, and at Nootka he bartered for 700 more, a statistic begging comparison with the assertion that Spanish officials at Nootka and San Blas left him without trade articles.[58]

Once his purposes at Mawina had been served, Colnett returned to Friendly Cove where, his journal notes, "I din'd daily with the Commandant; and sometimes my Officers." "They and myself treated with the greatest Politeness." He went to great lengths to persuade Eliza to deliver up the *Santa Saturnina*, which was constructed of materials from the *Northwest America* and the *Jason*. The commandant finally agreed, and Colnett's men began rigging the vessel for the trans-Pacific voyage, but later Eliza reversed his decision. As Colnett's journal explains it, "some evil dispos'd people had given out, I had bought her from him for 3000 Dollars, which accusation to falsify I must return the Boat, which my situation Obliged me to do."[59] Eliza's hospitality did not keep Colnett from trying to subvert Spanish relations with Ma-kwee-na, as he had with Wee-ka-na-nish. "They have driven Macquilla from two of his old residences and taken possession of them themselves," the English captain's journal remarks.

> This the Poor wretch timidly bears. Every artifice has been used to prejudice him against the English, but he has experienced too many Cruelties to believe all they say. I use the same arguments with him, I had done with Wickininish and he made the same application in return, requesting to see a larger ship. But he is a most miserable, cowardly wretch, at best, and flies whenever he sees the Spaniards.[60]

The chief's replies to Colnett's overtures evince the Indians' growing sophistication. The nation sending the largest warships would earn native deference. But Ma-kwee-na had much reason to fear Spanish hegemony. His alleged ritual cannibalism had become a major issue and threatened

---

58. "My Passport from the Vice Roy I secreted saying it was lost with Captain Hudson and only shewed him my Friendly Letter, which I receiv'd with it. In doing this it served two purposes: First, it kept them ignorant that I was expressly forbid trading on the Coast, and the Vice Roy's Ideas of Capturing us, and prevent their stopping any English that might arrive off the Coast." Colnett, *Journal*, p. 208.

59. Ibid., pp. 206–07, entry for March 1, 1791.

60. Ibid., pp. 208–09.

his continuance in power, whether or not he was guilty. Commander Eliza had received a report from some Indians to the effect that

> there are only two chieftains who eat human flesh: one lives in Tasis, at the foot of a very high mountain of this name, which one reaches by one of many arms of the sound and is about eight or nine leagues away; the other is one of the most prominent and closest to our establishment, called Macuina. This cruel man has eaten eleven children, which he bought for this purpose and raised to seven or eight years of age, executing this detestable act when it seemed to him they were ready, or his evilness prompted it. Placing the unfortunate victim before him and closing his eyes, as if to symbolize the horror that such an abominable deed caused his nature and humanity, he began to beat the air with a club until one of the blows struck its head. At once he quartered and cut it into strips, separating flesh from bones, eating it raw in great mouthfuls, shouting and making fearsome gestures and grimaces. After we had confirmed this with Englishmen of the *Argonaut* he came by and we gave him to understand, as well as we could, the great evil in this, and [we told him that] if we heard he repeated the practice we would go to his village, burn it, and kill everyone there. This admonition had the desired effect, although previously it had been determined he should be whipped, and this was not put in practice to avoid driving the Indians away. After three or four days he brought a little girl to sell, whom I bought for a sheet of copper, and gave the name Dolores. Since she was of the said age, I infer that she was being kept for such a depraved objective. This he denied and he assured was only a charge made against him by those of other villages. What is certain is that before this they brought the legs and arms of children to our ships in order to sell them to us.[61]

Later that year one of the children sold to Eliza confirmed that, "in effect Macuina liked human flesh, and that election of the child for this horrible banquet depended on the one to which his hand pointed while his eyes were blindfolded." [62] Such reports could be chalked up to the chief's enemies or to juvenile invention if the testimony were not so specific and from so many sources, year after year, giving details that correspond to little-known ritual among tribes elsewhere in the Americas. Whether true or not, the charge was a blot on Ma-kwee-na's reputation that he had to struggle mightily to dispel if he were to get back into Spanish graces and retain control over his tribal territory.

By spring, five members of the Spanish garrison had succumbed and many

61. Caamaño, "Diario," pp. 84–85, AT.
62. Malaspina, *Viaje*, p. 355.

more were gravely ill from the debilitating effects of scurvy and dysentery. Early in March the *Princesa* departed for California with thirty-two of the ailing as passengers, six of them in serious condition, in the hope that a benign climate would enable them to recover. Relief came on March 26 with the arrival of Ramón Antonio Saavedra and the *San Carlos* with a cargo of much-needed supplies from San Blas. Later in the season the *Aranzazú* made two trips to Nootka with provisions, once from San Blas and later from Monterey.[63]

Santa Cruz de Nuca was thrown into a state of alarm on April 3 when two Indians from Esperanza Inlet informed Eliza that they had sighted five vessels off their village. Certain that such a flotilla could not be Spanish and apprehensive of a British or Russian attempt to seize Nootka, Eliza commenced putting the settlement in a defensive posture. The fort was readied for action and two cannons hauled to the seaward side of the village to fend off a landing from that direction. "In order not to be surprised during the darkness of the night, which was one of ugly aspect and continual rain," Pantoja relates, "the commandant ordered sentinels to be doubled and make their rounds by sea and land and pass the word from one to another." [64] Eliza sent a boat to the headland north of Nootka, from which the entrance to Esperanza Inlet could be watched, but no sails were sighted, so he had Narváez, the *Santa Saturnina,* and eighteen armed men follow the passage around Mazarredo Island, scouting for signs of foreign presence. They learned from inquiries that four English trading vessels had been there as recently as two days before. Eliza's subsequent actions reveal his continuing apprehension of a concerted attempt to overpower the Spanish settlement.

Colnett's cooperation with Eliza for mutual survival did little to diminish the English captain's animus toward Spaniards in general. His disgust at not recovering the *Princess Royal* and the rebuilt *Northwest America* fueled this bellicosity. Having hoodwinked Eliza into letting him sweep Nootka of the season's pelts, he sailed from Friendly Cove with his valuable cargo on March 2, 1791, headed for the Sandwich Islands and Macao. The Spanish had not seen the last of him, however.

Since Quimper had not encountered Colnett, the viceroy ordered him to take the prize sloop directly to the Orient for delivery to its rightful owners. At Bodega's suggestion he carried the sea otter pelts gathered in 1790, plus the remainder collected under Vasadre's recently annulled contract, to be negotiated in Canton and the proceeds to be invested in a vessel for use in the fur trade, in which Quimper and crew would return to San Blas. Revillagigedo approved sending the furs—3,148 from California and 208

63. Pantoja, "Extracto," pp. 150–63; Eliza, "Extracto de la navegación," p. 142.
64. Pantoja, "Extracto," p. 157, AT.

from Quimper's cruise—but he was opposed to purchasing a vessel in Asia, since ships brought from there in the past had always required expensive repairs. Instead the furs should be sold for the benefit of the royal treasury by the Philippine Company, with Quimper and companions returning aboard the next vessel for Acapulco.[65]

Quimper left San Blas on February 11, with instructions to establish friendly relations with the Sandwich Islanders, en route, so that Spanish ships could call there in the future. He sighted Hawaii on March 20, and three days later dropped anchor in a bay on the western shore, only to be surrounded by great native canoes, each containing more warriors than Quimper had men in his entire crew. Fortunately, their attitude was peaceful, and for some pieces of metal they traded fresh fruit, hogs, and fowl. Several days later King Kamehameha came abroad and gave Quimper a handsome feather-covered helmet, cloak, and cape; the captain reciprocated with some big pieces of iron and an old pistol. The monarch, by now well acquainted with mariners of various nationalities, would be satisfied with nothing less than a fine musket, and Quimper eventually gave in. Thereafter Kamehameha was generous with provisions and many fine sea otter skins. Quimper wondered at this, knowing that the species had never been seen in the warm waters around Hawaii. On Oahu he would learn their source, the *Fair American,* overpowered by Kamehameha's warriors.[66]

While he was at anchor in Oahu's Kailua Bay, a letter came into Quimper's hand from Colnett to several Englishmen said to be residing on Hawaii. Translated by Juan Kendrick, it told of the *Argonaut's* arrest and detention and warned them of the impending Spanish arrival in Hawaii. No sooner had they learned of Colnett's presence in the islands than the *Argonaut* hove into sight, bearing down upon the *Princesa Real.* Quimper sent Kendrick in the ship's boat with a message manifesting his friendly intentions. Colnett's journal reveals the reception given these peaceful overtures.

> I called a council of my Officers, and it was unanimously agreed as the Spaniards had so often deceiv'd us and committed so many Piracies on us, to attempt to retake the Vessel by force of arms, which the Ship's Crew Joyfully agreed to. I hove to immediately, and clear'd the Decks and the Bore up.[67]

65. Revillagigedo to Floridablanca, November 26, 1790, and March 27, 1791; Revillagigedo to Pedro [López de] Lerena, March 31, 1791; all in MxAGN, cited from copies in CU-B by Ralph S. Kuykendall, "James Colnett and the 'Princess Royal,'" *OHQ* 25 (1924) : 44–46.

66. Quimper to Revillagigedo, Manila, July 15, 1791, SpAGI (Estado 20–68), in Francisco de las Barras de Aragón, *Reconocimiento de las Islas Hawai (Sandwich) por el marino español Quimper* (Madrid, 1954), pp. 4–11.

67. Colnett, *Journal,* p. 213; Colnett [to several Englishmen], April 1, 1791, Spanish trans. in SpAGI, retrans. in Kuykendall, "James Colnett, pp. 40–41.

By this time the *Argonaut* was broadside to the *Princesa Real,* at about a hundred yards distance. Quimper saw the English seamen preparing their artillery for action, so he ordered his men to do likewise, calling to Kendrick to return with the ship's boat. The American replied that Colnett said he was dressing and intended to come aboard the sloop. Minutes passed and the hurried preparations on both vessels continued. Again Quimper called across, protesting his peaceful intentions and asking why it appeared that the *Argonaut* was about to do battle. Colnett replied by dispatching Quimper's boat, without Kendrick but with an English officer carrying a letter stating:

> Your letter by Mr. Kendrik informs me that you are to convey the Sloop *Princess Royal* to Manilla and thence to Macao but as that is contrary to the Law of all Nations and particularly contrary to the Constitution of Great Britain whose Protection and License together with that of the Honble. Board of Marine I have now in possession and which I hope never to disgrace, I must act in conformity to it at the risk of my Life and will demand the Property of the Honble. South Sea Company—wherever I find it.
>
> For which reason I have detained Mr. Kendrik until I know your determination—this Business I hope will be amicably settled between us to the Honor of both Nations and ourselves—whatever terms or Conditions you can ask with reason will be agreed to by / Your Hble. Servant / James Colnett, Lieut. / of Royal Navy and Commander of all Vessels employd and to be employed for the time being for the Honble. South Sea Company of London.[68]

Since Kendrick had not returned, no one could make out the letter's meaning. The English officer, who spoke a little Spanish, said Colnett insisted that because of his superior rank, any interview must be held aboard the *Argonaut.* Quimper's orders were to avoid further friction with the English, so he complied, whereupon Colnett demanded that the sloop accompany him directly to Macao. Quimper's account asserts that he was ready to sacrifice his life and those of his men rather than depart from Revillagigedo's instructions to proceed to Manila, a determination that made Colnett desist and settle for copying Quimper's instructions, which specified that the vessel would be taken to Macao for delivery to its owners. The crisis past, they exchanged salutes, and for several days the two captains dined repeatedly as each other's guests. Quimper subsequently visited Kauai and Niihau, where he encountered the *Argonaut* once more before departing for the Philippines. The incident at Kailua is of interest to Pacific

68. Colnett to [Quimper], April 2, 1791, MxAGN (Prov. Internas 153), in Kuykendall, "James Colnett," pp. 48–49.

Northwest history in that it affords additional insight into Colnett's personality. Judge Howay, his principal biographer, says the episode shows him "at the best, a man who in emergency easily became unduly excited and acted in a precipitate, ill-judged, and un-balanced manner." [69] As paladin of British interests on the northwest coast, he left much to be desired.

Upon reaching the Philippines, the *Princesa Real* was taken to Macao by another crew. Before it appeared there, Colnett had begun legal action designed to refuse its restoration, on the grounds that it had been damaged when driven aground at San Blas during a storm; he was holding out for a large monetary settlement for all losses incurred by its seizure. His business associates backed him by refusing to take delivery, it was badly damaged by a typhoon, and Spanish authorities eventually sold the sloop in China for $2,000. The Spanish cargo of sea otter pelts was embargoed by Chinese customs as a result of strained relations between Peking and St. Petersburg. Assuming that all sea otter pelts came from Russian territory in North America, a Chinese edict in 1791 had prohibited their importation, and the *Princesa Real's* valuable cargo languished in Macao until the prohibition was lifted in May 1792. Colnett was even less fortunate with his 1,200 pelts. Proceeding to Japan, he found officials there unwilling to bargain, and he was obliged to take them to England, unsold. Ingraham, now master of the *Hope,* arrived in Macao in the autumn of 1791 and bribed local officials to smuggle his pelts ashore. "Incidents of this kind," Howay remarks, "throw light upon the vigour and determination of the American traders, and, whether admired or not, aid in accounting for the control which they obtained in such a short time over the maritime fur-trade." [70]

THE VICEROY'S SHIFTING PERSPECTIVE OF THE NORTHWEST COAST

At the Nootka controversy's inception, when a royal order warned that an Anglo-Spanish conflict seemed likely, Revillagigedo had notified the minister of war that there were "not enough forces in our South Sea and the Department of San Blas to counteract those which the English have at their Botany Bay, and I think therefore we should withdraw those we have in the pretended establishment of Nootka so that, instead of exposing them to be readily made prisoner, they can fall back to redouble the defenses

69. Quimper to Revillagigedo, July 15, 1791, p. 8; F. W. Howay, "Some Additional Notes Upon Captain Colnett and the 'Princess Royal,' " *OHQ* 26 (1925) : 16.

70. Howay, "Early Days of the Maritime Fur Trade," p. 41; Howay, "Some Additional Notes," p. 15; Howay, in Colnett, *Journal,* pp. xxviii, 229n; Alejandro Malaspina, "Extracto de lo que ha ocurido [sic] en las negociaciones de pieles de nutria emprendidas desde el año de 1784 hasta ahora por cuenta de S. M.." n.d., SpMN (335), fol. 44–45v; Kuykendall, "James Colnett," p. 52. Thurman, *San Blas,* pp. 324–25, traces the further complications of liquidating the *Princess Royal.*

of our older and established possessions, avoiding the great expense of subsisting at such a remote distance." [71] A day later he reiterated this advice to the minister of marine and Indies. Considering Britain's strength in Australia, Spain was outweighed on the northwest coast, and it should be anticipated "that any enterprise which they attempt in that area would put our ships in great risk, their capture being inevitable. Gathered together in San Blas," he suggested, "they would be of great importance to us, not only to protect this continent, and as auxiliaries of the presidios and missions of San Francisco and Monterey, but for any sudden alert, and as help for the Philippines, for which this port is well adapted." He considered the California coast too long to be occupied in its entirety or protected from foreign encroachments, with so few vessels at his disposal. "If the forces were augmented so as to make them respectable, the expense to the treasury would be enormous, and I would never dare guarantee that [foreign] navigation and commerce in those spacious distances could be checked." Hence he favored removing the troops and vessels from Nootka as soon as means could be found to send word northward. [72]

The Convention of 1790 allayed Revillagigedo's fears of a British attack. Shortly afterward he received the royal order (November 27, 1790) asserting Spain's right to prohibit foreign commerce or settlement south of Nootka and the equal right of Spanish and British subjects to traffic beyond Friendly Cove. Now he saw the northwest coast in a different light, and he relayed the ministry's commands to Nootka stipulating that, "in case the English solicit restoration of land which they never occupied in that Port or bring any other groundless pretension contrary or prejudicial to our rights, [you should] try to adjust everything suavely and amicably, but protest contravention of the recent adjustment between the two courts, providing me with the appropriate details," to be communicated to Madrid. [73] Two months later, responding to the royal order of December 25, 1790, Revillagigedo felt sufficiently confident of Spanish claims to the northwest coast to remind the ministry that "not in April of '89 . . . or at any other time were the English dispossessed of buildings or districts of land situated on the north coast of Californias [sic] and its adjacent islands." Since by the convention Spain promised to return lands that the English had never had, Madrid should offer to cede the rest of Nootka and transfer her base to a port on the north shore of the Strait of Juan de Fuca. By fixing a demarcation line from the strait's entrance to 60° north latitude, as the ministry had sug-

71. Revillagigedo to [Manuel José Antonio Hilario Negrete], conde de Campo de Alange, [minister of war], Mexico City, July 27, 1790, CU-B (Robbins Collection), Revillagigedo Papers, vol. 21, fol. 465–65v, AT. The royal order was dated May 24, 1790.

72. Revillagigedo to Valdés, Mexico City, July 28, 1790, ibid., fol. 482v–84v, AT.

73. As quoted in Revillagigedo to [Floridablanca], Mexico City, February 28, 1791, ibid., vol. 22, fol. 188v–190, AT.

gested, foreigners could be kept from penetrating to the "missions and province of New Mexico." This northernmost Iberian outpost could be used to keep watch over English activities and enable the Spanish to participate in the fur trade. South of Fuca, English vessels would be prohibited to traffic. The viceroy had a map of the northwest coast drawn, of which several copies were remitted to the ministry, on which such a boundary was designated. It embodied concepts that would guide forthcoming Spanish policy toward that area. Two points stand out from this new orientation: (1) Nootka Sound lay beyond the envisioned boundary and therefore its importance was lessened; (2) the Strait of Juan de Fuca and its unexplored interior waterways became of increased concern to Spanish strategy. Revillagigedo saw this as necessitating "discoveries overland from the Port of San Francisco and from the presidio of Santa Fé, New Mexico, to the Strait of Juan de Fuca, [which would require] sending two competent parties of troops commanded by men of bravery, prudence, and talent, each party carrying two able engineers as officers (even though they might not be from that corps), well instructed in mathematics in order to make the necessary observations, draw up maps, and compile perfect journals." While awaiting royal approval for such an effort, the viceroy intended to study papers of the Domínguez and Vélez de Escalante expedition northward from Santa Fé (1776) and acquire other information "on which to base the proposal which I will make to Your Excellency opportunely." [74] From favoring a timorous withdrawal to San Francisco, the viceroy had done an about-face and now took a position in line with that held by Madrid.

Revillagigedo instituted reforms intended to strengthen and make more effective Spanish efforts in the Pacific Northwest, but he was hindered by the necessity of getting prior permission from Madrid for expenditures of an unaccustomed nature. A case in point occurred at the height of the Nootka crisis, when the ministry actually took time to admonish that "in the future he put greater care in punctual observance of the laws, which prohibited removal of funds from the royal treasury, without express royal order, for expeditions of any kind, as he had done in providing 800 and more pesos for trading goods for the explorations of California." [75] This referred to the copper and cloth sent to Nootka in 1790—and used by

74. Revillagigedo to Floridablanca, Mexico City, March 27, 1791, ibid., fol. 192v–98, AT. There is no evidence, to date, that his plans for exploration by land toward the Pacific Northwest ever got off the ground. In 1776 a party of ten had set out from Santa Fe to discover a route to Monterey; they were led by friars Francisco Atanasio Domínguez and Silvestre Vélez de Escalante, with soldier-cartographer Bernardo de Miera y Pacheco. For six months they wandered northward into Colorado, across the Wasatch Mountains to Utah Lake, south into Arizona, and back to New Mexico, daunted by distance and winter, but having penetrated a vast, hitherto unknown area. The first edition of Miera's map is that of Yale University Library, 1970, from a MS in CtY-BWA.

75. Valdés to Revillagigedo, Madrid, July 30, 1790, AT, and Revillagigedo to López de Lerena, Mexico City, November 26, 1790, both in SpAGI (V, Aud. Guad. 492). Marginal

Martínez and Quimper that year as an experiment in promoting Spanish participation in the sea otter trade. A marginal notation on Revillagigedo's reply shows that the ministry accepted his explanation as satisfactory, but the reprimand probably discouraged other innovations.

One of the viceroy's reforms involving the northwest coast might be called "improved data control." In the fall of 1790 Revillagigedo appointed Francisco Antonio Mourelle to his secretariat especially to handle correspondence pertaining to the Nootka controversy. The chaotic state of the viceregal archives concerning previous voyages in that area led to Mourelle's assignment to the task of putting in order the enormous number of royal orders, instructions, journals, reports, and other classes of documents relating to the subject. Since his last visit to the northwest coast (1779), Mourelle had served as commandant of San Blas (1785) and made at least three trips to Manila and Canton. As a veteran of the expeditions of 1775 and 1779, the thirty-six-year-old frigate lieutenant ranked with Bodega, Martínez, and López de Haro in knowledge of the area and its history. He endeavored to assemble and condense all the pertinent documentation into one consecutive corpus, eliminating repetitions, and making a more readily comprehensible source. Volume one commenced, for example, with the warnings from St. Petersburg leading to the initial efforts northwestward. Motives for each successive expedition were enunciated, and Mourelle's summary of its accomplishments endeavored to show the consequences for subsequent Spanish policy, a mine of information not readily found elsewhere.[76]

### EXPLORATION OF HARO STRAIT, 1791

The effectiveness of Spanish strategy for the Pacific Northwest hinged upon more accurate knowledge of the coastline and, in particular, of the presence or absence of waterways giving access to the continental interior. The strait discovered by Quimper in 1790 and named after López de Haro tendered such a possibility and warranted immediate investigation. Such considerations underlay Spanish activities on the northwest coast in 1791. Eliza was ordered to provide for explorations from Mount St. Elias southward to examine Bucareli Sound and a number of other openings known to penetrate the continent. South of Nootka he should investigate the interior of Clayoquot Sound, the Strait of Juan de Fuca, and the coastline from Cape Flattery to Alta California.[77] Instructions for these efforts arrived in Nootka on March 26 aboard the *San Carlos,* commanded by

---

notation: "Satisfaze el cargo qe. se le hizo en real orden de 30 de Julio sobre un Libramiento pra. provin. de Nuca."

76. [Mourelle], "Compendio de noticias," SpMN (331). Commencing in February 1791, at least two other versions were compiled and are in CU-B. Wagner, *Spanish Explorations*, p. 70.

77. Bodega, "Secret instructions to Eliza," February 4, 1791, MxAGN (Hist. 69), trans. in Wagner, *Spanish Explorations*, pp. 137–41.

Ramón Antonio Saavedra y Guiralda. Eliza put Saavedra in command of Nootka, and, against orders, left the giant warship *Concepción* to guard the settlement, taking instead the much smaller *San Carlos.* By its very size the larger vessel would be better able to command the respect of foreigners arriving at Nootka. The schooner *Santa Saturnina* accompanied the *San Carlos,* in order to explore the channels demanding a craft of shallower draft and greater maneuverability. José María Narváez, Juan Carrasco, and a crew of twenty seamen manned the smaller vessel.[78]

The day before Eliza's departure, officers and sailors carried ashore the image of the Virgin of the Rosary, patroness of the settlement, placed it in the carpenter's shed on an altar made for the purpose and decorated with "the cleanest banners and a diversity of flowers." Following a mass "to implore her clemency for the happy success of the present expedition," the image was returned aboard ship in procession and saluted by the artillery.[79] Pious formalities were an essential element in preparing everyone for the unknown challenges ahead. Having sailed on May 4, his destination Alaska's Cape St. Elias, Eliza ran into several days of unfavorable north winds and elected instead to turn southward to examine the waterways south of Nootka. Any unexplored inlet might disclose the fabled northwest passage. He examined the innermost channels of Clayoquot and sent the *Santa Saturnina* to do the same for Barkley Sound, agreeing to meet the schooner later at Puerto de Córdoba (Esquimalt Harbor), near present-day Victoria.

Upon reaching the point of rendezvous, the *San Carlos* dropped anchor, and the longboat, commanded by ensign José Verdía, explored northward through Haro Strait; but Verdía was obliged by hostile war canoes to turn back before penetrating any great distance. After the schooner arrived, Verdía set out a second time, finding that the channel opened into a sound even broader than Fuca at its widest, a vast waterway stretching out of sight toward the northwest and dotted with islands, large and small. Named "Canal de Nuestra Señora del Rosario," honoring their patroness, it is now called the Strait of Georgia, a name bestowed by Vancouver a year later, while "Rosario Strait" applies solely to its southern extremity, a channel east of the San Juan Islands. After ten days Verdía returned to the flagship and Eliza transferred his base of operations to Puerto de Bodega y Quadra (Port Discovery), on the south side of Fuca, from where he dispatched the schooner and longboat to penetrate Haro Strait once more. Near the San Juan Islands war canoes again attempted to overpower the longboat, but the schooner succeeded in frightening them off by firing its cannons over their heads. For three weeks they followed the strait northwestward, to almost 50° of latitude and beyond the approximate parallel of Nootka, but they were forced by want of supplies to turn back before sighting any

78. Manifest of the *San Carlos* and the *Santa Saturnina,* May 1791, SpMN (332), fol. 62–63.
79. Pantoja, "Extracto," SpMN (331), fol. 228v.

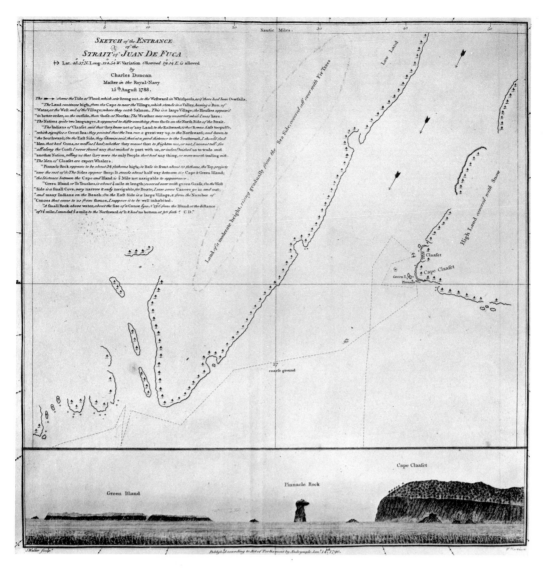

Publish'd according to Act of Parliament by Dalrymple Jan.ʳ 14.ᵗʰ 1790.

1. Captain Duncan's chart of 1788, showing the "pinnacle" identified by eighteenth-century mariners with that described in Fuca's account. Green Island (Tatoosh) and Cape Claaset (Flattery) are the northwestern tip of Washington State.

2. The natural stack called Fuca's Pillar today and Cape Flattery, as seen from the northeast.

3. Fuca's Pillar from the south, rising some 100 feet above the sea, with Tatoosh Island in the distance.

4. Spanish galleons such as plied the Manila-Acapulco route in the seventeenth-century.

5. Nehalem Beach, Oregon, where a galleon carrying beeswax met disaster.

6. A chunk of beeswax found by Nehalem resident Benjamin Lane and exhibited here by his daughter. It coincides with the standard dimensions of a *pieza* in a galleon's cargo. 7. A silver jar found within the hull of the beeswax vessel, 1898. 8. A chunk of beeswax stamped "67" (1679?), carbon-14-dated in 1961 as gathered some 280 years earlier.

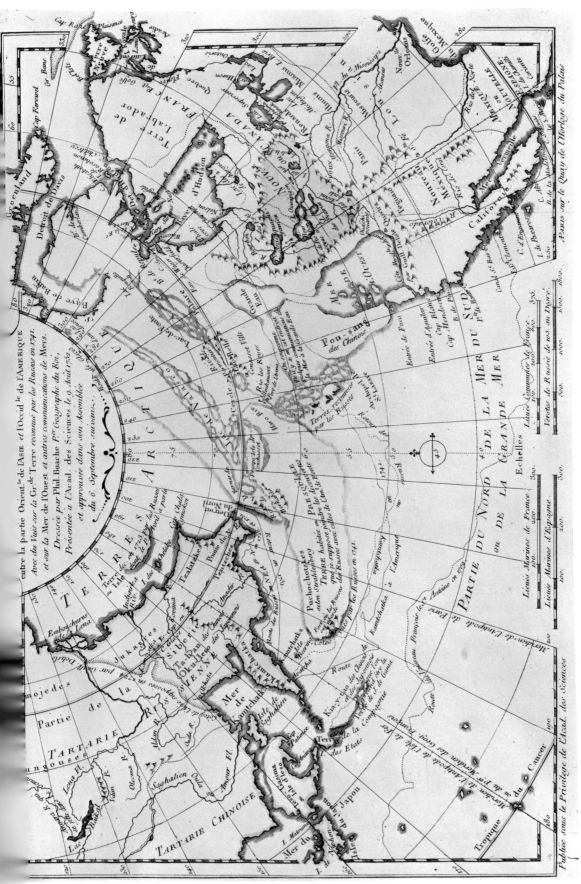

9. Philippe Buache's map of 1752: Fou-sang, Sea of the West, and the alleged discoveries of Fuca, Aguilar, and Fonte are placed near the actual routes of Bering and Chirikov.

10. A Russian map of 1758 that triggered Spanish efforts to protect western North America from Muscovite expansion.

12. Visitador José de Gálvez.   13. A Spanish stamp of 1967 honoring Juan Francisco de la Bodega y Quadra.

11. Goya's portrait of Carlos III.

14. Estéban José Martínez.

15. Francisco Antonio Mourelle.

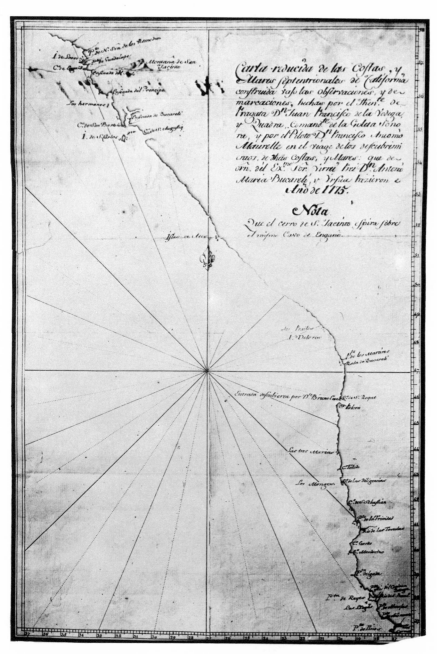

16. A version of the earliest map to record Spanish discoveries on the northwest coast, 1775. The upper part reflects the *Sonora*'s explorations along the Alaskan panhandle. Bruno Hezeta's *entrada* was later renamed by American captain Robert Gray after his ship *Columbia*.

17. The first chart of the Columbia River's mouth, 1775.

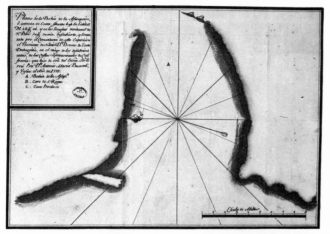

18. Puerto de los Mártires, in the lee of Point [ ] Washington, where five seamen from the *Son[ora]* killed. Nearby, Hezeta had just performed [ ] European act of possession on the northwest coas[t]

19. John Meares.

20. A drawing from John Meares's *Journal* showing his supposed settlement at Friendly Cove in 1788.

21. The Nootka chief Ke-le-kum (left) talking with his famous brother, Ma-kwee-na.

22. A London engraving of 1791 proclaiming that the Spanish "insult" at Nootka "and other aggravating circumstances raised the spirit of the English Nation, the event of which has been a speedy equipment of the most powerfull Fleet in the World, which by only shewing as the great bulwark of National liberty, the Spaniard has been reduced to reason, while surrounding Nations are held in awe."

23. Goya's portrait of Carlos IV, María Luisa, and their family. The future Fernando VII is in the left foreground. At far right are his sister, María Luisa Josefina, and the Duke of Parma.

24. Manuel de Godoy, as portrayed by Goya about 1802.

25. Louis XVI of France and Marie Antoinette.

26. The conde de Floridablanca. Goya placed himself in the portrait at the le

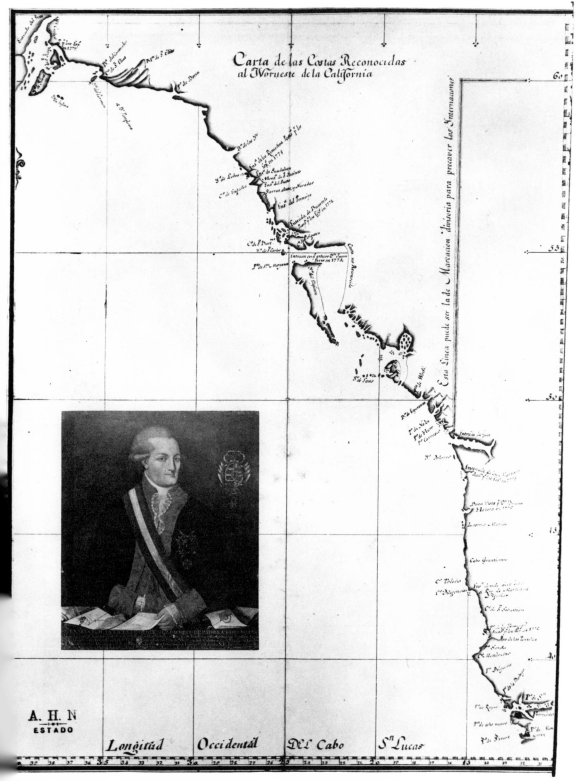

A map showing a proposed boundary from the mouth of Fuca's strait to 60° north latitude separating Spanish domain from territory open to both Spanish and British.   28. The second conde de Revillagigedo.

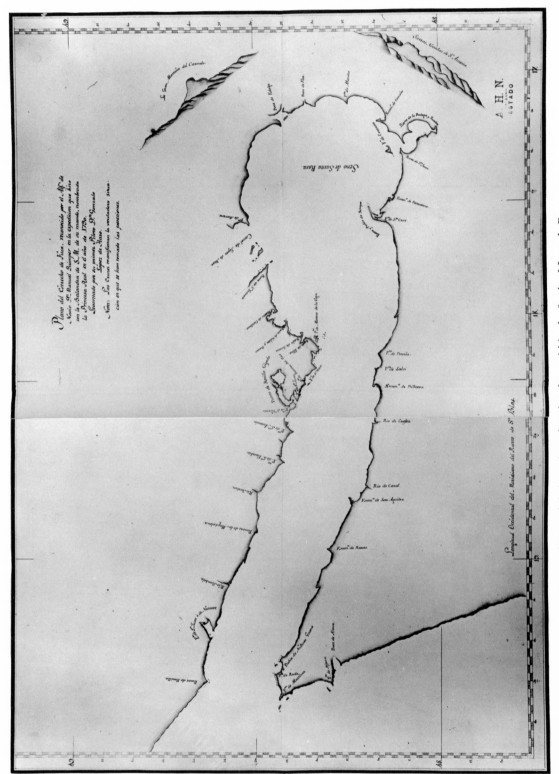

29. A map of Manuel Quimper's exploration deep within the Strait of Juan de Fuca, 1790.

30–34. Sketches by Suría and Cardero made at Yakutat Bay on Malaspina's visit in 1791. When a quarrel arose over pilfered clothing, a brave menaced the Spaniards with a knife. As they reloaded their equipment, one of the twin corvettes fired a cannon without shot. An aged chief waving stolen pantaloons restored peace. Sketches 33 and 34 show Indian clothing.

35. The sepulchre of a Tlingit chief.

36. Another Tlingit funerary monument.

37. The *Descubierta* and *Atrevida* at Yakutat, as seen from the tidal flat where seamen washed their clothing.

38. An Indian mother and child from Yakutat Bay.

40. Nootka chief Ma-kwee-na. The design woven into his hat alludes to his skill at hunting killer whales.

39. A Nootka Indian wearing the conical hat restricted to chiefs and their close relatives.

41. Suría's portrait of a young Nootka woman.

42. A Nootka chief and his wife.

43. Ma-kwee-na's prayer cubicle, in which he endured long fasts and uttered oracles.

44. A panorama of Friendly Cove as seen from the lighthouse in 1960.

45. An aerial view of Nootka Sound and Friendly Cove from the west.

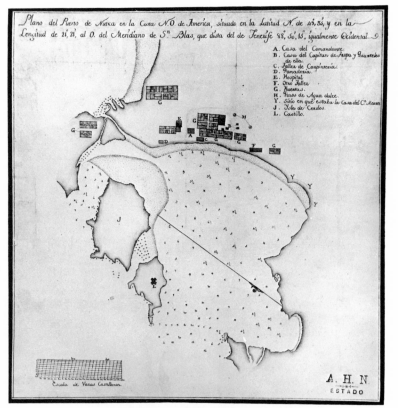

46. A chart of the Spanish base, labeled: A. Commandant's house, B. troop barracks, C. carpentry shop, D. bakery, E. infirmary, F. shop, G. gardens, H. wells, Y. site of Meares's camp, 1788, J. Hog Island, L. fort.

47. Cardero's sketch of Santa Cruz de Nootka and the frigate *Atrevida* in 1791.

48. The eastern sector of Friendly Cove. Tarpaulins shade the *Atrevida*'s deck as a British trader attracts native canoes.

49. Dances held by Chief Tlu-pa-na-nootl for Malaspina in 1791.

50. Dionisio Alcalá Galiano.

51. Cayetano Valdés.

52. The schooners *Sútil* and *Mexicana* and the frigate *Princesa* off the second Spanish base at Núñez Gaona in 17

53. The Spanish palisade being erected at Núñez Gaona (Neah Bay), the earliest white settlement in what is now Washington State.

54. Chief Te-ta-toos, of a village near present-day Victoria, B.C.

55. A chief from Gabriola Island (opposite Nanaimo, B.C.).

56. A Kwakiutl brave from Queen Charlotte Strait.

57. A tense moment in the Inside Passage as a Spanish boat explores a side channel.

58. The puberty ceremony for Ma-kwee-na's daughter.

59. Friendly Cove at its apex of activity, 1792.

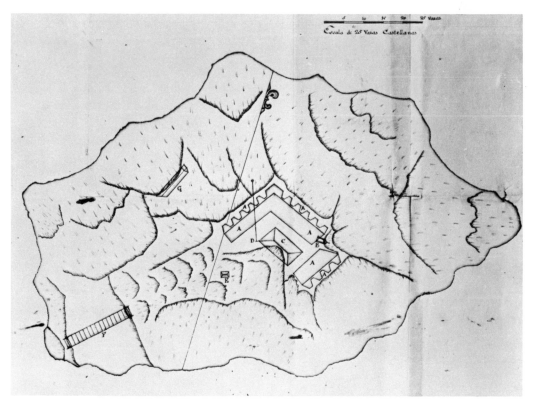

60. A chart of improvements made at San Miguel Fort by Salvador Fidalgo, 1792–93.

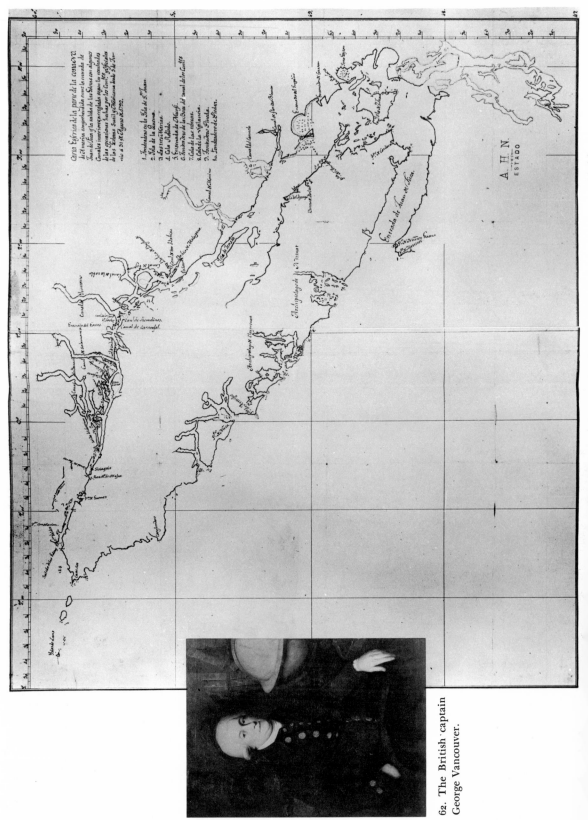

Carta Esferica de la parte de la costa N.O.
de America comprendida entre los Canales de
Juan de Fuca y la salida de las Salvas con algunos
Canales interiores arreglada segun las observaciones
de las Operaciones hechas por los Com.tes Españoles
de las Goletas Sutil y Mexicana desde 5 de Junio
hasta a 30 de Agosto de 1792.

1. Fondeadero en la Isla de S.n Juan.
2. Isla de la Palma.
3. Los tres Marias.
4. Cala Rallada.
5. Ensenada de Murfi.
6. Fondeadero de la Boca del Canal de los Gatts.
7. Cala de los rateros.
8. Caleta de la Vigilancia.
9. Fondeadero Fineda.
10. Fondeadero de Rodan.

A. H. N.
ESTADO

Entrada de Juan de Fuca

62. The British captain
George Vancouver.

terminus to the broad waterway. At one point on the eastern shore they noted an influx of fresh water, surmising correctly that the spot was the mouth of a large river—today's Fraser, named in 1808 by Simon Fraser, who found it by coming overland and descending by canoe to the tidewater. Near this river an Indian boy sold to the Spanish explorers told them of a site where tribes from the interior came to trade blue beads and pieces of metal for fish. The lad described four-footed creatures on which the tribes of the interior traveled, and when shown a sketch of a horse, confirmed it as what he had seen.

During the smaller vessels' absence, one of Eliza's men shot a huge ruminant—identifiable as an Olympia elk—of such size that its meat fed the seventy-man crew for three days. Upon the explorers' return, Eliza put Carrasco in charge of the schooner and transferred Narváez to the flagship to assist him in preparing maps of the area reconnoitered. Impressed with the significance of what had been found, the commander reported to the viceroy that "if there is anything of particular importance or consideration to be explored on this coast it is this large channel, as according to my method of thinking, and that of my pilot, it promises much." Its extent led him to predict that further explorations would show Nootka and Clayoquot to be inlets on a giant island, a conjecture proven true within the year. He was also prepared to affirm that "the passage to the Atlantic Ocean, which the foreign nations search for with such diligence on this coast, cannot in my opinion, if there be one, be found in any other part; it is either, I think, by this great channel, or it [i.e., the mainland] is [continuous] continent." [80]

While exploring the eastern end of the Strait of Juan de Fuca, Narváez had perceived that Quimper's "Ensenada de Caamaño" was an extensive inlet, not a bay, but, short of supplies that day, he rejoined the *San Carlos* fully expecting to return at a later date, since it was so close to Eliza's base of operations. Rosario Strait consumed their attention during subsequent weeks, and by the time they rejoined Eliza the commander wanted to start back toward Nootka, anticipating that considerable time would be lost beating upwind to emerge from the Strait of Juan de Fuca. Although on their maps they changed "Ensenada de Caamaño" to "Boca de Caamaño" (i.e., bay to inlet), once again Spanish explorers let knowledge of Puget Sound slip through their fingers. Carrasco is on record as noting: "It has also been determined that the *ensenada* named Caamaño is not an *ensenada* but an arm of the sea which flows toward the southeast." [81] The Spanish discovered the entrance to Puget Sound (Admiralty Inlet) but by neglecting to explore or publicize it, they failed to realize its extent or receive credit for the feat.

80. Eliza, "Extracto de la navegacion," p. 152.

81. Carrasco to Fidalgo, San Blas, November 9, 1791, in Wagner, *Spanish Explorations,* pp. 200–02. Eliza also specifically refers to Quimper's "Ensenada de Caamaño" as an inlet rather than a bay. See Eliza, ibid., p. 153.

As Eliza expected, they had much more difficulty leaving the strait than entering, because they had to sail against the prevailing winds. Proceeding along the south shore, they utilized the swift tide flowing seaward twice a day. En route Eliza examined a port that Quimper had missed, naming it Nuestra Señora de los Angeles, today's Port Angeles, an excellent harbor protected by a recurved spit. They also stopped at Núñez Gaona (Neah Bay). Pantoja's journal notes that it possessed serious defects as a port. The rocky bottom offered poor anchorage, and it was exposed to winds from the northwest, whence they prevail in summer. Vessels anchored there would be subjected to swells, and the beach had surf.[82] Although the journals make no mention of it, chaplain José Villaverde evidently proselytized the Indians whenever he had the opportunity. About a month later the *Columbia* anchored off "Ahshewat," a village on the seacoast a league south of Tatoosh Island, but not far overland from Neah Bay. Hoskins tells of a chief named "Clahclacko,"

> who from what I could understand wished to inform me the Spaniards had been here since us, endeavouring to convert them to Christianity, and that he and several others had been baptized, as also several of their children. This ceremony he went through, as also the chanting of some of their of their hymns with a most serious religious air, though it was in broken Spanish and Indian, yet he imitated the sounds of their voices, their motions and religious cants of their faces to a miracle, and at the same time condemned our irreligious manner of life.[83]

From Núñez Gaona the *San Carlos* and the *Santa Saturnina* headed toward Nootka, but it took the packetboat nineteen days to get there. The schooner was a poor sailer, and after two weeks of futile struggling to reach Nootka's latitude, Carrasco was forced by water shortage to head for Monterey and San Blas. Eliza had little to show for his summer of effort. He could not point to anything notable that Quimper had not seen the previous year, except Rosario Strait. He did not recognize Admiralty Inlet and the Fraser's mouth as significant. Although his plodding efforts filled in the details of Spanish charts, a more intrepid commander might have entered Puget Sound or followed the Inland Passage until its significance was ascertained. By not attempting such feats, Eliza handed Vancouver the opportunity to reap the benefits for Britain the following year.

### MALASPINA ON THE NORTHWEST COAST

Upon reaching Nootka, Eliza was disappointed to find that in his absence the Malaspina expedition had been there and had departed south-

---

82. Pantoja, "Extracto," p. 189.
83. Hoskins, "Narrative, p. 245. Perhaps this stemmed from Quimper's lengthier stay, in 1790.

ward a scant two days prior to his return. The *Descubierta* and the *Atrevida* had sailed from Cádiz coincidentally with the clash at Nootka in 1789, and the corps of scientists had conducted protracted studies in many parts of South and Central America. It was not until May 1791 that the expedition departed from Acapulco for the northwest Coast, sailing under new orders that had caught up with Malaspina in Mexico.

Three years earlier the publication of Lorenzo Ferrer Maldonado's account of an alleged voyage through the Strait of Anián had stimulated considerable interest in learned circles. Malaspina himself had expressed faith in the authenticity of the account; and when the renowned French cartographer Philippe Buache de Neuville endorsed it (November 1790), Floridablanca and Valdés were prompted to send Malaspina orders to explore the northwest coast between 59° and 60° with particular care, to ascertain whether a passage actually existed at the latitude stated by Ferrer Maldonado.[84]

Abandoning his original plan to sail from Acapulco to the Sandwich Islands (and spend the entire summer of 1791 examining and charting that archipelago), Malaspina decided to go directly to the northwest coast. By June 27 the twin corvettes were off the mouth of Yakutat Bay, which the Spanish, following the current practice among fur traders, called Port Mulgrave. The day dawned overcast and rainy, but when the clouds dissipated a deep cleft in the towering mountains was observed, just as the ancient account had led Malaspina to expect. Artist Tomás de Suría describes the imposing, snow-crowned panorama and the excitement of the moment. "Great was the joy of the commander and all the officers," he notes, "because they believed, and with some foundation, that this might be the much-desired and sought-for strait, which would form a passage to the North Sea of Europe and which has cost so much trouble to all the nations in various expeditions which they have made for simply this end, and for the discovery of which a great reward has been offered." [85]

The corvettes dropped anchor inside the bay, and Malaspina took two of the longboats and supplies for fifteen days and went to explore the tortuous channel penetrating the continent. Threading among increasingly frequent blocks of ice, they finally reached the front of a glacier, from which giant chunks were breaking off and falling into the bay with a thunderous, earthshaking roar. One seaman, reluctant to leave his curiosity unsatisfied and perhaps yearning for the fame his audacity might earn, stole

---

84. Malaspina to Valdés, Carraca, June 9, 1789, CtY-B; P. Buache de Neuville, "Memoria sobre el descubrimiento del paso norte ó del Mar Océano al del Sur por la parte septentrional de la América," in Malaspina, *Viaje*, pp. 144–49.

85. Suría, "Quaderno," pp. 246–47. It was named by Dixon (1787) for Constantine John Phipps (1744–1792), second Baron Mulgrave, lord of the admiralty (1777–82), commissioner of the boards of trade and control, and joint paymaster general of the forces. Aspinall, *Correspondence*, p. 15n.

away without leave and scaled a height above the bay, to a point where he could ascertain whether the channel continued as a transcontinental waterway on the other side of the glacier. At 10:00 P.M., still able to find his way in the northern twilight, he straggled into camp, dead tired and numbed with cold, but gratified at having established with certainty that a northwest passage did not exist in that vicinity. Malaspina named the inlet "Bahía del Desengaño" (Disappointment Bay), commemorating the sentiment at not finding the long-sought passageway. This was Malaspina's first acquaintance with the northwest coast, and Ferrer Maldonado's tale had led to excessive expectations. Veterans of previous explorations could have told him of many ice-carved gorges of similar aspect. After exploring several other fjords, to no better avail, he concluded that a northwest passage did not exist, at least at the latitude specified by Ferrer Maldonado, and that the account was apocryphal.

Malaspina remained within Yakutat Bay for more than a month while the longboats explored nearby channels and the scientists and artists performed their various labors on shore. As with the voyages of Cook and La Pérouse, the Malaspina expedition was very much a manifestation of the Enlightenment's enthusiasm for exploring, measuring, cataloguing, and depicting the least-known aspects of the world. This enthusiasm is borne out in the magnificent pictoral record and the scientific data assembled on the northwest coast. The many drawings made at Yakutat and Nootka are attributed to Tomás de Suría and José Cardero.[86] Diverse and detailed, these works posses a vigorous simplicity, great naturalness, and a high degree of ethnic fidelity.

The Indians of "Mulgrave" quite soon lost their initial reserve and timidity, swarming aboard the *Descubierta* and the *Atrevida* in numbers giving rise to fears that they might attempt to overpower the corvettes at a prearranged moment. When Malaspina sought to banish most of them to the beach, implying a certain mistrust, some of the braves reacted angrily. There had already been trouble over pilfered articles: the connecting pin of a launch rudder, a jacket, and a pair of trousers stripped from a seaman so incautious as to get within the Indians' grasp. When the argument grew heated, one brave drew a concealed knife and advanced toward a Spaniard. As officers and men hastened to load their equipment into the boats, one corvette fired a cannon without shot. Its roar stopped the warriors in their tracks, and while they looked about to see what damage had been done, the Spanish got away without bloodshed on either

86. Suría (b. 1761), a Valencian artist-engraver formerly employed at the Mexican mint, was a pupil of Jerónimo Antonio Gil, a Spanish artist of considerable renown, but Cardero was self-taught. Twenty-three years old in 1791, and an orderly to Alcalá Galiano, he stepped into the breach when drawings were needed, and his untutored talent produced works of great ethnological interest. Donald C. Cutter, "Early Spanish Artists," p. 151.

side. An aged chief who had come to trust Malaspina took it upon himself to reestablish harmony; he approached cautiously in a canoe, waving the stolen pantaloons, arms spread wide in the traditional gesture of friendship, and singing a peace chant. Malaspina rewarded the old man for his confidence with a number of gifts, and within several days native hostility disappeared.[87] The Spaniards were even taken to the tribe's burial ground, which, with its ornate funerary structures, inspired some of the artists' most unusual drawings.

Friction between Spaniards and Indians has repeatedly been noted to have occurred when seamen had their clothing stolen. An episode at Yakutat suggests why this tended to happen. Over a period of days several officers had been approached with offers to let them have access to Indian women. Malaspina cautioned against anything that might cause an incident, and there was some doubt whether the insinuations were correctly interpreted until an occasion when,

> importuned by this type of offer, an officer wanted to investigate its true meaning, especially since, if such a facility really existed as we supposed, it was important to take precautions regarding the crew's behavior, or if it were not true, we ought to dissipate this sinister idea about their character and customs. Led therefore by two young natives who with mysterious tone kept repeating the recognizable word "shout", the officer approached some trees next to the huts and it was easy to resolve any doubts, for at the foot of a tree were four or five women half covered with sea lion skins and immediately obedient to the will of almost all the tribe, who seemed unanimous in their intention of prostituting them. If morality and example had not sufficed to banish all ideas of this kind, that end would have been accomplished by the horrible aspect and abundant grease and filth with which the woman were covered, giving off an odor indescribably disagreeable.[88]

From their submissiveness, it can be assumed that the women were slaves captured in warfare with other tribes. In time the practice arose of prostituting slave women to white men of every nationality, as an additional source of revenue in a society inordinately concerned with wealth as the criterion of status.

The corvettes visited Prince William and Bucareli sounds before anchoring off Nootka at sunset on August 12, 1791. The launch of the *Concepción* came out to greet them, remaining alongside all night, and early the next morning they entered the cove, to a salute from San Miguel. Saavedra and Alberni came aboard to welcome Malaspina and he "regaled

---

87. Malaspina, *Viaje,* pp. 165–66, June 5, 1791.
88. Ibid., p. 157, AT.

them with a good breakfast." [89] At once the scientists took their instruments ashore and set up an observatory in several tents in order to conduct astronomical and geodesic experiments with greater accuracy than was possible aboard ship. The crew were put to work replenishing water and firewood.

Malaspina's description of the Nootka settlement mentions troops of the garrison living on land in barracks constructed of large planks, blacksmiths constantly at work at the forge, and a bake-oven that each morning produced fresh bread for everyone. Alberni's gardens were bearing in abundance. Having sent messages inviting the local chiefs to visit him, Malaspina wondered why so few natives were to be seen. The few fishermen approaching the corvettes behaved timidly. He concluded that Ma-kwee-na must be afraid. That chief's reticence (grounded perhaps on Spanish warnings about the consequences were he to indulge again in cannibalism), opened the way for rivals to displace him as the designated "sovereign" of Nootka Sound. The day after Malaspina arrived, a war canoe much larger than those customarily seen entered the cove; it was propelled by ten rowers on each side and had a broad space between them where the chief and his retinue stood. Tlu-pa-na-nootl (whom the Spanish called "Tlupanamibo"), aged leader of another village within the sound, had come to welcome the expedition. Alberni and a boy from Guadalajara who had learned some of the Nootka tongue acted as translators for the oration, recorded verbatim by Suría, who asserts that its eloquence and speciousness led Malaspina and his officers to form an elevated concept of the tribe's intelligence. After proclaiming Malaspina his superior, Tlu-pa-na-nootl declared that, having received the friendly summons,

> in compliance with it and with the friendship I profess for your nation and the great chief who sends you to our homes, I have come to see you and salute you. I am persuaded that you will be informed by Captain Alberni of the fidelity of my actions. . . . Don't assume that my age is an obstacle to serving in every way that you may be pleased to command. Although you may believe me a barbarian, I do not ignore the inviolable laws of friendship, which inspire me to tell you not to confide in, nor to feel safe from the dissimulated perfidy of, Macuina. He is crafty, overbearing, and looks on you with hatred and abhorrence. Shortly he plans to dislodge you from this place which you have founded in our domain, but he cannot do it while Tlupanamibo lives. Being experienced in this doublecrossing game, I will know how to oppose him, as I have his other malign projects up to the present. Since I am his subject, I could accompany him in his enterprises, but I forbear

89. Suría, "Quaderno," p. 273.

to do it because my heart is filled with integrity and justice. I know that you are men like us, but more civilized, and dedicated to the particular interests of yourself and your nation. I do not admire your manufactures and productions, so much esteemed among us. The common people do not yet think, and hence attibute to prodigies and enchantments those operations by which you conduct your great canoes. But in the end, if you wish to gain the entire confidence of all the tribe, proceed as the English do, who although more greedy, are upright, consistent, and in their treatment of us familiar and gracious.[90]

Tlu-pa-na-nootl saw in himself a replacement for Ma-kwee-na in the Spanish favor. The dances that he proceeded to stage on the beach and his nautical display in the cove had an ulterior motive: to play the Spanish off against rival nationalities. It would not be easy for the commandant at Santa Cruz de Nootka to maintain good relations with the rival chieftains as they jockeyed with one another for status in such a competitive hierarchy. Tlu-pa-na-nootl had camped on the beach right in front of the Spanish settlement and alongside Malaspina's tents and scientific equipment. "At certain hours of the day," Suría relates,

> he sang for us in company with his oarsmen about the glories of his nation and his ancestors, and at other times about his own feats and military exploits, all in a meter like the Anacreontic. When he got to these last songs this old man took on such vigor and enthusiasm that he was able to represent perfectly with his actions the struggles, the leaping, and the dismay of his enemies, and all that could give a true idea of his particular triumphs.[91]

Malaspina was not dissuaded by any of this from his desire to regain Ma-kwee-na's friendship. He sent geographer Felipe Bauzá and a survey party to conduct geodesic observations at a prominent headland northwest of Nootka, where the chief's summer village was then located. They found the lodges newly deserted, with the villagers hiding in the forest. Only one or two were willing to come and parley. For some time Tlu-pa-na-nootl alone among the chiefs from around the sound demonstrated any sign of friendliness. After four days of failing to get what he sought from Malaspina, the old chief said he would go in search of Ma-kwee-na, and left one of his own sons and a large box of treasured belongings, as security for his return with the other chieftain.

To reconnoiter the sound's interior, Malaspina placed José Espinoza and Ciriaco Cevallos in command of two longboats, with thirty armed men. At every village they were received "with the most disagreeable and tur-

90. Ibid., p. 274, AT.
91. Ibid., pp. 275–76, AT.

bulent visages," but no hostilities occurred. Ma-kwee-na was in residence when they approached his encampment at the head of Tahsis Inlet—ordinarily inhabited solely in the winter. When native sentries perceived their approach, warning was relayed ahead by musket shot, fishing canoes fled, and a great many armed warriors gathered on the beach, gesticulating and shooting firearms, as if to warn the Spaniards away. The officers came ashore alone and dispatched the launches to await them at some distance from shore. Ma-kwee-na received them coldly, his face revealing both anger and fear. By way of impressing the visitors with his power, he escorted them inside his lodge to show a chest containing fifteen additional muskets, over which an armed warrior stood constant guard. He also exhibited the contents of elaborate carved boxes holding his most treasured belongings, sheets and pieces of copper.[92] The callers' friendly behavior seems to have dispelled his doubts about Spanish intentions, however, and several days later the chief appeared at Friendly Cove with his entire retinue. He would not permit his three wives to come aboard the corvettes, however, and Malaspina noted a look of distrust in his countenance. The favorite spouse, a sister to chief Na-tsa-pā, was some twenty to twenty-five years of age, "and in affability, color, and features capable of standing out even where the ideas of beauty are well determined." [93] Ma-kwee-na came aboard each of the corvettes, where the officers served him tea. On his head he wore what is described as a reed cord into which some shiny "stars" of crystal were sewn. To dissipate any resentment still harbored toward the Spanish, Malaspina gave him two sails, four panes of window glass, a sheet of copper, a few yards of blue cloth, and some useful hardware. Immensely pleased, he responded by ratifying the cession of the site for the Spanish base, which had been made in previous years.[94]

The chiefs had become exceedingly choosy in bartering their pelts. The only items in which Ma-kwee-na showed any interest were window panes, firearms, and blue cloth, while Tlu-pa-na-nootl desired naught but gunpowder, sails, and hemp ropes for his canoes. "Macuina's character these days is difficult to decipher," Malaspina noted; "his temper seems simultaneously fierce, suspicious, and intrepid. The natural course of his inclinations is probably stirred up, on the one hand, by desire of the Europeans to capture his friendship, the treasure he has stored up in a few years, discords that have occurred among Europeans, and perhaps suggestions from one side or the other to secure a monopoly of pelts; on the other hand, consider the weakness of his forces, skirmishes suffered, profit from the traffic, and excessively frequent presence of European vessels in those

92. Malaspina, *Viaje,* pp. 193–94.
93. Ibid., p. 192, AT.
94. Ibid., p. 194.

regions." [95] The chieftain's physical attributes, Malaspina remarks, did not correspond to his dignity. Short but of well-developed musculature, Ma-kwee-na "attributed his present thin state to a scarcity of food since he had to abandon the port of Yucuat and, not without remorse or boasting, he reminisced . . . about the happy time in which, alone, he dared to harpoon a whale, when he enjoyed health and an uncommon robustness." [96] Other sources confirm that during recent winters the tribe had suffered unaccustomed famine, despite an abundance of marine life on the northwest coast.[97] The explanation that Ma-kwee-na offered, of having been displaced from Friendly Cove, may have been of less consequence than the fact that, after traders came with tempting wares, Nootka males became excessively preoccupied with sea otter hunting, whereas in former times they had dedicated more time to whaling, salmon fishing, and other pursuits connected with laying in a food supply for the lean season. The Europeans generated new wants and intensified old ones. The acquisition of Mexican copper, to be hammered into artistically-decorated *chipoks* and given away for status at some future potlatch, induced chiefs to keep their subjects hunting sea otters, rather than gathering a surplus of food.

Ma-kwee-na insisted on selling Malaspina a slave girl, which led the Parmesan to comment that purchasing children had become all too frequent at the Spanish settlement, although they were given as wards only to individuals of good conduct who had wives in the department of San Blas.[98] Upon their departure from Nootka, on the ships bound for San Blas,

> there were no fewer than twenty-two children of both sexes, sold indiscriminately by Macuina or lesser chieftains. They usually obtained for each child one or two copper sheets or at times a rifle or a few yards of cloth. Father Don Nicolás de Luera, chaplain of the frigate *Concepción,* distinguished himself particularly for his disinterested zeal in this kind of acquisition. Afterward he kept watch over their good habits and their social and Christian instruction. Ultimately he entrusted them for their dress, food, and subsequent instruction to those individuals of the crews who could take care of them and realize some benefit within their families from adopting these children.[99]

Although orphans were rescued in this manner, Malaspina felt that the practice should not be permitted to continue, "out of fear that those entrusted with these children might pretend, under guise of religion, to exert a kind of indelible mastery over these unfortunates." This judgment may

95. Ibid., pp. 354, 362, AT.
96. Ibid., p. 355, AT.
97. *Sútil y Mexicana,* p. 129.
98. Malaspina, *Viaje,* p. 192.
99. Ibid., p. 361, AT.

have been the product of subsequent observations, for at the time Malaspina accepted from Luera six boys acquired in exchange for guns. Luera had purchased them, Suría says, "for the purpose of teaching them the catechism and the doctrines of our sacred religion, and then baptizing them," and he adds that Luera's "Christian charity gave us much satisfaction and stimulated us to follow his commendable project." [100] At this point, obviously Suría had no hint of his commander's misgivings. The purchasing of slave children, ostensibly to save them from cannibalism, continued to be common. Following Eliza's return to Nootka, Pantoja noted:

> Since our arrival fifteen Indians of both sexes from four up to eight and ten years of age have been obtained in exchange for copper and Monterey shells, the principal land and sea officers having undertaken to raise and educate them. They are neither sons nor relatives of these natives but captives taken in wars which, as explained, they carry on. Some of the smallest they eat, an inhumanity for which the commandant, Don Francisco Eliza, has reprimanded them with great severity, indicating that it is something very bad and telling them that if he found out that they were continuing this abominable cruelty he would punish them severely.[101]

Later at least five more children were acquired, the price for all twenty being thirty-three sheets of copper, "the naval officers, caulkers, carpenters, and some of the gunners having taken charge of their education and training." In 1792 Eliza would report with satisfaction that during his three-year stay at Nootka no fewer than fifty-six children had been purchased there, at Clayoquot, or at Fuca. In addition, three adult men and a woman had voluntarily offered to accompany him to Spain.[102]

### MALASPINA'S RECOMMENDATIONS FOR THE NORTHWEST COAST

On August 28 the twin corvettes warped out of Friendly Cove, intending to explore the Entrada de Hezeta (Columbia River), as yet unseen by any

---

100. Among the slave children that Luera acquired, "there was one whom the sailors called 'Primo.' He displayed quite a little vivacity and already could pronounce some words in our language. He told us that he had been destined to be a victim and to be eaten by Chief Macuina together with many others, and that this custom was practiced with the younger prisoners of war, as well as in the ceremonies which were used in such a detestable and horrible sacrifice. Having discovered a way to escape he took refuge on the *Gertrudis*. This same day, when it was already night, two children arrived, a boy and a girl, brother and sister, who had also escaped from the fury of these barbarians. They said that they came from the country of the Nuchimas . . ." Suría, "Quaderno," pp. 274–75, entry for August 13, 1791, AT. The *Nuchimas* were the Kwakiutl, of the mainland and the northeast side of Vancouver island. The *Gertrudis* is presumably the schooner *Santa Saturnina*, which some still called by its earlier name, *Santa Gertrudis la Magna*. The frigate *Gertrudis* did not come to Nootka until 1792.

101. Pantoja, "Extracto," pp. 161–62, AT.

102. Ibid., p. 190; Eliza, "Extracto de la navegación," p. 154; Eliza, letter of July 7, 1792, cited by Wagner, *Spanish Explorations,* p. 154, who does not specify its location.

explorer since 1775. In Malaspina's opinion, although Hezeta's description conformed in some ways to Martín de Aguilar's river (1603), in other aspects it lent weight to theories of a passageway between the seas. When Malaspina reached that approximate latitude, fog obscured the coastline, and his search for the river was fruitless.

After a stopover in Monterey, Malaspina reached Acapulco in October, whence he sent Revillagigedo a letter addressed to the merchants of Mexico City, exhorting them, in the national interest, to participate in the sea otter trade. The Spanish possessed a special advantage, he declared, over other nationalities engaged in the traffic. An established trade route to the Orient already existed, by way of Manila. Mexico and California produced in abundance what the Indians most sought: copper, cloth, and abalone shells. None but the Spanish could compete in offering these commodities, much preferred to the pieces of iron offered by English traders. Whereas for very little compensation the Indians of Monterey would bring in all the abalone shells needed, on the northwest coast they were preferred above all other trade objects, and California was the sole source of supply. The gains might not be extraordinary, and the Merchants' Association must guard against excessive Spanish vessels reducing the margin of profit through overcompetition, but the traffic would benefit the colonies and national prosperity as well. Since other nations would be at a disadvantage, their trade would be weakened and foreign vessels would be driven from Spanish coasts by the competition, to the benefit of Madrid's commercial and political interests.[103]

The official account of his expedition gives additional details of Malaspina's plan for Spanish engagement in the fur trade. He urged that a private company be formed by a small number of stockholders in both Mexico City and Manila. The first expeditions should be independent of one another, and of the royal treasury. Using small ships, they should sail to ports near Mount St. Elias and cruise southward, trading at the appropriate spots. There must be no thought of making any outposts, which would be "the most destructive blow." He recommended that a commercial treaty be negotiated with Russia, enabling the companies to make additional profit by taking foodstuffs from Mexico and California to sell at Russian settlements in the Aleutians and Kamchatka. In no case should the enterprise be officially undertaken or put under the bureaucratic control of the Philippine Company. "Residence of the Philippine Company's administration in Madrid is sufficient in itself," he declared, "to destroy all advantages if these matters are delegated to that body; its decisions are tardy, its ideas overblown, employees too numerous, and deviations from the primary objective

---

103. "Carta de don Alejandro Malaspina al comercio de México convidándoles a un ensayo sobre el comercio de las pieles de Nutka," 1791, SpMN (335), fol. 53–5v.

entirely too easy." [104] Red tape and delay would surely stifle commercial success. His plan engendered no response in Mexican commercial circles. The reason, an Iberian historian diagnoses, is that it "signified incorporation of strange doctrines never put in practice by the Spanish," [105] that is, a free trade system.

Malaspina did not tarry long in Mexican waters; he departed in December 1791 for extended visits to the Marianas and the Philippines, returning home by way of Australia, New Zealand, Peru, Chile, the Malvinas (Falkland Islands), and Montevideo. Upon arrival in Cádiz (September 21, 1794) he was promoted to brigadier, and commenced editing a general account of his voyage, while the different specialists presented studies of their respective investigations in astronomy, physics, hydrography, and natural history. Since the manuscript containing his judgments about policy for the northwest coast includes specific recommendations to be carried out there in 1792, it must have been sent to the viceroy prior to Malaspina's departure from Acapulco.[106]

While in the Philippines, Malaspina gave the sea otter trade further attention. The traffic was then at a halt, due to the Chinese prohibition in effect from May 1791 to May 1792. His essay recounted Vasadre's misadventures and the unpredictability of Chinese policy toward the fur trade. As of 1792, the Spanish had sent 13,839 pelts to Canton, of which 3,953 remained to be sold, because of the embargo. Those already negotiated had yielded 46,960 pesos in cash and 152 tons of quicksilver, discounting one shipment in which they had been swindled and had received containers filled with less valuable lead. This accounting did not include shipping costs, commissions, salaries, risks, damages, and interest on money tied up in a business so intrinsically long and drawn out, and made more so by the infrequency of vessels from Mexico to Manila.[107] He did not paint a very encouraging picture of the gains to be secured by further Spanish participation in the trade. His views subsequent to arriving in Manila contrast with those he had held prior to leaving Acapulco and seem to reflect concepts held by Philippine Intendant González Carbajal, mentioned previously, who was seeking to discourage the sea otter traffic by way of Mexico in order to channel it directly through Manila.

Malaspina placed blame for the Nootka crisis upon Spain's defective policy toward the northwest coast. As soon as Madrid learned of the Russian

---

104. Malaspina, *Viaje*, p. 372n, AT.

105. Hernández, *Última Expansión Española en América*, p. 291, AT.

106. "Examen político de las costas del NO. de la América," SpMN (330), fol. 80–101v.

107. 2177 *picos*, a Philippine weight equivalent to 63.26 kilos or about 140 lbs. Malaspina, "Extracto de lo que ha ocurido [sic]," fol. 45v. Actually, the exchange of pelts for badly needed mercury earned a tidy profit, and the decline of the trade was due to factors other than financial failure. Ogden, "The Californias," p. 459.

presence there, he felt she should have inquired formally in St. Petersburg about the extent of Muscovite activities and objectives, and sought a treaty giving reciprocal rights in the North Pacific. Instead, with great expense and secrecy, Spanish expeditions had hugged the coast and accomplished little, instead of proceeding straight to Kamchatka for complete information. "A few crosses planted solemnly in places concerning which we did not know even whether they were islands or continent, and whether they were inhabited or not, dazzled our political outlook with the agreeable prospect of new conquests," he deplored, "and believing that it was not necessary to revalidate them in a treaty, we ruined even this small utility of our voyages in the eyes of Europe until, in 1788, we saw ourselves obliged to undertake once more the same explorations made in 1774." In his opinion, Spanish dominion north of Cape Blanco could hardly be considered to exist. Spanish activities there should be limited to the sea otter trade, in which they held the greatest potential advantages. Thanks to the Nootka Convention, Madrid might well rejoice that "our rights versus other European powers, insofar as those coasts and hinterlands are concerned, will be limited to demanding that no one possess them, without hesitating now as to whether this convention authorizes or invites us to assert custody." Thus Spain would avoid a repetition of past disturbances, brought about by occupying land not necessary or useful; there would be no further costly altercations.[108]

Malaspina suggested that Russia be party to the anticipated boundary treaty with Britain, the southern limit of Russian territory being set as Cook Inlet and the northern edge of Spanish domain as Cape Blanco. The intermediate area, as with the African coast, would belong to anyone wishing to establish there, it being understood that no mercantile establishment could be attempted until announcement had been made in Europe, to respect previous rights, with no enclave allowed to have jurisdiction over area larger than was necessary for a supply of lumber, firewood, and cultivated fields needed for its support. He cited the small area ceded by Ma-kwee-na to Meares as an example. In 1792 "it would be advantageous to substitute this method of purchasing specific tracts of land for the planting of many crosses, which do not receive the necessary validation in European treaties." [109]

In 1791 the Parmesan navigator's authority and opinion carried great weight in Spanish officialdom. He may be presumed to have influenced the perspectives of Revillagigedo, Valdés, Floridablanca, and possibly the king. His recommendations signified a complete reversal of policies instituted by José de Gálvez, continued under Bucareli and Flores, and implemented by a long series of explorers. Unhesitant at challenging the tremendous weight

108. Malaspina, *Viaje*, pp. 366–67, AT.
109. Ibid., p. 368n, AT.

of opinion habitually opposed to extensive institutional reform, Malaspina favored abandoning efforts to sustain and expand Spanish domain in North America by acts of possession, garrisons, missions, and evangelism—traditional methods that had created Spain's empire—and advocated means popular with the Russians, English, and Portuguese.

The extensive research conducted by Malaspina's scientists at every port of call made for an extremely slow pace and accumulated a burgeoning quantity of information. So voluminous and profusely illustrated were the reports of the various specialists that a cost estimate for the seven-volume work, with seventy maps and seventy plates of illustrations, ran to two million reales—an enormous sum for the time, but a minimum required to place their scientific accomplishments before the eyes of the world on a level to surpass the official publication of the findings of Cook's last voyage. Although financially hardpressed, the ministry approved Malaspina's request for the necessary funds.[110]

The scholarly project was well underway when a totally unforeseen factor put a stop to it, scattering its materials and those laboring on them to the four winds. Malaspina had returned from America enthusiastic about making radical changes in Spain's colonial policy and removing all burdens to the development of rich overseas possessions. In his impatience for reform, he became involved in a backstairs palace intrigue designed to accomplish no less a goal than topple from his pedestal the most potent figure in the government: Manuel de Godoy. To some degree Floridablanca and Aranda both owed their removal from office to the growing influence of the royal favorite. Those who resented Godoy for his sway over María Luisa and her husband were legion. Malaspina's rising star collided with that of the powerful prime minister when the Parmesan's New World exploits made him popular at court. Parma had always enjoyed the queen's particular affection, and Malaspina's personal qualities caught her eye. Those seeking means of undercutting Godoy saw in the illustrious navigator a possible replacement. The Spanish editor of Malaspina's narrative cites the conte di Greppi, a nineteenth-century ambassador to Spain whose father knew Malaspina intimately, who attributed the explorer's cooperativeness to acute political dissatisfaction. "This voyage impressed upon his passionate spirit the welfare of his fellow man, making him realize an absolute need for radical change in the system of government and legislation for the colonies," di Greppi asserts. Malaspina "insisted on the necessity of removing anything that would disturb free development, trying to unite that empire with more ample and reciprocal relations, so those far-off domains would not be considered as deposits of rich mines, but as an immense region yield-

110. Felipe Bauzá to José de Espinosa, Madrid, January 9, 1795, in Malaspina, *Viaje,* p. 683; Manuel Gil, "Defensa . . . hecha por él mismo," cited in Malaspina, *Viaje,* p. x.

ing all kinds of products and able to provide happiness for millions of individuals." [111]

In his preliminary report the spirited explorer severely criticized the defects of Spain's colonial policies. Given a chance to exercise greater influence by cultivating royal attention, he seized the opportunity. As Spanish historian Rafael Estrada delicately puts it, the intimacy with María Luisa "was born in the shadow of certain drawing lessons that Malaspina, with his finesse and keenness of spirit, made delightful for the sensitive and august lady." [112] At that moment she was at odds with Godoy and sought means of undermining his bond with her husband. Malaspina was induced to compose a letter exposing Godoy's incompetence, the purpose of which was to influence Carlos IV against his favorite. María Luisa hid the dangerous missive in her desk awaiting a proper occasion. Unable to suppress her satisfaction, she let fall an unguarded remark that made Godoy suspicious, and he pressed her co-conspirators, the marquesas of Matallana and Pizarro, until the latter yielded under coercion and revealed everything. Malaspina's letter and passionate writings on behalf of colonial reform served to construct a charge against him of conspiring against the state. Arrested (November 24, 1795), tried, and condemned, he was stripped of rank and sentenced to imprisonment for ten years and a day in the dungeons of Castle San Antón, La Coruña. His personal papers had been seized, the documentation from his expedition for the most part confiscated, and his associates disbanded. All plans for publication evaporated, and such papers and drawings as escaped seizure were hidden away by various of the scientists, many of them coming to rest in foreign repositories.[113]

Malaspina languished in confinement for eight years, until an Italian friend persuaded Napoleon to intercede for his freedom. Godoy's influence still prevailed, and the Parmesan's release was on condition that he never set foot again on Spanish territory, on pain of death. Estrada laments the famous navigator's personal eclipse, believing that the empire's fortune under his aegis would have been very different had he succeeded in re-

---

111. Malaspina, *Viaje*, p. xvii, AT.

112. Rafael Estrada, *El Viaje de las corbetas Descubierta y Atrevida y los artistas de la expedición, 1789–1794* (Madrid, 1930), p. 40, AT.

113. Malaspina, *Viaje*, p. ix, cites Joaquín Lorenzo Villanueva, a contemporary of Malaspina; Estrada, *El viaje*, pp. 40–41; B. del Carril, *La Expedición Malaspina*, p. 15. The trial record is in SpAHN (Estado 3025). Felipe Bauzá Cañas (1769–1833), the expedition's geographer who directed Malaspina's artists and preserved their works, eventually became director of the Depósito Hidrográfico, forerunner of today's Archivo del Museo Naval. As deputy to the Cortes in 1822, he voted against absolute monarchy, and when driven into exile by Fernando VII, he took with him many of the Malaspina drawings. Some of them were later found in collections in Great Britain, the United States, and Argentina, but most of those relating to the northwest coast remained the property of Bauza's heirs, until acquired recently by the Spanish government and deposited in Madrid's Museo de América. Cutter, "Early Spanish Artists," p. 152. Also see Cutter's review of B. del Carril's work in *HAHR* 43 (1963) : 154.

placing Godoy in the royal favor.[114] The economic and political reforms envisioned by Malaspina for Spanish America were anathema to Godoy, who instead chose a course that entangled Spain in Napoleon's web. When in 1808 the French emperor deposed Carlos IV, erecting a puppet government in Madrid, Spanish Americans seized the opportunity to attain a greater measure of self-government and economic independence, a trend that culminated in their throwing off the bonds that were stifling economic development, which Malaspina saw as essential to the contentment and loyalty of Spain's overseas subjects.

### ELIZA'S SECOND WINTER AT NOOTKA

Forty-eight hours after Malaspina sailed from Friendly Cove, the *San Carlos* returned from the Strait of Juan de Fuca, and Eliza resumed command of the Spanish base. Thereafter most of his attention seems to have been focused upon rescuing slave children from what he was convinced was an alimentary fate, hoping that the care and solicitude shown them would lead to evangelizing and making faithful subjects of the adults. In pilot Juan Pantoja's opinion it would have been easier to convert the natives to Christianity if they could have been persuaded to live in one spot the year around, but

> they have never been willing to bring their settlement to this cove, from which they retired upon the arrival of our vessels in April 1790, however much they have been invited. They thought our coming was to do them some harm, a vicious idea formed from being so assured by the English who were here, and through their rating of the commander of the previous expedition of 1789, Don Estéban Martínez, even though their experience has been contrary to this because, besides the good treatment given them, the commandant of the port, Don Francisco Eliza, has made them many presents.[115]

In September an incident occurred that did little to improve relations with the Indians. A cabin boy disappeared from the *San Carlos,* and after two days Saavedra and an armed party set out for Ma-kwee-na's summer village. Finding no trace of the lad, they seized two natives, who were brought back as hostages for the boy's safe return. It turned out that he had gone of his own free will to live with the aborigines, as two days later he was captured by a party of soldiers. The hostages were freed and presented with gifts of copper, cloth, and bread, while the youth was given "the proper number of lashes" for the trouble caused.[116]

114. Estrada, *El Viaje*, p. 47, AT. His health deteriorated, Malaspina returned to Italy, succumbing at Pontremoli on April 9, 1810 at the age of fifty-six.
115. Pantoja, "Extracto," pp. 161–62, AT.
116. Ibid., p. 195.

The *San Carlos* remained at Nootka until late October. When Narváez, Verdía, and Pantoja finished charts of the summer's explorations, the papers were rolled and sealed inside tin tubes with Eliza's reports to Revillagigedo and Bodega. The crew of sixty-four assigned to the packetboat (sixteen less than its complement upon arrival from San Blas) included those whose precarious state of health made their return south advisable. Of the sixty-four, eight, including the boatswain, were so ill that no service could be expected of them. "In view of our short crew and the advanced season," Pantoja comments,

> we were about to sail with some uneasiness, as there was a possibility in a storm of some accident during strong and frequent guests of wind which, accompanied by copious rainfall, rule in these latitudes during the beginning of winter. The rain is the worst—it and the great cold caused by wet clothes chill the body, particularly among those who own no other change of garments (as happens with most of those we have on board), and prevent the crew from working.[117]

Ill-clad and poorly fed, the peasants of Jalisco and Nayarit who comprised the bulk of the ordinary seamen were physically, culturally, and temperamentally at a disadvantage on the northwest coast. Small wonder that of the Spanish subjects visiting Nootka, few sought to remain any longer than necessary, or return there once away. Bodega, Mourelle, and Martínez are the only persons on record over the years as volunteering for repeated service there.

By the time Saavedra and the *San Carlos* warped out of the cove on October 24, winter was closing in about Eliza, Alberni, and the Nootka garrison, confining them to close quarters in clammy, bone-chilling cold. Not far from Nootka, and perhaps without Eliza's knowledge at the time, another nucleus of civilization endured the winter of 1791–92—Captain Robert Gray and the crew of the *Columbia,* at a cove in Clayoquot Sound.

### THE AMERICAN BID RENEWED

From the Spanish perspective, British traders seemed their prime rivals on the northwest coast. Not so obvious were the deleterious consequences for Spanish interests of the activities of the American captains Kendrick and Gray, who studiedly cultivated the successive commandants at Nootka while simultaneously developing techniques of evading Iberian controls. In 1790 most American traders as well as British (except for Colnett and his associates) had avoided the northwest coast for the first season since the inception of the fur trade. In 1791, however, Kendrick returned from Macao to the Queen Charlotte Islands with the *Lady Washington.* While

117. Ibid., pp. 195–96, AT.

anchored in Houston Steward channel, off Chief Koyah's village, at a moment when the Americans were absorbed by the confusion attending a busy trading session, Koyah's braves seized the vessel's arms chest and overpowered the entire crew. For several hours the old captain was in peril of losing both his ship and his life. By a stroke of luck, however, he and his men were not slain on the spot but confined below deck. They broke out an additional store of arms, retook the vessel, and slew many of the natives.[118]

On July 12 the *Lady Washington* entered Nootka Sound while Saavedra was in command there. Wary of the reception he might find, Kendrick armed his men to the teeth, loaded the cannons, and ordered matches lit, ready to open fire if need be. A sentinel hailed him through a speaking trumpet from atop the fort, warning him to stop. Kendrick pretended not to understand, and jauntily continued up the sound. Before he reached Mawina the wind fell off, and Saavedra sent an armed party to the vessel's side. Kendrick was told that the *Lady Washington* could have been sunk with the cannons of San Miguel, had the commandant so desired. Instead, Saavedra had sent his launches to tow them to Mawina, but with an official protest, since Nootka Sound was Spanish territory, and he informed the American captain that he could not enter or trade there without proper license. Kendrick's deferential answer, promising that he would soon depart, seems to have blunted any hostility, for he was sent a supply of fresh garden vegetables every day during the *Lady Washington's* stay. Kendrick said he would pay Saavedra an official visit, but somehow he never got around to it, although his officers came to Friendly Cove. Pantoja says Kendrick wrote that "he himself did not do so as he was satisfied of our friendship." To everyone's surprise, three officers of the *Lady Washington* gave Saavedra an official protest against their captain, "in which they said they desired to remain with us; a request which was not considered." [119]

Kendrick had several reasons to fear arrest or confiscation of his vessel. At Macao he had spent not only the $18,000 from the sale of his own furs from 1788–89 but also the money obtained from pelts received on consignment from Martínez, amounting to $8,000. By gross mismanagement the old man fell ever more deeply in debt, and in order to return had borrowed $3,000 more. Unpredictable Chinese restrictions and the graft rife at Canton and Macao may account for some of his difficulties. An eternal optimist, Kendrick hoped to recoup everything with his next cargo, and his audacity in exposing himself to Spanish arrest in 1791 paid off well, as he obtained upwards of 800 prime skins within Nootka Sound.[120]

118. Related by Gray to Menzies, in Menzies, *Journal*, pp. 14–15; see F. W. Howay, "The Ballad of the Bold Northwestman: An Incident in the Life of Captain John Kendrick," *WHQ* 20 (1929) : 114–23.

119. Pantoja, "Extracto," pp. 191–93; Haswell, "Log," pp. 298–99.

120. Kendrick to Joseph Barrell, Macao, March 28, 1792, DNA, in Howay, *Voyages of the "Columbia,"* pp. 470–73; Haswell, "Log."

Since the diplomatic collision between Madrid and London had been a stand-off, by 1791 Kendrick deemed it advisable to establish a claim to enclaves of territory for himself and for the United States of America, negotiating a purchase from Ma-kwee-na and five subaltern chiefs. In return for ten muskets the chiefs put their "X's" to a deed of sale of everything within a nine-mile radius of Chastacktoos harbor (Mawina Cove), including "all the land, rivers, creeks, harbors, islands, etc., with all the produce of the sea and land appertaining thereto," on condition that natives be allowed to continue residing and fishing there. This agreement also granted Kendrick free passage through the outlets to Nootka Sound. Ten of his crew signed as witnesses.[121]

The *Lady Washington* stayed in Nootka Sound less than two weeks on this occasion, but in that short time the area was stripped of the season's yield in peltry. When ready to leave, Haswell tells us, Kendrick "did not think it prudent to pass the garrison again." Instead, he threaded through the narrow exit to Esperanza Inlet, in the course of which he purchased additional enclaves at "New Chutleck, or Hoot-see-ess, alias Port Montgomery" (eighteen square miles, for two muskets, powder, and a sail), "Chenerkintau" (eighteen square miles, for six muskets, sailcloth, and an American flag), and "Tashees, the head of Nootka Sound" (nine miles around, for two muskets and powder). From there Kendrick proceeded southward to Clayoquot, without approaching the Spanish base, and resumed acquisition of land at strategic harbors. Wee-ka-na-nish was willing to deed him the land eighteen miles in every direction from Opitsat in return for four muskets, gunpowder, and a sail.[122]

A year later the Spanish would endeavor to secure a deed of purchase from Ma-kwee-na. Loyal to his agreement with Kendrick, in the new sale the old chief expressly exempted the land conveyed to his American friend. Although not then at Nootka, Kendrick heard about this; conceiving that his deeds possessed diplomatic importance, he registered them with the American consul in Canton and remitted duplicates to the American government. "I know not what measures are necessary to be taken, to secure the property of these purchases to me, and the government thereof to the United States," he wrote Jefferson,

> but it cannot be amiss to transmit them to you, to remain in the office of the Department of State. My claim to those territories has been allowed by the Spanish Crown: for the purchases I made at Nootka, were expressly excepted in a deed of conveyance of the Lands adjacent to, and surrounding Nootka Sound, executed in September last, to El Señor Don Juan Francisco de la Bodega, y Quadra, on behalf of

121. Indian deed to John Kendrick, July 20, 1791, in Felch, "Explorations," p. 168.

122. Haswell, "Log"; deeds formerly in archives of the U.S. Department of State, pub. in Felch, "Explorations," pp. 169–71.

His Catholic Majesty, by Macquinnah and the other chiefs of his tribe, to whom those lands belonged.

When I made these purchases, I did it under an impression, that it would receive the sanction of the United States, and, that should an act of the Legislature be necessary to secure them to me, I should find no difficulty in obtaining it. The future commercial advantages which may arise from the Fur Trade, besides many other branches which are daily opening to the view of those who visit the North West American Coast, may perhaps render a settlement there, worthy of the attention of some associated Company, under the protection of Government. Should this be the case, the possession of Lands, previously and so fairly acquired, would much assist the carrying the plan into effect. Many good purposes may be effected by the Union having possessions on that coast, which I shall not presume, Sir, to point out to you; and the benefits which have accrued to Individuals, by similar purchases to those I have made, in our own States, are too well known to need a remark.[123]

It warrants recalling that Kendrick's camp at Mawina antedated the Spanish settlement at Friendly Cove and that he had spent the winter of 1788–89 inside Nootka Sound.

When Captain Gray and the *Columbia* arrived on the northwest coast again, early in the summer of 1791, he carried a sea letter signed by President Washington and Secretary of State Jefferson. His instructions warned him "not to touch at any port of the Spanish dominions on the western continent of America, unless driven there by unavoidable accident, in which case you will stay no longer than is necessary, and while there, be careful to give no offence to any of the subjects of his Catholic Majesty, nor on any pretence whatever trade for a single farthing, unless for the supplies you may want, and let that be done under the immediate eye and sanction of authority." [124]

After trading profitably at Clayoquot, Gray gave the Spanish base at Nootka a wide berth and proceeded to the Queen Charlotte Islands. There his chief mate and several seamen were slain by the Haida when they went to fish in one of the sloop's boats and made the mistake of getting out of range of the *Columbia*'s guns. Returning to Clayoquot in August, Gray found that Kendrick had constructed a log house on an island in the area sold him by Wee-ka-na-nish, which he had fortified and christened "Fort Wash-

123. Kendrick to Jefferson, Port Independence, Hong Kong, March 1, 1793. In Felch, "Explorations," p. 168, who published it from state department archives.

124. John Barrell, Instructions to Robert Gray, Boston, September 25, 1790, in Howay, *Voyages of the "Columbia,"* pp. 443–47; George Washington and Thomas Jefferson, Sea letter to the *Columbia,* New York, September 16, 1790, in Felch, "Explorations," p. 174.

ington," honoring both the president and his own vessel. Relations between the two American captains were strained. Kendrick suspected that Gray might be carrying orders to seize the *Lady Washington,* since he had yet to remit a cent of earnings to his Boston backers, so he "kept himself always ready against attack." [125]

Because of his openhanded ways, Kendrick was the most popular trader with the natives. When Ingraham returned with his own vessel in 1792,

> every one of them inquir'd particularly after cap[tai]n Kendrick saying they had plenty of skins for him and they would not sell them to any one else. This they told us in Kyuquot—Indeed they all seem'd very fond of Cap[tai]n Kendrick for he ever treated them with great kindness —but I believe their principal view for wishing to see him at present was to dispose of their skins at an exorbitant price which none but Cap[tai]n Kendrick would give.[126]

Gray made no attempt to interfere with Kendrick and did not remain long at Clayoquot, but traded up and down the coast, always avoiding Nootka and the Spanish. Winter's approach obliged him, eventually, to return to Clayoquot to search for a likely cove to sit out the lonely months till spring. Shortly after Gray's return, Kendrick sailed for Macao. The *Columbia* anchored near the village of Clicksclocutsee, twelve miles from the sea, and a two-storied, fortified building was built on shore, which Gray named "Fort Defiance." The winter months were utilized to build a forty-ton sloop, named the *Adventure,* for use the following season in the fur trade. The site of their camp was at the entrance to Disappointment Inlet, opposite Opitsat. It was a poor choice, since on Gray's last visit to Wee-ka-na-nish an incident had occurred that the powerful chief was not likely to forgive or forget. In June 1791 Gray's Hawaiian cabin boy, a lad named Ottoo, went to a native village without the captain's knowledge. When his absence was noticed, Gray seized one of the chief's male relatives as hostage for Ottoo's safe return. The boy subsequently turned up, and the incident was seemingly smoothed over with a few gifts, but Wee-ka-na-nish was not one to allow his prestige to suffer any insult. His appetite for revenge was translated into action during the dead of winter, when the Americans were residing on shore. Calling together several allies, the chief plotted a surprise assault. To render the white men's arms ineffective, he endeavored to persuade Ottoo to wet their store of gunpowder. The latter's suspicious behavior led Gray to uncover the plot. The attack, on January 18, 1792, was

125. John Boit, "Log of the Second Voyage of the *Columbia,*" in Howay, *Voyages of the "Columbia,"* p. 379; Hoskins, "Narrative," pp. 242–48; Menzies, *Journal,* p. 14.

126. Joseph Ingraham, "Log of the Brigantine *Hope* from Boston to the Northwest Coast of America, and journal of events. 1790–1792," DLC, Ph in Cty-BWA (Coe 271), p. 182.

repelled successfully. According to the Americans, upward of 3,000 Indians were involved in the effort. The figure seems exaggerated, but there is no evidence to contradict it other than that the assault was weathered without any great difficulty.[127]

The ruthless tactics of the fur traders and the surprise attacks by the natives on unwary trading vessels brought an ever greater climate of violence to the fur trade. Increasingly, Friendly Cove with its sturdy fort and garrison seemed the only haven where fur traders could careen for repairs in comparative safety. The Spanish seemed securely ensconced there despite the Nootka Convention, which appeared to undermine their exclusive control. Ambiguities in the diplomatic accord had invigorated Iberian determination to retain sovereignty over the northwest coast—at least from exterior appearances—but the precise terms of a modus vivendi with the British remained far from settled. Madrid and London were sending representatives to the site to negotiate a practical settlement of remaining issues, but until details could be agreed upon, Anglo-Spanish rivalry for the northwest coast hung in balance, with the outcome difficult to foresee.

127. Hoskins, "Narrative," pp. 185–89; Boit, "Log" p. 370; Menzies, *Journal*, p. 14; Howay, *Voyages of the "Columbia"* p. 247n.

# 9  Confrontation at Friendly Cove, 1792

THE FIRST Nootka Convention fatally weakened Spain's claim to exclusive sovereignty over Nootka Sound. No matter how it was interpreted, the covenant returned a portion of Friendly Cove to Britain. Legal presence of foreign vessels within Nootka Sound destroyed its value to Madrid as a naval base. It had been hinted to London that Spain would consent to mutual "trade, navigation, and establishments" beyond 48° north (i.e., Strait of Fuca) in return for a boundary agreement at that latitude. Floridablanca had notified the Nootka commandant to anticipate Anglo-Spanish commissioners, who would iron out details on the spot. A royal order set forth the objectives of this negotiation, designed both to secure a boundary and to fulfill article five of the convention obliging restoration of lands purchased by British subjects on the northwest coast.[1] Revillagigedo chose the commandant of San Blas to handle the delicate mission. His instructions to Bodega admitted that although Spain must surrender the site of Meares's camp on the north side of Friendly Cove, there was no obligation to give up the Spanish settlement and coast to the south of it; nevertheless, he saw no utility in maintaining a base under such awkward circumstances, particularly if its cession could obtain a more valuable objective. The interior of Fuca was as yet only partially explored. The prospect of unknown passageways, interior gulfs, and navigable rivers in that area posed a threat of easy access to the heart of the continent. To guard against this danger, it was in Spain's interest to obtain a fixed boundary along easily ascertainable lines as a barrier to foreign encroachments upon Spanish California and New Mexico. To secure British agreement to an acceptable fixed boundary, Revillagigedo suggested that Bodega offer to abandon Nootka entirely.[2]

The viceroy's proposal grew out of the royal order of December 25, 1790, which suggested a line due north from Fuca's entrance to 60° north latitude. A fortified Spanish base on the strait could guard against foreign traffic entering any strategic waterway or river discovered later within its innermost reaches. No one as yet knew that it had another exit to the Pacific, north of Vancouver Island. The prominent natural feature was looked upon as an excellent permanent boundary between Spanish territory and

1. Dated May 12, 1791, its substance is given in Revillagigedo to Godoy, April 12, 1793, in Cavo and Bustamante, *Tres Siglos*, 3 : 135.

2. Revillagigedo to Bodega, Mexico City, October 29, 1791, MxAGN (Hist. 67), fol. 238–42v.

the coast which the convention obliged Madrid to share with Britain. The prospect of evacuating Nootka made the establishment of a base at Fuca quite urgent. Thus, Revillagigedo ordered occupation of the most appropriate harbor on the strait as soon as possible; He declared that a settlement should be planted and sustained with a garrison sufficient to equal that which the English might place at Nootka. Salvador Fidalgo and the frigate *Princesa* were designated to execute the task.[3]

The strategic importance of unexplored sections of Fuca, sighted by Quimper and his companions in 1790, was recognized in Madrid, and although Eliza's men currently were engaged in the task, the ministry ordered another expedition "to ascertain whether any of its channels penetrate to Hudson or Baffin Bay." [4] The impulse probably resulted from Martínez's references to such a hypothesis, but the need to explore that waterway to its extremities was obvious to anyone studying Quimper's charts. If such a passage existed, Revillagigedo thought it more likely in higher latitudes than within Fuca. Nevertheless, he replied, "no diligence should be spared on points of this grave nature, and if in effect there were a strait traversing the continent, it would be advantageous to have it discovered by a Spanish ship, in order to improve our situation accordingly." [5]

When the *Santa Saturnina* brought Bodega results of Eliza's explorations, it continued evident that many channels leading off the Strait of Juan de Fuca still remained to be explored. Responding to the ministry's concern about an intensified search for a northwest passage, Revillagigedo drew up plans for a new expedition, to be led by his secretary, frigate lieutenant Mourelle, whose rank, ability, prior experience on the northwest coast, and familiarity with the documentation of previous voyages commended him for the task. In choosing Mourelle, Revillagigedo passed over Martínez, who at that moment was petitioning cancellation of orders to return home and soliciting an opportunity to lead just such an effort.

Mourelle was told to proceed directly to 56° north in the newly constructed schooner *Mexicana,* and to explore from there southward to San Francisco, examining the inner reaches of Fuca "to determine whether they return to the western sea or penetrate to Baffin or Hudson Bay," and searching especially for the "River of Martín Aguilar." The royal intent was that "a detailed examination of all the bays, ports, rivers, capes, and inlets which enter the continent should give definitive knowledge for all time of that interesting region, today the principal object of European nations." Mourelle's search should "dissolve doubts and forestall the anxiety that

3. Ibid., fol. 243–45; Revillagigedo to Fidalgo, November 2, 1791, cited by Wagner, *Spanish Explorations,* p. 61.

4. Royal order, May 28, 1791, quoted in Revillagigedo to Floridablanca, Mexico City, September 1, 1791, CU-B (Robbins Collection), Revillagigedo Papers, vol. 22, fol. 200–13v.

5. Ibid., fol. 203v–04, AT.

such waterways would occasion at our court through general disturbance of commerce if they were discovered at some future time. "This exploration," Revillagigedo declared, "has another object still more important and necessary: the accuracy and adjustment of final agreements with officials of His Britannic Majesty depend on exact information which we may expect from it, and the dividing line with that nation will remain in suspense until the schooner's return, which I am confident will place me in a position to resolve with exactitude certain points of great importance." [6] With this in mind, Mourelle should ascertain the harbor on the north shore of Fuca best suited for a permanent Spanish base. If he should meet vessels of other nationalities, "urbanity and politeness will be the arms with which to capture the friendship of those navigators, making every effort to assist them where possible, especially those of His Britannic Majesty, with whom you will maintain the closest harmony, supplying each other with necessary aids." As to Indian policy, he warned,

> continuous contact with the natives of America will perhaps cause incidents, arising out of lack of vigilance or overconfidence, that may result in use of arms for purposes of defense. Such cases cause lamentable consequences: the blood of unfortunates who do not know the force of our arms is shed; some of our own die at their barbarous hands; continued explorations become impossible; and finally, their friendship is lost, for their aid contributes to success of the survey. . . . To prevent any such unfortunate accident, I am confident of your experience in dealing with them and of the spirit of humanity animating you. I hope that gifts, gentleness, and possibly pretending not to notice offenses they commit, as well as vigilance over your people so they do not insult the Indians in the slightest way, will be the bonds to link you with them, laying a foundation for a friendship perhaps very useful in the future to religion and the sovereign. Never use your weapons to offend them unless a crucial necessity obliges you to do so, in which case you must justify yourself upon your return to this capital.[7]

The instructions included a list of topics for inquiry with every tribe encountered. The influence of this ethnic inventory is evident in the valuable data for which the subsequent account of the expedition is renowned. The Spaniards were exhorted

> to neither take from the Indians nor permit taking anything belonging to them unless agreed upon and offered by their hand. It is of concern

6. Revillagigedo, Secret Instructions to Mourelle, September 9, 1791, MxAGN (Hist. 44), fol. 1v, AT.

7. Ibid., fol. 4–4v, AT.

to observe this so they may always comprehend that we profess good faith and are truthful, thus removing from their imagination any idea that we are capable of deceiving them. You will therefore punish any member of your crew committing the slightest infraction of this rule. You yourself will bear and make your men bear whatever treachery the natives commit, when this is not of such a character as to interfere with the essential duties of your commission. Always keep before you that I will be very pleased to see this service carried out without offending in the slightest degree those unhappy beings who in their ignorance clamor for my humanity and compassion.[8]

Far from being a platitudinous repetition of orders for previous expeditions, this unusual document embodies the viceroy's determination to avoid occurrences such as those which poisoned Martínez's relations with the natives. Revillagigedo's strictures on this occasion are as clear, emphatic, and eloquent a statement of Spain's Indian policy for the Pacific Northwest as exists. Enunciating principles and implementing them are hardly the same, but on the whole Iberian policy and practice toward the aborigines of the northwest coast compare quite favorably with those of other nationalities engaged in rivalry for that area. The Spanish in the eighteenth century had little in common with *conquistadores* of the widely diffused "Black Legend," which was derived from cruelties of sixteenth-century conquests, fueled by anti-Hispanic sentiment, and promoted by Spain's rivals to their own advantage.

By December 1791, the *Mexicana* and an armed longboat were prepared to depart northward for a headstart on the coming season. Malaspina's corvettes were at Acapulco, about to depart for the Orient. When the Parmesan explorer learned of vast waterways deep within Fuca, he became enthusiastic about the possibility of finding the long-sought northwest passage. He proposed that the expedition be enlarged to include another schooner, the *Sútil*, likewise just completed at San Blas, and pressed to have Mourelle replaced by two of his own men, Dionisio Alcalá Galiano and Cayetano Valdés. Revillagigedo consented, and Mourelle took the two identical schooners from San Blas to Acapulco and then resumed his secretarial post. Thus the last connection with the northwest coast was severed for this brave mariner, but a distinguished naval career awaited him elsewhere in the empire.[9] Alcalá Galiano's second officer was frigate

8. Ibid., fol. 6v–7v, AT.

9. Revillagigedo to Floridablanca, Mexico City, November 27, 1791, CU–B (Robbins Collection), Revillagigedo Papers, vol. 22, fol. 220v–23. Transferred to Spain in 1793, Mourelle was promoted to frigate captain (1799), ship's captain (1806), and commodore (1811). He became a member of the "Council of Generals" and a knight of the military Order of Santiago, commanded a series of warships and the naval installations at Algeciras, Málaga, and Ceuta, was

lieutenant Secundino Salamanca, and Valdés was accompanied by frigate lieutenant Juan Vernacci. Revillagigedo prepared new instructions altering somewhat the objectives set forth for Mourelle. Examining the coast from 56° southward was postponed in favor of concentrating upon northern and eastern branches of Fuca, "to obtain a complete knowledge of that interior part of the globe." If a northwest passage were disclosed, which now seemed more likely than ever, they should establish its location with great precision and "direct their course along it to Europe, if season and supplies permit, trying absolutely not to touch at any foreign ports, but if necessity obliges, attempt by any measures feasible to keep secret their derivation and undertaking, and above all the location of the passageway found." [10]

To escape malarial fevers plaguing Acapulco that time of year, Malaspina sailed for Asia before the *Sútil* and the *Mexicana* arrived there from San Blas. The twin schooners did not fulfill the requisites deemed necessary for their mission, and several months' labor was required to raise gunwales and decks. They were not able to depart until March 8. Meanwhile, an impressive flotilla of Spanish warships had got underway for the northwest coast.

### THE BOUNDARY EXPEDITION OF 1792

Spanish activities in the Pacific Northwest reached their peak in 1792, with (1) Bodega's "Expedición de Límites," to negotiate an accord with the British commissioner for Nootka; (2) Caamaño's explorations in Alaska; (3) Fidalgo's establishment of a settlement at Núñez Gaona (Neah Bay); and (4) the Alcalá Galiano and Valdés investigation of Fuca's secrets.

It was entirely fitting that Juan Francisco de la Bodega y Quadra be chosen to conduct the delicate negotiations for fulfilling terms on the

---

named *Vocal* in the junta for the defense of Cádiz (1809), and was placed in charge of a squadron being prepared to put down rebellion in the Río de la Plata (1818). It never got underway because of a revolt proclaiming anew the liberal constitution of 1812. Fernando VII was forced to acquiesce briefly, but he soon gained the upper hand, and the "Constitutionalists" were persecuted, banished, or executed. Mourelle came under attack for having taken an oath to the constitution, but at sixty-four death removed him from the scene (May 24, 1820). Dionisio Alcalá Galiano, born in Cabra, province of Córdoba, was twenty-nine years old when he sailed with Malaspina in 1789; he had seen service against Portugal in Brazilian waters and visited Colonia del Sacramento in the Río de la Plata, the Malvinas, and the Straits of Magellan. His participation in hydrographic charting of the Spanish coast (1783–85) proved valuable to him when he reached the northwest coast. Cayetano Valdés, a nephew of Minister Antonio Valdés, was born in Seville in 1767, entered the marine guard at Cádiz at fourteen, and a year later saw combat against the British at Gibraltar. *Enciclopedia General del Mar*, 4 : 701–2; 5 : 693–94; *Relación de los méritos y servicios del Capitán de Navío D. Francisco Mourelle* (n.d., n.p.), copy in SpMN (999).

10. Revillagigedo, Instructions to Alcalá Galiano and Valdés, Mexico City, January 21, 1792, SpMN (619), fol. 3–7v.

Nootka Convention. The most able naval officer on Mexico's west coast, the Peruvian-born commandant was, by reason of his personal experience on previous expeditions to the North Pacific, particularly qualified to know the historical grounds for Spain's claims in that area. He would proceed to Nootka aboard the frigate *Santa Gertrudis.* Commanded by ship's captain Alonso de Torres, the huge warship had been sent from Spain for the express purpose of reinforcing Spanish naval might during the crucial negotiations ahead. Bodega could also count upon the strength of the giant frigate *Concepción,* stationed at Nootka since 1790, and the brigantine *Activa,* newly constructed at San Blas, which followed him northward. The frigate *Aranzazú* also formed part of the expedition. Another frigate, the *Princesa,* would be at nearby Núñez Gaona, and the armed schooners *Sútil* and *Mexicana* would be operating in the neighborhood of Nootka all summer. The seven ships added up to a potent demonstration of Spanish naval power.[11] Although never sailing as a fleet, they constituted units in a coordinated plan, under Bodega's guidance. Considered as parts of a whole, they were the most impressive naval force sent by any nation to the North Pacific in the eighteenth century. Nevertheless, arrival and departure dates show that seldom were many of the warships anchored in Friendly Cove at once. Most of the time they were absent on explorations or en route to and fro with supplies from Monterey and San Blas. Significantly, Bodega's mission is referred to repeatedly as the *Expedición para la Entrega de Nootka* (Expedition for the Delivery of Nootka) in the instructions, journals, reports, and letters produced in the course of the effort; this corroborates the view that from the outset it was Revillagigedo's intention to yield Nootka to the British. The unsatisfactory trend of the negotiations, from Spain's point of view, explains why such a "delivery" did not take place.

On the eve of Bodega's departure northward, there came a hint of the wide gulf between Spanish and British viewpoints. Bodega received from an officer of the *Santa Gertrudis* a map published in London in 1790 showing the west coast of North America divided into British and Spanish possessions by a line falling just north of San Francisco Bay. The day he left San Blas, Bodega sent this chart to Revillagigedo, expressing concern that Britain might interpret the convention in a manner jeopardizing Spanish claims to everything north of San Francisco. Anticipating such a tack, he requested that additional instructions for meeting the challenge be sent him on the next ship north.[12]

The *Santa Gertrudis,* the *Princesa,* and the *Activa* sailed together on February 29, but mishaps sent two of the vessels back to port within several

11. An eighth vessel sailed under Spanish colors on the northwest coast in 1792 after Bodega purchased Gray's sloop *Adventure,* renamed *Orcasitas.*

12. Bodega to Revillagigedo, San Blas, February 29, 1792, MxAGN (Hist. 67).

days. Salvador Menéndez and the *Activa* set sail again on March 15; Fidalgo and the *Princesa* followed on March 23. Accompanying Bodega was José Mariano Moziño Suárez de Figueroa, a thirty-five-year-old naturalist of Spanish ancestry from Temascaltepec, a small town southwest of Toluca. Moziño had the services of a skilled assistant, artist Atanasio Echeverría y Godoy, of Mexico City's Academia de San Carlos; Echeverría's numerous sketches of plants, animals, Indians, and scenes in and around Nootka would so impress Revillagigedo that he would commission academy students to make multiple sets.[13] A summer at Friendly Cove enabled Moziño to compose a descriptive narrative rich in unique details. Of particular value are his insights into native acculturation from contact with various nationalities, and otherwise unknown aspects of Nootka mythology, deities, religious practices, marital customs, and political structure. By any standard this was the most valuable first-hand description of Spanish activities at Nootka Sound; but Moziño's readiness to offer an opinion, even when it differed from official policy, and to criticize where he felt warranted, may explain why it was not immediately published.[14]

Bodega reached Nootka in late April, four months before his opposite number appeared, although the British commissioner was not far off. As the giant *Santa Gertrudis* eased into Friendly Cove, the warships bringing his contender were approaching the Strait of Juan de Fuca.

### THE BRITISH COMMISSIONER FOR NOOTKA

The ink had scarcely dried on the Convention of 1790 when the Pitt ministry commenced preparations for a strong, well-armed, and well-equipped naval force to carry out terms of the accord extorted from Madrid. Leadership of the mission was conferred upon thirty-four-year-old Captain George Vancouver, a capable navigator already familiar with Nootka and the northwest coast as a veteran of Cook's expedition. Provided with two potent warships, the *Discovery* (with twenty cannons and a crew of 100) and the tender *Chatham* (with ten guns and twenty-five seamen), he sailed from England in April 1791, as soon as the vessels could be readied, expecting to take formal possession of the lands being returned to British subjects. The supply ship *Daedalus* would follow a short time later. Vancouver carried

---

13. A complete series is in CU-B (Robbins Collection), Revillagigedo Papers vol 30, with another complete set and truncated series in Madrid's ministry of foreign relations. Cutter, "Early Spanish Artists," p. 156.

14. His *Noticias de Nutka* appeared first in the *Gazeta de Guatemala* (1804–05), and then in Mexico City (1913), from a manuscript in the Sociedad Mejicana de Geografía y Estadística, both rare editions. Other manuscripts exist, with variant titles, in SpMN, CtY-B, and CU-B (Robbins Collection), Revillagigedo Papers. CaBViPA has translations by Ninian Bain (1926) and Charles Cotterell (n.d.). Iris Higbie Wilson's translation (Seattle, 1970), has at long last made this most important source readily accessible.

instructions to search for the alleged northwest passage, examine all inlets, ascend large rivers to the limit of navigation, and reconnoiter every European settlement on the northwest coast, endeavoring to learn the precise date when each was founded. He was "to avoid with the utmost caution the giving any ground of Jealousy or Complaint to the Subjects or Officers of His Catholic Majesty," and to make "reciprocally a free and unreserved communication of all Plans and Charts of Discoveries" with any Spanish officers and explorers met.[15]

Vancouver had scant means of knowing details of Iberian accomplishments on the northwest coast between 1774 and 1792. Prior to contact with Spanish officials, he had little idea of the extent of their explorations, or of Madrid's military strength in the area.

Having come by way of the Cape of Good Hope, New Zealand, Tahiti, and Hawaii, the British commissioner made landfall at 39° 20′ north latitude, near Cape Mendocino. As had Cook, he searched for Hezeta's "Entrada," recognizing from afar the headland just north of the Columbia that Meares had named Cape Disappointment, and he agreed with him that no such river existed. That very month the American Gray would sight what Cook, Meares, and Vancouver failed to find, and his discovery would have enduring political and diplomatic consequences for the Pacific Northwest. Vancouver encountered the *Columbia* near the Strait of Juan de Fuca on April 29, and Gray gave him his first up-to-date information about Spanish activities thereabouts. The American captain also told of sighting the Columbia's mouth a few days earlier.[16]

Instead of proceeding directly to Nootka and confronting his opposite number, Vancouver wanted to examine the Strait of Juan de Fuca and its interior waterways, to be in a better position to perceive what objectives he should pursue in negotiations at Friendly Cove. He arrived on the northwest coast expecting to secure Britain's rights to all the coast between the Russian outposts in Alaska and a point very near San Francisco Bay. Drake's claim to "Nova Albion" made him aspire to everything from "Drake's Bay" northward. His instructions were to begin explorations south of 40°, near the supposed site of Drake's landing. It is significant that upon performing his first formal act of possession on the northwest coast (June 4, 1792), near the present Everett, Washington, Vancouver claimed for George III all the coast from 39° 20′ (his first landfall) to that spot. Ferrelo's explorations in 1542–43, north of Drake's 1579 landing spot, were virtually unknown in Spain, to say nothing of England. From Britain's point of view, claims based on Spanish expeditions in 1774 and 1775 could scarcely compete with

15. Grenville to the Lords commissioners of the admiralty, February 11, 1791, in *BCPAD Report, 1913* (1914): 46–48.
16. Menzies, *Journal*, p. 14.

Drake's feat. Vancouver made his ambitious claim in good faith, convinced of its historical justification. The maps he prepared all depict a northern border for Spanish territory at about 39° north latitude, confirming Bodega's worst fears about British designs upon California.

Vancouver found important features within the Strait of Juan de Fuca that had eluded Quimper in 1790 and Eliza in 1791. He followed the "Boca de Caamaño," noted by Spanish explorers but neglected, into an intricate pattern of waterways and named it after Peter Puget, one of his officers. He examined and named the sound's many channels, eliminating the possibility that it led to a northwest passage. In the broad waterway that Vancouver named Gulf of Georgia (the Spanish Rosario Strait), the British explorers were surprised to encounter the *Sútil* and the *Mexicana*. Vancouver was disappointed to learn from Alcalá Galiano that Spanish expeditions had visited that area in 1790 and 1791. The four vessels continued their explorations together for a time, dividing the task of examining lateral openings and sharing findings. Eventually they pushed northward independently, through what came to be called the Inland Passage, to emerge into the Pacific. After a harrowing incident when the *Discovery* got stuck on a reef and very nearly capsized at low tide, the British warships arrived at Nootka on August 28, sharing with the Spanish schooners the credit for proving the vast land mass behind Nootka Sound to be truly an island.

### BODEGA AND MA-KWEE-NA

The Spanish presence at Friendly Cove, not unsurprisingly, was a prime factor in native acculturation. After Malaspina reinforced Ma-kwee-na's confidence in Spanish intentions, Eliza's relations with the Indians began to improve. The chieftains from around the sound continued to compete with one another, however, to secure preferential treatment, for the one receiving greatest recognition from the Spanish commandant stood to gain prestige over his rivals. Tlu-pa-na-nootl put his great dugout at Eliza's service for any purpose. And when Ma-kwee-na noted a shortage of supplies because of the delay of supply ships from San Blas, he kept the settlement provided with fresh fish, refusing any compensation for the service. Although Ma-kwee-na had an advantage in being chief of the band that claimed Uquot, he did not enjoy suzerainty over all the other chiefs of the sound, even though some recognized him as being of higher status. Ma-kwee-na revalidated the title inherited from his father, A-na-pā, said to have been killed in battle in 1778, by personally leading a campaign that desolated the villages of his father's enemies with what was described as "horrible butchery." [17]

Constant jockeying among the rival chiefs for hegemony did not prevent them from intermarrying, any more than it did among European rulers for

17. *Sútil y Mexicana*, pp. 17–19, 140.

centuries. Through the deceased Ke-le-kum, Ma-kwee-na retained a bond of kinship with the widow's brother, Wee-ka-na-nish, and Ma-kwee-na's favorite wife was a sister of chief Na-tsa-pā. There had been many wars between the Nootka and their Clayoquot neighbors, but the Nootka always lost, and therefore they recognized Wee-ka-na-nish as superior. By the time the Spanish established their settlement at Friendly Cove, Ma-kwee-na was at peace with his powerful neighbor—a peace in which Ke-le-kum's marital alliance perhaps played a part. The bond was further strengthened in 1792 when Ma-kwee-na betrothed his eldest daughter, A-pā-nas, to the oldest of Wee-ka-na-nish's sons. This followed closely upon proclamation, at the girl's coming-of-age ceremony, that her eldest son would assume Ma-kwee-na's name and inherit tribal leadership.[18] Having reached puberty, she was formally renamed Is-to-ko-tee-klā-mot. Near Ma-kwee-na's lodge a special platform was erected and decorated with a design portraying a creature with outstretched arms, signifying the chief's generosity. One of the Spanish sketches shows the girl standing between father and uncle, atop this platform. In the chief's name the uncle tossed a small wooden cylinder to twenty or thirty nude warriors assembled below, who wrestled frantically to seize it from one another. The one retaining it against all challengers received a prize of highly valued abalone shells. At one side some Spanish seamen are stripping, preparatory to ascending to the wrestling stage, and engaging in a similar contest. Gratified at having his daughter thus honored, Ma-kwee-na rewarded the winner with several prime sea otter pelts.[19]

Eliza's efforts to cultivate native friendship pale by comparison with Bodega's measures—so much so that one suspects a studied attention to this as a makeweight in the approaching confrontation with Vancouver. Reassured by the genial Peruvian's gestures, Ma-kwee-na moved his camp nearby and, at Bodega's invitation, dined at the commandant's table almost daily. "Since the chiefs are treated by us with extreme generosity, they present themselves always with an air of pleasure and self-assuredness," a Spanish source notes.

> Upon hearing the dinner bell Maquina comes daily, performs his courtesy with his hat and sits at the Commander's side. He asks for anything he pleases and uses a spoon, fork and glass very well. He asks for wine and sherry, coffee upon finishing if there is any, and chocolate in the mornings.[20]

18. "Apuntes, sin coordinar," SpMN (330), fol. 58. Handwriting comparison leads Cutter to believe the author was Secundino Salamanca, second officer of the *Sutil* (verbal communication, 1962); Vancouver, *Voyage*, 2 : 254. Presumably the boy proclaimed heir in 1789 had not survived.

19. *Sútil y Mexicana*, p. 143; Moziño, *Noticias*, pp. 34–37; Bodega, "Viaje a la Costa N. O. de la America Septentrion[al] . . . en las Fragatas de su mando Sta. Gertrudis, Aranzazu, Princesa, y Goleta Activa Año de 1792," CSmH (HM 141), fol. 24v–25.

20. "Apuntes, sin coordinar," fol. 58, AT.

Another Spanish account says Ma-kwee-na handled his cutlery "like the best-mannered European, allowing himself to be attended by the servants and amusing everyone with his festive humor." The chief was fond of wine, but he appointed one of his own people to gauge the limit, so as to avoid losing his dignity. Ordinarily accompanied at Bodega's table by his brother, Kwa-tla-tsa-pā, of whom he was extraordinarily fond, on occasion Ma-kwee-na brought with him numerous other relatives and subjects. "Our treatment has made them habituated to bread, chocolate, and other European foodstuffs, and in such a manner to beans, stewed in the style of New Spain, that they call this dish *Tays-frixoles*," [21] that is, "nobles' beans," which they are said to have preferred above all other food introduced to them. With *frijoles refritos,* Mexico's commonest dish, Bodega was as effective in catering to his native guests as in plying American and Englishmen with wines, brandies, and banquets served on sterling silver. In both cases, the result was tacit recognition and reinforcement of Spanish control over Friendly Cove.

Tlu-pa-na-nootl had the habit of coming once a week to enjoy Bodega's diningroom diplomacy, and always brought a freshly killed deer. He would be seated opposite his rival. Tlu-pa-na-nootl's "expressions were few, and mien stupid but kindly," this same Spanish source remarks. Ma-kwee-na, on the other hand,

> was endowed with a clear and sagacious talent, and knew very well the rights of sovereignty. He complained a great deal about treatment from foreign vessels trafficking on the coast, because of some outrages he claimed his people had received. He denied ever ceding the Port of Nutka to the English Lieutenant Meares, and confessed only to having permitted him to establish himself in it, repeating continually the cession made to the king of Spain of the same port and beaches corresponding to it with all their products.[22]

As for native response to his fraternal treatment, the Peruvian commandant remarks,

> I never had reason to be sorry; on the contrary I was able to corroborate with unequivocal proofs the confidence they have in me, and the love they profess for me, not only the plebeians, but the princes themselves, for they remain most nights to sleep in my house with the satisfaction that perhaps they would not receive in that of their most immediate relatives. Thus it has not been difficult to establish with them the humane system toward which my spirit is naturally inclined. I treat Macuina constantly as a friend, distinguishing him from all the rest

21. *Sútil y Mexicana,* pp. 17, 130, AT.
22. Ibid., pp. 17–18, AT.

with the clearest demonstrations of appreciation. He always occupies the first place when he eats at my table, and I myself take care to serve him and give him everything he might wish, and he makes a public show of my friendship and esteems it greatly when I visit his villages.[23]

Bodega's openhandedness was not abused. "None of the chiefs ever stole any of the many furnishings that they had within their reach in my house," he comments; "on the contrary they restored several things pilfered by commoners, whose inclination toward theft either has weakened to the extreme, or was never as great as others have stated." [24] The commandant's readiness to fraternize with the natives was not shared by Vancouver's officers, one of whom describes the people of Nootka, whether chiefs or plebeians, men or women, as being "extremely filthy and dirty in their persons, dwellings, manner of living and in short in everything whatever. . . . They seldom or ever wash themselves, and they beautify themselves highly in their opinions by besmearing their faces with Red Ochre and white paint mixed with Fish Oil, in different figures, which at times renders their appearance frightful." Only the women ever combed their hair, but "the combs they make use of are only for the purpose of combing the Hair smooth and straight and not for destroying vermin." "These they conceive too precious to run the risk of loosing by using small combs therefore they pick them out with their fingers from each others heads and not willing to go unrewarded for their pains—eat them." [25]

Nonetheless, there is ample evidence that Ma-kwee-na's behavior was rapidly changing under Spanish influence. Although he never is mentioned as replacing or complementing his cutsark with pantaloons, on special occasions he took great pride in wearing a handsome steel helmet and coat of mail given him by Bodega. The Limeño tendered him recognition as sovereign, a rank he did not actually hold among his peers. Since Ma-kwee-na was paid such deference, it is hardly surprising that he sought every means of remaining in Bodega's good graces, fulfilling every wish insofar as possible. Not content to be displaced, Kee-o-ka-ma-sha staged an elaborate masked dance in Bodega's honor, in which he took the principal part, imitating a series of animals. Similarly, Tlu-pa-na-nootl endeavored to enhance his own image with an aquatic spectacle. In what Bodega described as the largest dugout he had ever seen, the chief made three quick turns around all the vessels in the cove, his rowers rhythmically beating the sides of the craft with their oars, singing the customary chant in praise of friendship. None of these efforts altered Bodega's preference for Ma-kwee-na.[26]

23. Bodega, "Viaje," fol. 23–23v, AT.
24. Ibid., fol. 25v–26, AT.
25. Bell, *Journal*, p. 36.
26. Moziño, *Noticias*, p. 16; Bodega, "Viaje," fol. 23–25.

The latter's acculturation engendered problems in his personal life and tensions within the tribe, because of his dual role as chief and religious leader. His very name meant "Chief of the Sun," and he had prime responsibility for preserving and handing down secrets of his tribe's religion, making sacrifices to the Creator, Kwa-ootl, and seeking oracles. Part of the veneration accorded Ma-kwee-na derived from the concept that, after death, he would become a member of a class of supernatural beings with power to control the elements. His duties as chief priest required him to observe periodic fasts, shut within a rectangular box, grotesquely painted on the inside. In compassion for the chief's sleepless suffering within the prayer cubicle, his family would sit around in a ring, consoling him constantly, until he entered a trance and commenced to shout and howl; his utterances were regarded as portents of the future and of the deity's will. That Cardero was permitted to sketch this sanctuary and that Moziño learned as much as he did about Nootka religion suggest little effort to hide the chief's religious role, and scant interference from the Spanish with native ritual.[27] But Ma-kwee-na's old status as intercessor with the Creator inevitably was eroded by his subservience to Bodega and the Spanish priests, and by his fondness for and growing dependence upon goods solely obtainable from the white man.

Ma-kwee-na's chiefly duties included acting as supreme judge over his subjects in cases of wrongdoing. Bodega could not avoid becoming involved, to the detriment of the chief's authority. An anonymous Spanish account relates that a native

> came to us for refuge, we told Maquina, and when it was learned his crime was merely cheating in the sale of furs we asked for his life. It was conceded, on condition that we strip him, dress him in our manner, and let him remain with us, because he could no longer live among them. The chief said he would also request us to punish some of those [white men] who deserved it.[28]

Four years of contact with the Spanish had so altered Nootka behavior that, upon returning in 1792, Joseph Ingraham would exclaim:

> Most of the chiefs of any consequence were quite polish'd by the Spanish gentlemen for when any of them met or parted with me it was a great deal of ceremony as bowing scraping adieu senior etc. The Commodore even admitted Maquinna and his brothers to dine at table with him and they behav'd with great decency. I veryly believe if the Spaniards had the tuition of these people but a few years longer they

27. Moziño, *Noticias*, chapters 3–5; *Sútil y Mexicana*, pp. 136–40, 145–46; Bell, *Journal*, p. 36; "Apuntes, sin coordinar," fol. 57.

28. "Apuntes, sin coordinar," fol. 57v, AT.

would be quite civiliz'd. These people can never wish to have among them a better Friend than Don Quadra—nothing can exceed his attention and kindness to them; they all seem sensible of it and are extravagantly fond of him.[29]

Wooing native favor was an important part of the astute commandant's strategy for furthering Spanish interests. Although Bodega's Indian policy was studied in its humanity and coincided with ulterior motives, it was no less sincere. His log remarks: "I can perhaps flatter myself that treating these Indians as men ought to be treated, and not like individuals of inferior nature, I have lived in the very breast of tranquility." [30]

Moziño resented oft-heard white remarks about Indian thievery and perversity—belied by the five months he and Bodega had lived among them—since they had impressed him with their general honesty and gentleness. "What a pity that they could not in general say the same about us," he exclaims.

> The sailors, either as a result of their almost brutal upbringing or because they envied the humane treatment the commandant and other officers always gave the natives, insulted them at various times, crippled some and wounded others, and did not fail to kill several. Humanity is the greatest characteristic of civilization. All the sciences and arts have no value if they serve only to make us cruel and haughty.[31]

### GROWING VIOLENCE IN THE SEA OTTER TRADE

Strengthening Indian friendship was crucial at a time when the sea otter trade was witnessing increasing violence. Since Spanish policy no longer proscribed foreign vessels on the northwest coast, by 1792 competition for peltry had swollen to include, besides an unknown number of Russian vessels operating from Prince William Sound westward, nine British traders, four American, four of Portuguese registry (probably owned principally by British subjects), one French ship, and one operating under the Swedish flag. The plethora of traders and increasing Indian sophistication led to a growing number of incidents stemming from guile on both sides. Moziño places much of the blame upon the elder Kendrick's shoulders. Kendrick succeeded in gaining Indian friendship and confidence as did no other trader, by giving them gifts, amusing them with fireworks, speaking their tongue, and wearing their dress, while showing them how to use firearms and trading them great quantities of guns and ammunition.[32] His gener-

---

29. Ingraham, "Log," p. 182.
30. Bodega, "Viaje," fol. 25.
31. Moziño, *Noticias,* p. 84.
32. "I cannot say whether it was self-interest or rivalry with the English that suggested to the Americans the perverse idea of teaching the savages the handling of firearms—a lesson

osity was legendary, but it inflated what other traders would have to pay for pelts. Bell asserts that as of 1792 the price brought by sea otter pelts in China had dropped from an average of forty to fifteen dollars apiece, whereas native demands had quadrupled. "Muskets were early given them in Barter which they could not use without Power and Ball," he complains.

> These they demanded for the Skins and got them and for a length of time no skins could be purchased without ammunition & Fire Arms. Some of the first Muskets that were sold procured 6 and seven Skins, now, two skins, but more commonly one, is the price. At the district of Wicananish that chief can turn out four hundred men arm'd with muskets and well found with ammunition, a considerable part of which have been given him in barter by a Mr. Kendrick, Master of an American Vessel call'd the Washington. Their former weapons, Bows and Arrows, Spears and Clubs are now thrown aside & forgotten. At Nootka it was the same way everyone had his musket. Thus are they supplied with weapons which they no sooner possess than they turn against the donors. Few ships have been on the Coast that have not been attack'd or attempted to be attacked and in general many lives have been lost on both sides.[33]

Although Bell might be suspected of anti-American bias, his story is corroborated by Spanish and American sources. After the clash between Martínez and Colnett, American traders sought to exploit the furry wealth with few scruples and little regard for the future, believing that whatever the diplomatic outcome, Americans would not be allowed to traffic on that coast no matter which nation emerged as victor. "The eagerness of some of these desperate Traders," Bell remarks, "has in more than two or three instances urged them to infamous practices for procuring their cargoes for where the Indians have refused disposing of their Skins either from disliking the articles or from the quantity offered being too small in their opinions, some of these Traders have by force of Arms made them part with the skins on their own terms, nay have in some places forcibly taken their skins from them without making any return whatever." [34]

Gray's incident-filled cruise in 1792 is illustrative of this increased resort to violence. The winter of 1791–92, it will be remembered, he remained at anchor in Clayoquot Sound, building the sloop *Adventure*. There he had learned in advance of the vengeful attack being prepared by Wee-ka-na-nish,

---

that could be harmful to all humanity. He [Kendrick] gave Maquinna a swivel gun; he furnished Wickinanish with more than two hundred guns, two barrels of powder, and a considerable portion of shot, which [the Indians] have just finished using on the unhappy sailors of Captains Brown and Baker." Ibid., p. 71.

33. Bell, *Journal*, pp. 40–41.

34. Ibid., p. 41.

and had repelled it with considerable slaughter. After launching the sloop (February 23), Gray abandoned "Fort Defiance," leaving it standing. He probably did not expect to use it again, for prior to departing he anchored off Opitsat and sent an armed party to repay Wee-ka-na-nish's assault. The town was deserted; its inhabitants had fled in such haste that many domestic utensils were still in place or hidden in nearby bushes. "I am sorry to be under the necessity of remarking," Boit states,

> that this day I was *sent* with three boats, all well manned and armed, to destroy the Village of Opitsatah. It was a command I was no ways tenacious of, and am grieved to think Capt. Gray should let his passions go too far. This village was about a half a mile in diameter, and contained upwards of 200 houses, generally well built for *Indians*. Every door that you entered was in resemblance to a human and beasts head, the passage being through the mouth, besides which there was much more rude carved work about the dwellings some of which was by no means inelegant. This fine village, the Work of Ages, was in a short time totally destroyed.[35]

From Clayoquot the *Adventure* traded to the north while the *Columbia* went southward. In April, Gray sighted the great river discovered by Hezeta in 1775 and named it after his vessel, although it could not have escaped him that Hezeta deserved the credit, as his "Entrada" appeared at that latitude on Spanish maps. For seventeen years mariners had sought Hezeta's passageway and, when it eluded them, had denied its existence. Since Spanish policy had endeavored, without success, to keep it a secret, there was some justice to its being renamed by Gray. As with the *Santiago* in 1775, the *Columbia* was prevented from crossing the dangerous bar on its first attempt by strong currents and menacing surf. Unlike Hezeta, Gray immediately spread word of his discovery among other nationalities, and his achievement obtained international recognition, providing the United States with one of its most impressive claims to the Pacific Northwest. A few days later he discovered another large estuary, today called Gray's Harbor. He then returned to the Columbia, succeeded in crossing the bar, ascended the river some twenty-five miles, and remained there for ten days to trade with the natives before returning northward. Upon reentering Clayoquot, knowing that Wee-ka-na-nish would surely seek to avenge Opitsat's destruction, Gray had his crew in readiness. "At 10 in the evening," Boit relates,

> a number of large Canoes full of People, came into the Cove, they halted near some rocks about Pistol shot from the Ship, and there waited about ten minutes, during which time all hands was brought

---

35. Boit, "Log," pp. 390–91, entry for March 25, 1792, Punctuation and spelling emended.

to arms upon deck in readiness to receive them. Soon a large War Canoe, with above 25 Indians, paddled off for the Ship, We hail'd them, but they still persisted, and other Canoes was seen following, upon which Capt. Gray order'd us to fire, which we did so effectually as to kill or wound every soul in the Canoe. She drifted along side, but we push'd her Clear, and she drove to the North side of the Cove, under the Shade of the trees. 'Twas bright moon light and the woods *echoed* with the dying groans of these unfortunate Savages. We observ'd many Canoes passing and repassing the Cove at a small distance, in all probability they was after the poor dead Indians. They soon after ceas'd groaning, and we neither see nor heard any thing of them after.[36]

The attack was not renewed. Since the Spanish made it a practice to offer the healing power of their medicine to anyone requesting treatment, on June 3 a party of braves came to Nootka bearing a gravely wounded companion, and Ma-kwee-na brought him to Bodega. The surgeons extracted two bullets from his thigh and offered to let him recuperate in their infirmary. "Although Maquina concurred, assuring him of our good treatment and friendship," an anonymous Spanish source relates, "the wounded man could not overcome his suspicions because of the recent memory of the evil handling he had received from Europeans and had himself carried away." [37] The natives complained bitterly of Gray's cruelty, but neglected to say that the injury had occurred during an assault on the *Columbia*. Allegedly the incident took place at Esperanza Inlet, where Gray was said to have attacked a village that refused to trade with him. Both Spanish and British accepted at face value the tale about Gray's unprovoked onslaught.[38]

Another clash occurred at Clayoquot about this time, this one involving the British. A group of merchants had obtained a grant from London permitting them to establish trading posts and settlements on the northwest coast, and they sent out three vessels: the *Jackal* (commanded by Alexander Stewart, second mate of the *Princess Royal* in 1789), the *Butterworth* (under Captain William Brown), and the *Prince Le Boo* (under a Captain Sharp). Brown, commander of the effort, had instructions to plant three "factories," one in the Queen Charlotte Islands and two on the mainland. When he anchored off Opitsat, an argument with Wee-ka-na-nish ensued because (as American traders from the *Thomas Jefferson* were told) the chief had not reciprocated with the number of pelts deemed equivalent to presents handed out. Wee-ka-na-nish's brother and two subordinate chiefs were slain. In June the *Jefferson* entered Clayoquot, unaware of this incident, and Wee-ka-

36. Ibid., p. 401, entry for May 29, 1792.
37. "Apuntes, sin coordinar," fol. 59, AT.
38. *Sútil y Mexicana,* p. 24.

na-nish was so wary that he refused to come aboard unless Captain Josiah Roberts sent two officers ashore as hostages. He excused his behavior by telling of the trouble with Brown. He did not mention assaulting the *Columbia,* but he complained that Gray had threatened to fire upon his people unless paid in pelts for a coat lent the chief.[39] The native version of these episodes cannot be taken as the full story; what is significant nevertheless is the growing incidence of force in the peltry traffic. Clayoquot was a more important source of furs than Nootka, but Wee-ka-na-nish was audacious, quick to take offense, and implacable in seeking revenge. When vessels needed repairing, most captains preferred putting in at Nootka, since Ma-kwee-na was uncommonly eager to hobnob with any and all European visitors.

Analyzing the reasons for such acute distrust between traders and Indians, Howay points out that the trading cruises were by and large individual efforts, with little cooperation or identification of mutual interests between rival vessels. Since captain and crew might never again have occasion to visit the same spot, there was a temptation to make the most of every opportunity, disregarding future relationships with a particular village. The Indian reaction to such behavior was to seek revenge upon the perpetrator where possible, and otherwise, on the next vessel of the same nationality to visit that locality.[40]

Some traders resorted to ingenuity rather than force, endeavoring to overcome native sales resistance. In 1792 Ingraham found that trade articles highly appreciated in previous years were now disdained. Noting the fondness of Indian women for bracelets, he had his blacksmith fashion pieces of iron into round rings, nicely burnished, which were purveyed as proper items for female attire. Soon the fad spread, and Ingraham found he could extract three prime pelts for each one. As competition between rival vessels heightened, the natives became increasingly choosy and shrewd in driving a bargain. Adapting, American traders made their vessels into floating emporiums, stocked with merchandise of every kind to entice the eye and satisfy the whim of the most particular customer. Yankee traders enjoyed another advantage, destined in the long run to make them predominant in the trade. Licenses required of British fur traders from the South Sea and East India Companies contained stringent prohibitions against using revenue from fur cargoes to purchase luxury items in China for sale in England. Americans operated under no such handicap and, as Howay points out, "made fortunes while the traders of Old England lost them." [41]

39. Ingraham, "Log," pp. 170–71; Bodega, "Viaje," fol. 19–19v; Howay, "Fur Trade in Northwestern Development," p. 277; F. W. Howay, "A Yankee Trader on the Northwest Coast, 1791–1795," *WHQ* 21 (1930): p. 85.

40. Howay, "Ballad of the Bold Northwestman," p. 122.

41. Howay, *Voyages of the "Columbia,"* p. xxvi; Ingraham, "Log," extract pub. in *WHQ* 12 (1921): 10–12.

The Convention of 1790 encouraged commercial circles in London to think of British rights to traffic and settle on the northwest coast as fully secured, to the exclusion of Americans. Captain Brown anchored at Nootka on the same day as Captain Magee of the *Margaret,* out of Boston. At once the Englishman undertook to prevent the American from continuing his cruise, on grounds that Britain had an exclusive right to trade in that area. To prevent an altercation, Bodega was obliged to intervene, and Magee went undisturbed. Whether because of continued Spanish presence on the northwest coast, deadlock in the Bodega-Vancouver negotiations, or Bodega's allowing Americans to skim the cream from the sea otter trade, none of Brown's three factories was ever established.[42]

The growing ruthlessness and violence, increased financial risks, and unpredictability of the profit margin when pelts reached China did not escape notice of those in a position to recommend or discourage Spanish participation. Nor was it lost on the chieftains that the Spanish had more interest in obtaining political hegemony than in exploiting peltry. Although American and British goods were much sought after, rival chiefs competing for status within the potlatch system came to appreciate that the successive Spanish commandants at Nootka habitually offered tea and sympathy, medical care, and valuable presents to anyone willing to come to the commandant's house—which English-speaking traders called the Big House—and pay deference to Spanish sovereignty, tell a tale of woe, or complain about the cruel and unjust behavior of other nationalities. Bodega's open-handedness fostered a rapid improvement in Spanish relations with the natives. As the memory of specific offenses by Martínez and Eliza faded, the chiefs evinced a growing preference for the Iberians to continue in control of Friendly Cove, seeing them as palpably less greedy and unscrupulous than other nationalities. When British subjects insinuated that Spanish dominion over Nootka might soon come to an end, Ma-kwee-na's reaction—at least ostensibly—was one of regret, mixed with anxiety about the difficulties a change might portend.[43]

### CAAMAÑO'S ALASKAN EXPLORATIONS

Jacinto Caamaño and the *Aranzazú* brought additional supplies for Nootka on May 13. To eliminate gaps in cartographical knowledge beyond Nootka, Bodega required a more navigable vessel than the huge *Concepción.* To free the *Aranzazú* for this purpose, the cargo destined for California ports was transferred to the *Concepción,* which would return southward.

---

42. Boit, "Log," pp. 412–13; George Vancouver, "A Narrative of My Proceedings in His Majesty's Sloop Discovery from 18th of August to the 26th. September 1792, Particularly Relative to Transactions with Sigr. Quadra, Respecting the Cession of Certain Territories on the N. W. Coast of America," in "Papers Relating to Nootka Sound and to Captain Vancouver's Expedition," *BCPAD Report, 1913* (1914): p. 18 (hereafter referred to as Vancouver, "Narrative").
43. Vancouver, *Voyage* 1 : 385–86.

On June 12 Caamaño departed to fulfill the viceroy's instructions to Bodega for charting the coast from Bucareli Sound southward, an area as yet insufficiently examined but known to contain a maze of islands, channels, and inlets, one of which might conceal the Strait of Bartholomew Fonte, a legendary waterway still finding some credence. If such a passageway existed, it behooved Spain to ascertain its exact location before making a boundary settlement, because of the threat it might pose of easy penetration to the continental interior. Even if existence of such a strait were disproven, Bodega and Caamaño anticipated that a useful purpose would be served in completing cartographical representation of the coastline.

Formal acts of possession were performed on Graham Island, in the Queen Charlotte archipelago, on various islands along the mainland, and on the continent itself. Despite the treacherous reputation acquired by the Haida among the fur traders, Caamaño found the reception friendly wherever he called. At a port he named "Floridablanca," near Dixon Entrance, he was gratified,

> to note the natives' disappointment when he announced his departure, as they accompanied him constantly. He was no less impressed by the determination of one Indian of about sixteen or eighteen years of age, of good appearance who, having requested permission to stay and sleep on the corvette, the next day asked to remain and accompany him on his voyage. Caamaño suspected that the decision originated from a desire to see a foreign country and that, once the whim were satisfied, he would request being returned to his birthplace, as had occurred with several taken by some Englishmen to Macao and returned. He tried to make it understood that there was no objection to taking him if homeland, relatives, and friends were renounced forever. Surprised by this proposition, the Indian was moved to say he desisted from his pretension, but before long he declared himself resolved to leave everything ever possessed, including his robes of sea otter which, replaced with shirt, breeches, etc., he tossed into the last canoe alongside the corvette. He was so set in his resolve that pleas of his compatriots could not shake him and he refused to talk with them.[44]

The *Aranzazú* proved too deep in draft and difficult to maneuver to enter many of the inlets sighted; this was accomplished by using longboats and

---

44. Jacinto Caamaño, "Expedición de la corbeta Aranzazú al mando del Teniente de Navío D. Jacinto Caamaño á comprobar la relación de Fonte," in *Colección de documentos inéditos para la historia de España* (Madrid, 1849), 15 : 331, AT, entry for July 21, 1792. Perhaps it was to this youth whom Menzies referred in December 1792, at Monterey: "An Indian Boy whom the Spaniards brought from Charlotte Island in the Ship Aranzazu, though from a much colder climate died here after a short & severe illness." Menzies, *Journal*, November 1792 to December 1793, in *CHSQ* 2 (1924) : 293.

depending upon brawnier members of the crew to man the oars. Caamaño was determined to explore every single fjord, for each winding channel held the enticement of being the gateway to an inland passage. The typical gorge was enclosed by walls from one-half to two miles apart and so steep that men taking soundings near shore felt the weight slide deeper along the precipitous bottom. Even eighty fathoms of cord did not suffice to plumb in the center. Often a channel penetrated so far that the Spaniards felt they were about to discover the fabled passage to the opposite sea, or at least a route leading deep within the mainland. Instead, upon rounding a bend, they found it terminated by an arc of unbroken mountains with scarcely enough flat beach to walk on. At San Roque roadstead, on Pitt Island, the longboats were being readied to explore nearby channels when a chieftain approached and asked where they were going. When their intentions were explained, he warned that the waterways were very long, and in them dwelt "very large animals capable of throwing all of their bodies up out of the water, that assaulted canoes and ate their occupants." [45] They gave the chief a number of presents, but greeted his tale with considerable skepticism. The description suggests *Orca gladiator,* a species playing a large role in northwest coast myths and art forms. Killer whales often make such leaps, cavorting or seizing seals or polar bears asleep on iceflows, and their fearsome reputation stems from alleged assaults on small boats.

During the longboats' absence, Caamaño gave some of his men permission to go ashore in a canoe, the only craft remaining with the frigate, in order to bathe and wash clothes. After several hours the lookout spied one of them swimming back toward the frigate, but obviously tiring and about to drown. A hatch cover was thrown over the side, and a sailor paddled atop it to the swimmer's side. When brought aboard he told how a great many armed natives had suddenly approached the bathing site. Caught by surprise, the sailors abandoned their clothes and fled into the forest or jumped into the water, except for the boatswain and a pilot's apprentice, who were seized. With no boat to go to their rescue, it looked as if the others, some of whom were seen struggling against waves and current to reach the frigate, would surely perish. On a makeshift raft of barrels and planks, four men paddled toward them with staves. A rope played out from aboard the frigate could pull the raft back once the swimmers were reached. Several had been rescued when two great canoes came into view, approaching from a distant cove and heading on a course certain to intercept the raft. Fearful for swimmers and rescuers alike, Caamaño had no choice but to order it pulled back. Abandoning hope of saving the rest, he implored the chaplain to give them absolution. Another canoeload of warriors put out from the beach and warned the approaching canoes away from the frigate, dashing hopes of seizing hostages. Suddenly, to everyone's surprise, another

45. Caamaño, "Expedición," p. 338, AT.

dugout started moving furiously toward the frigate. As it drew near, an Indian stood up in the bow and indicated by signs that he intended to help those about to drown. Astonished and grateful at this turn of events, Caamaño was even more relieved when he saw the ship's canoe returning with the two captured sailors. Once aboard, they told a harrowing story. Ja-ma-sit, aged father of the chieftain whom Caamaño had laden with gifts, had interceded for their lives when braves of another group wanted to shoot and club them to death. Opposing sides had threatened each other with lances, guns, and bows and arrows, until Ja-ma-sit prevailed by urging his own people to rally. He took the men to his lodge, covered their heads with fine white feathers, and gave them some berries to eat, after which he brought them to the canoe and sent along some of his braves to protect them against further attack. Another canoe brought two more of the missing men, pulled from the water semiconscious and carried to the frigate wrapped in sea otter robes. Caamaño invited the rescuers to come aboard, gave them a number of gifts, and tried to make it understood that two more were still missing. They offered to leave behind the presents being sent to Ja-ma-sit as bond for the remaining seamen, and they shortly returned with them.

The next morning Ja-ma-sit, his brother, son, and seven other braves came toward the frigate, singing the peace chant. An eyewitness describes the old chief's efforts, in the canoe's stern, to "force his body, bent with the weight of eighty years, to accompany his brother who was trying to do a dance at the other end of the canoe, and to jump around, managing to do little more than some feints that threatened to become dangerous falls." [46] Both chiefs wore elaborate feather and fur headdresses decorated with mother-of-pearl buttons and eagle claws. Arms spread wide, they sprinkled the customary feathers on the water and, once aboard, insisted on releasing a handful of down over the heads of Caamaño and everyone else aboard ship. The captain was given a sea otter pelt, and at his order the visitors were fed a great quantity of bread and a liberal amount of wine. By the time they departed, all were happily chanting songs of peace. Later that day the launches returned, having followed every channel in the neighborhood without discovering a northwest passage.

Subsequently Caamaño encountered a large strait which he followed northward for over 100 miles. Later Vancouver was told that the Spanish conceived it "to be the Straits of Admiral de Fonte, & traced it as far as 55½° North Latitude, where its capaciousness had so little diminished, that there were reasons to conclude from its appearance that it must penetrate a considerable way inland, but the unfavorableness of the weather prevented their pursuing it further." [47] This channel, which Vancouver would

46. Ibid., pp. 338–43.
47. Menzies, *Journal*, p. 121.

name Clarence Strait, temporarily added enthusiasm to the expectations of finding the legendary passage. More importantly, it revealed that much of what previously had been considered mainland, including the surroundings of Bucareli Sound, was in actuality an archipelago. Caamaño's explorations continued all summer, following heretofore uncharted inland waterways northward until unfavorable weather persuaded him to head toward Nootka, where he rejoined Bodega on September 8.

### THE SPANISH SETTLEMENT AT NEAH BAY

Upon giving Malaspina's officers command of the exploration of Fuca's interior, the viceroy removed from his instructions to Mourelle the stipulation that he seek the best harbor on the north side of that waterway. The change reflects Revillagigedo's decision to occupy Núñez Gaona, or Neah Bay, on the south shore, just inside the strait's entrance. Salvador Fidalgo, to whom command of the project was entrusted, set out from San Blas with the *Princesa* on March 23, 1792. His first pilot and second-in-command was Antonio Serantes, the mariner who had run afoul of Martínez in 1788. Second pilot Hipólito Tono, chaplain José Alejandro López de Nava, surgeon Juan de Diós Morelos, seventy seamen, and thirteen soldiers made up the balance of the company. Fidalgo proceeded directly to his destination, without calling at Nootka, and dropped anchor there on May 29. Although Núñez Gaona's deficiencies as a harbor had been noted, its proximity to the ocean and command of the strait gave it strategic importance. Port Angeles and other harbors reconnoitered deeper within the strait would be much less accessible for sailing vessels. Until a better harbor was selected, Fidalgo was to seek a spot affording the best anchorage, fresh water, and flat land for cultivation. After taking possession with the usual ceremonies, he should erect a battery for mounting his cannons on the mainland, with a palisade for protection against Indian attack. Appropriate buildings were to be constructed as shelter for the soldiers, as well as an infirmary and storehouses. Before the supply of biscuit was depleted, there must be in operation an oven big enough to provide Spanish ships calling there with bread and hardtack. The Indians should be treated with kindness in order to avoid trouble and gain their assistance in tending crops. Generous treatment must also be accorded any foreigners visiting Núñez Gaona, but they were to be informed that terms of the convention prohibited trading south of the settlement. The buildings, fortifications, and ceremonial salutes on days of fiesta would serve to remind the Indians and foreign vessels of Spain's intention to defend the establishment and insure due respect for the flag.[48]

48. Bodega to Fidalgo, February 29, 1792, MxAGN (Hist. 67). An opinion that the Spanish buildings at Neah Bay were of brick may have originated from the fact that occasional bricks have been disinterred there, probably from this oven; see O. B. Sperlin, "Washington Forts of the Fur Trade Regime," *WHQ* 8 (1917) : 102.

Revillagigedo contemplated colonizing the new settlement by garrisoning it with married men, accompanied by their families, so they would not have to be replaced with frequency and would put down roots, but no wives and children accompanied the first contingent. Since the convention permitted English vessels to call there, and the inhabitants would be tempted to trade with them, he proposed paying the men of the garrison in paper money, supplies, and trade articles, to avoid a drainage of specie into foreign hands. Any goods the English wished to trade should be received on two years credit, offering in return only the products of that area. In this fashion, the viceroy believed, Spain's rivals "would become our tributaries while they find out they cannot extract the advantages they have imagined, and will abandon their establishment [at Nootka] entirely, or will keep it in such a fashion as to give us no concern." [49] He suggested that such a policy might even permit abandoning the presidios of California, which each year were proving more expensive to maintain.

The fort established at Neah Bay in 1792 was the first white settlement in the future United States territory west of the Rockies and north of San Francisco, excepting those in Alaska. The site chosen was a rocky terrace near the beach, on the west bank of a small creek. The palisade extended to the stream's mouth at one corner, providing access to fresh water and the beach, where a longboat remained in readiness should an Indian assault necessitate retreat to the *Princesa*. To Fidalgo's disappointment the bay's rocky bottom and surf prevented anchoring within musket-shot of the beach. Around the perimeter trees and brush were cut away in a swath more than a musket-shot wide, creating a broad, safe clearing to discourage sneak attacks, and at the same time providing lumber. Roofs were thatched with grass. Atop a barracks in the center, Fidalgo placed four cannons, in readiness to repel any assault, with a guards' keeping watch around the clock. Corrals were built for the cows, sheep, goats, and pigs, and ground was broken for vegetable gardens. To secure an earlier harvest, shoots had been started in San Blas and were ready for transplanting. The elaborate precautions against Indian attack were prompted by the fact that there were numerous villages nearby, and by the reputation of tribes south of the strait for treachery. Fidalgo made it a rule to fire a cannon at retreat and another at reveille, and he let it be known that between dusk and dawn no natives were to approach the settlement or the *Princesa*.[50]

When the *Sútil* and the *Mexicana* called there on June 6, en route to the interior of Fuca, palisade and buildings were just taking shape. José Cardero

49. Revillagigedo to Floridablanca, Mexico City, September 1, 1791, CU-B (Robbins Collection), Revillagigedo Papers, vol. 22, fol. 200–15v, AT.

50. *Sútil y Mexicana*, pp. 29–31.

made several sketches, providing us with an idea of what the settlement looked like at the time. The ships' journals comment on the friendly relations then reigning with the Indians, although the braves had little esteem for abalone shells and Fidalgo was reluctant to give them the knives they demanded.[51] None but chiefs were allowed aboard the schooners, a precaution not only against being overpowered but also against petty thievery and incidents it might provoke. "This was necessary," one account notes, "since we had noted their inclination toward theft, in cases where they could hide the object before we saw it; one lad offered to bring us women so we might use them for our pleasure, but since many were there with him, I inferred those destined for this service were probably slaves, just as the children they sell, much as done at Nootka and Mulgrave."[52] The women wore small grass aprons and a skin over their shoulders, fastened at the neck. Faces and hair were daubed with grease and pigment, and from earlobes and septums hung pendants of shell. Numerous bracelets and necklaces of deer horn, whale bone, shells, and pieces of copper completed their adornment.

If we are to believe a surviving tradition, one of these women occasioned Fidalgo's first incident with the natives. Captain Henry Shepherd and the British brigantine *Venus* anchored off the Spanish base on July 2, and Fidalgo paid the captain a visit. Upon returning to the *Princesa* he learned that Antonio Serantes, the first officer, had gone ashore at 2:00 P.M. and soon afterward went off into the forest alone, but had not returned. Since Serantes carried a musket there was no undue alarm until night fell without word of him. The next morning a party of twenty armed men, with some dogs, tried to track the missing officer, but at dusk they returned without having found a trace. Pressing the inquiry, Fidalgo was told by an Indian that Serantes had been slain by chief Ta-toosh. In his ire, the commandant seized on the first means at hand: two canoes happened to be approaching the frigate, and he ordered a cannon fired. With disastrous accuracy the cannonball ripped through one of the canoes, killing all its occupants except a boy and a girl.

Several days later the stench of decomposition led the Spaniards to a clump of thick underbrush not far from the palisade where they found the missing officer's naked and mutilated cadaver, pierced by several wounds. His clothing and musket were gone. As told and retold, the incident may have acquired embellishments. One of Vancouver's officers heard that the natives had lain in ambush, waiting until Serantes fired his gun and rush-

51. Anonymous account of the cruise of the *Sútil* and the *Mexicana*, 1792, SpMN (33), fol. 22, AT; "Apuntes, sin coordinar," fol. 60.
52. Ibid.

ing him before he could reload. Another heard that the murderers "were afterwards seen rejoicing in their Savage Cruelties by placing part of his remains on a stick & dancing round it in a Ring."[53]

The day before the macabre find, Fidalgo wrote Bodega by means of Captain Shepherd, telling of Serantes's disappearance and presumed death at the hands of Ta-toosh, and noting the revenge taken on the Indian canoes. The *Venus* arrived at Nootka on July 20, and words of the violence spread quickly throughout the sound. For several days the canoes ordinarily seen were notably absent. Indian sources said Ta-toosh had come northward seeking aid from Wee-ka-na-nish and other chieftains to obtain vengeance. Bodega summoned Ma-kwee-na and asked him to send a canoe with a letter to Fidalgo. The chief offered to take it personally, to demonstrate his affection and loyalty to the Spanish. Bodega abhorred what he called a reprisal "out of all proportion" to the situation, which could only result in turning the natives against the Spanish. "It does not seem right to me for you to have taken vengeance on those who perhaps were innocent when the assassin is unknown," Bodega wrote, and he counseled refraining in the future from acts of revenge, exhorting Fidalgo "to give the Indians by example the best lessons in kindness, and only endeavor to protect yourself." Fidalgo later received a severe reprimand from Revillagigedo and eventually from the king himself.[54]

After several weeks had passed, Ma-kwee-na appeared one day at the Big House while the commandant was dining with a number of foreign captains. The chief's visage betrayed his agitation, and he said there was much to tell Bodega in private. When the strangers left, Ma-kwee-na handed back the letter for Fidalgo, explaining with considerable emotion that due to the incident at Clayoquot in which Brown had slain a canoeload of people, Wee-ka-na-nish and his allies were planning to join Ta-toosh in a concerted retaliation upon whites in general. They had shamed Ma-kwee-na for carrying a message to Fidalgo, and endeavored to dissuade him from believing in Bodega's friendship. His defense of the Spanish proved fruitless, and he had been obliged to turn back to avoid aggravating them. A report came that Brown had abducted two sons of "Captain Hanna," a prominent chieftain whose sobriquet honored the earliest fur trader. The aggrieved father came to Ma-kwee-na, who persuaded him to complain to Bodega. The

53. Thomas Manby, "Journal of the voyage of H.M.S. *Discovery* and *Chatham* under the command of Captain George Vancouver, to the Northwest Coast of America, February 10, 1791 to June 30, 1793," CtY-BWA (Coe 325), fol. 34; Menzies, *Journal*, p. 127. Johnny Markishtum, in 1960 the oldest Makah and reputedly the most knowledgeable about tribal traditions, told the author that the Spaniard was slain because of his advances to an Indian woman and that the perpetrator was her enraged native suitor.

54. Fidalgo to Bodega, July 4, 1792, and Bodega to Fidalgo, August 6, 1792, both in MxAGN (Hist. 67), Ph in DLC; Revillagigedo to Valdés, November 30, 1792, CU-B (Robbins Collection), Revillagigedo Papers vol. 19; Bodega, "Viaje," fol. 16–16v.

sources contain no hint of any action against Brown, but after two days of residing with Bodega, "Captain Hanna" agreed to convey the letter to Fidalgo and endeavor to quiet the thirst for vengeance among the other chieftains. Upon returning some days later with Fidalgo's answer, the willing chief received an appropriate reward.[55]

### THE SÚTIL AND THE MEXICANA PENETRATE THE INLAND PASSAGE

The cruise of the *Sútil* and the *Mexicana* is the best known of all Spanish voyages to the northwest coast because of an account of it published in 1802. Donald Cutter recently established that this narrative, often attributed to others, stems from the talented José Cardero, whose many excellent sketches further document the effort.[56]

While at Nootka, the officers of the two schooners, Bodega, and Captain Torres of the *Santa Gertrudis* paid a courtesy visit to the village of chief Kee-o-ka-ma-sha. In their honor Ma-kwee-na's rival staged an impressive welcoming ceremony, complete with powdered feathers tossed into the air and dances in which he imitated a series of animals with various elaborate masks, with appropriate sounds and movements. He laid eight handsome sea otter pelts at Bodega's feet, and one each before the other Spanish officers. Other chiefs witnessed the ceremony, and Kee-o-ka-ma-sha explained with some embarrassment that they were not given presents because the visit took him by surprise, when he did not have sufficient pelts on hand. One of his own garments had been unsewn to provide sufficient gifts for the Spanish guests, who were puzzled that he did not request anything in return, not comprehending that that would have violated the ceremony's intent—to enhance the giver's prestige. When on the following day the chief visited Bodega and was given a "sumptuous present of copper, axes, abalone shells, etcetera," he accepted the articles without hesitation.[57]

During the twin schooners' visit, "in the evenings some amatory scenes could be noted between our people and the Indian women, but nothing that caused very much public scandal." John Jewitt, who early in the nineteenth century spent several years as a captive at Nootka, would protest that, from the prostitution of female slaves to white seamen, "an opinion ap-

---

55. Bodega, "Viaje," fol. 19v–20.

56. Dionisio Alcalá Galiano was long considered the narrative's author, although it may have been assembled from various journals by José de Espinosa y Tello. Cutter establishes authorship of the basic account from a version in Cardero's own handwriting in SpMN (1060) and from internal evidence that it was not written by any of the four principal officers. Donald Cutter, "Early Spanish Artists" p. 153, who cites "Estado de la Goleta . . . Sútil," SpAHN (Estado 4290). The twin schooners arrived on May 13, almost simultaneously with the *Aranzazú*, finding there the frigates *Santa Gertrudis* and *Concepción* and the brigantine *Activa*. These would be the six vessels in Cardero's well-known sketch, since upon his return in August the schooners stayed only a matter of hours.

57. "Apuntes, sin coordinar," fol. 58.

pears to have been formed by some of our navigators, injurious to the chastity of their females, than which nothing can be more generally untrue, as perhaps in no part of the world is that virtue more prized." [58] Jewitt notwithstanding, although Nootka men were zealous about the conduct of their own wives, the white man's tools and trinkets proved a powerful attraction, and those Indians who owned slaves soon learned that pandering could be as remunerative as hunting and trapping, with little or no effort involved. Many months separated mariners from home, the fleshpots of Macao, or the charms of Hawaii. The result was a commerce that loosed a crippling blight on the northwest coast, for the diseases contracted by slaves soon spread to their masters. The consequences were already visible in 1792. "They are beginning to feel the terrible ravages of the venereal evil which threatens them with the unhappy fortune of the inhabitants of Old California, whose race has been almost extinguished by effects of that illness," Cardero remarks, "and since the population of Nutka today consists of not more than 2,000 inhabitants, it may be feared that within a few years the greater part will disappear, and the tribe that we describe will lose its political existence." [59]

The *Sútil* and the *Mexicana* arrived off the new settlement at Núñez Gaona on June 6, where they encountered a friendly chief named Te-ta-koos, from a village deep within Fuca (near the present Victoria), who offered to accompany them to his home as guide and ambassador. The explorers welcomed the offer, and, his alert intelligence grasping at once the usage of their charts, he pointed to channels and islands ahead. Of the European captains of his acquaintance, he remembered "Meas," Cook, "Kimpair," and to the Spaniards' surprise "Wancoobair" and "Bolton," the first hint that Vancouver and Broughton had already reached the northwest coast, for the British warships had entered Fuca about a month before Fidalgo's arrival at Núñez Gaona.

While examining what is today Bellingham Bay, they recognized in the ominous rumbling and flashes of fire to the east that continued day and night signs of a volcanic eruption. Under clear conditions the volcano (Mount Baker, which last erupted in 1852) is a prominent feature on the eastern horizon. Quimper had placed it on his maps in 1790 as the *Gran Montaña del Carmelo*, but the name that prevailed honors Joseph Baker, an officer with Vancouver. Threading northward through the San Juan Islands, near the present city of Vancouver, the twin schooners encountered the *Discovery* and the *Chatham* on June 21. Each pair of vessels carried

58. John Rodgers Jewitt, *Narrative of the Adventures and Sufferings of John R. Jewit; Only Survivor of the Crew of the Ship Boston, During a Captivity of Nearly Three Years Among the Savages of Nootka Sound: With an Account of the Manners, Mode of Living, and Religious Opinions of the Natives* . . . [Middletown, Conn., 1815], unnumbered.

59. *Sútil y Mexicana*, p. 147, AT.

orders to treat the rival nationality with civility, so there was no hesitation in establishing a friendly relationship and readily exchanging information about their respective explorations. For a time they continued not far from one another, cooperating in the laborious task of examining every single channel and opening. Archibald Menzies, the *Discovery*'s surgeon and naturalist, remarks: "We continued visiting one another during our stay on the most cordial terms of friendship which was mutually cultivated on both sides by frequently spending our convivial hours together in a most social manner." [60]

Having emerged into the Pacific at Queen Charlotte Strait, the *Sútil* and the *Mexicana* arrived in Nootka again on August 31, three days after Vancouver. Once and for all it could be asserted that the Strait of Juan de Fuca offered no passageway to the Atlantic. Examination of the interior channels led the Spaniards to conclude: "One does not find there terrestrial or marine products whose examination or acquisition is worth exposing oneself to the consequences of a protracted voyage." They had not observed any sites appropriate for a Spanish settlement. Sea otters were never found deep within the strait, so trading vessels would not be likely to frequent it. They also emphasized the deficiencies of Núñez Gaona as a harbor, portraying in vivid terms the peril to which the little settlement would be subjected during the approaching winter.[61] Fidalgo's recent trouble made the outpost's survival that much more difficult and hazardous.

The two schooners did not tarry, sailing at midnight the day of their arrival. Five days later they were off the mouth of Hezeta's "Entrada," newly discovered by Gray. The American captain had given Bodega a chart of the great river's mouth, and since Alcalá Galiano and Valdés found that it conformed with what they had observed, the schooners did not attempt to cross the hazardous bar, but hurried southward. The renown their cruise acquired was due less to its actual achievements than to Cardero's powers of observation and the detailed journal he compiled. Part of the credit for its ethnological quality must go to the viceroy's original instructions to Mourelle, probably drawn up by that intelligent mariner himself, which alerted Cardero to the importance of gathering such data. Returning to Mexico City and the Academia de San Carlos, the young artist finished his drawings, eventually accompanying Cayetano Valdés back to Spain, where he was assigned to the naval supply corps at Cádiz. There is no evidence that his artistic and narrative talents were ever again put to use.[62]

Since Alcalá Galiano, Valdés, and Cardero had been detached from Malas-

60. Menzies, *Journal*, p. 78.

61. *Sútil y Mexicana*, p. 110.

62. Valencian cartographer Fernando Selma prepared the engravings from Suría and Cardero's drawings. Cutter, "Early Spanish Artists," pp. 155–57.

pina's service in 1792, they escaped the taint attached to many of their associates following the illustrious navigator's imprisonment. The ministry used Cardero's narrative as a cornerstone for a more modest effort, substituted for Malaspina's grandiose but discredited opus, to demonstrate Spanish accomplishments on the northwest coast of America. Cardero's humble rank may account for the fact that his authorship of the basic account was not specified in the published version. The renowned geographer-historian Martín Fernández de Navarrete undertook the task of preparing an introduction describing Spanish voyages prior to 1792, a labor that could not be accomplished without considerable research. The maps and engravings accompanying the publication entailed considerable expense and testify to Madrid's continuing concern with documenting her claims in the Pacific Northwest. Editing, engraving, printing, and binding consumed many months, and the finished work did not appear until 1802. As for its effect upon Spain's territorial claims, the effort was tantamount to locking the barn door after the proverbial theft.

### BODEGA'S INQUEST INTO THE EVENTS OF 1788–89

The frigate *Daedalus* arrived in Nootka on July 4 with supplies for Vancouver; but the British commissioner and his vessels were still in the Inland Passage. Captain Thomas New brought an order from Floridablanca requiring that the bearer be put in possession of lands and buildings occupied by British subjects prior to the Nootka incident. Bodega was able to persuade him that it would be preferable to await Vancouver. New's compliant attitude led to expectations of similar comportment from Vancouver. Russian expansion, previously such a bugaboo, now seemed in abeyance. The Americans were no danger, so it no longer appeared necessary to keep the garrison in a constant state of readiness to repel a surprise naval attack. The *Santa Gertrudis* was old, ungainly, slow, and relatively useless for exploration. Since its large crew placed an undue strain upon supplies, Bodega resolved to send it to Monterey. Torres departed on July 19 with orders to call at Núñez Gaona and to inspect the coast, at any risk (*a todo riesgo*), from 47° to 41° north latitude; having done so, he was to await Bodega in California. His instructions stressed the importance of insuring that no river or strait along the coast elude discovery.[63]

The *Concepción* and its large complement likewise constituted an unnecessary burden upon Bodega's stores, now that hostilities seemed remote. After two consecutive winters at Nootka, the huge warship departed southward on July 24, under Francisco de Eliza, who had served on the northwest coast without respite since 1790. Bodega also ordered Alberni and his

63. Bodega, "Viaje," fol. 13v–15v.

Catalán volunteers to return to their former garrison at Guadalajara. The surviving members—for a number had succumbed to various complaints—were all back in Mexico by the end of the season.[64] With the *Concepción*'s departure, only the *Activa* remained on duty at Nootka. The Limeño dissipated the powerful flotilla available to him at the season's inception, preferring to use means other than force to protect Spanish interests in the presence of the many well-armed British, American, and occasional Portuguese, French, and Swedish trading vessels frequenting the coast that season. Anticipating Vancouver's appearance, he commenced gathering information about events at Nootka preceding and during the Anglo-Spanish clash. To his good fortune, there were a number of persons currently on the northwest coast who had witnessed some of the crucial episodes. Among the vessels entering Friendly Cove while Bodega resided there was the *Feliz Aventureira*, still flying the Portuguese flag, but now commanded by Francisco José Viana, captain of the *Ifigenia Nubiana* in 1788–89. Responding to Bodega's inquiry, Viana gave testimony, already cited in chapter 4, to the effect that the *Ifigenia* had flown the Portuguese banner at Nootka in 1788–89, and that the hut that Meares's carpenters had built on shore was not only inconsequential but had been dismantled prior to their departure.[65]

Another opportunity for first-hand information arose on July 23 with the *Columbia*'s appearance. Gray's vessel had struck a submerged rock while under full sail, extensively damaging bow and hull, and the Captain was obliged to put in at nearby Clayoquot, knowing full well the reception to be expected from Wee-ka-na-nish. The brig was beached at high tide in a secluded spot, without opposition, and upon the ebb they found the keel split and the planking rent in various places. A few boards were quickly replaced, but bow and keel could not be repaired without careening and extensive new timbering. Clayoquot was out of the question for a protracted stay, and Gray was forced to put to sea again and make for the safety of the Spanish base. The brig skirted Point Estéban so closely that a current carried it onto the rocks. Several cannons were fired in the desperate hope that they might be seen from San Miguel. Happily, the signal of distress was recognized as such, and Bodega sent every small boat in the cove to their assistance. Not until 10:00 P.M. was the vessel liberated from its dangerous perch. Taking water badly, it limped into Friendly Cove the next morning. Gray was provided with the "second best house" as a residence, and a storehouse was put at his disposal so the *Columbia* could be unloaded and

64. Pedro Alberni to Revillagigedo, San Blas, November 22, 1792, CSmH (HM 327).

65. Viana to Bodega, [June] 1792, in *BCPAD Report, 1913* (1914) : 13–14. The *Feliz Aventureira* was at Nootka from June 11 to June 20, 1792; Bodega, "Viaje," fol. 12–13.

drawn up on the beach for major overhauling. Assisted by Spanish and English carpenters, the Americans completed their repairs in a short time, and the brig was refloated.[66]

A third valuable source of information became available with the arrival of the *Hope,* out of Boston, captained by Joseph Ingraham, first mate of the *Lady Washington* in 1788–89. Still later, and while Bodega's negotiations with Vancouver were underway, another participant appeared: Robert Duffin, an officer aboard the *Feliz Aventureira* in 1788 and the *Argonaut* during 1789–91. This time Duffin came as supercargo of the *São José o Fénix,* a brig operating out of Macao under Portuguese colors but for the benefit of British investors.[67] Gonzalo López de Haro also revisited Nootka in 1792 as an officer of the *Santa Gertrudis.* Outranked by a number of others, his name hardly ever appears, and there is no record of his testifying, although he probably provided data informally. Other "old timers" revisiting Nootka in 1792 were Charles Barkley and his wife, who returned with the *Halcyon* from Calcutta. Alexander Stewart, captain of the *Jackal* on the northwest coast in 1792, had been second mate of the *Princess Royal* upon its seizure in 1789. Then, too, Vancouver himself had visited the area with Cook in 1778, and Menzies had been Colnett's surgeon aboard the *Prince of Wales* in 1787–88. There was a plethora of eyewitnesses to the events of previous years. "It would seem that coincidence tried to contribute as many measures as possible to help clarify everything," Bodega's aide Felix de Cepeda remarks. "With the exception of only Captain Colnet, all the individuals who might have participated in what happened in the year '89 were found in Nutka for this occasion either before or after." Not quite! Martínez and the elder Kendrick were absent; Hudson and his companions had gone to a watery grave off Hesquiat; and the Metcalfes were dead. But the reunion of principals was nevertheless remarkable. Cepeda notes that "the Americans defend Martínez absolutely, making an effort to vindicate entirely his conduct, *which they see criticized with the greatest pain.*"[68]

Responding to Bodega's request, Gray and Ingraham answered jointly with an account of Meares's activities in 1788 and Martínez's actions in 1789. As seen from citations in previous chapters, their perspective favored

66. Boit, "Log," p. 408; Bodega, "Viaje," fol. 16v–17; John Hoskins to Joseph Barrell, Nootka Sound, August 21, 1792, MHi (Barrell Letters), in F. W. Howay, "Letters Relating to the Second Voyage of the Columbia," *OHQ* 24 (1923) : 141–47.

67. Ingraham was at Nootka from August 1 through 6 and from September 11 through 20, returning again on October 2, after Bodega had departed. Ingraham, "Log," pp. 188 ff. Duffin arrived on September 18. Bell, *Journal,* p. 25; Vancouver, *Voyage,* 1 : 404–06.

68. ". . . defienden absolutamente los Americanos á Martínez, esforzándose á vindicar del todo su conducta *que ven tachada con el mayor dolor.*" Félix de Cepeda, as cited in "Noticias y apuntamientos sacados del Extracto Historico Sobre la Costa N. O. de America Septentrional por Dn. Felix de Cepeda año de 1792," UKLBM (Add. 13,974), fol. 346v.

Spanish claims over those of the British, and Martínez over Colnett. The missive closed with an expression of their hope that, "when things are represented in truth as they are, it will rescue our friend Dn. E: J: Martinez from any censure; at least that he may not be deemed an imposter and a pirate, which many from only hearing one part of the story supposed he was." [69] Ingraham's journal summarizes the advice offered Bodega:

> In my opinion agreeable to the 1st article of the convention if our information was his guide he was to cede nothing as no subject of His Britannic Majesty was ever dispossessed of any land or buildings—but of ships only. The land when the Spaniards arrived was occupied by the Indians only and buildings there were none, but had been long dispos'd of.[70]

Since Gray, Ingraham, and their compatriots were guests at Bodega's table every day during their stay, it followed that their opinions made some impression on him, and vice versa. Martínez's and Bodega's solicitude for the Americans had not been wasted. When it came time for the *Columbia* to depart, Boit reflected:

> It is but doing Justice to the Spaniards at Nootka Sound to observe that during our tarry among them we was treated with the greatest hospitality, and in fact they seem'd to exert themselves and to feel interested in our behalf. May such fine fellows Never be in want of the like assistance shou'd they ever stand in need of it from the hands of any American. The Governor wou'd Not allow Capt. Gray for to pay one farthing.[71]

The base hummed with activity, as a constant flow of trading vessels called there to avail themselves of a safe refuge to replenish water and firewood and make needed repairs. There is some disagreement in the sources as to the size of the settlement. Ingraham described it as consisting of sixteen houses in 1792, all temporary structures built for convenience and comfort rather than for beauty and regularity. In addition there were storehouses, a bakery, an infirmary, and animal sheds. He lamented that the convention had made it probable that Spain would soon retire from the site: "In short it seem'd a pity to disturbe people in so fair a way to establish a good settlement and who to me seem'd above any best calculated for such purposes." [72] Boit says that Nootka consisted of some fifty houses, "indifferently built (except the Governors, which was rather *grand* than

---

69. Gray and Ingraham to Bodega, Nootka, August 5, 1792, MxAGN (Hist. 70), in Vancouver, "Narrative," pp. 15–17, and Howay, *Voyages of the "Columbia,"* pp. 474–79.
70. Ingraham, "Log," p. 198.
71. Boit, "Logs," p. 413, entry for August 24, 1792.
72. Ingraham, "Log," p. 180.

otherways),'' with about 200 inhabitants, between Spaniards and "Peru Indians" (Mexican mestizos?). "Their fort was no great thing, mounted with 6 Twenty four and Thirty six pounders," and he notes, "the platforms would not bear the weight of metal." [73] His count must have included even the outhouses, sheds, and huts. Thomas Manby, of the *Chatham*, says there were five houses of different sizes in addition to the main building, which was capable of housing 100 persons and was well constructed to repel the cold of winter. Two-storied, with a balcony on the front, the house had a guard room at one end of the ground floor and a kitchen and servants' room at the other, while upstairs a large dining area referred to as the "great hall" separated a number of smaller rooms for the commandant and his officers. The walls were whitened with lime from crushed, burned oyster shells.[74]

Because the Spanish maintained tranquil relations with the local tribes, traders arriving in Friendly Cove could relax their constant vigil, escape the confinement of cramped quarters, and go ashore to sample such attractions as the place afforded. Bodega established a tradition of hospitality, and officers of all nationalities found a welcome change from their habitual diet at his bounteous table. Nevertheless, he let it be known that deference must be paid to Spanish authority. Ingraham says every captain was expected to send his ship's papers ashore for inspection, which "I supposed was only right and proper." Observance of such formalities gave tacit confirmation of Spain's effective sovereignty. What Martínez had tried to accomplish with arguments and threats, Bodega secured through helpfulness and generosity. The day Ingraham departed, he records that Bodega sent him "40 fresh salmon, some fresh pork, eggs, butter, 50 loaves new bread, some wine, brandy, and a great supply of cabbages, sallad, etc., which considering the part of the world we were in I thot a very handsome present." "Not a day pass'd during our stay in this port," he continues, "but every ship without respect to nation or person received marks of Don Juan's Hospitality." [75] Vancouver confirms that each morning every vessel in the cove was supplied at no cost with hot rolls, milk, and vegetables.[76]

Captains and supercargoes of any and all visiting vessels had a standing invitation at Bodega's table while anchored in Friendly Cove. Boit tells of one sumptuous meal; impressed by the luxury with which the fifty-four guests were served, he calculated that a total of 270 sterling silver plates had been used. "Dishes, Knifes and forks, and indeed every thing else was of Silver and always replaced with spare ones," he insists. "There could

73. Boit, "Log," pp. 410–11.
74. Manby, "Journal," pt. 2, fol. 35; Menzies, *Journal*, p. 111; Bodega, "Viaje," fol. 22v.
75. Ingraham, "Log," p. 188, 190–91.
76. Bell, *Journal*, p. 17.

be no mistake in this as they never carried the dirty plates or Dishes from the Hall where we dined." [77] Among Lima's artistocracy, sterling table service was not unusual, given the abundance of silver in Peru, but it understandably awed the Americans and Englishmen encountering such opulence at remote Nootka. Ingraham corroborates the elegance of Bodega's table, and remarks that even the siesta had become a custom at the port, following such hearty meals. Vancouver would find it difficult to dislodge from Friendly Cove a man so universally respected, firmly entrenched, and endeared to the tastes of natives and traders alike. The Americans had nothing but praise for Bodega. "I tho't him one of the most agreeable men I ever met with," Ingraham remarks.[78] John Hoskins, supercargo of the *Columbia*, characterized him as "really a gentleman, a friend to all the human race, a father to the natives, who all love him & a good friend to the Americans in general." [79] Captain Gray did not take this regard lightly; soon he would sail from Nootka for the last time, return to Boston, marry, and in November 1794 name his first-born son Robert Don Quadra Gray.[80]

It would do the warmhearted commandant less than justice to assume that his generosity was always motivated by political considerations. Witness the succor given one Captain Weatherhead and his companions, shipwrecked on Tahiti, rescued by a British trader, and put ashore at Nootka, penniless and stranded. Bodega took them under his wing, provided transportation to San Blas, and gave Weatherhead 200 dollars from his own pocket to help them get back to England.[81] That the Limeño's gentlemanly approach to human relations did much to assuage Anglo-Spanish rancor is shown by Ingraham's observation that even the English prisoners carried to San Blas commended him,

> and the Englishmen here speak equally well of him at present. The Commander of the English store ship who was a jocose old gentleman said the stories his grandmother had related to him in his infancy respecting the Spaniards were yet fresh in his memory and excited such horror that for some time he could scarce reconcile to himself that the people who were treating him with such attention and Hos-

77. Boit "Log," pp. 411–12.

78. ". . . as usuall with Spaniards of any rank everything was served on silver—as I knew it was a generall custom with the Spaniards to sleep after dinner I took leave early." Ingraham, "Log," p. 182.

79. Hoskins to Barrell, August 21, 1792, in Howay, "Letters," p. 146.

80. The boy died shortly before his seventh birthday; his father contracted yellow fever on a voyage to South Carolina about 1809 and died at sea. F. W. Howay and Albert Matthews, "Some Notes Upon Captain Robert Gray (1755–1809)," *WHQ* 21 (1930) : 12.

81. Menzies, *Journal*, p. 113; Bell, *Journal*, pp. 118–19. Bell calls this individual "Mr. Wetherell," master of the *Matilda*, and says he was put ashore at Nootka by Captain Baker of the *Jenny*.

pitality were Spaniards. Such are the effects of prejudice impress'd on young minds that they are extremely hard to conquer. Reasoning without experience I believe will seldom effect a change. I will remember as no doubt many thousands more must, in America, when we were taught to despise the French and Spaniards that they were little better than the vilest savages. The revolution has no doubt chang'd the sentiments of most people yet I dare believe there are this day many remaining in America who cannot intirely divest themselves of the early prejudice imbib'd against the French and Spaniards.[82]

Under Bodega's aegis Friendly Cove became worthy of its name. That some foreign guests may have abused his hospitality, however, is suggested by an episode involving Captain Magee, of the American trader *Margaret,* whose complaints of ill health led Bodega to grant his request to move into the house left vacant upon Gray's departure, while the *Margaret* continued to cruise for furs. The old man took advantage of the opportunity to carry ashore a large store of New England rum, and he soon had a flourishing enterprise going in grog, finding no lack of thirsty customers for his highly adulterated wares. With the arrival of Vancouver's warships, Magee's business augmented to the point where it menaced the health of some of the tars. Spirits estimated to have originally cost two shillings or half a crown were bringing four dollars a gallon. "Our seamen," Bell relates, "were continually drunk which from the badness of the liquor threw them into fits of sickness; and Captn. Vancouver was at last oblig'd to take measures that prevented any further trade of that nature with our people." [83] The enterprise could not have escaped Don Juan's notice, and his permissiveness toward Magee may reflect still another measure to gain an ally in the approaching confrontation with Vancouver. Perhaps Bodega's willingness to permit a technically illegal business to exist was due to the fact that, as a creole, he shared a widespread colonial resentment of mercantilist policies that prohibited traffic with foreigners. Sentiment was growing in Spanish America that the area might benefit from a relaxation of regulations proscribing trade with non-Spanish parts of the globe.

### NEGOTIATIONS OF THE NOOTKA COMMISSIONERS

The *Discovery* and the *Chatham* arrived off Friendly Cove on August 28, fired a thirteen gun cannonade, and were saluted in turn by the Spanish flagship. Upon landing, Vancouver and his officers were received ceremoniously by the Spanish troops, assembled on the beach. Bodega and his officers awaited them at the door of the large house, whence they were

82. Ingraham, "Log," p. 192. The reference is to Capt. Thomas New, of H.M.S. *Daedalus.*
83. Bell, *Journal,* pp. 17–18; Bodega, "Viaje," fol. 21.

conducted to the salon on the second floor. The tension of the moment, for both sides, is revealed in the stiff formalities. Neither Vancouver nor Bodega knew the other's tongue, but Thomas Dobson, mate of the *Daedalus,* spoke Spanish. John Howell, supercargo of the American trader *Margaret,* is also mentioned as interpreter during the voluminous exchange of correspondence in days to follow.

Don Juan offered his guests every convenience the settlement could provide, and insisted that they regard his dwelling and table as their own during their stay. His hospitality, Menzies remarks, "seemed to have no other bound than the limited sphere of supply to which his present situation confined him." Formal amenities concluded, the Englishmen spent the remainder of the day reconnoitering the settlement. "There was a well-stocked poultry yard," Menzies notes,

> & Goats Sheep & Black Cattle were feeding round the Village. Blacksmiths were seen busily engaged in one place & Carpenters in another, so that the different occupations of Building & repairing Vessels & Houses were at once going forward. In short the Spaniards seem to go on here with greater activity & industry than we are led to believe of them at any of their other remote infant Settlements.[84]

The next morning Bodega breakfasted aboard the *Discovery* and visited the *Chatham.* That evening he reciprocated with a banquet. "As many officers as could be spared from the vessels with myself dined with Senr. Quadra, and were gratified with a repast we had lately been little accustomed to, or had the most distant idea of meeting with at this place," Vancouver remarks. "A dinner of five courses, consisting of a superfluity of the best provisions, was served with great elegance."[85] The meal consisted largely of products from Nootka—vegetables from the gardens, fish, and game. Salutes resounded from the guns of the *Activa* as the diners toasted their respective sovereigns and the successful termination of Vancouver's expedition. "In short," Menzies relates, "the evening was spent with that unreserved conviviality that made us forget we were strangers, in the mutual pleasure which each individual seemed to enjoy." Upon learning of the corps of distinguished scientists visiting Nootka with Malaspina, Menzies concluded that "the Spaniards mean to shake off now entirely that odium of indolence & secrecy with which they have been long accused."[86]

The morning after Vancouver's arrival, Ma-kwee-na tried to visit him, but the sentry and officer on deck kept him from coming aboard, there being nothing distinguishing about his dress. He took great affront and went

84. Menzies, *Journal,* pp. 111–12; Ingraham, "Log," p. 198.
85. Vancouver, *Voyage,* 1 : 385.
86. Menzies, *Journal,* p. 128.

straight to Bodega to protest. Only after receiving a number of presents was the irate chief persuaded to join them at the table. Several glasses of wine later, he commenced his tirade anew, complaining that the Spanish intended to leave Nootka to the English, and that the British might eventually surrender it to a third nation, with the result that he and his people would be constantly disturbed by adjusting to new masters. Bodega endeavored to sooth and reassure him that he would be treated by the English with the same consideration he now received. At this Ma-kwee-na seemed somewhat mollified. "I could not help observing with a mixture of surprize and pleasure," Vancouver notes, "how much the Spaniards had succeeded in gaining the good opinion and confidence of these people; together with the very orderly behavior so conspicuously evident in their conduct towards the Spaniards on all occasions." [87] Judging by this episode, Bodega was still giving every appearance of preparing to turn over the Spanish base. The Indians demonstrated great inquisitiveness about Vancouver's motives in coming to Nootka, and wanted to know whether the English intended to take revenge upon the Spanish for Martínez's actions. Ma-kwee-na made discreet inquiries on both sides to ascertain the state of relations between the rival nationalities. [88]

With Bodega's consent, Vancouver set up a camp on shore to perform astronomical observations. Two buildings were put at his disposal, one for an infirmary and another as a storehouse for supplies from the *Daedalus*. The *Discovery* and the *Chatham* both needed repairs below the waterline and would have to be careened. A camp for carrying this out was established on the site of Meares's 1788 house.

The principal purpose of the British commissioner's mission was now at hand—securing from his opposite number compliance with the terms extracted from Madrid by the Convention of 1790. "His Britannick Majestys Officer who will deliver this letter," Floridablanca had ordered, "shall immediately be put into possession of the Buildings and Districts or parcels of Land which were occupied by the subjects of that Sovereign in April 1789 as well in the Port of Nootka or of St. Lawrence as in the other said to be called Port Cox and to be situated about sixteen Leagues distant from the former to the southward and that all such parcels or Districts of Land of which the English subjects were dispossessed be restored to the said officer." [89] With such a document, Vancouver anticipated no difficulty in taking over Nootka. He had arrived on the northwest coast with scant knowledge of previous Spanish activities or accomplishments there, and his let-

---

87. Vancouver, *Voyage*, 1 : 385–86.

88. Menzies, *Journal*, pp. 114–15.

89. Portion copied in Vancouver to Evan Nepean, Monterey, January 7, 1793, in *BCPAD Report, 1913* (1914) : 36–38; Vancouver, "Narrative," p. 19.

ters to friends and superiors show his astonishment at finding his rivals so well established, their settlement a beehive of activity and his opponent disarmingly hospitable and genial beyond measure.

No one knew better than Bodega the details of Spanish efforts on the northwest coast, and he quickly acquainted Vancouver with the extent of Spanish explorations from 1774 to date, defending Madrid's claims by citing acts of possession performed at many spots along the coast since 1775. That Vancouver respected such rituals is shown by his own performance of them. "If such acts of possession had any validity the Spanish right to the country, aside from that actually in the possession of the Russians, was about as clear as it could have been made," Wagner remarks. "Actual occupation by them was in evidence at Nootka Sound in fortifications, buildings, consisting of houses, warehouses, etc., and a considerable body of armed men besides the continuous presence since 1790 of men of war." [90] To justify British claims, Vancouver would have to take some other tack than citing Drake and Cook, for in Bodega, fifteen years his senior, he faced an amiable but determined and well-informed adversary, capable of countering every argument with weighty historical evidence in Spain's favor. Yet there is every indication that until late in the summer Bodega expected to cede the settlement shortly. Before July was out he had sent a portion of the soldiers and livestock to California and San Blas. All but two of San Miguel's cannons had been taken aboard the same vessel. In keeping with this intention, the day after Vancouver arrived Bodega sent him a letter narrating events of 1788 and 1789 as pieced together from eyewitness testimony, declaring that Nootka would be turned over to the British, even though it could be demonstrated with unequivocal proof that the "injuries, prejudices and usurpations which Captain Mears represents, are chimerical." Attached to the missive were affidavits obtained from the various witnesses, testifying that Meares had not purchased any land, that the only habitation he built was little more than a temporary shelter, and that no edifice at all existed upon Martínez's arrival in 1789. The viceroy had restored the English vessels and cargo and had provided wages for the crew. Hence Bodega opined that Spain was not obliged to deliver up anything at Nootka, but,

> comprehending that the spirit of the king, my master, is to establish a solid and permanent peace with all nations, in order to remove obstacles which might cause discord, far from intending to continue in this port, I am ready (without prejudice to our legitimate right, nor that of the courts' better informed decisions) generously to cede to England the houses, offices, and gardens which have with so much labor been

90. Wagner, "Creation of Rights of Sovereignty," pp. 320–21.

cultivated here, removing myself to Fuca. And so that the subjects of both nations will never be disturbed or molested, it [Fuca] ought to be our last establishment, where the dividing point ought to be fixed, from which [all land] to the northward should be in common the free entry, use, and commerce conformable to article 5 of the convention. No others should be allowed, unless by permission from the respective courts, nor should the English be permitted to the south of Fuca.[91]

The keystone of Bodega's stance was that he would evacuate Nootka "without prejudice to our legitimate right," that is, without surrendering the principle of Spain's ownership of the balance of Nootka Sound, aside from Meares's tract. It is significant that between the date of this first letter to Vancouver and the reply three days later, the *Sútil* and the *Mexicana* arrived for a stay of less than twenty-four hours. The twin schooners brought information confirming Núñez Gaona's poor quality as a harbor. Moreover, continued trouble with the large Indian villages nearby made it hazardous to attempt a permanent settlement there. The opinions of Alcalá Galiano and Valdés weighed heavily with Bodega, strengthening his growing conviction that it was in Spain's interest to retain its base at Nootka, the most convenient and strategic harbor yet discovered on the northwest coast.

Bodega's confident statement of Spanish rights evoked a comparably assertive response from Vancouver, who took a position from which he could not be swerved during subsequent negotiations: that the convention gave British subjects a right to unmolested access at any spot on the coast beyond the northernmost Spanish settlement made previous to April 1789. "I should suppose," he declared, "the Establishment His Catholic Majesty has made in the mouth of Fuca to come under the denomination of a port of free access, as well as such as may have been, or may hereafter be made from thence south to Port St. Francisco, conceiving that port to be the Northernmost port of the said Coast then occupied by Spain." [92] He made it quite clear that London intended to challenge Spain's title to everything north of San Francisco Bay. Since he was unauthorized to enter into any negotiations other than those required to received possession of lands once occupied by British subjects, which he understood as meaning the the total circumference of the ports of Nootka and Cox (Clayoquot), he refused to be drawn into any discussion of boundaries.

Bodega's efforts to obtain a boundary at the Strait of Juan de Fuca were thus stymied from the outset. His reply suggested that until the matter could be referred to their respective courts for settlement, he would be

91. Bodega to Vancouver, August 29, 1792, in Bodega, "Viaje," fol. 35, AT; also trans. in Vancouver, "Narrative," pp. 12–13; Ingraham, "Log," p. 180; Bell, *Journal,* pp. 17–18.
92. Vancouver to Bodega, September 1, 1792, in Vancouver, "Narrative," p. 17.

willing to yield possession of the tract where Meares made his encampment and would remove Spanish forces from Nootka, placing the settlement under Vancouver's command until their respective governments decided what should be done. This would not signify, he emphasized, surrendering Spanish ownership of the settlement.[93] To underline the attractiveness of this offer, he escorted Vancouver around the settlement to display the labor recently devoted to readying storehouses, putting buildings in excellent repair, constructing a new bake oven, improving gardens, and building up a stock of cattle, swine, and poultry for the coming winter.

Vancouver's narrative indicates that he was "at a considerable loss at first what measures to pursue," since a Spanish evacuation of Nootka without yielding the principle of ownership entailed a number of perils. "Considering the principal object His Majesty had in view in directing the undertaking of this Expedition was for facilitating and acquiring commercial advantages, . . . and [seeing] the nature and quantity of articles of traffic and other stores sent out in the Daedalus, from the Secretary of State's Office, together with such conversation as I had formerly been present at in that office, induced me to believe an establishment was in contemplation shortly to take place some where on this coast, though I had not received a single line from that office on that or any other subject." He was certain "that this place would not long remain unoccupied by some one of the trading nations . . . in which case a probability of involving my Country in fresh disputes, &ca., might be laid to my charge." [94]

As an indication of the trouble that might ensue were Spain to evacuate Nootka, Vancouver mentioned the Anglo-American incident that would have resulted but for Bodega's intervention, when Captain Brown endeavored to check the American trader Magee's cruise. To avoid such incidents, Vancouver decided to unload his store ship and proceed with plans to leave Lieutenant Broughton and the *Chatham* at Nootka during the coming winter.

After several communications had been exchanged without further progress, Don Juan proposed taking advantage of pleasant weather to visit Makwee-na's village at the head of Tahsis Inlet, "that he might have the pleasure of recommending the English commanders & their Officers to the particular notice of the Chief & his Tribe," Menzies records, "& thereby do away any alarm they might prepossess about our quarreling by convincing them of the friendship that subsisted between the two Nations, & likewise as the place was so soon to be given up to the English, he wishd for their own happiness to do away any bias they might have formed in favor of the Spaniards from their residing so long amongst them." [95]

---

93. Bodega to Vancouver, September 2, 1792, in Ibid., p. 21.
94. Ibid., p. 18.
95. Menzies, *Journal*, p. 115.

A messenger hurried ahead with word of their visit, and they set out bright and early on September 4 in three English pinnaces and a large Spanish launch. Bodega and Vancouver traveled together in the most commodious craft. "Winding inland by a deep Valley between very high steep mountains," Menzies relates, "the Water was smooth & the day was uncommonly favorable for our excursion, [and] we therefore proceeded at an easy rate, with drums beating & Fifes playing to the no small entertainment of the Natives, as it gave a martial solemnity to our Visit, highly gratifying to their feelings in thus imitating their own customs on similar occasions, for in their friendly Visits their approach is always announced by vociferous songs & plaintive airs." At dusk they sighted Ma-kwee-na's village, but postponed a formal arrival for the morrow, camping for the night "in a fine Meadow delightfully skirting a small Bay a little short of the Village, but while the Tents were pitching & dinner getting ready, a party of the Officers walked along the Beach & paid their respects to the Chief at his own House in a short visit, which he & several of his Attendants returned by coming to the Encampment to dine with us." [96]

The next day the boats paraded in front of the village, accompanied by fife and drum, before pulling in to the beach, where Ma-kwee-na and his warriors were waiting to escort them to the chief's great lodge. His four wives and numerous children, all very cleanly dressed for the occasion, were seated on a platform at one side of the central room, described as being thirty yards long. Before seating themselves upon benches covered with soft furs and fine mats, the guests paid their respects to the wives and to Ma-kwee-na's eldest daughter, whose issue would inherit his name and title. The princess conducted herself, Vancouver remarks, "with much propriety and decorum." [97]

Bodega opened the parley by recommending as his personal friends Vancover, Broughton, and the other British officers and by assuring Ma-kwee-na "of the friendship & good understanding which subsisted between the English & Spaniards, & that the latter were only to quit his Territories by a mutual agreement between the two Nations, but that they would ever continue steadily their friendship & respect for him and his Tribe." [98] The chief assented to receiving the English as his friends, but he lamented that Bodega planned to depart. To cement a bond of good will, Vancouver and Broughton presented Ma-kwee-na, his daughter, wives, and brothers with gifts of cloth, copper, blankets, beads, and trinkets. The chief responded by inviting them to join in a feast he had prepared. "In a corner of the house was the Royal Kitchen," Bell notes,

96. Ibid., p. 116.
97. Vancouver, *Voyage*, 1 : 395–96; Bell, *Journal*, pp. 20–22.
98. Menzies, *Journal*, p. 118.

where the Cooks were busily employed in boiling Oil of different kinds, preparing Stews arnd Fricasees of Porpoise, Whale, Seal, and such delicious Meats. But the Cooks' trouble & skill was thrown away upon us for we had a far better dinner to sit down to. It was agreed on setting out that Don Quadra shou'd furnish the Eatables and Captn. Vancouver the Drinkables but one would have imagined that Seigr. Quadra's whole Household had been there. A Table was soon raised which was one of the broad planks from the roof of Maquinna's House and we were served up two Courses, *on Plate,* in a style little inferior to what we met with at the Governor's own house.[99]

Menzies confirms the sterling service, and says the elegance made them forget they were dining under the roof of a Nootka chief. "Maquina and his Wives & Daughter, together with other Chiefs sat at the head of the Table," he adds, "partook of the Entertainment & joined us in drinking a convivial glass of wine after dinner, while the rest of the Natives entertained themselves at a Mess not less gratefull to their palate." "It consisted of a large *Tunny* & a Porpus cut up in small pieces entrails & all into a large Trough with a mixture of Water blood & fish Oil, & the whole stewed by throwing heated Stones into it."[100]

After the meal, at a signal from Ma-kwee-na, his warriors commenced a bizarre dance. Some wore elaborate Indian dress, while others imitated Europeans, Chinese, or Sandwich Islanders, all heavily armed with muskets, spears, or clubs. Part of the attire was recognizably European. Bell noted the chief's brother wore "a complete suit of Stage Armour that very likely was often the property of Hamlet's Ghost," probably a reference to Bodega's gift of a helmet and coat of mail. Warpaint covered the dancers' faces and their hair was daubed with fish oil, powdered with red ochre, and sprinkled with bird down. Twenty warriors with muskets and an equal number bearing spears danced singly and then in unison, stamping, shouting, gesticulating, and beating the stocks of their weapons against the ground. While not devoid of harmony, Bell remarks, their songs were all "of the Fierce & Warlike style and subject and one or two of them ended with a frightful Yell that to a strangers ear was truly terrific." Dancers represented "the different evolutions of attacking an enemy, sometimes crouching down, sometimes retreating, at other times advancing with firm steps & eyes steadily fixed on the Commanders who were seated in the middle of our group, & to whom all their feigned aims & motions were directed, sometimes with much pointed archness as to occasion some alarm of their intentions being real."[101] Bodega and Vancouver retained their composure, masking what-

99. Bell, *Journal,* pp. 20–21.
100. Menzies, *Journal,* p. 120.
101. Ibid., pp. 118–19.

ever qualms they may have had at being surrounded by an overwhelming force of well-armed warriors, far from protection of the garrison and warships at Friendly Cove. Ma-kwee-na had stolen away under pretense of giving some orders. Suddenly he jumped into the center of the arena, draped with an exceptionally large and exquisite sea otter robe, wearing a round, black hat, and grotesquely masked. From a belt at his waist dangled small, hollow tubes of copper and brass which in swinging against his muscular loins "made a wonderful tingling noise" as he pranced. As his dance evolved, the chief "play'd some dextrous Pantomimical tricks with his Hat & Mask." [102] Elaborate northwest coast masks from recent times reveal how this was done; the Masks were manipulated by cords from within so that they would open and disclose as many as three successive faces, one within the other, dramatizing particular legends.

An attendant laid presents of sea otter skins before both Vancouver and Bodega, proclaiming in a loud and solemn voice that they were gifts from "King" Ma-kwee-na. By way of contributing to the entertainment and demonstrating his own country's way of amusement, Vancouver had his men perform a rustic dance and reel, to the accompaniment of the fife, a source of great merriment for the natives. Ma-kwee-na made no attempt to conceal his delight at the personal compliment of the commanders' visit, and he promised to reciprocate within several days. Vancouver offered to put on a display of fireworks in his honor.

The native entertainment, Bell remarks, "was something grand and curious and well worth coming the distance from Nootka to see alone." But by the finale it was late evening and "it would not only have been imprudent but unpleasant to pass the night here." Some miles down the channel tents were pitched at an appropriately isolated spot, and the unusual day concluded with an "excellent supper and much conviviality & pleasantry." The mutual esteem between the two commanders, despite disagreement upon official matters, was much enhanced by this shared outing. Late the next afternoon, before they reached Friendly Cove, Vancouver was asked by his Peruvian friend if he would mind if, "in the course of my farther exploring this country I would name some port or Island after us both, in commemoration of our meeting and the friendly intercourse that on that occasion has taken place; which I promised to do; and conceiving no place more eligible than the place of our meeting, I have therefore named this land, (which by our sailing at the back we have discovered to be an extensive Island) the Island of Quadra and Vancouver: which compliment he was excessively pleased with." [103]

102. Bell, *Journal*, p. 21.

103. Ibid.; Vancouver, "Narrative," p. 19. The compound name appeared on Spanish and English maps for a few years, but being difficult to pronounce, that portion honoring the amiable Limeño fell into disuse.

The next day Ma-kwee-na, his relatives, and his subjects visited Friendly Cove en masse, eager to behold the promised fireworks. To his dismay, Vancouver found it impossible to refuse permission for the principal braves to clamber aboard ship. "I could not avoid noticing them to be the greatest beggars I had ever seen, and expressing the most excessive impatience on all occasions," he remarks,

> and indeed that kind of disposition seems generally very prevalent among them, which I attribute to be in a great measure owing to the vast indulgence the Spaniards have shewn them: as anything they take a fancy to, if not immediately given, though probably not in our power to spare, they affect to be greatly offended, and remain sulky for two or three days. It was fortunate I had at hand everything to satisfy Maquinna's requests which were upon the whole very moderate: probably the number of things I had given himself and family so recently at Tasheers had not quite escaped his memory: his impatience was however almost beyond bearing in soliciting the amusement I had promised him: he could not, or would not be prevailed on to believe that night was necessary for such an exhibition, accusing us of telling falsities &ca. &ca. Sr. Quadra however at length prevailed on him to stay the night on assuring him all we had said was true.[104]

Vancouver describes the native reaction to the rockets, pinwheels, and other novelties as a mixture of fear and admiration. The chief was persuaded to light a few himself, and, enormously gratified by the event, he reciprocated with chants and dances lasting late into the night, until everyone within earshot had reached the point of utter exhaustion.

### DEADLOCK IN THE BOUNDARY NEGOTIATIONS

Despite their mutual admiration, the commissioners got nowhere with their negotiations because of the convention's ambiguous wording and the mutually exclusive claims of each side. Bodega continued willing to restore the land that Meares was said to have occupied. He maintained his offer of the use of buildings, storehouses, and gardens on condition that this did not entail relinquishing Spanish sovereignty over the rest of the sound. Vancouver again declared himself ready to take possession of Meares's "territories" but declined any retrospective discussion of rights—meaning Madrid's claim to the coastline north of San Francisco. He preferred avoiding any discussion of restitution not giving Britain ownership of all of

---

104. Vancouver, "Narrative," p. 20. Bell received quite a different impression: "Captn. Vancouver according to his promise . . . exhibited in the evening some Fireworks on shore, that astonished the natives though in a much less degree than I expected, for such is their frigid inanimate disposition that nothing will alter the Muscles of their Countenances, and the greater part of those that were present at this sight showed as much unconcern and were as little moved by it as if nothing of the kind was going on." Bell, *Journal*, p. 23.

Nootka Sound, in view of the principle that such recognition would establish. After several more communications back and forth without any further progress, on September 11 Vancouver came earlier than usual to the
big hall for the evening meal and expressly said that he would not accept
possession of anything at Nootka with the slightest restriction, since the
preamble of the convention, article one, and Floridablanca's letter both
authorized the turning over of everything. If this was not to be done, Vancouver felt compelled to depart and report accordingly to his court.[105]

Bodega countered with a denial that the cited documents obliged him
or gave him the power to alienate the property or abandon the settlement
belonging to His Catholic Majesty; that if it were to be evacuated it would
be because he considered that that was the best means of avoiding renewed
incidents—and that he was persuaded that London would not be opposed
to locating the dividing line at Fuca, or to "the possibility that we should
return to establish ourselves here if someday it were considered necessary."
He pointed out that if it had been their respective sovereign's intention
to hand over the terrain in question without any inquiry into the subject,
as Vancouver insisted, then there would have been little purpose in sending
commissioners to negotiate the matter. At that point servants announced
dinner, and Bodega suggested they continue the discussion after eating,
with the understanding that the subject could be freely debated, in an
attempt to reach some kind of agreement. As usual Dobson served as translator, and Broughton and Moziño spoke French, so the principals could resort to alternative methods of insuring complete understanding. Bodega
vindicated Martínez's conduct and stressed Ma-kwee-na's consent to Spanish
occupation of Friendly Cove. The site of Meares's camp was outside the
Spanish settlement, and Vancouver could take possession of it whenever he
pleased. The Englishman held that Martínez's conduct and Ma-kwee-na's
donation of land for the Spanish settlement were immaterial to his mission.
"I could not enter into any argument or discussion to that effect," he
informed Bodega,

> nor in our final conclusion of this negotiation could any subject of
> right or pretentions appear. This being finally understood, it was
> agreed that we should respectively represent our transactions to our
> different Courts, who possessing such information would decide on
> the Subject of right &ca. in the mean time he would leave me in
> full possession of these territories, which he would quit so soon as
> his Vessel was ready to receive him; and on his departure the Spanish
> flag should be hauled down and the British flag hoisted in its room;
> which he would salute, provided I would return an equal number

105. Bodega, "Viaje," fol. 42–42v.

of guns, which being likewise agreed to, matters seemed perfectly settled to the wish and desire of all parties.[106]

Such terms were embodied in a letter which Vancouver wrote at Bodega's table. At once the Limeño penned a short reply: "I am ready to deliver to you agreeable to the 1st. article of the Convention the territories which were occupied by the British subjects in April 1789, and to *leave ours* until the discussion of the courts; which is as far as my powers extend." [107] Bodega says that the note was translated into French for Vancouver's easier understanding, and he supposed it was their mutual view that the negotiations had been satisfactorily concluded. Vancouver's narrative agrees that, "this negotiation being brought to so pleasant a conclusion he requested we would remain on shore in order to pass the evening with him, which we accordingly did." From Bodega's account it would appear that his note was not handed to Vancouver's interpreter until they bid each other goodnight. Vancouver declares that upon receiving its translation, the following morning, he was greatly astonished. His esteem for Don Juan did not prevent an exasperated reply at having to reopen the subject.

> What I understand to be the territories of which His Britannic Majesty's subjects were dispossessed of, and to be restored to them by the 1st. article of the convention, and Count Floridablanca's letter, is this place, in toto, and Port Cox: of which, if it is not in your power to put me in full possession, I can have no idea of hoisting the British flag on the Spot you have pointed out in this cove, of but little more than an hundred yards in extent any way. If therefore that is your situation I must decline receiving any such restitution on the part of His Britannic Majesty: and so soon as His Britannic Majesty's Vessels under my command are in readiness, I shall proceed to Sea, until I receive further directions. . . .[108]

Eager as Vancouver was to take over the base at once, one can perceive his reluctance to let slip through his fingers the larger fruits of Pitt's diplomatic tour de force—which would happen if he occupied the settlement on Bodega's terms. The Peruvian's response was moderate but adamant.

> I repeat, I will leave you in possession not only of the territories which were taken from His Britannic Majesty's subjects in April 1789, but

106. Vancouver, "Narrative," p. 22.

107. Bodega to Vancouver, September 11, 1792, in ibid., pp. 21–22; Vancouver's letter to Bodega, "Aboard the *Descubierta,*" dated September 12, is found in Bodega, "Viaje," fol. 43–43v, where the circumstances under which it was written are related. Having come by way of the Cape of Good Hope, the Englishman's log was a day ahead, and for reasons of his own he chose to give the impression that this missive was written aboard his flagship.

108. Vancouver to Bodega, September 13, 1792, in Vancouver, "Narrative," p. 23.

also that which was then occupied by the natives of the place, and now by the Spaniards in consequence of the cession made in their favor by Maquinna. But you have not the power to controvert, nor I to adjudge, the property of this land; thus I hope it will be convenient to you to have the possession of the whole; and [we] will inform our Sovereigns; and they will decide the most just. . . . I am ready to deliver all that was occupied by the English in that epoch, as a thing belonging to Great Britain, and to leave you in possession of the remaining land, reserving only the right of property, which I have not the power to alienate, and according to my method of thinking ought to be preserved jointly with the British subjects, and to comply in this manner with the sense of the treaty.[109]

As to Vancouver's suggestion that he had gone back on his word to cede the entire settlement, Bodega countered, "I in nothing vary from my first expressions, which were always limited with these words, 'without prejudice to our legitimate right, or what the courts [when] better instructed [i.e., informed] may resolve.' This is without renouncing the property which I comprehend ought to remain in favor of the king my master."[110]

By now Bodega was fully aware of the peril to Madrid's interests of retreating from a claim to at least a portion of Nootka Sound. English maps and his discussions with Vancouver made it apparent that London aspired to defining Spain's undisputed claims as extending no farther northward than San Francisco Bay. From all appearances, the British intended to use the convention as grounds for frequenting unoccupied spots along the coast anywhere north of ten leagues from San Francisco. But if Madrid sustained a claim to its settlement at Friendly Cove, however embarrassed she might be by the presence of foreigners, the convention made it illegal for British vessels to visit the coast south of Port Cox (Clayoquot), except in cases of emergency. Bodega had good reason to fear that if Spain surrendered her claim to Friendly Cove, historically defensible by virtue of Pérez's discovery and Martínez's occupation, there might be difficulty in finding convincing arguments for a boundary at the Strait of Juan de Fuca, or for prohibiting British activities short of Alta California.

Bodega had come prepared to evacuate the settlement, and prior to the start of negotiations he went so far as to set a date for its delivery.[111] Subsequent to his arrival, however, the testimony accruing from a number of sources had intensified his conviction that Spain had a valid title to Nootka Sound. Now he was convinced that to fulfill the convention, Madrid would

109. Bodega to Vancouver, September 13, 1792, in ibid., pp. 23–24.
110. Ibid.
111. Menzies, *Journal,* p. 123.

not have to deliver up more than the area actually occupied by Meares. The British were convinced that Bodega's American friends had a hand in stiffening his resolve. "The Arrival of an American Brig stopped the intended plans," Manby asserts, "the Master of her having sufficient influence with the Spaniards, persuaded them that the treaty between the two nations, only gave the English, the spot of which they were dispossessed of, by Sen. Martínez." [112] The brig in question was the *Columbia*, since Manby goes on to say that it had been present when Martínez made his seizures. Gray and Ingraham spoke as one voice in their advice to Bodega. Ma-kwee-na's testimony, and Viana's, added weight to Bodega's conviction that Spain was justified in placing the narrowest construction upon article one of the convention. His friendship with Vancouver was insufficient to bridge the enormous gap between their retrospective points of view—a breach indeed empires apart.

### MURDER AT FRIENDLY COVE

That the Indian warranted consideration as a fellow human being was not a widely shared assumption on the northwest coast in 1792. A cross-cultural comparison in this regard is nowhere better seen than in an incident on September 14 which threw Nootka into the biggest uproar since Ke-le-ken's death. As Bell describes it:

> A fine little Spanish Boy—one of Mr Quadra's servants, who had been missing about eight & forty hours, was found most barbarously murdered in a small bight within the Cove where the Ships lay. A bloody knife was found lying near him. It is supposed he was decoyed thither by some of the Indians, under the pretence of gratifying an illicit intercourse with one of their women, but no reason could be assigned whatever for the taking away his life. No quarrel was known [to have] happened between the Indians and him or any of the Spaniards, on the contrary the Indians enjoyed a happier time since the Spaniards had been first there. None of his Cloathes were to be found but he was left naked with his throat cut in a dreadful manner from ear to ear. He had several stabs and cuts in his arms and on the backs of his hands, and the calves of his legs, and the fleshy parts of his thighs were most Butcherly cut out and supposed to be eaten by the savage perpetrators of this act.[113]

Surgeon Archibald Menzies found the lad's "throat & the right side of his neck had been cut & mangled in a dreadfull manner; there were some deep gashes on the inside of his thighs, & apparently a small piece cut out

112. Manby, "Journal," pt. 2, fol. 34.
113. Bell, *Journal*, p. 25.

of the Calf of each Legg, though it is probable that the contraction of the strong Muscles composing that part might occasion the Vacuity." "This would be of very little consequence," he says, "had it not been afterwards urged as proof that the Natives who were supposed to be the Murderers were Cannibals & cut out these pieces for the purposes of eating them." [114] A Spanish account adds that a handkerchief lay near the body and that the lethal weapon was an English razor.[115] Bell relates that when the Indians learned of the murder, "those that were in the Cove took instantly to their Canoes, and made out of the Cove, and in a few minutes not a canoe was to be seen, except one, which with four Natives happened to be on Board the Hope Brig, but hearing the alarm, and observing the Spanish Boats coming in haste towards them, three of them jump'd into the canoe and got off, the remaining poor fellow had jump'd overboard from the Brig, and was endeavoring to escape by swimming, but he was taken up and carried on shore." [116]

Describing the incident in a report to his superiors, Vancouver remarked that "on this occasion all the Indians in our neighbourhood departed, which seemed rather to support the opinion of some of them having committed the crime." His journal repeats his conclusion that "the immediate departure of all the inhabitants of the sound from our neighborhood became a strong presumptive proof of their delinquency." [117] The brunt of suspicion fell upon Ma-kwee-na's people, as being most numerous in the vicinity. A Spanish source relates what happened aboard the *Hope* somewhat differently.

> Word spread among all foreign vessels then found at the anchorage, and their respective captains promised to join us in avenging this atrocity. Ingraham, of Boston, consequently the following day arrested two of Macuina's servants, named *Frijoles* and *Agustín,* sent word of it, and asked for troops to transfer them to the stocks of our brigantine of war, the *Activa.* Taking fright at this, they jumped into the water where, despite their dexterity in swimming, our launch caught up to them, and they were conducted, with arms tied, to Don Juan de la Bodega y Quadra. He was well satisfied that they were innocent, since they were not absent an instant from our house the night the little page was killed. Therefore he let them go free, charging that in his name they supplicate Maquina to investigate who had been the aggressor.[118]

Two days later, Ma-kwee-na came to the cove and berated the whites for arresting two of his people without any evidence of their guilt. Although

114. Menzies, *Journal,* p. 122.
115. *Sútil y Mexicana,* p. 149.
116. Bell, *Journal,* p. 25.
117. Vancouver, "Narrative," p. 24; Vancouver, *Voyage,* 1 : 402.
118. *Sútil y Mexicana,* p. 149, AT.

grateful that Bodega had freed them, the chief was dismayed that "your soldiers, when mine were leaving, told them I had suggested such evil." Persuaded that Bodega did not share such an opinion, Ma-kwee-na recited the many gifts he had received from the commandant, and remarked:

> Our reciprocal confidence has reached the point where we have slept alone in the same chamber, a place in which, finding you without arms or men for defense, I could have taken your life, if a friend were capable of betrayal. It would do me and my dignity an injustice to imagine that if I wanted to break the peace I would order the assassination of a boy less able to defend himself than if he were a woman. Don't you presume that a chief like myself would commence hostilities by killing other chiefs and throwing the force of his subjects against that of your soldiers? You would be the one whose life would be in greatest danger if we were enemies.[119]

Wee-ka-na-nish and other chiefs were his allies and had many guns and bullets. "All of us united," Ma-kwee-na pointed out, "would comprise a number so incomparably greater than the Spanish, English, and Americans together that there would be no fear of engaging in combat." Bodega and his officers had gone among them lightly escorted, yet never were harmed or even insulted. "Far from doing damage to the Spanish," Ma-kwee-na proclaimed himself "ready to avenge that which they have received." He asked to borrow a launch and six swivel guns so that, allied with relatives, he could "destroy those bandits" from across the sound whom he conjectured were responsible. If Bodega would send Spanish soldiers along, "our enemies will know Macuina is the same as Quadra, and Quadra is the same as Macuina."

Bodega listened politely, but he was no readier to unleash violence against another tribe than he had been to do so against Ma-kwee-na. Vancouver and Ingraham were of the opinion that he should have taken more vigorous action, or at least hold Ma-kwee-na hostage until the murderer was delivered up. "It is surely to be regretted," the Englishman Bell comments,

> that Mr. Quadra's mildness and lenity would not suffer him proceeding further, and with more rigour in this inhuman affair, as it was thought by many, and even by all his own officers he ought, and might have done. But though I myself have not the most distant idea that the murder was committed by any person but of the Native Indians, and that those parts of the Flesh cut out of the Legs & Thighs were eaten by them, it seems some of the Spaniards had their doubts of this, and did not think it improbable but that it was committed by a Mexican Indian,

119. Ibid., pp. 148–51, AT.

and had formerly belonged to the Spanish Brig but had deserted some time back and had not been heard of a good while. But this was far from being the general opinion, for the accounts of all that saw the Boy last pretty generally agreed that he was walking along the Beach towards the corner of the Cove with two Indians, and some of these said they saw him embark in a canoe from that place with these Indians and a woman and paddle towards the little Cove where he was afterwards found. But these good qualities, mildness and Lenity, that I have observed Mr Quadra possessed so considerable a share of, are often too mistaken, and are as frequently carried to as great extremes by some as the opposite qualities are by others. Here we may say Mr Quadra was *too good* a man, he even treated the Indians more like companions than people that should be taught subjection. His house was open to them all and a considerable number of them were fed there every day. But such goodness is thrown away on these wretches, they are possessed of no affection, nor gratitude and the man that would profess himself your warm friend today would cut your throat & dine off you tomorrow.[120]

Vancouver also refers to a suspect among the Spanish seamen, "a black man, of a very infamous character, who had deserted much about that time," and Bodega confirms the desertion of an ordinary seaman, noted on the same day that the page's corpse was discovered.[121] Although Ingraham concurred with those who thought Ma-kwee-na should have been detained until the guilty parties were surrendered, he understood Bodega's reasons, commenting, "Señor Quadra made some enquiry about the matter but as he could not with certainty ascertain the guilty person he rather chose to look over it than to risk punishing the innocent therefore the matter was dropt and the natives returned to the cove with their usuall confidence." [122] In the absence of concrete evidence, Bodega did well to smooth over the matter. His sense of justice was keen; even assuming the killer to have been an Indian, vengeance was purposeless, and retaliation would have hampered relations with the natives, so assiduously cultivated as a means of advancing Spanish political objectives.

This incident inevitably stirred up the cannibalism issue, the most aggravating factor in Spanish-Indian relations at Nootka. The mutilation murder was sure confirmation for Bell, who remarks, "Knowing well in what light we consider this species of Barbarity, of course, when questioned on the subject they will not own it." He adds that, "During the time we were at Nootka Mr Hanson in passing from the Daedalus to the Chatham had a

120. Bell, *Journal*, p. 25.
121. Vancouver, "Narrative," p. 24; Bodega, "Viaje," fol. 47v–48.
122. Ingraham, "Log," p. 200.

human hand thrown into the boat to him from some Indians in a Canoe that had not been a very long time cut from the Body." [123]

After painstaking study of the Nootka language and customs, Moziño concluded:

> From the consistent reports that the Spaniards and Boston men have given us, it appears to be proved in an uncontestable manner that these savages have been cannibals. In fact, they came on board the packet boat *San Carlos,* commanded by Lieutenant Don Salvador Fidalgo, with the cooked hand of a child, and took other limbs prepared in the same manner to other vessels. Certainly the abhorrence which they immediately preceived on our part, and the threats of punishment which they were promised for such execrable cruelty, have made them remove this viand from their tables; or, better yet, the precious peace which they have enjoyed has not permitted them to be supplied with prisoners, the unfortunate victims who became entombed in their stomachs. Hauitl assured me that not everyone had eaten flesh, nor did they all the time, just the fiercest warriors when they prepared to go to war. I doubt the truth of this story, because this wise Indian knew very well how much we detested this custom, and now that he could not contradict what so many honest men had said, he wanted at least to diminish the gravity and circumstances of a crime that makes even nature shudder.[124]

Promoting a climate for harmony between cultures having such different values posed no small problem at Friendly Cove. Don Juan's tolerance for Ma-kwee-na's customs drew the line at anthropophagy, but the patience, wisdom, and justice displayed in his treatment of the Indians contrasts notably with the behavior of his contemporaries, and added measurably to Spain's hold over Nootka Sound.

### NEGOTIATIONS BROKEN OFF

Shortly after Bodega and Vancouver reached a deadlock in their negotiations, an additional element entered the situation with the arrival on September 16 of the *São José o Fénix,* out of Macao and flying Portuguese colors. João Barros de Andrade captained the brig, but the supercargo and actual boss of the cruise was Robert Duffin, an officer aboard both the *Feliz*

---

123. Bell, *Journal,* pp. 39–40.

124. Moziño, *Noticias,* pp. 22–23. Elsewhere he identifies Ha-witl as a "Prince," (p. 20), i.e., of the noble class. The informant's credibility is enhanced in that it was not in his interest to admit the existence of anthropophagy. Nor would Moziño denigrate gratuitously the people in whose study he lavished such devoted, painstaking effort. Moziño's editor, faced with modern opinion, dismisses this testimony as baseless, but it warrants evaluation in the light of other firsthand eighteenth-century sources.

*Aventureira* in 1788 and the *Argonaut* in 1789–91. Duffin provided Vancouver with a statement bolstering British claims to Nootka by reason of Meares's activities there in 1788. Duffin claimed that Meares had purchased all of the land occupied by Ma-kwee-na's village at Friendly Cove, not just the small area where his camp had stood.[125] The British commissioner took this new evidence into his next conference with Bodega. "My response," Don Juan relates, "reduced to a few words, was to say that he ought not to judge by one sole testimony, above all when it was corroborated that Meares had behaved irresponsibly in compromising two friendly nations, perhaps thinking that without further inquiry he would be rewarded with the imagined sum that he charged against Spain." [126] Bodega held that, since Duffin was Meares's associate, with a vested interest in the matter, his testimony was prejudiced and had to be discounted. Gray and Ingraham had departed, so to shed light upon the contradictions, Duffin's affidavit was read to Ma-kwee-na, and several foreign captains and Spanish officers were asked to be witnesses.

> About the sale he [Ma-kwee-na] made to Mr. Meares, he responded that he had not done any such thing, using the word *Huic;* I insisted to him that Captain Meares had assured it, but he repeated that nevertheless it was false, for he had never sold anything other than skins, at the rate of ten for each sheet of copper. [He added] that in effect he had sold to the American Captain Kendric a portion of land in Marbuina, for ten rifles and a little powder; that the place where the Spaniards have erected their houses was donated by himself to D. Francisco Eliza, and afterward to me, the said commandant, under condition that it be returned in case the Spaniards retired from here.[127]

To further bolster the Spanish title, Bodega had Ma-kwee-na execute a deed of gift for the land on which the settlement was located. The information that Gray, Ingraham, Viana, and Ma-kwee-na gave Bodega probably was not the decisive factor inducing him to back away from a compromise with Vancouver. Much of this testimony had been assembled before the British commissioner arrived, yet until the moment negotiations ground to a halt, Bodega was preparing to evacuate Nootka, on condition Spanish removal not be taken as admission that Madrid was conceding its title. But Vancouver would accept all or nothing. When Bodega confirmed Vancouver's intention of using the convention as a wedge to give British subjects

125. Duffin to Vancouver, [Nootka, between September 18 and 21, 1792], in Bell, *Journal,* pp. 27–29, and Vancouver, *Voyage,* 1 : 404–05.

126. Bodega, "Viaje," fol. 53v, AT.

127. Moziño acted as translator, and Ma-kwee-na's deposition was signed by Bodega, Magee, Howell, Barros Andrade, José Antonio Ximénez, and Salvador Menéndez. See Bodega, "Viaje," fol. 60v–62, AT; Ingraham, "Log," p. 199.

access to everything north of San Francisco Bay, he was forced into a holding strategy. In view of Vancouver's designs on the entire coast, it behooved Madrid to retain Nootka and renegotiate with London a specific settlement on terms more favorable than the British commissioner was disposed to allow. The letters that followed only reiterated previous positions, without conceding a particle. Vancouver refused to discuss boundaries and would only accept delivery of Nootka and Clayoquot Sounds as a whole. Perhaps to undermine his opposite number's resolve, Vancouver expressed surprise at noncompliance with the gentlemen's agreement that Nootka would be turned over entirely, an agreement that had led to their unloading the *Daedalus* and *Chatham* and storing their supplies ashore. If Nootka were not relinquished, these would all have to be reloaded. Bodega would not be shaken; he regretted that Vancouver had not understood "the expressions which were manifested in my first letter, where I was ready to cede the houses, gardens, lands &c. but under these restrictions." Missives between the commissioners became increasingly curt, but Vancouver's report notes that "this difference in opinion had however no effects on the rights of hospitality and friendship: we visited as usual." His insistence upon demands that Bodega was unwilling to concede finally led them to suspend negotiations until London and Madrid could arrive at a more specific agreement regarding respective rights on the northwest coast.[128]

Whether because of the number of Spanish warships in the area, the extent of Spanish activity on the northwest coast in 1792, or Bodega's amiable and generous treatment, Vancouver chose not to take a belligerent position or negotiate from a position of force by bringing into play his frigates' powerful armament. His temperate remonstrances evoked a correspondingly amiable response from his diplomatic opponent. Don Juan's fraternal bond with Vancouver not only avoided the rancor that might otherwise have been generated by such mutually exclusive pretensions, but fostered a mutual benefit through the generous exchange of cartographic information from Spanish and British explorations on the northwest coast. Vancouver gleaned much of his data from Iberian explorers, and since his journal and maps were soon published and widely disseminated, Spanish contributions to charting the complexities of that region have gone unappreciated for the most part. Because of Bodega's openhandedness, Vancouver had access to many Spanish charts executed prior to 1792. Traces of his use of those charts are evident in such Spanish names as persist today, because Vancouver chose to respect and copy a small fraction of those found on Bodega's charts; but for every Spanish toponym preserved, dozens were disregarded, and the British nomenclature has prevailed.

128. Vancouver to Bodega, September 20, 1792, and Bodega to Vancouver, September 20, 1792, both in Vancouver, "Narrative," pp. 26–27; see also p. 24.

Since no satisfactory settlement with Vancouver appeared possible, necessity obliged Bodega to return to his duties as commandant of San Blas. When the time came for departure, there was considerable mutual regret, despite the failure to reach an accord. The day before Bodega left, he and his subordinates were invited to a farewell dinner aboard the *Discovery*. Bell relates that afterward the Limeño "insisted on our all going on shore, and spending the last evening with him which we did exceedingly pleasantly with Singing, Music, Dancing and all kinds of amusements," and he lamented:

> Never was the departure of a man more regretted than that of Mr. Quadra's. He was universally belov'd and admired and the only consolation we had was that we should see him again at Monterrey (whither 'twas reported we were to go from this) there he said he wou'd wait for us and make it his business to receive us. In such a place as Nootka, so remote from all civilized places (except the small settlements in California) and after having been so long there, he lived in a style that I should suppose is rarely seen under such circumstances, and supported the dignity of his Court in a very becoming manner. His house was open to every gentleman, he gave few particular invitations, they were general. He was fond of society and of social amusements and the Evening parties at his house were among the pleasantest I have spent since leaving England.[129]

Bell adds that once Bodega and Vancouver resolved to refer their differences to Madrid and London for solution, they "parted on as good terms as they met."

#### ABANDONMENT OF THE SETTLEMENT AT NEAH BAY

Bodega's inability to reach a boundary agreement with Vancouver doomed the Spanish naval base on the Strait of Juan de Fuca. Initially, it had been anticipated that Núñez Gaona would eventually replace Santa Cruz de Nootka in importance, by reason of its accessibility to the sea and command of the strait. But the justification for this second Spanish settlement on the northwest coast was questioned even before its establishment was begun. Fidalgo's party was not yet upon the site when Revillagigedo had misgivings about the expediency of a base there, and he decided to cancel the effort unless it were judged essential. Bodega replied that in his opinion a base there had never seemed a good idea. Fidalgo had been sent only because of the viceroy's orders, but the endeavor would not be prolonged, unless it proved necessary or advantageous. Alcalá Galiano and other officials would be con-

129. Bell, *Journal*, p. 30.

sulted as to the advisability of continuing or abandoning the new settlement.[130]

The *Santa Gertrudis*'s departure on July 19 offered an opportunity to evaluate Nuñez Gaona's importance. Captain Torres was ordered to stop there and conduct a junta with Fidalgo and his fellow officers to ascertain their views. At the close of the meeting, each participant offered his written opinion. Torres, Ensign Félix de Cepeda, and Lieutenants José Quevedo and Ramón Abad had not been to the port previously; hence they deferred to Fidalgo, the only member of the junta who had lived there. He admitted that the surrounding terrain was flat and appropriate for a settlement and that the fortification had the necessary number of barracks and sheds, a ready source of fresh water, and a nearby stand of thick, tall timber. The gardens, as well as the surrounding vegetation, indicated fertile soil. In good weather no vessel could enter or leave the strait without being seen from the fort. Despite these advantages, the settlement could scarcely subsist or serve any purpose unless a warship was permanently stationed there. The bay had a rocky bottom and was exposed to winds from the first and fourth quadrants, and the surf was considerable, making it dangerous to anchor closer than about a cannon-shot from shore. Exposed as any ship would be to northwest, northerly, and northeast winds, it could remain only in good weather. Lack of shelter would oblige all vessels to leave during winter months. The others agreed with Fidalgo that want of a sheltered anchorage was crucial. No warship could hope to ride out the winter and guard the settlement or keep vigil over the strait. It was too late to build a structure large enough to protect the sizable force that would be needed there against Indians and elements. The advantages gained from the base would not be commensurate with the expense and danger involved, but the junta abstained from pronouncing a definitive verdict, leaving the matter to superior resolution.[131]

Núñez Gaona's fate hung in suspension until September, when the stalemate between Bodega and Vancouver postponed indefinitely the intended "delivery" of Nootka to Britain. Since Spain would retain Friendly Cove until the impasse could be resolved by direct dickering between Madrid and London, the urgency of having a naval base at Fuca abated, at least for the

130. Revillagigedo to Bodega, March 7, 1792, MxAGN (Hist. 67). Probably conveyed to Nootka by the *Aranzazú* (dep. San Blas, March 20; arr. Nootka, May 13), last vessel to reach Nootka before Bodega began to act upon it in July. Letter from Bodega to Revillagigedo, cited by Wagner, *Spanish Explorations*, p. 64, without specifying date or location.

131. Acts of the junta at Núñez Gaona, July 22, 1792, MxAGN (Hist. 67); "Extracto de noticias," SpMN (575bis), fol. 130v–31. Contrary to what some authors have stated, Alcalá Galiano and Valdés were not present, but were exploring the Inland Passage. Their written opinions on the matter, dated October 22, 1792, were submitted to Bodega at Monterey, MxAGN (Hist. 67). Ingraham probably carried the junta's results to Bodega. The *Hope* called at Núñez Gaona the second week in August, bringing dispatches from Bodega to Fidalgo, and performed the same service again in September; see Ingraham, "Log," p. 188 and Bodega, "Viaje," fol. 49v.

moment. The bay also declined in strategic importance when the possibility of finding the entrance to a northwest passage somewhere within the Strait of Juan de Fuca was eliminated. The scarcity of sea otters deep within that waterway and the difficulties of bucking prevailing winds to emerge reduced the value of Puget Sound and other interior waterways. As soon as it seemed evident that he could reach no satisfactory boundary agreement with Vancouver, Bodega advised Fidalgo to abandon the effort at Núñez Gaona. When Ingraham left for the strait on September 15, he conveyed instructions to dismantle the fort at once and prepare to bring armament, animals, and men to Nootka aboard the *Princesa,* as soon as Bodega himself arrived.

Jacinto Caamaño was put in temporary charge of Nootka, where the *Aranzazú* would remain on guard until Fidalgo and the *Princesa* came. As Bodega and the *Activa* put to sea on September 21, the *Columbia* happened to be approaching, and hove to, in order that the captains might speak. Gray knew that the Spanish suffered a perennial shortage of bottoms. The *Columbia* was shorthanded, and he hoped to dispose of the *Adventure* at a profit, rather than take her to China. Boit notes that Bodega "appear'd anxious to have the Sloop and Haswell was not backward in displaying her to the best advantage." [132] Bodega agreed to Gray's price of seventy-five prime sea otter pelts, if the ship was delivered to Núñez Gaona. He told the Americans that the vessel would be a gift for the viceroy. Presumably, it was purchased with pelts given to Bodega by the Indians, and in the viceroy's name it would be added to the flotilla operating out of San Blas.

The *Activa* and the *Columbia* arrived off the strait simultaneously as darkness fell on September 25. Since Gray was well acquainted with the area, he kept right on to Núñez Gaona and anchored there by dawn, alongside Ingraham and the *Hope.* Salvadore Menéndez, captain of the Spanish brig, was unfamiliar with the waterway's swift currents. At first light the Americans could see the *Activa* in the distance, becalmed and anchored dangerously near Cape Flattery, so Ingraham and Gray sent their longboats to tow the ship to safety. Boit, among those going to its succor, comments that "when I came on board, instead of using every effort to get clear of the threatening Danger, they was performing Mass." [133] The peril of the moment may explain the habitually amiable commodore's pique upon his rescuer's arrival. Ingraham, who usually had nothing but praise for his revered friend, remarks that "Don Juan Francisco seem'd displeased we had not sent our Long Boats off to him the preceding Evening but we inform'd him the long boats of both vessels were hoisted in besides that the distance was too great to risk our boats with few men where the savages

132. Boit, "Log," p. 414; Robert Gray and John Hoskins to Joseph Barrell, "Ship Columbia, Straits of de Fuca," September 28, 1792, MHi (Barrell Letters), in Howay, "Letters," pp. 147–48.
133. Boit, "Log," p. 416.

were so numerous and by no means to be trusted having not long before murder'd the first Lieutenant of [the] *Princessa* not far from the ship —these well grounded reasons apparently satisfied Don Juan that our not sending our boats did not proceed from inattention or neglect which it is certain his kind treatment to us did not merit." Tide and winds did not permit bringing them in at once, and the Americans stayed to dine with Bodega. At nightfall they started back to their own vessels, and as they were passing a large village near the cape, the natives "set up a most hidious yelling." "We had musketts in the boat and a small brass swivel in the bow in case of an attack," Ingraham relates, "yet were the[y] resolute as they are generally esteem'd to be we should scarce have an opportunity of firing above once ere they would have boarded us[;] severall canoes were lurking about, perhaps fishing, however we did not choose to trust them for if they approached us we fir'd a musket ball over them which had the desire'd effect." [134]

These populous villages had kept the little settlement in a constant state of wariness all summer long. Natives visiting the *Columbia* complained of disliking the Spanish. By night, canoes prowled around ships anchored in the bay, despite Fidalgo's twilight cannon shot warning them away. Ingraham presumed they sought some opportunity to avenge Fidalgo's indiscriminate retaliation for Serantes's murder. "This circumstance seem'd to have a very sensible effect on these people for when ever any thing relative to the affair was mention'd it would occasion a tremour and every one was ready to say it was none of their tribe etc.," the American relates. "If the innocent were punish'd and the guilty escaped it was a pity but how was any one to ascertain the guilty person as no one would come forward to acuse him or them hence Señor Fidalgo to convince them such enormities would not be passed over with impunity thought proper to make an example of the first he met with after the death of his unfortunate officer and much esteem'd friend." [135] Such reasoning notwithstanding, Fidalgo's act made eventual Indian retaliation a certainty, given the native code that damage to a tribe had to be avenged.

Bodega relates that, desirous of inquiring into the cause of Serantes's murder, he gave a number of gifts to Chief Ta-tla-ku, who persuaded his brother Ta-toosh and other chieftains to come to a conference.

> All were in agreement that Indians of a neighboring village assassinated the pilot to rob him, and fled thereafter in fear of being punished. But despite their efforts in pretense of sincerity, I was not well satisfied of their innocence, nor am I far from believing that Tutusi and Tatlacu

134. Ingraham, "Log," pp. 201–02.
135. Ibid.; Boit, "Logs," p. 416.

are themselves capable of doing as much to others careless enough to trust them or the women who come to the ships. Withal I gave them the greatest show of friendship, and I ceded them the barracks constructed on land, without permitting a single stick to be taken away.[136]

The little settlement never had amounted to much. Boit described it as having about ten houses, but Ingraham says it was no more than "a few Huts and a tollerable good garden." [137] Gray's invitation to the officers of the *Activa, Princesa, Hope,* and *Adventure* to dine with him aboard the *Columbia* was the little settlement's dying gasp; within a few hours it would be desolate of white inhabitants.

By the next morning, September 29, everything useful had already been loaded aboard the *Princesa*, which sailed for Nootka. Ingraham and the *Hope* departed almost simultaneously. The *Activa* left for Monterey later that day with all that remained of the little establishment. The *Adventure,* renamed *Orcasitas* and commanded by López de Haro, followed Bodega southward. The next morning Gray weighed anchor, leaving the site deserted. Its Spanish name, so awkward for those of another tongue, was soon forgotten and "Ne-ar," the Indian designation, prevailed to become today's Neah Bay.

### THE STRENGTHENING OF SPANISH RESOLVE TO KEEP NOOTKA

Bodega's decision or the opinions of participants in the junta at Núñez Gaona notwithstanding, the little settlement's extinction had been determined before it was even founded, and by events occuring in Europe, not in America. As will be recalled, Floridablanca was banished to Murcia in February 1792 and replaced by the francophile Aranda. At the change in ministries, an experiment in conciliating revolutionary France, Aranda sought political mileage by criticizing Floridablanca's handling of the Nootka Crisis and adopting a more bellicose stance toward Great Britain. It is hardly coincidence that, the day after Floridablanca's dismissal, a royal order countermanded Revillagigedo's plan for retreating to a boundary at Fuca, declaring that His Catholic Majesty would never consent to the entire cession of Nootka. The Spanish commandant there should be given to understand that the convention did not entitle subjects of any nation but Spain and England to frequent the area or carry on commerce there, a privilege to be obtained by negotiation directly with Madrid, and subject to its interests and the state of relations with that other nation.[138]

This new stance put Revillagigedo in a difficult position, for the instruc-

---

136. Bodega, "Viaje," fol. 66v, AT.
137. Ingraham, "Log," p. 203.
138. Royal order of February 29, 1792, cited by Revillagigedo to Godoy, April 12, 1793, p. 157; *Compendio histórico*, pp. 52–53.

tions that Bodega had carried northward in the spring of 1792 permitted ceding Nootka if the British commissioner was amenable to a boundary at Fuca. Now the retreat had to be prevented, if it had not already taken place. The viceroy cast about for means of getting word to Bodega, but he was hampered by the scarcity of vessels. The Nootka-built *Santa Saturnina,* hardly a craft to undertake such a long voyage alone, was the only available bottom in San Blas at the time. Commanded by first pilot Juan Carrasco, it hurried northward in June in an effort to reach Friendly Cove before irreversible concessions were made. Carrasco did not reach San Francisco until September, and was still there when the *Activa* anchored at Monterey on October 10.[139] Following their instructions, the *Santa Gertrudis,* the *Sútil,* and the *Mexicana* were awaiting Bodega there. A shortage of supplies had discouraged Torres from making an adequate survey of the Columbia's mouth, but from what was known of its characteristics, Bodega concluded that the river was not a northwest passage and held no immediate importance as a site for a Spanish settlement. Within a few days the new orders from Madrid and Mexico City came overland from San Francisco. Putting to good use the schooner purchased from Gray, Bodega sent López de Haro and the *Orcasitas* hurrying northward to advise Fidalgo to exclude traders of other than Spanish and British nationality from Nootka unless their nation signed a particular convention with Spain allowing reciprocal benefits to Spanish subjects. The schooner started for Nootka on October 21, despite the lateness of the season, and, although rough weather was encountered, it made the round trip by December 23.[140]

The situation at Friendly Cove, meanwhile, had undergone a change; the warmhearted Limeño was scarcely out of sight when the natives noted a difference in their reception at the Big House. As soon as Fidalgo took over, Caamaño prepared to take the *Aranzazú* to San Blas. Shortly before departing southward he gave what Menzies describes as an "elegant entertainment" for his successor, to which Vancouver, his officers, and other captains there at the time were invited. Ma-kwee-na and some of his relatives visited the cove that day, expecting the same benevolent welcome as when Bodega presided there, but they were abruptly turned away. Plainly, the fraternization of Don Juan's time was a thing of the past. Following Serantes's death, Fidalgo had little trust or patience for Indian ways, and the page's mysterious fate probably hardened other convictions in this regard. The new commandant resolved to keep the chiefs and their people at a distance, and he ordered his men to warn them away from the settlement except at specified times, and then to watch carefully when they approached. Offended at not being received as usual and at being the butt of suspicion, Ma-kwee-na left

139. Bodega, "Viaje," fol. 79–80, 88v.
140. Ibid., fol. 80, 88v.

the cove in a huff, but before departing he took the opportunity to express to Vancouver his dislike for all Spaniards except his revered friend, Bodega. Singling out Martínez for particular complaint, he charged the Sevillano with coming ashore accompanied by an armed guard and obliging him by threats to cede Nootka to Spain. He deplored Vancouver's imminent departure, saying that "his people would always be harrassed and ill-treated by new-comers, [and] intreated that [the British commander] would leave some persons behind for their protection. Very little dependence, however, is to be placed in the truth or sincerity of such declarations," Vancouver felt, "since these people, unlettered as they are, possess no small share of policy and address, and spare no pains to ingratiate themselves, by the help of a little flattery." [141]

Friendly relations continued between the English and Spanish. Prior to the *Aranzazú*'s departure, on October 4, Vancouver offered a farewell banquet, to which all of the Spanish officials were invited. Twenty-one-gun salutes accompanied toasts to both sovereigns. What with the arrival and departure of so many ships and the coming and going of the Spanish commandant visiting each vessel, the cannonades were a constant disturbance to tranquility. "Saluting was so common among the Trading Vessels that visited the Cove," Menzies comments, "that there was scarcely a day past without puffings of this kind from some Vessel or other, & we too followed the example, & puffed it away as well as any of them, till at last we were become so scarce of ammunition to defend ourselves from the treacherous Indians, that we were obliged to get supplies of Powder from both the Spaniards & Traders before we left the Coast." [142]

Vancouver sent his government a report of the deadlock with Bodega, explaining that he had refused to accept the corner of the cove on which Meares's house was located, "whose whole extent is scarce more than a musquet shot in any direction," because in doing so he would have betrayed the trust put in him.[143] The missive was dispatched with one of his officers, Lieutenant Zachary Mudge, who sailed for Macao as a passenger aboard the *São José o Fénix*. The British commissioner's departure for Monterey was delayed until supplies could be reloaded from the storehouses on shore, where they had been placed in expectation of Nootka's cession. He canceled plans for sending the *Daedalus* to the penal colony at Australia's Botany Bay to obtain colonists for Nootka. Instead, Captain New was sent to New South Wales for provisions to supply the *Discovery* and the *Chatham* until further orders came from London. Meanwhile, Vancouver hoped to fulfill those portions of his instructions relative to surveying Spanish settlements in Cali-

141. Vancouver, *Voyage*, 1 : 409; Menzies, *Journal*, p. 127.
142. Menzies, *Journal*, p. 127.
143. Vancouver, "Narrative," p. 27; Menzies, *Journal*, p. 123; Ingraham, "Log," p. 195.

fornia, charting the farther reaches of the northwest coast and possibly discovering a northwest passage.

October's cold, driving rain and heavy winds from the southeast tumbled great swells into the harbor, foretelling miserable winter months ahead. Shortly before Vancouver was to leave, Captain James Baker and the British trader *Jenny* put in at Friendly Cove. Baker intended sailing directly for London, and so two Hawaiian girls who had been accompanying him disembarked. Since the *Discovery* and the *Chatham* were to winter in the Sandwich Islands, Vancouver offered to return the damsels to their home. The occurrence hints at one reason why Hawaii was so popular a way station and watering place for vessels operating on the northwest coast.[144]

The British warships got underway for California on October 12, but during their attempt to round San Miguel Island a sudden gust drove the *Chatham* onto jagged rocks. Surf breaking about the vessel threatened to pound it to pieces, but the *Daedalus* and a Spanish launch managed to haul it into deep water before the hull received much damage. Fidalgo went out in one of his longboats to bid Vancouver adieu. "It was but natural to feel some reluctance at parting," Menzies remarks,

> as during our stay at Nootka the Spanish Officers & we lived on the most amicable footing. Our frequent & social meetings at Sr. Quadra's hospitable mansion afforded constant opportunity of testifying our mutual regard & friendship for each other, by that harmony & good understanding which always marked our convivial hours. In short even in this distant sequestered gloomy region we passed our time together chearfully & happy.[145]

Vancouver arrived off the Columbia on October 19, but heavy surf over the bar discouraged him from taking the *Discovery* inside. Lieutenant Broughton succeeded in getting the *Chatham* safely through the turbulence, and he sailed up the estuary until navigation became hazardous. Casting anchor, he took a well-armed party of hefty rowers and ascended the swift-flowing river to a point where dangerous rapids obliged them to turn back, a spot over 100 miles from the ocean, near the present Washougal, Washington.

#### BODEGA AND VANCOUVER IN CALIFORNIA

As a result of his deadlock with Vancouver, the commandant of San Blas was prompted to make a number of recommendations for strengthening Spain's position on the northwest coast. Since he was to remain at Monterey

144. Menzies, *Journal*, p. 131; F. W. Howay and T. C. Elliott, "Voyages of the 'Jenny' to Oregon, 1792–94," *OHQ* 30 (1929) : 197.

145. Menzies, *Journal*, pp. 130–31; Manby, "Journal," pt. 2, fol. 37.

for some months (October 9 to January 13), it was urgent that his suggestions be conveyed to Revillagigedo without delay, and they were dispatched late in October aboard the *Santa Gertrudis.*

Bodega was convinced that "England had no right to reclaim ownership of the Port of Nuca, nor was Spain obliged to make that cession." He was persuaded that Nootka constituted the only good port north of San Francisco. As for the impasse with Vancouver, which had prevented Bodega's abandoning Nootka, "if the King, as obliged by other political motives, should want to give it up, nothing has been lost by postponement, for besides the fact that Vancouver did not come to this coast for that alone, and he has to return next year to conclude his reconnaissance, he and all sixteen French, English, Portuguese, and American vessels touching that Port during my residence will spread word of assistance for which they are indebted to me." [146] The comment is revealing; his openhandedness had had a purpose. Bodega entertained no illusions about the ease of maintaining Spanish dominion over the northwest coast, and he suspected that there was not a point between Cape Mendocino and 52° north latitude but had been visited by hyperactive American and British traders. English vessels outnumbered Spanish ships there in 1792 by three to one. Means had to be found to counteract the commercial success of foreign fur traders, or soon British subjects would be forming permanent outposts there. He conceived the northwest coast as strategically important to the defense of California and New Mexico. Preventing such settlements would be easier than eliminating them, once made. "If someday we should think to eject them from the ports beyond San Francisco, our efforts would be useless, and perhaps they would invade [Nootka] and other ports of New California, which I shall not be able to fortify at present." [147] Maintenance of a moderate sized squadron of armed warships would be exorbitantly expensive, yet fruitless, since such a force would be insufficient to defend such an extended coastline. The sole alternative was to drive foreign trading vessels from the area by making their traffic unprofitable. If Spanish subjects were allowed to trade freely for sea otter pelts, they would be in a position to pay better prices than other nationalities, since Mexico and California produced in quantity the trade articles most desired by Indians: copper, abalone shells, and cloth. The requirements of Spanish

146. Bodega to Revillagigedo, Monterey, October 24, 1792, MxAGN (Hist. 71), Ph in DLC; copy in Bodega, "Viaje," fol. 82, AT.

147. "La experiencia que he recibido me ha hecho ver que en el dia está expuesto nuestro Pabellón, pues los Buques de San Blás son los únicos que navegan con poca, ó ninguna Artillería, y todos juntos no componen la tercia parte de solo los Ingleses que surcan por aquí, y si algún día se pensase en desaloxarlos de los Puertos abanzado a S(a)n. Fran(cis)co. sería inútiles nuestros esfuerzos, y á caso podrían invadir este, y los demás de la nueva California, que Yo no podré fortificar á la presente." Bodega, "Viaje," fol. 28v, entry made in late August, at Nootka.

fur traders would in turn invigorate copper mining in Mexico, gathering of shells in Monterey, and textile manufacturing in Querétaro, Puebla, Cholula, and elsewhere, providing jobs for innumerable unemployed. By outbidding competitors, Spanish traders could reduce foreign profits to a point where the foreigners would cease frequenting the northwest coast. Spanish trading activities could be combined effectively with exploration, to reconnoiter unknown portions of the coast at little or no expense. To implement this plan, the department would need additional swift frigates. Such settlements as already existed should be fortified against the possibility of attack. Nootka's retention was important, since it was situated in the midst of areas yielding the most pelts and could serve as base from which smaller vessels would make trading cruises to Fuca, Clayoquot, the Queen Charlotte Islands, Bucareli Sound, and Port Mulgrave (Yakutat). Bodega suggested provisioning trading vessels at the California settlements, from whence pelts could be dispatched to Asia, "bringing back in exchange inexpensive yet excellent fabrics of that continent and silver which originally came from our mines and went to stagnate for so many centuries in coffers of the Chinese, Japanese, etc." [148] Bodega's good judgment has never been disputed; the fact that his suggestions differ little from those of Martínez in 1789 is a testimonial to the oft-maligned Sevillano's ingenuity.

The commandant's expectation of extending the sphere of Spanish activities beyond Nootka is also reflected in a conversation he had with Ingraham at Núñez Gaona; the latter relates that when he mentioned the excellent qualities of an inlet in the Queen Charlotte Islands, "Don Juan said as he supposed they would form a settlement there he would make a point of having Hancock's River examin'd for the purpose." [149] While his remark may have been uttered calculatedly, and may not have reflected a serious intent, the deed to Nootka that Bodega sought and secured from Ma-kwee-na after negotiations with Vancouver ground to a halt suggests that the commandant was preparing to hold the sound permanently, excepting the site of Meares's camp, which was useless to the British without possession of the entire cove.

Bodega's stay at Monterey was very productive cartographically. He compiled the results of all explorations to date and prepared a map indicating the areas still needing exploration. He suspected that all the land heretofore sighted between 50° and 60° north latitude was not really part of the continent, but a vast archipelago, and he drew up plans to explore the remaining area, using the *Concepción,* the *Activa,* and the *Orcasitas,* although he acknowledged that the necessary preparations would not permit carrying

148. Ibid., fol. 29–30, AT; these are concepts repeated in his letter to the viceroy of October 24, 1792.
149. Ingraham, "Log," p. 203.

this out until 1794.[150] The fact that Bodega contemplated sending Spanish explorers on missions far to the north of Nootka confirms that, pursuant to Madrid's latest directives, he now envisioned sustaining rather than withdrawing Spanish claims to the area north of the Strait of Juan de Fuca and hoped to promote Iberian fur trading activities far beyond Nootka.

Having decided upon a strategy for strengthening Spain's position upon the northwest coast, Bodega turned to examining means of making Alta California an asset rather than a drain upon the royal treasury. He foresaw with accuracy the importance that hides would have in its economy, and he suggested encouraging the traffic in pelts from California's abundant sea otters, bears, and sea lions, as well as fostering the cultivation of hemp. If a triangular trade with Nootka and the Orient were initiated, he predicted that the Alta California settlements would flourish richly within a few years, and attract in proportionate measure colonists needed to secure the region for Spain.[151]

When Vancouver entered San Francisco Bay, he was received with great courtesy by the presidio's commandant, for Bodega had ordered that if the Briton's vessels arrived there, they were to be supplied with every accommodation the small settlement had to offer. When the British commander proposed to pay for supplies provided, he was informed that Bodega's orders expressly prohibited taking a penny for anything the British vessels needed.[152]

Menzies describes San Francisco as an unpretentious, rectangular fort of adobe, with thatched huts around the inside of three walls, where the commandant, thirty-six soldiers, and their families lived. The presidio had no artillery of any kind, its defense being a squad of able cavalry. Some distance away was a small two- or three-pound cannon, installed on an eminence dominating the entrance to the bay—today's Golden Gate. The Spanish had taken considerable pains to keep foreigners from knowing how weakly defended the California settlements were. The valuable intelligence that Vancouver gathered about California ports amounted to espionage, from the Spanish point of view, but when the Englishmen reached Monterey, Don Juan received them as warmly as ever. Taking their cue from him, the townspeople entertained their British guests lavishly. Always the genial host, Bodega gave several parties in their honor, and the pleasant sojourn was enlivened by trips into the country, a grizzly bear hunt, and even a bullfight. On an excursion to Mission Carmelo, Menzies was impressed at the beautiful pastures "swarming" with herds of feeding cattle and horses. That evening Vancouver and his officers were invited to a fiesta at the governor's

150. Bodega, "Viaje," fol. 83v–84.
151. Ibid., fol. 85.
152. Menzies, *Journal*, November 1792 to December 1793, in *CHSQ* 2 (1924) : 269–84.

house. "It was to begin at seven," Menzies relates, "but the Ladies had such unusual preparations to make that they could not be got together till near ten." "Most of them had their Hair in long queues reaching down to their waist," he notes, and "even in this remote region they seemed most attached to the Spanish exhilarating dance the *Fandango,* a performance which requires no little elasticity of limbs as well as nimbleness of capers & gestures." "Wheeling about, changing sides & smacking with their fingers at every motion," the couples danced so close to each other and "with such wanton attitudes & motions, such leering looks, sparkling eyes & trembling limbs, as would decompose the gravity of a Stoic." At Vancouver's request, Menzies adds, the two Hawaiian women from the *Jenny* "exhibited their manner of singing and dancing, which did not appear to afford much entertainment to the Spanish Ladies, indeed I believe they thought this crude performance was introduced by way of ridiculing their favorite dance the Fandango, as they soon afterward departed." [153]

Broughton was allowed to accompany Bodega to San Blas, so as to proceed to London by way of Mexico City with important dispatches. Peter Puget replaced him as captain of the *Chatham.* One of Vancouver's letters was to an influential friend, Sir Evan Nepean, under secretary of state for home affairs, to be presented to the ministry in case his conduct fell under censure. Vancouver explained the particulars that had been "the cause of placing me in a very embarrassed situation respecting such of my transactions as have taken place at Nootka." He voiced his disappointment at arriving in Nootka to find that the *Daedalus* had failed to bring sufficiently detailed instructions regarding objectives to be pursued with the Spanish commissioner. Floridablanca's instructions were likewise too imprecise about what should be restored, and, as a consequence, Bodega would consent to recognize as legitimately British only "a small chasm in the rockey shores of the spacious Port of Nootka; *which chasm not a hundred yards in extent in any one direction* being the exact space which the house and brestwork of Mr. Mears occupied." In the absence of instructions, Vancouver said he had been forced to guess what expedient would prove least liable to censure, and that "there can be little doubt I should either [have] proved myself a most consumate fool or a traitor to have acceeded to any such cession without positive directions to that effect." Since Bodega had been unwilling to restore more than "that small pittence of rocks and sandy beach," Vancouver preferred to refuse any restitution at all until their respective courts could agree upon the exact terms of settlement.[154]

Bodega refused Vancouver's offer to pay for the many things supplied to the British warships at Monterey. Despite being at loggerheads over settle-

153. Ibid., p. 284.
154. Vancouver to Nepean, January 7, 1793, in *BCPAD Report, 1913* (1914) : 36–38.

ment of the Nootka question, the men parted as the warmest of personal friends when the *Activa* sailed for San Blas on January 13, 1793. The British vessels shortly afterward headed toward the Sandwich Islands, to spend the balance of the winter there before returning northward for further explorations on the northwest coast while awaiting new orders from London.

Bodega's recommendations from Monterey had reached San Blas aboard the *Santa Gertrudis* on November 13, and until they could be relayed to Mexico City, Revillagigedo had no means of knowing whether Spain still occupied Friendly Cove or not. The Viceroy had been obliged to comply with Madrid's order to retain Nootka, despite his own inclinations. He superimposed his views upon summaries to the ministry of the latest reports from Bodega. His digest of messages received in Mexico City on November 8 closes with an affirmation that, if word came that the *Santa Saturnina* had not reached Bodega in time to prevent abandonment of the Spanish settlement at Nootka, Bodega would be ordered "to return immediately to comply with the said Royal resolution of February 29th." The viceregal "extract" added, however, that Nootka should not be retained; it would be more convenient to have the dividing line drawn at Fuca, "and the English locating themselves at Nuca, there [would] remain a neutral space of thirty leagues intermediate, for in this manner a proximity between Spanish and English would be avoided, as well as the damage that would originate easily from frequent contact between vassals of the two powers." [155]

Shortly afterward, Bodega's reports from Monterey reached Mexico City, revealing that, far from having relinquished Nootka, he now looked toward strengthening Madrid's dominion there by encouraging Spanish participation in the fur trade. Although Bodega's ideas were consonant with the Aranda ministry's newly adopted stance, they met with scant enthusiasm in the viceregal place. Revillagigedo was opposed from the outset to Bodega's recommendations regarding the sea otter trade, for the same reasons that had led him to veto Martínez's project: the recent Chinese prohibition of such trade, the sinking prices to be obtained for prime pelts, and the risks involved, which would repel the merchants of Mexico City. Word had not yet reached Mexico about the repeal of the Chinese embargo. Although Bodega's suggestions coincided with those of Malaspina, Revillagigedo dismissed them with the excuse that when Martínez proposed similar measures in 1789, "confidential inquiry revealed the merchants of New Spain are little inclined to a business in which they would obtain no certain and known profit." Although Bodega claimed that Nootka was the best port on the northwest coast, the viceroy judged that "if our Crown tries to embrace

155. "Extracto de las noticias de nuestros expediciones al N. de Californias recividas en Mexico la noche del 8 de Noviembre de 1792. por cartas de los Comandantes de los Buques destinados á ellas," SpMN (575 bis), fol. 133–34, AT.

settlements that distant, the treasury will be burdened anew with swollen expenses, without obtaining the benefits that Quadra thinks, because the Port of Nuca is not as good as he states, to judge by the opinion of other practical and intelligent mariners." [156] The document, deceptively titled "News Lately Received," is clearly a draft of the policy that Revilla-gigedo had decided to push in regard to the northwest coast. He would obey, albeit reluctantly, the ministerial order to sustain Spanish claims to Nootka and prohibit trade there by other nationalities than the British, but in the interest of economy, Madrid's pretensions in the Pacific Northwest would be asserted in the minimal way necessitated by the royal order. He shunned a project for official participation in the fur trade for the benefit of the royal treasury, and brushed aside suggestions for a calculated program of encouraging the merchant class of Mexico to engage in such a trade by means of monopolies, privileges, tax exemptions, and other such devices. Instead, he suggested a hybrid scheme of his own devising, with elements drawn from previous plans. To diminish profits of foreign traders, he intended to have every vessel sailing for Nootka take along a quantity of copper plates, abalone shells, cheap cloth, and trinkets. While engaged in explorations, Spanish captains could collect a sufficient share of the annual yield of peltry to ruin the profits of foreigners.[157]

Revillagigedo's modest plan may have seemed promising in theory, but in practice—as, for example, was the case with Quimper in 1790—Spanish explorers were too preoccupied with exploration and cartography to offer British and American traders much competition. Spanish trading efforts scarcely made a dent in the supply and had little impact on foreign profits—and the yield to the royal treasury was far from sufficient to reimburse the cost of Spanish expeditions. The viceroy's project was designed to give an appearance of activity; it excused his not adopting more ambitious measures, but it was inadequate for achieving Madrid's principal political objective: making it unprofitable for foreign fur traders to frequent the northwest coast. By dragging his feet, Revillagigedo had annulled the plan drafted by Martínez, and elaborated upon by the Philippine Company, calling for a series of missions and presidios and a fleet of sloops to dominate the northwest coast fur trade. Now he undercut Bodega's strategy for enlisting Mexican merchants in that commerce. By failing to institute an effective policy that would give Spanish activities on the northwest coast a self-supporting basis and at the same time drive away foreign competitors, Revillagigedo contributed significantly to the ultimate exclusion of Spain from that area.

156. "Noticias que se han recibido ultimamente de Monterrey por la fragata 'Santa Gertrudis' a continuación de las que se dieron de Nutka 1792," ibid., fol. 112–12v, AT.

157. Revillagigedo to López de Lerena, Mexico City, November 26, 1790, T in CU–B cited by Ogden "The Californias" p. 466.

When Bodega returned to San Blas in the spring of 1793, the British effort to pry Spain from Nootka Sound appeared to have suffered a setback, and the trend of Iberian activities on the northwest coast seemed to be on the upswing. Few of those involved could have perceived that superficial aspects were deceptive; the outcome would depend on realities in Europe, not on the face of events in the Pacific Northwest.

FROM 1790 THROUGH 1792, Spanish warships and officialdom enjoyed hegemony over the northwest coast by dint of superior firepower and available military force, although they were usually numerically overmatched at any one site by English and American trading vessels. No foreign force, or combination of forces, challenged Spanish pretensions by following a course leading to a clash. Instead, all vessels seeking refuge within Nootka's confines paid deference to His Catholic Majesty's flag. In 1793, however, a noticeable ebb commenced in Spanish activities on the northwest coast which forecast the eventual retreat of that banner from the Pacific Northwest. The direction of the tide had been determined in Europe in 1790, but recession from the high water mark of floodtide was scarcely perceptible at first. By the summer of 1793 the retreat would gain velocity and become obvious to other nationalities jockeying for advantage on the northwest coast.

During the winter of 1792–93, Fidalgo employed his men in strengthening the fortification atop San Miguel Island. The legend on a chart that he prepared of the fort describes the barracks there as capable of housing thirty-five to forty men and as built so low as to be invisible from beyond the exterior walls, which were two yards high and equally wide. Care was taken to place the corridors and gun emplacements over a grill of logs and ditches so precipitation would drain away. To reduce fatalities in case of accidental explosion, the magazine was located on the opposite side of the island's rocky crest from the guns and barracks. Within the fort's confines was a small kitchen to prepare meals for those on duty. Ingraham's sketch of San Miguel in 1793 confirms the faithfulness of Fidalgo's chart. The care bestowed upon perfecting such defenses manifests Bodega's preparedness to retain Nootka, should his policy recommendations be adopted.

Despite experience gained in previous winters, the little settlement was again in dire circumstances by spring. When the *Chatham* arrived from Hawaii on April 15, Puget found Fidalgo and his men in deplorable health. "Two thirds of the Crew, of the *Princessa* was down with the Scurvy," Manby relates,

> several had died, and one was buried the Night previous to our arrival
> —For three Months scarce an hour was free from Rain—the attendant
> damps and bleak produced every malady, on the human frame, and
> destroyed the few Vegetables they had stored up during the Summer, in

short they were destitute, of nearly every thing that could possibly check the raging sickness.—The humidity of the atmosphere had destroyed their flour, bread they were quite deficient of and a greater mortification than all to a Spaniard was the total want of Tobacco—Fortunately our arrival in a small degree, tended to lull their wants, as it enabled us to supply them with Flour and pease and plenty of Tobacco. The Sick soon recover'd and every Spaniard with a grateful Heart, acknowledged us their deliverers, from the jaws of Death.[1]

In gratitude Fidalgo invited Puget and his officers to take up quarters in the main building and share his table while they remained in Friendly Cove. Puget accepted, as the *Chatham* needed careening. The staples that he contributed were a catalyst to friendly cooperation between the Spanish and English carpenters in accomplishing the work on the ship, despite the linguistic barrier. The translator could not be everywhere at once, and "when this Man is not at hand," Manby remarks, "curious scenes, repeatedly ensue as our Conversation is generally carried on, by a few words, of all Languages—& signs—altho' the 'Nootka Lingo,' forms the greatest part— some times, we understand each other—at other times not: The honest Don, slaps his forehead, shrugs his Shoulders, and exclaims: Diable[,] What a pity; what a misfortune . . . that so many Languages should prevail in this little World. This burle[s]qing the Planet." [2] Manby greatly regretted their not being able to speak the same tongue: "How gratifying would it prove at this moment. I could then converse with Don Fidalgo, An intelligent Man. A man of learning, science, and great abilities, his mouth would never open, but most likely, I should acquire knowledge." [3]

Such obviously sincere and candid portraits of individual Spaniards on the northwest coast, aside from the universally admired Bodega, are rare in the sources, and totally absent in the formal content prevailing in Spanish documents. Were it not for British and American logs, many of the most interesting details about life at Nootka during Spanish dominion would have been lost. Manby conveys some idea of the conviviality still prevailing between Spanish and English at Friendly Cove in 1793. Fidalgo's relations with the natives were less amiable. Upon assuming command his initial stance had been to reject fraternization with Ma-kwee-na and other chieftains—a reflection of the recent trouble with Ta-toosh—but a winter of tranquil coexistence softened this attitude. The settlement's dependence upon fish and game obtained from the natives probably contributed to the mending of former ties. Come spring, Ma-kwee-na once again took up resi-

1. Manby, "Journal," pt. 2, fol. 83–84.
2. Ibid., fol. 84–85.
3. Ibid., fol. 85.

dence at the village site northwest of town, directly on the ocean. He and
other chiefs resumed visiting Fidalgo, and as they seldom came empty-
handed, but always brought a newly killed deer or fresh salmon, they were
sure of a welcome. The degree of familiarity between mariners and natives
is revealed by a passage in Manby's journal:

> Canoes from the upper part of the Sound often attend us to the number
> of fifteen, or twenty at a time, each carrying four or five Indians the
> most part Women: We found the Ladies, very liberal, with their favors
> and by no means, so bashful, as in our last visit to Nootka. When di-
> vested of their abominable filth, they are by no means bad looking. I
> had once interest enough, with one, to prevail on her using Soap and
> hot Water, the alteration it occasioned was beyond conception, How-
> ever the fair one, found herself uncomfortable, in being clean'd of her
> filth and nastiness, and took the first opportunity to Equip in the
> fashion of the country, by smearing herself over with Grease, Train oil
> and red ocre, and decorating her Jetty locks, with the white down of sea
> fowl, Thus beautified, she again appeared, with the idea of fascinating,
> and could not be prevailed on to believe, that cleanliness, was the
> chief attraction, with us, which led admiration.[4]

Repairs on the *Chatham* were completed in less than a month, and Puget
departed northward several days before the *Discovery* arrived at Nootka on
May 20. Vancouver tarried briefly; and, encountering Puget several days out
of Nootka, he spent the summer with the *Chatham*'s captain exploring the
coastline north of Vancouver Island. By scant weeks they missed witnessing a
milestone in the exploration of the Far Northwest when Alexander Mackenzie, agent of the North West Company, became the first explorer to cross
the continent north of Spanish settlements. From central Canada he ascended the Peace River to the Continental Divide. After following due
south for a time the river that would later be called the Fraser, he concluded that it flowed into the Pacific too far south of Nootka, so he ascended
one of its western tributaries to the summit of the coastal range, and then
descended another stream until he reached an arm of the sea at Bella Coola.
One of the *Discovery*'s boats had been there just six weeks before. At the
western terminus of their odyssey, a point on Dean Channel, on a huge rock
he painted with a mixture of vermilion pigment and grease: "Alexander
Mackenzie, from Canada, by land, the twenty-second of July, one thousand
seven hundred and ninety-three." Disappointed at finding no means of con-
tacting his compatriots, Mackenzie returned eastward.[5]

4. Ibid., fol. 86.
5. Mark S. Wade, *Mackenzie of Canada* (Edinburgh and London, 1927), p. 197.

THE INQUEST INTO POLICY FOR THE NORTHWEST COAST

Revillagigedo's frugal inclinations made him anything but enthusiastic about retaining Nootka, much less over following Bodega's recommendation to expand activities on the northwest coast. The arrival in Mexico City of the officers of the *Sútil* and the *Mexicana* afforded the viceroy an opportunity to inquire into important questions confronting Spain in the Far North, but the questionnaire directed to them reveals that he sought confirmation of his opinions rather than unbiased views. For example, to aid him in deciding whether additional reconnaissance was necessary between 50° and 60° north latitude, the explorers were asked to designate which ports, entrances, and anchorages needed more detailed examination. But their answers were somewhat predetermined by Revillagigedo's declaration that "These repeated expeditions lead one to believe we have achieved as much nautical knowledge as is needed of those seas, about which I suppose you to be well informed, from having navigated them yourselves." [6] By asking negative questions on each point, he could expect replies that would justify overruling Bodega's plan for additional Spanish settlements on the northwest coast as a means of dominating the sea otter trade.

Despite the viceroy's patently negative attitude, Dionisio Alcalá Galiano and Juan Vernacci favored further Spanish explorations north of Fuca, insisting upon the need to examine every possible channel in still unexplored areas on the western fringe of North America, to settle once and for all the speculation as to whether any passageway existed between the Atlantic and the Pacific, while recognizing that such a channel existed, it would lie so far north as to offer little advantage over existing navigation routes. The only benefit from its disclosure would be the honor of making the discovery. Vancouver still persisted in the search, and Vernacci feared that his diligence "might well give them the glory, and we could not listen without covering ourselves with shame, if they should find the much desired passage to the other sea." [7] Cayetano Valdés and Secundino Salamanca opposed further explorations, judging that Vancouver's charts would fulfill the scientific need.

Although intensified competition had diminished profits in the sea otter trade, all four officers inferred that peltry must still be worthwhile, since so many captains returned season after season. The only peaceful means of combatting the foreign traffic would be to weaken it through competition. The Spanish controlled the source of abalone shells and had an adequate supply of copper sheets and woven cloth. Vernacci proposed that supply

6. Revillagigedo to Alcalá Galiano, Valdés, Vernacci, and Salamanca, Mexico City, March 2, 1793, MxAGN (Hist. 71), fol. 20–20v, AT.

7. Vernacci to Revillagigedo, Mexico City, March 5, 1793, MxAGN (Hist. 71), fol. 25–28v, AT.

ships for Alta California go directly to the northwest coast each year, search for the northwest passage until August, trading all the while, and then head for California ports. In such fashion, within two years a complete and accurate chart of the coastline could be completed.[8] Valdés advised an annual reconnoitering of the coast between Fuca and San Francisco Bay, visiting every port and anchorage, so as to note the proximity of any foreign threat and assess the risk from such incursions.[9]

Salamanca thought the sea otter trade "would continue to attract men to those coasts for many years; this alone should not be feared if the foreigners would limit themselves to exploiting an aspect which we neglect and to affirming chimerical pretensions over a portion of land which we cannot guard, possess, or even survey, separated from our territory by an invincible barrier of many leagues of rivers and impenetrable wilds." Nevertheless, he believed that Spain should take steps to prevent the peltry from serving as an excuse for foreign vessels to frequent and survey the coastline closer to California settlements; he warned of the risk that foreign officers might develop practical experience "which might be directed against us in the interests of their own nation." Even with Spain's advantage in the Manila route, Salamanca doubted whether the merchants of Mexico could ever get their costs down to the level reached by foreigners, who did it "at the cost of hard work, and exposing their crews to illness and evident risks, and at the expense of repeated violence and injustices to the miserable savages." [10]

Another opinion voiced at this juncture was that of ensign Félix de Cepeda, Bodega's assistant in 1792. His report, transmitted to the viceroy and ministry, advised against maintaining any settlement north of San Francisco. He thought permitting foreign settlements there was preferable to making great expenditures to occupy the entire coastline and risk a quarrel with Britain. He interpreted the convention to mean that any new Spanish settlement founded north of San Francisco would automatically become a port of free access to the English. "What advantage," he demanded, "can we hope for in establishments of that kind?" Instead, all ideas for expeditions, bases, or activities on the northwest coast should be abandoned.[11]

Revillagigedo probably was also influenced by Moziño's detailed and well-conceived arguments. A manuscript of *Noticias de Nutka* is among the viceroy's personal papers.[12] Moziño judged Nootka to be of no advantage to Spain, yet exorbitantly expensive. The Spanish carried on an insignificant

8. Alcalá Galiano to Revillagigedo, Mexico City, March 5, 1793, MxAGN (Hist. 71), fol. 21–24.
9. Valdés to Revillagigedo, Mexico City, March 6, 1793, MxAGN (Hist. 71), fol. 29–32.
10. Salamanca to Revillagigedo, Mexico City, March 6, 1793, MxAGN (Hist. 71), fol. 33–37, AT.
11. "Noticias y apuntamientos," fol. 362–64v, AT. Cepeda's original report is known only through this extract.
12. Revillagigedo Papers (Robbins Collection), CU–B.

commerce in furs at Friendly Cove, which produced fewer pelts than were taken from many other localities at some distance. Profits in the fur trade were not dependent upon dominion over Nootka, as proven by American trading activities. Mexico and California did not enjoy greater security because of Spanish control over Friendly Cove. Two hundred leagues of unoccupied territory between there and San Francisco offered ample opportunity for any enemy to undertake an invasion of Spanish territory. Circumstances prevented fortifying Nootka to resist any concerted attack, for the settlement would require a garrison of at least battalion strength. Judging from recent experience, this would cost nearly a million pesos annually for the four or five years needed to clear forests and raise crops necessary for its maintenance. Even if the Spanish succeeded in taking over the fur trade entirely, profits probably would be insufficient to maintain the warships and supply vessels and the 6,000 to 8,000 men needed to dominate the extended coastline.[13]

In Moziño's opinion, California should be the first object of Spain's attention, as it offered greater hopes of being of some advantage to the nation. San Francisco was the best port on the Pacific coast of North America. Climate and fertility made California far more important than the Nootka area. San Francisco had but fifteen soldiers to defend it, Monterey scarcely twice that number, and either might be readily taken over by Spain's enemies. Spreading Spanish military strength along the northwest coast in small garrisons would merely weaken the nation's power. "Not only Nutka," Moziño declared, "but all those posts of the north ought to be abandoned to protect California," which would pay for its own expenses if properly developed. In the fur trade competition he recognized Spain's natural advantages, and he suggested further that the trade should be carried on in vessels purchased in China, where they could be acquired for less, and manned by Chinese seamen, who demanded smaller salaries. As Spanish trading vessels augmented in numbers, other nationalities would be excluded. Spanish subjects would benefit from the profits of the fur trade, and Spain's possessions along the Pacific coast would be secured and would thrive from the ensuing traffic.[14]

13. Moziño, *Noticias*, pp. 90–93.

14. Ibid., pp. 94–97. Moziño never saw his treatise on Nootka receive official recognition. In 1803, the year it appeared in a Guatemalan gazette, he emigrated to Madrid, finding use for his talents as a member of the supreme junta of sanitation. After the Napoleonic occupation (1808) he was appointed director of the Royal Cabinet of Natural History and professor of zoology, but when patriots reoccupied Madrid (1812) he was arrested. Set free after a time, he took exile in France, leaving behind the results of years of scientific labor. Permitted to return in 1817, he spent his remaining years in obscurity in Barcelona, dying there in 1820. Iris Higbie Wilson, "Scientific Aspects of Spanish Exploration in New Spain During the Late Eighteenth Century" (Master's thesis, University of Southern California, 1962), pp. 271–84, 281–82, 287.

Most of the opinions available to the viceroy (excepting that of Bodega) reinforced his convictions about the doubtful utility of further Spanish explorations and settlements on the northwest coast. All those questioned were dubious of achieving a favorable balance in the sea otter trade after discounting the cost of retaining Nootka, although most saw participation in that traffic as the sole means of discouraging foreigners from frequenting that coastline. If they did not sway Revillagigedo toward what was already his inclination, they led him to feel justified in advising major changes in Madrid's policy for the northwest coast, modifications in a direction contrary to that of the most recent orders from the conde de Aranda.

The aged prime minister's eight-month tenure in office came to a sudden close in November 1792, as a consequence of the deteriorating situation in France. Upon receiving word of Aranda's replacement by Godoy, Revillagigedo composed a lengthy memorial for the edification of his new superior. It shows the viceroy's rationale for what he had done and would henceforth recommend regarding Spanish aspirations in the Pacific Northwest. In it he summarized the explorations northward from San Blas between 1769 and 1792, offered his personal opinions on decisions made by his predecessors with respect to that coastline, and commented on the conduct of Martínez in 1789 and upon recommendations made by Martínez, Bodega, and others for the northwest coast. Most importantly, the missive set forth his own deliberations and suggested modifications in policy toward the northern perimeter of Spanish domains in America. His chief concern since assuming office and the principal object of his attention, Revillagigedo declared, had been the measures to be taken with regard to the northwest coast, where there existed a delicate and dangerous situation inherited from his predecessor. The costly and profitless explorations and supply ships needed to sustain Nootka particularly mortified him. He regarded with dismay the prospect of continued or enlarged operations in that area. "From now on a halt should be called to all projects obliging us to make great expenditures, even though recommended with the greatest certainty as promising advantageous results, for these are always understood as for some time in the future, whereas it has to come from a treasury which, pressed by urgent requirements, is being burdened by considerable debts. Once its funds are exhausted, and those of the moneylenders, those projects will be unsustainable, their advantages will evaporate, it will be difficult to recoup expenses made, and it may perhaps become necessary to continue others even greater, with the almost certain risk that they would be fruitless." [15]

Revillagigedo acknowledged that Spain could no longer pretend to absolute possession of the Pacific coast of North America. He lacked the forces, ships, and funds to uproot Russian settlements in the north, and he feared

15. Revillagigedo to Godoy, April 12, 1793, in Cavo and Bustamante, *Tres Siglos*, 3 : 147, AT.

that the Muscovites might soon attempt to establish outposts closer to Nootka. As for Britain's motives in the Nootka controversy and her demanding a right to settle anywhere north of San Francisco Bay, he was convinced that there was a conspiracy to penetrate the Pacific with illicit commerce and partake of commercial opportunities in the trade between New Spain and the Orient. Possession of Nootka had been worse than useless because of the expenses incurred. In the future it would be still more costly, and perhaps even cause trouble with Britain. For this reason it should be ceded entirely, which would satisfy what the English were determined to make a point of honor.[16]

In essence, the viceroy's long missive was an assemblage of arguments for reversing the royal order (February 29, 1792) specifying Nootka's retention. As an alternative, Revillagigedo reaffirmed his plan for setting up a boundary from the mouth of Fuca to 60° north latitude. He suggested one more expedition to the far north in 1794 in search of a northwest passage, if its nonexistence still remained unproven. Beyond that, he announced suspension of explorations at high latitudes, believing it more important to examine the coastline from 48° southward, in order to ward off English attempts to carry out their designs upon the area closer to San Francisco. He intended to improve the defenses of San Francisco, Monterey, and San Diego, and he expected to occupy and make a defensible establishment at Bodega Bay and also, if it became necessary, at the mouth of the Columbia. He also stressed the importance of exploring that great river to its source.[17]

Revillagigedo repeated for Godoy's benefit his previous disparagement of Spanish participation in the fur trade. Intensified competition by so many vessels had made the supply of pelts diminish to the point where each season would be decreasingly lucrative. The Indians were becoming more astute, audacious, and bellicose as a result of contact with unscrupulous traders, and this made trading cruises highly dangerous ventures. Spanish subjects should be allowed to compete in the traffic, although he doubted any would do so, because of opportunities of getting a greater return, with less risk, from investments in mines and placer beds of New Spain.[18] Although Revillagigedo had been voicing some of these opinions ever since assuming office in 1789, this report signifies a watershed—a decisive reorientation in his objectives. Henceforth the concentration would be upon exploring and protecting territory from Fuca southward; Bodega's plans for strengthening Spanish control over Nootka and cornering the fur trade along the coast beyond were overruled.

Revillagigedo never shared Gálvez's vision of a new Spanish realm in

16. Ibid., pp. 150, 161.
17. Ibid., pp. 134–35, 144–48, 152.
18. Ibid., p. 149.

western North America stretching to the Arctic. In his opinion, the ambition to extend Spanish dominion over the coastline beyond California had proven illusory, exorbitantly costly, and infeasible. From Godoy's perspective Revillagigedo's reasoning seemed impeccable, and the long memorial doubtless had a profound effect upon the ministry's subsequent attitude toward the northwest coast. Concern in Madrid and Mexico City for claims over Nootka was supplanted by suspicion of British designs upon Alta California. Nootka Sound and everything north of Fuca was written off as a loss.

### THE ACTIVA AND THE MEXICANA ON THE WASHINGTON-OREGON COAST

The impasse between Bodega and Vancouver, together with the supposed threat to Alta California, obliged Revillagigedo to send out further expeditions in 1793, directed henceforth toward the area between Fuca and San Francisco Bay. The garrison at Nootka also had to be maintained until a satisfactory boundary settlement with Britain could be reached. It was decided that the commandant at Nootka should be relieved every year. Thus, Ramón Saavedra and the *San Carlos* were sent to replace Fidalgo and the *Princesa*.[19]

There was every indication that the Pitt ministry interpreted the convention to mean that British subjects had a right to settle at any unoccupied spot north of San Francisco. To counteract such moves, it was important to have accurate cartographical information about the coastline south of Fuca. The task of gathering it had been entrusted to Torres and the *Santa Gertrudis* in 1792, but with little result. Previous Spanish explorers, in their concern over the fjords of British Columbia and Alaska, had given only slight attention to the shores of the present states of Oregon and Washington. Vessels from San Blas had habitually headed straight for high latitudes and, pressed by a perennial shortage of rations, had hurried to Alta California on the return journey. Bad weather or adverse currents had discouraged several Spanish attempts to investigate the estuary sighted by Hezeta in 1775, and they had possessed no knowledge whatsoever of the hinterland to which the great river gave access until Broughton's reconnaissance in 1792.

The expedition that Revillagigedo sent northward in the spring of 1793 was for the particular purpose of exploring the coastline from Fuca southward. He knew that Gray and Broughton had entered the Columbia, and he was desirous of learning more about the area where the great river had its source. As he had informed Godoy, he now contemplated the eventual establishment of an Iberian settlement near the strategic estuary's mouth.[20]

---

19. The *San Carlos* left San Blas on March 23, 1793, and arrived in Nootka on May 9; the *Princesa* sailed for New Spain on June 9. *Compendio Histórico*, pp. 82–83.

20. The viceregal order, of March 17, 1793, is cited by Revillagigedo to Godoy, April 12, 1793, p. 148.

Francisco de Eliza—he of the lethargic meandering about Fuca's interior in 1791—was given command of the *Activa*, which left San Blas on April 30, accompanied by Juan Martínez y Zayas with the *Mexicana*. Many weeks of adverse winds and a water shortage were Eliza's excuses for turning southward when he was midway up the present Oregon coast, and he accomplished next to nothing. The *Mexicana* had awaited the flagship off the extinct settlement at Neah Bay until August. When Eliza failed to appear, Martínez y Zayas was obliged to attempt to accomplish alone the objectives of their mission. From Cape Flattery southward he explored carefully. He examined Gray's Harbor, crossed the Columbia's dangerous bar, and penetrated the silt-laden estuary some fourteen miles before running aground. The difficulties of navigation and the menace of war canoes hovering nearby eventually persuaded him to turn seaward. Because of its dangerous entrance and sizable populations of seemingly unfriendly Indians, the estuary did not appear to be a likely spot for a Spanish base.[21]

Every protected anchorage between Fuca and San Francisco was a potential toehold for foreign encroachments. Some forty miles north of the Golden Gate, dagger-like Puerto de la Bodega (today's Tomales Bay) presented the most immediate danger. Since its discovery by Bodega and the *Sonora* in 1775, the long, narrow inlet had been reputed to be the best anchorage within a hundred leagues of San Francisco; but it had been neglected in favor of securing control over harbors much farther north. Colnett's brief sojourn thereabouts in 1790, on the way northward after his release, gave rise to a rumor in Alta California that the English were frequenting the place. Bodega had heard this from some Indians during his stay in Monterey and considered it unlikely, but from his conversations with Vancouver he feared that Britain entertained a special interest in possessing a port close to the northernmost Alta California settlement. It was important to block any English move to occupy the strategic inlet, and Bodega's plans for such an endeavor seem to have gotten underway in February 1793, a month before Revillagigedo gave the order for its colonization.[22]

In command of the effort was Juan Bautista Matute, with the *Sútil*. The *Aranzazú* would follow latter with troops and artisans. If Matute encountered the British in possession of the site, he was instructed not to use force but to make the proper protest and give an immediate and full report to his superiors. The governor of California was ordered to provide the necessary assistance. Supplies were to be sent overland from San Francisco Bay. On May 26 Matute's schooner anchored off the tidewater inlet today

21. Juan Martínez y Zayas, "Viage a la costa comprehendido entre la boca sur de Fuca, y el Puerto de San Francisco . . . 1793," trans. in H. R. Wagner, "The Last Spanish Exploration of the Northwest Coast and the Attempt to Colonize Bodega Bay," *CHSQ* 10 (1931) : 321–33.

22. Revillagigedo to Bodega, March 17, 1793, MxAGN (Hist. 71), Ph in DLC; "Reconocimiento del Puerto de la Bodega for el Teniente de Fragata D. Juan Bautista Matute," SpMN (575 bis), no. 9.

called Bodega Bay, several miles beyond the opening discovered in 1775. Reconnaissance disclosed a number of tree stumps (probably left by Colnett's men in 1790), which persuaded Matute that foreigners had been there in the not too distant past. His examination of Puerto de la Bodega revealed its entrance to be so shallow as to prevent entry of vessels of more than fifteen feet in draft. With a northwest wind, breakers across the bar became extremely hazardous. When the *Aranzazú* arrived, it dared not enter, so Matute ordered the frigate's men and armaments disembarked within San Francisco Bay and sent to him overland. They ran into many difficulties which hindered construction of a settlement. Matute's own ill health seems to have been the prime reason, however, for discontinuing the work. When the *Activa* arrived there on August 9 after Eliza's failure to reach Fuca, Matute embarked his men aboard the *Sútil* and followed the brigantine to San Francisco. Their objective had not been renounced entirely. Arriving in San Blas on November 4, Matute remitted to Revillagigedo a new plan for accomplishing the purpose; this plan called for two schooners of shallow draft, a large launch, sailors, a troop of cavalry, five skilled carpenters, and fifty mules with which to establish an overland supply route. He suggested that two missions be founded near Bodega Bay, to aid in bringing the area under Spanish dominion.[23] This ambitious and expensive project was never put into action, for by then the tumultuous course of events in Europe had brought about a radical shift of alliances, mitigating fear of British designs —the prime motive for Matute's activities.

Word of such developments took many months to reach California and the northwest coast, where suspicions of Vancouver's intentions were mounting. Following replacement by Saavedra as commandant of Nootka, Fidalgo wrote Revillagigedo from San Francisco to warn of the danger from weaponry aboard Vancouver's warships, and to relay rumors that the English commander might attack Monterey or San Diego.[24]

Vancouver called at the Nootka settlement in October, on his way southward after a fruitful season of explorations. The *San Carlos*, the only vessel there, was laid up for the winter, and Commander Saavedra was residing ashore. Puget was sent to reconnoiter Bodega Bay, while the *Discovery* proceeded directly to San Francisco. To Vancouver's considerable surprise, upon anchoring in front of the presidio he encountered a much less cordial reception than he had found in 1792. Several weeks previously Governor Arrillaga had received orders, relayed to every presidio along the coast, to be on guard in case any British vessels arrived.[25] Only Vancouver and two of

23. "Resultas del viaje en las goletas *Activa* y *Mejicana,* al mando del teniente de navío don Francisco Eliza, en el reconocimiento de la costa de California desde los 41° a 47° de latitud y boca del rio La Columbia," 1793, SpMN (331), fol. 282; Ybarra, *De California á Alaska,* pp. 162–64.

24. Fidalgo to Revillagigedo, Puerto de San Francisco, July 20, 1793, SpAHN (Estado 4290).

25. Arrillaga to presidio commandants of the Californias, Monterey, September 23, 1793. For a calendar and résumé of this and other manuscripts in SpAGI (Sec. V) resulting from Van-

his officers were allowed ashore; he was refused permission to erect tents or shelters, and watering parties could land only under the eyes of a Spanish guard. Nor was Vancouver's request to ride to Mission San Francisco granted. Menzies noted eight cannons on the beach, and he saw laborers leveling a terrace overlooking the bay's mouth, presumably for a battery, "and a more suitable situation could not be fixed on, as it perfectly commanded the entrance." [26]

Vancouver subsequently visited Arrillaga in Monterey, and although the governor gave him some domestic animals, the reception was again cool. Despite his manifest suspicion, Arrillaga provided the Britons with needed supplies free of charge—a token, they were told, of the friendship existing between Spain and England. Vancouver's funds were practically exhausted after several years without additional support from England, but he insisted upon giving a personal note in payment for values received. Arrillaga's report of Vancouver's visit indicated that the Spaniard had ordered all the presidio commanders to give only such aid to their English visitors as was absolutely necessary.[27]

The British commander assumed that Arrillaga's hostile attitude derived from personal prejudices, imposed on his subordinates, rather than from official policy emanating from the viceroy. Local officials elsewhere displayed no undue signs of suspicion or unfriendliness. At San Diego the British seamen roamed the settlement and entered the presidio without restriction, sightseeing and procuring riding horses. Only when the Spanish commandant noted that his own men were outnumbered was it stipulated that they were "to take their walk any other way as it was against his orders to admit so many into the Presidio." Thereafter Vancouver forbade anyone but officers from going as far as the fort.[28] There was justification for looking upon the Englishman's scientific investigations as a genteel excuse for what amounted to espionage, as he specifically sought information about ports, anchorages, numbers of ships, and the strength of Spain's tiny garrisons. Worried warnings circulated to and fro, and there was much speculation about British designs. To Vancouver's disappointment, new instructions still had not arrived from London about the settlement to be sought with the Spanish commissioner for Nootka. Therefore, having tarried as long as he dared in California waters without invoking Spanish restrictions, he set sail for the Sandwich Islands and his customary wintering place.

---

couver's visit, see Charles E. Chapman, *Catalogue of Materials in the Archivo General de Indias for the History of the Pacific Coast and the American Southwest* (Berkeley, 1919), pp. 661–62.

26. Menzies, *Journal*, pp. 305–07.
27. Chapman, *Catalogue*.
28. Menzies, *Journal*, pp. 316–17, 335.

EUROPEAN TURMOIL AND THE SECOND NOOTKA CONVENTION, 1793

The execution of Louis XVI and Marie Antoinette (January 21 and October 16, 1793) and the Reign of Terror (1793–94) had profound repercussions south of the Pyrenees and across the English Channel. When French radicals declared war against Britain in February 1793, and against Spain the following month, the erstwhile enemies found themselves united by a common cause. Negotiations for an Anglo-Spanish alliance began just four days after Louis went to the guillotine, and the formal signing took place four months later. Fear and disgust over Parisian excesses brought the traditional rivals toward an adjustment of outstanding differences. One consequence was to open Spanish Louisiana to British trade. Incensed at the alliance, the French Republic sent Citizen Edmund Gênet as minister to the United States, still formally allied with Paris, in the expectation of organizing an American effort to strike at Spanish settlements in Florida and Louisiana. The notorious consequences of Gênet's machinations created an atmosphere of distrust between Spain and the United States that eventually reached Spanish officials and American fur traders in the Pacific northwest. It was against this altered backdrop of alliances and enmities that subsequent negotiations between London and Madrid over Nootka took place. Motives for amicable relations accelerated the pace at which the differences that had plagued Bodega and Vancouver were settled.

Following presentation of Meares's Memorial to Parliament in April 1790, the sum that the English trader claimed in indemnity ballooned along with the international crisis. The initial claim was for 653,433 Spanish dollars, but within six months the bill stood at £469,865 (roughly two and a quarter million dollars)—a fourfold increase.[29] Meares arrived at this elevated sum by estimating a yield in sea otter skins greater than any that a trading vessel had ever collected on the northwest coast—over six times what his own vessels had gathered in 1788—and assigned each pelt a value far above that received even for prime skins in China. For many months the Spanish consul in London (Manuel de las Heras) dickered with the British commissioner (Sir Ralph Woodford) before reaching an agreement on the sum to be paid Meares's firm. Some idea of Pitt's technique in pushing his terms is obtained from the Spanish ambassador's report to Madrid:

> During all the course of conferences between commissioners Las Heras and Woodford relative to indemnification over Nootka Sound, these people have proceeded so vexatiously and precipitately, since it is such

29. "A Recapitulation and General Account of the Losses and Damages Sworn to Have Been Sustained by the United Company of British Merchants Trading to the North West Coast of America," London, September 7, 1790, UKLPRO (F. O. Miscel. 5, App. 9), in "Papers Relating to Nootka Sound," *BCPAD Report 1913* (1914) : 35.

a notorious wrong and injustice, that it was almost a scandal. Without allowing an hour of time to examine any point, they harassed and forced the said Spanish consul to respond at once in writing to their specious demands, which they had made up among themselves at their whim. And to excuse as far as possible such a strange procedure they posed as being compelled to do so by the phantom (used here all the time) *that the public, the Parliament, and commercial circles of London* were resentful over the delay and it was urgent to quiet them.[30]

A second Nootka Convention was signed at the British Foreign Office on February 12, 1793, by which Spain agreed to pay for lands, ships, and cargoes seized at Nootka to the sum of 210,000 Spanish dollars.[31] Meares's preposterously padded claim probably was recognized as such by Whitehall, as the indemnification finally required of Madrid cannot be regarded as excessive, if it be conceded that Martínez was unjustified in arresting the ships in question. In Spanish eyes this was not the case, however, and the payment was considered an extortion exacted under duress in 1790, as the sole means of avoiding war. This second convention had no direct connection with the dispute between Bodega and Vancouver over a restitution at Nootka. Word of their inability to reach an accord took several more months to reach Madrid and London. Differences on that score still remained to be negotiated, and promised to be considerably more thorny than the indemnifications.

THE DIPLOMATIC CLIMATE OF THE THIRD NOOTKA CONVENTION, 1794

An Anglo-Spanish alliance was in total contrast to past relations between the rival empires; it grew out of the common sentiment that impelled Holland, Austria, and Prussia to join the First Coalition against revolutionary France. The unnatural embrace between Madrid and London would be brief, but it prompted peaceful adjustment of grave issues arising from ambiguities in the Convention of 1790. Confronted with the dire trend of events beyond the Pyrenees, Carlos IV and his ministers deemed the formation of defensive alliances to be more important than the defense of national honor or claims over far-off regions of dubious economic value.

The remaining points of difference as to which nation possessed a more

---

30. Bernardo Marqués del Campo to the conde de Aranda, London, November 2, 1792, Spain, Archivo de Simancas (Estado 8148), vol. 13; cited by Angel Santos, S.J., *Jesuitas en el Polo Norte: La Misión de Alaska* (Madrid, 1943), p. 75.

31. "Convención entre sus Majestades católica y británica para arreglar definitivamente la restitución de los buques británicos apresados en Nootka: concluida y firmada en Whitehall el 12 de febrero de 1793," in Alejandro del Cantillo, ed. *Tratados, convenciones y declaraciones de paz y comercio que han hecho con las potencias estranjeras los monarcas españoles de la casa de Borbón* (Madrid, 1843), p. 646; English trans. in Manning, "Nootka Sound Controversy," pp. 467–68. See appendix B for the text in Spanish.

solid title to Nootka could be resolved following arrival of Revillagigedo's long missive of April 12, 1793, advising Godoy of the futility of retaining Friendly Cove. Moreover, Whitehall no longer looked upon Nootka with the fervor of 1790; a foreign office memorandum set the stance which London would henceforth take. "Vancouver was very naturally induced from the Nature of his instructions and a Recollection of the original Ground of Quarrel to hesitate and ultimately to decline closing the transaction on the terms suggested by the Spanish Commandant," the memorialist recognized. "I regret however that it was not closed on those terms," he continued,

> for we would have been in Possession and under those Circumstances would have been on a better footing for Negotiating at home, than when the Spaniards are in possession, and when they may feel a point of honour not to depart from the Ground assumed by their Commandant. All that We really are anxious about in this particular part of the Business is the safety of our National honour which renders *a Restitution* necessary. The extent of that *Restitution* is not of much moment, and in truth the only Evidence to which either Party can resort, will justify the claim of either side. The true state of the fact appears to be that Mears never was in possession of more than the Hut where the tent now stands in the Drawing made by Mr. Humphrys, and therefore in a narrow and literal sense Restitution is complied with by restoring that spot. But we are justified in maintaining that the transaction cannot admit of so narrow a Construction, the Place being so small as not to admit of a divided Property. I think this last Circumstance may afford a good way of terminating the Dispute for instead of insisting *solely* upon our Right let us mix with it in our statement the obvious inconvenience of a Division, and by negotiating upon it in that Manner, I daresay Lord St Helens will find no great difficulty in persuading the Spanish Minister to make the Concession absolute which the Spanish Commandant at Nootka did not think himself at liberty to do. The use of the Harbour must of course remain common to both Parties.[32]

The observations served as a basis for instructions to Alleyne Fitzherbert, now Baron St. Helens and ambassador to Spain, to approach Godoy with a modified offer for resolving the remaining issues over the northwest coast. Britain's honor would be satisfied if Spain restored Meares's tract, however small, and yielded claims to exclusive sovereignty over lands *immediately adjacent,* the lack of which made restitution worthless.[33] Such terms, however, would be a major concession for Madrid. To maneuver Godoy to the

32. Memorandum, n.d., UKLPRO (F. O.), in "Papers Relating to Nootka Sound," *BCPAD Report, 1913* (1914): 38–39.

33. Grenville to St. Helens, August 9, 1793, copy in CaBViPA, cited by Mills, "Nootka Sound Incident," p. 122.

point of yielding, how logical to employ the envoy so successful in 1790! St. Helens's proposal for a third convention recognized that the first Nootka Convention did not give Britain

> any right to sovereignty or exclusive possession of all that Port, but on the other hand neither does it seem just that restitution be limited to the small space of land occupied by Mr. Meares and his companions, and that Sovereignty and possession of the remainder of the port be left for Spain; above all, it should be considered that when that tract was occupied, the neighboring lands (of which the English always have pretended they were the first purchasers) were not in possession of the Spanish, who only acquired them after the necessary withdrawal of the former; so that if restitution is limited to the small corner in question, its use would be null; and consequently the value would be so inferior to that which it held when the English enjoyed free access to adjacent lands, restitution along boundaries pretended by the Spanish official could not be looked upon as fulfilling in good faith obligations contracted in said Convention.[34]

St. Helens discounted the importance of Nootka, in view of the revelation that it was not on the mainland of North America, and suggested that, to settle the dispute, new orders be given to officials on both sides stating in substance that His Catholic Majesty would restore tracts of land of which British subjects were dispossessed,

> without any mention, in the Declaration to this end, of any reservations about rights of the Spanish Crown or any fixing of boundaries; and that the British official will accept that restitution as complete and satisfactory by a Counter-Declaration on his part; and that he, according to procedure, will hoist the British flag on the site which Mr. Meares once occupied. Afterward the two officials will withdraw their respective nationals from said port, which will be open in the future to subjects of both crowns to put in there and construct temporary edifices for use during their stay but without either nation being able to make a permanent establishment or claim any territorial sovereignty to exclusion of the other.[35]

Although this proposal required an unpalatable renunciation of Spain's claim to exclusive sovereignty over the area not included in Meares's tract, it seemed to tie British hands with regard to future settlements there. Since Revillagigedo had recommended ceding Nootka, an accord was soon reached

---

34. [St. Helens to Godoy, September 1793], SpAHN (Estado 4291 bis), AT; author and date are established from citations in another letter to Godoy of December 29, 1793, in the same *legajo*.
35. Ibid.

over the text of a "Convention for the Mutual Abandonment of Nootka," signed on January 11, 1794.[36] That it differed little from St. Helens's proposal is no surprise, considering Godoy's engrossment during those months with countering the French invasion of Spain's northern provinces, an experience whose horrors were to be burned into Iberian memory for all time by Goya's *Disasters of War*.

Godoy turned to securing through diplomacy what had proven too costly and ineffective to secure by means of maritime expeditions. The Spanish ambassador in St. Petersburg was instructed to seek a treaty of commerce entailing a boundary settlement on the northwest coast that would circumscribe British activities there. Ambassador José de Onís's reply was that anti-French sentiment in Russia made for more friendly relations with Britain, and "this matter cannot be fulfilled with the same facility, now that this court has seriously contemplated uniting with that of London."[37] Godoy's hope of thwarting Pitt through a boundary agreement with Catherine came to nothing.

### ISOLATION OF THE NOOTKA SETTLEMENT

The turmoil in Europe produced not a ripple at Nootka, where the scene was altered only by the change of seasons. Life at the Spanish base was quickened solely by occasional visits from foreign trading vessels and perennial contact with the aborigines, whose life style was inevitably altered by the introduction of firearms, sails, knives, and other elements of European culture. Despite the varied temptations to which his subjects were exposed, Makwee-na managed to keep at peace with the white man as long as the Spanish remained at Nootka, although the loss of his traditional summer residence at Yuquot disturbed tribal economy. He complained to visitors of other nationalities that being dislodged from Friendly Cove kept him from dwelling close to his customary fishing grounds. The reorientation of masculine activities from fishing to procuring sea otter pelts for barter curtailed normal provision of food. As a result, the winter of 1793–94 witnessed great hardship among the natives. Whether from a poor fishing season, or improvidence in laying in an adequate supply of dried fish and whale oil, before spring arrived the specter of famine stalked the Indian villages. "Had not Senr. Saavedra administered to their relief, many of them would probably have fallen a sacrifice to the scarcity," Vancouver relates, "and although

36. "Acuerdo ó convenio entre España é Inglaterra para la ejecución del artículo 1.° de la convención de 28 de octubre de 1790; firmado en Madrid el 11 de enero de 1794," in Cantillo, *Tratados*, pp. 653–54; English trans. in Manning, "Nootka Sound Controversy," pp. 469–70. See appendix B for the text in Spanish.

37. Onís to the ministry, St. Petersburg, March 31, 1795, SpAHN (Estado 4669), cited by Mario Hernández y Sánchez-Barba, "Españoles, Rusos e Ingleses en el Pacífico Norte, durante el siglo XVIII," *Información jurídica* 121 (Madrid, 1953): 554, AT.

the provident care he had taken was inadequate to all that was demanded of him, yet the assistance he had been able to afford them, was, much to the credit of the natives, acknowledged by them with the most grateful expressions."[38]

In May a three-day hurricane-like storm hit the northwest coast. The great wind was reported by trading vessels as far south as the Columbia River. At Friendly Cove enormous trees were uprooted, and a furious surf rocked ships anchored there until their yardarms touched the waves. The natives proclaimed it the worst windstorm ever known.[39]

The *Aranzazú* made two round trips to the northwest coast in 1794. José Tovar y Tamáriz brought the annual quota of supplies from San Blas early in the spring, and then, probably because of the extreme shortage due to the Indian famine, he sailed for Monterey to bring back additional provisions. In Monterey command of the frigate devolved upon Juan Kendrick. Fray Magín Catalá, one of the Franciscan chaplains at Nootka, who had accompanied Tovar to Monterey, was unable to return, and Kendrick refused to start northward until another priest was named in replacement, an incident interpreted as evidence of Kendrick's solicitude for the Indians and of the sincerity with which he embraced the religion of the monarch he now served.[40] The details of events on the northwest coast in the remaining months before Spain retreated from Nootka are scanty and derive mostly from non-Spanish sources. There is a dearth of logs and reports from the mariners and priests involved, and many questions remain unanswered.

Iberian participation in the sea otter traffic never got into high gear, despite several tentative starts. To encourage Spanish subjects, and "in order that foreigners may not profit so easily," in February 1794 a special decree removed all duties previously levied on pelts exported from Spanish ports to the Orient.[41] Since this reversal of policy contrasts so completely with Revillagigedo's consistently negative reports to Madrid, it may be that his opinions were eventually outweighed by cumulative recommendations from Vasadre, Martínez, Malaspina, Bodega, and others. At once Ramón Pérez and Nicolás Manzaneli, two affluent residents of San Blas, applied for permission to engage in bartering Mexican and Chinese goods for sea otter pelts. Both requests received royal approval, but their projects involved solely Alta California.[42]

38. Vancouver, *Voyage*, 3 : 304.

39. Journal of the *Jefferson*, DLC, cited by F. W. Howay, "The 'Resolution' on the Oregon Coast, 1793–94," 34 (1933) : 212.

40. Vancouver, *Voyage*, 3 : 300–01, 305; Bancroft, *History of the Northwest Coast*, 1 : 296; Howay, "John Kendrick," pp. 295–96.

41. Revillagigedo to Diego de Gardoqui, Mexico City, April 30, 1794, MxAGN (Corr. Virreyes 174), cited by Ogden, "The Californias," p. 468.

42. Pérez to Revillagigedo, San Blas, April 24, 1794, MxAGN (Prov. Internas 165); Viceroy Branciforte to Diego de Borica, Mexico City, February 28, 1795, CU-B (Prov. State Papers 13–12), cited by Ogden, "The Californias."

There is no evidence that a private Spanish trading vessel ever visited the northwest coast. The most important inhibiting factor was the abundance of sea otters in Alta and Baja California waters. Acquiring or constructing appropriate vessels on the west coast of Mexico and outfitting them for voyages to the northwest coast entailed the risk of large sums of money. There were also cultural impediments to Iberian participation in the trade. Schurz points out that "Spanish society was long dominated by an aristocratic sentiment which discriminated against those who trafficked, and in a people so sensitive to personal dignity this prejudice barred a mercantile career to the ambitious or the socially aspiring."[43] Nonetheless, by 1791 a total of 14,139 pelts had reached the Chinese market in six shipments under Spanish auspices, selling for 180,085 Spanish dollars. Of this, $32,682 went for expenses and $112,515 was invested in quicksilver.[44] The mercury would be vastly more valuable upon reaching New Spain. This balance represents the results of Vasadre's official venture and the pelts obtained by Martínez, Quimper, and others on the northwest coast. But Vasadre's project was killed by opposition from the Philippine Company. The halfhearted measures substituted by Revillagigedo failed to sustain the pace initiated so vigorously when Vasadre was in Alta California. By the time it became official policy to remove obstacles to private traders, in 1794, Mexican or Spanish merchants could not be expected to send private vessels to the northwest coast, for Madrid had agreed to abandon Nootka, the only safe refuge for any ship along that coast. Obviously the traffic would be more difficult and hazardous, hence less inviting to investors, once there was no Spanish outpost beyond San Francisco and Iberian warships were no longer stationed on the northwest coast.

## THE FIRST ÁLAVA MISSION TO "DELIVER" NOOTKA

Two days after the signing of the Third Nootka Convention, a commission was remitted to Bodega, or in his absence to the official designated by the viceroy, to execute the terms for "delivering" Nootka to Britain. The commandant did not live to learn of his new commission. He had begged off coming to Mexico City to report to the viceroy personally "because my broken health does not permit me at present to tire myself much, nor my excessive expenses allow me to enter into other new ones."[45] Weary of the

---

43. Schurz, *Manila Galleon,* p. 388.

44. "Liquidación en extracto del producto por venta de pieles de nutria," Mexico City, May 20, 1797, Cty-BWA (Coe). See appendix C.

45. Bodega to Revillagigedo, Tepic, February 15, 1793, MxAGN (Hist. 70), T in CaBViPA; "Instrucciones del Duque de la Alcudia para la entrega de Notka a Inglaterra, según el acuerdo firmado por ambas Cortes," Madrid, January 13, 1794, SpAHN (Estado 4291 bis); Bodega to Revillagigedo, San Blas, May 4, 1793, and Revillagigedo to the Conde de Campo Alange, Mexico City, May 29, 1793, SpAGI (V), cited by Chapman, *Catalogue,* p. 659. Despite a period of seclusion in Guadalajara, Bodega suffered a seizure and died in Mexico City on March 26, 1794. Revillagigedo to Alcudia, April 30, 1794, SpAHN (Estado 4290), cited by Michael E.

deprivations inherent to the department of San Blas, he petitioned for a promotion which would have taken him back to Peru, soliciting appointment
as governor of the port of Callao, or some equally good post. In consideration of his merits and services, Revillagigedo approved, but Bodega succumbed before the ministry took any action.

Thereupon Brigadier General José Manuel de Álava became the new commandant of San Blas and commissioner for Nootka. Revillagigedo anticipated a satisfactory resolution to the negotiations between Godoy and St.
Helens before word of the third convention actually arrived from Madrid,
and Álava left Mexico City in May 1794 to prepare an expedition to meet
Vancouver at Nootka before the summer was out. The viceroy was impatient
to plug without further ado the hole that was draining royal funds. When
Álava was ready to sail northward with Fidalgo and the *Princesa,* the long-
awaited news of a final accord still had not arrived. If they did not depart
soon, Álava risked missing the rendezvous with his opposite number at
Nootka. There was also the chance that Vancouver might have received instructions directly from Spain by means of a British vessel, as had happened
in the case of Floridablanca's initial order for the restitution of Meares's
tracts. Under these circumstances Álava and Fidalgo sailed on June 16, leaving another vessel ready to bring the new orders, expected hourly, if and
when they arrived. Álava would wait at Nootka until October 15, and if the
orders were not delivered to him there, they were to be taken to him at
Monterey.[46]

The *Discovery* and the *Chatham* returned from Hawaii to the northwest
coast for the third consecutive season in 1794. Vancouver still hoped to meet
Bodega and receive delivery of Nootka. Word had not yet reached the northwest coast of the recent accord, or of Don Juan's death. To accomplish some
gainful purpose while awaiting further orders, the British commander spent
the summer charting the coast north of his previous explorations; he examined Cook inlet and visited Russian establishments in several places. Finally
satisfied, after exhaustive search, that no passage to the Atlantic existed, he
set course toward Nootka for the last time.

On August 31 the *Princesa* arrived at the Spanish base. The next day
Álava took over formal command from Saavedra, and that evening the *Discovery* hove into sight. Vancouver was surprised to find six vessels riding at
anchor in the little cove: the warships *Princesa, Aranzazú,* and *San Carlos,*
two British traders (*Phoenix* and *Prince Le Boo*), and Kendrick's *Lady
Washington.* At the news about Don Juan he was moved to remark that it

---

Thurman, "Juan Bodega y Quadra and the Spanish Retreat From Nootka, 1790–1794," in
*Reflections of Western Historians: Papers of the 7th Annual Conference of the Western
History Association . . . 1967* (Tucson, 1969), p. 62.

46. Álava to Godoy, May 18, 1794; Vancouver, *Voyage,* 3 : 301–02.

"produced the deepest regret for the loss of a character so amiable, and so truly ornamental to civil society." [47]

To their mutual dismay, the commissioners found that neither had specific instructions about settling the issues at stake, but since further orders might arrive at any time, there was little to do but wait, at least until October 15. Vancouver's investigations were completed, and only the expectation of taking formal receivership of all or part of Nootka Sound detained him from commencing the long voyage homeward. In the meantime, Spanish carpenters and caulkers assisted Vancouver's men in making much-needed repairs to the hulls of his two vessels. While marking time, the two commanders paid a formal visit of adieu to Ma-kwee-na at his winter residence, taking along a party of fifty-six. "Notwithstanding that we were well persuaded of the Friendly disposition of the natives," Vancouver remarks, "yet I considered it necessary that the boats should be equipped for defence, as on all other such occasions." [48] Overlooking any evidence of distrust, Ma-kwee-na received his visitors with a great ceremony in their honor and the customary oratory and dances. The party also visited the villages of two lesser chiefs deep within the sound. Everywhere they were greeted amicably. Vancouver notes, however, that on the return journey to Friendly Cove, as the boats passed through wild, inhospitable gorges whose densely forested walls or sheer cliffs rose to immense height, Álava registered his astonishment that the region "could ever have been the object of contention between our respective sovereigns." [49] From an Iberian perspective, it had little to offer.

## THE DEATH OF KENDRICK

Captain Juan Kendrick eased the ungainly *Aranzazú* out of Friendly Cove on September 11, 1794, and set a course for Monterey and San Blas. He had taken leave of his father for the last time. The elder Kendrick, veteran of many a close brush with death, would be felled within weeks by a friendly hand. Heading for China once again, the *Lady Washington* anchored off present-day Honolulu on December 12 alongside the British trader *Jackal*, itself arrived from Nootka not long before. The two vessels witnessed a celebration by the king of Oahu of his triumph over invaders from another island. Captain Brown, who had aided in the victory, fired a broadside with his guns as a salute, but one of the *Jackal*'s guns still contained a lethal charge, which raked the side of Kendrick's ship, unintentionally killing the captain and several sailors.[50]

47. Vancouver, *Voyage*, 3 : 300–01; Vancouver to a Mr. Sykes, Nootka, October [September] 2, 1794, in *WHQ* 18 (1927) : 55–56.

48. Vancouver, *Voyage* 3 : 307; George Vancouver to J. G. Vancouver, his brother, Nootka, "or board the *Discovery*," September 8, 1794, CtY-BWA (Coe 491).

49. Vancouver, *Voyage* 3 : 312.

50. Howay, *Voyages of the "Columbia,"* p. xii.

John Howell assumed command, continued to China, and attempted to settle the old trader's disordered affairs, but debts far exceeded assets. His report to the original stockholders mentions the $8,000 still due Martínez; there was no expectation of settling this account, but the corresponding papers were given to some Spanish supercargoes in Canton, to be taken to their countryman.[51]

Howell remitted to owner Joseph Barrell the deeds for Kendrick's territorial purchases on the northwest coast, but warned, "If you knew the lands as well as I do, you would not be very anxious about the fate of them." This did not discourage the firm of Barrell and Servantes, 24 Threadneedle Street, London, from issuing a circular dated August 31, 1795, and printed in four European languages, soliciting immigrants, "such as may be inclined to associate for settling a Commonwealth on their own Code of Laws, on a spot of the globe nowhere surpassed in delightful situation, healthy climate, and fertile soil; claimed by no civilized nation; and purchased under a sacred Treaty of Amity and Commerce, and for a valuable consideration, of the friendly natives." [52] It described a tract comprehending 4° of latitude, of 240 square miles.

Subsequent to a successful trading cruise to Nootka in 1796, Howell softened his judgment. "I have had an opportuity of seeing most parts of Capt. Kendrick's purchases on the No. Wt. Coast of America," he wrote,

> and cannot flatter you with any hopes of profit from them even to your great, great grand children. They cost but little, it is true; and when the Millenium shall arrive and all the nations of the earth shall be at peace, your Posterity may, perhaps, settle them. That Captain Kendrick considered his title a good one I had sufficient proof of, when he one day told the Commandant at Nootka Sound, that he bought his territories, whilst other nations stole them; and that if they (the Spaniards) were impertinent he would raise the Indians and drive them from their settlements. This, altho' a bold, was nevertheless a moderate project, for a mind like his. Two of his favorite plans were to change the prevalence of the westerly winds in the Atlantic Ocean, and turn the Gulf Stream into the Pacific, by cutting a canal through Mexico. But with all his fooleries he was a wonderful man, and worthy to be remembered beyond the gliding Hours of the present generation. He was ruined by his appointment to the Columbia. Empires & fortunes broke on his sight. The paltry two-penny objects of his expedition were swallowed up in the magnitude of his Gulliverian Views. North East America was on the Lilliputian, but he designed N. W. America to be on the Brob-

51. John Howell to Joseph Barrell, Canton, May 11, 1795, DNA, in Nellie B. Pipes, ed., "Later Affairs of Kendrick; Barrell Letters," *OHQ* 30 (1929) : 99–101.

52. Felch, *Historical Magazine* 8 (1870) : 173.

dingnagian scale. Had you known him as well as I did, you would have sent some Glumdalclitch or other as nurse with him.[53]

There is no other reference to Kendrick's threat to organize an Indian uprising to evict the Spanish from Nootka. Such a scene in Martínez's time is unlikely, as the two cooperated closely. After 1793, however, when it became Spanish policy to warn vessels of other than Spanish or British nationality away from Nootka, Kendrick was bitter at being denied access to his favorite anchorage at Mawina. Despite his failure to turn a profit, John Kendrick emerges from the sources as a more sympathetic figure than his famous associate. Gray and Kendrick were opposites in character, the one practical, consistent, and ruthless—the other a benevolent and improvident dreamer. Both were courageous, but only Gray would accomplish his purposes. In contrast to the cruel and vengeful captain of the *Columbia*, Kendrick sought and earned the affection and respect of Indians and Spanish alike. The omnipresent old trader's activities are enmeshed inextricably in the warp and woof of the history of Spain in the Pacific Northwest, and although his dawdling impracticality frustrated associates and subordinates, yielding nothing but losses to his financial backers, his support and deference toward the successive Spanish commandants at Nootka measurably eased the way for his compatriot traders.

### THE COMPLETION OF VANCOUVER'S MISSION

Álava and Vancouver cooled their heels at Nootka until mid-October, awaiting the anticipated instructions. None had arrived by October 15, and the British vessels were in readiness to sail that midnight. Álava, Fidalgo, and the *Princesa* followed them southward the next morning. The two commissioners agreed to meet at Monterey. Saavedra had been restored as commandant and the *San Carlos* remained for another winter to protect the garrison. Three summers earlier, Vancouver had come to the northwest coast expecting to take possession of Nootka for His Britannic Majesty, but on his many visits to Friendly Cove he had to be content with the role of honored guest, feted cordially but denied his aspiration. Upon his final departure, the Spanish banner still flew over San Miguel.

Soon after Fidalgo anchored at Monterey, the long-awaited orders from Madrid arrived there. Vancouver had received no further messages, but Álava disclosed the pertinent parts of his own instructions, stating that a convention had been signed and that a special British envoy would come to

---

53. Howell to Barrell, Macao, December 23, 1796, DNA, in Pipes, "Later Affairs," pp. 101–02. In 1838 the heirs of Kendrick's Yankee backers endeavored to get Senate confirmation of their ownership of his land purchases. Again in 1840, 1851, and 1852 there was Senate discussion of these claims, but in April 1854 a negative report on their worth discouraged official action to assert American ownership. See Felch, *Historical Magazine*, passim.

the northwest coast to execute its terms.[54] The English commander received this news with mixed feelings—disappointment at losing the personal satisfaction of taking possession of Nootka, and relief at knowing he could return home in honor, as the Spanish settlement there would soon be extinct. For many a month he had been short of supplies and funds, dependent upon personal notes and the willingness of his rivals for food, gunpowder, and other necessities. He took the admiralty's neglect as humiliating. On his last visit to Nootka he had to request of Álava that he be allowed to skip the usual ceremonial salutes for want of gunpowder, which Vancouver says "was very politely excused and dispensed with by the whole party." [55] After four years at sea, his men longed for home, and he sailed from Monterey as soon as the two warships could be replenished with supplies for the long voyage.

They arrived in England in September 1795. Vancouver's broken health was attributed to the prolonged exploration, and he succumbed to his infirmities at age forty, three years later. The time left to him did not suffice to ready his journal for the press. A brother put the final touches to the excellent work, published posthumously, which presented Vancouver's meticulous explorations to the world and described the northwest coast in a manner never surpassed.

### REVILLAGIGEDO REPLACED

The year 1794 saw another principal figure removed from the scene. When Godoy ascended to the apex of power in Madrid, his avaricious brother-in-law coveted the viceroyalty of New Spain. Five days after the Marqués de Branciforte landed in Veracruz, his predecessor presumed to offer him some suggestions for the northwest coast. "I have always been of the opinion, and have proposed to the court," Revillagigedo wrote,

> the advisability of withdrawing our boundaries to the Strait of Juan de Fuca, which seems to be the demarcation line indicated by Nature itself; and it would be most fortunate for our nation if there remained an intermediate zone not belonging to anyone, to block clandestine commerce and motives for dissensions, the most to be feared; for Your Excellency must already know the cost of those past, despite the good treatment I gave the English prisoners and the outfitting I ordered done for them to make up for all their losses, which straightened out a lot of difficulties.[56]

54. Vancouver, *Voyage*, 3 : 331–32.
55. Ibid., p. 304.
56. Revillagigedo to Branciforte, Mexico City, June 20, 1794, SpBN (MS 11, 003), fol. 294–95, AT.

He cited a recent royal order which would permit such an adjustment between the Spanish and British commissioners who had been sent to carry out the abandonment of Nootka. There is no evidence, however, that his advice was heeded. Despite Revillagigedo's scrupulous honesty, upon arrival in Spain he was arraigned on charges of inefficiency and corruption, but the detractors were unable to amass sufficient proof of their accusations, and he was entirely cleared. A fair evaluation of the conde's influence on the history of Spain in the Pacific Northwest is not so readily made. From Madrid's point of view his impact was detrimental if, as Gálvez insisted, her claims there warranted being maintained, even at considerable expense, as a western anchor for a perimeter of defense around the northern edge of Spanish Louisiana, New Mexico, and California. Not only did Revillagigedo encourage withdrawal from Nootka, but he neglected to take effective measures to establish a base somewhere else in the Pacific Northwest to bolster the boundary that he envisioned at the Strait of Juan de Fuca. He acted wisely, on the other hand, if one concludes that Spain, rather than assert disputable territorial claims over vast portions of unexplored hinterland, should have ensured more efficient and profitable dominion over Mexico proper, with its all-important silver mines.

Branciforte exceeded Revillagigedo in his disinclination to support Spanish claims to the Pacific Northwest. He arrived in Veracruz loaded down with luxury items brought as personal baggage, exempt from duties and restrictions, which were immediately sold at speculative prices. His scandalous peculation while in office included such acts as exporting pearls that, as viceroy, he had ordered devalued in Mexico. How could imperial interests be protected effectively by an administrator whose major preoccupation was self-enrichment?

### NOOTKA EVACUATED

Lieutenant Thomas Pearce, the British commissioner appointed to replace Vancouver at the restitution of Meares's tracts at Nootka, came by way of Cádiz and Veracruz, aboard Spanish vessels, rather than at the head of a costly British expedition—a measure of the concern the Pitt ministry now held for the northwest coast. On January 13, 1795, Pearce sailed northward from San Blas on the *Activa*, now captained by Cosme Bertodano. The brig called at Monterey, where Pearce first met General Álava, his opposite number, and the two continued northward together with Bertodano. Upon their arrival at Nootka on March 16, Álava ordered Saavedra and his men to dismantle the fort and prepare to abandon the settlement.[57]

57. Pearce to the Duke of Portland, Tepic, April 25, 1795, in *BCHA, Annual Report* 2 (1924) : 34–35; reprinted from *London Gazette,* no. 13813 (September 12–15, 1795).

The Third Nootka Convention prescribed that the commissioners meet "in the same place, or near, where the buildings stood which were formerly occupied by the subjects of His Britannic Majesty." Following the restitution, "the British official shall unfurl the British flag over the land so restored in sign of possession." Pearce was not satisfied with accounts of the limited extent of Meares's land, and he requested that Ma-kwee-na and other chieftains of the area be called together for questioning about such subjects. Juan Kendrick, a witness to the events there in 1788 and 1789, was among the officers present. Pearce describes him as "perfectly conversant" in the Nootka language, and he served as interpreter for the interrogation. The chiefs were told that because of the good reports given of them by Captain Cook and subsequent British subjects trading at Nootka, His Britannic Majesty had determined to take them under his protection. "With this Account they all seemed much pleased," Pearce reported, "observing that the English had ever been their good Friends—but were very Anxious to know if the Spanish should return, whether they were to be friends with them; from which I inferred that they had not been treated very kindly by them." [58] Once Pearce's questions had been answered, he and Álava reached terms agreeable to both sides about the extent of land to be restored.

By March 28 everything of value had been stowed aboard the *Activa* and the *San Carlos*. "General Álava and myself then met," Pearce relates, "agreeable to our respective instructions, on the place where formerly the British Buildings stood; where we Signed and Exchanged the Declaration and Counter Declaration for restoring those Lands to His Majesty, as agreed upon by the two Courts—after which ceremony I ordered the British Flag to be Hoisted in token of Possession and the General gave directions for the Troops to Embark." There were no trading vessels present to witness the brief but significant ceremony, and Pearce's account is our sole source for the scene. The Spanish delivered over to him the site of Meares's camp, and the British flag was hoisted on a flagpole, whereupon the commissioners prepared to depart, in compliance with the terms never to make a permanent settlement there again. Pearce commended the flag to Ma-kwee-na's care, instructing that it be hoisted whenever a sail appeared. "This mark of confidence gratified him very much," Pearce reports. He and Álava both left letters to be shown to visiting fur traders, explaining the terms of the evacuation. Immediately following these formalities, the lone representative of His Britannic Majesty and last vestige of His Catholic Majesty's forces went aboard the two Spanish warships, which eased out to sea leaving cove and sound to the natives and the elements.[59] An unimpressive finale to a drama that had almost sparked a global conflict!

58. Ibid.
59. Ibid.

The vessels were scarcely out of sight when Ma-kwee-na's people stripped the village of everything that had not been taken away. The search for highly prized nails doomed every structure to quick demolition; the natives were in quest of even the tiniest scraps of metal, which could be fashioned into fishhooks. Although the chieftain had been promised possession of the main building once the Spanish left, he had no interest in moving in, and it went the way of the others, the choicest pieces doubtless ending up in the chief's lodge. Ransackers even dug up the little cemetery to remove the nails from coffins.[60] Soon there was little evidence that civilization had ever tried to plant an outpost on the site. Later that summer, lodges were built again in the location favored by Ma-kwee-na's ancestors as a residence, and the cove regained much of its aspect of twenty-one years earlier, when Pérez and Martínez in the *Santiago* had first cast anchor off the sound's entrance.

### RENEWED ANGLO-SPANISH ENMITY

The circumstances under which Madrid's and London's differences over Nootka could be resolved were brief in duration, indeed. The very month that Álava and Pearce evacuated Friendly Cove, Godoy sent Branciforte a warning of an imminent break with Britain, cautioning the viceroy against possible English attempts to invade weak points in Spain's American colonies. Branciforte's reply set forth in detail various reasons why he judged that some of the anticipated English attacks would be directed toward California and Louisiana.[61] Godoy's measure was in preparation for his proximate desertion of the first anti-French coalition in order to make a separate peace with the republicans. The shift came about as a result of Spain's vicissitudes in the war. Early in the conflict, its army invading southern France found those provinces so preponderantly monarchist as to welcome the Spanish as deliverers. An Anglo-Spanish force captured the naval base at Toulon and, assisted by royalist sympathizers, secured control of a large portion of the French fleet, with the expectation that it would be kept in trust for the French Bourbons. Months later republican forces retook the city, and the British put the torch to these vessels to keep them from being evacuated to Spain. Madrid looked upon the French fleet as important to Spanish interests, and this act, more than any other, is judged to have revealed to her that London's goals in the struggle were incompatible with her own. As Bemis deftly remarks, "Spain had been affrighted by the apparition of the republican ogre into marrying a selfish spouse with whom she had really nothing in common." [62]

60. F. W. Howay, "The Spanish Settlement at Nootka," *WHQ* 8 (1917) : 170.

61. Royal order of March 9, 1795, cited in Branciforte to Godoy, July 3, 1795, SpAGI (Estado 23–7).

62. Bemis, *Pinckney's Treaty*, p. 200.

The campaigns of 1793–94 were but a long series of failures; Spanish commanders appear to have had no coordinated plan of action. The defenders of monarchy could not muster supplies to march upon Paris, and the Republic gained the initiative, concentrated its efforts on the most vulnerable opponent, and pushed the Spanish back across the Pyrenees. As a consequence of the invasion that followed, the northern provinces of Spain suffered greatly. Popular resentment over the burdens of war and taxation came to such a pass that the royal favorite scarcely dared appear in public. On one occasion, while he was en route from one royal residence to another, the threat to his person became so acute that he abandoned his own vehicle to take refuge in the royal carriage with Carlos and María Luisa.[63] Spain's misfortunes under the British alliance motivated a revaluation of such an untraditional foreign policy. After the Thermidorean Reaction against Robespierre (July 1794), Godoy began secret negotiations with the Directory for a truce. The resultant Treaty of Basel (July 22, 1795) restored occupied provinces in northern Spain in return for cession to France of eastern Hispaniola, Spain's oldest colony in North America. Hoping to rebuild France's former empire in North America, Paris also tried to pressure Madrid into ceding Louisiana, but was unsuccessful.

Godoy knew that the Franco-Spanish treaty would alienate London, but, compared with invasion from across the Pyrenees, English assaults were the lesser evil. Carlos IV was so gratified by the achievement that he bestowed upon Godoy, already elevated to nobility as the Duke of Alcudia, the additional title of "Prince of the Peace." Although the favorite ranked ever higher in his master's esteem, some elements in Spanish society hated him. These were the months of Malaspina's downfall; implicated with the famous mariner were the royal couple's personal confessors and Minister of the Marine Antonio Valdés, who was forced to resign. Godoy then set about clearing himself of charges of incompetence in a memorial read to the council of state. The peaceful adjustments engineered with France and the United States (Pinckney's Treaty) were his self-justification, and he emerged from the crisis stronger than ever within the royal household.[64]

Many nations have paid a high price in territorial losses only to learn that appeasing an aggressive neighbor with cessions in peripheral areas merely stimulates his yen for a more important prize. Nootka's evacuation, contrary to Madrid's expectations, did not lessen the danger that the British would plant outposts nearer San Francisco Bay, or attempt to seize Spanish

63. Bute to Grenville, July 19, 1795, "Most secret & private," UKLPRO (F. O. Spain, 72/41), cited by Whitaker, *Spanish American Frontier*, p. 208.

64. Ibid., pp. 208–09; Whitaker cites the acts of the Consejo de Estado, November 22 and 27, 1795, in SpAHN, and Bute to Grenville, October 31, 1795, no. 30, "Most Secret," UKLPRO (F. O. Spain, 72/39).

ports in Alta California. Those settlements remained uneasy, worried about rumors of possible British attacks. Memories of Vancouver's recent careful inspection of the bays and garrisons helped nourish such suspicions. The British frigate *Resolution*'s unexpected visit to California ports in 1795 did nothing to assuage these fears.[65] Spanish apprehensions that London coveted territory in Spanish America were justified. In October 1795 Colonel John Graves Simcoe, lieutenant governor of Upper Canada, was instructed to promote an effort among settlers and Indians in the American West for a concerted attack upon New Spain.[66] Another episode in the long series of frontier intrigues, it never got underway, but it reveals that Madrid's distrust was not gratuitous.

The alliance between Madrid and Paris was sealed with the Treaty of San Ildefonso (August 1796), and within little more than a month Spain declared war upon Britain. One of the justifications cited was that London had abused the First Nootka Convention to open the Pacific shores of America to British trade, and that English vessels frequented isolated spots on the coast of Peru and Chile, under pretext of whaling, but actually to carry on contraband trade. Warnings sped to New Spain, Yucatán, and Caracas to anticipate attacks by Francisco de Miranda and others whom Madrid knew to be engaged in fomenting incursions, with British encouragement. Branciforte's reaction as far as the Pacific coast was concerned was largely limited to taking precautions against assaults on Acapulco and San Blas.[67]

Effective action to preserve Spanish claims over the northwest coast was made even less likely by Madrid's decision to transfer administration of the department of San Blas from that port to Cavite, in the Philippines. However inadequate the mosquito-ridden, sand-filled Mexican port was, moving the center of operations so far away could only hinder sustaining California settlements. Branciforte's reply pointed this out; he would comply despite his opinion to the contrary, but San Blas should continue to be used by supply vessels sent to California.[68] Bodega's suggestion that Acapulco supplant San Blas as administrative center for the department was either ignored or forgotten.

As a consequence of the break with London, Madrid found it difficult to protect lines of communication to America against attack. She suffered a

65. Antonio de Grajera to Branciforte, San Diego, September 6, 1795; Branciforte to Grajera, Mexico City, November 7, 1795; and Branciforte to Godoy, Mexico City, November 30, 1795; all in SpAGI (Estado 23–57).

66. William S. Robertson, "Francisco de Miranda," p. 310.

67. "Manifiesto contra Inglaterra," San Lorenzo del Escorial, October 7, 1796, in Modesto Lafuente y Zamálloa, *Historia general de España, desde los tiempos más remotos hasta nuestros días* 30 vols. (Madrid, 1850–69), 22 : 36–40; William S. Robertson, "Francisco de Miranda," p. 312; Branciforte to Jacobo Ugarte y Loyola, Mexico City, November 9, 1796, SpAGI (Estado 43–22).

68. Branciforte to Pedro Varela, and Branciforte to Godoy, Mexico City, December 29, 1796, SpAGI (Estado 25–93).

resounding defeat off Cape San Vicente (February 14, 1797), and Minorca and Trinidad fell to British task forces. From the latter, Commander Thomas Picton encouraged revolt in Spanish America with a proclamation issued on June 26, 1797, promising British support for any popular movement for independence from Spain. Copies of the edict circulated widely on the Spanish Main, and it is known to have fed the fires of revolt that eventually broke out there.[69] The baneful consequences of these developments eclipsed for a time all concern in Madrid and Mexico City for the dormant Spanish claims over the northwest coast.

FRIENDLY COVE IN NATIVE HANDS

In September 1795, five months after the extinction of the Spanish settlement at Nootka, Captain Charles Bishop, of the British trader *Ruby,* called at Friendly Cove and found the American snow *Mercury* riding at anchor there. As yet only a small party of Indian fishermen had moved back to the site of the former village. Ma-kwee-na visited the *Ruby,* although "extremely ill of an ague." After a few gifts had been exchanged, he showed Bishop the letters left by Pearce and Álava, addressed to Captain Broughton of the British warship *Providence.* "Hence we conclude that the Spaniards have given up this place and that Captain Broughton is expected to settle it," Bishop notes, and says he told the chief so. Ma-kwee-na and his people "expressed much satisfaction on hearing it, and were very ready to 'peeshac' [curse?] the Spaniards, who had killed their favorite, 'Canningham' [Ke-le-kum]." "Wacush-wacush Englies, peeshac-peeshac Hispannia, cocksuttle Canningham, peeshac Hispannia," they exclaimed, which Bishop translates as: "Friends, friends the English; bad, bad the Spaniards; they killed Canningham; bad the Spaniards." [70]

Consistent with his past comportment, Ma-kwee-na's strategy was to remain on good terms with whatever nation seemed most likely to gain hegemony over Nootka, and Iberian determination patently was in ebb.

On the site of the erstwhile base, Bishop's men picked up a number of planks still lying about and took them aboard. Prior to departing Bishop recorded that the chief "continues very ill of an ague, which will probably soon dismiss him to the shades," and several weeks later, at Clayoquot, Wee-ka-na-nish told him that Ma-kwee-na had died, and that he had just been to Nootka for the obsequies, a report not corroborated by other sources.[71]

69. William S. Robertson, "Francisco de Miranda," p. 314.

70. Charles Bishop, "Journal of the *Ruby,* 1794–96," CaBViPA (A/A/20.5/R82B), p. 74, punctuation supplied.

71. Ibid., pp. 84–86, entry for October 5, 1795. A distinguished name did not disappear with its possessor; it could be assumed by a candidate of the proper lineage who validated his claim with feats of prowess and a potlatch where guests, by participating, gave tacit acknowledgment. Hence subsequent references to Ma-kwee-na may not refer to the same individual. See Drucker, *Cultures of the North Pacific Coast,* p. 55.

Other accounts mention him as continuing as Nootka's chief for many years; however, his successor may have assumed the famous name.

In April 1796, Lieutenant Broughton and the *Providence* arrived off Nootka. He and Zachary Mudge, whom Vancouver had sent home by different routes for further instructions, had returned with credentials from London and Madrid enabling them to take delivery of Nootka from its Spanish commander. They were unaware that the site had been evacuated more than a year earlier. The *Providence* had urgent need to reach a safe harbor, as its hull was leaking badly. In the face of heavy winds, Broughton anchored some eight miles off the sound, and Mudge set out for the cove with a well-armed party. Five hours of rowing later, they were enveloped in a thick snowstorm, the temperature dropped well below freezing, and the gale was increasing. When Mudge caught a glimpse of the cove's interior, during a brief let-up in the storm, he realized instantly that the lodges he saw were not the familiar Spanish buildings. Knowing the native population to be numerous, and fearing the worst, he returned to the *Providence*. For three days Broughton waited at anchor until the offshore gale had subsided, debating what to do. When the wind shifted to onshore, he ascended the sound to Mawina Cove, judging it a safer place for careening and major repairs. No sooner had he cast anchor than the ship was surrounded by canoes. The visitors proved friendly. Broughton was presented with the letters from Álava and Pearce, and he was disappointed to learn that he had come halfway around the world on a wild goose chase. The British remained at Mawina for a month making much-needed repairs, and then visited Núñez Gaona, finding it equally deserted. At Monterey, Broughton was at a loss to understand the icy reception he received, such a contrast to the fiestas and hospitality of his sojourn in 1792. He sent the viceroy his credentials from Godoy, and Mudge remitted an account of their visit to Nootka, to be transmitted to the admiralty, by way of Spain. Since the original is now in the Archives of Indies, Spanish authorities evidently decided that its contents should not reach London.[72]

### THE LAST SPANISH EXPEDITION TO THE NORTHWEST COAST

Although by the Convention of 1794 Madrid gave up exclusive sovereignty over Friendly Cove, Spanish territorial claims to the rest of the coast were not abandoned, contrary to what many authors have assumed. The viceroy decided that an expedition should be sent as far as Bucareli Bay every six months to scout for suspicious foreign activities. José Tobar y Tamáriz commanded the first of these expeditions, using the schooner *Sútil,* which departed northward from San Blas on March 16, 1796. Unfavorable weather prevented his reaching the latitude specified in his in-

72. Mudge to the admiralty, aboard the *Providence,* Monterey Bay, June 20, 1796, SpAGI (Estado 39–14); Branciforte to Godoy, Mexico City, October 28, 1796, SpAGI (Estado 25–28).

structions. He arrived at Friendly Cove on June 19, encountering the American trader *Otter*. Captain Ebenezer Dawes (or Dorr?) had as passengers five English seamen and thirty-one-year-old Thomas Muir, a lawyer from Glasgow who was something of a celebrity. A parliamentary reformer arrested in 1793 for reading seditious matter aloud and recommending Thomas Paine's *Rights of Man,* Muir had been sentenced to fourteen years of exile and was transported to the penal colony at Botany Bay. His case aroused considerably sympathy in the United States, and Dawes had visited Australia for the express purpose of rescuing him.[73] Muir requested Tobar's help in getting to the United States quickly, to see President Washington. Before they reached Monterey, Muir's remarks gave the Spanish captain second thoughts about the wisdom of taking the six foreigners aboard. Soon after anchoring in San Blas, Tobar found himself arrested and court martialed for his unauthorized deed. He was sentenced to exclusion from future positions of command. Muir petitioned to proceed to Havana and the United States, but Branciforte sent him to Spain as a prisoner.[74]

As a side effect of the viceroy's anxiety about both Broughton's intentions and the threat of British attacks on the Pacific coast, Juan Kendrick fell under suspicion, despite his faithful service to Spain for seven years, often in positions of command. Schurz believes that it was feared he would be sympathetic to the United States, which was now suspected of designs upon California, possibly in league with Britain. Kendrick was sent to Spain, ostensibly to act as interpreter for Muir and his companions. The experience appears to have soured him on remaining a Spanish subject, for three years later he was back on the northwest coast as supercargo of the American trader *Eliza*. His last known contact with Spanish officials was in May 1799, when the *Eliza* put into San Francisco under a plea of necessity. Upon learning that his acquaintance of years before was aboard the vessel, Governor Borica became suspicious, conceiving the real purpose of the stop to be contraband trade.[75] After this episode, the younger Kendrick drops from sight in contemporary records.

No other person, except possibly Ma-kwee-na, was eyewitness to so much of early northwest coast history. Valuable as the young American should have been as a source of information, not a single document from his hand

73. Wagner, "The Last Spanish Exploration of the Northwest Coast," p. 322; Marjorie Masson and J. Franklin Jameson, "The Odyssey of Thomas Muir," *AHR* 29 (1923) : 49–72. See items in the bibliography, pp. 905, 908, under Hosie and McDonald.

74. Tobar to Jacinto Caamaño, San Blas, August 12, 1796, SpAGI (Estado 25–45); deposition against José Tobar y Tamáriz, 1796, SpAGI (Estado 25–56). Tobar's punishment for having shown charity toward Muir received royal approval; minute of a message to the viceroy of New Spain, Aranjuez, May 21, 1797, SpAGI (Estado 37–32).

75. Schurz, *Manila Galleon,* p. 208; Branciforte to Godoy, Mexico City, September 26, 1796, SpAGI (Estado 25–46), and October 27, 1796, SpAGI (Estado 25–56); Diego de Borica to Viceroy Miguel José de Azanza, Monterey, June 3, 1799, copy in CU-B, cited by Ogden, *California Sea Otter Trade,* p. 34.

is known. Although his education may have been limited by his having put to sea with his father at an early age, the Spanish are not likely to have conferred command of the *Aranzazú* upon an illiterate. Sufficiently taciturn to remain unquoted in the sources, Juan Kendrick nonetheless earned the esteem of a succession of Iberian commandants. He was an important link in the bonds of friendship that long endured between Spanish and American nationals on the northwest coast, virtually without a contrary incident.

At the outbreak of war between Madrid and London in 1796, Godoy became increasingly entangled in the turmoil afflicting western Europe. Spanish efforts to retain a measure of sovereignty over the northwest coast were reduced to attempts to determine the extent of foreign activities there. In 1797 the schooner *Mexicana* is alleged to have sailed northward on a cruise similar to that of the *Sútil* the previous year, but the archives have not yet yielded logs or accounts of the voyage, if indeed it took place.[76] Official Spanish naval activities on the northwest coast ceased entirely after 1797. Although Spanish subjects may have sighted or visited the coastline beyond Cape Mendocino at a later date, no trace of such occurrences has come to light in Iberian archives. Following curtailment of Spanish voyages to the northwest coast, San Blas went into swift decline, despite its role in supplying Alta California and providing occasional repair services for galleons in the Manila trade. Its prosperity had depended largely upon the enormous outlay of funds sunk into shipbuilding, repairing, and other activities generated by the outfitting of expeditions to the northwest coast. Mourelle, Valdés, and Alcalá Galiano went on to positions of great responsibility in Europe. Some of the lesser figures remained assigned to the department of San Blas, serving aboard vessels bound for California and the Philippines. In 1794 Alberni was named commandant of the presidio at San Francisco, and he was accompanied there by seventy-eight of the Catalonian volunteers. Fidalgo remained at San Blas, reached the rank of frigate captain, and died there on September 27, 1803. Pantoja was still attached to the department in 1803.[77] López de Haro served out of San Blas for many years, mainly captaining supply ships to Alta California. He was promoted to frigate lieutenant in 1805 and frigate captain in 1818, and sometime after 1805 his cartographic talents warranted his assignment to a topographic survey of the boundaries of Spanish territory in Louisiana. Mexico's revolution against Spanish dominion engulfed his last years; he was imprisoned as a *peninsular,* and expired in a Puebla dungeon in 1823.[78]

---

76. Wagner, "The Last Spanish Exploration of the Northwest Coast," pp. 321–22.

77. Biographical record of Spanish naval officers in the Indies, SpMN (1250), fol. 9v; Wagner, *Spanish Explorations,* p. 29; Thurman, *San Blas,* p. 355n.

78. López de Haro's 1808 map of the interior provinces, SpAHN (Estado. Carpeta de Mapas de América del Norte, no. 30), is reproduced in Luís Navarro García, *Las Provincias Internas en el siglo XIX* (Seville, 1965), plate IV.

PROJECTS FOR REOCCUPYING NOOTKA

As a consequence of the rupture between Madrid and London, after 1796 English freebooters commenced stalking sea-lanes in the Pacific and became a cause of constant preoccupation for the viceroys and governors. The few warships in the department of San Blas were powerless to check contraband runners along the California coast. In January 1799, officials in San Diego questioned four American sailors left on a California beach by a brigantine. They testified that to their knowledge the English had no settlements on the northwest coast. The viceroy's continued concern over the northwest coast is reflected in his letter remitting this testimony to the ministry. Five months later, he would again communicate his concern for counteracting the danger to the California coast from English corsairs "infesting" the Pacific. He also voiced a fear of Russian incursions.[79]

Renewed fears of Muscovite encroachments originated from the state of war existing between Russia and Spain during 1799–1801. Tsar Paul I had assumed the title of Protector and Grand Master of the Order of St. John in Jerusalem. His Catholic Majesty conceived it his duty to refuse recognizing investiture in that post of a sovereign outside the Roman communion, a quixotic gesture leading the tsar to declare war on Spain. The gauntlet was taken up at once in Madrid, and for many months each nation awaited attack from the other. Distant as their capitals were, it did not escape either monarch that the vulnerable backside of his far-flung domains was dangerously exposed to surprise attack from the opponent. Rumors reached Madrid of a plan for Russo-British operations on the Pacific Coast, with the design of seizing Spanish California. A royal order on January 27, 1800, warned against such a possibility.[80]

Perhaps as a result of this apprehension, within several weeks the ministry received a memorial drawn up by Nicolás Pérez de Santa María. Designed to deflect a much-feared British attack on Spanish colonies, it recommended that Spain take the offensive and ally herself with France and Holland to form a strong naval force and threaten British colonies. The enemy would be forced to send troops to defend its territories in the New World and India. With English forces thus deployed and diluted, the combined fleet would provide the shield necessary to recover Gibraltar, Jamaica, and Nootka Sound. Pérez also envisioned an attack upon Portugal and the trans-

79. Manuel Rodríguez, "Deposition given by four American sailors concerning the northwest coast and Sandwich Islands, San Diego, January 8, 1799," and Viceroy Miguel José de Azanza to Prime Minister Mariano Luís de Urquijo, Mexico City, June 26, 1799, SpAGI (Estado 28–39); Azanza to Urquijo, Mexico City, December 20, 1799, Pedro Cevallos to the Secretario del Despacho de Guerra, Aranjuez, February 21, 1802, and José Antonio Caballero to Pedro Cevallos, Aranjuez, March 10, 1802, all in SpAGI (Estado 28–62), cited by Chapman, *Catalogue*, p. 689.

80. Royal order to the viceroy of New Spain, January 27, 1800, MxAGN (Reales Cedulas 176), cited by W. S. Robertson, "Francisco de Miranda," p. 345.

fer of Brazil to French ownership.[81] This memorial is significant in that it reveals that Nootka had become, along with Gibraltar and Jamaica, a thorn in the Spanish side, a festering wound in the nation's sense of honor that would be slow in healing. Upon visiting New Spain in 1803–04, Alexander von Humboldt learned that during this crisis,

> for some time it was meditated in Mexico, and plans were even made, for a daring project of preparing in the ports of San Blas and Monterey a maritime expedition against the Russian colonies in America. If that endeavor had gotten underway, we would have witnessed a struggle between the two nations that, occupying the opposite extremes of Europe, are neighbors in the other hemisphere, on the eastern and western edges of their spacious empires.[82]

As Greenhow pointed out over a century ago, when Spain declared war upon Britain in 1796 "the Nootka Convention, with all its stipulations, of whatsoever nature they might have been, expired, agreeably to the rule universally observed and enforced among civilized nations, that *all treaties are ended by war between the parties*." [83] Madrid could honorably renew its claim to exclusive ownership of Nootka Sound. It was this reasoning that allowed Spain to think once again of reoccupying Friendly Cove. Before the catastrophe at Trafalgar in 1805, plans for ambitious Franco-Spanish naval operations did not seem as unrealistic as they now do, but Madrid never succeeded in employing the combined navy to pull any of its chestnuts out of the fire. Napoleon's efforts were focused on France's aggrandizement, at Spain's expense when necessary.

Instead of taking the offensive, as Pérez de Santa María suggested, Madrid appears to have been thrown back upon the defensive by a memorial which —significantly—is found in the same file of secret state papers in Madrid. Dated June 5, 1800, and written by Simón Orueta in London, it warned of emissaries from Peru who were negotiating with Pitt for aid in setting up a movement in their homeland to achieve independence from Spain. British representatives had already been sent to Peru and estimates had been arrived at as to the men, ships, and munitions that would be needed to promote a revolution there.[84] The importance of Peruvian revenues to Spain's economy was indisputable, and it is easy to understand Madrid's preference

81. Pérez de Santa María to the Spanish ministry, February 10, 1800, SpAHN (Estado 4219), cited in ibid.

82. Alexander von Humboldt, *Ensayo político sobre el reino de la Nueva España*, 4 vols. (Mexico City, 1941), 2 : 378–79, AT.

83. Robert Greenhow, *The History of Oregon and California, and Other Territories on the North-west Coast of North America* (Boston, 1844), p. 258.

84. Simón Orueta, Memorial, London, June 5, 1800, SpAHN (Estado 4219), cited by W. S. Robertson, "Francisco de Miranda," p. 346.

for defending proven resources over pursuing evanescent objectives that in past decades had consumed vast sums without tangible results.

It was well known that Miranda continued his efforts at revolutionizing the Spanish Main. A royal order of July 3, 1800, declared the death penalty for him or anyone else caught in a filibustering expedition. Robertson sets forth in detail the intrigues of the years that followed, by which Pitt continued to assist Miranda and other representatives of republican factions in New Granada, Peru, Mexico, and elsewhere. It was not lost on Madrid that, in encouraging antimonarchical movements in Spanish America, London was not displaying an enthusiasm for republicanism, but seeking client states that could give economic access to areas and peoples heretofore denied Britain by Spanish policy. Year after year Spanish espionage uncovered British projects for attacking Spanish Florida and Louisiana, an aspect of the continuing Anglo-French conflict.[85] By giving Miranda and his collaborators sporadic encouragement that was sufficient to keep Madrid on the defensive, Pitt prevented Spain from regaining territories that had been pared from her colonial empire.

Following Bonaparte's victory over Austria at Marengo (June 14, 1800), Russia left the Second Coalition and became a French ally. As a consequence the tsar and Carlos IV patched up their differences with a treaty signed on October 4, 1801. Plans contemplated in Madrid and Mexico City for reoccupying Nootka and dislodging Russian establishments in Alaska were perforce shelved.

### MASSACRE AT NOOTKA

Once in a great while news arrived in California concerning the northwest coast. The *Boston* had called at Nootka in March 1803, but instead of putting in at Friendly Cove, it anchored farther up the sound in the lee of an island. Captain John Salter began to trade at once with Ma-kwee-na (or another chief so called), who borrowed a double-barreled shotgun. When the gun was returned several days later with a present of a brace of ducks, Salter saw that one of its flintlocks was broken. Flying into a rage, he called the chief abusive names and hit him over the head with the stock.[86] Hiding his wrath, Ma-kwee-na went ashore. Upon his return four days later, elaborately painted and wearing a bear mask, he was accompanied by many fellow chiefs and warriors but he maintained a semblance of amity. After dining at Salter's table, the wily leader suggested sending a boat to Friendly Cove, where the salmon were running. The pinnace had scarcely disappeared from sight when the captain asked several of the braves to assist in

85. W. S. Robertson, "Francisco de Miranda," pp. 336, 346, 352–53.

86. Samuel Hill, "Loss of the Boston (Communicated by Captain Hill from Canton)," *Columbian Sentinel*, Boston, May 20, 1807; reprinted by F. W. Howay, "An Early Account of the Loss of the Boston in 1803," *WHQ* 17 (1925): 282–87; Jewitt, *Narrative*, unnumbered. Jewitt's account saw many subsequent editions, in this country and abroad.

hoisting a launch over the side, so that he might sail as soon as the fishing party returned. When the Americans were off guard, Ma-kwee-na gave a signal and, leading the fray himself, grappled with Salter and hurled him overboard, where some women in a canoe beat his brains out. All of the crew above deck were soon overwhelmed and slain.

Two sailors escaped the brief and bloody carnage. John Jewitt, a young Englishman who had shipped on as armorer, was wounded while attempting to climb out of the hold. The natives shut the hatch on him until all was over. The dead were beheaded, their bodies dumped into the bay, and the severed heads lined up in a row on deck. Then Jewitt was compelled to tally the grisly trophies to see that all were accounted for. His life was spared only because Ma-kwee-na knew he was a blacksmith and wanted to utilize his skill. Later an older man appeared who had been hiding in the hold. A Philadelphian named John Thompson, he escaped execution solely because Jewitt, with a show of grief, succeeded in passing the old fellow off as his father. The chief required their aid to sail the *Boston* into Friendly Cove, where it was beached. Knowing the utility of cannons, he forced them to help him set up a battery in front of the village.

Three days later the American traders *Juno* and *Mary,* whose captains had learned of the massacre, dropped anchor off the cove's mouth and fired several broadsides into Ma-kwee-na's lodges, but they did little damage. Not long afterward the *Boston* caught fire and burned to the waterline. Jewitt's captivity and bizarre experiences prior to rescue in 1805 would provide him with grist for a small book so popular that it saw many editions in the first half of the nineteenth century.

Shortly after the *Boston* burned, Captain John Brown of the *Alexander,* out of Boston, sought to anchor in Friendly Cove and narrowly escaped Salter's fate. Later, at the entrance to the Strait of Juan de Fuca, Brown learned some of the details by which Nootka had become such a dangerous cul-de-sac. When the American captain called at Monterey in August, Spanish officials sent a long account of his tale to San Blas, subsequently relayed to Mexico City, warning that "the Indians of Nuca had set up a battery of 24 cannons of 4- and 6-inch calibre on the same spot where we the Spanish had them; that the cannons of the battery are those of the overpowered frigate; and that they allowed to live three of the most intelligent [seamen]for that purpose." [87]

The news that Ma-kwee-na and his people had reverted to savagery can be assumed to have given pause to those who heard of it in Mexico City or Madrid and still entertained illusions of reoccupying Nootka Sound.

87. Benito Vivero y Escaño, "Noticias de Nootka y Californias," San Blas, October 22, 1803, MxAGN (Californias 62), fol. 304. He quotes a letter, fol. 306, from Braulio de Otalora y Oquendo, Monterey, August 31, 1803.

## 11  Spanish Defense of Oregon's Eastern Perimeter, 1796–1807

MOST ACCOUNTS of Spanish activities in the Pacific Northwest leave the impression that after Nootka's evacuation Madrid lost all interest in the area and that her paper claims to it were unassociated with any real sentiment. This traditional perspective ignores numerous documented episodes testifying to a continued Spanish concern with that region. What has not been sufficiently appreciated is that, under Godoy's influence, Madrid's traditional dependence upon naval forces to protect her interests there was abandoned in favor of overland efforts from St. Louis and Santa Fe. The objective of such activities remained the same: to retain sway over the area west of Louisiana, soon to be called Oregon, and to exclude rival nationalities from an unexplored region in which Spanish strategists hypothesized potential avenues of penetration to Mexico's mining centers.

At the close of the eighteenth century the immense area west of the Mississippi appeared on most maps of North America as His Catholic Majesty's territory, but little was known about the interior of that broad region. Despite decades of exploration along the Pacific coast, Spain had cloaked her findings in such a blanket of silence that her own subjects in the upper Mississippi basin, called "Spanish Illinois," had little knowledge of the measures their government had taken to counter Russian, English, and American activities along the western edge of the continent.

Reports about the course of the upper Missouri made Spanish officials apprehensive that it stemmed from tributaries close to other streams leading to the Río Grande and the Colorado—fears corresponding to geographic reality, since South Pass (alt. 7,500 ft.) offers a broad and easy gateway from tributaries of the Big Horn and North Platte to the Green River, the Colorado, and the Gulf of California. Their concern was that foreigners might find easy access to the interior provinces' weakly defended northern perimeter and endanger the silver mines of Chihuahua and Sonora. In 1789 Floridablanca had been warned of such danger by the Spanish minister to the United States. Diego de Gardoqui told of conversing with a young Englishman, just returned from Hudson's Bay Company outposts in the upper Mississippi basin, who claimed to have reached the mountains from which streams flowed into the Pacific and to have learned from the most distant Indian nation visited that "about 100 miles from that place there was a river which empties into the Pacific Ocean." Gardoqui urged that officials in

Spanish Illinois be ordered to locate sources of the reported rivers, explore the country westward, and find a route to the Pacific. He suggested that the wealth in furs revealed by Cook's expedition be opened up for exploitation. If Britain's colony at Botany Bay failed, the English might seize on the reported route across the Rockies to establish a colony north of San Francisco, "on some coast of our continent from which they could ship contraband goods to our ports which is the general purpose of everybody." [1]

Spain's maximum known penetration toward the northwest occurred in 1790, when Santiago la Iglesia (Jacques d'Église) reached the Mandan Indians, of present-day North Dakota. From them he learned of British outposts not far to the north, western prongs of penetration of the Hudson's Bay Company. Spanish officials were well justified in fearing that British traders, then actively pushing westward, might soon challenge Spanish claims in territory farther south.

CLAMORGAN AND THE MISSOURI COMPANY

Spain's subjects on the upper Mississippi were a motley lot. Often the Spanish governor of Louisiana was dependent upon local officials of French, Canadian, Scottish, or English origin rather than Iberian or Mexican. Spanish participation in fur trading activities was negligible until invigorated by measures instituted by the Baron de Carondelet as a means of counteracting foreign penetration. In 1794 he warned Madrid that, if not checked, the Americans would in time "demand the possession of the rich mines of the interior provinces of the very kingdom of Mexico." [2]

A direct result of Carondelet's preoccupation with this threat was the formation of a "Commercial Company for the Discovery of the Nations of the Upper Missouri," incorporated by a group of merchants in St. Louis (San Luís de Ilinueces). The stockholders elected as director Santiago (Jacques) Clamorgan, the prime mover among them. Born on Guadeloupe of Welsh, French, Portuguese, and possibly African ancestry, Clamorgan was a self-made man who had become a rich and respected member of commercial circles in New Orleans and St. Louis.[3] One of the declared ob-

1. Gardoqui to Floridablanca, [Philadelphia], June 25, 1789, SpAHN (Estado 3893), trans. in Abraham P. Nasatir, ed., *Before Lewis and Clark: Documents Illustrating the History of the Missouri, 1785–1804*, 2 vols. (St. Louis, 1952), 1 : 130–31 (hereafter cited as *Before Lewis and Clark*). Spanish preoccupation with pushing westward from St. Louis is extensively discussed in Nasatir's introduction. Foreign threats to New Mexico's northeastern perimeter are examined in detail by Noel M. Loomis and Abraham P. Nasatir, *Pedro Vial and the Roads to Sante Fe* (Norman, Okla., 1967) (hereafter cited as *Vial*).

2. Carondelet, as cited by James Alexander Robertson, *Louisiana Under the Rule of Spain, France, and the United States, 1785–1807*, 2 vols. (Cleveland, 1911), 1 : 297.

3. Articles of incorporation, St. Louis, May 12, 1794, SpAGI (Papeles de Cuba 2363), trans. in *Before Lewis and Clark*, 1 : 217–25. Of the other founders, Benito Vásquez was Galician, and Joseph Motard, Antoine Reilhe, and Louis Chauvet Dubreuil were born in France. Laurent

jectives of the Missouri Company, as it is usually called, was to seek a route to the Pacific by pushing up the Missouri to its headwaters and extending trading activities to Indian nations along another river, believed to lie not far beyond the divide, that was assumed to flow into the Pacific somewhere between Nootka and California. From St. Louis, the lieutenant governor of Spanish Illinois, Zenón Trudeau, urged that the company be granted an exclusive right of trade on the upper Missouri, to defray heavy expenses necessitated by the planned transcontinental journey. He also told of talking personally with an old man who had traveled to the Missouri's headwaters and had seen, at a certain distance farther on, a large river flowing westward.[4]

Carondelet granted the exclusive concessions requested. To stimulate rapid achievement of the most important objective, he offered a reward of 2,000 Spanish dollars, later raised to 3,000, to the first subject of His Catholic Majesty to reach the Pacific by traveling overland from the Missouri. His lack of accurate knowledge about the coast is evinced by his expectation that Russian settlements would be encountered there, and he declared that a certificate should be secured from the Russian commandant as proof of reaching the Pacific.[5] South of Yakutat there were no Muscovite activities until an outpost was planted at Sitka in 1799. Carondelet subsequently wrote the captain general of Havana (remitting a copy to the ministry) emphasizing the importance of exploring the Missouri to its headwaters and finding a route to the Pacific in order to thwart the Americans, whom he described as "advancing with an incredible rapidity." [6]

At a cost of $47,000 the Missouri Company sent out its first expedition in the summer of 1794. Leader of the party was Jean Baptiste Trudeau (or Truteau), no relation to the lieutenant governor of St. Louis. A Montreal-born teacher turned trader, Trudeau had come to St. Louis in 1774 as its first schoolmaster. The company's directors anticipated that his education would fit their unusual objectives: gathering geographical knowledge as well as laying the basis for fur trading activities. His instructions were to establish friendly relations with the *Serpientes* (Snake Indians), a tribe said to dwell on the western slopes. He was to inquire about a route to the Sea of the West and learn whether rivers on the other side of the "Rocky

Durocher, Charles Sanguinet, and Hyacinthe St. Cyr were French-Canadians, and Joseph Robidou a Canadian of French and Spanish extraction. Abraham P. Nasatir, "Jacques Clamorgan: Colonial Promoter of the Northern Border of New Spain," *NMHR* 17 (1942) : 104.

4. Zenón Trudeau to Carondelet, St. Louis, May 31, 1794, SpAGI (Papeles de Cuba 2363), trans. in *Before Lewis and Clark,* 1 : 228–29.

5. Carondelet to Zenón Trudeau, New Orleans, July 12, 1794, SpAGI (Papeles de Cuba, 2363), trans. in ibid., pp. 235–36.

6. Carondelet to Luís de las Casas, New Orleans, November 24, 1794, UKLBM (Add. MSS. 17,567), fol. 22–63v, trans. in ibid., pp. 253–59.

Chain" flowed westward.[7] The party consisted of ten men in a pirogue, the standard craft for ascending shallow, turbid streams of the trans-Mississippi region. Bands of Sioux stopped them and demanded the better part of their cargo long before Trudeau reached the tribes that were his objective. He was powerless to keep the remaining articles from being pilfered during the first winter, spent among the Ponca, and the second, among the Pawnee. In 1797 he returned in utter failure.

To back up Trudeau's effort, in 1795 the company outfitted a second expedition at even greater expense ($54,000). Clamorgan hoped it would reach the Pacific by the following spring. Commanded by one Lecuyer, it departed from St. Louis in April, but Lecuyer's mismanagement and Ponca raids defeated the group before it reached Trudeau.

La Iglesia, discoverer of the Mandan, kept aloof from Clamorgan's enterprise, and aspired to crossing the continent independently. He intended to spend the winter of 1795 among the Arikara and head for the Pacific in the spring. "He seems determined to make this discovery and, since he is full of courage and ambition, he is capable of so dangerous an undertaking," the lieutenant governor in St. Louis wrote Carondelet. "It is a pity that he should not have instructions that would make [it] easy for him to secure all the benefit of a trip which might [also] be of interest to the [Spanish] government." [8] How far westward La Iglesia penetrated on his trek in 1796 has never been ascertained, but that he survived the effort is known, as years later he visited Santa Fe.

Word that Trudeau and Lecuyer had failed took some time to reach St. Louis. Meanwhile, Clamorgan and his associates continued their efforts to obtain governmental subsidies for the ambitious project that they envisaged: protecting the northern perimeter of Spanish territory by discovering a route and establishing a chain of forts to the Pacific. Having described British encroachments among the Mandan, they warned:

> If you believe it of importance to preserve the possessions of His Majesty from invasion which is rapidly moving forward to the frontiers of the Californias, crossing a territory which belongs to us, we ought not to permit this occasion to pass by without beseeching you to arouse your intelligence, your patriotism, and your talent to make known your observations to the Governor-General, pointing out to him the

7. Clamorgan to Jean Baptiste Trudeau, St. Louis, June 30, 1794, SpAGI (Papeles de Cuba 2363), trans. in ibid., pp. 243–53.

8. Zenón Trudeau to Carondelet, St. Louis, July 15, 1795, CU-B, and Trudeau to Carondelet, July 20, 1795, SpAGI (Papeles de Cuba 214A), both trans. in ibid, pp. 341–45. La Iglesia was murdered in New Mexico, sometime before November 1806. Lansing B. Bloom, "The Death of Jacques d'Eglise," *NMHR* 2 (1927) : 369–79.

necessity of maintaining a militia to protect and defend the line which our Company is extending from the Maha [Omaha] nation to beyond the Rocky [Mountain] Chain about 50° north latitude to approach the Sound of Nootka.

This distance, which is not less than seven or eight hundred leagues, demands a chain of forts located at intervals which our Company has already begun to build, and which ought to continue in the same direction.[9]

To bind the tribes to their "Great Chief," the king of Spain, perforce a great many presents would have to be distributed. A third expedition would be needed, and Clamorgan requested a subsidy of $100 anually for each soldier maintained in the forts to be erected and twelve swivel guns or little cannons for their protection. Lieutenant Governor Trudeau remitted the request to his superior in New Orleans but added that several members of the company had resigned because Clamorgan "has at heart his own interests rather than those of the others." His objectives were economically hazardous, and the partners' resources would be exhausted before any profit could be expected, "returns which, I believe, will exist some day, but a little too late for those who do not have sufficient means." [10]

Impressed by the political significance of Clamorgan's goals, Carondelet discounted Trudeau's pessimism and remitted the directors' report to Godoy, recommending the matter's importance in that it "directly concerns the boundaries of the possessions of Spain towards the North and Northeast of Louisiana and the New Kingdom of Mexico, extending to the South Sea by Nootka Sound, within which [boundaries] the English are making their way secretly and forming settlements which in a short time will secure them possession of that same territory which they do not at present dare to claim by the least right of ownership." He justified offering a sizable reward, in the king's name, for finding a route to the Pacific, because "such a discovery was important to the state; for it would determine its boundaries in a permanent fashion by founding a settlement with all the necessary arrangements to prevent the English or the Russians from establishing themselves or extending themselves on those coasts, remote from the other Spanish possessions and near Nootka Sound." He predicted that the Spaniards would have to move fast in order to prevent Britain from dominating the Missouri's headwaters. If British subjects were not checked, "Spain will find herself quite unable to prevent the commerce that their trading houses will carry on with the *Provincias Internas* and California, whose inhabitants, in addition, will find themselves plundered by the savage tribes which will then be

9. Clamorgan and Reilhe to [Zenón Trudeau], St. Louis, July 8, 1795, SpAGI (Papeles de Cuba 2364), trans. in *Before Lewis and Clark*, 1 : 335–41.

10. Trudeau to Carondelet, July 20, 1795, trans. in *Before Lewis and Clark*, 1 : 343–45.

dependent on the English and will be provided with firearms by them." He suggested supplying the Missouri Company with $10,000 a year to maintain 100 armed men in the line of forts, eventually to become settlements and a buttress against English and American penetration of the Interior Provinces.[11]

Ten months after the evacuation of Friendly Cove, with its hands tied by the diplomatic standoff over Nootka, the council of state decided to pursue its continuing interest in the Pacific Northwest by approving the $3,000 reward to a Spanish subject for discovering a route to the Pacific and by encouraging the construction of a chain of posts from St. Louis to the ocean. In contrast with the maritime efforts upon which Ministers Gálvez and Valdés had relied, the new technique for excluding foreigners from that area would be carried out by private enterprise, with a minimum of expense to the royal treasury.[12]

The Missouri Company's third expedition set out in August 1795, led by John Mackay, a Scottish highlander of Catholic persuasion. A former employee of the North West Company, after fifteen years in Canada he had moved to St. Louis and become a Spanish subject. Accompanying Mackay was John Evans, a young Welshman who had come to America to search for an alleged tribe of "Welsh Indians," which he expected to find on the upper Missouri. The party consisted of thirty men in four pirogues; they carried merchandise worth 50,000 Spanish dollars. At the approach of winter they established a blockhouse on the Missouri, not far from Omaha, to which Mackay gave the name Fort Charles, honoring Carlos IV. As spring approached, he gave Evans instructions to continue up the Missouri and onward to the Western Sea, with directions as to route and objectives that antedate by more than seven years Meriwether Lewis's orders, and anticipate Jefferson's ideas to a marked degree. Mackay was atypical among those of his calling—by and large an unlettered bunch—and in reference to his instructions to Evans, F. J. Teggart has commented: "Written by an inconspicuous fur trader, in the wilderness, in the depth of a Nebraskan winter, it is worthy of comparison, as well in thought as in expression, with the finished product of President Jefferson."[13] Evans departed from Fort Charles fully expecting to reach the Pacific, and Mackay returned to St. Louis to report that the Welshman was well on his way. Clamorgan relayed

11. Carondelet to the duque de Alcudia, New Orleans, January 8, 1796, "reservada," SpAHN (Estado 3900), trans. in *Before Lewis and Clark*, 2 : 385–95.

12. Minutes of the Consejo Supremo de Estado, Madrid, May 27, 1796, SpAHN, trans. in ibid., pp. 432–39.

13. Frederick J. Teggart, "Notes Supplementary to Any Edition of Lewis vand Clark," *AHA Annual Report, 1908* (1909) : 191–92; Mackay, Instructions to John Evans, January 28, 1796, contemporary copy (in French), CU-B (Pinart MSS), trans. in *Before Lewis and Clark*, 2 : 410–14; an account of the expedition, from SpAGI (Papeles de Cuba 2364), is trans. in ibid., 1 : 356–64.

the good news to Carondelet, who remitted Mackay's journal to Godoy with a renewed warning about English encroachments on the upper Missouri.[14] In acknowledging Clamorgan's letter, Carondelet expressed satisfaction with Mackay's measures and the instructions given to the party headed for the Pacific. "It is confidently reported that a Spanish squadron has sailed from Europe in order to go and dislodge the English from Nootka Sound," he declared, "and it would be a curious fact if our people were to arrive at the same point at the same time." [15] This is puzzling, for in 1796 there were no white settlements of any nationality between San Francisco Bay and the Russian outposts in Alaska. Other than Pérez de Santa María's project of 1800, no plans have come to light for the reoccupation of Nootka.

Evans and his scantily outfitted party had little chance of completing the gigantic task undertaken. Continuing up the Missouri, they traversed Arikara territory, searching for the Mandan, whose language was reputed to possess similarities to Welsh. Arriving at a Mandan village in September 1796, Evans had this hope dashed upon finding their tongue incomprehensible. Here he encountered a small fort that Canadian traders had constructed. After distributing presents, Evans delivered a speech about the benefits of becoming His Catholic Majesty's subjects, took possession of the fort, lowered the British flag, and replaced it with Spanish colors. A rival trader witnessing the scene endeavored to incite the Indians against them, but a sufficient number favored the Spanish for Evans to prevail. Leaving a flag with the chiefs, he turned back to warn of the British threat, reaching St. Louis on July 15, 1797.[16]

Clamorgan had invested all of his once-considerable resources in the effort entrusted to Mackay and Evans, but he received little help and less approval from Lieutenant Governor Trudeau. In December 1795, several months after the third expedition's departure, he sent another memorial to Carondelet via Trudeau, who took the occasion to comment that Clamorgan's suggestions might contribute to the design for counteracting foreign encroachments—"if I believed I could count on his plan; but stripped of means, I believe that ambition makes him promise more than he will be able to execute." [17] Nonetheless, Clamorgan succeeded in obtaining a large investment from Andrew Todd, an Irish trader formerly of Michilimackinac who had shifted allegiance to Spain and moved to New Orleans after London—by the terms of Jay's Treaty—had promised to evacuate its posts on American territory north of the Ohio. Todd's $8,000 temporarily renewed hope in St. Louis that the enterprise would rally. Such expecta-

14. Carondelet to the Prince of the Peace, New Orleans, June 3, 1796, SpAHN (Estado 3900), trans. in *Before Lewis and Clark*, 1 : 354–56.

15. Carondelet to Clamorgan, New Orleans, July 9, 1796, MoHi, trans. in ibid., 2 : 422–43.

16. David Williams, "John Evans' Strange Journey," *AHR* 54 (1948–49) : 525.

17. Zenón Trudeau to Carondelet, St. Louis, December 19, 1795, SpAGI (Papeles de Cuba, 211), trans. in *Before Lewis and Clark*, 1 : 373–75.

tions were short-lived, however; the Irishman fell victim to a yellow fever epidemic ravaging New Orleans in 1796, and this brought Clamorgan's aspirations crashing to earth, for the deceased merchant's heirs had little confidence in the speculation in which the Missouri Company had already dropped so considerable a sum.

Although Clamorgan's petition for a subsidy of $10,000 gained royal approval, the Missouri Company failed to receive a cent because of differences with Trudeau about fulfillment of the compact. As a consequence, the expeditions served only to impoverish the partners, who grew dissatisfied with Clamorgan's management and eventually dropped out. After protracted litigation and compromise, the company evolved into a firm known as Clamorgan, Loisel, and Company. Régis Loisel was still trading on the Missouri when Lewis and Clark ascended it in 1804 to fulfill Clamorgan's dream. Manuel Gayoso de Lemos, Carondelet's successor as governor of Louisiana, catered to Mackay and Evans after the Missouri Company's failure in order to prevent their defection to some other country; he named the older man governor of the post at San Andrés, near St. Louis, and invited Evans to dwell in his own residence in New Orleans. Gayoso hoped their experience might be put to use in establishing a satisfactory boundary between Spanish and British territory. In November 1798, he asked the ministry to send a surveyor to establish the boundary of Spanish territory on the north. He suggested a tentative limit to Madrid's claims along a line running by water, insofar as possible, between the Mississippi's source and Lake Winnipeg, from there to Great Slave Lake, then due west to the crest of the Rocky Mountains, south along that range to the latitude of Nootka, and then due west to the Pacific.[18] Such expansive borders would never be surveyed by Spanish explorers, as events in Europe soon overshadowed all else. Diplomatic pressure from Paris presently caused boundaries in North America to be shifted with little regard for discoveries, explorations, or far-flung outposts.

## SPAIN LOOSENS ITS GRIP UPON LOUISIANA

As author of the Franco-Spanish alliance of 1796, the "Prince of the Peace" received the brunt of blame for the defeat shared with the French off Cape San Vicente in 1797. Adding to Godoy's difficulties, the Directory pressed for his dismissal because of his stance, taken at María Luisa's behest, against treatment accorded her brother, the Duke of Parma, during the

---

18. Gayoso to Francisco Saavedra, November 22, 1798, SpAHN (Estado 3900), trans. in ibid., 2 : 583–86 (see also 1 : 93). Gayoso wrote Mackay in May 1799 that Evans was seriously ill; a month later he was dead. Mackay lived on in Missouri to become an American citizen, a judge, and in 1816 a representative to the Missouri territorial legislature. Williams, "John Evans' Strange Journey," p. 528; Louis Houck, *Spanish Régime in Missouri*, 2 vols. (Chicago, 1908), 2 : 252.

invasion by French armies in the Italian campaign of 1796. Fernando had been obliged to repurchase a life interest in his title with six million lire and twenty-five of the finest paintings in the ducal collection, renowned throughout Europe. Another factor in Godoy's eclipse appears to have been a falling-out with the queen. Such influence as he continued to exercise came about more through his sway over Carlos IV. Resigning from the ministry in March 1798, he nonetheless continued as the king's closest adviser. Francisco Saavedra, Godoy's replacement as secretary of state, was himself displaced in February 1799, supposedly because of illness, by Mariano Luís de Urquijo.

During the brief period that Godoy was out of office, a maneuver that he had initiated radically altered Madrid's policy and options regarding the area between St. Louis and Nootka: the bartering of Louisiana to France. An understanding of how Napoleon ostensibly gained title to that colony, but failed to make good on the bargain prior to selling it to the United States, is essential to comprehending Madrid's bellicose reaction to the purchase itself, to the Lewis and Clark expedition, and to other American maneuvers on the Louisiana frontier, which propelled Spain and the United States to the edge of war in 1806–07.

The Directory regarded the former French colony of Louisiana, ceded to Spain in 1763, as vital to rebuilding a colonial empire. Prior to the revolution, fully two-thirds of France's overseas interests had concerned Saint Domingue. To vanquish Toussaint L'Ouverture, leader of the Haitian rebels, and restore the western half of Hispaniola to the wealthy colony of yore, a nearby continental granary was needed to supply the sugar plantations with products of a temperate climate. By contrast, Louisiana was never lucrative in Spanish hands. Madrid's annual expenditures to administer the colony, woo Indian nations, and bribe "Men of the Western Waters" exceded by five times the revenue garnered from Louisiana. Therefore, Godoy decided to make a strategic retreat from the Mississippi valley. Whitaker has shown that the policy change evolved from pressures and frustrations leading to Pinckney's Treaty in 1795. In December of that year, realizing that concessions to the United States on the Mississippi lent an aspect of futility to further Spanish efforts to make Louisiana a colony to rival New Spain, Godoy approached Paris with a proposal to barter Louisiana for Santo Domingo, ceded to France six months earlier as part of the price of the Treaty of Basel. Such a pact was signed (1796) but never ratified by the Directory, on grounds that Madrid was asking too much. As Whitaker comments, the episode points to Godoy's strategy: shortening Spanish lines of defense in North America.[19] Significantly, this maneuver coincides with the Spanish

19. Arthur P. Whitaker, *The Mississippi Question, 1795–1803; A Study in Trade, Politics, and Diplomacy*, 2d ed. (Gloucester, Mass., 1962), pp. 53, 177.

retreat from Nootka. In 1797 the French ambassador addressed Godoy a letter enumerating Pitt's objectives in America: possession of Nootka, Mississippi navigation, and seizure of Spanish provinces. Predicting an English declaration of war upon Spain and an effort to secure these goals, the ambassador urged the cession of Louisiana and Florida in order to interpose France in the aggressor's way.[20]

Godoy's pragmatic approach to the difficulties of preserving Madrid's claims over uncolonized areas on the northern perimeter of New Spain is enunciated most clearly in his marginal comment to a report from the Spanish minister to the United States about word of an American incursion into Louisiana: "You can't put doors on open country" (*No es posible poner puertas al campo*). Unable to barter Louisiana to Paris at an advantage, Godoy recommended relying upon "reciprocity and guile" (*reciprocidad y maña*) to fend off invasion by American frontier elements.[21] In subsequent years the number and intensity of these threats would grow beyond his most pessimistic expectations. During John Adams's administration, Federalist influence brought closer contacts with London, and Franco-American relations deteriorated to the point of the "Quasi-war" of 1797–99. As France's ally, Spain feared becoming involved, conscious of her vulnerability to an Anglo-American campaign in North America. Hamilton and Miranda were collaborating on plans for subverting Spanish America, and the professional revolutionary from Caracas was still being abetted by Pitt.[22]

Bonaparte's elevation to first consul was a turning-point in Spanish history. Madrid soon found that Napoleon drove a harder bargain than the Directory. While Urquijo headed the ministry, the queen's efforts to help Parma became linked to France's desire for Louisiana. Madrid was willing to part with Louisiana if the price was right—French assistance in regaining Trinidad or Minorca and substantial accretions to Parma—but the negotiation took on compulsory overtones. Knowing full well María Luisa's devotion to Parma, which her daughter and son-in-law stood to inherit, Napoleon ordered his minister in Madrid to propose that in return for Louisiana, Parma would be enlarged somewhat. More than that he would not offer. Urquijo was warned: "I declare to you formally that your action will decide the fate of the Duke of Parma, and should you refuse to cede Louisiana you may count on getting nothing for that Prince." It was suggested that in Napoleon's hands vast and relatively vacant Louisiana would be an effective buffer to aggressive Americans with antimonarchical ideas and a fascination

20. General Dominique-Catherine de Perignon to the Prince of the Peace, Madrid, January 1, 1797, SpAHN (Estado 3891), cited in *Vial*, p. 104.

21. Casa Irujo to the Prince of the Peace, Philadelphia, August 5, 1797, with Godoy's marginal comment, SpAHN (Estado 3891), cited by Whitaker, *Mississippi Question*, p. 180.

22. Whitaker, *Mississippi Question*, chapter VII, passim.

for Mexican silver. The growth of the United States and her enduring bonds of interest with England, Bonaparte's envoy warned,

> may and must some day bring these two powers to concert together [in] the conquest of the Spanish colonies. If national interest is the surest foundation for political calculations, this conjecture must appear incontestable. The Court of Spain will do, then, at once a wise and great act if it calls the French to the defence of its colonies by ceding Louisiana to them and by replacing in their hands this outpost of its richest possessions in the New World.[23]

By the secret treaty signed at "La Granja" on October 1, 1800, Bonaparte promised to enlarge Parma to become the "Kingdom of Etruria," adding to it either Tuscany or the Roman Legations, and securing its recognition by the Holy Roman Emperor "and all other interested states." Retrocession of Louisiana, "with the same extent that it now has in the hands of Spain, and that it had when France possessed it," was not to take place until six months after Napoleon fulfilled his part of the bargain.

For two years, knowledge of this pact was kept from the Spanish people, an indication of the sensitive issues it entailed. Napoleon found its terms not as easy to meet as he had anticipated, for some of the "interested states" refused to cooperate. Eager to proceed with his plans in America, the first consul pressed Madrid for Louisiana's retrocession anyway. To this end His Catholic Majesty was promised, in Napoleon's name, that the colony would never be alienated to a third power; if France wished to divest herself of it at some future time, the only receiver could be Spain. Accepting at face value Bonaparte's pledge that the original terms of the exchange would be met, Carlos IV yielded. On October 15, 1802, orders were sent to Louisiana's delivery to France. Fernando, duke of Parma, died in 1802, and a year later his successor, Luís, María Luisa's nephew and son-in-law, also succumbed. "Etruria" as a political entity soon vanished from the map.[24]

Godoy did not head the ministry at the moment Louisiana was bartered away, but as the king's chief adviser he was a full party to the fateful step. Although the first consul and the "Prince of the Peace" were profoundly suspicious of one another, Bonaparte recognized in Godoy's ambitious character and sway over the Spanish sovereigns a tool useful for his own ends, and behind the scenes he sought the favorite's restoration to power. The Corsican's wish was gratified with the appointment of Godoy's kinsman, Pedro Cevallos, as foreign secretary in December 1800, while Godoy received a newly created and anomalous title making him the real power behind the

23. Cited by Henry Adams, *History*, 1 : 363–64; ibid., p. 176.
24. Whitaker, *Mississippi Question*, pp. 254–55; Izquierdo, *Antecedentes*, p. 85.

ministry.[25] With Godoy again at the helm, Madrid followed a course ever more subservient to Napoleon's will. The Convention of Aranjuez (1801) placed Spain once more at France's side to confront the Second European Coalition—Great Britain, Austria, and Russia. As part of Napoleonic strategy, Godoy led an army into Portugal to subdue that traditional British partisan and close its ports to English vessels. France's enemies sued for peace (Treaty of Amiens, 1802). Napoleon's regard for Spanish interests became evident when the preliminary treaty, drawn up without consulting Madrid, recognized British ownership of Trinidad. Spain was obliged to be consoled with regaining Minorca. The Peace of Amiens proved merely a truce, for Napoleon would not rest content until he had humbled England. In 1803 war erupted, and once again Spain was pressed to France's side.

Louisiana had never included lands west of the Mississippi basin, and its retrocession to France did not terminate Madrid's concern for her claims over the area beyond the Rocky Mountains, in California and the Pacific Northwest. Evidence of this continued interest in sustaining her prerogatives over the northwest coast is the officially subsidized publication in 1802 of the famous *Relación del viaje hecho por las goletas Sútil y Mexicana,* an account of the explorations of Alcalá Galiano and Valdés in 1792. This work contained an extensive introduction by Martín Fernández de Navarrete, one of the most prominent geographer-historians of the time, offering a succinct history of Spanish voyages to the northwest coast and vindicating Madrid's territorial claims there by right of prior discovery. The little volume was accompanied by an atlas in larger format with handsomely engraved maps and scenes. The sum invested in preparing and publishing the work evinces an official determination to demonstrate that the northwest coast belonged to Spain by right of discovery and exploration, and was not a part of the territory ceded to France.[26]

A graphic idea of the concepts then being taught to young Spanish noblemen and officers about Madrid's claims in western North America is provided by a map printed in Madrid in 1802 by Isidro de Antillón y Marzo to accompany his course in geography, taught "by order of His Majesty" (see end pocket). A cartographic rarity, little known and never republished until now, it is astonishingly well proportioned and complete, considering that it antedates the Lewis and Clark expedition, as well as Alexander von Humboldt's publications. A yellow color superimposed on California and the northwest coast as far as the northern tip of Vancouver Island delimits Antillón's concept of the extent of Spanish claims, whereas the coastline

25. André Fugier, *Napoléon et l'Espagne, 1799–1808,* 2 vols. (Paris, 1930), 1 : 119, 183–84. In August 1801 Godoy was named "Generalísimo de los Ejércitos," and two months later "Generalísimo de las Armas de Mar y Tierra." Izquierdo, *Antecedentes,* pp. 52–53.

26. A conclusion first asserted in 1844 by Greenhow, *History of Oregon and California,* 241n.

beyond, as far as the Aleutians, is pink. Louisiana was depicted as Spanish territory, since Bonaparte's promises with regard to Etruria had not been fulfilled, and the treaty of retrocession was not yet in effect.

### SPAIN AND THE LEWIS AND CLARK EXPEDITION

As early as 1782 Thomas Jefferson suggested to George Rogers Clark the possibility of participating in an expedition into Spanish territory to discover a route to the Pacific.[27] Clark turned down the feeler because of his own financial problems, but he warned that a large party would "never answer the purpose," as it would alarm the Indian nations.[28] To a certain extent Jefferson was following this advice when two years later he proposed that John Ledyard attempt to cross Siberia and North America alone. Clark's brother William, younger by eighteen years, would eventually achieve the feat. Although Jefferson contemplated having a route to the Pacific explored as a prologue to future territorial acquisitions, he recognized that the United States did not yet possess the strength to proceed beyond the Mississippi, and in the meantime he preferred to have Spain retain that area, rather than see it come under British, French, or Russian sway. In 1786 he confided to a friend:

> Our confederacy must be viewed as the nest from which all America, North and South is to be peopled. We should take care too not to think it for the interest of that great continent to press too soon on the Spaniards. Those countries cannot be in better hands. My fear is that they are too feeble to hold them till our population can be sufficiently advanced to gain it from them peice by peice [*sic*].[29]

Jefferson's acquaintance with Ledyard, later that year, heightened his appreciation of the importance of northwest coast resources for the United States. As Washington's secretary of state the Virginian was sent the deeds to Kendrick's land purchases on Vancouver Island, and by undisclosed means he acquired Ingraham's log of the *Hope*, 1790–92. In 1793 he found another candidate for his transcontinental project in André Michaux, a French botanist of renown then residing in the United States. While still secretary of state, Jefferson commenced organizing an expedition, led by Michaux, to ascend the Missouri and continue onward in an endeavor to reach the Pacific. Washington, Hamilton, and many other prominent men contributed to the American Philosophical Society's fund to finance Michaux. Jefferson wrote his instructions, which suggested crossing from the

27. Jefferson to Clark, November 26, 1792, and one other date, in Jefferson, *Papers*, 6 : 204–06, 371.
28. Clark to Jefferson, Richmond, Va., February 8, 1784, in Donald Jackson, ed., *Letters of the Lewis and Clark Expedition, with Related Documents, 1783–1854* (Urbana, Ill., 1962), pp. 655–56.
29. Jefferson to Archibald Stuart, Paris, January 25, 1786, in Jefferson, *Papers*, 9 : 217–19.

Mississippi to the Missouri well above Spanish outposts, to avoid being stopped. From the Missouri's headwaters he should search for a river to carry him to the Pacific at a temperate latitude.[30] The plan aborted when Michaux became entangled in Edmund Gênet's web and allowed his expedition to serve as camouflage for a projected assault against Spanish territory. Gênet's activities soon became a public scandal. Michaux had not even crossed the Mississippi when an order arrived from Paris for his recall.

Jefferson's disappointment with Michaux did not dissipate his concern for the scheme. Not long after he became president, rumors of Louisiana's retrocession to France gave the dream new urgency. An American expedition must reap the benefits accruing from the discovery of a route to the Pacific before Napoleon's forces had an opportunity to occupy upper Louisiana. If not, the achievement would surely fall to French explorers, with foreseeable political consequences. Jefferson could not have ignored the danger that his project would be an offense to Madrid, but it was a risk that he was willing to take. Spain's reaction to the effort triggered a new phase in Iberian measures to keep foreigners out of the hinterland between Nootka and New Mexico, an exciting story that has yet to be adequately told.

The president had qualms about the constitutionality of allocating funds to support an expedition outside national territory, but his attachment to the idea overcame his scruples on this point. Before broaching to Congress the subject of a federally sponsored expedition to the Pacific Northwest, he probed the extent of Spain's concern with that area through Carlos IV's ambassador to the United States, the marqués de Casa Irujo. Following their conversation, Casa Irujo informed the ministry that in a "frank and confident tone" Jefferson had inquired whether the Spanish court "would take it badly" if Congress sent a "group of travelers" in what he called "a small caravan" with "no other view than the advancement of geography," to explore from the Missouri to the Pacific Ocean. "I replied to him that making use of the same frankness with which he honored me, I would take the liberty of telling him, that I persuaded myself that an expedition of this nature could not fail to give umbrage to our Government." Casa Irujo thought he had impressed Jefferson with the impracticality and inadvisability of such an effort, but he warned: "The President has been all his life a man of letters, very speculative and a lover of glory, and it would be possible [that] he might attempt to perpetuate the fame of his administration not only by the measures of frugality and economy which characterize him, but also by discovering or attempting at least to discover the way by which the

---

30. Jefferson to Michaux, April 30, 1793, in Jackson, *Letters*, pp. 669–72 (see also pp. 667–69); Reuben Gold Thwaites, ed., *Original Journals of the Lewis and Clark Expedition, 1804–1806*, 8 vols. (New York, 1904–05), 7 195–96.

Americans may some day extend their population and their influence up to the coasts of the South Sea." [31] A marginal notation shows that on February 19, 1803, Carlos IV signified his satisfaction that the president had been persuaded to abandon the project.

Casa Irujo's negative reaction did not dissuade Jefferson from asking Congress for an appropriation for the project, a request originally to have appeared in the president's regular message to Congress on December 15, 1802. But when a draft was presented to the cabinet, Secretary of the Treasury Albert Gallatin counselled that it be made in secret; this was accomplished in a confidential message on January 18, 1803, and discussed in Congress behind closed doors. There were precedents for foreign scientific expeditions being permitted to carry out studies in the Spanish Empire, as with La Condamine's expedition and von Humboldt's visit to South and Central America. It is within this frame of reference that Jefferson's message remarked: "The nation claiming the territory, regarding this as a literary pursuit which it is in the habit of permitting within it's dominions, would not be disposed to view it with jealousy, even if the expiring state of it's interest there did not render it a matter of indifference." Casa Irujo's response had suggested Madrid's position on such a matter, and what Jefferson told Congress was something less than the truth. He asked that the $2,000 appropriation be designated "for the purpose of extending the external commerce of the U.S." This would "cover the undertaking from notice, and prevent the obstructions which interested individuals might otherwise previously prepare in it's [sic] way." [32] The maneuver did not escape Casa Irujo's knowledge, for in less than two weeks we find him notifying Madrid of it, but he said that the Senate "does not see the advantages that the President proposes in this expedition," and he predicted, erroneously, that the request would be defeated.[33]

Congress was induced to make the appropriation because Jefferson emphasized the need to counteract British traders on the upper Missouri. It became law on February 28. To head the expedition Jefferson designated Meriwether Lewis, his twenty-nine-year-old private secretary, who had seen army duty on the western frontier. Lewis selected as his assistant William Clark, four years his senior, whose military service in the West during the

31. Casa Irujo to Pedro Cevallos, December 2, 1802, SpAHN (Estado 6530), trans. in *Before Lewis and Clark*, 2 : 712–14. In the marqués de Casa Irujo's time, Spanish usage often employed the "Y" as initial letter in names now correctly spelled with an "I," and he signed his name "Casa Yrujo," and sometimes merely "Yrujo." The simplification appears in American historiography, but in Spanish indices one must look for him under "C."

32. Jefferson to Congress, January 18, 1803, confidential, DLC (Jefferson Papers), in Jackson, *Letters*, pp. 10–13.

33. Casa Irujo to Cevallos, January 31, 1803, SpAHN (Estado 5630), trans. in *Before Lewis and Clark*, 2 : 715–16.

Revolution and travels on behalf of his older brother recommended him greatly for the purpose. In an effort to acquaint Lewis with all available information about previous explorations, the president provided reproductions of Spanish and French maps and copies of the journals of Jean Baptiste Trudeau, John Mackay, and John Evans.[34]

A passport was requested for the expeditionaries from Edward Thornton, British chargé in Washington, who reported to Whitehall his opinion that "the apprehended occupation of Louisiana by the French seems to have accelerated the determination of the President, as he thinks it certain that on their arrival they will instantly set on foot enterprizes of a similar nature."[35] The passport from Thornton was used as leverage to secure a similar document from French chargé André Pichon, who complied but reported to Talleyrand that he had inquired whether the Spanish ambassador was also granting a passport, to which Jefferson replied "that he ought to give it" (*qu'il devait le donner*).[36]

There is no record of the president's requesting such a document from Casa Irujo. Their conversation of the preceding December made it inadvisable to do so. Despite assurances to Congress, Jefferson knew that the expedition would step on Spanish toes. To camouflage preparations, he informed Lewis, "the idea that you are going to explore the Mississippi has been generally given out; it satisfies public curiosity and masks sufficiently the real destination."[37] His instructions to Lewis were less than candid: "Your mission has been communicated to the ministers here from France, Spain and Great Britain, and through them to their governments; & such assurances given them as to it's objects, as we trust will satisfy them."[38] On the contrary, every effort had been made to keep the expedition a secret from Casa Irujo, aside from the initial sounding-out of his attitude toward a "literary pursuit" in the Far West. Jefferson knew that Lewis would penetrate an area still claimed by Spain. That he did not conceive the region beyond the crest of the Rocky Mountains as a part of Louisiana is shown in further instructions sent to Lewis at the latter's first wintering spot: "The boundaries of interior Louisiana are the high lands inclosing all the waters which run into the Mississippi or Missouri directly or indirectly, with a greater breadth on the gulph of Mexico." "The object of your mission is single," the same letter emphasized, "the direct water communication from

34. Teggart, "Notes," p. 192.

35. Thornton to Robert Banks Jenkinson, Lord Hawkesbury, British secretary of state for foreign affairs, Philadelphia, March 9, 1803, UKLPRO (F. O. 5/38), in Jackson, *Letters*, pp. 25–27.

36. Pichon to Talleyrand, Georgetown, 13 Ventose Year 11 (March 4, 1803), FrMAE (Corr. Pol., E. U. 55 : 318), trans. in ibid., pp. 22–23.

37. Jefferson to Lewis, April 27, 1803, DLC (Jefferson Papers), in ibid., p. 44.

38. Jefferson to Lewis, Washington, D.C., June 30, 1803, DLC (Jefferson Papers), in ibid., pp. 61–66.

sea to sea formed by the bed of the Missouri & perhaps the Oregon," and he sent along an "act for taking possession." [39]

It should be underscored that Jefferson's project was set in motion several months before there appeared the slightest inkling that the United States would be able to purchase all of Louisiana. Hearing rumors of the retrocession of that colony to France, the president had conceived the idea of purchasing the "island" on the east bank of the lower Mississippi upon which New Orleans is located, and also, if possible, the Floridas, East and West, which he erroneously thought were included in the retrocession. Jefferson sent James Monroe as minister extraordinary to France to advance the matter. Whitaker makes a persuasive case that Monroe's appointment was made more to placate Western sentiment on the issue than from a conviction that the desired territory could be acquired, for which end prospects of success were slender.[40]

Louisiana had not been formally occupied by France, for mosquitoes, yellow fever, and Toussaint L'Ouverture's army of former slaves had destroyed the forces with which Napoleon intended to rebuild a colonial empire in the heart of North America. In 1802 Pitt had offered Louisiana to the United States if the latter would not take offense at the area's being invaded by British forces. If Napoleon could not protect the colony, it behooved him to place it in American hands. To Monroe's amazement, upon arriving in Paris he found the first consul disposed to sell all of it. When Bonaparte's plans in Haiti bogged down and an unusually cold winter detained the fleet intended to reoccupy New Orleans, he suddenly decided to convert the entire colony into cash, even though the terms with regard to Etruria had not been fulfilled and he had promised Spain not to transfer Louisiana to a third power. As a recent work points out, whatever Louisiana's economic promise to Napoleon, 'it was outweighed by the military value to him of the price paid by the United States and prevention of the colony's seizure by Britain." [41] The treaties of purchase and cession were signed at once (April 30, 1803), before the president or Congress could be consulted.

The Spanish ministry was understandably dismayed when word arrived that Louisiana had been sold to the very republic against which Carlos sought a buffer. A protest lodged with the United States claimed that the transfer was illegal, since the terms ceding it to France prohibited alienation to any power but Spain. The protest went no further than that, for Casa

39. Jefferson to Lewis, Washington, D.C., November 16, 1803, DLC (Jefferson Papers), in ibid., pp. 136–38.

40. Whitaker, *Mississippi Question*, p. 208.

41. Francis S. Philbrick, *The Rise of the West, 1754–1830* (New York, 1965; paperback ed., 1966), p. 217, citing Napoleon's statement to François Barbé-Marbois, as related in the latter's *History of Louisiana* (Philadelphia, 1830), pp. 263–64.

Irujo advised from Philadelphia that if Madrid tried to retain Louisiana the United States surely would attempt to seize it anyway, and as indemnification for the expense might invade and annex East and West Florida.[42]

Meriwether Lewis left the capital on July 5, 1803, shortly after word of the Louisiana Purchase arrived. Upon reaching the Mississippi, in December, he made a short side trip downstream to visit Lieutenant Carlos Dehault Delassus, Spanish governor at St. Louis.[43] No orders had arrived there regarding an American takeover, and, although the reception was polite, after examining passports and papers the governor told Lewis that "he was sensible [that] the objects of the Government of the U. States as well as my own were no other than those stated in my Passports or such as had been expressed by myself; that these in their execution, would not be injurious to his royal master, the King of Spain, nor would they in his opinion prove in any manner detrimental to his Majesty's subjects with whose interests he was at that moment particularly charged, that as an individual he viewed it as a hazardous enterprize, but wished it every success, nor would he from his personal inclinations obstruct it[s] progress a single moment." Nevertheless, Dehault Delassus concluded that "his feelings as a man, his duty as an Officer, and his orders as such, strengthened also by the undeviating policy of the Spanish Government, with regard to the nonadmission of foreigners into the interior of their provinces, equally forbad his granting me permission at this time to ascend the Missouri river; however he would if permitted by me take a transcript of my Passports, and send them immediately by an express to New Orleans to the Govr. Genl. of the Province, and that he would with cheerfulness give the aid of his influence with that officer, to promote my wishes." [44] Lewis was advised to remain at Cahokia until such time as the governor-general gave consent for them to ascend the Missouri.

Dehault Delassus's report to his superiors in New Orleans gives quite another perspective: "I have hinted to him that my orders did not permit me to consent to his passing to enter the Missouri River and that I was opposing it in the name of the King, my master." Lewis had replied, the Spaniard wrote, that "my opinion sufficed and that from now he would not go to the said river, I having observed to him that he surprised me for not having provided himself with a passport from our Spanish Minister in Philadelphia; that if he had had a passport in the name of the King my master, he could have removed all difficulty." To this the American responded that upon leaving Philadelphia "it was already at the beginning of

42. Bemis, *Diplomatic History*, pp. 182–83.

43. Pierre Charles du Hault Delassus de Luzière, a landed aristocrat from Flanders, left France because of the revolution. Reaching New Orleans in 1794, two years later he was named Spanish commandant at Nuevo Madrid, and lieutenant governor of Upper Louisiana in 1799. *Vial*, pp. 124n, 186n.

44. Lewis to Jefferson, Cahokia, December 19, 1803, T in PHi, in Jackson, *Letters*, pp. 146–47.

July, that he thought he would find the French here, that for that reason, he had not believed it necessary to carry a passport from Señor Marqués de [Casa] Yrujo." Lewis said he would remain on the American side of the Mississippi until spring, awaiting orders from New Orleans permitting him to pass, but Dehault Delassus warned, "I believe that his mission has no other object than to discover the Pacific Ocean, following the Missouri, and to make intelligent observations, because he has the reputation of being a very well educated man and of many talents." [45]

The marqués de Casa Calvo, the governor's superior in New Orleans, replied that if St. Louis had not already been transferred to the appropriate American representative, "you will not put any obstacle to impede Capt. Merry Weather Lewis's entrance in the Missouri whenever he wishes; nevertheless Your Excellency did right in taking the dispositions of which your official letter no. 213 treats." [46] The warning had been shoved aside. More than a month elapsed before Dehault's Delassus's stance invoked correspondingly zealous measures to protect Spanish claims over the area beyond Louisiana. That sudden turnabout, following weeks of inaction, appears to have been triggered by a covert act of the highest ranking officer in the United States army, Brigadier General James Wilkinson. A man of exceeding ambition and considerable energy, Wilkinson never allowed military responsibilities to distract his attention for very long from schemes to achieve personal pecuniary benefit. During the Revolutionary War he had a part in the Conway Cabal, an unsuccessful attempt to remove Washington from supreme command. Habitually involved in deception and intrigue, in 1787 he had begun to receive a sizable but irregularly paid pension from the Spanish governor in New Orleans in return for information provided in a series of memorials and, by his own offer, for promoting pro-Spanish sentiment in Kentucky. A veteran of the Battle of Fallen Timbers (1794), as his rivals for military prominence faded from the scene Wilkinson became the nation's ranking general, commander of the army in the West, and one of the most influential men in the country.[47]

At word of Louisiana's acquisition, Jefferson disposed that Wilkinson share with the first American governor of that new territory the honor of taking possession. They received formal delivery of New Orleans on December 20, 1803, and the general was still there as Lewis and Clark prepared to break winter camp and start up the Missouri. Ready as ever to take ad-

45. Dehault Delassus to Manuel Salcedo and the marqués de Casa Calvo, St. Louis, December 9, 1803, SpAGI (Papeles de Cuba 2368), trans. in *Before Lewis and Clark*, 2 : 719–20.

46. [Casa Calvo] to Dehault Delassus, New Orleans, January 28, 1804, SpAGI (Papeles de Cuba 141), in Jackson, *Letters*, p. 167.

47. Bemis, "Pinckney's Treaty," pp. 109–125; James Ripley Jacobs, *Tarnished Warrior, Major-General James Wilkinson* (New York, 1938), pp. 205–06; Thomas Perkins Abernethy, *The Burr Conspiracy* (New York, 1954), passim.

vantage of his position to glean any tangential rewards, Wilkinson submitted to Spanish authorities another of his secret reports, at least by early March 1804. Titled "Reflections on Louisiana," it suggested means whereby Spain might protect her territories from American encroachment. The original in English probably was destroyed; the Spanish translation is signed by Vicente Folch, governor of West Florida, to whom it was attributed when first published in 1911.[48] That Folch's signature attested to its authenticity, and that Wilkinson submitted it to him for translation were subsequently demonstrated by Isaac Joslin Cox.[49]

The general was privy to Lewis's objectives and revealed them to his Spanish cronies. He recommended that "an express ought immediately to be sent to the governor of Santa Fe, and another to the captain-general of Chihuagea [Chihuahua] in order that they may detach a sufficient body of chasseurs to intercept Captain Lewis and His party who are on the Missouri River, and force them to retire or take them prisoners." [50] In (West) Florida, he asserted, bets were being offered that within five years the Americans would have established a port on the Pacific coast. Having underscored American aggressiveness, he emphasized the importance of checking their infiltration into Texas and the Interior Provinces by insisting upon a boundary along the Mississippi. He also suggested that action be taken to break up Daniel Boone's settlement on the Missouri. On March 12, 1804, Wilkinson cautioned these same officials that his name must never be used in their correspondence, just the number "13," and that his letters must be destroyed after translation.[51]

On the basis of this seemingly treacherous action one cannot assume that Wilkinson "betrayed" Lewis and Clark, for his Spanish contacts probably questioned him about Lewis's mission after the warning from St. Louis. He did not tell the Spaniards anything about the expedition that they did not already know. On the other hand, the measures that he suggested would endanger Jefferson's endeavor. The web spun by the general's covert activities in the period of the alleged Burr Conspiracy (1804–07) is so complex that the possibility must not be overlooked that, rather than aiding Madrid,

48. [Wilkinson], "Reflections on Louisiana," SpAGI (Papeles de Cuba 2355), T in Miss. State Dept. of Archives and History, Jackson, Miss., trans. in James A. Robertson, *Louisiana Under Spain*, 2 : 325–47. West Florida and Louisiana had different governors, resident in Baton Rouge and New Orleans, and both were subordinate to the captain general of Cuba.

49. I. J. Cox, "General Wilkinson and His Later Intrigues With the Spaniards," *AHR* 19 (1913–14) : 798n. He cites Folch's description of the circumstances surrounding translation of Wilkinson's memorial in Folch to [Salvador de Muro y Salazar, Marqués de] Someruelos, Captain General de Cuba, April 10, 1804, "reservada No. 3," SpAGI (Papeles de Cuba 1574).

50. [Wilkinson], "Reflections," p. 342.

51. Wilkinson to Casa Calvo, March 12, 1804, SpAHN (Estado 5545), excerpt in Abernethy, *Burr Conspiracy*, pp. 11–12.

he may have been setting the stage for incidents that would provide an excuse to declare war and invade Spanish borderlands.

This ostensible service to Spanish interests gave Wilkinson an opportunity to request that his former annual pension of $2,000, unpaid for some ten years, not only be paid, but be doubled henceforth. The marqués de Casa Calvo thought so highly of the general's memorial that he forwarded it to the ministry acompanied by additional suggestions, paid Wilkinson $12,000, and granted his request for valuable commercial privileges.[52] Most of the sum was invested in sugar, which the general shipped to New York City.[53] Proceeding there himself, he commenced machinations with Aaron Burr that led to one of the most intriguing chapters of American history. As we shall see, the affair would have a profound effect upon the Spanish reaction to the American challenge in the Pacific Northwest. Interestingly, more than a year and a half after delivering his memorial to Spanish officials—and when it was too late to recall or warn Lewis and Clark, or protect them from ambush—the general covered himself by informing Secretary of War Henry Dearborn about Spanish plans to intercept the American expedition, without ever going into detail as to how he found them out.[54] As far as the general knew at that late date, the encounter might have already taken place.

Sebastián Calvo de la Puerta y O'Farril, marqués de Casa Calvo, had been designated to determine the boundaries of Louisiana preparatory to turning it over to France, only to learn of its alienation to the United States. His answer to Dehault Delassus's warning about the danger from Jefferson's "literary pursuit" was, as mentioned, that no obstacle be placed in "Capt. Merry Weather Lewis' " path. On March 5, following Wilkinson's suggestions to the letter, Casa Calvo took a decisive step toward thwarting the American expedition by sending a warning overland by special courier to Nemesio Salcedo, commandant general of the Interior Provinces in Chihuahua:

> This step on the part of the United States at the same time that it took possession of the province of Louisiana [and] its haste to instruct itself and to explore the course of the Missouri whose origin they claim belongs to them, extending their designs as far as the South Sea, forces us necessarily to become active and to hasten our steps in order to cut off the gigantic steps of our neighbors if we wish, as it is our duty, to preserve undamaged [intact] the dominions of the King and to prevent

52. **Casa Calvo to Cevallos,** March 30, 1804, SpAHN (Estado 5545), cited by ibid., p. 12.

53. Deposition of John McDonough, Jr., 1807, cited by Abernethy, p. 254; Cox, "General Wilkinson," p. 800.

54. Wilkinson to the secretary of war, October 19, 1805, DNA, cited by John Bakeless, *Lewis and Clark, Partners in Discovery* (New York, 1947), p. 475.

ruin and destruction of the *Provincias Internas* and of the Kingdom of New Spain.

The only means which presents itself is to arrest Captain Merry Weather and his party, which cannot help but pass through the nations neighboring New Mexico, its presidios or *rancherías*.[55]

After remarking on other matters, Casa Calvo reemphasized the need for counteracting the American menace:

In view of what has been said above I do not doubt that Your Excellency will give orders that the most efficacious steps be taken to arrest . . . Captain Merry and his followers, who, according to notices, number twenty-five men, and to seize their papers and instruments that may be found on them. This action may be based upon the fact that without permission of the Spanish government they have entered its territory. Since the line of demarcation has not been determined as yet, they cannot infer that [the area] already belongs to the United States. It is fitting to the confidential intentions of the ministry, by which I am instructed to stop the progress of these investigations, that although there be no motive or pretext whatsoever, nevertheless it is absolutely necessary for reasons of state to carry out the arrest of the said captain.[56]

Nevertheless, for unknown reasons, Casa Calvo waited almost a month before sending Madrid a copy of this missive, with a covering letter stressing his fear that the United States, in "hasty and gigantic steps," was attempting to form a chain of establishments to the South Sea, by ascending the Missouri and "making themselves masters of our rich possessions, which they desire." "It is painful to acknowledge it and experience it," he wrote, "but it will be much more painful not to use all our forces, while there is still time to remedy [the situation] even though it be at the cost of continual vigilance and no small expense." [57]

Lewis and Clark did not start up the "Big Muddy" until May 14, 1804. Their party was now enlarged to some fifty men. Not long after leaving winter camp, they met another party going downstream, led by Régis Loisel, Clamorgan's associate in the venture stemming from the defunct Missouri Company. Loisel provided them with valuable information about the territory and the Indian nations ahead, but upon arriving in St. Louis he presented Dehault Delassus with a memorial pointing out the American expedi-

55. "El único medio que se presenta es arrestar el Capitan Merry Wheather, y su Partido que no puede menos de Pasar por entre las Naciones vecinas de Nuestro Mexico, por sus Presidios o rancherías." Casa Calvo to Nemesio Salcedo, New Orleans, March 5, 1804, SpAHN (Estado 5542), trans. in *Before Lewis and Clark*, 2 : 731–32.

56. Ibid.

57. Casa Calvo to Pedro Cevallos, New Orleans, March 30, 1804, SpAHN (Estado 5542), trans. in ibid., 2 : 727–28. The message was received in Madrid on July 18, 1804.

tion's menace to Spanish interests, and he offered to serve as a Spanish agent to counteract the Americans on the Missouri.[58] His report was forwarded at once to Casa Calvo.

Even before the alarming reports about Meriwether Lewis were relayed to Madrid, the ministry was engaged in debating the stance to be taken along the western perimeter of American territory. As to Louisiana's boundaries on the north and west, the Junta for the Fortifications and Defenses of Indies decided that

> since those that ought to be established on the north side are so doubtful and little known, we must trust the prudent discretion and careful investigations of our commissioners, stipulating that they obtain in the boundary adjustment every advantage possible conforming with equitable reasoning, it being beyond controversy that the Misuri and Misisipi confluence ought to belong to Spain because, among other reasons, . . . if both banks of the Misuri belong to Spain, this would avoid giving the neighboring power any pretext of navigating that voluminous river, whose course curves around north of New Mexico.[59]

Several weeks later a letter was entered into the supreme council's record that reflected Godoy's thoughts upon an appropriate boundary. "Our commissioners should maintain that the new possessors of Louisiana who enter from the Misisipi to navigate the Red River may not go farther upstream than the precise point where the dividing line, which ought to pass between Los Adaes and Nachitoches, cuts the said river near the latter post, and also that they may not pretend the slightest right to navigate the Misuri River, for that never had any relation to Louisiana." [60] Whereas in the American capital it was assumed that the Louisiana Purchase doubled the national area, Godoy sought to restrict it to the present state of Louisiana (minus that portion east of the Mississippi and north of the "island" of New Orleans), eastern Arkansas, and eastern Missouri.

Casa Calvo's urgently worded warning to the commandant general of the Interior Provinces took almost two months to cross the vast plains, mountains, and deserts between New Orleans and Chihuahua. Salcedo's response was to remit the missive on May 3, 1804, to Fernando de Chacón, governor of New Mexico, together with an order stating that "as the views of this expe-

58. Loisel to Dehault Delassus, May 28, 1804, MHi (Houck Papers), trans. in ibid., 2 : 735–40; Bakeless, *Lewis and Clark*, pp. 117–18.

59. "Consulta de la Junta de Fortificaciones y Defensas de Indias," Madrid, March 17, 1804, copy in MxAGN (Prov. Internas 200), fol. 267–68v, AT.

60. Francisco Gil to Pedro Cevallos, Madrid, April 6, 1804, copy in MxAGN (Prov. Internas 200), fol. 265–66v, AT; quotes a letter from Antonio Sampes, jefe del estado mayor, communicating opinions of the Prince of the Peace.

dition [Merry] may be directed to the ends which the said Marqués [Casa Calvo] affirms, it is very prudent and necessary that on our part they may be impeded and [if] it may not be possible, either on account of the weather which they have had since the cited date, or on account of the considerable distances, let us take at least some knowledge of its progress and state of being." To accomplish these purposes, Chacón was instructed to "come to an agreement with the chief of the Comanches or with the Chief of any other [Indian nation] which you judge more *á propos,* [to] send a party of individuals which you may collect to reconnoitre the country which lies between those villages as far as the right bank of the Missouri, with instructions and necessary provisions so that they examine if there are traces or other vestiges of the expedition of Merry and so that they acquaint themselves with the direction that it has taken and of their operations upon the territory, if they do not succeed in finding any other Indian village which may have seen it and may be able to give these notices." He suggested that Chacón "inform Don Pedro Vial of the object of this voyage in case he may desire to join the expedition, as he is the most experienced in those territories." Salcedo stressed that "nothing would be more useful than the apprehension of Merry, and even though I realize it is not an easy undertaking, chance might proportion things in such a way that it might be successful, for which reason it will not be superfluous for Your Excellency to give notice of this matter to the Indians, interesting their friendship and notions of generosity, telling them that they will be well compensated." [61]

The *Diccionario* of the Real Academia Española defines *aprehensión* as "Acción y efecto de aprehender" (action or effect of seizing), *aprehender* being "Coger, prender a una persona, o bien alguna cosa, especialmente si es de contrabando" (to catch, to seize a person, or else something, especially if it is contraband). Followed to the letter, Salcedo's order meant that Merry should be seized or arrested.

On the same day as his order for Merry's "apprehension" went out, Salcedo answered Casa Calvo's warning, commenting that the passage of five months since the message from St. Louis made it difficult to attain the success that he would have desired. Some eight months earlier he had sent governors of the border provinces orders which would be quite opportune "even in the very case that Your Excellency speaks of." Until he received more exact news, the information "that I now have will suffice and I am protecting myself by repeating to you the punctual observance of my cited orders." Salcedo's letter is tinged with indignation. He chided Casa Calvo

61. "Nada sería más útil que la aprehensión de Merry, y aunque conozco es empresa no fácil pudiera la casualidad proporcionar las cosas de modo que se consiguiera . . ." Salcedo to the governor of New Mexico, Chihuahua, May 3, 1804, SpAHN (Estado 5542), trans. in *Before Lewis and Clark,* 2 : 734–35.

for not having made a protest about Merry to the United States through the general in command of Louisiana.[62]

In a third letter, written the same day, Salcedo sent the viceroy of Mexico an account of his measures with regard to Merry, enclosing copies of Casa Calvo's letter and his reply, and five days later he remitted a similar set, including Chacón's orders, to Madrid. "Your Excellency will recognize," he noted,

> that the expedition is directed to territories under my command and that it is a step of the said United States which indicates its ambitious views in the same act . . . [as] taking possession of Louisiana. I am unable to dictate any other precautionary step than the orders already communicated to the governors of Texas and New Mexico relative to their preventing the introduction of foreigners in[to] the districts of both provinces, and to their refusing permission to such foreigners." [63]

These orders would be reiterated, he declared, and a party of Indian allies had been sent to reconnoiter as far as the Missouri, "to examine if the expedition of Merry has penetrated into these territories, to acquire all possible knowledge of its progress, and even to stop them, making efforts to apprehend it." He added that he was sending an account of the matter to Casa Irujo in Philadelphia for proper action there. The viceroy acknowledged Salcedo's letter, requesting that he be kept informed of developments and results of measures taken, "it being very important to the service of the king." The ministry replied four and a half months later that Salcedo's conduct received His Majesty's full approval.[64]

Upon receiving Salcedo's criticism that he had procrastinated in warning Chihuahua about Captain "Merry" in time for effective countermeasures to be taken, Casa Calvo was incensed. He sent the ministry Salcedo's reply, accompanied by a full account of the matter, protesting that he had tried to hasten measures "which must be taken to contain the ambitious designs and extraordinary intentions of our neighbors." "In these parallel documents," he suggested, "Your Excellency will surely observe the indifference with which so important a message has been treated." With obscure reasoning Salcedo had refrained from taking "efficacious and prompt measures which might have been followed upon receipt of my letter in order to compensate

62. Salcedo to Casa Calvo, Chihuahua, May 3, 1804, SpAGI (Papeles de Cuba 2368), trans. in ibid., pp. 732–34.

63. Salcedo to Pedro Cevallos, Chihuahua, May 8, 1804, SpAHN (Estado 5542), and Salcedo to Viceroy José de Iturrigaray, Chihuahua, May 3, 1804, MxAGN (Hist. 200), both trans. in ibid., pp. 728–31.

64. Iturrigaray to Salcedo, [Mexico City] June 2, 1804, MxAGN (Hist. 200), and [Cevallos] to Salcedo, San Ildefonso, September 24, 1804, SpAHN (Estado 5542), both trans. in ibid., pp. 729, 735.

for the time and distance," and as a consequence the Americans had covered considerable distance already. Since Spain had no establishments on the upper Missouri, there was no means of knowing exactly where they were. He deplored the fact that Salcedo had not taken "more active measures because of an erroneous confidence, and I fear that this same confidence will injure the promptness of the dispositions which should be taken to stop the progress of Merry." [65] Shortly afterward Casa Calvo must have received Loisel's warning, for we find him suggesting that Loisel be employed as a Spanish agent on the upper Missouri to counteract the American threat.[66]

Casa Calvo's irate reports about the danger of an inadequate response to the American challenge on the upper Missouri struck a responsive chord in Madrid. He was commended for insisting that Salcedo take effective measures to stop "the expedition of the American Captain Merry Weather directed to reconnoitre the territory which belongs to His Majesty." "I am informing you," Minister of State Pedro Cevallos wrote, "that His Majesty has ordered me to instruct his Minister Plenipotentiary in the United States that he complain to that government against so manifest an offense against the sovereignty of the King." [67] The recommendation that Loisel be employed as a Spanish agent on the upper Missouri was approved. Unfortunately, the trader had succumbed in New Orleans the preceding October.

A Spanish note to Secretary of State Madison (March 12, 1805) represented the Lewis and Clark expedition as violating the status quo in the disputed territory, since its true boundaries had yet to be established.[68] Jefferson did not respond, formally or informally. American unwillingness to give some sort of answer increased Madrid's determination to thwart the president's project. The ministry's anger over the matter jeopardized negotiations in Madrid with Jefferson's envoy, James Monroe. After successfully acquiring Louisiana, Monroe had been named ambassador to London. At the outbreak of war between Spain and Britain in 1803, Jefferson had sent him on a special mission to Madrid to assist Charles Pinckney, the American representative there. Consistent with his ideas in 1790, Jefferson hoped to profit from Spain's embarrassments by pressing for both the inclusion of West Florida as part of the Louisiana Purchase and the cession of East Florida in return for renunciation of certain pecuniary claims against Spain.

65. Casa Calvo to Cevallos, New Orleans, September 15, 1804, SpAGI (Papeles de Cuba 2368), trans. in ibid., pp. 750–52.

66. Casa Calvo to Cevallos, and Casa Calvo to the Prince of the Peace, New Orleans, September 30, 1804, SpAGI (Papeles de Cuba 2368), trans. in ibid., pp. 754–58.

67. Cevallos to Casa Calvo, January 17, 1805, SpAGI (Papeles de Cuba 176B), trans. in ibid., p. 752; see also pp. 736n, 755–58.

68. Casa Irujo to Madison, Washington, D.C. March 12, 1805, SpAHN (Estado 5542). A copy formerly in Department of State is cited by I. J. Cox, *The Early Explorations of Louisiana* (Cincinnati, 1906), pp. 23, 134.

The president also sought to establish a western boundary for Louisiana at the Río Grande.[69] Monroe found the discourteous treatment he received at Godoy's hands difficult to understand. Word reaching Madrid about the president's "literary pursuit" did not improve the climate for Monroe's bold objectives. Negotiations were eventually broken off and, on May 22, 1805, Monroe took leave of Carlos IV and returned to London. That very day Madrid warned Viceroy Iturrigaray that "the political situation with regard to the United States of America is darkly uncertain, because the negotiations which were undertaken with Mr. Monroe have been broken off on account of the fact that the claims he advanced were as ambitious and exorbitant as they were prejudicial to the rights of the Crown." The viceroy was instructed that "the defenses of our possessions will, therefore, be looked to with utmost care." [70] The warning was formulated into a royal order (June 5, 1805) to Salcedo, duly relayed to Santa Fe.[71] The plan seeded by Wilkinson, taken up by Casa Calvo, approved in Madrid, and to be executed by the governor of New Mexico by now showed every indication of maturing into an incident of considerable dimensions.

### THE FIRST SPANISH ATTEMPT TO APPREHEND LEWIS AND CLARK

The fact that orders to check Meriwether Lewis actually got beyond the planning stage and that four successive expeditions set out from Santa Fe for this purpose between 1804 and 1806 has virtually eluded historians, including the authors of the most recent and complete studies of the Lewis and Clark expedition. Documents in Madrid, Seville, Mexico City, and Santa Fe permit the reconstruction of this campaign to its curious and significant culmination.[72]

69. I. J. Cox, *The West Florida Controversy, 1798–1813* (Baltimore, 1918), pp. 102–38; Bemis, *Diplomatic History*, pp. 183–85.

70. Francisco Gil to Iturrigaray, May 22, 1805, MxAGN (Reales Cédulas 195), excerpt trans. in Walter Flavius McCaleb, *The Aaron Burr Conspiracy* (New York, 1936), p. 94.

71. Royal order, June 5, 1805, NmSRC (Span. Arch. 1841a); see Ralph Twitchell, *The Spanish Archives of New Mexico*, 2 vols. (Cedar Rapids, Ia., 1914), 2 : 471. In 1963 the document had disappeared.

72. Some of the pertinent material has been catalogued by Twitchell, *Spanish Archives*, pp. 480–89, and by Herbert Eugene Bolton, *Guide to Materials for the History of the United States in the Principal Archives of Mexico* (Washington, D.C., 1913), pp. 308–09, but its relevance is not indicated in either work. In 1906 I. J. Cox, in *Early Explorations*, pp. 24, 65–66, 85–87, mentioned an expedition northward from Santa Fe in 1804, but he did not identify Captain "Merry" as Lewis. Cox was cited by Thomas Maitland Marshall, *A History of the Western Boundary of the Louisiana Purchase, 1819–1841* (Berkeley, 1914), chapter II, passim, but again the connection with the famous expedition went unnoticed. Carl Irving Wheat, *Mapping the Transmississippi West, 1540–1861*, 2 vols. (San Francisco, 1957–58), 1 : 127–28n, concluded that the projected expedition to intercept Lewis and Clark did not take place. In 1960 the author's doctoral dissertation at Yale cited the documentation indicating that such attempts did occur. Donald Jackson's masterful edition of *The Journals of Zebulon Montgomery Pike, With Letters and Related Documents*, 2 vols. (Norman, Okla., 1966), 2 : 109–10n, 377n (hereafter cited as

The very day the American explorers left winter camp on the Mississippi's east bank and started poling up the Missouri (May 14, 1804), the plan to thwart them began taking shape with the arrival in Santa Fe of two Apaches bearing a packet of letters from Chihuahua for Governor Chacón. Among the letters was a copy of Casa Calvo's warning to Salcedo (March 5, 1804) and Salcedo's order to Chacón (May 3, 1804) for the "apprehension" of Captain Merry. "Taking into account the projects and ideas of Mr. Merry," Chacón replied two days later, "I shall inquire of the allied [Indian] nations what they know about the matter, encouraging them to preserve and defend the lands they inhabit and upon which depends their subsistence and commerce with tribes friendly to them; and if from the said heathens I cannot learn anything, I will send a party to reconnoiter the terrain between this province and the cited Misury River, employing Bernardo Castro's project of searching for the Mountain of Gold [a legend of Coronado's time], by this means avoiding any suspicion on the part of Merry or the barbarous tribes that might aid him." [73] There is nothing in the letter, beyond the natural assumption, to prove that Chacón passed on to Pedro Vial the order for Merry's "apprehension." June and July would elapse before the projected expedition set forth.

Pedro Vial was relatively unknown until the recent biography by Loomis and Nasatir. Born sometime between 1746 and 1755 in Lyon, the French explorer-guide had acquired extensive and unique geographic knowledge of the uppermost Missouri before coming to trade along Texas's Red River, as early as 1779. Virtually singlehanded he opened Santa Fe to the outside world—until his time the only route being by way of El Paso and Chihuahua. In 1786–87 he found an overland route from San Antonio de Bexar to Santa Fe, and two years later he established a more northerly route from Santa Fe to Natchitoches. In 1792, at Revillagigedo's instigation, he discovered a way from Santa Fe to San Luís de Ilinueces, the famed Santa Fe Trail. During the latter exploit, Vial and companions were captured by a

Jackson, *Pike*), includes or cites several of these items, but specifically as they illuminate Spanish reactions to Pike, not to Lewis and Clark. In *Pedro Vial and the Roads to Santa Fe* (1967), Noel Loomis and Abraham P. Nasatir cite some of the pertinent documents in the course of chronicling Vial's life, but without piecing together the panoply of efforts to intercept Lewis and Clark. While noting the Spanish desire to stop Captain "Meri," they conclude: "It seems too that they might well have done so, but, although everybody talked about it, nobody had the courage to pull the string." (p. 109). By way of explanation they suggest: "A skeptic might think the Spaniards had waited long enough to be thoroughly safe, but it rather looks as if there were too much caution, too much red tape, and too much of that venerable pastime sometimes spoken of as passing the buck" (p. 203).

Closer examination of the extant documentation suggests quite a different conclusion, that is, that the Spanish made repeated efforts of considerable magnitude to intercept Lewis and Clark, and came surprisingly and dangerously close to achieving their objective.

73. Chacón to Salcedo, Santa Fe, May 16, 1804, NmSRC (Span. Arch. 1730), AT.

Kansas war party, stripped of clothing and supplies, and would have been killed on the spot had Vial not been recognized by a brave as a friend from previous years, presumably in Spanish Illinois. Six weeks later, Vial and his captors reached a friendly village on the Kansas River, where the explorers were succored and clothed by a French trader and permitted to continue on to St. Louis.[74]

In 1795 the governor of New Mexico sent Vial to make peace with the Pawnee tribe. Eight days out of Santa Fe he reached one of their villages on the Kansas, meeting traders who were only ten days by canoe from St. Louis, which made Spanish officials realize that they could no longer count upon the intervening wastelands as a secure barrier against foreign penetration of New Mexico.[75] Two years later Vial left New Mexico for upper Louisiana, apparently as a result of repressive measures taken against inhabitants of French origin, a consequence of royal orders in response to the French Revolution. In 1799 he was residing at Portage des Sioux, north of St. Louis. With the relaxation of Franco-Spanish tensions, Vial gave up his efforts to discover and exploit lead mines around St. Geneviève, and by 1803 he was back in Santa Fe, serving as a guide and interpreter.[76]

As second in command on the 1804 effort to "apprehend" Captain Merry, Vial would be accompanied by José Jarvet, a soldier-interpreter with a long familiarity with the Pawnee. Jarvet passed as a "Frenchman" but was actually a Protestant from Pennsylvania. His original patronymic, perhaps Harvey or some such name, is not known, but Spanish documents refer to him variously: Jarvet, Jarvay, Jarvai, Jarbet, Tarvet, Tanvert, Charvet, Chalvet, Chalvert, Calvert, and Calbert. Jarvet is the spelling ultimately used by Vial, the only author of extant writing who knew the young American intimately.[77]

Vial, Jarvet, and a column of soldiers left Santa Fe on August 1, 1804, and

---

74. *Vial,* pp. x, 328, 376–78, 384–88.

75. Trudeau to Carondelet, no. 229. St. Louis, July 4, 1795, SpAGI (Papeles de Cuba 22), trans. in *Before Lewis and Clark,* 1 : 329–30.

76. *Vial,* pp. 412–17.

77. See Bloom, "Death of Jacques d'Eglise," p. 371n; Jackson, *Pike,* 2 : 109n, suggests that he may have been the trader Joseph Calvé, who once owned property at St. Charles, and Portage des Sioux. Jarvet is often called a "Frenchman," but Pedro de Nava, Salcedo's predecessor, learned that he was born in Philadelphia, of Presbyterian stock, and in 1794 left Fort Pitt and came to Natchez, New Orleans, and Natchitoches. The youth lived some fourteen months among the nomadic tribes, making his way by repairing firearms. During the alarm over radical "Frenchmen," Jarvet was ordered brought to Coahuila and prevented from "penetrating to the Indians, as he might attempt to do, since this class of wandering men love greatly the opportunity that facilitates their living among the barbarians in order to give free reign to their passions." Pedro de Nava to the Duke of Alcudia, Chihuahua, November 3, 1795, SpAGI (Estado, Santo Domingo 37), cited by *Vial,* pp. 171–72, 412. That Jarvet sired a child by a Pawnee woman is borne out by a reference that in 1806 the lad, then 10, was brought to Santa Fe. Real Alencaster to Salcedo, Santa Fe, October 8, 1806, NmSRC (Span. Arch. 2022). Keeping Jarvet away from Indian country proved difficult. In 1804 traders Baptiste LaLande and Jeanot Meteyer were said to be going from St. Louis to the Pawnee, "with the idea of meeting another,

at Taos the mayor provided them with ten citizens and an equal number of Indians. The entire company numbered fifty-two. Following the Río de las Ánimas Perdidas en el Purgatorio (Purgatoire) to the Napestle (Arkansas) and traveling rapidly, by September 3 they had reached the Río Chato (Platte). They followed the Platte for two days and on the 6th arrived at a Pawnee village in central Nebraska. "A great many of their captains came to meet us," Vial's diary relates.

> They gave us a great reception; after arriving at their villages I found about twenty Frenchmen from whom I learned how the Americans had taken over the government. They told me there had been numerous parties (*compañías*) with four carriages (*carruajes*) very loaded with articles for all the nations of the Misury that they might encounter in the interior. In every village they pass, large gifts are made to all chiefs and principal men and said chiefs are induced to surrender medals and patents in their possession, given by the Spanish government. I have charged the aforementioned chiefs of the country not to give up the medals or patents, telling them they still do not know the Americans but in the future they will.[78]

Although Vial exhorted them against dealings with the Americans, his diary makes no reference to having asked for any overt action against Captain "Merry." Many miles separated the Spanish from their quarry. The Niobrara, next major river to the north, joins the Missouri at the Nebraska–South Dakota border. On September 4 Lewis and Clark passed its mouth as they slowly poled up the "Big Muddy." Whether the Frenchmen's report of heavily encumbered parties ascending the Missouri referred to Lewis and Clark cannot be ascertained, for other American trading parties set out to win over Indian allegiance about this time. There is no indication that Vial

named Josef Gervaes who they say is waiting for them in the nations and is to guide them to Mexico. This Gervaes, it is said, knows the road very well. He is the same one who last year conducted the Panis nation to make peace with the governor of Santa Fe or with the commandant of the frontiers and it seems that he has also conducted them this spring. He is returning from this latter trip and is waiting for the said Meteyer." Dehault Delassus to Casa Calvo, St. Louis, August 10, 1804, SpAGI (Papeles de Cuba 141), trans. in *Before Lewis and Clark*, 2 : 742–45. Few knew the route at that early date, and it has been suggested that "Gervaes" and Jarvet are the same man. Donald Nuttall, "The American Threat to New Mexico, 1804–1822," M.A. thesis, San Diego State College, 1959, p. 54, cited by *Vial*, p. 172, whose authors do not concur, as they knew of no other evidence that Jarvet had accompanied the Pawnee to Santa Fe. Vial's diary for the expedition of 1804 (entry for September 15), cited at length below, shows that Vial and Jarvet had previously escorted five Pawnee chiefs to visit the governor of New Mexico. As we shall see, Vial and Jarvet did meet Babtiste LaLande among the Pawnee in the fall of 1804. Vial's diary, crucial to clarifying efforts to "apprehend" Lewis and Clark, was not known to Loomis and Nasatir (see *Vial*, p. 423n). The author is indebted to Dr. Luís Navarro García, of the Universidad de Sevilla, for knowledge of its location in SpAGI (Aud. Guad. 398).

78. Diario de Dn. Pedro Vial a la nación Panana, Santa Fe, November 23, 1804, SpAGI (Aud. Guad. 398), fol. 3v–4, AT.

received any information that he identified as pertaining to "Merry." He may have assumed that the expedition had already gone up-river and out of his reach, leaving him no ready means of carrying out his instructions.

That Vial and Jarvet had previously escorted five Pawnee chiefs to Santa Fe is disclosed in Vial's account of his speech on September 15 before a council of Pawnee and Oto leaders.[79] After receiving Governor Chacón's presents, the renowned chief "Sartariche" (Sharitarish, "White Wolf") responded that he and his people were content to have Spanish representatives come to them as brothers. Chief "Caigie" and eleven of his braves were willing to accompany Vial back to Santa Fe. On September 20 they resumed the homeward trek. After a brush with a Comanche war party near the Purgatoire, they reached Santa Fe on November 5, where "Caigie" was presented with gifts of clothing, a horse, rifle, powder, bullets, and a medal bearing the royal bust.[80] A month elapsed before Chacón remitted Vial's diary to Salcedo, with a letter stating

> that it contains no particulars about discoveries or other inquiries of which he was forewarned in his instructions. The only thing I have been able to learn from the Frenchmen from San Luis de los Ylanuez who on this last occasion accompanied [read: came back with] him is that the Americans had sent an expedition to reconnoiter the Misury River to its origin, with an order to attract to their side all heathen nations they might encounter; that the nearest and best-known had been convoked and [the Americans] had taken from them medals and patents from officials in New Orleans, giving them others from the American republic, with flags of the same nation, and that only the Pawnee nation refused to admit them or recognize as allies any but the Spanish.[81]

Chacón reported that, to offset this influence, he had given the Pawnee chief who came to Santa Fe a new patent, a medal, and a handsome gift, so as to perpetuate the alliance.

79. Ibid., fol. 4–4v, AT. Vial's command of Spanish left much to be desired. Since Jarvet's identification with Gervaes is corroborated by a grammatically defective sentence in this passage, and translation requires emendation, it warrants consideration in the original tongue.

> El dia 15 se juntaron todos los Capitanes y todos los Guapos del Pueblo en una Casa, por el Consejo, y por saver á que fin era mi llegada yo les digo yo soy enbiado del Gran Capitan D. Fernando Chacon, a venir á conducir los Pananas que havian quedado entre los Españoles para que no se vinieran solos el Gran Capitan embía un vestido largo y un sombrero de tres picos y lo demas correspondiente al vestido, el Gran Capitan Español está contento de haver conocido toda su Nacion Panana como ha venido con Pedro Vial y José Jarvay que habla de la lengua Panana hicieron la Paz con migo, yo les encargo que se mantengan todos bien al Capitan Panis Caigie que ablo con migo de los cinco que vinieron aser la Paz con migo y que fueron todos bien vestidos y fueron todos muy contentos. . . .

80. Ibid., fol. 5v.

81. Chacón to Salcedo, Santa Fe, December 13, 1804, SpAGI (Aud. Guad. 398), AT.

Vial's objectives are corroborated in Salcedo's letter forwarding the guide's diary to Madrid. The effort had been sent out in response to Casa Calvo's warning about Captain "Merri" ascending the Missouri, "so as to simultaneously ratify the peace and friendship with the Panana (Pawnee) Indians, and to reconnoiter dissimulatively the country to the edge of the said river." Salcedo added that Vial "did not acquire news of Captain Merri, but from some Frenchmen residing in Ylinoa who at that season were found in those remote habitations, it was learned that the government of the United States had sent another expedition with the object of reconnoitering the Misuri to its origin, and to win over all the heathen nations that it might encounter." (That Merry and this latter expedition were the same seems not to have been recognized by Vial, Chacón, or Salcedo.) Salcedo warned that the Americans would leave no stone unturned to undermine Spain's alliance with Indian nations north of New Mexico, "for in their procedures and the reconnaissance they are undertaking in order to carry out their ambitious designs of enlarging their territory, it seems they have as their objective no less than facilitating for the future their commerce to Asia by making a port on the South Sea between 40° and 45° latitude, at which parallels the Misuri has its sources, in case they find them navigable." [82] He requested further instructions on how to proceed.

### THE SECOND EXPEDITION TO COUNTER LEWIS AND CLARK

Spring and summer passed without an answer. Governor Chacón was replaced, for reasons of health, by Joaquín del Real Alencaster. Salcedo received word in September of the "darkly uncertain" situation following the failure of Godoy's negotiations with Monroe. The ministry ordered measures taken against the Americans' "ambitious and exhorbitant" designs on Spanish territory (see p. 460). This directive triggered Salcedo's second endeavor to thwart "Captain Merry."

The commandant general's instructions for this effort show that, because of the big southward bend in the upper Missouri, he considered its upper tributaries to be close to those of the Rio Grande and the Colorado, and therefore an avenue to the heart of New Mexico. The increasing frequency of American activity on the Missouri made it vital that Real Alencaster adopt every means possible "to prevent all risk, insofar as the nature of the country permits; and this is required by our indisputable Rights over those territories." Salcedo was determined to place impediments to such traffic; alliances with tribes along the Missouri seemed the most feasible instrument. Real Alencaster was warned "to take the most efficient measures to improve the friendship" of the Panana, Oto, and Lobo (Loup Pawnee) nations, and get their chiefs to come to Santa Fe every year, to win their favor with gen-

82. Salcedo to Pedro Cevallos, Chihuahua, February 5, 1805, ibid., AT.

erous gifts. A new expedition should go out, this time under Jarvet's leadership, to invite the chiefs to Santa Fe for a parley. Then, by means of friendly treatment and presents Real Alencaster ought to "infuse them with a horror" of the English and Americans, and persuade them to refuse any contacts with those whose sole object was to expel them from their lands. Once the chiefs accepted this idea, the governor should get them to promise that "when Captain Merri's expedition returns . . . they will intercept it, apprehending its members." If this should prove difficult, Salcedo added, "you may induce them with assurances of such rewards as they might desire, at least to do everything possible to take from them any coffers and papers that the expedition itself might be carrying." He stressed that, "if by this means we could acquire them, considerable advantages would result without our having to use the alternative of stationing troops in spots where the expedition might pass, since perhaps that would cause resentment and agitation among the Indians." [83] That Jarvet, not Vial, was suggested to lead this second effort may well be a measure of Salcedo's displeasure at the old guide's failure to locate his quarry the first time out.

Real Alencaster replied at once, declaring that he would take great pains to gain the friendship of tribes along the Missouri, if their chiefs could be persuaded to come to Santa Fe. Within several days an expedition led by

---

83. Salcedo to Real Alencaster, Chihuahua, September 9, 1805, MxMDN, Archivo de la Biblioteca (Legajo 1787–1807, Cuaderno 15), fol. 20–21, T in DLC, T in IU-H (Cunningham Transcripts), trans. in Jackson, *Pike,* 2 : 104–08. Jackson acknowledges problems from the defective transcript in IU-H. The crucial portion deserves publication from the T in DLC.

> Si en el tiempo que há tenido Vm a su inmediacion al nuevo Ynterprete de los Pananas Jose Calbert, lo há calificado por de buen porte, berdad y deseos de dár pruebas de la utilidad de sus Servicios, considero oportuno q(u)e aprovechando lo faborable de la estacion presente en que los Yndios se retiran de las Cazerias, le previniese Vm. se trasladará al **Pais** de los Pananas llevando algun corto regalo para los Caudillos, y que les hicese entender q(u)e habiendo ocurrido asuntos de importancia que tratar, quiere Vm que se le presenten en esa Villa, donde p(o)r medio de su comoda asistencia y del obsequio que tiene resuelto hacerles les dará una nueva prueba del afecto que les deben, y que en el caso de verificarse su concurrencia ahi procediera Vm. no solo a infundirles horror a los Yngleses y Americanos, sino a persuadirlos a que abiertamente se nieguen a su comunicacion, en inteligencia de que no tienen otras miras que las de arrojarlas de sus terrenos para poseerlos; cuya idea exhornada con la viveza q(u)e corresponde seria utilisimo comprometerlos a que quando regrese la expedicion de Capitan Merri que llevó el obgeto de reconocer el Misuri hasta su origen y de regalar a las Naciones en nombre del Gobierno Americano la interceptaran, aprehendiendo a sus Individuos, lo qual si se les dificulta conseguir, podrá Vm. inducirlos a que a lo menos baxo el seguro de la recompensa que quisieren, hicieran todo lo posible por quitarles qualesquiera Cofres y papeles que conduzca la misma expedicion, mediante a que de adquirirlos nosotros resultarian considerables ventajas sin que para ellos podamos valernos del arvitrio de situar Tropas en los parages donde aquella pueda tocar, por quanto tál vez induciria recelos y alteraciones en los Yndios.

In 1915 Bolton catalogued this and related documents in Mexico's Secretaría de Guerra y Marina, now Ministerio de Defensa Nacional. In 1963, at the author's request, ministerial personnel made an unsuccessful attempt to locate the volume in question. Others' efforts have been equally futile. See Jackson, *Pike,* 2 : 108n.

Vial and Jarvet, with two carabineers and fifty other armed men, would depart in search of the Pawnee, to see why their chiefs had not visited Santa Fe that year. Having encountered them, the troops would return, but the two guides intended to remain with the Indians all winter, investigating the progress of the American expedition and cultivating the friendship of the "Lobos" and other nations. In the spring of 1806 Jarvet would return to Santa Fe with whatever chiefs were willing to come, while Vial was to "remain and penetrate farther, in order to acquire the friendship of others, approach those nearest the Misuri, and examine the state and progress of Captain Merri's expedition, as well as to see if something can influence against them and their conclusion, fulfilling totally or in part the project and undertaking which your excellency insinuates in the fourth paragraph, especially at its conclusion, of the cited official letter of September 9, a point that I very much recommend to Vial and Chalvet." The paragraph referred to (in terms so guarded as to emphasize its secrecy) had ordered the apprehension of Captain Merry and his coffers and papers. To justify retaining Vial as commandant, the governor explained that

> although Chalvet has particular ascendency over the Pananas and assuredly was the one who persuaded them not to accept the friendship of the Anglo-Americans, to whom he would not present himself, having been summoned, he does not have all the talent and disposition nor knowledge of old man Vial for negotiating and obtaining advantages from the different nations of interest to us. Therefore I thought it advisable that both go, considering that at some time it will be very essential to have a spy among the Panana or other nations.[84]

They would take with them a quantity of gifts for the chiefs, but Real Alencaster asked Salcedo to order from Mexico City a half dozen 7 or 8 ounce and two dozen $1\frac{1}{2}$ ounce silver medals bearing the royal portraits on one side, and on the reverse a laurel wreath and meritorious inscription, as well as a dozen large, silver-headed canes. The American practice of distributing such gifts made emulation a matter of necessity.

The governor's instructions for this second expedition are specifically entitled "to acquire news and knowledge of the state of Captain Merri's expedition." Vial was ordered to spend the winter among the Pawnee, "in order to inform himself, as prearranged, of the progress of the Anglo-Americans in the Missouri, especially in the spring." Jarvet should accompany those chiefs coming to see the governor in the spring, whereas Vial ought to "approach the tribes nearest the Missouri, and examine the state and progress

---

84. Real Alencaster to Salcedo, Santa Fe, October 11, 1805, MxMDN, Archivo de la Biblioteca (Legajo 1787–1807, Cuaderno 15), fol. 39–40, T in DLC, original draft in NmSRC (Span. Arch. 1903), AT.

of the expedition of Captain Merry, in case it should be possible for him to have any influence against the aforementioned progress and expedition, at its conclusion." Vial was to remain "through the spring, not returning until summer has started; this is so necessary and useful that it may be necessary that Chalvert return when Vial leaves in order that one of them may always be among the Pawnees or any other nation nearest to the Missouri because of the news which may concern us." Guardedly he added: "Vial will bear in mind the interesting confidential charge that I have entrusted to him, for which accomplishment he will not omit any necessary step, being confident that the accomplishment and the success of this expedition which I entrust to him will furnish him a just reward and a real compensation." [85]

Salcedo had been obliged to specify that Merry should be arrested (see p. 466), since the governor was hundreds of miles away. Real Alencaster could acknowledge this order by referring to the corresponding paragraph in Salcedo's letter (see p. 467). But it was wise not to spell out here Vial's most important objective, lest something befall the expedition and this paper end up in American hands. So the "interesting confidential charge" entrusted to Vial had been communicated verbally. The secrecy underscores its delicacy.

This second attempt to counter Captain Merry left Santa Fe on October 14, 1805. Accompanying Vial and Jarvet were carabineers Juan Lucero, Francisco García, forty-eight soldiers, traders Baptiste LaLande and Laurent Durocher, three other "Frenchmen," and James Purcell, an American. The governor sent these traders along with the understanding that they would continue on to St. Charles, near St. Louis, gather news of American activities, and return eventually to report to him.[86] Three days later the column doubled in size when fifty militiamen from Taos joined the expedition. They crossed the Sangre de Cristo range without difficulty, despite the lateness of the season, and on November 5 made camp near the junction of the Purgatoire and the Arkansas, amid signs of recent Indian presence in great numbers. Fearing a night ambush, Vial took every precaution for defense. The next morning, on the north bank of the Arkansas they saw six braves of unrecognizable tribe, who avoided Jarvet's endeavor to parley. At midnight on November 6, Vial's diary relates,

> they attacked us in three bands, one group going for the horses, and two for the camp. It was necessary to protect the horses, and most of the

85. Real Alencaster, Instructions to Vial and Chalvert [Jarvet], Santa Fe, October 13, 1805, MxMDN, Archivo de la Biblioteca (Legajo 1787–1807, Cuaderno 15), fol. 61–63, T in DLC, trans. in *Vial*, pp. 430–33. A footnote comments: "It sounds as if perhaps he has suggested that Vial organize the Indians to stop Lewis and Clark," but Loomis and Nasatir fail to pursue the topic.

86. Ibid.; Real Alencaster to Salcedo, October 11, 1805.

men went to save them. Only six remained in camp, which had to be abandoned because of the enemy's superiority. . . . They got possession of our supply of goods, taking the greater part, both those of the men and those destined for presents. I had divided the latter into separate groups so if we met tribes, as we went along, we could give each what was suitable. They took more than two of the three shares, leaving only what was in a trunk. The attackers must have been some 100 or more in number. Having pillaged the camp, they gathered to take the horses and make their escape, but our militia, carabineers, and the Frenchmen proved courageous, recovering the animals from the enemy three successive times. After three hours, seeing their ineffectiveness, nothwithstanding their force being three times ours, they withdrew from sight, taking only interpreter Jarvet's horse, which had left the herd, and we rushed them until they were thrown into the river, shrieking, from which it is thought some harm was done them.[87]

Because of his disadvantageous position, Vial gathered up the remaining baggage and provisions, seeking more favorable terrain. As soon as he began to leave, the still-unrecognized enemy returned to the onslaught, attacking on foot and horseback, following the retreating column three leagues before finally desisting. Despite the ferocity of the skirmish, only one man suffered a serious wound, having been hit in the leg by a bullet. The elaborately attired assailants employed firearms, not arrows, and despite all the shouting, they had not used any recognizable tongue. Vial discounted their being either Pawnee or Kiowa.[88] His munitions exhausted, the baggage pillaged, and his provisions gone, Vial had no alternative but to turn back. The expeditionaries reached Santa Fe in safety, their mission an utter failure. Vial's diary closes with a recommendation that a fort be established on the banks of the Napestle (Arkansas).

The governor attributed the fiasco to the circumstance that "the Americans have had more than enough time to regale and attract to their friendship various tribes." He decided, therefore, that the friendly chiefs should be summoned "in order to acquire important news without exposing an expedition that may have to sustain the functions of arms [that is, fight] until we know who are the true enemies and whether it will be best or not to attack them." He commended the valor of Lucero, García, the soldiers, and the Frenchmen, but praise for Vial and Jarvet is notably absent from the

---

87. Pedro Vial, "Diario," October 14–November 19, 1805, MxMDN, Archivo de la Biblioteca (Legajo 1787–1807, Cuaderno 15), fol. 64–67, T in DLC, AT, variant trans. in *Vial,* pp. 433–38. Loomis and Nasatir alter Vial's reference to "Jarvet" to the spelling they prefer, "Chalvert," as used by Real Alencaster.

88. From what the Republican Pawnee told trader George Sibley in 1808, the assailants of 1805 were the Skidi, or Loup Pawnee. Jackson, *Pike,* 2 : 373, 377n.

report. In an accompanying letter to Salcedo he requested $8,500 to cement Indian alliances on the northern frontier.[89]

How could tribes on the far-off Missouri be persuaded to "apprehend" American explorers if those nearer Santa Fe had been drawn into the American embrace or were hostile to Spanish expeditions? Scarcely a week after Vial and his companions returned, the governor sent carabineer Juan Lucero northward from Taos (on November 27) with a force of twenty-five militiamen to learn who the assailants had been. In eleven days he made contact with the "Caigua" (Kiowa), who received him amicably and offered to bring the Comanche and ten other tribes to parley once again with the Spanish. The results of Lucero's mission were in Real Alencaster's hands by Christmas.[90] There is no indication that Lucero found a clue as to the attackers, but his report underlined the increasing difficulty of insuring that the Plains tribes would resist American penetration. During the expedition with Vial and Jarvet he had observed them arguing with the "Frenchmen." Understanding something of their tongue, he had queried Vial at greater length and learned that LaLande, Durocher, and the others disparaged Spanish chances of competing with the Americans in winning over tribes with gifts. They had chided Vial and Jarvet for serving for small wages, saying that the Americans paid interpreters half again as much. Called before the governor, the two guides confirmed Lucero's testimony.[91]

Spanish officials had no way of knowing the exact position of the American transcontinental expedition. After spending the winter of 1804–05 among the Mandan, Lewis and Clark had continued up the Missouri the following spring, moving much faster. By October, when Vial and Jarvet left Santa Fe the second time in search of them, the explorers were already on the lower Columbia. They sighted its mouth in November 1805, spent the winter near present day Astoria, and started homeward on March 23, 1806.

### VIAL'S THIRD SALLY AGAINST CAPTAIN MERRY

Real Alencaster interpreted the Pawnee chiefs' failure to visit him in the fall of 1805 and the skirmish that crippled and cut short Vial's second expedition as signs that the Indians were "in complete agreement and commerce with the Americans." [92] Pondering the royal order of June 5, 1805,

89. Real Alencaster to Salcedo, Santa Fe, November 20, 1805, NmSRC (Span. Arch. 1925), trans. in *Vial*, pp. 438–39, and November 20, 1805, NmSRC (Span. Arch. 1926).

90. Salcedo to the governor of New Mexico, Chihuahua, January 16, 1806, NmSCR (Span. Arch. 1953), trans. in *Vial*, pp. 443–45.

91. Real Alencaster to Salcedo, January 4, 1806, NmSRC (Span. Arch. 1942), in *NMHR* 2 (1927) : 376–77.

92. Real Alencaster to Salcedo, Santa Fe, Jaunary 4, 1806, likewise in NmSRC (Span. Arch. 1942), trans. in *Vial*, pp. 441–43.

and Salcedo's insistence upon a redoubled effort to check Captain Merry (see pp. 460, 465), and taking into account the "ambitious ideas" of the Americans, the governor recommended a series of measures. He considered it "indispensable to show that there exist more forces in this province, both in order that our allies may appreciate our friendship more and so that they will not be so easily seduced." Bands that waged war on the Spanish should be punished, "an object that cannot be carried out with those forces that exist here, because they are too small." Interpreters should be sent to live with the friendly tribes to gather information. He seconded Vial's proposal for a fort and settlement on the Arkansas River, as a means of sustaining trade and alliances with the Pawnee and other plains nations. "Upon the completion of the suggested expedition of Vial and Chalvert," he concluded, "the following spring, depending upon its results, if it should be necessary, let me go out in command of another expedition for purposes that may interest the State; I am ready to carry it out in case your Excellency approves and orders it." [93]

In another letter, three days earlier, Real Alencaster had confirmed that he was outfitting another expedition to Pawnee country, this time of 300 men, which Vial would lead northward in April.[94] They set out, as scheduled, on April 24, 1806. Since no additional set of orders has come to light, presumably those of October 13, 1805 (see p. 467), were still in force. Although Vial's mission may have been solely to construct the fort recommended on the Arkansas, this seems unlikely, since there is no evidence that Salcedo ever consented to such a measure.

Vial and his column could not have gotten very far onto the Great Plains, for in less than a month Real Alencaster would report that Vial and Jarvet had returned because their men had deserted.[95] There is no known diary of the effort, and our knowledge of what occurred is derived from Salcedo's curt reply to Real Alencaster:

> Informed by Your Excellency's letter number 269 of May 20th last, that disobeying the sergeants and corporals in charge of Vial and Chalvert's second [*sic*] expedition, the militia and Indians named for their escort abandoned it, returning to their towns, I approve the step that as a consequence you say you have taken, whereby there be conducted to that capital the tenth part of the number of said individuals in order to initiate the respective judicial inquiry into the matter and once con-

93. Ibid.

94. Real Alencaster to Salcedo, Santa Fe, January 1, 1806, MxMDN, Archivo de la Biblioteca (Legajo 1787–1807, Cuaderno 15), fol. 95–99. Given their present inaccessibility, our knowledge of this document and those cited in the following footnote is limited to Bolton's résumé, p. 309.

95. Real Alencaster to Salcedo, Santa Fe, May 20 and May 30, 1806, MxMDN, Archivo de la Biblioteca (Legajo 1787–1807, Cuaderno 15), fol. 146, 148–51.

cluded, I instruct Your Excellency to give me an account of it, to resolve what is fitting.[96]

That the men were brought to trial is confirmed by a subsequent document.[97] As a trailbreaker, Vial had few peers, but his reputation appears not to have survived the disgrace covering this third attempt to check Captain "Merry." The old explorer's biographers do not make this point, but it is evident from the way his name suddenly ceases to appear in the governor's papers.

### DUNBAR AND BURR DISTRACT ATTENTION FROM MERRY

At this juncture, word reached Madrid and Chihuahua of another probe into Spanish domains prepared under Jefferson's aegis by William Dunbar, a well-known Scottish plantation owner in Natchez. Dunbar had led an exploring party up Arkansas's Ouachita River in 1804–05. Subsequently, at the president's request, he set about organizing an expedition to examine the Red River. Although it was under nominal command of Captain Richard Sparks, it would actually be led by civilian surveyor Thomas Freeman, accompanied by Dr. Peter Custis, a party of soldiers, and a servant, making a total of twenty-four men. Dunbar did not go along.[98] The Freeman-Sparks expedition possessed no other connection with Lewis and Clark than that it, too, was sponsored by Jefferson to explore the western fringe of Louisiana. But it would be bracketed by Spanish officials with the threat from Captain Merry and would have the result of decoying Spanish attention away from the earlier expedition.

Dunbar had asked Louisiana's Governor Claiborne to obtain a passport for the Red River explorers from Casa Calvo, in case they encountered Spanish officials. The marqués somewhat reluctantly complied, offering his superiors the excuse that the Americans would have departed without it in any case. By conceding it, he was able to extract the condition that several

96. Salcedo to Real Alencaster, Chihuahua, July 18, 1806, NmSRC (Span. Arch. 2001), AT. As trans. in *Vial*, p. 447, the onus falls upon Vial and Jarvet, an impression not conveyed by the original text:

> Enterado por oficio de Vm numero 269 de 20 de Mayo ultimo, de que desovedeciendo a los Sargentos y cabos encargados de la segunda expedición de Vial y Chalvert, la abandonaron retirandose a sus Pueblos los vecinos é Indios nombrados para su escolta, apruevo la disposicion que en consecuencia me dice Vm. ha tomado relativa á que sea conducida á esa Capital la decima parte del numero de dichos Individuos con el fin de formar la respectiva causa sobre el asunto y concluida, prevengo a Vm. me dé cuenta con ella, para resolver lo que corresponda.

97. Real Alencaster to Salcedo, Santa Fe, June 16, 1807, NmSRC (Span. Arch. 2058), trans. in *Vial*, p. 447.

98. I. J. Cox, "The Exploration of the Louisiana Frontier, 1803–06," *AHA Annual Report, 1904* (1905): 160–64; William H. Goetzmann, *Army Exploration in the American West* (New Haven, 1960), pp. 35–36.

Spanish subjects go along. One of these was Tomás Power, a Canary Islander, who had ample experience in the Interior Provinces and spoke English well, having served in a secret capacity on previous occasions, most importantly as courier to Wilkinson.[99] Power was given confidential instructions to keep Casa Calvo informed, as the marques's immediate reaction toward Dunbar's investigation was to rank it with that of Meriwether Lewis as an ill-disguised measure for encroaching upon Spanish domains.

Upon hearing of the new American threat, Salcedo shot off a stiffly worded reply that he would not honor the passport given Dunbar nor permit the Americans to enter Spanish territory. There was no need for more geographic knowledge of that area, and the information garnered "can be put to dangerous use in the Future, in case of hostilities between Spain and the United States." He pointed out that "the expedition of Mr. Merri along the River Misuri, besides its reconnoitering to the first sources from which it [the river] rises, had the concealed [*doble*] end of capturing the good will of the heathen Nations which live on both sides." [100]

When word reached Madrid of Jefferson's insistence on sending probes into Spanish territory, patience wore thin there as well. Months had passed since the initial protest about "Merry," and the United States had not deigned to answer. A royal resolution to the minister of war (September 4, 1805), sent to Salcedo as a royal order, declared that, although another protest would be lodged, peremptory action could not be postponed. "Although there is no record, nor does [Casa] Yrujo mention that the secretary of state has answered him about Captain Merry's commission, it is evident that, after having given due notice, our government is sufficiently authorized to check the progress of Captain Merry's commission, if he tries to carry it forward within the dominions of the king; all of which His Majesty has ordered me to bring to Your Excellency's attention, so that the ministry in your care can advise the commandant general of the Interior Provinces of whatever is warranted, while charging him always to use appropriate moderation." [101] A copy in Santa Fe shows that this order reached Salcedo in Feb-

99. Casa Calvo to Nemesio Salcedo, New Orleans, July 18, 1805, NmSRC (Span. Arch. 1856). In 1796 Power carried $9,000 from New Orleans to Wilkinson in Cincinnati; the money was concealed in barrels of coffee and sugar. Affidavit of Peter Derbigny, August 29, 1807, cited by Abernethy, *Burr Conspiracy*, pp. 254, 265; Casa Calvo to Pedro Cevallos, New Orleans, July 18, 1805. NmSRC (Span. Arch. 1856), AT.

100. Salcedo to Casa Calvo, Chihuahua, October 8, 1805, NmSRC (Span. Arch. 1856), copy made at Chihuahua, April 12, 1806, T in IU-H (Cunningham Transcripts), trans. in Jackson, *Pike*, 2 : 111–12.

101. "Aunque no consta ni Yrujo menciona que el Secretario de Estado le hubiese contestado sobre el asunto de la comision del Capitan Merry, es evidente que despues de haber representado en su debido tiempo, está nuestro Gobierno suficientemente autorizado á impedir al Capitan Merry el progresso de su comision, si intentase llebarla adelante dentro de los Dominios del Rey. Lo que me ha mandado S. M. poner en noticia de V. E. a fin de que por el Ministerio

ruary 1806, and was relayed to Real Alencaster without modification or comment.

While Madrid's concern was growing over the threat from the Lewis and Clark expedition, her suspicions that Americans in high places contemplated encroachments upon Spanish domain, west of Louisiana were heightened by Aaron Burr's mysterious activities. The former vice-president's western tour in the summer of 1805 provoked a spate of rumors about a British-supported expedition to invade Spanish territories. Messages circulating between Madrid, Mexico City, Chihuahua, and Santa Fe in the fall of 1805 show that in official thinking the threat from "Merry" was associated with the portent of Monroe's precipitate departure from Madrid and with reports about Burr. In the expectation of trouble, in October 1805, 600 troops were transferred from Havana to Pensacola to reinforce West Florida. Small reconnoitering outposts were established at Bayou Pierre and Nana, east of the Sabine and west of Natchitoches, to watch for signs of American penetration. Salcedo warned the viceroy that "the pretensions and encroachments of the frontier of the United States of America upon territories of this commandancy general may proliferate in such a manner that, even overcoming obstacles, it will be impossible to counter all of them, since that government at all appearances is directing a large portion of its attention to these domains. This is testified," he asserted, "by the fact that in addition to efficacious diligence practiced to garner the friendship of Indian nations known to them in Texas, they have resorted to similar methods with those that inhabit the banks of the navigable rivers Misuri, Napest[l]e, Arcanzas, Colorado [Red] and Chato [Platte] which surround the province of New Mexico." [102]

Burr arrived back in Washington from his wideranging tour in mid-November 1805 and commenced simultaneous negotiations with the British and Spanish ministers, seeking assistance for his plans in the West, which varied according to the listener. In December, Jefferson delivered a message to Congress that was widely interpreted as almost a declaration of war against Spain over West Florida and the western boundary of Louisiana. Any assessment of Burr's objectives must take into account the heightened state of tension between Washington and Madrid. The literature on the alleged Burr Conspiracy is prodigious; our only concern in the pages that follow is for

---

de su cargo se prevenga lo conveniente al Comandante General, de las Provincias Internas, bien que encargandole siempre la moderacion correspondiente." [Cevallos] to José Antonio Caballero, minister of war, San Ildefonso, September 4, 1805, transcribed in Salcedo to the governor of New Mexico, Chihuahua, February 11, 1806, NmSRC (Span. Arch. 1967). Salcedo's copy is faithful to the original in SpAHN (Estado 5542); Royal order of October 12, 1805, NmSRC (Span. Arch. 1905).

102. Salcedo to Iturrigaray, Chihuahua, October 6, 1805, MxAGN (Prov. Internas 200), fol. 269–72v, AT; McCaleb, *Aaron Burr Conspiracy*, p. 94; Abernethy, *Burr Conspiracy*, p. 35.

its impact upon Spanish efforts to exclude Americans from the Pacific Northwest.

From Philadelphia the marqués de Casa Irujo kept Madrid informed of Burr's movements, as revealed by the ambassador's own dickering with Burr's agents and by a spy whom Casa Irujo sent to dog Burr's steps.[103] One of the marques's assistants, Valentín de Foronda, sent the ministry several newspaper clippings to document his warning that the Americans aspired to boundaries on the Rio Grande and the Pacific Coast. "These men are prideful: they have the impudence to look upon us as weak: to look upon us with disdain," Foronda wrote.[104] That his letter and the clippings are found in a ministerial *legajo* alongside Godoy's angry reaction to word of Lewis and Clark's progress shows the tenor of discussions at the highest level.

A royal order castigated Casa Calvo for having provided Dunbar's party with a passport, stating that he should have resisted the project from the outset.[105] As for Lewis and Clark, an irate message fired off to Salcedo complained:

> His Majesty orders me to tell you that he is surprised that you have not kept him informed of progress of the said expedition; likewise His Majesty desires to know how the said expedition has been permitted in territory of his domains, being well known that its designs ought to cause suspicion although disguised with the appearance of being purely scientific.[106]

The order is unequivocal evidence of the ministry's concern about the area into which Meriwether Lewis and his companions were penetrating—particularly because of its supposed strategic importance for areas farther south.

Thanks to José de Gálvez's half-realized dream of empire, on Salcedo's shoulders rested the responsibility for defending an enormous region, larger

103. Lengthy excerpts from Casa Irujo's reports are trans. by McCaleb. The best analysis of Wilkinson's connections with the affair is in Abernethy's *Burr Conspiracy*, although some aspects remain to be clarified. For many of the pertinent documents, see V. B. Reed and J. D. Williams, eds., *The Case of Aaron Burr* (Boston, 1960).

104. Valentín de Foronda to Cevallos, Philadelphia, November 4, 1805, SpAHN (Estado 5542), AT.

105. Minute of a royal order, February 7, 1806, ibid.

106. "Habiendo llegado a noticia del Rey, que en las Gacetas Americanas se ha publicado que el Capitan Merry Weather y su expedicion que entró por el Misury, se hallaba ya a "1609" millas rio arriba, y con esperanzas de invernar en la Costa del Mar Pacifico; me manda S. M. decir a V. S. ha extrañado que V. S. no haya dado parte de los progresos de dicha expedición; y asimismo que desea S. M. saber como se ha permitido la citada expedición en territorio de sus Dominios, siendo bien conocido que los designios de ella deben hacerse sospechosos por mas disfrazados que vayan con la apariencia de ser puramente científicos." [Minister of state] to the commandant general of the interior provinces, El Pardo, February 12, 1806, ibid.

than that administered by any other Spanish commandant in America. Hampered by attenuated lines of communication and supply, he had been reprimanded by superiors unable to appreciate the hindrances to be overcome. He would be blamed should the American expedition to the Pacific return successfully. Salcedo's correspondence at this point shows him devoting considerable attention to countering Captain Merry before the transcontinental mission could succeed.

The commandant's problems were compounded, however, when the frontier situation took a new turn. On February 5, 1806, the Spanish garrison of thirty men at Los Adais, fourteen miles west of Natchitoches, was persuaded by an American force twice as large to relinquish its post without a fight. In a special message to Congress (March 19), Jefferson warned anew of the possibility of war with Spain because of frontier incidents. Salcedo reacted by reinforcing his outposts along the Sabine. He was of the opinion that, in sending troops beyond Arroyo Hondo, near Natchitoches, Washington had broken faith with Madrid. "Ever since France sold Louisiana to the United States," he advised Governor Cordero, of Texas,

> nothing has been left undone to extend the limits [of American territory] into the Spanish possessions of the Missouri (*Misuri*) and Arkansas (*Napestle*), and to secure the twenty-two leagues of land lying between Arroyo Hondo and the Sabine, the former of which marks the boundary of Louisiana, as the Americans well know. They are also massing troops without question of expense to hold by force their spoils. They are also intriguing with the Indians, have built a storehouse at Natchitoches and have filled it with gifts for them. It has not been possible for us to oppose them in force, but in order to counteract their influence among the Indians I have dispatched expeditions to the various tribes, our dependencies—some to the far Northwest.[107]

Salcedo had just finished setting in march his fourth and most ambitious attempt to check Captain "Merry"—the Melgares expedition. The message to Governor Cordero shows the extent to which the Sabine crisis intruded upon Salcedo's design for intercepting Lewis and Clark. From his perspective the threats on the Arroyo Hondo, the Red River, and the upper Missouri were components of a total picture, all of which had to be dealt with simultaneously. The likelihood of conflict increased still further when, late in July, a body of 400 poorly equipped Spanish troops advanced to positions at Bayou Pierre, some fifty miles northwest of Natchitoches and sixty miles east of the Sabine. Word that the Spaniards were recrossing the Sabine spread like wildfire in Louisiana. It became General Wilkinson's

---

107. Salcedo to Antonio Cordero, Chihuahua, April 15, 1806, TxU (Bexar Archives), excerpt trans. in McCaleb, *Aaron Burr Conspiracy,* p. 95; Abernethy, *Burr Conspiracy,* p. 48.

responsibility to evict them. Jefferson fully expected war to ensue from the anticipated encounter.[108] It is in the context of this ongoing crisis that the next expedition toward the Missouri, the largest Spanish force ever sent onto the Great Plains, must be considered.

### MELGARES AND CAPTAIN MERRY

Until now, the Melgares expedition's connection with previous efforts to thwart Lewis and Clark has never been suggested. Salcedo had responded to Real Alencaster's expressed need for additional troops to overawe the Plains Indians (see p. 470) by sending a force of sixty dragoons under the leadership of Lieutenant Facundo Melgares, his most capable officer. From Chihuahua the latter brought an order (April 12, 1806) that, as summarized by Bolton, "reports the sending of Melgares with 60 men to assist the governor and states that the promised expedition has been turned into one designed to reconnoitre the Colorado (Red) and Arkansas, to watch the Dunbar expedition, drive it back, or capture it and take it to Santa Fe." [109] The original document's present inaccessibility prevents knowing whether Bolton's résumé discloses all of this effort's objectives. That it also was directed against Captain Merry is suggested by subsequent circumstances. Melgares and this message did not arrive in the New Mexican capital until after Vial, Jarvet, and 300 men had departed northward on the third endeavor directed against Merry, to be hamstrung by mutiny and desertions (see p. 471).

Upon reporting Vial's fiasco, Real Alencaster endeavored to lessen the blow by telling Salcedo of the measures being taken to send out Melgares and the dragoons, presumably to complete Vial's mission. They were scheduled for departure on June 15—105 soldiers, 400 New Mexico militiamen, and 100 Indian allies. They would proceed down the Red River as far as the "Rio de las Arcas," and then go northward to the Arkansas and the land of the Pawnee, Lobo, and Oto.[110] Melgares's instructions and diary have never been found. It is likely that Vial and Jarvet went along in subordinate roles because of their previous experience and knowledge of Indian tongues, but there is no evidence that this was the case. The Melgares expedition has never been adequately described or studied, a task exceedingly difficult from the few available Spanish sources, and at present most of our knowl-

108. Jefferson to Caesar Rodney, attorney general of the United States, December 5, 1806; Jefferson to John Langdon, governor of New Hamphire, December 22, 1806, cited by Abernethy, *Burr Conspiracy*, p. 138.

109. Salcedo to Real Alencaster, Chihuahua, April 12, 1806, MxMDN, Archivo de la Biblioteca (Legajo 1787–1807, Cuaderno 15), fol. 108–09. See Bolton, *Guide*, p. 309, our only means of knowledge, for the present, of this crucial letter. Melgares was New Mexico's last Spanish governor, 1818–22.

110. Rea Alencaster to Salcedo, Santa Fe, May 30, 1806, MxMDN (Legajo 1787–1807, Cuaderno 15), fol. 148–51, summarized by Bolton, *Guide*, p. 309; Real Alencaster to Salcedo, Santa Fe, October 8, 1806, NmSRC (Span. Arch. 2022).

edge of it comes from references by Zebulon Pike and his companions, who entered Pawnee country less than a month after Melgares departed. They heard the chiefs talk about the giant expedition, and subsequent to his capture by the Spanish Pike got to know Melgares well.

Pike says the Spanish lieutenant was the nephew of a royal judge in New Spain and "a man of immense fortune, . . . generous in its disposal, almost to profusion." The American explorer corroborates the 600 mounted men in the expedition, adding that each led two horses and a mule, for a total of 2,075 beasts. Melgares was accustomed to taking along every convenience that a gentleman required. His mode of living, Pike observed, "was superior to any thing we have an idea of in our army; having eight mules loaded with his common camp equipage, wines, confectionary, &." [111] In Pike's subsequent observations on New Spain, he tells of an episode during Melgares's trek, the significance of which he could not have known:

> The whole male population [of New Mexico] are subject to military duty, without pay or emolument, and are obliged to find their own horses, arms and provision. The only thing furnished by the government is ammunition, and it is extraordinary with what subordination they act when they are turned out to do military duty, a strong proof of which was exhibited in the expedition of Malgares [*sic*] to the Pawnees. His command consisted of 100 dragoons of the regular service and 500 drafts from the province. He had continued down the Red river until their provision began to be short: they then demanded of the lieutenant where he was bound and the intention of the expedition? To this he haughtily replied, "wherever his horse led him." A few mornings after he was presented with a petition, signed by 200 of the militia, to return home. He halted immediately, and caused his dragoons to erect a gallows; then beat to arms. The troops fell in: he separated the *petitioners* from the others, then took the man who had presented the petition, tied him up, and gave him 50 lashes, and threatened to put to death, on the gallows erected, any man who should dare to grumble. This effectually silenced them, and quelled the rising spirit of sedition; but it was remarked that it was the first instance of a Spaniard receiving corporal punishment ever known in the province. [112]

The incident reveals Melgares's determination not to have a recurrence of the disobedience that had ruined Vial's mission earlier that year. In late August or early September Melgares arrived at a Pawnee village that, from archeological evidence and Pike's maps and tables, can be located on the south bank of the Republican River, between today's Red Cloud and Guide

---

111. Jackson, *Pike*, 1 : 324, 406–07.
112. Pike's observations on New Spain, Washington, April 12, 1808; Jackson, *Pike*, 2 : 57–58.

Rock, Nebraska, some 140 miles short of the Missouri.[113] Although Melgares had no means of knowing it, he was very close to Lewis and Clark, who were rapidly descending the Big Muddy. On September 1 they passed the Niobrara's mouth, and ten days later reached the Platte, their nearest approximation to the huge Spanish force.

From that same Pawnee village, on October 1, Pike wrote Secretary of War Henry Dearborn that upon their arrival they "were much surprised to learn, that it was not more than three or four weeks, since a party of Spanish troops (whose number were estimated by the Indians of this town, at 300) had returned to Santa Fe." The main body of soldiers had remained on the Arkansas, after a tribe with whom they had just signed a treaty had stolen a large number of their horses. The Pawnee had reported "that the officer who commanded said party, was too young to hold councils, &c. that he had *only* come to open the road, but that in the spring his superior would be here, and teach the Indians what was good for them; and that they would build a town near them." [114]

An important clue to Melgares's ultimate objective is provided by another Pike letter at this juncture:

> "We were . . . strongly urged by the head chief [Sharitarish], to return the way we came, and not prosecute our voyage any further; this brought on an explanation as to our views towards the Spanish government; in which the chief declared, that it was the intention of the Spanish troops to have proceeded further towards the Mississippi, but, that he objected to it, and they listened to him and returned; he therefore hoped we would be equally reasonable; but finding I still determined on proceeding, he told me in plain terms (if the interpreter erred not) that it was the *will of the Spaniards we should not proceed.*" [115]

The Spanish expedition's purpose, Pike says in a lengthy footnote to his journal obviously written after his release, was to search for *him*. Word of

---

113. Donald Jackson, "How Lost Was Zebulon Pike?" *AH* 16, no. 2 (1965) : 14n. Other opinions, not reckoning with Pike's tables and maps, place it farther east, near Republic, Kansas, where a monument to that effect was erected in 1901; see Jackson, *Pike*, 1 : 325–27n.

114. Pike to Secretary of War Henry Dearborn, Pawnee Republic, October 1, 1806, in Jackson, *Pike*, 2 : 148–49.

115. Pike to General J. Wilkinson, Pawnee Republic, October 2, 1806, in Jackson, *Pike*, 2 : 150–53. It might be hypothesized that the chief lied in saying that he had denied the Spanish passage, as it would have been a natural ploy to justify refusing Pike, yet make the American feel he was getting equal treatment. If the chief's story was true, however, and Sharitarish *had* opposed Melgares going onward, this would not be mutually exclusive with the chief's subsequent tack—that he had promised Spanish officials to oppose American penetration westward. The latter would be in accord with what Spanish officials were seeking: an Indian barrier.

his coming had been forwarded from "Spanish emissaries" in St. Louis. "This information was personally communicated to me, as an instance of the rapid means they possessed of transmitting the information relative to the occurrences transacting on our frontier." He had been given to understand that Melgares's first objective was "to descend the Red river, in order, if he met our expedition, to intercept and turn us back, or should major Sparks and Mr. Freeman have missed the party from Nacogdoches, under the command of captain Viana, to oblige them to return and not penetrate further into the country, or make them prisoners of war." Lesser objectives, they told Pike, were to explore from the Platte to the Missouri and to cement alliances with the Pawnee and other tribes.[116] Pike does not seem to have questioned the excuse of such explorations in an area that held no mysteries for the Spanish. After descending the Red River 233 leagues, Pike relates that the large force headed northward toward the Arkansas River,

> where lieut. Malgares left 240 of his men, with the lame and tired horses, whilst he proceeded on with the rest to the Pawnee republic; here he was met by the chiefs and warriors of the Grand Pawnees; held councils with the two nations, and presented them the flags, medals, &c. which were destined for them. He did not proceed on to the execution of his mission with the Pawnee Mahaws and Kans, as he represented to me, from the poverty of their horses, and the discontent of his own men, but as I conceive, from the suspicion and discontent which began to arise between the Spaniards and the Indians.[117]

That Melgares was searching the Red River for Dunbar's probe is confirmed by Salcedo's letter to Real Alencaster of April 12, 1806 (see p. 477), but there is no mention in the commandant general's letters of Pike prior to his capture. The Freeman-Sparks expedition would be turned back farther downstream by a force sent out from Nacogdoches, also at Salcedo's orders.[118]

Historians—to a man—have accepted at face value Pike's belief that he was the object of Melgares's search. It should be recalled that, before leaving Chihuahua in April 1806, Melgares had been ordered to mount a combined mission to the Red River and the Pawnee country. Moreover, there

---

116. Jackson, *Pike,* 1 : 323–24.

117. Ibid., p. 324.

118. In response to an order from Salcedo to Antonio Cordero, governor of Texas, dated October 8, 1805, TxU (Bexar Archives), the Spanish force set out from Nacogdoches (July 12, 1806) under Francisco Viana. I. J. Cox, "The Exploration of the Louisiana Frontier, 1803–06," *AHA Annual Report, 1904* (1905): p. 164. The Americans left Fort Adams, on the Mississippi, in April and proceeded approximately 635 miles up the Red River before being turned back on July 29. See *An Account of the Red River in Louisiana, Drawn up from the Return of Messrs. Freeman and Custis to the War Office, in the United States, Who Explored the Same in the Year 1806* (n.p., 1817).

is no mention in known Spanish documents, prior to Pike's capture, of an overland probe from St. Louis other than the ventures of LaLande, Durocher, and other traders. Melgares's expedition was ponderous, and it could not have been organized, outfitted, and dispatched on a moment's notice; yet it departed from Santa Fe in mid-June, whereas Pike and his men did not get away from St. Louis until July 15. Granted, if Wilkinson had wished to inform Spanish officials of Pike's coming, there was ample time for him to have done so, as he was the intellectual author of the venture. Pike himself had known as early as May 3, 1906, that he was going on the mission.[119] But until there is some other evidence that Salcedo had received prior warning about Pike, we are entitled to question the assertion. The hypothesis that Melgares's endeavor was, at least in part, a continuation of Vial's efforts to "apprehend" Captain Merry has a more solid basis in Spanish documents.

It proved easy for the Americans to follow the Spanish track, chewed into the sod, to the banks of the Arkansas. There Pike dispatched his letters back to civilization with his second in command, Lieutenant James B. Wilkinson, the general's son. Melgares and his men had ascended the Arkansas to the Purgatoire, and arrived back in Santa Fe about October 1.[120]

The circumstances under which the American explorer was given to understand that word of his coming had reached Santa Fe, and that he was the object of Melgares's search, warrant examination. The Americans' presence in New Mexico became known to Spanish officials when Dr. John H. Robinson, one of Pike's companions, purposely went on to Santa Fe. The day of Pike's capture, at the fort that his men had erected on the Conejos, an upper tributary of the Río Grande, the force coming in search of him was preceded by two "Frenchmen," one of whom told him two days later

> that the expedition which had been at the Pawnees, had descended the Red River 233 leagues and from thence crossed to the Pawnees expressly in search of my party (this was afterwards confirmed by the gentleman who commanded the troops.)[.] He then expressed great regret at my misfortunes, as he termed them[,] in being taken, and offered his services in secreting papers &c. I took him at his word, and for my amusement I thought I would try him and give him, a leaf or two of my journal (copied) which mentioned the time of my sailing from Belle

119. Pike to Daniel Bissell, Garrison St. Louis, May 3, 1806. Mercantile Library Association, St. Louis, Mo., in Jackson, *Pike,* 1 : 274–75.

120. Real Alencaster to Salcedo, Santa Fe, October 8, 1806, Museum of New Mexico, Santa Fe (Photostat, No. 2022), cited by Abernethy, *Burr Conspiracy,* p. 126; Salcedo to Cevallos, Chihuahua, September 9, 1806, SpAHN (Estado 5542). The ministry replied that "obliging the expedition which the President of the United States had sent to reconnoitre the course of the Colorado [Red] River to leave His Majesty's dominions" had received the royal approval and accredited Salcedo's "zeal and love for the Royal service." [Cevallos] to Salcedo, Aranjuez, January 26, 1807, SpAHN (Estado 5542), AT.

Fontaine, and our force. This I charged him to guard very carefully and give to me after the investigation of my papers at Santa Fe.[121]

Several days later, upon his first interview with Governor Real Alencaster, Pike's journal notes:

> At the door of the government house, I met the old Frenchman, to whom I had given the scrap of paper on the 27th February. He had left us in the morning, and as I suppose, hurried in to make his report, and I presume had presented this paper to his excellency. I demanded with a look of contempt, if he had made his report? to which he made reply in an humble tone, and began to excuse himself, but I did not wait to hear his excuses.[122]

Thus there had been an opportunity for the "old Frenchman" to inform Real Alencaster and Melgares of what Pike had been told regarding Melgares's reason for being in Pawnee country. On the same pages Pike identifies Baptiste LaLande by name, and it is clear that he was not one of the two "Frenchmen" encountered on the Conejos. They were guides entrusted with the mission of leading a column of fifty dragoons and fifty militiamen in search of the party with which Dr. Robinson had crossed the Sangre de Cristo Mountains in the dead of winter. Vial and Jarvet were the most experienced guides of the time. When Pike asked about Spanish purposes in sending such a large force onto the Great Plains as had accompanied Melgares, the "old Frenchman" could hardly have been expected to admit to an effort directed against Captain "Merry," particularly since the transcontinental expedition had been crowned with success the previous fall. While still at the Pawnee village, on October 4 Pike had received word of the American explorers' return.[123] News of the feat soon reached Madrid, Mexico City, Chihuahua, and Santa Fe. Spanish authorities had a compelling reason to hide Melgares's objectives behind a ready excuse, Pike's coming.

While Wilkinson's maneuvers at this point may have included letting Spanish authorities know about Pike before he left St. Louis, it is significant that Pike's name does not appear in Spanish documents, bracketed with those of Merry and Dunbar, prior to his arrest on the Conejos. The "apprehension" of Captain Merry, one suspects, was at least one purpose of the huge Spanish force that advanced northward toward the Missouri but was hamstrung by horse thieves and stalemated by determined Pawnee opposition. Admittedly, the evidence is circumstantial, but it suggests that Melgares's objectives on the Missouri included those of the previous sallies

121. Pike's Journal, entry for February 28, 1807; Jackson, *Pike*, 1 : 386.
122. Ibid., entry for March 3, 1807; Jackson, *Pike*, 1 : 393.
123. Ibid., entry for October 4, 1806; Jackson, *Pike*, 1 : 330.

headed by Vial and Jarvet, and that his intent was to fulfill the ever more censorious orders raining upon Salcedo's head from Madrid to thwart Jefferson's transcontinental effort (see pp. 473, 475). Real Alencaster wanted to awe the Plains Indians, and Melgares's force was well suited for that purpose. It was too unwieldy for a surprise attack on Lewis and Clark, but astride the Missouri at an appropriate spot it could have arrested their progress homeward. It was overkill, in the modern sense, and that proved a part of Melgares's undoing. His force was too big to travel swiftly, live off the land, keep from offending Indian allies, and succeed in its hypothetical objective. With 240 of his men in one spot and 360 in another, his lines of supply were nonexistent, and it would have been difficult for him to push on to the Missouri, fend off the Pawnee, and remain there for a protracted time until Merry's problematical return. Vial's previous expeditions had not led him to expect Pawnee opposition. Moreover, the "apprehension" of Lewis and Clark, as originally envisaged, was dependent on using Indian allies as cats' paws. Without their cooperation, the objective of checking Merry was fraught with problems. Although Pike soon proved that the Pawnee could be bluffed, and would yield rather than fight to impede his passage, Melgares chose not to make the attempt. Pike's conviction that Melgares was searching for him has kept historians from perceiving that Melgares and his troops came very close to intercepting President Jefferson's "literary pursuit."

#### MADRID'S REACTION TO THE RETURN OF LEWIS AND CLARK

News of Lewis and Clark's arrival in St. Louis on September 23, 1806, spread quickly, thrilling the American people and surprising many who had given the explorers up for lost in the trackless wilds beyond the Rockies. Word of their success profoundly disgusted the marqués de Casa Irujo, in Philadelphia, who had been the first to warn of the threat that the president's project represented to Spanish interests. At once he composed an angry message to the viceroy of Mexico, remitting a copy to Madrid. "Although this exploration of territory recognized as belonging to the King Our Lord and without his consent will not immediately provide this [American] government with any other advantages than the glory of having accomplished it," the marqués opined,

> nevertheless the circumstance that in the territories near the Missouri's origin abundant furs of very fine quality are found, and the facility with which they can be exported to China by the Kooskooske and Columbia, may encourage some attempts by individuals in this country, whose business spirit and mercantile sagacity are well known. It seems to me advisable for Your Excellency to examine ways of making some

establishment, with the corresponding means of defense, at the mouth of the cited Columbia River, and to issue strict orders not to permit arrival there, by land or sea, of any American or foreigner of any nation whatever. For if we do not stop in time and in a decisive manner the evils that may occur in the future to the interests of the king or his vassals, prejudicial consequences may follow to both. Also it is my opinion that by this means we will pluck the fruit from their discoveries, for in time of peace it will be very easy for the Philippine Company, or private individuals, to organize there a commerce with the tribes of Indians occupying those territories, and with those inhabiting the Missouri's headwaters, and establish with China an advantageous commerce that the acquisitive industry of these people will inevitably wish to take over.[124]

Casa Irujo's covering letter to the ministry recalled his prediction, three years before, of the danger from President Jefferson's search for a route to the Pacific. Hence, he remonstrated, his suggestions for countering the American threat ought to be given the government's full attention. Madrid should complain once again to Washington that "without our consent and with its sanction, explorations had been attempted and executed in regions belonging exclusively to Spain." [125]

A résumé of papers presented for royal perusal on November 29, 1806, including a translation of an account of the Lewis and Clark expedition published in New York, has the royal reaction recorded in its wide left margin. Carlos IV disapproved "the lack of vigilance by those charged with maintaining it so as to detain those explorers, and they are ordered anew to do so if, as expected, the United States repeats the exploration." Also, the king declared that "it would not be amiss to caution prudence and not call upon force except as a last resort, and record all occurrences and answers in the most satisfactory and authentic manner." These sentiments were embodied in a royal order sent that same day to Salcedo.[126]

The series of futile expeditions sent to "apprehend" Lewis and Clark show that Madrid still entertained illusions of sustaining claims over the

---

124. Casa Irujo to Viceroy José de Iturrigaray, Philadelphia, November 3, 1803, SpAHN (Estado 5542), AT.

125. Casa Irujo to Cevallos, Philadelphia, November 8, 1806, SpMN (567), AT. Attached to that letter is a translation of Clark's letter to his brother from St. Louis, September 23, 1806.

126. "Desapruebese la falta de vigilancia a quienes se encargó la tuviesen para detener a estos exploradores, y encargueseles de nuevo para si como es regular repiten los estados unidos la exploracion. No es ocioso encargarles la prudencia para no llegar a vias de hecho sino en el ultimo extremo, y formalicen todas las ocurrencias y contestaciones del modo mas satisfactorio y fehaciente." Resumen de cartas recibidas, presentada al Rey, November 29, 1806, SpAHN (Estado 5542), AT; Royal order to the commandant general of the Interior Provinces, San Lorenzo [del Escorial], November 29, 1806, SpAHN (Estado 5542).

Pacific Northwest. Spanish officials unanimously conceived Jefferson's project as a threat to His Catholic Majesty's interests, but defending that area by overland sallies from New Mexico was an impossibility. Although the Pacific Northwest fell within Salcedo's jurisdiction, Chihuahua was too remote from California, the Columbia basin, and the Strait of Juan de Fuca. Problems closer at hand, in Texas and New Mexico, demanded his immediate attention. Casa Irujo's suggestion for a fort at the Columbia's mouth would have been difficult to implement. Acapulco, San Blas, or Manila, from which naval operations had to depart, were outside Salcedo's purview. So far as can be determined, the measure never reached the planning stage. Even so, it is surprising how close the Spanish came to intercepting Lewis and Clark, in 1804, and again in 1806. A matter of several days' march, in each case, prevented an encounter that could have resulted in a major incident between the two nations, at a moment when both sides were anticipating a conflict arising from other issues. An assault upon Lewis and Clark, had it become public knowledge, would have provided the excuse that many Americans sought for an invasion of West Florida and Texas.

Disgust and dismay characterize Madrid's reaction to the triumph of Lewis and Clark. Plainly, the feat damaged Spain's chances of retaining sway over the vast hinterland between New Mexico and Nootka. It portended, as Wilkinson had predicted, that the Americans would soon be attempting to plant a settlement at the mouth of the Columbia. Although Spain no longer considered Nootka a worthwhile objective, she had not yet resigned herself to forgoing the territory between San Francisco, Fuca, and the upper Missouri. But throughout the preceding chapters, the evidence has accrued that Spain's primary interest in the Pacific Northwest was in retaining it as an unexplored buffer zone of protection for Mexico's mines. Spanish officials did not rise to the challenge from Lewis and Clark's feat with plans for garrisoned outposts, missions, Indian alliances, expeditions, explorations, a diplomatic effort, or other conventional measures employed in the past to forestall further erosion of His Catholic Majesty's claims. The explanation is that at this moment officials in the Floridas, the Interior Provinces, and even Mexico City and Madrid were in suspense about the implications of Burr's ominous activities, which threatened to strike at more important possessions than Oregon. Their utter absorption in preparing for a possible assault upon the Floridas, Texas, and New Mexico postponed efforts to protect Spanish interests farther west—despite evidence that Wilkinson's design may have included Spanish-claimed territory in the Pacific Northwest, as well.

Although Burr took pains to assure Casa Irujo that his plans were solely secessionist and did not include an attack upon Spanish territory, the marqués was dubious, and he warned the governor of West Florida and his superiors in Madrid to be on guard.[127] Harmon Blennerhasset's mansion, on an island in the Ohio not far from Marietta, was the staging point for those persuaded to join Burr's ranks. Mobilization took place under the guise of a "Mexican Association" for the "liberation" of Spanish colonial territories. Many influential men in the West were eager to entertain Burr and offer encouragement, although volunteers to go along did not appear in the numbers anticipated, for a public clamor was mounting, censorious of the government's inaction in the face of widespread rumors about Burr's objectives, in which some saw a danger of national dismemberment. In West Florida and Texas, Spanish officials prepared to repulse what they conceived to be an officially encouraged assault, disguised as a secessionist movement to keep Spain off guard.

For the governor of New Mexico, Pike's probe seemed a harbinger of an American invasion. One of Pike's men had approached José Jarvet, upon hearing that several parties were being sent northward to scout for Americans. He told Jarvet "that they would be exposing themselves [to capture]," for General Wilkinson had promised that if Christmas 1806 passed without Pike's return, he would assume that Pike was a prisoner of the Spaniards and would send forces "of three to four thousand men each, that they would go along the principal Rivers [tributary to the Mississippi], and that he thought it beyond doubt that those parties would now be near." [128] Real Alencaster hastened to guard passes on the approaches to New Mexico. Whatever Pike's role in Wilkinson's larger design, Spanish officials concluded that he had been gathering data for military purposes.

By the time word of Pike's arrest reached the United States, Burr's scheme had come apart at the seams. Several days before General Wilkinson arrived at Natchitoches (September 22, 1806), Spanish commander Simón de Herrena exercised his own power of discretion and withdrew his forces from Bayou Pierre to west of the Sabin. The excuse for invading Spanish territory had evaporated. Soon afterward, Wilkinson ceased coordinating his actions with Burr and negotiated a neutral-ground truce with Herrera, dissipating the chances of war (November 5, 1806). Then, moving quickly, the general prepared an ostensible defense of New Orleans, arrested Burr's collaborators there, and acted to check the irregular force descending the Mississippi. Since Burr's associates included many of Jefferson's friends, the president made no move against their activities until revelations directly

---

127. Casa Irujo to Cevallos, November 10, 1806, excerpt trans. in McCaleb, *Aaron Burr Conspiracy*, pp. 82–83.

128. Real Alencaster to Salcedo, Santa Fe, April 15, 1807, IU-H (Cunningham Transcripts), trans. in Jackson, *Pike*, 2 : 197–200.

from Wilkinson's hands made further delay impossible.[129] A presidential proclamation (November 27, 1806) forbade preparation on American soil of an expedition against Spanish territory.

Spanish authorities in West Florida had learned that in New Orleans a "strong party" was fomenting a plan to "revolutionize the kingdom of Mexico," a plot said to include many ecclesiastics and other subjects who were already won over.[130] Governor Folch informed the viceroy that Burr planned to have an army of 28,000 to 30,000 march upon Baton Rouge, Pensacola, the Río Grande, and Mexico.[131] Until Burr's arrest, escape, and final capture (February 19, 1807), Spanish officialdom continued to worry about counteracting his activities. Wilkinson, meanwhile, had turned his attention to assembling testimony of Burr's involvement in an alleged secessionist movement.[132]

Whatever the general and his associates were up to, there is suspicion that Wilkinson's designs on Spanish borderlands may have included territory still claimed by Madrid in the Pacific Northwest. There is evidence that in the fall of 1806, as Lewis and Clark descended the Missouri and Pike headed for New Mexico, a mysterious party of Americans started for the Columbia basin. In August 1807, shortly after David Thompson had planted Kootenai House in eastern British Columbia for the North West Company of Montreal, the Kootenai Indians brought him word "that about 3 weeks ago the Americans to the number of 42 arrived to settle a military Post, at the confluence of the two most southern & considerable Branches of the Columbia & that they were preparing to make a small advance post lower down on the River." [133] Aliases were used in the several messages that the

129. Records of a cabinet meeting on November 25, 1806, suggest that a letter from Wilkinson, dated October 21, triggered Jefferson's proclamation; excerpt in McCaleb, *Aaron Burr Conspiracy*, pp. 125–26.

130. Juan Ventura Morales to Viceroy Iturrigaray, Pensacola, May 12, 1806, TxU (Bexar Archives), cited by McCaleb, *Aaron Burr Conspiracy*, p. 61. The report coincides essentially with objectives of the "Mexican Association" of New Orleans, which included the mayor, sheriff, Catholic bishop of the diocese, mother superior of the Ursuline Convent, and other important officials and merchants. The plan was to seize Spanish West Florida, raise the banner of an independent Mexico, stage a coup in New Orleans, and, with British assistance, invade Texas and Mexico. Abernethy, *Burr Conspiracy*, pp. 24–30.

131. Folch to Iturrigaray, October 1, 1806, excerpt trans. in McCaleb, *Aaron Burr Conspiracy*, p. 88.

132. Consistent with his long-time previous service to Spain, at this point Wilkinson sent a personal courier to the viceroy, requesting a large reward for his part in putting a stop to the Burr peril. Iturrigaray thanked him but declined to forward the requested sum without a definite order from Madrid. Iturrigaray to Cevallos, March 12, 1807, MxAGN, excerpt trans. in ibid., pp. 144–45.

133. David Thompson, "Narrative of the Expedition to the Kootanae & Flat Bow Indian Countries, on the Sources of the Columbia River . . . 1807," ed. T. C. Elliot, *OHQ* 26 (1925): 43. A series of articles on this topic appeared in the *OHQ*: J. N. Barry, "Lieutenant Jeremy Pinch,"

Roseman-Perch-Pinch expedition subsequently exchanged with Thompson. The formal protest from "Fort Lewis, Yellow River, Columbia, July 10, 1807," warning Thompson away from American territory is so similar to a document previously used by Pike under comparable circumstances on the upper Mississippi as to implicate General Wilkinson with this otherwise unrecorded project. Alvin Josephy, Jr., author of the fullest reconstruction of the episode, is persuaded that these Americans had reached the Nez Perce Indians. He points to a skein of evidence that Captain John McClallen, "an ex-artillery officer who had served Wilkinson in public and private ventures, may have gone to the Northwest and been wiped out by Blackfeet." [134] But Josephy warns that no proof of such events has yet been found. "The total absence of all evidence," in his opinion, "suggests not only that McClallen never came back but that Wilkinson in time was able to destroy any papers he owned that referred to this secret venture." [135]

This curious episode implies that for Wilkinson, no less than for Jefferson, the Pacific Northwest constituted part of the territory where Madrid's "expiring interest" invited American attention. The disappearance of all American documentation for the effort invites a comparison with Pike's mission. If Pike and his men had frozen to death in the Colorado Rockies, as nearly was the case, would their endeavor have been shrouded in comparable silence? As with Pike's expedition, the Roseman-Perch-Pinch effort wore a military aspect. Was it likewise aimed at scouting Spanish borderlands preparatory to an anticipated war? McClallen started up the Missouri before Wilkinson had any word as to whether Lewis and Clark were still alive. For all the general knew until the latter's return, they had been intercepted by the Spanish, as his memorial had suggested and as he had predicted to Dearborn a year and a half after their departure westward.

Although it was unknown to Spanish authorities, the "Roseman-Perch-Pinch" expedition must be taken into account in any assessment of Wilkinson's intentions in the West. In 1806 Madrid still considered that she had an interest in the Pacific Northwest, for strategic reasons. Spain—always jealous of her prerogatives—was susceptible to being triggered into reasserting herself. Wilkinson's memorial to his Spanish contacts advocating Lewis's arrest did just that. What the general intended to accomplish is of

---

38 (1937) : 223–27; J. B. Tyrell, "Letter to Roseman and Perch, July 10, 1807," 38 (1937) : 391–97; J. S. Douglas, "Jeremy Pinch and the War Department," 39 (1938): 425–31; T. C. Elliott, "The Strange Case of David Thompson and Jeremy Pinch," 40 (1939) : 188–99; and W. J. Ghent, "'Jeremy Pinch' Again," 40 (1939) : 307–14. The subject receives its best treatment to date in Alvin M. Josephy, Jr., *The Nez Perce Indians and the Opening of the Northwest* (New Haven and London, 1965), pp. 41–42, 652, 656–62.

134. Josephy, *Nez Perce*, p. 42.
135. Ibid., p. 660.

less concern here than the impact of his machinations upon Spanish officialdom. Salcedo's orders to "apprehend" Merry—spawned in Wilkinson's
mind—fell short of realization and escaped American notice. When Madrid
did not do the expected and respond to either the Louisiana Purchase or
the bold probes on the frontier with some "casus belli," a stirring justification for invading Spanish territory failed to materialize.

Since Spanish officials had been alerted to the danger from Burr's activities, and exaggerated rumors of the gathering of a formidable force rico-
cheted back and forth, their attention perforce was focused upon the most
likely places to be invaded. Melgares, at his confrontation with Sharitarish,
was probably more concerned with the threat behind him, on the Sabine
and Red rivers, than with the situation beyond the Pawnee Republic, on
the Missouri. Preserving Indian alliances under such circumstances may
have seemed more important than the problematical chance of finding
Captain Merry.

Lewis and Clark returned from the Pacific unhindered. Few could foresee the nationalistic consequences of their feat. Little remained that Madrid
could do to repair the damage. Establishing outposts among the Pawnee,
along the Missouri, or at the Columbia's mouth entailed a host of difficulties. Salcedo's resources had to be devoted to protecting more vital areas.
The Freeman-Sparks probe had been blunted and Pike and his companions
arrested, but Spanish authorities dared not relax their guard, for they suspected Jefferson of being intent upon promoting more of the same.

Indeed, one factor in the process leading to Burr's debacle was Jefferson's covert encouragement of a series of encroachments upon territory
claimed by Spain. Since the Nootka Crisis of 1790, Jefferson had looked
upon "western restlessness" as useful leverage in securing concessions from
Madrid. If a boundary incident offered a pretext for war, or a filibuster
raising the banner of an independent Mexico in Baton Rouge touched off
a conflict, Burr and his collaborators assumed that their endeavor would
have Jefferson's sympathy, or at least passive cooperation. While Burr was
awaiting trial, the president wrote of the affair to the American minister in
Madrid.

> Never did a nation act towards another with more perfidy and in-
> justice than Spain has constantly practiced against us; and if we have
> kept our hands off her till now, it has been purely out of respect to
> France, and from the value we set on the friendship of France. We
> expect, therefore, from the friendship of the Emperor that he will
> either compel Spain to do us justice, or abandon her to us. We ask
> but one month to be in possession of the City of Mexico. No better
> proof of the good faith of the United States could have been given

than the vigor with which we have acted and the expense incurred
in suppressing the enterprise meditated lately by Burr against Mexico,
although at first he proposed a separation of the western country, and
on the ground received encouragement and aid from [the marqués de
Casa] Yrujo, according to the usual spirit of his government towards
us, yet he very early saw that the fidelity of the western country was
not to be shaken and turned himself wholly toward Mexico, and so
popular is an enterprise on that country in this, that we had only to
lie still and he would have had followers enough to have been in the
City of Mexico in six weeks.[136]

"To lie still" had been Jefferson's attitude toward Miranda's preparations
in New York City for an expedition to revolutionize Caracas. McCaleb
suggests that this may have been the president's plan with regard to Burr,
until the cry of treason resounded throughout the land and made inaction
impossible.[137] When the administration was forced to act, it was to its interest to convict Burr in order to disassociate the government from his objectives and thus avoid ruining chances of acquiring the Floridas by diplomacy.

Distantly related as all this may seem at first glance to the history of
Spanish concern with the Pacific Northwest, its significance is that Madrid—
so aroused by the feat of Lewis and Clark—was deflected by the Burr affair
from reasserting her claims to Oregon and was drawn instead to protecting
the Texas–West Florida frontier. Spanish officials watched with morbid fascination as the threat from Burr's furtive activities grew. Rumors made the
danger seem especially great. An effective response to the challenge raised
by Lewis and Clark's feat was not forthcoming. Before any measures were
taken in the direction suggested by Ambassador Casa Irujo of securing control over the Columbia and anticipating the Americans in the fur trade
there, the Spanish empire was plunged into turmoil by events on the
Iberian Peninsula in 1808. A period of eclipse of national power ensued
from which Spain emerged—years later—with her overseas dominions
threatened in many places more vital than the still largely unassessed wilds
of the Pacific Northwest.

136. Jefferson to James Bowdoin, April 2, 1807, excerpt in McCaleb, *Aaron Burr Conspiracy,*
p. 263.
137. Ibid., p. 263.

## 12   *The Spanish and "Manifest Destiny," 1808–1819*

SPANISH STATESMEN were so accustomed to thinking in terms of the strategic relevance of the hinterland west of upper Louisiana to imperial interests that this concern survived the period of Bourbon dethronement, 1808–14. Madrid's persistence in claiming the Pacific Northwest for herself would have considerable consequences upon international rivalry for that area and would determine the location of a number of state boundaries.

Spain's failure to realize her objectives on that perimeter of her empire resulted from events in Europe and the United States, rather than from occurrences in what the English-speaking world was beginning to call Oregon. Carlos IV's predicament grew in proportion to the rise of Napoleon's star. The entire western world became increasingly entangled in the coils of struggle between France, dominant on the continent, and Britain, preeminent on the seas. Spain, caught between the two great contestants, but contiguous with France, was particularly vulnerable to Bonaparte's armies. Carlos IV's course of appeasement, paying in excess of a million dollars a month to remain neutral, had the effect of hastening rather than avoiding war. London resented the support provided her enemy's military machine, and British warships commenced attacking Spanish fleets bringing silver from America. Drawn into the conflict and pitted against the Third Coalition (Britain, Austria, Prussia, and Russia), the Spanish saw their fleet destroyed off Cape Trafalgar in 1805.[1] Having lost the better part of her naval forces, Madrid found it ever more difficult to maintain communications with and fend off encroachments upon the New World territory that she claimed but had inadequately colonized.

Godoy's increasing subservience to Bonaparte brought more trouble overseas. Harried officials in Spanish America could spare little attention to preserving Carlos IV's claims in western North America. In 1796, 1804, 1806, and 1808, London pondered plans for assaults upon Louisiana, Mexico, Chile, and Peru. Lord Castlereagh and Sir Arthur Wellesley (the future duke of Wellington) met repeatedly with Francisco de Miranda, William Jacobs, and others ambitious to revolutionize or seize valuable colonies

---

1. Fugier, *Napoléon et l'Espagne*, 1 : 395. As commander of the *Bahama*, Dionisio Alcalá Galiano lost his life at Trafalgar. Cayetano Valdés, captain of the *Pelayo* in the battle of Cape San Vicente (1797) and defender of Cádiz against Nelson (1797), commanded the *Neptuno* at Trafalgar. Gravely wounded, he survived to become squadron chief and lieutenant general. After a decade of exile in England (about 1823–33) he was given command of the Department of Cádiz. *Enciclopedia General del Mar*, 6 : 693–94.

from Spain. William Spence Robertson, who chronicles these efforts, remarks that they "show clearly that the English Government designed the
ultimate conquest of a large part of the Spanish dominions in America."[2]
Some of the plans got underway: Miranda landed in what is now Venezuela;
for a short time Captain Home Popham occupied Buenos Aires (1806); a
similar landing that same year in Chile met with little success. In each case
Britain's military commitment was either unofficial, incomplete, or publicly
denied, but the numerous plans and actual attacks show that Spanish fears
were justified. Godoy's agents often were able to learn of such projects in
time for defensive measures.

As long as Spain was allied with France, weak spots in Spanish America
were fair game for Britain. Nowhere were Madrid's claims more vulnerable
than in the western North America, an area coveted by important men in
commercial and governmental circles in London. But when Napoleon deposed the Bourbons and drove the Spanish into an alliance with Britain,
London's plans for further encroachments upon Spanish territory had to be
deferred.

### BOURBON CAPTIVITY

Bonaparte's victories on the continent, at Jena and Friedland, made him
even more disposed to exploit his Spanish ally. It was an uphill battle for
Godoy to do other than tailor Madrid's policy to harmonize with the emperor's purposes. Napoleon insisted upon sending French troops across
northern Spain to crush Britain's Portuguese ally. Spanish resentment over
this drift of events coalesced in a faction that played up to the twenty-four-
year-old heir apparent, Fernando, who lent himself to an intrigue culminating in his arrest. When, in a secret trial within the Escorial, it developed
that the Prince of Asturias had been in surreptitious contact with Napoleon's envoy (Eugène de Beauharnais, the emperor's stepson by Josephine),
Fernando was acquitted, lest the emperor have an excuse to make himself
an arbiter in the quarrel and gain even greater sway over the nation. For
the public, this outcome seemed to corroborate the prince's innocence and
confirm the tales cultivated by Godoy's enemies. With 100,000 French
troops on Spanish soil and the flower of Carlos IV's army fighting in Denmark, the king was in a tenuous position, and he moved to the greater
safety of the Palace of Aranjuez, south of Madrid. Godoy's advice that Spain
oppose entry of additional French troops was unanimously rejected by the
rest of the royal council, for that would have signified war.

The abortive *fernandino* intrigue invited a Napoleonic power play.
Early in March the emperor demanded that he be given all the provinces
bordering France, in exchange for the cession of Portugal to Spain. At this

2. W. S. Robertson, "Francisco de Miranda," p. 393. See also pp. 355, 357, 392–93, 400.

it became evident to those privy to the situation that the policy of accommodating Bonaparte had failed. Godoy counseled Carlos and María Luisa to withdraw to Seville, preparatory to moving the court temporarily to Mexico City, if necessary. To Napoleon's envoy in Madrid it was evident that Godoy's power was in full ebb. "As luck would have it," he reported to the emperor, "the hatred of the Spanish for the Prince of the Peace is so extreme as to make him solely responsible for all their tribulations." [3]

The evening of March 17, 1808, word circulated at Aranjuez that the sovereigns were fleeing to Andalusia and that Fernando, against his will and compelled by Godoy, would be taken with them. A ranting mob sacked Godoy's residence. Fernandinos enlarged upon rumors of additional violence and constrained Carlos IV to abdicate in favor of his son. The turmoil accompanying these events gave French troops, under Napoleon's brother-in-law, Prince Joachim Murat, an opportunity to occupy Madrid on March 23 with scarcely any resistance.

As soon as he dared, Carlos secretly annulled his abdication, declaring that it had been done "in the midst of the tumult and forced by critical circumstances." A declaration to this effect was spirited to Murat. Once away from Aranjuez and within the relative safety of the Escorial, Carlos asked his brother to communicate the fact to the junta of government. Fernando and his collaborators were unwilling to incline themselves once again to Carlos's rule, as the son's succession to the throne had been proclaimed throughout the country. However, Carlos IV's protest cast grave doubts upon the legality of Fernando's claim to the crown. At Napoleon's order, Murat persisted in addressing the son as Prince of Asturias and referring to the father as sovereign. The junta decided that Carlos IV's message would be transmitted to Fernando but not made public for fear of provoking an uprising. As Carlos desired, he would meet with the emperor, who led everyone to believe that he intended to visit Spain. Hoping to gain Napoleon's recognition of his own sovereignty, Fernando hurried northward to greet him, but from Burgos onward he became a virtual prisoner of the French general and troops that were his escort.

In his eagerness to beat his parents to Bonaparte's presence, Fernando was induced to cross onto French territory of his own free will.[4] Only then did he perceive that the emperor had Bourbon dethronement in mind. Yet he did not warn his parents away! Carlos IV arrived in Bayonne on April 30. Day after day they were kept in the dark as to their host's next move. Far from being discredited in his subjects' eyes by this course of action, the

3. Claude Philippe, comte de Tournon-Simiane, to Napoleon, Burgos, March 16, 1808, FrAN (AF *4*, 1680); Spanish trans. in Izquierdo, *Antecedentes*, pp. 298–99, AT. The count had left Madrid on March 13.

4. For the stratagem by which this was accomplished, see Napoleon to Fernando VII, Bayonne, April 16, 1808, in Izquierdo, *Antecedentes*, pp. 379–80.

son's popularity grew. As Fernando's most recent biographer remarks, Napoleon "put in his hands the palm of martyrdom, for the Spanish did not see in this act of their king ingenuousness, but rather the loyalty of an *hidalgo* for whom perfidy in a friend is impossible." [5]

On May 2 Bonaparte's emissaries attempted to remove to Bayonne the youngest of Carlos IV's sons, fourteen-year-old Francisco de Paula Antonio. Word spread quickly, and at one corner of Madrid's Palacio de Oriente the populace clashed with Murat's troops, who were escorting the infante's carriage. Soon the entire capital was enveloped in violence. The bloody riots of "Dos de Mayo," 1808, still commemorated as a hallowed national holiday, marked the beginning of a five-year struggle against French domination. Napoleon summoned Fernando and obliged him to recognize his father as sovereign or be treated as a rebel, which would have meant his execution. Carlos refused to return to Spain, where his own authority seemed to have evaporated. He held his son responsible for the situation and made it clear that he would not relinquish his crown to Fernando. The emperor ruled out a regency in favor of younger sons. England had to be prevented from "infecting the Peninsula." Napoleon issued his ultimatum: "If Your Majesty does not want, or does not dare, to take part in this effort, I will give him asylum in my states and Your Majesty will make a renunciation in my favor of his own." [6]

With every other alternative unpalatable, the broken-spirited sixty-year-old monarch acquiesced in Napoleon's intention to install a Bonaparte dynasty in Madrid, hoping to keep the empire intact by a treaty that stipulated its nonabsorption by France (as had been sought and achieved when the Bourbons had replaced the Hapsburgs a century before). The emperor pledged Carlos and María Luisa a substantial pension and a palatial residence in France (promises fulfilled in a minimal fashion). Fernando and his retinue were interned under military guard at Valençay, Talleyrand's handsome château in the Loire valley. "There would be no inconvenience," Napoleon instructed their involuntary host, "in having the Prince of Asturias become attached to some pretty woman, above all if one can be sure of her." [7] There Fernando would remain until his captor was en route to Elba.

In short order juntas convened all over Spain to combat the French. There was no central government, for most of Fernando's men had compromised themselves with Murat's regime. As a consequence of the struggle that ensued, in which ambush and surprise assault replaced conventional combat, the word "guerrilla" entered the English language. Before Joseph

---

5. Izquierdo, *Antecedentes*, p. 53.
6. Conversation related by Carlos IV to Godoy, cited in ibid., pp. 412–13.
7. Napoleon to Talleyrand, Bayonne, May 9, 1808; Spanish trans. in ibid., p. 535, AT.

Bonaparte, formerly puppet king of Naples, even arrived in Madrid to assume the throne as José I, he expressed doubts of finding there a single sincere partisan, and his worst suspicions were soon confirmed.[8] Everywhere beyond the radius of French armies, Fernando VII was hailed as the true sovereign. When the juntas appealed to Britain for aid, an army being assembled in Ireland by the future Duke of Wellington for an attack on Spanish colonies was sent instead to help the Spanish people expel the French.

The Bonapartist regime in Madrid was a major factor in dissolving the bonds of Spain's overseas empire. During the Spanish-American gravitation toward independence (1810–24), Britain's alliance with the Spanish juntas against Napoleon kept London from taking full advantage of the power vacuum in America. Instead, the colonies there evolved into independent, Spanish-speaking republics or became a part of the United States, as in the case of the Southwest and the Pacific Northwest.

The struggle against Napoleon had the effect of diverting British attention away from California and the Columbia basin, an interest that had been enlivened by the Nootka controversy and publication of the results of Vancouver's examination of that coast, from Alaska to San Diego.

### THE RUSSIAN ADVANCE TOWARD CALIFORNIA

With Carlos and Fernando languishing in Napoleonic captivity, Madrid's claims to the northwest coast hardly needed to be reckoned with in St. Petersburg. Russia, more active than ever in Alaska, seized the opportunity to strengthen her colony in America, at Spain's expense.

During the eighteenth century Russian fur trading activities in North America were confined almost entirely to the area west of Prince William Sound, but the reproductive rate of the sea otter could not keep pace with the numbers killed by Aleut hunters in the Russian service. In area after area the species became too scarce to be worth hunting. Muscovite traders and Aleut fleets of bidarkas pushed ever eastward, seeking better hunting areas.

The Russian expedition to occupy Nootka that Zaikov and Martínez had looked for in 1789 did not get underway, and the diplomatic imbroglio of 1790 discouraged Muscovite intentions in that direction for a time. When Aleksandr Andreevich Baranov came to Alaska in 1791 as chief manager of the Russian fur trading company and of the colony, he carried instructions for a probe toward Nootka to ascertain the point where the Spanish placed their boundary. On the northern side of that spot he was to plant an outpost and establish friendly relations with the natives. In 1795 he reconnoitered the harbor where Sitka is now located and took

8. Joseph's letters to the Emperor are cited in ibid., p. 486.

formal possession for Russia, but he made no attempt at planting an out-post, content for the time with establishing a fort at Yakutat Bay (Port Mulgrave to other nationalities). From European gazettes Baranov learned of Friendly Cove's evacuation in 1795. In 1796 he informed St. Petersburg of his intention to establish a settlement there at the earliest opportunity, taking advantage of Spanish and British preoccupation with the war against France. His plans were delayed, however, by want of vessels and means, and until 1799 there were no Russian outposts south of Yakutat.[9] That year, accompanied by a great flotilla of bidarkas, Baranov and a party of settlers arrived at the first of his intended settlements, present-day Sitka. The direc-tion of his aspirations is revealed in a stanza of the chant that he composed for the dedication of the strong fort which was soon completed. Known as the "Song of Baranov," its recitation became a feature at the inauguration of every Russian outpost founded thereafter in America:

> Buildings are raised on New World ground,
> Now Russia rushes to Nootka Sound,
> The Peoples wild are Nature's child,
> And friendly now to Russian rule.[10]

Tsar Paul I chartered the Russian-American Company in 1799, giving it exclusive rights for trading in Russian America, thus eliminating the ruth-less competition between small, rival companies. Baranov was named *Glavnyi Pravitel*, a title borne by all his successors, sometimes translated as chief factor or manager, but more aptly as governor.[11] Various disasters hampered plans for expansion to Nootka. The perennial shortage of ships, loss of several vessels at sea, and utter annihilation of Sitka itself caused the project to be postponed again and again. Russian and Aleut intrusion upon ancestral hunting grounds was greatly resented by the Tlingit, who in 1802 attacked the settlement and fortress. After fearful carnage, the defenders were slain and their severed heads impaled at beachside to warn off future colonizers. Two years later a heavily armed Russian-Aleut ex-pedition personally headed by Baranov reoccupied the site, but only after a week of siege and a furious battle costing many lives. The new establish-ment, named Novo Arkhangelsk, became capital of Russian America.

The decline of Spanish fur trading efforts allowed the sea otter to multi-ply in California waters. Yankee Captain Joseph O'Cain conceived a

---

9. Petr Aleksandrovich Tikhmenev, *Istoricheskoe Obozrenie Obrazovaniia Rossiisko-Amerikan-skoi Kompanii*, 2 vols. (St. Petersburg, 1861–62), 1 : 34. Excerpt translated in C. L. Andrews, "Russian Plans," p. 84; Poniatowski, *Histoire*, p. 90; Semen Bentsionovich Okun', *The Russian-American Company* (Cambridge, Mass., 1951), p. 53.

10. C. L. Andrews, "Russian Plans," p. 86.

11. Hector Chevigny, *Russian America: The Great Alaskan Venture, 1741–1867* (New York, 1965), p. 100n.

scheme for exploiting this untapped wealth. He had been to Kodiak on two previous occasions as an officer on vessels which had profited from Baranov's chronic shortage of supplies by trading him much-needed items for sea otter pelts. In 1803 O'Cain returned with his own vessel, expecting to secure pelts without the risks inherent in dealing directly with tribes farther south. Baranov had no furs awaiting shipment but was eager for the supplies. O'Cain negotiated for a flotilla of Aleut hunters to operate off unpopulated stretches of Baja California, where there were no Indians capable of posing a serious obstacle and little danger of Spanish patrols. After the Aleuts were paid, the catch would be divided equally between the American captain and Russian company. In 1802 Baranov had been ordered to extend Russian settlements farther toward the southeast, and he seized upon this arrangement as a practical and inexpensive means of penetrating the California area. O'Cain's hunters were commanded by one Shutzov, whom Baranov secretly instructed to examine the coast of California with care and find a propitious site for a permanent Russian settlement. The venture, which yielded the Russian-American Company a share worth $80,000, was the first of a number of similar compacts with other American vessels, with returns for Baranov running as high as $100,000 a voyage. Every such expedition carried a Russian agent to direct the Aleut hunters. The contract system with American captains tapped sea otter resources in California at a time when Baranov lacked sufficient ships of his own to exploit the Alaskan coastline, let alone areas farther south. As soon as circumstances permitted he chose to reap 100 percent of the yield by using only Russian ships.[12]

In the course of a journey intended to lead him around the world, Nikolai Petrovich Rezanov visited Novo Arkhangelsk in 1805. Through his deceased wife, Grigori Shelikhov's daughter, Rezanov was virtually director of the Russian-American Company's affairs, and his visit to Alaska was of capital importance. A protégé of Chief Minister Count Nikolai Rumiantsev, Rezanov held the titles of grand chamberlain, privy councilor, and procurator general of the senate, and his views commanded attention at home as well as in Alaska. What he saw at the tiny Russian outposts soon dispelled grandiose images cultivated by his late father-in-law. He found the capital of Russian America to be a small settlement on the brink of starvation, because of the chronic shortage of vessels and tenuous supply lines from Siberia. To counteract the increasing scarcity of sea otters north of Sitka, Rezanov proposed establishing additional Russian establishments farther south, on the mainland opposite the Queen Charlotte Islands, in the Strait of Juan de Fuca, and at the mouth of the Columbia River. Rezanov's letter to Tsar Alexander I making these recommendations commented that the

12. Ibid., pp. 101–02, 130; Poniatowski, *Histoire,* p. 144.

Spanish were "very weak in his country," and lamented that upon the 1798 declaration of war against Spain, Russia had not seized the California coast from 34° northward, as it might "profitably have been held and always by us kept afterward." [13] He pointed out the importance of acting speedily, while Napoleon had Europe distracted. Baranov shared Rezanov's interest in the coastline north of San Francisco Bay, and in 1806 reported to the Russian ministry: "Today there subsists even yet an unoccupied portion that would be very useful to us and even indispensable. . . . If we should permit it to escape us, what will posterity say?" [14]

After enduring a rugged winter at Novo Arkhangelsk, during which a number of his compatriots perished from scurvy, Rezanov decided to explore means of providing an adequate supply of temperate zone products. Purchasing the *Juno* from Rhode Islander John D'Wolf, he and his suite set out for Spanish California. On the journey southward he sought to cross the bar at the Columbia's mouth and survey the estuary as a site for a settlement envisioned there. Adverse winds and a shortage of able hands among the scurvy-ridden crew discouraged the attempt, and he continued on to San Francisco.

Rezanov's polish and diplomatic behavior impressed the Californians, and he in turn was attracted by María de la Concepción Marcela Argüello, fifteen-year-old daughter of José Darío Argüello, commandant at San Francisco—although it has been suggested that Rezanov's attentions were "more the wiles of a politician than the wooing of a lover." [15] In the words of Georg Heinrich von Langsdorff, Rezanov's German physician-companion, the Russian aristocrat "conceived the idea that through a marriage with the daughter of the Commandante . . . a close bond would be formed for future business intercourse between the Russian-American Company and the province of Nueva California." [16] Rezanov's confidential report to the Russian ministry admitted that the romance had "not begun in hot passion," but his words evince a felicitous coincidence between the interests of sentiment and shrewd diplomacy. Fair Conchita accepted the forty-two-year-old widower's proposal, despite her family's initial objections. The wedding could not take place, everyone agreed, until permission had been obtained from both pope and king for them to marry outside her religion.

The courtship tends to obscure the fact that Rezanov came to California on a mission amounting to espionage, inimical to Spanish interests, for he cherished the dream of expropriating for Russia a goodly portion of Alta

13. Rezanov to the tsar, Novo Arkhangelsk, 1805, in Tikhmenev, *Istoricheskoe*, 2 : 232 ff.; trans. in C. L. Andrews, "Russian Plans," pp. 88–89.

14. Baranov to the minister of commerce, June 17, 1806, cited by Poniatowski, *Histoire*, p. 144, AT.

15. Andrews, "Russian Plans," p. 89.

16. Langsdorff, as cited by Allan Temko, "Russians in California," *AH* 11, no. 3 (1960) : 9.

California. His sojourn (April 5–May 21, 1806) yielded specific information about the province's weaknesses, confirming the complete absence of Spanish control over the area north of San Francisco Bay, and it underscored advantages to be gained from a Russian settlement at that latitude. The *Juno* was loaded to capacity with a cargo of California jerky and grain, a godsend to Sitka. On the voyage northward, Rezanov composed a report to the ministry in which he anticipated the day when "all this country could be made a corporal part of the Russian Empire." [17] Before departing for Siberia and St. Petersburg he left Baranov a series of recommendations concerning the contemplated expansion southward. The poignancy of Rezanov's idyll—for the Spanish never learned of his designs upon California—was enhanced when he died after falling through the ice of a Siberian river. No one in Russia sent word of this to Conchita. The faithful maiden rejected all other suitors and, when the first convent in California was founded, she became a nun. The larger significance of the episode is that it persuaded Rezanov to recommend establishing a Russian settlement at strategic Bodega Bay, just beyond Spanish control but close enough to facilitate trading for much-needed foodstuffs.

The first documented Russian land activities south of Sitka occurred in 1807 when, operating under contract with Baranov, Captain Oliver Kimball and the American trader *Peacock* came to California waters with a group of twelve Aleut bidarkas, commanded by veteran Vasilii Petrovich Tarakanov, one of the few persons to be rescued after the Sitka massacre of 1802. A man with an ear for Indian languages, Tarakanov had already been to California with O'Cain. [18] Kimball put in at Bodega Bay in March 1807, remaining there until May, and a few crude huts were erected ashore. The Aleuts ranged up and down the coast and a few even entered San Francisco Bay, where the sea otter swam in great, unmolested herds. The bidarkas hugged the far shore of the Golden Gate, away from the presidio's cannons, but did not escape notice. On one occasion, when five of the skin boats tried to slip out of the bay, a cannonball came so close that two were abandoned and the hunters fled overland. O'Cain and others frequented the Farallons and Santa Catalina Island. Soon, groups of Aleut hunters were remaining the year around at isolated bays in Baja California. The governor of Alta California, José Joaquín de Arrillaga, learned of such activities, but he was powerless to capture the mother vessels or the bidarkas at sea. His measures were limited, for want of warships, to clashes with Aleuts encountered on the mainland.

17. Rezanov, as cited by Temko, "Russians."

18. Chevigny, *Russian America*, pp. 135, 270, who sometimes refers to him as Timofei Tarakanov; Adele Ogden, "Russian Sea-Otter and Seal Hunting on the California Coast, 1803–1841," *CHSQ*, 12 (1933): p. 221.

Over the years Russian aspirations along the Pacific coast grew as Spain's ability to defend her claims atrophied. Russian cartographers acquired the habit of claiming for the tsar everything north of the Columbia, a point underscored (significantly, considering his subsequent role in formulating the Monroe Doctrine) by John Quincy Adams, American minister to St. Petersburg, in communications to President Madison's secretary of state.[19] As a consequence of Rezanov's recommendations, Baranov received instructions (1807) to set in motion the deceased aristocrat's vast projects for Russian settlements in California, Hawaii, and at the mouth of the Columbia. That same year an expedition set out from Novo Arkhangelsk, composed of the *Juno* and the *O'Cain,* captained by Americans and accompanied by a fleet of bidarkas commanded by Baranov's right-hand man and successor-designate, Ivan Alexandrovich Kuskov. Their objective is unknown, but they were headed somewhere south of the present Alaska-Canada boundary. At that latitude, however, a pitched battle ensued with the local Indians, who had been incited to resist the invasion by Captain Samuel Hill of the American brig *Lydia.* After eight Aleuts fell before the onslaught, Kuskov ordered a retreat to Novo Arkhangelsk.[20]

Baranov would not be dissuaded. In 1808 he sent southward a more ambitious effort, again under Kuskov's direction, to reconnoiter sites for Russian settlements at Bodega Bay and the Columbia's mouth, in anticipation of a rumored American attempt to occupy the latter spot. This expedition, so potentially important had it succeeded, is little known and seldom mentioned in the standard works. It should be emphasized that at this time there were no white outposts between Sitka and San Francisco, nor had any been attempted since the 1795 evacuation of Nootka. If Kuskov had carried out his intent, the tsar would have had a solid basis on which to justify a claim to the entire coast, to the very neighborhood of San Francisco. Captain Nikolai Isakovich Bulygin and the *Saint Nicholas,* a brig that Baranov had purchased from an American trader, sailed from Novo Arkhangelsk on September 28, unexplainably late in the season. As supercargo and boss of the *promyshlenniki* came Vasilii Tarakanov, veteran of Kimball's sojourn at Bodega Bay the previous summer. Kuskov and a second vessel, the *Kadiak,* were to examine Bodega Bay and meet Bulygin at Gray's Harbor in December.[21]

Off today's Washington coast, near where the *Sonora* had been ambushed in 1775, the *Saint Nicholas* got becalmed while too close to shore. Bulygin

19. J. Q. Adams to Secretary of State [Robert Smith], no. 27, St. Petersburg, October 12, 1810, cited by S. F. Bemis, *John Quincy Adams and the Foundations of American Foreign Policy* (New York, 1949), p. 174.

20. C. L. Andrews, "Russian Plans," pp. 89–90.

21. C. L. Andrews, "The Wreck of the St. Nicholas," *WHQ* 13 (1922): 27; Chevigny, *Russian America,* pp. 135–37.

put out three anchors, but during the night a wind came up and the cables chafed against submerged rocks and snapped. The foreyard broke, making it impossible to maneuver against the wind, and soon the brig was aground. Everyone reached the beach safely, and some of the arms, ammunition, tents, and provisions were removed before waves battered the ship apart. Among the castaways were the captain's young and attractive wife and several Aleut women. It was decided that all should try to reach Gray's Harbor, some seventy miles to the south, in time to meet the *Kadiak*. They had scarcely made contact with the natives when a fracas ensued, in which several of the Russians were injured. Subsequently, they persuaded some other Indians to ferry them across a deep, swift river, but they were attacked at the most disadvantageous moment. The three women, in the lead canoe, were carried away as captives. Everyone in the second canoe was wounded by a volley of arrows, but all managed to rejoin their companions. Two of the wounded later died. Eventually the others all fell prisoner or surrendered voluntarily to the Makah, to the north, into whose possession Bulygin's wife had come. She persuaded her compatriots that they would receive better treatment there than at the hands of other tribes. In 1810, Captain Brown of the *Lydia* rescued thirteen of those surviving by offering a respectable ransom for their delivery to the village where he lay at anchor—probably Neah Bay—and he took them to Novo Arkhangelsk. Bulygin and his wife died before rescue came, but Tarakanov survived to record their sufferings. The tragedy probably dampened interest at Novo Arkhangelsk in the potentialities of a settlement at the Columbia's mouth, as the project was not revived.[22] Soon Americans would occupy the spot.

When the *Saint Nicholas* failed to appear at Gray's Harbor, the *Kadiak* continued to Novo Arkhangelsk. Early in 1809 Kuskov returned to Bodega Bay and ordered temporary buildings erected to house his men on shore. The force consisted of forty Russians and 150 Aleuts, twenty of them women. The establishment was named "Fort Rumiantsev" in honor of the Russian chancellor. To reach sea otter herds within San Francisco Bay, yet escape the murderous cannons at its entrance, the Aleuts made a short portage across the Marin Peninsula with the light boats in which they accompanied the ship. As a result of their rich harvest, the *Kadiak* returned northward after five months with 2,000 pelts. American ships with Aleut hunters made Bodega Bay their base the following year, and once again bidarkas boldly roamed San Francisco Bay; some of the Aleuts were killed by the Spanish and others captured, but the fabulous catch within the great estuary tempted them to continue taking the calculated risk. Kuskov returned to Bodega with the *Chirikov* in 1811, and a half dozen American

22. Chevigny, *Russian America*.

vessels with Aleut hunters also were based there that season. The area fairly swarmed with Aleuts. At one time there were 130 bidarkas hunting clandestinely within San Francisco Bay. Commander Argüello sent a party to the north shore of the bay to seize the hunters when they came there at nightfall, but they eluded capture. Eventually he resorted to posting a continual armed guard at the few spots around the bay where fresh water might be obtained.[23]

For a permanent settlement Kuskov selected a cove—today's Kuskov Bay—thirty miles north of Bodega. Despite its inferior anchorage, it lay at a safer distance from Spanish retaliation. For a trifling sum in blankets, tools, and beads, he purchased from the Pomo Indians a tract for a fort atop a promontory protected on three sides by the sea. A permanent establishment obviated sharing 50 percent of the peltry with Yankee captains. On this site, in 1812, he founded "Rossiya"—an archaic term for Russia—called "Fuerte Rusa" in Spanish, and "Fort Ross" in English. The force brought southward that year numbered ninety-five Russians and eighty Aleuts. A strong palisade of redwood planks, surmounted by spikes, encompassed the settlement. It provided a toehold for Russia within walking distance of strategic San Francisco Bay, the finest harbor on the Pacific coast, and it represented a key move in Rezanov's plan for extending Russian dominion over everything to at least that latitude. That same year Kuskov established an outpost on one of the Farallon Islands, where a crew of men would remain the year around, exploiting large herds of seals and sea lions frequenting the spot in order to supply Fort Ross with salted meat and provide the Aleuts with skins for clothing and boats, as well as much-appreciated blubber and oil.[24]

Despite the American and British fur trading establishments that were planted at the Columbia's mouth in 1811, Russia now enjoyed a superior position on the Pacific coast. At the outbreak of the War of 1812, many American traders sold their vessels to Baranov rather than expose themselves to British capture. Rezanov's recommendation for a base in Hawaii was carried out in 1815 with the founding of a Russian fort at Honolulu.[25] The international situation bid fair to make the Muscovites masters of the North Pacific and the sea otter trade—a threat quickly comprehended in Monterey and Mexico City, if not yet in London or Washington. Fort Ross caused immediate alarm and mortification in California, but there were not enough soldiers and arms in that province to take on the Russians while the motherland grappled with Napoleon and Mexico itself was torn by

23. Ogden, "Russian Sea-Otter and Seal Hunting," p. 229.

24. E. O. Essig, "The Russian Settlement at Ross," *CHSQ* 12 (1933).

25. C. L. Andrews, "Russian Plans," p. 91. See Richard A. Pierce, *Russia's Hawaiian Adventure, 1815–1817* (Berkeley and Los Angeles, 1965).

revolt. Local officials were impotent to dislodge the Slavs from their easily defended fort. To all protests and demands that he and his men leave, Kuskov responded politely but firmly that his superiors' orders could not be disobeyed. Secure behind his stockade, he proceeded to develop the enclave as a base for peltry, shipbuilding, and raising the crops and cattle needed to supply Alaskan settlements.

From the beginning, sub rosa commercial dealings existed between the Russians and Spanish subjects. Each side soon became dependent upon the other for certain supplies, and California authorities for a time made a pretense of overlooking the illegal trade. In 1815 a new governor, Pablo Vicente de Solá, instituted a more rigorous policy; thereafter, Russians slipping ashore south of San Francisco to engage in illegal bartering or poach upon Spanish cattle ran an increased risk of being captured. Aleuts could no longer hunt south of Bodega Bay with impunity, and those who dared were often seized and imprisoned. Although the Iberian colonists needed supplies obtainable through Fort Ross, in his negotiations to secure provisions for his military forces Solá stoutly resisted all entreaties that Aleuts be permitted to hunt the sea otter on an equal-share basis in the areas from which they were being excluded. The California governor's position was that he would not be justified in asking the viceroy to consent to such a pact unless the Russians first abandoned their intrusion upon Spanish territory. In 1818, following Bourbon restoration, the viceroy ordered Solá to expel the Muscovite enclave. The governor had no alternative but to answer that he lacked the necessary military strength to comply.[26] In 1821, when Mexico cut its ties with Spain, California's defenses against Slavic encroachment were still further weakened.

The Russian senate ratified a ukase (September 4, 1821) intended to make the North Pacific a Russian preserve, forbidding foreign vessels to approach within 100 miles of the continent, from 51° of latitude northward, upon pain of confiscation. This pronouncement, made at the urging of the Russian-American Company to increase its profit margin, was interpreted by Russia's rivals as evidence of the increased belligerency of her imperialism. Fears of Muscovite designs upon all of California were justified. One of the directors of the Russian-American Company, after inspecting Fort Ross in 1824, presented a plan whereby Russia would side with Spanish monarchists in California against Mexican republicans, using armed force if necessary. He suggested that once California declared its independence of Mexico, Russia doubtless would be able to subject California to its tute-

26. Clarence John Dufour, "The Russian Withdrawal from California," *CHSQ* 12 (1933) : 241; Pablo Vicente de Solá to Viceroy Juan Ruiz de Apodaca, conde del Venadito, Monterey, April 3, 1818, and viceroy to the minister of state, Mexico City, September 30, 1818, SpAGI (Estado 32–32), cited by Ogden, "Russian Sea-Otter and Seal Hunting," pp. 321–33.

lage. José Altamira, commandant in San Francisco, was receptive to the design, but the plans collapsed following the director's recall to St. Petersburg to stand trial for complicity in the Decembrist plot of 1826.[27]

Since Mexico's new government found it impossible to keep Russian poachers from California waters, in 1823 it agreed to allow Muscovite vessels to operate there and retain a 50 percent share of their catch, with the remainder sold to the Mexican government at a fixed price in return for wheat. Thereafter, great quantities of pelts were harvested by Aleut hunters in the San Francisco Bay area with the complete cooperation of Mexican authorities. Furs thus obtained by the Mexicans were bartered with the Russians for European manufactured goods, in growing demand in California. The market for pelts at Fort Ross prompted Mexican companies to enter the competition, and in 1831 Governor Manuel Victoria advised Baron Ferdinand von Wrangell, governor of Russian America, of discontinuation of the contract system. Mexico was eager to obtain Russian diplomatic recognition, and Von Wrangell saw in this wish a possibility of obtaining valuable concessions. In 1832 he suggested bartering recognition for cession of additional territory contiguous to Fort Ross. He hinted to his superiors that Russia might even secure everything north of San Francisco Bay. Tsar Nicholas was unwilling, however, to extend diplomatic relations to the infant republic, and the concessions that Von Wrangell desired were never obtained.[28]

Fort Ross is pertinent to Spanish aspirations in the Pacific Northwest in that the existence of the Russian enclave indicates the weakness of Iberian dominion over the coast north of San Francisco after the turn of the century. Von Wrangell's successor, Captain Ivan Kouprianov, ordered all the Fort Ross Aleuts brought to Kodiak in 1838, telling evidence of the base's decline.[29] In 1841 the Russian-American Company sold its buildings and equipment there to John Sutter, the prominent Swiss pioneer, for the sum of $30,000. The colony was abandoned because of economic factors, not Mexican pressure. The sea otter population could not withstand intensive hunting indefinitely, and it was nearing extinction. When the yield in pelts fell off, the base produced an increasing annual deficit. It had failed as a shipbuilding center, its anchorage was poor, and the cultivated area was too restricted and cool to produce enough to fulfill its complementary function for Alaska. To the good fortune of the eventual heirs to Cali-

27. Poniatowski, *Histoire*, p. 153. For the complex motives behind the ukase, not of the tsar's making and contrary to his impulses, and the effect of the liberal "Decembrist" plot upon the Russian-American Company, see Chevigny, *Russian America*, pp. 175–88.

28. Ogden, "Russian Sea-Otter and Seal Hunting," p. 236; Poniatowski, *Histoire*, p. 154; Temko, "Russians," p. 84.

29. A. P. Kashevaroff, "Fort Ross, An Account of Russian Settlement," *Alaska Magazine* 1 (1927) : 235 ff.

fornia, Rossiya was evacuated by its founders a scant six years before the discovery at Sutter's Mill changed the world's attitude about California's promise.

### GROWING AMERICAN INTEREST IN THE PACIFIC NORTHWEST

As a consequence of the sea otter trade, there was considerable knowledge in some circles in the United States about the northwest coast long before Lewis and Clark reached that far-off shore. Despite competent studies of the maritime fur trade, the number and importance of the early American voyages to the northwest coast are seldom appreciated. Appendix E indicates the nationalities of vessels visiting that shore from 1774 to 1825 and shows a preponderance of American over British ships even before 1800. By 1805, when Lewis and Clark reached the Pacific, the recorded number of American trading cruises exceeded 120, as compared with 80 British and 43 Spanish visits, the latter being for strategic rather than trading purposes. By 1825, more than 300 American vessels had visited the area, and the trade constituted one of our merchant marine's most important activities. Trade between the Atlantic seaboard, the northwest coast, and China influenced business circles and acquainted sufficient numbers of Americans with the opposite edge of the continent to attract their gaze toward the promise of Oregon, making it one of the objectives of America's "Manifest Destiny."

John Jacob Astor sent his first vessel to the northwest coast in 1809, and in 1811 his men founded Astoria, at the Columbia's mouth, to serve as an emporium for trade with the interior, Russian Alaska, and China. It was the first white settlement between Fort Ross and Sitka since Nootka's evacuation, sixteen years before.

Significantly for future diplomatic rivalry over Oregon, Astor's men were already ensconced in their palisade when, four months later, David Thompson and a party of North West Company men arrived on the site from the interior. Apprised by his superiors of Astor's plan, Thompson had been instructed to beat the Americans to the spot. Hazardous canyons on the Pend Oreille River had delayed Thompson and his companions on their downstream journey. He had established Kullyspell House on Lake Pend Oreille (1809), and his associates founded Spokane House (1810). The following season Thompson hurried down the Columbia, leaving a marker at the mouth of the Snake River asserting Britain's claim over that watershed, to find the Americans well established at Astoria.

American activities in the Columbia basin came to an abrupt halt when word arrived that war had broken out between Washington and London. Rumor had it that a British man-of-war was coming to blast Astoria off its foundations. The little stockade could not hope to resist, so in October 1813 it was sold to the North West Company. American posts in the interior were likewise taken over. Many of Astor's men entered British service rather than leave the area. The report about a British frigate soon proved true. Captain Black of the *Raccoon* was somewhat disgruntled to find his objective already in British hands, and he performed a formal act of possession on December 13 in the name of His Britannic Majesty, renaming the spot Fort George. By doing so he gave the episode an aspect of military conquest, a circumstance with lasting consequences. The Treaty of Ghent at war's end provided for a return to status quo ante bellum, and in 1818 representatives of the British government were obliged to lower the British ensign, hoist the American flag, and salute it in the presence of an American commissioner. Astoria's restoration weakened Britain's position in Oregon to the point that soon London was willing to accept the Columbia as the southern boundary to its claims.

Spanish officials in Monterey and Chihuahua had scant means of knowing about American and British activities in Oregon. Iberian apprehensions about the northwest coast yielded to concern about the threat from Fort Ross and the flotillas of Aleut hunters frequenting California waters. Foreigners operated with impunity north of San Francisco after 1808, and Spanish officials were unable to oppose them effectively, for the motherland was totally occupied with the struggle against Napoleon.

REVOLUTION AND COUNTERREVOLUTION IN THE SPANISH EMPIRE

In 1814 Fernando regained his throne. His parents never returned to Spain, but resided in Italy, with Godoy at their side until they succumbed, within weeks of each other, in 1819.

The Bourbon eclipse was, if not actually the cause, surely the immediate catalyst to disintegration of Spain's vast empire. During the period that José I occupied the throne, 1808 through 1813, Spanish America was thrown into turmoil by a series of revolts that had a telling effect on Spanish colonials of every persuasion. When news of Bourbon captivity reached Mexico City, creole elements protested against the Napoleonic puppet and declared in favor of Fernando VII, but the *gachupines,* or peninsula-born, gave their support to the junta in Cádiz. Viceroy Iturrigaray sided with the creoles, and he was deposed by a militia organized by judges of the Audiencia. In 1810 a new viceroy arrived, the junta's appointee. In less than a month, with the famous "Grito de Dolores," curate Miguel Hidalgo raised his cry of protest under the standard of Our Lady of Guadalupe, igniting a popular revolt that took on the aspect of a radical effort to destroy not only the government but the entire power structure. His widespread initial gains eventually foundered. Attempting to flee toward the United States, Hidalgo and many other leaders of the revolt were captured and executed in Chihuahua in 1811 by forces under Nemesio Salcedo, commandant general of the Interior Provinces. The violence of class war disrupted life in much of Mexico, and the Californians could take some satisfaction from their isolation. Small wonder that the northwest coast and hinterland were almost forgotten.

In 1810 revolts also flared in Caracas, Cartagena, Bogotá, Santiago de Chile, and Buenos Aires, but only in the latter case did the effort result in independence for the region involved. The almost universal failure of the initial rebellions in Spanish America and the return of Fernando VII to the throne in 1814 ushered in a period of counterrevolution and reaction in the Spanish Empire. Restored to power, Fernando not only expelled or imprisoned those who had collaborated with the puppet regime, but he repudiated liberal measures instituted during his exile by the Cortes in Cádiz, initiating a systematic persecution of all members of that body. His actions strengthened the hand of democratic leaders in Spanish America. Despite Fernando's repeated appeals for reconciliation with his subjects, the insurrectionists were able to export revolution with considerable success. In 1817 José de San Martín's army crossed the Andes into Chile. At Boyacá in 1819, Simón Bolívar broke the back of Spanish power in present-day Colombia, but his forces and those of San Martín were separated by thousands of miles of territory over which Madrid still ruled unchallenged. Despite loss of the Río de la Plata, Chile, and New Granada, the empire was still largely intact. Spanish armies prevailed in Mexico, Central America, Cuba, Venezuela, Ecuador, Peru, and the Philippines. But it is against this background of revolt and uncertain loyalties that the final episodes in the history of Spain and the Pacific Northwest must be depicted, for that turbulence, more than any other factor, determined the particular outcome of the diplomatic liquidation of Madrid's claims over the northwest coast.

### SPANISH EXPLORATIONS IN OREGON'S INTERIOR

His Catholic Majesty's subjects were conspicuously lax in examining the interior of North America north and west of New Mexico and upper Louisiana, in striking contrast to Hispanic activity in South and Central America during the sixteenth century, where hardly a valley, mountain range, or potential mineral deposit went unnoticed. The Domínguez and Vélez de Escalante expedition of 1776 may not have been the only Spanish effort to penetrate the hinterland northwest of New Mexico, but evidence of other probes in that direction is scanty. Archival destruction accompanying the political turmoil that ripped to shreds Spain's colonial bureaucracy prevents an assumption that nothing has escaped historians.

In 1919 Henry Wagner published, without editorial comment, a purported account of one such feat, in which Spanish friars were said to have crossed overland from the Colorado's headwaters in 1810–11 and descended a river in Oregon to the Pacific. Wagner never returned to the topic, and it has not been followed up by subsequent scholars.[30] The mystery is enhanced when one pieces together the biography of William Davis Robinson, the little-known American responsible for the account. Robinson was an enthusiastic proponent of what a later generation would call "Manifest Destiny." His nine years of adventure in what is now Venezuela led him to publish a pamphlet in 1815 advocating an "early connection" between the United States and an independent Spanish America.[31] In 1816 he went to Mexico, allegedly to collect upon debts owed by Mexican revolutionaries for munitions acquired in the United States. At General Guadalupe Victoria's headquarters he was provided with a narrative of the friars' wanderings in Oregon and was asked to impress upon President Madison the importance of that area, so as to obtain American help in preventing Russia from securing control of the coast between Fort Ross and Alaska. As Robinson returned toward Veracruz with a rebel force, he was ambushed and he lost his baggage. The royalists condemned him to death, taking him to be John Hamilton Robinson of the Pike expedition, who had gone on to become a brigadier general with the revolutionaries. Although the businessman disassociated himself from the doctor, it was held that he knew too much about conditions within Mexico for release. After three years of confinement at Oaxaca, Veracruz, Havana, and Cádiz, Robinson escaped to an American ship. Once home, he published his *Memoirs of the Mexican Revolution* (Philadelphia, 1820; London, 1821), which refers briefly to the expedition in question. In 1821 he sent a more detailed account, the letter which concerns us, to John Eaton, U.S. senator from Tennessee.

Robinson argued that maritime explorations had not disclosed everything of strategic importance on the Pacific coast between 42° and 49° of latitude, "that part of the coast which most particularly interests the United States." To substantiate that the area had good bays and rivers of consequence, he cited the manuscript of the friars' explorations, furnished him in 1816 "by one of the revolutionary chiefs, for the express purpose of being communicated to our government." He claimed that the lost manuscript's contents were "still fresh in my recollection." He had been given to understand that one or two priests were dispatched annually to the interior of Alta California to evangelize the natives and gather topographical information, but

---

30. Charles L. Camp's revised edition of Wagner's *The Plains and the Rockies* (Columbus, Ohio, 1953), p. 42, remarks: "From the description which Robinson gives of the country it is hardly possible that this tale can be true."

31. William Davis Robinson, *A Cursory View of Spanish America, Particularly the Neighboring Viceroyalties of Mexico and New Granada, Chiefly Intended to Elucidate the Policy of an Early Connection Between the United States and These Countries* (Georgetown, D.C., 1815).

their reports were "transmitted with great care to the City of Mexico, and there locked up in the ecclesiastical archives, except such portion of it as the Archbishop of Mexico thought proper to communicate to the viceroy." For critical evaluation, the rest of the tale warrants perusal in its entirety:

> In the years 1810 and 11, two friars made an excursion up the River Colorado. This noble river discharges itself in the Gulf of California, about the latitude 32,40. The bar at its mouth has six to nine fathoms water on it, and the river may be ascended with a line of battleship at least one hundred miles. The friars followed the course of this river nearly six hundred and fifty miles; they found the current gentle, with scarcely any impediments to its navigation by large vessels nearly the whole distance. Several fine streams emptied into the Colorado, but they did not explore their sources. They state the principal source of the Colorado, to be in the Rocky or Snowy Mountains, between latitude 40 and 41. The description they give of the country through which the Colorado flows, would induce the reader to believe that it is the finest region in the Mexican empire. They represent the banks of the river as being, in many places, one hundred feet above its surface; that the whole country is a forest of majestic trees, and that they had never seen such exuberant vegetation. When they came to the ridge of mountains where the Colorado has its source, they proceeded a few miles on the eastern declivity of the ridge, and, to their astonishment, found several streams pursuing a course nearly opposite to these, on the western side of the ridge. I presume, from the descriptions of the friars, that the streams which thus excited their surprise, were the head waters of the Arkansas, La Platte, and some others of our great rivers, which have their sources in those regions.
>
> The friars spent several days on the eastern side of the ridge—they passed over six distinct rivers, all of which, they say, were of considerable depth and width—they met several roving bands of Indians, who treated them with kindness, and conducted them, by a short route, on their return, over the ridge to the River Colorado. The distance between the sources of the respective rivers on each side of the ridge, they represent as very trifling, not exceeding 22 or 25 leagues. They represent the ridge as full of deep ravines, and have no doubt that it would be easy to open a water communication by canals, between the rivers before mentioned. They gave a glowing description of the beauty of the country, comparing it to the hills and vales of Andalusia and Grenada! They dwell particularly on the mildness of the climate, and recommended the immediate establishment there of two missionaries.

The original intention of the two friars, was to return to Monterey, by descending the Colorado, but learning from the Indians that, at a short distance to the west, there were two other rivers as large as the Colorado, they determined on exploring the country, and accordingly, after traveling two days, they came to a spacious lake, which they described to be about forty leagues in circumference; from this lake issued two fine rivers. They descended what they considered the largest stream, whose general course was about W. N. W.. After descending about fifty leagues, they represented the river to be deep, and in many places, a mile in width. They continued their route until the river discharged itself on the coast of California, at about the latitude 43 30. They state the bar at the mouth of the river to have on [it] at least twenty feet water. They procured a large canoe from the Indians, and went leisurely along the coast until they reached Monterey. It is possible, some portion of the remarks of these friars may not be correct, but of the fidelity of their general statements, I have no doubt, particularly as to the important fact of their having descended a river which disembogues on the California coast, at the latitude before mentioned.[32]

On his way from San Blas to Mexico City in 1812, one of the friars had been intercepted by a party of revolutionaries, whence his account came into Robinson's possession. No one, Wagner included, has ever cited a clue to the identity of one of the friars offered by Robinson's *Memoirs of the Mexican Revolution,* which states: "We have perused some interesting manuscripts respecting the Californias, and the provinces of Sinaloa and Sonora: one in particular, written by *Padre Garcia,* who travelled from the mouth of the Colorado to its source, a distance of more than six hundred miles." [33]

The account's details are so far from corresponding to actual Colorado River geography as to suggest that the entire story was invented for the purpose of bringing American diplomatic pressure to bear upon Russia to prevent further Muscovite encroachments in northern California. As Robinson's letter declares, "There is no circumstance which has excited more indignation among the Mexican people, than that of the Russians having made an establishment at Badoga [Bodega] Point, and if the Mexican revolutionists had succeeded in their struggle for independence, one

32. Robinson to Senator John H. Eaton, January 15, 1821, *Daily National Intelligencer,* January 25, 1821; reprinted in *Niles' Weekly Register,* March 10, 21, and 25, 1821; reprinted from the latter in *WHQ* 10 (1919): 145–46. Extracts from Robinson's *Memoirs* were then appearing serially in the *Daily National Intelligencer* (journalistic voice of the government), which printed this letter to Eaton, whence it was reprinted in the influential *Niles' Weekly Register.*

33. W. D. Robinson, *Memoirs of the Mexican Revolution: Including a Narrative of the Expedition of General Xavier Mina* (Philadelphia, 1820), p. 366. The italics are Robinson's.

of the first acts of the new government would have been the expulsion of the Russians from that post." [34] Robinson's letter to Eaton was to urge that the United States forestall further Russian settlements by establishing a base somewhere between 42° and 49° north latitude. Since such a settlement would facilitate a productive trade with Japan, the Philippine Islands, and all of Asia, he predicted it "would speedily become a great commercial emporium."

Within two years Robinson was dead, his career cut short in his early thirties, possibly as a consequence of his long confinement in Spanish jails.[35] This may help explain why Padre García's tale was not more widely publicized. Interestingly, Robinson's letter coincided with an effort by Dr. John Floyd, chairman of a committee in the House of Representatives that, as a consequence of a resolution by Floyd, was inquiring into the expediency of occupying the Columbia River basin. With Thomas Hart Benton's backing, Floyd was trying to document a charge that Secretary of State John Quincy Adams had been neglecting western interests. Eaton was also among Adams's political opponents. To Robinson's letter, as published in the *National Intelligencer,* was added a communication from Commodore David Porter to President Madison urging simultaneous naval and overland expeditions to explore the Pacific coast. Porter's letter, with three hundred signatures, was submitted to President Monroe in 1821.[36] These efforts to promote American occupation of the Pacific coast caught the attention of the Russian government and are part of the background for the famous ukase issued later that year, warning other nations away from the North Pacific. Pressure from the political opposition and the Russian threat obliged Adams to come to grips with the "Oregon Question." One consequence was the administration's firm stance against further European colonization in the New World, as expressed in Monroe's annual message to Congress in 1823. This was a key portion of the Monroe Doctrine.[37]

Padre García's tale may well be spurious, but its geographical errors might have been created when Robinson reconstructed it from memory after his sojourn in Spanish dungeons. The story cannot be brushed aside lightly, although the hypothesis that the route which the friars supposedly followed included Klamath Lake and the river of the same name runs aground on geographical reality. Several hundred miles of basins and ranges separate upper tributaries of the Colorado from the Klamath, which enters the Pacific at about 41° 30', two degrees south of where Robinson says the friars emerged. A course due west from the upper Colorado intersects,

34. Robinson to Eaton, January 15, 1821, in *WHQ* 10 (1919) : 148.

35. His probable birthplace was Georgetown (then Maryland), about 1775, and he died before 1823. *National Cyclopedia of American Biography,* 18 : 185.

36. Bemis, *Adams,* pp. 485–89, 494–96. Porter's letter is dated October 31, 1815.

37. Ibid., pp. 494–96.

within a short distance, the basin of the Snake and Columbia, which indeed forms a mile-wide river before reaching the ocean, at about 46° 30′. Until the García account is independently corroborated, it remains in the same limbo as earlier narratives of questionable visits to the Pacific Northwest.

Historians of Colorado River exploration do not mention a Padre García, but as a recent work on trans-Mississippi discoveries points out, one of the great and virtually unknown stories of exploration in the American West is that of Spanish penetration northwestward from the outermost fringe of New Mexico.[38] In 1811 an expedition set out from Santa Fe to investigate reports of an unknown Spanish settlement which Ute Indians said lay north of their territory and was supposedly surrounded by wild tribes. Leader of the effort was Don José Rafael Serracino, postmaster of New Mexico. A three-month trek brought him to a large river, probably the Grand but possibly the Snake, where many articles of Spanish manufacture were found. Judging it impossible to cross, Serracino turned back, learning only that the artifacts had come from somewhere north and west of the great river.[39]

Unlikely as it seems that Padre García and his companion could follow the Colorado River from delta to source, James Pattie claimed to have achieved such a feat in 1826.[40] Whether Spanish friars traversed present-day Oregon in 1810 begs further investigation in appropriate archives, but even if the expedition did take place it had no influence upon Spanish attitudes toward the Pacific Northwest in that period of revolutionary turmoil. Nor did the better-documented Serracino probe have any impact upon subsequent history of that area.

38. William H. Goetzmann, *Exploration and Empire: The Explorer and the Scientist in the Winning of the American West* (New York, 1966), p. 68. There is no mention of such an expedition, nor a clue to the identity of Padre García, in Herbert Priestly, *Franciscan Explorations in California* (Glendale, Calif., 1946). José García, a Cantabrian ordained in Mexico City (1797), served the Alta California missions from 1800 to 1808, when for reasons of health and "a very poor disposition" he was permitted to return to Mexico. He sailed from San Diego in November 1808, and in 1810 he requested permission to join the Franciscan province of the Holy Gospel (Mexico City). On March 27, 1811, he asked for readmission to San Fernando College. Maynard Geiger, *Franciscan Missionaries in Hispanic California, 1769–1848: A Biographical Dictionary* (San Marino, Calif., 1969), pp. 97–98.

39. Pedro Bautista Pino, "Exposición sucinta y sencilla de la Provincia de Nuevo Mexico," in H. B. Carroll and J. Villasana Haggard, eds., *Three New Mexico Chronicles* (Albuquerque, 1942), p. 134, cited by Goetzmann, *Exploration*, p. 69, who suggests that Robinson's account may be a confused version of Serracino's expedition. A local legend in Idaho of a seventeenth-century Spanish silver mine on the St. Maries River is not corroborated by known Spanish documents. See Conrad McCall, "The Lost Mine of the Coeur d'Alenes," *Spokane Spokesman-Review*, March 6, 1910, sec. 4, pp. 1, 4; discussed by Hult, *Lost Mines*, pp. 171–77, 246.

40. James Ohio Pattie, *The Personal Narrative of James Ohio Pattie of Kentucky* (Cincinnati, 1831). Despite an admixture of fiction in his account, that Pattie followed the Colorado to its headwaters is generally accepted. Joseph J. Hill, "New Light on Pattie and the Southwestern Fur Trade," *SHQ* 26 (1922–23) : 243–54.

From the foregoing, we should not assume that Spanish authorities were indifferent to what was occurring in the Pacific Northwest once the Napoleonic shadow abated. Facundo Melgares, governor of New Mexico from 1818 to 1822, fortified a string of posts along the northeastern edge of his jurisdiction. In 1818 a warning arrived from the Spanish consul in New Orleans that a battalion of 300 Americans commanded by Lieutenant Colonel Talbot Chambers had left St. Louis, headed up the Missouri for the Roche Jaune, or Piedra Amarilla (Yellowstone). Madrid and Washington had not yet agreed upon a boundary, and that area was still considered by Spanish officials to be within the domain of His Catholic Majesty. Melgares hastened to equip and send out an expedition to reconnoiter the Yellowstone, make contact with representatives of the Hudson's Bay Company, and ascertain what could be done to repel the Americans. To lead the effort, Melgares turned "to the only individual in the province who had made that trip before." [41] José Jarvet, Vial's companion of former years, was placed in command of a fifteen-man column, purposely kept small so as to be able to sustain itself by hunting. Jarvet reached the area of the Yellowstone without encountering anything of import. The Chambers battalion corresponds to the so-called Yellowstone Expedition, Secretary of War Calhoun's project for bringing the upper Missouri under American influence. One thousand men, six steamboats, and a corps of explorers led by Major Stephen H. Long started up the Missouri in the spring of 1819, but scurvy, fever, and a congressional cutback in funds kept the effort from getting beyond Council Bluffs. Subsequent incidents

41. Navarro García, *Las Provincias Internas,* p. 100, cites Melgares to Alejo García Conde, commandant general of the interior provinces, Santa Fe, April 1, 1819, and Viceroy Conde del Venadito to the minister of state, Mexico City, June 30, 1819, SpAGI (Estado 33). See also Melgares to García Conde, Santa Fe, July 9, 1819, SpAGI (Estado 33), cited in *Vial,* pp. 455–56; and Venadito to the first secretary of state, Mexico City, September 30, 1819, SpAGI (Estado 33), trans. in Alfred Barnaby Thomas, "The Yellowstone River, James Long and Spanish Reaction to American Intrusion Into Spanish Dominions, 1818–1819," *NMHR,* 4 (1929) : 170–77.

Navarro García does not suggest when Jarvet might have visited the upper tributaries of the Missouri, prior to 1819. Was Melgares referring solely to the expeditions with Vial (1804–05)? Perhaps not. Kenneth L. Holmes, "Joseph Gervais," in LeRoy Hafen, *Mountain Men and the Fur Trade,* 9 vols. to date (Glendale, Calif., 1965–69), 7 : 131–45, traces the life of a French Canadian known as Joseph "Gervais," "Jervé," and "Jarvay," a buffalo hunter on the Arkansas prior to joining Wilson Price Hunt's overland party to Astoria in 1811. Gervais returned eastward in 1814 and does not reappear in Oregon until 1821.

Our Jarvet drops from sight in New Mexican records between 1810 and 1819. The governor of New Mexico sent for him in 1810—the intent unknown (*Vial,* p. 455). It bears asking whether he was entrusted with a mission to scout American activities in the Pacific Northwest. Hunt was eager to hire men with experience on the frontier. Events derived from the War of 1812 brought "Gervais" eastward, possessed of valuable geographic knowledge. If he went back to his old haunts on the Arkansas, this may account for Melgares' remark, and putting Jarvet to use once again. Subsequent revolutionary turmoil in Spanish colonies would make life on the Willamette seem much more inviting. An accomplice in an attempt to thwart Lewis and Clark would have good reason to keep much of his biography a secret from his Oregon neighbors, and posterity.

along the Spanish-American frontier closer to Santa Fe diverted Melgares's attention from the Yellowstone and upper Missouri.[42]

### THE TRANSCONTINENTAL TREATY OF 1819

Although Fernando VII and his ministers were confronted by grave matters elsewhere, Madrid was not yet resigned to loss of the northwest coast and the hinterland between Nootka and the Missouri. This fact was amply demonstrated by negotiations in 1817–19 leading to the Florida Treaty, more aptly named Transcontinental Treaty, of 1819. The American declaration of intent to reoccupy Astoria triggered anxiety among Spanish officials for Madrid's claims over that area. Fernando's government could ill afford a dispute with the United States over the western perimeter of Louisiana, considering the need to counteract rebellion in Spanish America. What Madrid desired was a boundary settlement that would put a permanent check upon American expansion toward Mexico's mineral resources, which were as important as ever to the motherland.

To secure American recognition of a fixed boundary, Fernando VII was willing to make concessions. The ministry perceived that American expansionists looked upon East Florida as a territory destined to come under American dominion eventually. In 1810, while revolts were occurring in many colonies against José I, colonists in West Florida who were predominantly American in origin had seized Baton Rouge, the provincial capital, proclaimed an independent republic, and requested annexation to the United States. After the Bourbon restoration, it became obvious to Madrid that Spain could not defend East Florida's exposed northern perimeter and that the peninsula was a liability. During Madison's administration, while Monroe was secretary of state, the Spanish minister in the United States, Luís de Onís, approached Monroe with an offer to recognize American ownership of West Florida if the United States would agree to a mutual boundary along the Mississippi River. As this would have annulled the Louisiana Purchase, Monroe put him off. Relations also were aggravated by claims of American citizens against Spain arising out of losses suffered by American (neutral) shipping in Spanish waters during the Napoleonic wars.[43]

Madrid's pressing need to transfer her troops to more crucial colonies made a boundary settlement much to be desired, even if it had to be purchased by territorial concessions. Narciso de Heredia, a former secretary of the legation in Washington, who was regarded as the ministerial expert on American affairs, drew up a memorandum outlining various approaches to the problem. Common to all of them was the suggestion that west of the

---

42. Goetzmann, *Exploration*, pp. 58–64; Navarro García, *Las Provincias Internas*, pp. 101–02.
43. Bemis, *Diplomatic History*, p. 184.

Missouri's headwaters the boundary be left undetermined, for want of precise geographical data. Heredia predicted that the Americans would not be dissuaded from striving for a trade route overland to the Columbia and the Pacific. He recommended seeking British support by reminding London of the competition that the Americans would give the British in the North Pacific. Secretary of State José García de León y Pizarro heeded Heredia's advice and sought aid from London, but to little avail.[44]

These antecedents are important to understanding the diplomatic climate when, late in 1817, in the first year of Monroe's presidency, Luís de Onís renewed negotiations for a boundary that would make Spanish territory secure against American expansion. His opponent, the most sophisticated American diplomat since Franklin, was Secretary of State John Quincy Adams, an ardent expansionist. As minister to Russia in 1811 Adams had revealed his dreams for the future in a letter to his mother in which he criticized New England Federalists for separatist tendencies. If that party were not put down, he warned, "instead of a nation, coextensive with the North American continent, destined by God and nature to be the most populous and most powerful people ever combined under one social compact, we shall have an endless multitude of little insignificant clans and tribes at eternal war with one another for a rock or a fish pond, the sport and fable of European masters and oppressors." [45] Two months later he elaborated on the subject to his father. "The whole continent of North America appears to be destined by Divine Providence to be peopled by one *nation,* speaking one language, professing one general system of religious and political principles, and accustomed to one general tenor of social usages and customs," he opined. "For the common happiness of them all, for their peace and prosperity, I believe it indispensable that they should be associated in one federal Union." [46]

A diplomat steeled by such convictions would not overlook an opportunity to profit from Spain's plight. It was in the American interest not only to secure East Florida in payment for a boundary settlement but to place the border as far toward the southwest as possible. Conversely, it behooved Spain to parlay the sacrifice of Florida into an easily ascertainable boundary, as far to the northeast as feasible. With the same bait, Madrid

44. Narciso de Heredia, "Exposición hecha al Rey Nuestro Señor y a su Consejo de Estado sobre nuestras relaciones políticas y diferencias actuales con el gobierno de los Estados Unidos de América," Madrid, June 4, 1817, in José García de Léon y Pizarro, *Memorias,* 2d ed., 2 vols. (Madrid, 1953), 1 : 188–223; Philip Coolidge Brooks, "The Pacific Coast's First International Boundary Delineation, 1816–1819," *PHR* 3 (1934) : 66–67.

45. J. Q. Adams to Abigail Adams, St. Petersburg, June 30, 1811, in J. Q. Adams, *Writings,* ed. Worthington C. Ford, 7 vols. (New York, 1913–17), 4 : 128, cited by Bemis, *Adams,* p. 182.

46. J. Q. Adams to John Adams, St. Petersburg, August 31, 1811, in J. Q. Adams, *Writings,* 4 : 209. Cited by Bemis, *Adams,* p. 182.

hoped to gain a promise from the United States to maintain a policy of nonrecognition toward governments proclaimed by revolutionists in some parts of Spanish America.

The maximum American claim sought to place the western boundary of Louisiana at the Rio Grande, thus embracing all of Texas. The maximum Spanish pretension rejected the legality of the Louisiana Purchase and placed the eastern boundary of Spanish territory at the Mississippi. Madrid considered cession of the Floridas a fair payment for American acceptance of a boundary along the Mississippi.[47] Eager as he was to obtain East Florida, Adams was not prepared to renounce fully one-half of the territorial extent of the United States. Madrid would consent to retreat from the Mississippi only in return for the nonrecognition pledge, but this offer, once made, yielded terrain that Onís could not recover in subsequent haggling, although Adams never did agree to the pledge that Fernando sought.

As a compromise, Adams suggested a boundary along Texas's Colorado River to its source, and from there to the "northern limits of Louisiana." While this would have given the United States over half of Texas, it would have sealed Americans off from the Rocky Mountains. As Bemis has pointed out, here was a unique chance to counter American expansionists, "by taking advantage of Adams' rather careless offer, to halt their westward march, to lock them up, if not east of the Alleghenies, then at least east of the Rocky Mountains.[48] Even if Onís recognized the opportunity, however, he was not authorized to accept a boundary that far west.

Among Adams's papers is a memorandum of February 1818, in Monroe's hand, containing the first indication of a plan to push for a boundary running from the headwaters of the Arkansas due west to the Pacific. Bemis, Adams's biographer, accepts the secretary of state's claim that the inspiration for this maneuver was his own and not Monroe's: "It is not difficult to believe that the President was recording and sanctioning what the two men had agreed to in previous discussions, in which the Secretary of State had come out for a boundary line all the way through to the other ocean." [49] But Onís was far from ready to relinquish Spanish claims to the northwest coast. Indeed, the following month we find him suggesting to Madrid that, "there being at a very short distance from the mouth of the River Columbia on the Pacific Ocean an island situated in the middle of said river which offers an excellent position for a military establishment, it is of the highest importance that it be occupied as soon as possible, with the purpose

47. Philip Coolidge Brooks, *Diplomacy and the Borderlands: The Adams-Onís Treaty of 1819* (Berkeley, 1939), p. 85; Bemis, *Adams*, p. 305.

48. Bemis, *Adams*, p. 309.

49. Ibid., pp. 310–11.

of protecting the possessions and the commerce of the Monarchy in that region, as the United States will not delay in carrying out its project of opening a route by that river to the South Sea." [50] The idea struck a chord of response in Madrid. The viceroy of Mexico was ordered to fortify the island in question, "without giving the slightest motive of complaint to the United States; it being your responsibility to justify this project as you find it most convenient." [51] The viceroy set the order aside, however, saying that it would necessitate a naval force on the Pacific coast, whereas he could only master a single brigantine, and that in a sad state of disrepair. The most surprising aspect of this chimerical scheme is that it secured approval in Madrid and was not shot down until reaching Mexico City.

Simultaneously with the Adams-Onís negotiations, in 1818 Richard Rush and Albert Gallatin represented Monroe and Adams in talks held in London to determine a boundary with Canada westward from the Lake of the Woods. The Castlereagh ministry agreed to a line due west along the 49th parallel as far as the crest of the "Stony Mountains." The British would not, however, consent to any delineation beyond the Rockies, where they were reluctant to concede that the United States had any claims at all. Unable to arrive at a satisfactory boundary there, the negotiators agreed to disagree. For ten years, they decided, the subjects of both parties to the treaty would have "free and open" access to territory beyond the mountains, without prejudice to the claims of either nation. Bemis believes that it was in composing instructions for Rush and Gallatin that Adams and Monroe first realized the significance of the negotiations with Spain over claims that the United States wished to assert beyond the Rockies.[52]

Although Madrid endeavored to persuade Britain to bring her influence to bear on the boundary negotiations in Spain's behalf, the Castlereagh ministry refused to be drawn into the matter, even when a force under General Andrew Jackson invaded East Florida in pursuit of Creek and Seminole raiders, seized the provincial capital of Pensacola, and executed Alexander Arbuthnot and Robert Ambrister, two Britons believed to have been inciting the Indians. By the terms of Pinckney's Treaty, Madrid had promised to restrain Indian nations within her territories from depredations onto American soil, but Spain's military weakness in East Florida made this pledge impossible to keep. Although in the cabinet's secret discussions Adams defended Jackson, the general was tried for exceeding his instructions. Repudiation of his acts was sufficient to dissuade London from making

50. Onís to García de León y Pizarro, March 3, 1818, SpAHN (Estado 5562), trans. in Brooks, "Pacific Coast's First Boundary," pp. 69–70.

51. Francisco de Eguía (minister of war) to the Conde de Venadito, quoted in Eguía to García de León y Pizarro, July 6, 1818, SpAHN (Estado 5562), trans. in ibid., p. 70; Conde de Venadito to minister of war, Mexico City, December 31, 1818, SpAHN (Estado 5562).

52. Bemis, *Adams*, p. 309.

an issue of the Arbuthnot-Ambrister incident, but British acquiescence was an affront to Spain and underscored the difficulty of holding onto Florida much longer. Adams found his position vis-à-vis Onís considerably improved by the whole matter. Quite naturally Onís was furious about Jackson's acts, and demanded indemnities for Spain, threatening to break off negotiations for American acquisition of East Florida. It was obvious, however, that since the area was slipping from Madrid's grasp, it should be bartered for a boundary settlement.

At a meeting not long after the uproar over Jackson's sally into Florida, Adams told Onís that if the Floridas were ceded, the United States would pay the claims of American citizens against Spain, and a western boundary could remain in suspension. At this point Onís made a tactical error; he admitted that his instructions precluded any agreement that did not establish a definitive boundary: "That is the sole object of the sacrifices which His Majesty is disposed to make of the Floridas, and I will not advise His Majesty to make any settlement unless it fixes safe and permanent limits west of the Mississippi." Seizing the advantage, Adams replied, "If that's the way it is, we can take the Rio Bravo [Rio Grande] del Norte for a frontier." With matching cynicism Onís retorted, "Better still the Mississippi." [53]

Adams's bold maneuvering eventually edged Onís toward important concessions beyond the Mississippi. As a basis for deliberations, they employed John Melish's *Map of the United States and Contiguous British and Spanish Possessions,* in the 1818 edition. Adams suggested drawing the boundary along Texas's Colorado River to its source, northward to the Missouri's source, and then due west to the Pacific. "So you are trying to dispossess us also of the whole Pacific Coast which belongs to us, and which Juan de Fuca took possession of in the King's name up to 56°!" Onís exclaimed with more feeling than accuracy.[54] Adams countered references to Spanish discoveries by citing English and Russian activities and claims along the same coastline. Of greater significance, he stated, was the fact that the United States had establishments on the Columbia which needed routes of communication to the Missouri.

The American offer of July 16 varied only slightly from the ultimate settlement in the treaty signed seven months later, but it took that long to press the Spanish diplomat for such sweeping concessions. From his talks with Adams, Onís became convinced that the United States entertained expansionist intentions far beyond the claims being asserted by the secretary of state. "Here are their views, clear enough, and the truth is they are less exaggerated than their real ones," he advised Madrid. "If His Majesty can't get the support of any Power, and hasn't sufficient forces to make war on

53. Adams papers, as cited in ibid., pp. 317–18.
54. Ibid., pp. 318–19.

this country, then I think it would be best not to delay making the best settlement possible, seeing that things certainly won't be better for a long time." [55]

Onís made a counteroffer on October 24 of a boundary along the 93rd meridian from the Gulf of Mexico to the Missouri River (bisecting the present states of Louisiana and Arkansas), up the Missouri to its source, and from there onward to be fixed by a joint commission, with navigation of the Missouri and Mississippi open to subjects of both nations. This would have cut the United States off from the Pacific Northwest by all but a narrow strip between the Missouri and the 49th parallel. Monroe instructed Adams to break off negotiations unless Onís agreed to more reasonable terms. On October 31 the Spaniard was tendered a "final offer," in which the Louisiana border was shifted to the Sabine but the boundary demands along the Pacific were lowered from 41° 30′ north latitude to the 41st parallel. "As the session of Congress is at hand," Adams warned, "I am directed to request your immediate and frank reply to this communication." [56]

Onís reacted by retreating to a proposal for a boundary along the Sabine, to 32° north, and from that point due north to the Missouri, up the middle of that river to its source, with a joint commission determining the border to the north and west, "in a manner conformable to the titles and documents and possession respectively exhibited." [57] Conceivably this would have enabled Spain to prove her title to the northwest coast as far as Nootka, and that would have spelled trouble for American claims in the Pacific Northwest. Monroe's response was an angry message to Congress in which he reviewed the entire negotiations. He instructed Adams to retract all previous offers, and the secretary of state returned to the initial American stance: that the western boundary of Louisiana was the Rio Grande.

On November 28, 1818, in reply to propaganda pamphlets that Onís had been publishing in Philadelphia,[58] Adams sent a message to the American minister in Madrid, defending Jackson's activities in Florida and asserting that if Spain could not keep order there the area should be ceded to the United States.[59] So effective was Adams's defense of the American position

55. Onís to García de León y Pizarro, Bristol, Pa., July 18, 1818, SpAHN (Estado 5643), trans. in ibid., p. 319.

56. Adams to Onís, October 31, 1818. *ASP, Foreign Relations,* 4 : 531; J. Q. Adams, *Memoirs,* ed. Charles Francis Adams, 12 vols. (Philadelphia, 1874–77), 4 : 144 cited in ibid., p. 323.

57. Onís to Adams, November 16, 1818. *ASP, Foreign Relations,* 4 : 531–32, cited in ibid., p. 324.

58. [Luís de Onís y González], [Observations on West Florida,] and *Observations on the Conduct of our Executive Towards Spain* (both n.p., n.d.), signed: Verus; also *Observations on the Existing Differences Between the Government of Spain and the United States, by Verus. No. III* (Philadelphia, 1817).

59. Adams to Erving, November 28, 1818, *ASP, Foreign Relations,* 4 : 539–612, cited by Bemis, *Adams,* pp. 326–29.

that, upon publication, the message profoundly influenced opinion not only in America but also in London and, above all, in Madrid. The impression it made in the Spanish capital virtually laid the Florida question to rest.

José García de León y Pizarro resigned from the ministry in October 1818, leaving on his desk a draft that his successor, the Marqués de Casa Irujo, former ambassador to the United States, used as a basis for further instructions to Onís. Priority should go to securing an eastern boundary for Texas at the Sabine, gaining a pledge not to recognize rebel governments, and avoiding a break with the United States and an invasion of Mexico. Onís was to strive for the best northern boundary that circumstances would permit. If feasible, it should follow the Missouri to its source, and from these run to the Pacific "as far north as possible." [60] Accordingly, Onís proposed a boundary westward from the Missouri's source, by way of the Snake River, to the Columbia's mouth. Adams rejected the offer, as it would have deprived the United States of territory west of the Missouri. He made a counteroffer that differed not one whit from his ultimatum of October 31.

The Melish map showed a "San Clementini" river, labeled "Multnomah" on its lower course, flowing northwest across Oregon and entering the Columbia where the Willamette does today. Onís fell back to a line that followed the Arkansas to its source, extended along a parallel due west to the source of the "San Clemente" (*sic*) or Multnomah, and descended that river to the Columbia and the ocean—a tremendous concession. For the first time he acquiesced to the surrender of all the Mississippi watershed; that is, the Louisiana Purchase. Monroe and his cabinet, except for Adams, were inclined to accept this proposal, if the boundary ran from the Multnomah along the 43rd parallel to the sea. The secretary of state held to his insistence on a more southerly parallel. His counteroffer was for a border up the Red River to a "great bend" between 101° and 102° west longtitude, thence due north to the Arkansas, up the Arkansas to its source, and to the Pacific along the 41st parallel, a concession allowing a larger zone of protection north of Santa Fe, Taos, and other Spanish towns on the upper Río Grande.

Onís was willing to accept Adams's proposal, if it were altered to read that from the Arkansas's source the boundary should follow the 42nd parallel to the Multnomah, descend it to 43° latitude, and thence to the sea. Again Monroe and all his cabinet but Adams were willing to close the deal. The secretary of state held out for the 41st parallel and countered with a demand for additional territory in Texas on the upper Red River. At this the Spaniard capitulated. The final treaty line, as signed on Washington's birthday, 1819, was a compromise between Adams's 41st parallel and Onís's 43rd. From the Gulf of Mexico it ran up the Sabine to 32° north, along that meridian to the Red River, up the Red to the hundredth meridian, north to

60. Instructions dated October 10, 1818; Brooks, *Diplomacy and the Borderlands*, p. 155.

the Arkansas, up that river to its source, due north to 42°, and west along that parallel to the Pacific. In jockeying for advantage, the two negotiators determined today's boundaries between Texas and Louisiana, Texas and Oklahoma, Utah and Idaho, Nevada and Idaho, Nevada and Oregon, and California and Oregon. The treaty also ceded East and West Florida to the United States. Of greatest importance to the history of the Pacific Northwest was article three, by which His Catholic Majesty ceded to the United States all "rights, claims, and pretensions to any territory east and north of the agreed boundary, and reciprocally, the United States renounced all titles to the west and south of it." The American government assumed responsibility for paying the claims of its citizens against Spain, up to a total of $5 million —the so-called purchase of Florida.

The secretary of state's coup in obtaining a boundary that extended to the Pacific greatly strengthened the nation's claim to Oregon by making the United States heir to prerogatives derived from Spanish discoveries on the northwest coast. As for Spain, the Treaty of 1819 conceded what for many years had been evident—that her territorial pretensions in the Pacific Northwest could no longer be implemented. Madrid, in an excess of optimism, had hoped to trade the Floridas for nullification of all or most of the Louisiana Purchase; but Adams, while gaining the former and holding on to the latter, also won the legacy of Spanish claims to Oregon. Bemis calls the treaty "the greatest diplomatic victory won by any single individual in the history of the United States." [61]

Although Adams's political opponents and the southern elements in Congress grumbled about his failure to gain Texas and charged him with having traded that rich province for the lesser-known wastes of Oregon, the Senate gave immediate approval to the treaty. When its exact terms became known in Madrid, the council of state found them highly dissatisfying, particularly the concessions on the northwest coast. Onís reported that a better bargain could not be struck and that the sacrifices were preferable to war.[62] An excuse to postpone ratification was found in a claim regarding certain land titles in Florida. The king delayed a full year and a half before consenting to the accord, attempting to exact a promise not to recognize the rebel governments—one of his original objectives. Adams put him off with the statement that, "as a necessary consequence of the neutrality between Spain and the South American provinces, the United States can contract no engagement not to form any relations with those provinces." [63] It was by now obvious that the United States could not be persuaded to make such a pledge,

---

61. Bemis, *Adams*, p. 340.

62. Minutes of the Council of State, May 1, 1819, SpAHN (Estado 5661), cited by Brooks, "Pacific Coast's First Boundary," p. 75.

63. J. Q. Adams to Francisco Dionisio Vivés (Onís's successor), Washington, May 3, 1820, in Adams, *Writings*, 7 : 8–14.

and Fernando's need for a fixed boundary forced him to sign the treaty anyway.

The skilled maneuvering of John Quincy Adams hastened liquidation of Spain's dormant claims in the Pacific Northwest. Had the United States accepted one of Onís's earlier offers—as Monroe and the rest of his cabinet were willing to do—American expansion to the Pacific would undoubtedly have been delayed or even thwarted, allowing some other power to gain entry there. The consequences could have been "Balkanization" of the trans-Mississippi region or conflict with Spain, Mexico, Britain, or Russia over Oregon.

THE CLAIMS INHERITED FROM SPAIN AND THE DIMENSIONS OF OREGON

In 1819 Madrid retreated from the contest for the Pacific Northwest once and for all. Prior to the Transcontinental Treaty, American pretensions in Oregon rested on Gray's alleged discovery of the Columbia, Lewis and Clark's feat, and Astoria—none of which pertained to the area north of the Columbia. From 1819 onward, the United States could assert a claim to the coastline as far as Spain's previous title had extended. Adams proceeded to do just that. His self-confident stance, expressed in the Monroe Doctrine of 1823, bore fruit a year later in a Russo-American treaty, by which the tsar proscribed his subjects from making additional settlements in America south of 54° 40′ north latitude. In turn, Americans could not colonize north of that parallel, the present southern boundary of Alaska.

That same year Adams commenced negotiations with the Canning ministry in London, using the reinforced American claims to Oregon as grounds for settlement of an Anglo-American boundary to the Pacific. Canning had always deplored Castlereagh's restoration of Astoria, and was unwilling to see Britain retreat from the Columbia. He claimed that the Nootka Convention gave Britain an equal right with Spain to all of the northwest coast. Adams contended that the Anglo-Spanish declaration of war in 1796 had voided the 1790 Convention; he was not aware of the exact terms of the second and third Nootka conventions, which were not published until 1843. If, as London maintained, the 1790 Convention was still in force, then the other two accords had equal vigor.[64] Either way, the United States inherited Spain's title to Nootka; the Third Nootka Convention restored only Meares's small tract of land, and both sides agreed never to make a permanent settlement there. Had Adams known this, it would have strengthened his hand in negotiating with Canning. Instead, the British and the Americans renewed the agreement of 1818 to postpone designating a boundary west of the Rockies. In 1827 an Anglo-American Convention extended these terms indefinitely but provided for cancellation by either na-

64. David Hunter Miller, ed., *Treaties and Other International Acts of the United States of America,* 8 vols. (Washington, D.C., 1931–48), 5 : 17, cited by Bemis, *Diplomatic History,* 274–75n.

tion upon one year's notice. The Oregon question was reopened during Tyler's administration—the Webster-Ashburton negotiations (1841–42)—but Washington still labored under the misconception that Madrid had renounced her claim to Vancouver Island because the Spanish settlement at Friendly Cove had been withdrawn as a consequence of the Third Nootka Convention.

The mission to the Pacific Northwest of U.S. Navy Lieutenant Charles Wilkes resulted in a report (1842) that the United States should seek every means of getting the boundary moved north of the 49th parallel in order to include the Strait of Juan de Fuca, Puget Sound, and as much of Vancouver Island as possible. In 1843 the Third Nootka Convention was published in Madrid as part of a general collection of Spanish treaties, but there is no indication that its relevance on this point was recognized by Webster's successors as secretary of state. Calhoun assumed the office in 1844, the last year of Tyler's administration, and his policy of "masterly inactivity" studiously avoided a boundary settlement until time and American immigration into Oregon could favor the U.S. position. The growing flood of migrants made "Fifty-four forty or fight!", implying possession of all the coast south of Russian Alaska, a factor in Polk's election in 1844. Despite campaign oratory, the impending crisis over Texas's annexation led Polk's secretary of state, James Buchanan, to retreat from the maximum claim. Polk preferred to resolve the Oregon question with Britain peaceably in order to clear the decks for war with Mexico. Washington and London agreed to extend the boundary along the 49th parallel from the Rockies to tidewater, and to the Pacific by way of the Strait of Juan de Fuca. The Oregon Treaty was signed in Washington on June 15, 1846, a scant month after the outbreak of the Mexican War.

Although Americans profited from Madrid's historical claims to the northwest coast, it is evident that the Spanish voyages, discoveries, and treaties justifying such claims were scarcely known in the United States, even among our best-educated statesmen. Perhaps because of the time lapse between Spanish withdrawal and American colonization, the saga of Iberian activities in the Pacific Northwest never won a place in the historical awareness of the average American—even among inhabitants of the area. Today little remains of that early chapter in the region's history save for a host of Spanish place names from Oregon to Alaska, and tons of futile documentation, carefully preserved in Mexican and Spanish archives.[65]

65. As the nineteenth century advanced, Britain ruled the seas, English charts prevailed, and place names on Spanish charts were forgotten. Such Iberian toponymy as remains was preserved because Vancouver carried a number of Spanish charts and sometimes retained nomenclature previously assigned by them. But for his generosity in this regard, there would be even less today to remind us of Spain's erstwhile presence. Wagner, *Cartography*, vol. 2, lists alphabetically the Spanish place names still in use on the northwest coast, with the chronology and derivation of each.

# *13  Atrophy of Empire: The Factors*

Under Carlos III, Spain ranked among the leading powers of the globe. In 1789, when Martínez planted the Spanish flag at Nootka Sound, Carlos IV could claim the largest empire of his time—from Naples, Sicily, and enclaves in Africa westward to the Philippines, and from Tierra del Fuego to Prince William's Sound in Alaska—a veritable flood tide of empire. Within thirty years, however, Spain found herself shorn of much of her colonial realm, and struggling frantically to retain the remainder. If Madrid's efforts on the northwest coast were the apex of her colonial expansion, what factors proved her undoing in the abrupt ebb that followed? The hindsight of two centuries provides a clearer perspective than was available to the protagonists—of the dream, the fact, the nightmare, and the residue.

## THE DREAM

The spurt of activity that carried Spanish explorers to Alaskan waters in 1774 and 1775, after more than a century and a half of ignoring the northwest coast, stemmed from José de Gálvez's dream for western North America. It had little to do with religious zeal or pecuniary ambitions. Spanish subjects went there in the course of military service to protect Madrid's claim to that area. Her concern was with the threat from that direction by Russia, Britain, and later the United States. Every renewal of Spanish activity from 1769 onward was a reaction to foreign intrusion, real or imagined.[1] When no immediate threat was disclosed, Madrid attempted little or nothing in the area beyond San Francisco.

The instructions for the various expeditions and their resulting charts show that Spanish attention focused primarily on finding potential ports for defending the Pacific Northwest, rather than on discovering arable lands or mineral resources. The Spanish never really appreciated the region for itself. The ministry's interest in the northwest coast never progressed beyond the concept of excluding rivals from those shores and retaining the hinterland in its pristine, unexplored state as a buffer against penetration of Mexico. Such a passive pattern, geared to countering foreign aggression,

---

1. The expeditions of 1774 and 1775 had the objective of scouting the Russian threat. That of 1779 was to counteract Cook. In 1788 Martínez was investigating reports of Russian outposts in Alaska. In 1789 he hoped to forestall Russian colonization of Nootka. From 1790 until 1795, every expedition northward—including that of Malaspina—was intended to supply the Nootka garrison or explore an area posing a threat of an undisclosed waterway penetrating the continent and menacing New Spain's northern flank.

proved ineffective. Spain failed to retain the northwest coast because she waited until emergencies occurred before laying the groundwork for effective political dominion. Therefore, her tardy remedial measures were inadequate to the challenge.

Gálvez's dream was doomed by geophysical realities: the inadequacies of San Blas as a base of operations; the lack of an administrative capital for the Interior Provinces farther toward the northwest than Chihuahua, from whence effective government was impractical; the impediments to overland communications with Nootka, Puget Sound, and the Columbia. But these difficulties are easier to perceive in retrospect. His was the nation that had subdued much of the New World in half a century. What obstacles could western North America offer to exceed those of the Andes or the Amazon? Gálvez's judgments were formulated without any knowledge of the terrain and tribes between upper Louisiana and the Pacific. The length of the coastline and the intricate waterways and fjords made it difficult for any nation to maintain dominion over the area if faced with a determined challenger. Attenuated lines of supply exposed any northwest coast settlements to easy capture or blockade.

In hindsight it seems foolish for Madrid to have wasted her resources on trying to exert dominion over the northwest coast. But when Spanish expeditions were first sent there, it was commonly believed that they would find a Sea of the West, and channels and rivers that might offer access to New Spain's vulnerable northern perimeter. Thus, it behooved Madrid to acquire the necessary geographical knowledge about that area.

### THE FACT

If Spain had chosen to stand firm on the northwest coast in 1790, her strategic advantages in Mexico and California would have made the British position in North America untenable. It was not the vigor of foreign activities that loosened Carlos IV's grip upon Nootka; indeed, Martínez nipped in the bud the sole attempt in the eighteenth century to plant a settlement south of Russia's Alaskan ouposts.

An examination of Madrid's shifting stance from 1790 onward, through successively weaker positions regarding the northwest coast, shows that each move in the direction of less resistance came not from Spanish officers in Nootka or San Blas but from the highest levels of government in Mexico City and Madrid. Martínez, Bodega, and other principals in Spanish activities on that coastline were consistently firm in defending Spain's interests there; they made Madrid's claims to the northwest coast a fact to be reckoned with. Until 1795, British and American fur traders considered it the better part of wisdom to pay deference to the red and yellow banner flying over Santa Cruz de Nootka. When a softening occurred in Spain's stance in the area, it did not proceed from a weakness there, relative to other powers, but from a vulnerability in Europe. Spain yielded on the northwest coast because of decisions made in Madrid and Mexico City to protect the motherland.

Later, when Godoy turned to protecting Madrid's claims in the Pacific Northwest by overland efforts from St. Louis and Santa Fe, Melgares demonstrated Spanish ability to take onto the Great Plains an army sufficient to awe the Indians or any Americans in the area at that time; but he chose to preserve Indian alliances and avoid a clash rather than proceed with the problematical search for "Captain Merry." Bourbon dethronement, a year later, was of more consequence in hampering Spanish measures to check the westward push of Americans than the problems inherent in doing so. Geographic obstacles hindered Spanish officials from carrying out their objectives, but political decisions at the highest level were of more consequence in determining the course and effectiveness of Spanish participation in the contest for the Far West.

The northwest coast under Spanish dominion was a parasitical colony, a white elephant that, despite its latent wealth, required a gigantic annual subsidy at New Spain's expense. Spanish officials were appalled at the tremendous drain on viceregal coffers. The British, Russian, and American governments suffered no such expenditures in establishing their respective claims. Madrid never developed a self-supporting means of promoting her political objectives at Nootka, on the upper Missouri, or in the Columbia basin. Furs, fish, timber, and gold—resources that might have underwritten the cost—were never successfully exploited. With her existing network of colonies and ports in the Philippines and on mid-Pacific islands, at San Diego, San Francisco, Núñez Gaona, and Nootka, united by a functioning trade route to China, Spain was better equipped than her competitors to send ships to the northwest coast and bid for skins at prices that would drive other nationalities from the trade. But Vasadre's defeat at the hands of the Philippine Company dissuaded other entrepreneurs. In the absence of viceregal encouragement, the commerce never got underway. Mexico's mineral wealth received preferential attention.

The anticipation of a share in a valuable cargo of furs gave a compulsive vitality to the efforts of fur traders on the northwest coast, whereas Spanish seamen in the area stood to gain nothing but a dubious recognition of merit, a subsistence salary, and perhaps a promotion as reward for the deprivations and anxiety endured there. The Iberians faced exceedingly energetic and persistent rivals, self-sufficient in the extreme, who did not depend upon governmental subsidies, a protective fleet of warships, or a costly network of garrisons. Except for Martínez's single experiment with Kendrick, Spanish officials never tried the device, used by Baranov, of contracting with foreign fur traders to exploit furry resources, under Spanish supervision and taxation, with the revenue earmarked to subsidize the cost of maintaining Iberian sovereignty.

Endemic disease and a high infant mortality rate prevented Spain and Mexico from having surplus population that might have been induced to migrate to latitudes beyond San Francisco Bay and engage in the fur trade or farm the fertile earth. Alexander von Humboldt perceived this disadvantage, predicting that north of the 38th parallel the tribes of independent Indians "probably will be subdued gradually by Russian colonists, who since the close of the last century have advanced from the eastern extremity of Asia to the American continent." He warned:

> The progress of the Siberian Russians toward the south naturally will be more rapid than that which the Mexican Spanish will make toward the north. A hunting people, accustomed to living under cloud-filled skies in an excessively cold climate finds agreeable the temperature reigning on the coast of New Cornwall [Pacific Northwest]. And this same coast, on the other hand, seems an uninhabitable land, a polar region, to colonists coming from a moderate climate, from the fertile and delicious plains of Sonora and New California.[2]

Unless transported there under duress, the average Spanish-American disdained such northern latitudes, a reality acknowledged by officials who advocated colonizing the northwest with vagrants and felons. The colonization societies that in the mid-nineteenth century promoted American immigration to Oregon had no parallel in Spanish America.

Explorations along the coast did not readily disclose the vast resources that today support a mushrooming population in the Pacific Northwest. In a persistent search to eliminate the possibility of a northwest passage, the Spanish gave most of their attention to examining fjords in Alaska and British Columbia that even today continue sparsely inhabited. Spain wearied of that fruitless effort, and European factors cut short her activities there before the revelation of interior areas of less rainfall and greater agricultural promise, more similar climatically to northern Spain and the Mexican highlands. In a day when navigation depended upon sail, Spanish explorers could not appreciate the importance of harbors deep within the waterways that now support such cities as Victoria, Vancouver, and Seattle. By failing to complete reconnaissance of the Pacific Northwest, to recognize its natural advantages, or to establish permanent settlements in fertile spots, Madrid lost the area by default.

Spanish explorations northward along the Pacific coast in the sixteenth century followed the pattern of Iberian exploits elsewhere in the New

2. Humboldt, *Ensayo político*, 2 : 378, AT.

World at that time—a saga of intrepid fortune seekers led by wealthy men who required no expenditures by the government, so great was their expectation of plunder in gold, silver, and pearls. But superficial visits to the California coast turned up no precious metals. In contrast to the Aztec and the Inca, the Indians of the Pacific Northwest ignored the auriferous wealth in the beds of their swift rivers and lacked the golden ornaments that would have induced explorers to seek out the mother lodes. Only time and chance would reveal the nuggets of the Fraser and the Yukon. Given the importance of mining in Spanish America, it is surprising that so little attention was given to assessing such resources in the Pacific Northwest.[3] This underscores a contrast between Iberian culture in the sixteenth and the eighteenth centuries: whereas under the early Hapsburgs the Spanish had been aggressive and exploitative, under the Bourbons they were protective, concerned with preserving what had already been gained, and not disposed to respond belligerently, except in self-defense.

Madrid's claims to northwest America were undermined by a propagandistic failure. If the expeditions of 1774 and 1775 had been adequately publicized before the courts and scientific circles of Europe, Cook's visit to that same shore several years later would have received its proper chronological rank—that is, preceded by the visits of Bering, Chirikov, Pérez, Hezeta, and Bodega. But for centuries a mantle of silence had proven the least costly means of protecting Spain's interests in the Pacific, and the practice was not easy to discredit or abandon. By contrast, narratives of the voyages of English and American mariners to the northwest coast circulated widely, in German and French as well as in English. That Spain did not make known her accomplishments on the northwest coast explains, in part, the occurrence of the Nootka Sound controversy. British fur traders came to those shores knowing little or nothing about Spanish feats in that area, and they were unprepared to pay any deference to Madrid's territorial claims, which seemed unreasonable and preposterous. The laws of Indies made Martinez dutybound to arrest foreigners who persisted, in the face of warnings, in establishing settlements on Spanish territory. If Madrid's claim had been better known in Europe, a British attempt to colonize Nootka would have appeared no more legitimate than English intrusions on the Mosquito coast of Nicaragua and Honduras. The Pitt ministry would have had difficulty taking the self-righteous pose it assumed in 1790 to coerce Carlos IV into appeasement over events at Friendly Cove.

Goaded by the examples of Cook and La Pérouse, Madrid perceived the political and scientific advantages of shedding light upon its overseas establishments. But Malaspina's undoing at Godoy's hands relegated his ex-

---

3. An exception is a reference by Moziño to rock samples taken to Mexico City for analysis. *Noticias,* pp. 4–5.

pedition's efforts to limbo. Several superficial historical surveys discussing the northwest coast were written by private individuals, but never published.[4] Moziño's able description of Nootka was all but lost in an obscure Guatemalan periodical, 1803–04. Madrid's policy of secrecy about her activities was a great handicap for contemporary Spanish historians, unless they were part of the government itself, in which case their talents were focused upon furthering official objectives and policies, rather than on making objective historical investigations. Martín Fernández de Navarrete's officially subsidized publication of the journals of the *Sutil* and the *Mexicana* in 1802 was a belated effort to show the extent of Spanish achievements on the northwest coast, but it had no discernible impact upon rivalry for Oregon.

While in Mexico in 1803–04, Alexander von Humboldt talked with Jacinto Caamaño a number of times, and in his summary of Spanish activities on the northwest coast remarks: "In my opinion it is necessary to gather all these materials in a work that would embrace everything pertaining to the political and commercial affairs of Mexico."[5] The task was never attempted in his own publications.

There are a number of monographs on individual expeditions and leaders, but Spanish and Mexican scholars have yet to assess the full panorama of the subject, as it influenced the larger history of Spanish America or the North Pacific.[6] To affect the course of events it is not sufficient that the

---

4. "Descripción geográphico histórica de la Californa, y tierras situadas al nord-ouest de la América hasta el Estrecho de Anián, según las últimas observaciones: y de las Islas de Anadir, Eleuteras, y de Bering," CtY-BWA (Coe 139); Fray Iñigo Abbad y Lasierra, "Descripción de las costas de California Septentrional y Meridional hasta el Estrecho de Anián; su descubrimiento, variedad de nombres que se le han dado, geografía de las costas del mar del Sur desde el cabo de San Lucas hasta el Círculo Artico, viajes hechos a ella, temperamento y calidad de la tierra, puertos, misiones y descubrimientos de los rusos . . . y comercio de estos," SpBP (1480). Iris Higbie Wilson notes the series of tragedies befalling Spanish research, which "allowed a disorganized mass of information to be buried in archives, lost, given away, or sold to foreign collectors. . . . If Spain contributed little to science," she asserts, "it was not for lack of ideas and worthwhile experiments but rather because of events which defeated her ambitious undertakings." I. H. Wilson, "Spanish Scientists in the Pacific Northwest, 1790–92," in *Reflections of Western Historians: Papers of the 7th Annual Conference of the Western History Association . . . 1967* (Tucson, 1969), p. 47.

5. Humboldt, *Ensayo político*, 2 : 376–77.

6. The directors and staff of Madrid's Archivo del Museo Naval and Mexico City's Archivo General de la Nación are well aware of the extent of Spanish activities on the northwest coast, have been responsible for a number of important catalogues and monographs of pertinency, and extend a hospitable and helpful reception to scholars interested in their documentary treasures. In 1967 a set of eight Spanish postage stamps portrayed northwest coast subjects, in a continuing series of "Builders of the New World," commemorating achievements in Spain's erstwhile colonies. Depicted are Bodega, Mourelle, Martínez, Cayetano Valdés, the Spanish settlement at Nootka, the Malaspina chart of Friendly Cove, Bodega's 1792 map of the northwest coast, and "San Elías, Alaska" (actually the *Sutil* and the *Mexicana*, with Mt. Baker, Washington, in the background).

people of a nation believe their position to be historically justified; that conviction must be backed by adequate physical strength, and the idea must be conveyed to other nationalities in order to discourage rivals. Obviously Madrid failed in this regard, primarily as a consequence of her habit of secrecy.

Not only Spanish historians, but viceroys, ministers, diplomats, and explorers were seriously handicapped by the tremendous obstacle of inadequate data control that stemmed from difficulties in consulting accounts of earlier explorations. Charts, logs, and accounts of explorations often were not available to guide subsequent expeditionaries, bolster claims during diplomatic negotiations, or aid in composing detailed, accurate historical works to publicize the achievements of Ferrelo, Vizcaíno, and the long list of later expeditionaries who sailed northward along the Pacific coast. Once the prime documents on each voyage entered the precincts of Spanish bureaucracy, they seldom reappeared, for none were deemed safe for publication. Explorers of later decades never had more than a vague idea of previous discoveries. Even Malaspina, for example, was unable to consult original accounts of the efforts of 1774 and 1775 prior to setting out for the Pacific in 1789.[7] It is testimony to José de Gálvez's perspicacity that he endeavored to overcome this handicap by creating in Seville a central repository for all records pertaining to Madrid's overseas possessions, the renowned Archive of Indies.

Spain's defeat in the rivalry for the Pacific Northwest can also be attributed in some measure to the failure of her missionary efforts there. Elsewhere in Spanish America a prime factor in creating a basis for empire was the Christianizing of the aborigines. The labor of the Church had political consequences everywhere in the Spanish empire but on the northwest coast. Referring to California, Chapman notes that "the government did not undergo expense for missions, unless it had some other object in view."[8] A mission was never founded at Nootka because, from the very beginning, Viceroy Flores meant the settlement to be *fingida,* merely pretended. Four men of the cloth were sent to Nootka in 1798 to give the place the appearance of a permanent settlement, but it was not intended that they should remain all winter. After the First Nootka Convention, it appeared only a matter of time until the establishment would be evacuated. Such missionary activities as took place were not of sufficient intensity or duration to be very effective. This shortcoming provoked the outspoken Moziño, who commented:

> Several of the natives, especially Nana-quius, Nat-zape, Quio-comasia, and Tata-no, learned to speak quite a bit of our language. The facility

---

7. Malaspina, *Viaje,* p. 364.
8. Chapman, *Founding of Spanish California,* p. 15.

with which they grasped most of the things we wanted to explain to them should make us very sorry that the ministers of the Gospel have not taken advantage of such a fine opportunity to plant the Catholic faith among them. I know that the cross-bearers [priests] reported that a mission could not be established here because there was a lack of land that could be cultivated. What a small obstacle! As if a mission and improved land were synonymous! And could not a doctrine that was taught by fishermen in the first place be communicated to those who out of necessity, ignorance, and a lack of resources follow this profession? [9]

The priests' diaries shed little light on the subject. Their main concerns were attending to the spiritual needs of Spanish and Mexican personnel, participating in the formal acts of possession, and taking care of slave children purchased from the Indians. The practice of adopting Indian waifs had little acculturative effect upon their respective tribes, however, because instead of being schooled at Nootka and remaining as a nucleus of a Christian settlement—the method used elsewhere in Spanish America to win over pagan tribes—all were brought to Monterey, San Blas, or Tepic. There is no record that any returned to the northwest coast to propagate their adopted culture.

Near the close of the nineteenth century a Belgian priest made inquiries at Nootka to determine how much had been retained in tribal memory about the time of Spanish occupation. "Oh yes," he was told, "there were priests—two priests, very heavy and corpulent—they had no hair, were almost completely bald, and when the sun stops [winter solstice] they had two babies." "My grand uncle used to go to see the people in church (indicating the place where the chapel was erected, close to where the chief has his house now) and the people would go on their knees and get up." [10] Enough was remembered of hymns learned from the Spanish that on one occasion the priest had an Indian woman sing them before the archbishop. "Tradition points out the site of the governor's house, the church, and the burial ground," Howay noted in 1917. "Spanish numbers up to ten can be counted by many Indians of the neighborhood, though only a linguist could recognize their identity." [11]

Spanish presence on the northwest coast influenced the aboriginal population in a multitude of ways, but did nothing to create a bulwark for Madrid's political dominion, even though an impartial assessment suggests that Spanish policy was sincere in seeking Indian welfare—as that welfare was defined and perceived by Iberian officials and priests. No Spanish or

9. Moziño, *Noticias*, pp. 84–85.
10. Rev. Augustin J. Brabant, *Vancouver Island and Its Missions, 1874–1900: Reminiscences* (Hesquiat, B.C., 1900), as cited by Howay, "Spanish Settlement," pp. 170–71.
11. Howay, "Spanish Settlement."

Spanish-Americans "went native," or took Indian wives, as with many Frenchmen in Canada or conquistadores and their descendants in Spanish America, to sire a mestizo class that would feel a sense of identification with Spain. There were enduring consequences from the Iberian arrival, however, seen most vividly in the copper and abalone that assumed such a prominent place thereafter in native art. Less obvious, but more insidious, from dealings with the Spanish a fondness developed for numerous articles, foodstuffs, and beverages—artificial needs that made the Indian dependent upon commerce with traders.

The Spanish were not alone to blame, but their presence at Nootka had an evil effect on the Indians as a consequence of the juxtaposition of natives desirous of European manufactures with seamen and soldiers long away from home and deprived of female companionship. There was no official discouragement of fraternization; Martínez and Bodega set an example by their familiarity with the chiefs. Aside from efforts to abolish cannibalism and warfare, Spanish officials abstained from imposing their own standards upon the natives, or from tampering extensively with indigenous concepts and practices. Although the seeds of change had been sown, Indian culture survived the brief period of Iberian presence relatively intact.

The terms of the Third Nootka Convention may not provide the entire explanation, but Friendly Cove was never again to be a white settlement. It remains the exclusive domain of the tribal council, save for the larger of the two islands at its entrance, which has a government lighthouse. Descendants of the original inhabitants no longer migrate each winter to the head of Tahsis Inlet, today occupied by a sawmill. There is no store or pier in the village, and steamships that often pass the cove's entrance never stop as they head for mills and canneries deep within the sound. In the vestibule of the Roman Catholic church an illuminated stained glass panel, a recent gift of the Spanish government, commemorates friendly relations between Iberian explorers and the Indians of the northwest coast—sole reminder of Spain's erstwhile presence at Nootka. Canadian government employees manning the lighthouse seldom come ashore, and then only after receiving permission from Chief Ambrose Ma-kwee-na, a man in his forties who is directly descended from the celebrated chieftain. Tribal prerogatives, which are strictly observed, include consent to land.

### THE NIGHTMARE

Spain's chief handicap in rivalry for the Pacific Northwest lay in her debilitating involvement in the crises of the French Revolution and the Napoleonic wars. Claims based on prior discovery and symbolic acts of possession were of scant value to Madrid when they could not be supported in Europe from a position of strength.

When Madrid found herself pushed toward war and Floridablanca could no longer procrastinate while awaiting additional information to bolster the Spanish position, Carlos IV had to choose between conflict or appeasement. He elected to yield rather than to plunge into a war in which Spain would be fighting without allies. Floridablanca resorted to the tactic of seeking a convention sufficiently ambiguous in wording to permit escape from a dangerous and untenable situation. The price of compromise was surrender of claims to exclusive dominion over the northwest coast. No matter what loopholes Floridablanca thought he perceived in its terminology, the Nootka Convention of 1790 drove a fatal wedge into Spain's position in the Pacific Northwest.

One of the first cracks in Spain's colonial empire appeared on the northwest coast. The Nootka Sound controversy, the initial setback there, has sometimes been designated the beginning of the end of the Spanish Empire. Pride and *pundonor* took Carlos IV to the very brink of war before he yielded. The French Revolution and Napoleon's advent affected in the most profound degree the history of the Pacific Northwest. If it had not been for events in France: (1) Pitt would not have been able to make such bold use of the Nootka incident to extort his objectives from Madrid in 1790, and Spain would have persisted in endeavoring to retain exclusive control over Nootka, Bucareli Sound, and the adjacent coast; (2) the United States would not have gained Louisiana as effortlessly as she did, an opportunity stemming from Carlos IV's submission to Napoleon; and (3) it is unlikely that Madrid would have ceded her claims in the Pacific Northwest to the United States in order to stabilize the Spanish-American boundary, obtain a non-recognition pledge, and quell the rebellions originating during Bourbon captivity.

The clash at Nootka, and its consequences, brought an abrupt awakening from the long-sustained dream of keeping the Pacific a Spanish lake and the west coast of the Americas a preserve off limits to other nationalities. Spain had nurtured this illusion against inroads by other powers for several centuries. The latter part of the eighteenth century saw it shattered. On land, too, Madrid's cherished concepts collided with reality. Despite a rallying of Spanish energies under able Carlos III, his uxorious successor was no match for events confronting the nation from across the Pyrenees. No sovereign in Europe was safe from the guileful Corsican. Bourbon captivity, 1808–14, weakened Spain's American empire beyond repair and doomed Madrid's pretensions in western North America. An edifice in ruins, a machine abandoned to rust, a human body stretched out in death lose so vital a portion of what they once were that it is difficult to appreciate the impressiveness they formerly possessed. So it is with the Spanish Empire in the closing decades of the eighteenth century, before it was laid low. In hindsight we perceive those years through the dust raised by the Napoleonic era, when Madrid's fortunes suffered so drastically. Too readily we forget how formidable His Catholic Majesty's image seemed to Kendrick, Ingraham, and other Americans of the time.

To a certain extent Madrid's claims over the Pacific Northwest were victim of the circumstance that the Spanish had as rivals for North America the most aggressively expansive nations of the time, which found historic and geographic justification for challenging Spanish pretensions to exclusive ownership of the Far West. The feats of Drake, Cook, Gray, and Lewis and Clark fueled sentiments of indignation against papal bulls and hoary acts of formal possession without actual settlement. Centuries of religious struggle conditioned Protestant countries to hatred of the Spanish "Dons." Since Elizabethan times England's economic growth was often at Spain's expense, and the British were ethically accustomed to prying economic advantages from incursions at weak spots in the Spanish Empire. After breaking away from the mother country, the United States was aware that survival depended upon the pursuit of her own interests, not the benign openhandedness of European imperial powers. As Spain's grip over the western portion of the continent loosened, it behooved American leaders to prevent Britain and Russia from moving into the vacuum. Jefferson and John Quincy Adams saw this clearly; both were predisposed to exploit any advantage. Henry Adams's metaphor of Spain's empire in the West as a beached whale, to be carved up at will by the Americans, is valid after 1808.[12] That it was not yet a carcass prior to that date is the import of Melgares's powerful sally onto the Great Plains in 1806 in search of Captain "Merry." Yet territorial concerns seem to be a compulsive aspect of human behavior, and following Fernando's return to the throne in 1814, Madrid again maneuvered to preserve what she could of erstwhile pretensions to western North America, only to have those aspirations finally throttled by the shrewd diplomacy of John Quincy Adams, taking advantage of Spain's embarrassments elsewhere.

### THE RESIDUE

Just as one perceives the high water mark on a beach by the debris, so the Iberian attempt to gain sway over the far northwest is recalled by the Spanish place names that linger on from Alaska to Oregon. Like deadwood,

12. "If the Southern and Western people, who saw the Spanish flag flaunted every day in their faces, learned to hate the Spaniard as their natural enemy, the Government at Washington, which saw a wider field, never missed an opportunity to thrust its knife into the joints of its unwieldly prey. In the end, far more than half the territory of the United States was the spoil of Spanish empire, rarely acquired with perfect propriety. To sum up the story in a single word, Spain had immense influence over the United States; but it was the influence of the whale over its captors,—the charm of a huge, helpless, and profitable victim." Henry Adams, *History,* 1 : 339–40.

beached and weathered, on some remote shore—so it was with the dreams and efforts of the Iberian explorers and statesmen who expended so much energy and concern, apparently for naught. Or did something worthwhile result from so much expenditure, such physical discomfort, deprivation, and even death? So remote does the time of Spanish exertions seem upon visiting today's modest villages at Nootka and Neah Bay that the heated eighteenth-century contest for those shores seems incongruous and at best a trivial part of the remote past, with little more than academic interest. Yet the consequences of that rivalry determined the ultimate nationality of a vast area in western North America. The Nootka Sound controversy was one of the most resounding diplomatic crises in the eighteenth century, with a baneful effect on Spain and France. Friendly Cove was the point of intersection between mutually exclusive imperial trajectories. For a brief period Nootka seemed to hold the key to control of all western North America north of San Francisco Bay. After the discovery that it was merely a bay on an offshore island, the sound lost its strategic importance. Madrid and London, in their need to present a united front against revolutionary France, had to abstain from occupying the site. The Nootka conventions inhibited both Britain and Spain from proceeding with plans for outposts, missions, settlements, and garrisons elsewhere on the northwest coast—as any new settlement would automatically become a port of free access to the resented rival. Americans cannot regret that the Nootka crisis took the precise turn that it did, for the conventions dissuaded both Madrid and London from planting naval bases along the contested coast. A generation later, American migrants to Oregon would be ready to drive home the wedge inserted into that area by Gray, Kendrick, Lewis and Clark, and Astor's men.

At best, Spain's position in the Pacific Northwest was extremely vulnerable, but had the Nootka crisis and Bourbon dethronement been averted, it is not improbable that the area could have remained in Latin American hands. Strange as a Spanish colony in that cool latitude might seem at first glance, a comparison with southern Chile removes the incongruity. Such a colony would have posed a considerable obstacle to westward expansion for both the United States and Canada—and would no doubt have considerably altered the history of the Far West. The power struggle between London and Madrid resulted in an Iberian retreat from Nootka and Louisiana, and the expanding American republic thus avoided a conflict with Spain or her heirs over the trans-Mississippi area and the Pacific coast. If the creation of a transcontinental republic was our "manifest destiny," Americans can take satisfaction from the fact that the republic fell heir to the territory claimed by Madrid in the Oregon country without taking a single Spanish life or leaving a residue of resentment.

After the Transcontinental Treaty of 1819, rivalry for that wild coast and hinterland was between Britain and the United States. American statesmen, merchants, missionaries, and farmers saw great promise in an area where Madrid had seen only incalculable expenditures, motives for international disputes, the risk of war, hardships, cold, scurvy, and frustration. The region that the Spanish had not appreciated enough to give any other name than that of "the coast to the north of California" became "Oregon," lodestone for immigrant Americans, who built there a home for grateful millions and opened a doorway to Alaska, Hawaii, and the Orient.

Nor should it be overlooked that Spain's vigorous occupation of Friendly Cove in 1789 dampened the tsarina's scheme to extend Muscovite claims from Nootka to Hudson Bay. Otherwise, the contest for the northwest coast might have been between Madrid and St. Petersburg. Spain's stance in 1790 checked Muscovite expansion eastward until the turn of the century. Had Catherine's projects matured without discouragement, Russian America would have extended much farther south than it did. Had it included more temperate areas, Slavic outposts in Alaska would have been easier to sustain. If Alaska and Ft. Ross were not successfully enlarged, it was to a great degree because of Spain's oft-expressed hostility.

After the beaver had been virtually swept from successive areas in Oregon, London's concern for retaining the lower Columbia basin diminished, especially since the area's retention involved a risk of war with the United States—given strengthened American claims and convictions following the Transcontinental Treaty. The United States enjoyed the most favorable position for filling the geopolitical vacuum with a growing stream of self-reliant colonists who, not needing protective fleets or official subsidies and monopolies, relied upon agriculture, lumbering, mining, and fishing to build a thriving economic basis for population expansion. Spanish claims to the northwest coast by prior discovery kept Britain from having clear title to Oregon. The principal significance of Spain's earlier presence there is that in retiring from the contest, Madrid ceded its claims to the United States. John Quincy Adams's achievement in 1819 and the geographical contiguousness that enabled American settlers to migrate overland made Washington, Oregon, and Idaho a part of the United States rather than Canada. As Bemis remarks, "Surely the creation of the Continental Republic from Atlantic to Pacific represents the greatest single achievement of American nationality, the basis of all subsequent accomplishments." [13] A knowledge of Spanish efforts to hold sway over the Pacific Northwest helps to understand that process. The relative ease with which the area was acquired by the United States, without recourse to arms, is in large measure due to Spain's efforts there, with the checks it placed upon Russia and Britain.

13. Bemis, *Adams,* p. 300.

Although Americans were not the first to frequent the Pacific shore of this continent, they eventually acquired its choicest portion through the combined effects of European rivalry, geographical proximity, vigorous statesmanship, and aggressive personal achievements of intrepid frontiersmen and missionaries, hardy pioneer settlers, and enterprising investors. Spain failed in the Pacific Northwest by reason of the inverse of each of these factors. The United States possessed a burgeoning population able to overflow into the virgin agricultural lands of the Oregon Territory, succeeding where Spain, Russia, and Britain fell short because settlers became the fulcrum for political dominion.

By midcentury, when Americans by the tens of thousands began streaming into the Pacific Northwest, Spanish participation in earlier chapters of its history had faded from collective memory. The names linger on— Juan de Fuca Strait, Port Angeles, San Juan Islands, Cordova, Valdez— vestiges of that distant time when the yellow and red banner of His Catholic Majesty waved over Friendly Cove, and genial Don Francisco held forth at the great house, welcoming one and all to his table, dining off silver plate on king salmon, venison, refried beans, and vegetables fresh from Pedro Alberni's gardens. This scene of international camaraderie, so studiously cultivated by the Limeño's fine wines and brandies, inevitably dissolves into one of Colnett and Martínez in a shouting match. A musket shot echoes across the cove and Ke-le-kum's body pitches from his canoe, tinting the azure water an ugly shade of red. Then a vision of the disembodied heads of the *Boston*'s crew, lined up in a row, being counted by John Jewitt, jolts one back into the twentieth century with a shudder. But Estéban Point, Fidalgo Island, Haro Strait, Port Alberni, and a host of other places endure—relics of men long gone, their names immured like fossils in the sediment of time past—bearing witness to a stirring and significant period in the history of the American West.

# Appendix A  Lok's Account of Fuca's Voyage, 1592

A NOTE made by me Michael Lok the elder, touching the Strait of Sea, commonly called Fretum Anian, in the South Sea, through the North-west passage of Meta incognita.

When I was at Venice, in April 1596, happily arrived there an old man, about three-score yeares of age, called commonly Juan de Fuca, but named properly Apostolos Valerianos, of Nation a Greeke, borne in the Iland Cefalonia, of profession a Mariner, and an ancient Pilot of Shippes. This man being come lately out of Spaine, arrived first at Ligorno, and went thence to Florence in Italie, where he found one John Dowglas, an Englishman, a famous Mariner, ready comming for Venice, to be Pilot of a Venetian Ship, named Ragasona for England, in whose company they came both together to Venice. And John Dowglas being well acquainted with me before, he gave me knowledge of this Greeke Pilot, and brought him to my speech: and in long talke and conference betweene us, in presence of John Dowglas: this Greeke Pilot declared in the Italian and Spanish languages, thus much in effect as followeth.

First he said, that he had bin in the West Indies of Spaine by the space of fortie yeeres, and had sailed to and from many places thereof, as Mariner and Pilot, in the service of the Spaniards.

Also he said, that he was in the Spanish Shippe, which in returning from the Ilands, Philippinas and China, towards Nova Spania, was robbed and taken at the Cape California, by Captaine Candish Englishman, whereby he lost sixtie thousand Duckets, of his owne goods.

Also he said, that he was Pilot of three small Ships which the Vizeroy of Mexico sent from Mexico, armed with one hundred men, Souldiers, under a Captaine, Spaniards, to discover the Straits of Anian, along the coast of the South-Sea, and to fortifie in that Strait, to resist the passage and proceedings of the English Nation, which were feared to passe through those Straits into the South Sea. And that by reason of a mutinie which happened among the Souldiers, for the Sodomie of their Captaine, that Voyage was overthrowne, and the Ships returned backe from California coast to Nova Spania, without any effect of thing done in that Voyage. And that after their returne, the Captaine was at Mexico punished by justice.

Also he said, that shortly after the said Voyage was so ill ended, the said Viceroy of Mexico, sent him out againe Anno 1592, with a small Caravela, and a Pinnace, armed with Mariners onely, to follow the said Voyage, for discovery of the same Straits of Anian, and the passage thereof, into the Sea which they call the North Sea, which is our North-west Sea. And that he followed his course in that Voyage West and North-west in the South Sea, all alongst the coast of Nova Spania, and California, and the Indies, now called North America (all

539

which Voyage hee signified to me in a great Map, and a Sea-card of mine owne, which I laied before him) untill hee came to the Latitude of fortie seven degrees, and that there finding that the Land trended North and North-east, with a broad Inlet of Sea, betweene 47. and 48. degrees of Latitude: hee entred thereinto, sayling therein more then twentie dayes, and found that Land trending still sometime North-west and North-east, and North, and also East and South-east-ward, and very much broader Sea then was at the said entrance, and that hee passed by divers Ilands in that sayling. And that at the entrance of this said Strait, there is on the North-west coast thereof, a great Hedland or Iland, with an exceeding high Pinacle, or spired Rocke, like a piller thereupon.

Also he said, that he went on Land in divers places, and that he saw some people on Land, clad in Beasts skins: and that the Land is very fruitfull, and rich of gold, Silver, Pearle, and other things, like Nova Spania.

And also he said, that he being entred thus farre into the said Strait, and being come into the North Sea already, and finding the Sea wide enough every where, and to be about thirtie or fortie leagues wide in the mouth of the Straits, where he entred; hee thought he had now well discharged his office, and done the thing which he was sent to doe: and that hee not being armed to resist the force of the Salvage people that might happen, hee therefore set sayle and returned homewards againe towards Nova Spania, where hee arrived at Acapulco, Anno 1592. hoping to be rewarded greatly of the Viceroy, for this service done in this said Voyage.

Also he said, that after his comming to Mexico, hee was greatly welcommed by the Viceroy, and had great promises of great reward, but that having sued there two yeares time, and obtained nothing to his content, the Viceroy told him, that he should be rewarded in Spaine of the King himselfe very greatly, and willed him therefore to goe into Spaine, which Voyage hee did performe.

Also he said, that when he was come into Spaine, he was greatly welcommed there at the Kings Court, in wordes after the Spanish manner, but after long time of suite there also, hee could not get any reward there neither to his content. And that therefore at the length he stole away out of Spaine, and came into Italie, to goe home againe and live among his owne Kindred and Countri-men, he being very old.

Also he said, that hee thought the cause of his ill reward had of the Spaniards, to bee for that they did understand very well, that the English Nation had now given over all their voyages for discoverie of the North-west passage, wherefore they need not feare them any more to come that way into the South Sea, and therefore they needed not his service therein any more.

Also he said, that in regard of this ill reward had of the Spaniards, and under-standing of the noble minde of the Queene of England, and of her warres main-tayned so valiantly against the Spaniards, and hoping that her Majestie would doe him justice for his goods lost by Captaine Candish, he would bee content to goe into England, and serve her Majestie in that voyage for the discoverie perfectly of the North-west passage into the South Sea, and would put his life into her Majesties hands to performe the same, if shee would furnish him with onely one ship of fortie tunnes burden and a Pinnasse, and that he would performe it in thirtie dayes time, from one end to the other of the Streights. And he willed me so to write into England.

And upon this conference had twise with the said Greeke Pilot, I did write thereof accordingly into England unto the right honourable the old Lord Treasurer Cecill, and to Sir Walter Raleigh, and to Master Richard Hakluyt that famous Cosmographer, certifying them hereof by my Letters. And in the behalfe of the said Greeke Pilot, I prayed them to disburse one hundred pounds of money, to bring him into England with my selfe, for that my owne purse would not stretch so wide at that time. And I had answere hereof by Letters of friends, that this action was very well liked, and greatly desired in England to bee effected; but the money was not readie, and therefore this action dyed at that time, though the said Greeke Pilot perchance liveth still this day at home in his owne Countrie in Cefalonia, towards the which place he went from me within a fortnight after this conference had at Venice.

And in the meane time, while I followed my owne businesse in Venice, being in Law suit against the Companie of Merchants of Turkie, and Sir John Spencer their Governour in London, to recover my pension due for my office of being their Consull at Aleppo in Turkie, which they held from me wrongfully. And when I was (as I thought) in a readinesse to returne home into England, for that it pleased the Lords of her Majesties honourable Privie Counsell in England, to looke into this Cause of my Law suit for my reliefe; I thought that I should be able of my owne purse to take with me into England the said Greek Pilot. And therefore I wrote unto him from Venice a Letter dated in July 1596. which is copied hereunder.

Al Mag.<sup>co</sup> Sig.<sup>or</sup> Capitan Juan De Fuca Piloto de Indias, amigo char<sup>mo</sup>. en Zefalonia.

Muy honrado Sennor, siendo yo para buelverme en Inglatierra dentre de pocas mezes, y accuerdandome de lo trattado entre my y V.M. en Venesia, sobre el viagio de las Indias, me ha parescido bien de scrivir esta carta á V.M. paraque si tengais animo de andar con migo, puedais escribirme presto, en que maniera quereis consertaros. Y puedais embiarmi vuestra carta, con esta nao Ingles que sta al Zante (sino hallais otra coientura meier) con el sobrescritto que diga, en casa del Sennor Eleazar Hycman Mercader Ingles, al tragetto, de San Thomas en Venisia. Y Dios guarde la persona de V.M. Fecha en Venesia al primer dia de Julio, 1596. annos.

Amigo de V. M. Michael Lok Ingles.[1]

---

1. To the Magnificent Señor Captain Juan de Fuca, Pilot of the Indies, dear friend in Zefalonia.

Very honored Sir: Since I am ready to return to England within a few months, and remembering what we had discussed in Venice, about a voyage to the Indies, it seemed advisable for me to write to you, in case you want to go with me, so that you can write to me at once about what manner of contract you would desire. You can send your letter to me by this English ship, which is in Zante (unless you find some better means), addressed on the outside to the house of Signor Eleazar Hycman, English merchant, at the ferry of St. Thomas in Venice. God guard the person of Your Grace. Done in Venice on the first day of July, of the year 1596.

The friend of Your Grace, Michael Lok, Englishman

And I sent the said Letter from Venice to Zante, in the ship Cherubin. And shortly after I sent a copie thereof in the ship Mynyon. And also a third copie thereof by Manea Orlando Patron de Nave Venetian. And unto my said Letters he wrote mee answere to Venice by one Letter which came not to my hands. And also by another Letter which came to my hands, which is copied here-under.

Al Ill^mo. Sig^or. Michal Loch Ingles, in casa del Sig^or. Lasaro Merca. der Ingles, al tragetto de San Thomas en Venesia.

Muy Illustre Seg^or. lo carta de V.M. recevi á 20. dias del Mese di Settembre, por loqual veo Loche V.M. me manda, io tengho animo de complir Loche tengo promettido á V.M. y no solo yo, mas tengo vinte hombres para lievar con migo, por che son hombres vaglientes; y assi estoi esperando, por otra carta che avise á V.M. parache me embiais los dinieros che tengo escritto á V. M. Porche bien save V. M. como io vine pover, porche me glievo Captain Candis mas de sessanta mille ducados, come V. M. bien save: embiandome lo dicho, iré a servir á V. M. con todos mis compagneros. I no spero otra cossa mas de la voluntad é carta de V.M. I con tanto nostro Sig^or. Dios guarda la Illustre persona de V. M. muchos annos. De Ceffalonia á 24. de Settembre del 1596.

Amigo & servitor de V. M.

Juan Fuca [2]

And the said Letter came to my hands in Venice, the 16. day of November, 1596. but my Law suite with the Companie of Turkie was not yet ended, by reason of Sir John Spencers suite made in England at the Queenes Court to the contrarie, seeking onely to have his money discharged which I had attached in Venice for my said pension, and thereby my owne purse was not yet readie for the Greeke Pilot.

And neverthelesse, hoping that my said suite would have shortly a good end; I wrote another Letter to this Greeke Pilot from Venice, dated the 20. of November, 1596. which came not to his hands. And also another Letter, dated the 24. of Januarie 1596. which came to his hands. And thereof he wrote me answere, dated the 28. of May, 1577. which I received the first of August 1597. by Thomas Norden an English Merchant yet living in London, wherein he promised still to

2. The defective Spanish of Fuca's letter to Lok is approximately the linguistic blend that might be expected from a poorly educated Levantine pilot; in approximate translation it reads:

Very Illustrious Sir: I received your letter of the month of September, by which I see what your worship orders me. I am eager to fulfill what I promised you, and not only me, but I have twenty men to take with me, because they are brave men; and thus I am waiting, because in another letter I advised your worship so that you would send me the money which I wrote you about. Your worship knows how I became poor, because Captain Candis took away from me more than sixty thousand ducats, as you well know. Upon sending me what I have written, I will go to serve your worship with all of my companions. And I await nothing more than the will and letter of your worship. And so may our Lord God preserve the illustrious person of your worship many years. From Ceffalonia on September 24th, 1596.

The friend and servant of your worship.

Juan Fuca.

goe with me into England, to performe the said voyage for discoverie of the North-west passage into the South Sea, if I would send him money for his charges according to his former writing, without the which money, he said he could not goe, for that he said he was undone utterly, when he was in the Ship Santa Anna, which came from China, and was robbed at California. And yet againe afterward I wrote him another Letter from Venice, whereunto he wrote me answere, by a Letter written in his Greeke language, dated the 20. of October, 1589. the which I have still by me, wherein he promiseth still to goe with me into England, and performe the said voyage of discoverie of the North-west passage into the South Sea by the said streights, which he calleth the Streight of of Nova Spania, which he saith is but thirtie daies voyage in the streights, if I will send him the money formerly written for his charges. The which money I could not yet send him, for that I had not yet recovered my pension owing mee by the Companie of Turkie aforesaid. And so of long time I stayed from any furder proceeding with him in this matter.

And yet lastly, when I my selfe was at Zante, in the moneth of June 1602. minding to passe from thence for England by Sea, for that I had then recovered a little money from the Companie of Turkie, by an order of the Lords of the Privie Counsell of England, I wrote another Letter to this Greeke Pilot to Cefalonia, and required him to come to me to Zante, and goe with mee into England, but I had none answere thereof from him, for that as I heard afterward at Zante, he was then dead, or very likely to die of great sicknesse. Whereupon I returned my selfe by Sea from Zante to Venice, and from thence I went by land through France into England, where I arrived at Christmas, An. 1602. safely, I thanke God, after my absence from thence ten yeeres time; with great troubles had for the Company of Turkies businesse, which hath cost me a great summe of money, for the which I am not yet satisfied of them.[3]

3. Lok's account is reproduced from Purchas, *Hakluytus Posthumus, or Purchas His Pilgrimes,* in Hakluyt Society, *Works,* ex. ser. 14 (Glasgow, 1906) : 415–21.

# *Appendix B   The Nootka Conventions*

THE FIRST NOOTKA CONVENTION, 1790 [1]

ESTANDO dispuestas sus Majestades católica y británica á terminar por un convenio pronto y sólido las diferencias que se han suscitado últimamente entre las dos coronas; han hallado que el mejor medio de conseguir tan saludable fin sería el de una transaccion amigable, la cual dejando á un lado toda discusion retrospectiva de los derechos y pretensiones de las los partes, arreglase su posicion respectiva para lo venidero sobre bases conformes á sus verdaderos intereses y al deseo mútuo que anima á sus Majestades de establecer entre sí en todo y en todas partes la mas perfecta amistad, armonia y buena correspondencia. Con esta mira han nombrado y constituido por sus plenipotenciarios, á saber: su Majestad católica á don José Moñino, conde de Florida Blanca, caballero gran cruz de la real órden española de Cárlos III, consejero de estado de su Majestad y su primer secretario de estado y del despacho; y su Majestad británica á don Alleyne Fitz-Herbert, del consejo privado de su Majestad en la Gran Bretaña y en Irlanda, y su embajador estraordinario y plenipotenciario cerca de su Majestad católica; quienes despues de haberse comunicado sus respectivos plenos poderes, han convenido en los articulos siguientes.

### Artículo 1.º

Se ha convenido que los edificios y distritos de terreno situados en la costa de noroeste del continente de la América setentrional, ó bien en las islas adyacentes á este continente, de que los súbditos de su Majestad británica fueron desposeidos por el mes de abril de 1789 por un oficial español, serán restituidos á los dichos súbditos británicos.

### Artículo 2.º

Además, se hará una justa reparacion, según la naturaleza del caso, de todo acto de violencia ó de hostilidad que pueda haber sido cometido desde el dicho mes de abril 1789 por los súbditos de una de las dos partes contratantes contra los súbditos de la otra; y en el caso que despues de dicha época algunos de los súbditos respectivos hayan sido desposeidos por fuerza de sus terrenos, edificios, navíos, mercaderías ó cualesquiera otros objetos de propiedad en dicho continente y en los mares ó islas adyacentes, se les volverá á poner en posesion, ó se les hará una justa compensacion por las pérdidas que hubieren padecido.

### Artículo 3.º

Y á fin de estrechar los vínculos de amistad, y de conservar en lo venidero una perfecta armonía y buena inteligencia entre las dos partes contratantes, se ha convenido que los súbditos respectivos no serán perturbados ni molestados, ya sea navegando ó pescando en el *Océano Pacífico ó en los mares del Sur;* ya sea desembarcando en las costas que circundan estos mares, en parages no ocupados ya, á

---

1. Cantillo, *Tratados, convenios y declaraciones,* pp. 623–25.

544

fin de comerciar con los naturales del pais, ó para formar establecimientos, aunque todo ha de ser con sujecion á las restricciones y providencias que se especificarán en los tres artículos siguientes.

### Artículo 4.º

Su Majestad británica se obliga á emplear los medios mas eficaces para que la navegacion y la pesca de sus súbditos en el *Océano Pacifico ó en los mares del Sur* no sirvan de pretesto á un comercio ilícito con los establecimientos españoles; y con esta mira se ha estipulado ademas espresamente, que los súbditos británicos no navegarán ni pescarán en los dichos mares á distancia de diez leguas marítimas de ninguna parte de las costas ya ocupadas por España.

### Artículo 5.º

Se ha convenido que así en los parages que se restituyan á los súbditos británicos en virtud del artículo 1.º, como en todas las otras partes de la costa del norteoeste de la América Setentrional ó de las islas adyacentes, situadas al Norte de las partes de la dicha costa ya ocupadas for España, en cualquiera parte donde los súbditos de la una de las dos potencias hubieren formado establecimientos desde el mes de abril de 1789, ó los formaren en adelante, tendrán libre entrada los súbditos de la otra y comerciarán sin obstáculo ni molestia.

### Artículo 6.º

Se ha convenido tambien por lo que hace á las costas tanto orientales como occidentales de la América Meridional y á las islas adyacentes, que los súbditos respectivos no formarán en lo venidero ningun establecimiento en las partes de estas costas, situadas al Sur de las partes de las mismas costas y de las islas adyacentes ya ocupadas por España. Bien entendido que los dichos súbditos respectivos conservarán la facultad de desembarcar en las costas é islas así situadas, para los objetos de su pesca, y de levantar cabañas y otras obras temporales que sirvan solamente á estos objetos.

### Artículo 7.º

En todos los casos de queja ó de infraccion de los artículos de la presente convencion, los oficiales de una y otra parte, sin propasarse desde luego á ninguna violencia ó via de hecho, deberán hacer una relacion exacta del caso y de sus circunstancias á sus córtes respectivas, que terminarán amigablemente estas diferencias.

### Artículo 8.º

La presente convencion será ratificada y confirmada en el término de seis semanas, contado desde el dia de su firma, ó antes si ser pudiere.

En fé de lo cual, nosotros los infrascritos plenipotenciarios de sus Majestades católica y británica, hemos firmado en su nombre y en virtud de nuestros plenos poderes respectivos la presente convencion, y la hemos puesto los sellos de nuestras armas. En San Lorenzo el Real á 28 de octubre de 1790.—El conde de Florida Blanca.—Alleyne Fitz-Herbert.

#### ARTICULO SECRETO.

Como por el artículo 6.º del presente convenio se ha estipulado por lo que mira á las costas así orientales como occidentales de la América Meridional é islas adyacentes, que los súbditos respectivos no formarán en adelante ningun establecimiento en las partes de estas costas, situadas al Sur de las partes de las mismas costas ya ocupadas for España, se he convenido y determinado por el presente artículo, que dicha estipulacion no estará en vigor mas que entre tanto que no se forme algun establecimiento en los lugares en cuestion por súbditos de otra potencia. El presente artículo secreto tendrá igual fuerza que si estuviere inserto en la convención. En fé de lo cual, nos los infrascritos plenipotenciarios de sus Majestades católica y británica hemos firmado el presente artículo secreto, y le hemos puesto los sellos de nuestras armas. Hecho en San Lorenzo el Real á 28 de octubre de 1790.—El conde de Florida Blanca.—Alleyne Fitz-Herbert.

### THE SECOND NOOTKA CONVENTION, 1793 [2]

Deseando sus Majestades católica y británica en virtud de las *declaraciones* cangeadas en Madrid el 24 de julio de 1790 y convenio firmado en el Escorial en 28 de octubre siguiente, arreglar y resolver definitivamente todo lo que mira á la restitucion de los navíos británicos apresados en Nootka, como tambien á la indemnizacion de las partes interesadas en dichos buques; han nombrado para este fin y constituido por sus comisarios y plenipotenciaros, á saber; de parte de su Majestad católica, *don Manuel de las Heras,* comisario ordenador de los ejércitos de su dicha Majestad, su agente y cónsul general en los reinos de la Gran Bretaña é Irlanda; y por parte de su Majestad británica el señor *Rodulfo Woodford,* caballero baronet de la Gran Bretaña; los cuales despues de haberse comunicado sus plenos poderes respectivos han convenido en los artículos siguientes:

Artículo 1.º

Su Majestad católica ademas de haber restituido el navío *Argonauta,* cuya entrega se hizo en el puerto de San Blas en el de 1791. conviene en pagar por via de indemnizacion á dichas partes interesadas la cantidad de doscientos diez mil pesos fuertes en especie: bien entendido que esta suma ha de servir de compensacion y completa indemnizacion de todas sus pérdidas, sean las que se quieran, sin escepcion alguna, y sin que por ningun pretesto ó motivo pueda hacerse en lo sucesivo reclamacion sobre este objeto.

Artículo 2.º

Dicho pago se hará el dia en que se firme la presente convencion por el comisario de su Majestad católica al comisario de su Majestad británica, el cual le dará al mismo tiempo una carta de pago concebida en los términos enunciados en el anterior artículo, firmada por el mismo comisario por sí y á nombre y por órden de su Majestad británica y de dichas partes interesadas. Y se unirá al presente convenio una copia espresiva en buena y debida forma de dicha carta de pago, é igualmente de los respectivos plenos poderes y escrituras de poder de las citadas partes interesadas.

Artículo 3.º

Las ratificaciones de la presente convencion se cambiarán en esta ciudad de Londres en el término de seis semanas desde el dia de la fecha ó antes si fuere posible. En fé de lo cual, nos los infrascritos comisarios y plenipotenciarios de sus Majestades católica y británica, hemos firmado en su nombre y en virtud de

2. Ibid., p. 646.

nuestros respectivos plenos poderes la presente convencion, poniendo en ella los sellos de nuestras armas. Hecho en Whitehall á 12 de febrero de 1793.—*Manuel de las Heras.—R. Woodford.*

### THE THIRD NOOTKA CONVENTION, 1794 [3]

Deseando sus Majestades católica y británica remover y obviar toda duda y dificultad relativa á la ejecucion del artículo 1.º de la convencion concluida entre sus dichas Majestades el 28 de octubre de 1790, han resuelto y convenido en mandar que se envien nuevas instrucciones á los oficiales que respectivamente han comisionado para llevar á debido efecto el dicho artículo, cuyas instrucciones serán del tenor siguiente:

"Que dentro del término mas corto que sea posible, despues de la llegada á "Nootka de los dichos oficiales, estos se juntarán en el lugar ó cerca de el en que "estaban los edificios que antes fueron ocupados por los súbditos de su Majestad "británica, á cuyo tiempo y en cuyo lugar cangearán mútuamente la *declaracion* "*y contra-declaracion* siguientes:"

#### Declaracion.

"Yo N... N..., en nombre y de órden de su Majestad católica, por estas presentes "restituyo á N... N... los edificios y distritos de terreno situados sobre la costa "del Norueste del continente de la América septentrional ó en las islas adya- "centes á este continente, de los cuales los súbditos de su Majestad británica fue- "ron desposeidos hácia el mes de abril de 1789 por un oficial español. En fé de "lo cual he firmado la presente *declaracion,* sellándola con el sello de mis armas. "Fecho en Nootka á.... de.... de 179..."

#### Contra-declaracion.

"Yo N... N..., en nombre y de órden de su Majestad británica por estas pre- "sentes, declaro que los edificios y distritos de terreno situados sobre la costa del "Norueste del continente de la América septentrional, ó en las islas adyacentes á "este continente, de los cuales los súbditos de su Majestad británica fueron des- "poseidos hácia el mes de abril de 1789 por un oficial español, me han sido res- "tituidos por N... N..., cuya restitucion declaro ser plena y satisfactoria. En fé de "lo cual he firmado la presente *contra-declaracion,* sellándola con el sello de mis "armas. Fecho en Nootka á.... de.... de 179..."

"Que entonces el oficial británico hará enarbolar la bandera británica sobre "el terreno asi restituido, en señal de posesion. Y que despues de estas formali- "dades, los oficiales de las dos coronas retirarán respectivamente su gente del "dicho puerto de Nootka."

Ademas han convenido sus dichas Majestades en que los súbditos de ambas naciones tendrán la libertad de frecuentar en las ocasiones que les convenga el referido puerto, y de construir allí edificios temporales para su acomodo durante su residencia en dichas ocasiones. Pero que ni la una ni la otra de las dos partes hará en el dicho puerto establecimiento alguno permanente, ó reclamará allí derecho alguno de soberanía ó de domin[i]o territorial con esclusion de la otra. Y sus dichas Majestades se ayudarán mutuamente para mantener á sus súbditos

3. Ibid., pp. 653–54.

en el libre acceso al dicho puerto de Nootka contra otra nacion cualquiera que intentare establecer allí alguna soberanía ó dominio.

En fé de lo cual, nos los infrascritos primer secretario de estado y del despacho de su Majestad católica, y embajador estraordinario y plenipotenciario de su Majestad británica, en nombre de de órden espresa de nuestras soberanos respectivos, hemos firmado el presente acuerdo, sellándolo con los sellos de nuestras armas. Fecho en Madrid á 11 de enero de 1794.—El duque de Alcudia.—St. Helens.

# Appendix C   A Balance Sheet of the Spanish Sea Otter Trade, 1786-1797

*Liquidacion en Extracto del producto por venta de Pieles de nutria y Lobos Marinos en el Reyno de China, sus gastos en Canton, Macao y Manila, compra de azogues de la Asia y sus costos hasta embarcarse para N[ueva] E[spaña].—Mexico, 20 de Mayo de 1797.*[a]

| [Year] | Numero de pieles | Venta | Gastos en Macao y Canton | Compra en Azogues | Liquido en Canton | Gastos en Manila | Sobrantes | Deficientes |
|---|---|---|---|---|---|---|---|---|
| [1786] | 1,054[b] | 16,060 | 6,571.5 | | 9,488.3 | 3,450. | 6,038.5 | |
| [1787] | 1,749[c] | 33,000 | 2,397.3 | 13,500 | 17,102.5 | 494.6.7 | 16,607.6.5 | |
| [ca. 1790] | 7,127[d] | 106,025 | 1,890.0 | 99,015.7.11 | 5,118.6.1 | 5,502. | | 383.1.11 |
| [1791] | 3,356[e] | 21,000 | 10,515.6.8 | | 10,484.1.4 | 17.2.6 | 10,466.6.1 | |
| [1791] | 353[f] | 4,000 | 1,843.4 | | 2,156.6 | | 2,156.6 | |
| | 14,139 | 180,085 | 23,218.2.8 | 112,515.7.11 | 44,350.5.5 | 9,464.1.1 | 35,269.6.3 | 383.1.11 |
| *Princesa Real*[g] | | | | | | 12,530.3.3 | | 12,870.0.3 |
| *Fragata San José* | | 1,014 | 1,353.5 | | | 35,765.5.8 | | 35,765.5.8 |
| Totales: | 14,139 | 181,099 | 24,571.7.8 | 112,515.7.11 | 44,350.5.5 | 57,760.2 | 35,269.6.3 | 49,018.7.10 |

SOURCE: Anonymous eighteenth-century manuscript, heretofore unpublished, from the the Western Americana Collection, Beinecke Rare Book Library, Yale.

NOTE: The columns tabulate, respectively, the number of pelts, their value upon sale, expenses in Macao and Canto, purchases in mercury, cash in Canton, expenses in Manilia, profits, and losses. Values are in pesos, reales, and cuartos.

a "Liquidation in extract of the product by sale of sea otter and sea lion pelts in the Kingdom of China, their expenses in Canton, Macao, and Manila, the purchase of mercury in Asia and its expenses until embarcation for New Spain.—Mexico, May 20, 1797."

b Collected in California by Vicente Vasadre and taken to Manila on the *San Andrés*.

c Brought to San Blas from the California missions by the *Favorita* and *San Carlos*; taken to Manila by the *San José*.

d See A. Ogden, in *Pacific Historical Review* 1 (1932) : 459.

e Sent from San Blas on the *Princesa Real*.

f Sent from Acapulco to Manila on the *San Andrés* (Malaspina, "Extracto de lo que ha ocurido [sic] en las negociaciones de pieles de nutria," in Archivo del Museo Naval, Ministerio de Marina, Madrid [335], fol. 45v.).

g The erstwhile *Princess Royal*, sold in China when the British refused repossession.

# Appendix D    Spanish Vessels on the Northwest Coast, 1774–1797

| Name | Class | Place and year of construction | Physical description | Years it visited the northwest coast |
|---|---|---|---|---|
| *Activa* | brigantine | San Blas, 1791 | 213.5 tons | '92, '93, '95 |
| *Nuestra Señora de Aranzazú* | frigate | ? | 205 tons | '89, '90, '91, '92, '94 |
| *Atrevida* | corvette | Cádiz, 1789 | 120' long; 31'6" beam; 14'2" draft; 306 tons | |
| *Nuestra Señora de la Concepción* | frigate | Realejo, (Nicaragua) | | '90, '91, '92 |
| *Descubierta* | corvette | Cádiz, 1789 | same as *Atrevida* | '91 |
| *Favorita* (alias *Nuestra Señora de los Remedios*) | frigate | Guayaquil, 1778 | 72' long; 25' beam; 16' draft; 193 tons | '79 |
| *Mexicana* (alias *Nuestra Señora de la Asunción*) | schooner | San Blas, 1791 | 46'10" keel; 13'10" beam; 6'2" draft; 46 tons | '92, '93, '97 (?) |
| *Orcasitas* (erstwhile *Adventure*) | sloop | Clayoquot, 1791–92 | 34 tons | '92 |
| *Princesa Real* (erstwhile *Princess Royal*) | sloop | ? | 43' keel; 16' beam; 8' draft; 65 tons | '90 |
| *Princesa* (alias *Nuestra Señora del Rosario*) | frigate | San Blas, 1778 | ca.91' long; ca.25' beam; ca. 15' draft; 189 tons | '79, '88, '89, '90, '91, '92, '93, '94 |
| *San Carlos* (alias *El Filipino*) | packetboat | Manila | 92' long; 24' beam; 15' draft; 196 tons | '88, '89, '90, '91 '93, '94, '95 |
| *Santa Gertrudis* | frigate | Spain (?) | ? | '92 |
| *Santa Gertrudis la Magna* (alias *Northwest America*, alias *Santa Saturnina*) | schooner | Nootka, 1788; enlarged, 1789; reassembled, 1790 | 39' long; 13' beam; 5'6" draft; 32 tons | '88, '89, '90, '91, |
| *Santiago* (alias *Nueva Galicia*) | frigate | San Blas, 1773 | ca.62' long; ca.20' beam; 225.5 tons | '74, '75 |
| *Sonora* (alias *La Felicidad*) | schooner | ? | ca.33' long; 8'4" beam; 8' draft; 59 tons | '75 |
| *Sútil* (alias *Nuestra Señora del Carmen*) | schooner | San Blas, 1791 | 46'10" keel; 13'10" beam; 6'2" draft; 46 tons | '92, '96 |

# Appendix E  Nationality of Vessels Visiting the Northwest Coast, 1774–1820

| | Spanish | British | American | French | Portuguese | Russian | Austrian | Swedish | Unidentified | Total |
|---|---|---|---|---|---|---|---|---|---|---|
| 1774 | 1 | – | – | – | – | – | – | – | – | 1 |
| 1775 | 2 | – | – | – | – | – | – | – | – | 2 |
| 1776 | – | – | – | – | – | – | – | – | – | – |
| 1777 | – | – | – | – | – | – | – | – | – | – |
| 1778 | – | 2 | – | – | – | – | – | – | – | 2 |
| 1779 | 2 | – | – | – | – | – | – | – | – | 2 |
| 1780 | – | – | – | – | – | – | – | – | – | – |
| 1781 | – | – | – | – | – | – | – | – | – | – |
| 1782 | – | – | – | – | – | – | – | – | – | – |
| 1783 | – | – | – | – | – | – | – | – | – | – |
| 1784 | – | – | – | – | – | – | – | – | – | – |
| 1785 | – | 1 | – | – | – | – | – | – | – | 1 |
| 1786 | – | 8 | – | 2 | – | – | – | – | – | 10 |
| 1787 | – | 5 | – | – | – | – | 1 | – | – | 6 |
| 1788 | 2 | 2 | 3 | – | 3 | – | – | – | – | 10 |
| 1789 | 4 | 2 | 4 | – | 2 | – | – | 1 | – | 13 |
| 1790 | 6 | 2 | 3 | – | – | – | – | 1 | – | 12 |
| 1791 | 7 | 5 | 5 | 1 | – | – | – | 1 | – | 19 |
| 1792 | 8 | 13 | 5 | 1 | 4 | – | – | 1 | – | 32 |
| 1793 | 4 | 9 | 8 | 2 | 1 | – | – | – | – | 24 |
| 1794 | 3 | 9 | 5 | – | – | – | – | – | – | 17 |
| 1795 | 2 | 3 | 3 | – | – | – | – | – | – | 8 |
| 1796 | 1 | 6 | 3 | – | – | – | – | – | – | 10 |
| 1797 | 1? | 2 | 4 | – | – | – | – | – | – | 7 |
| 1798 | – | 2 | 4 | – | – | – | – | – | 1 | 7 |
| 1799 | – | 3 | 6 | – | – | – | – | – | – | 9 |
| 1800 | – | 1 | 8 | – | – | – | – | – | – | 9 |
| 1801 | – | 3 | 20 | – | – | – | – | – | – | 23 |
| 1802 | – | 2 | 17 | – | – | – | – | – | – | 19 |
| 1803 | – | – | 11 | – | – | – | – | – | – | 11 |
| 1804 | – | – | 6 | – | – | – | – | – | – | 6 |
| 1805 | – | – | 8 | – | – | 2 | – | – | – | 10 |
| 1806 | – | – | 12 | – | – | – | – | – | – | 12 |
| 1807 | – | 1 | 11 | – | – | 1 | – | – | 1 | 14 |
| 1808 | – | 1 | 7 | – | – | 2 | – | – | – | 10 |
| 1809 | – | 1 | 8 | – | – | 1 | – | – | – | 10 |
| 1810 | – | – | 10 | – | – | 2 | – | – | – | 12 |
| 1811 | – | – | 15 | – | – | 1 | – | – | – | 16 |
| 1812 | – | – | 15 | – | – | – | – | – | – | 15 |
| 1813 | – | 1 | 12 | – | – | – | – | – | – | 13 |
| 1814 | – | 3 | 3 | – | – | 1 | – | – | – | 7 |
| 1815 | – | 2 | 6 | – | – | 2 | – | – | 1 | 11 |
| 1816 | – | 2 | 9 | – | – | – | – | – | – | 11 |
| 1817 | – | 1 | 15 | 1 | – | – | – | – | – | 17 |
| 1818 | – | 1 | 12 | 1 | – | 1 | – | – | – | 15 |
| 1819 | – | – | 8 | – | – | – | – | – | – | 8 |
| 1820 | – | – | 9 | – | – | – | – | – | – | 9 |
| Total | 43 | 93 | 275 | 8 | 10 | 13 | 1 | 4 | 3 | 450 |

SOURCE: F. W. Howay, "A List of Trading Vessels in Maritime Fur Trade," *Proceedings of the Royal Society of Canada*, 3d ser., 24 (1930): 111–34; 25 (1931): 117–49; 26 (1932): 43–86; 27 (1933): 119–47; 28 (1934): 11–49.

NOTE: Not enough is known of Russian vessels in Alaska to show them here with accuracy. Only those on record as coming south of Sitka are included.

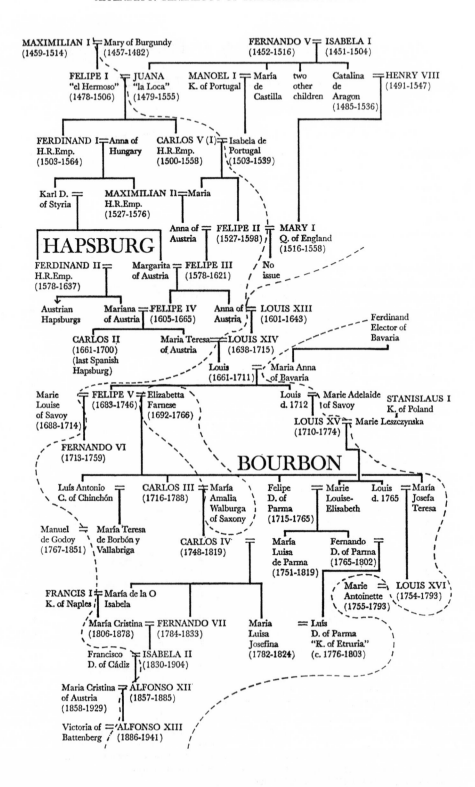

# Bibliography

BIBLIOGRAPHICAL AIDS

Bemis, Samuel Flagg, and Griffin, Grace Gardner. *Guide to the Diplomatic History of the United States, 1775–1921.* Washington, D.C., 1935.

. Bermúdez Plata, Cristóbal, ed. *Catálogo de documentos de la sección novena del Archivo General de Indias.* Vol. 1, series 1ª and 2ª. *Santo Domingo, Cuba, Puerto Rico, Luisiana, Florida y México.* Seville, 1949.

Bolton, Herbert Eugene. *Guide to Materials for the History of the United States in the Principal Archives of Mexico.* Washington, D.C., 1913.

Bromberg, Eric. "A Bibliography of Theses and Dissertations Concerning the Pacific Northwest and Alaska." *PNQ* 40 (1949) : 203–52; 42 (1951) : 147–66; [Supplement], *OHQ* 49 (1958) : 27–84.

Burrus, E. J. "An Introduction to Bibliographical Tools in Spanish Archives and Manuscript Collections for American History." *HAHR* 35 (1955) : 443–83.

Butler, Ruth Lapham. *A Checklist of Manuscripts in the Edward E. Ayer Collection.* Chicago, 1937.

Chapman, Charles Edward. *Catalogue of Materials in the Archivo General de Indias for the History of the Pacific Coast and the American Southwest.* Berkeley, 1919.

Cowan, Robert Ernest. *A Bibliography of the History of California and the Pacific West, 1510–1906.* Columbus, Ohio, 1952.

Domínguez Bordoña, Jesús. *Catálogo de la Biblioteca de Palacio.* Vol. 9. *Manuscritos de América.* Madrid, 1935.

Eberstadt, Edward and sons. *The Northwest Coast: A Century of Personal Narratives of Discovery, Conquest and Exploration . . . 1741–1841.* New York, 1941. Catalogue No. 119.

Essig, E. O. "Bibliography Relating to the Russians in California." *CHSQ* 12 (1933) : 210–16.

Fisher, Mary Ann. *Preliminary Guide to the Microfilm Collection in the Bancroft Library.* Berkeley, 1955.

Golder, Frank A. *Guide to Materials for American History in Russian Archives.* 2 vols. Washington, D.C., 1917–37.

Gómez Canedo, Lino. *Los Archivos de la historia de América. Período colonial Español.* 2 vols. Mexico City, 1961.

Griffin, Grace Gardner. "Foreign American History MSS Copies in Library of Congress." *Journal of Documentary Reproduction* 3 (1941) : 3–9.

Guillén y Tato, Julio Fernando. *Repertorio de los m.ss., cartas, planos y dibujos relativos a las Californias, existentes en este museo.* Madrid, Museo Naval, 1932.

Hill, Roscoe R. *Descriptive Catalogue of the Documents Relating to the History*

of the United States in the Papeles Procedentes de Cuba, Deposited in the
Archivo General de Indias at Seville. Washington, D.C., 1916.

Howay, Frederick William. "The Early Literature of the Northwest Coast."
*Proceedings of the Royal Society of Canada,* 3rd ser., 18 (1924) : sec. 2, 1–31.

Hussey, Roland D. "Manuscript Hispanic Americana in the Ayer Collection of
the Newberry Library, Chicago." *HAHR* 10 (1930) : 113–18.

*Índice histórico Español.* Barcelona, 1953–.

Jones, Cecil Knight. "Hispano-Americana in the Library of Congress." *HAHR*
2 (1919) : 96–104.

Judson, Katherine Berry. *Subject Index to the History of the Pacific Northwest
and Alaska as Found in the United States Government Documents, Congressional Series, in the American State Papers, and in Other Documents, 1789–
1881.* Olympia, Wash., 1913.

Kerner, Robert J. "Russian Expansion to America: Its Bibliographical Foundations." *Papers of the Bibliographical Society of America* 25 (1931) : 111–29.

Lada-Mocarski, Valerian. *Bibliography of Books on Alaska Published Before
1868.* New Haven, 1969.

London. British Museum. *Catalogue of the Manuscripts in the Spanish Language in the British Museum,* by Pascual d Gayangos. 4 vols. London, 1875–77.

Martin, Thomas P. "Transcripts, Facsimiles, and Manuscripts in the Spanish
Language in the Library of Congress, 1929." *HAHR* 9 (1929) : 243–46.

———. "Spanish Archive Materials and Related Materials in Other National
Archives, Copied for the Library of Congress, Project 'A' Gift Fund, 1927–
1929." *HAHR* 10 (1930) : 95–98.

Mecham, J. Lloyd. "The Northern Expansion of New Spain, 1522–1822: A Selected Descriptive Bibliographical List." *HAHR* 7 (1927) : 233–76.

Medina, José Toribio. *Biblioteca Hispano-Americana (1493–1810).* 7 vols. Santiago de Chile, 1898–1907.

———. *La Imprenta en México (1539–1821).* 8 vols. Santiago de Chile, 1908–12.

Millares Carlo, Agustín, and Mantecón, José Ignacio. *Repertorio bibliográfico
de las colecciones diplomáticas fundamentales para la historia de México.*
Mexico City, 1948.

Morgan, Dale L., and Hammon, George P. *A Guide to the Manuscript Collections of the Bancroft Library.* Vol. 1. *Pacific and Western Manuscripts (Except
California).* Berkeley and Los Angeles, 1963.

Paris. Bibliothèque Nationale. Département des Manuscrits. *Catalogue des manuscrits Espagnols et des manuscrits Portugais,* by M. Alfred Morel-Fatio. 2 vols.
Paris, 1881–92.

———. *Catalogue des manuscrits Mèxicains de la Bibliothèque Nationale.* Paris,
1899.

Paso y Troncoso, Francisco. *Índice de documentos de Nueva España existentes
en el Archivo de Indias de Sevilla.* 4 vols. Mexico City, 1928–31.

Paz, Julián. *Catálogo de la Colección de documentos inéditos para la historia de
España.* 2 vols. Madrid, 1930–31.

———. *Catálogo de manuscritos de América existentes en la Biblioteca Nacional.*
Madrid, 1933.

Peña y Cámara, José María. *Archivo General de Indias de Sevilla: Guía del Visitante.* Valencia, 1958.

Phillips, P. C. *The Lowery Collection. A Descriptive List of Maps of the Spanish Possessions Within the Present Limits of the United States, 1502–1820.* Washington, D.C., 1912.

Read, Benjamin Maurice. *Chronological Digest of the "Documentos Inéditos del Archivo de las Indias."* Albuquerque, 1914.

*Relaciones diplomáticas entre España y los Estados Unidos Según los Documentos del Archivo Histórico Nacional.* 2 vols. Madrid, 1944–46.

Sánchez Alonso, Benito. *Fuentes de la Historia Española e Hispano-Americana.* 3d ed. 3 vols. Madrid, 1952.

Schäfer, Ernesto. *Índice de la Colección de documentos inéditos de Indias.* 2 vols. Madrid, 1946–47.

Shepherd, William Robert. *Guide to the Materials for the History of the United States in Spanish Archives (Simancas, the Archivo Histórico Nacional, and Seville).* Washington, D.C., 1907.

Smith, Charles Wesley. *Pacific Northwest Americana: A Checklist of Books and Pamphlets Relating to the History of the Pacific Northwest.* 3d ed. Portland, 1950.

Steck, Francis Borgia. *A Tentative Guide to Historical Materials on the Spanish Borderlands.* Philadelphia, 1943.

Taylor, Alexander Smith. *Bibliografica Californica, 1510–1863.* San Francisco, 1891.

Torres Lanzas, Pedro, ed. *Relación descriptiva de los mapas, planos, &, de México y Floridas existentes en el Archivo General de Indias.* 2 vols. Seville, 1900.

———. *Catálogo de legajos del Archivo General de Indias, secciones primera y segunda, Patronato y Contaduría General del Consejo de Indias.* Seville, 1919.

Tudela de la Orden, José. *Los Manuscritos de América en las bibliotecas de España.* Madrid, 1954.

Twitchell, Ralph Emerson. *The Spanish Archives of New Mexico.* 2 vols. Cedar Rapids, Ia. 1914.

Vela, V. Vicente. *Índice de la colección de documentos de Fernández de Navarrete que posee el Museo Naval.* Madrid, 1946.

Wagner, Henry Raup. *Bibliography of Printed Works in Spanish Relating to Those Portions of the United States Which Formerly Belonged to Mexico.* Santiago de Chile, 1917. Supplement: Berkeley, 1918.

———. *The Spanish Southwest, 1542–1794: An Annotated Bibliography.* 2 vols. Albuquerque, 1937.

———. *The Plains and the Rockies: A Bibliography.* Rev. ed. by Charles L. Camp. Columbus, Ohio, 1953.

Winther, Oscar Osburn. *A Classified Bibliography of the Periodical Literature of the Trans-Mississippi West (1811–1957).* Bloomington, Ind., 1961.

Withington, Mary C. *A Catalogue of Manuscripts in the Collection of Western Americana Founded by William Robertson Coe . . . Yale University Library.* New Haven, 1952.

SPAIN AND SPANISH AMERICA

*La Administración de D. Frey Antonio María de Bucareli y Ursúa, cuadragésimo sexto Virrey de México.* Mexico City, 1936.

Aiton, Arthur S. *Antonio de Mendoza, First Viceroy of New Spain.* Durham, N.C., 1927.

———. "The Diplomacy of the Louisiana Cession." *AHR* 36 (1931) : 701–20.

Arco, Ricardo del. "El Almirante Pedro Porter y Casanate, explorador del Golfo de California. Noticias Inéditas." *Revista de Indias* 8 (1947) : 783–844.

Armas Medina, Fernando de. "Luisiana y Florida en el Reinado de Carlos III." *Estudios Americanos* 19, no. 100 (Seville, 1960) : 67–92.

Barras y Aragón, Francisco de las *Apresamiento del Galeón de Acapulco "Nuestra Señora de Covadonga" por el Comodoro Inglés Anson (30 de Junio de 1743).* Madrid, 1947.

Bécker, Jerónimo. *Historia de las relaciones exteriores de España durante el siglo XIX.* 3 vols. Madrid, 1924–26.

Berte-Langereau, Jack. "Marie-Louise de Parme et les Siens." *Hispania* 18 (Madrid, 1958) : 237–78.

Beruete y Moret, A. de. *Goya as Portrait Painter.* (Boston and New York, 1922).

Bobb, Bernard. "Bucareli and the Interior Provinces." *HAHR* 34 (1954) : 20–36.

———. *The Viceregency of Antonio María Bucareli in New Spain, 1771–1779.* Austin, 1962.

Brand, Donald Dilworth. "The Development of Pacific Coast Ports During the Spanish Colonial Period in Mexico." Sociedad Mexicana de Antropología. *Estudios antropológicos publicados en homenaje al Doctor Manuel Gamio* (Mexico City, 1956) : 577–91.

Burriel, Andrés Marcos. *Noticia de la California, y de su conquista temporal, y espiritual hasta el tiempo presente. Sacada de la historia manuscrita, formada en Mexico año de 1739 por el Padre Miguel Venegas, de la Compañia de Jesús; y de otras noticias, y relaciones antiguas, y modernas.* Madrid, 1757. 2d ed. 3 vols. Mexico City, 1943–44.

Burney, James. *A Chronological History of the Discoveries in the South Sea or Pacific Ocean.* 5 vols. London, 1803–17.

Cantillo, Alejandro del, ed. *Tratados, convenios y declaraciones de paz y de comercio que han hecho con las potencias estranjeras los monarcas españoles de la casa de Borbón.* Madrid, 1843.

Castillo Ledón, Luis. "El Puerto de San Blas. Su fundación y su historia." *Boletín de la Sociedad Mexicana de Geografía y Estadística* 60 (1945) : 583–95.

Cavo, Andrés, and Bustamante, Carlos María. *Los Tres Siglos de México durante el gobierno Español, hasta la entrada del ejército trigarante.* 4 vols. Mexico City, 1836–38.

Chadwick, French E. *The Relations of the United States and Spain: Diplomacy.* New York, 1909.

Chapman, Charles Edward. "The Difficulties of Maintaining the Department of San Blas, 1775–1777." *SHQ* 19 (1915–16) : 261–70.

————. *The Founding of Spanish California: The Northwestward Expansion of New Spain, 1687–1773*. New York, 1916.

————. *A History of California: The Spanish Period*. New York, 1921.

Chaumié, Jacqueline. "La Correspondance des agents diplomatiques de l'Espagne en France pendant la Révolution." *Bulletin hispanique* 37 (Bordeaux, 1935) : 189–95; 38 (1936) : 502–36.

Corona, Carlos. *Revolución y reacción en el reinado de Carlos IV*. Madrid, 1957.

Cuevas, Mariano. *Monje y marino: La vida y los tiempos de Fray Andrés de Urdaneta*. Mexico City, 1943.

Dahlgren, Erik Wilhelm. *Were the Hawaiian Islands Visited by the Spaniards Before Their Discovery by Captain Cook in 1778?* Stockholm, 1916 [1917].

Danvilla y Collado, Manuel. *Reinado de Carlos III*. 6 vols. Madrid, 1893–96.

*Diccionario marítimo Español*. Madrid, 1864.

*Enciclopedia general del mar*. 6 vols. Madrid and Barcelona, 1957.

*Enciclopedia vniversal ilvstrada evropeo-americana*. 70 vols. in 72. Barcelona, [1907?–30]; appendix, 10 vols. 1930–33. Usually referred to as *Enciclopedia Espasa*.

Fernández Duro, Cesáreo. *La Armada Española desde la unión de los reinos de Castilla y de Aragón*. 9 vols. Madrid, 1895–1903.

Ferrer del Río, Antonio. *Historia del reinado de Carlos III en España*. 4 vols. Madrid, 1856.

Floridablanca, José de Moñino y Redondo, Conde de. *El Testamento político del Conde de Floridablanca*. Edited by Antonio Rumeu de Armas. Madrid, 1962.

Fugier, André. *Napoléon et l'Espagne, 1799–1808*. 2 vols. Paris, 1930.

García de León y Pizarro, José. *Memorias*. 2d ed. 2 vols. Madrid, 1953.

Geiger, Maynard, *Franciscan Missionaries in Hispanic California, 1769–1848: a Biographical Dictionary*. San Marino, Calif., 1969.

Gemelli Careri, Giovanni Francesco. *Giro del Mondo*. 9 vols. Venice, 1791. English translation: "A Voyage Round the World." In vol. 4 of *A Collection of Voyages and Travels*, edited by Awnsham Churchill. 3d ed. 6 vols. London, 1744–46.

Gerhard, Peter. *Pirates on the West Coast of New Spain, 1565–1742*. Glendale, Calif., 1960.

————. *Pirates in Baja California*. Mexico City, 1963.

Godoy Alvarez de Faría Ríos Sánchez y Zarzoza, Manuel de. *Cuenta dada de su vida política por Don Manuel Godoy, Príncipe de la Paz, ó sean memorias críticas y aplogéticas para la historia del reinado del Señor D. Carlos IV. de Borbón*. 3 vols. Madrid, 1836–42. Most recent edition: *Memorias. Edición y estudio preliminar de Carlos Seco Serrano*. 2 vols. Madrid, 1956.

Gómez de la Puente, Eusebio. *Iconografía de gobernantes de la Nueva España*. Mexico City, 1921.

Gómez del Campillo, Miguel. *Relaciones diplomáticas entre España y los Estados Unidos, según documentos del Archivo Histórico Nacional*. 2 vols. Madrid, 1944–46.

Gutiérrez Camarena, Marcial. *San Blas y las Californias. Estudio histórico del puerto.* Mexico City, 1956.

Gutiérrez de los Ríos y Rohan-Chabot, Carlos José, Conde de Fernán-Núñez. *Vida de Carlos III.* 2 vols. Madrid, 1898.

Hernández y Sánchez-Barba, Mario. "Individualismo y colectivismo en la pacificación de una 'perisferia de tensión' Americana del siglo XVIII." *Revista de estudios políticos* 59 (Madrid, 1957) : 169–98.

Humboldt, Alexander von. *Essai politique sur le royaume de la Nouvelle Espagne.* 4 vols. and atlas. Paris, 1811; Spanish translation: *Ensayo político sobre el reino de la Nueva España.* 4 vols. Mexico City, 1941.

Humphreys, Robin A. "Richard Oswald's Plan for an English and Russian Attack on Spanish America, 1781–1782." *HAHR* 18 (1938) : 95–101.

Inskeep, Edward L. "San Blas, Nayarit: An Historical and Geographic Study." *JW* 2 (1963) : 133–44.

Izquierdo Hernández, Manuel. *Antecedentes y comienzos del reinado de Fernando VII.* Madrid, 1963.

Kinnaird, Lucia Burk, ed. "Creassy's Plan for Seizing Panama." *HAHR* 13 (1933) : 46–78.

Lafuente y Zamálloa, Modesto. *Historia general de España, desde los tiempos más remotos hasta nuestros días.* 30 vols. Madrid, 1850–69.

Leonard, Irving A. "An Attempted Indian Attack on the Manila Galleon." *HAHR* 11 (1931) : 69–76.

Longstaff, F. V. "Spanish Naval Bases and Ports on the Pacific Coast of Mexico, 1513–1833." *BCHQ* 16 (1952) : 181–89.

Madol, Hans Roger. *Godoy. Das Ende des Alten Spanien. Der Erste Diktator Unserer Zeit.* Berlin, 1932. Spanish translation: Madrid, 1943.

Majó Framis, Ricardo. *Vidas de los navegantes y conquistadores Españoles del siglo XV, XVI, XVII y XVIII.* 3 vols. Madrid, 1950–54.

Manfredini, James Manfred. *The Political Role of the Count of Revillagigedo, Viceroy of New Spain, 1789–1794.* New Brunswick, N.J., 1949.

Mange, Juan Matheo. *Luz de tierra incógnita en la América Septentrional y diario de las exploraciones en Sonora.* Mexico City, 1926.

Martí, Francisco, *El Proceso de El Escorial.* Pamplona, 1965.

Moñino y Redondo, José, Conde de Floridablanca. *Obras originales del Conde de Floridablanca.* Madrid, 1887.

Mosk, Sanford Alexander. "Spanish Voyages and Pearl Fisheries in the Gulf of California: A Study in Economic History." Ph.D. dissertation, University of California, 1931.

———. "The Cardona Company and the Pearl Fisheries of Lower California." *PHR* 3 (1934) : 50–61.

———. "Spanish Pearl-fishing Operations on the Pearl Coast in the Sixteenth Century." *HAHR* 18 (1938) : 392–400.

———. "Capitalistic Development in Lower California Pearl Fisheries." *PHR* 10 (1941) : 461–68.

Mousset, Albert. *Un Témoin ignoré de la Revolution, le Comte de Fernán Núñez, ambassadeur d'Espagne à Paris (1781–1791).* Paris, 1924.

Muriel, Andrés. *Gobierno del Señor Rey Carlos III*. Madrid, 1839.

———. *Historia de Carlos IV*. 6 vols. Madrid, 1893–94.

Navarro García, Luís de. "El Norte de Nueva España como problema político en el siglo XVIII." *Revista estudios americanos* 103 (Seville, 1960) : 15–31.

———. *Don José de Gálvez y la Comandancia General de las Provincias Internas del Norte de Nueva España*. Seville, 1964.

———. *Las Provincias Internas en el siglo XIX*. Seville, 1965.

Navarro Latorre, José, and Solano Costa, Fernando. *¿Conspiración española? 1787–1789: Contribución al estudio de las primeras relaciones históricas entre España y los Estados Unidos de Norteamérica*. Zaragoza, 1949.

*Official Correspondence Between Don Luis de Onís . . . and John Quincy Adams . . . in Relation to the Floridas and the Boundaries of Louisiana*. London, 1818.

Ogden, Adele, "The Californias in Spain's Pacific Otter Trade, 1775–1795." *PHR* 1 (1932) : 444–69.

———. "Russian Sea-Otter and Seal Hunting on the California Coast, 1803–1841." *CHSQ* 12 (1933) : 217–39.

———. *The California Sea Otter Trade, 1784–1848*. Berkeley and Los Angeles, 1941.

Onís y González, Luís de [Verus]. *Observations on the Conduct of our Executive Towards Spain*. n.p., n.d.

——— [Verus]. *[Observations on West Florida.]* n.p., n.d.

——— [Verus]. *Observations on the Existing Differences Between the Government of Spain and the United States, by Verus. No. III*. Philadelphia, 1817.

Onís y González, Luís de. *Memoria sobre las negociaciones entre España y Estados Unidos de América, que dieron motivo al tratado de 1819*. Madrid, 1820. 2d ed. Mexico City, 1826. English translation: *Memoir Upon the Negotiations Between Spain and the United States, Which Led to the Treaty of 1819*. Baltimore, 1821. 2d ed. Washington, D.C., 1821.

Orozco y Berra, Manuel. *Historia de la dominación española en México*. 4 vols. Mexico City, 1938.

Palacio Atard, Vicente. *El Tercer Pacto de familia*. Madrid, 1945.

Palóu, Fray Francisco. *Historical Memoirs of New California*. 4 vols. Berkeley, 1926.

Pavía, Francisco de Paula. *Galería biográfica de los generales de Marina*. 4 vols. Madrid, 1873–74.

Pérez de Guzmán y Gallo, Juan. *Las Relaciones políticas de España con las demás potencias de Europa al caer el Conde de Floridablanca en 1792*. Madrid, 1906.

———. *Embajada del Conde de Fernán Núñez en París durante el primer período de la Revolución Francesa*. Madrid, 1907.

———. "La Embajada de España en París en los comienzos de la Revolución Francesa." *España Moderna* 228 (1907) : 5–22; 229 (1908) : 59–71; 230 (1909) : 87–101. 2d ed. *Memorias de la Academia de la Historia* 12 (Madrid, 1910) : 1–132.

———. *Estudios de la vida, reinado, proscripción y muerte de Carlos IV y María Luisa de Borbón, Reyes de España*. 2d ed. Madrid, 1909.

Perkins, Dexter. "Russia and the Spanish Colonies, 1817–1818." *AHR* 28 (1923) : 656–73.

Pi y Margall, Francisco, and Pi y Arsuaga, Francisco. *Historia de España en el siglo XIX.* 9 vols. Barcelona, 1902.

Portillo y Diez de Sollano, Álvaro del. *Descubrimientos y exploraciones en las costas de California.* Madrid, 1947.

Powell, Philip W. *Soldiers, Indians & Silver: The Northward Advance of New Spain, 1550–1600.* Berkeley, 1952.

Priestly, Herbert Ingram. *José de Gálvez, Visitor-General of New Spain (1765–1771).* Berkeley, 1916.

————. *Franciscan Explorations in California.* Glendale, Calif., 1946.

Ramírez de Villa-Urrutia, Wenceslao, Marqués de Villa-Urrutia. *Relaciones entre España é Inglaterra durante la Guerra de Independencia: Apuntes para la historia diplomática de España de 1808 á 1814.* 3 vols. Madrid, 1911–14.

————. *La Reina María Luisa, esposa de Carlos IV.* Madrid, 1927.

Renaut, François Paul. *Le Pacte de famille et l'Amérique: La politique coloniale Franco-Espagnole de 1760 à 1792.* Paris, 1922.

Rivera Cambas, Manuel. *Los Gobernantes de México.* 2 vols. Mexico City, 1872.

Robertson, William Spence. "Francisco de Miranda and the Revolutionizing of Spanish America." *Annual Report of the American Historical Association, 1907* 1 (1908) : 189–539.

————. *The Life of Miranda.* 2 vols. Chapel Hill, N.C., 1929.

Robinson, William Davis. *A Cursory View of Spanish America, Particularly the Neighbouring Viceroyalties of Mexico and New Granada, Chiefly Intended to Elucidate the Policy of an Early Connection Between the United States and These Countries.* Georgetown, D.C., 1815.

————. *Memoirs of the Mexican Revolution: Including a Narrative of the Expedition of General Xavier Mina.* Philadelphia, 1820.

————. Letter to Senator John H. Eaton, January 15, 1821, in *Daily National Intelligencer,* 25 January 1821. Reprinted in *Niles' Weekly Register,* March 10, 21, and 25, 1821. Reprinted from the latter in *WHQ* 10 (1919) : 141–49.

Rodríguez Casado, Vicente. "El Pacífico en la política internacional española hasta la emancipación de América." *Estudios americanos* 2, no. 5 (Seville, 1950) : 1–30.

————. *La Política y los políticos en el reinado de Carlos III.* Madrid, 1962.

Rodríguez de Montalvo, Garci. *Las Sergas de Esplandián.* Madrid, 1510.

Rubio Mañé, Jorge Ignacio. "Síntesis histórica de la vida del II Conde de Revilla Gigedo, Virrey de Nueva España." *Anuario de estudios americanos* 6 (1949) : 451–96.

————. *Introducción al estudio de los virreyes de Nueva España, 1535–1746.* Mexico City, 1955.

Sales, Fray Luís de. *Noticias de la provincia de Californias.* Valencia, 1794.

Seco y Serrano, Carlos. "Godoy: El hombre y el político." In Manuel de Godoy. *Memorias.* 2 vols. Madrid, 1956. 1: vii–cxxxvii.

Schurz, William Lytle. "The Manila Galleon and California." *SHQ* 21 (1917) : 107–08.

————. "Mexico, Peru, and the Manila Galleon." *HAHR* 1 (1918) : 389–402.

————. "The Spanish Lake." *HAHR* 5 (1922) : 181–94.

————. *The Manila Galleon.* New York, 1939.

Soldevila Zubiburu, Fernando. *Historia de España.* 7 vols. Barcelona, 1952–59.

Sorel, Albert. "La Diplomatie Française et l'Espagne de 1792 à 1797." *Révue historique* 11 (1878) : 298–333; 12 (1879) : 279–313; 13 (1880) : 41–80, 241–78.

Stokes, John F. G. "Hawaii Discovered by the Spaniards: Theories Treated and Refuted." *Hawaiian Historical Society Papers* 20 (1939) : 38–113.

Tate, Vernon Dale. "The Founding of the Port of San Blas." Ph.D. dissertation, University of California, 1934.

Thomas, Martin, ed. "Creassy's Plan for Seizing Panama." *HAHR* 22 (1942) : 82–103.

Thurman, Michael E. "The Establishment of the Department of San Blas and Its Initial Naval Fleet: 1767–1770." *HAHR* 43 (1963) : 65–67.

————. *The Naval Department of San Blas, New Spain's Bastion for Alta California and Nootka, 1767 to 1798.* Glendale, Calif., 1967.

Tratchevsky, Alexandre. "L'Espagne à l'époque de la Revolution Française." *Révue historique* 31 (1886) : 1–55.

Vallentin, Antonina. *This I Saw: The Life and Times of Goya.* New York, 1949.

Vásquez de Acuña, Isidoro. "El Ministro de Indias Don José de Gálvez, Marqués de Sonora." *Revista de Indias* 19 (Madrid, 1959) : 448–73.

Velasco Ceballos, Rómulo. "Bucareli. Su Administración." *Publicaciones del Archivo General de la Nación* 30 (Mexico City, 1936) : vii–cix.

Wagner, Henry Raup. "Pearl Fishing Enterprises in the Gulf of California; the Expedition of Sebastián Vizcaíno." *HAHR* 10 (1930) : 188–220.

————. "Urdaneta and the Return Route from the Philippine Islands." *PHR* 13 (1944) : 313–16.

————. "The Descent on California in 1683." *CHSQ* 26 (1947) : 309–19.

Watson, Douglas Sloane. *The Spanish Occupation of California.* San Francisco, 1934.

Whitaker, Arthur P. *The Spanish-American Frontier, 1783–1795: The Westward Movement and the Spanish Retreat in the Mississippi Valley.* Boston and New York, 1927. 2d ed. Gloucester, Mass., 1962.

————. *The Mississippi Question, 1795–1803: A Study in Trade, Politics, and Diplomacy.* New York and London, 1934. 2d ed. Gloucester, Mass., 1962.

————. *The United States and the Independence of Latin America, 1800–1830.* Baltimore, 1941. 2d. ed. New York, 1964.

## THE SPANISH ON THE NORTHWEST COAST

### Sources

Bodega y Quadra, Juan Francisco de la. "Navegación hecha por Don Juan Francisco de la Bodega y Quadra, Teniente de Fragata de la Real Armada y comandante de la goleta "Sonora": A los descubrimientos de los mares y costa septentrional de California." *Colección de diarios y relaciones para la historia de los viajes y descubrimientos* 2 (Madrid, 1943) : 102–33.

Bodega y Quadra, Juan Francisco de la. "Primer Viaje hasta la altura de 58°
. . . 1775." *Anuario de la Dirección de Hidrografía* 3 (Madrid, 1865) : 279–93.
———. "Segunda Salida hasta los 61 grados en la fragata Nuestra Señora de
los Remedios (a) la Favorita . . . 1779." *Anuario de la Dirección de Hidro-
grafía* 3 (Madrid, 1865) : 294–331.
———. "Méthodo de la navegacion que congeturo combendrá se observe para
seguir los descubrimientos de la costa septentrional de la California . . ."
*Anuario de la Dirección de Hidrografía* 3 (Madrid, 1865) : 331–34.
Caamaño, Jacinto. "Expedición de la corbeta Aranzazú al mando del Teniente de
Navío D. Jacinto Caamaño á comprobar la relación de Fonte." *Colección
de documentos inéditos para la historia de España* 15 (Madrid, 1849) : 323–63.
———. "Extracto del diario . . . 1792." English translation: *BCHQ* 2 (1938):
195–222, 265–301.
Campa Cos, Fray Miguel de la. *A Journal of Explorations: Northward Along the
Coast From Monterey in . . . 1775.* Edited by John Galvin. San Francisco, 1964.
[Cardero, José,] *Relación del viaje hecho por las goletas Sútil y Mexicana en el
año de 1792.* 1 vol. and atlas. Madrid, 1802.
Carrasco y Guisasola, Francisco, ed. *Documentos referentes al reconocimiento
de las costas de las Californias, desde el Cabo de San Lucas al de Mendocino.*
Madrid, 1882.
Crespi, Juan. "Diario." [1774]. *PHSSC* 2 (1891) : 143–76. English translation : 177–
213. 2d ed. Donald C. Cutter, ed. *The California Coast: A Bilingual Edition of
Documents from the Sutro Collection.* Norman, Okla., 1969. Pp. 203–278.
Eliza, Francisco de. "Extracto de la navegación . . . 1791." English translation
in H. R. Wagner. *Spanish Explorations in the Strait of Juan de Fuca.* Santa
Ana, Calif., 1933. Pp. 141–54.
———. "Extracto de los acaecido en la navegacion . . ." English translation in
H. R. Wagner. "The Last Spanish Exploration of the Northwest Coast and
the Attempt to Colonize Bodega Bay." *CHSQ* 10 (1931) : 333–36.
Espinosa, Rafael. "Breve Relación del viaje que hizo el Capitan Sebastian Vizcaíno
en el año de mil seiscientos dos, a reconocer la costa exterior y occidental de la
California sobre el mar del Sur, y algunas noticias acerca de la Baja-California."
*Boletín de la Sociedad Mexicana de Geografía y Estadística* 5 (1857) : 429–46.
Ferrer Maldonado, Lorenzo. "Relación del descubrimiento del Estrecho de Anian
que hice yo . . . el año de 1588 . . ." In Alejandro Malaspina. *Viaje político-
científico alrededor del Mundo . . .* Madrid, 1885. Pp. 137–44.
Fonte, Bartholomew de. "A Letter from Admiral Bartholomew de Fonte the
Admiral of New Spain and Peru and Now Prince of Chile." *Monthly
Miscellany; or Memoirs for the Curious* 2 (London, 1708): April and June.
García Riobó, Fray Juan Antonio. "An Account of the Voyage Made by Father
John Riobó, as Chaplain of His Majesty's Frigate la Princesa and la Favorita
[in 1779] to Discover New Lands and Seas North of the Settlements of the Ports
of Monterey and of Our Father, San Francisco." *Catholic Historical Review* 4
(1918–19) : 222–29.
Goycoechea, Felipe. "Diario" [1793]. English translation in H. R. Wagner. "The

Last Spanish Exploration of the Northwest Coast and the Attempt to Colonize Bodega Bay." *CHSQ* 10 (1931) : 342–45.

Lok, Michael. "A Note Made by Me Michael Lok the Elder, Touching the Strait of Sea, Commonly Called Fretum Anian, in the South Sea, Through the Northwest Passage of Meta Incognita." In Samuel Purchas. *Hakluytus Posthumus, or Purchas His Pilgrimes. Vol. 3.* (London, 1625. Pp. 849–52. Hakluyt Society, *Works,* extra ser. 14 (Glasgow, 1906) : 415–21.

M. . . . C. . . . , R. . . . "Sobre Exploraciones y fundaciones de la costa septentrional de las Californias en tiempo del Excmo. Sr. Virrey Don Martín de Mayorga." *Boletín del Archivo General de la Nación* 14 (Mexico City, 1943): 409–21.

Malaspina, Alejandro. *Viaje político-científico alrededor del Mundo por las corbetas Descubierta y Atrevida.* Madrid, 1885.

"Manifiesto que el Discretorio del Apostólico Colegio de San Fernando hizo al Rey, en 26 de febrero de 1776, sobre los nuevos descubrimientos de la Alta California." In *Las Misiones de la Alta California.* Mexico City, 1914. Pp. 27–84. 2d ed. *Informe de el Appco. Colegio de San Fernando de México, sobre los descubrimientos entre los 30 y 60 grados de latitud.* Mexico City, 1948.

Martínez, Estéban José. "Diario de la Navegacion que Yo el Alf(ere)z. de Navio de la R(ea)l. Arm(a)da. D(o)n. Estevan Josef Martinez boy a executar al P(uer)to. de S(a)n. Lorenzo de Nuca, mandando la Frag(a)ta. Princessa, y Paquebot S(a)n. Carlos . . . 1789." Edited by Roberto Barreiro-Meiro. *Colección de diarios y relaciones para la historia de los viajes y descubrimientos* 6 (Madrid, 1964) : 19–148.

Martínez y Zayas, Juan. "Viage a la costa comprehendido entre la boca sur de Fuca, y el Puerto de San Francisco . . . 1793." English translation: H. R. Wagner. "The Last Spanish Exploration of the Northwest Coast and the Attempt to Colonize Bodega Bay." *CHSQ* 10 (1931) : 321–33.

Morse, William I., ed. *Letters of Alejandro Malaspina (1790–1791).* Boston, 1944.

Mourelle, Francisco Antonio. "Journal of a Voyage in 1775." In Barrington, Daines. *Miscellaines.* London, 1781. Pp. 469–534. 2d ed. *Voyage of the Sonora in the Second Bucareli Expedition to Explore the Northwest Coast . . . 1775.* San Francisco, 1920.

———. "Diario, 1779." Extract in Jean François Galaup de la Pérouse. *Voyage de La Pérouse autour du Monde.* Vol. 4. Paris, 1797. Pp. 324–42.

Moziño Suárez de Figueroa, José Mariano. *Noticias de Nutka. Diccionario de la lengua de los Nutkeses y descripción del volcán de Tuxtla.* Mexico City, 1913; *Noticias de Nutka, an Account of Nootka Sound in 1792.* Translated and edited by Iris Higbie Wilson. Seattle, 1970.

Pantoja y Arriaga, Juan. "Extracto de la navegación . . . 1791." *Colección de documentos inéditos para la historia de España* 15 (1849) : 111–21. English translation in H. R. Wagner. *Spanish Explorations in the Strait of Juan de Fuca.* Santa Ana, Calif., 1933. Pp. 155–98.

"Papers Relating to Nootka Sound and to Captain Vancouver's Expedition." *BCPAD Report, 1913* (Victoria, B.C., 1914) : 11–48.

Peña Saravia, Fray Tomás de la. "Diario" [1774]. *PHSSC* 2 (1891) : 83–11; English translation, 111–43. 2d ed. Donald C. Cutter, ed. *The California Coast. A Bilingual Edition of Documents from the Sutro Collection.* Norman, Okla., 1969. Pp. 135–201.

Quimper, Manuel. "Diario, 1790." Partly translated in H. R. Wagner. *Spanish Explorations in the Strait of Juan de Fuca.* Santa Ana, Calif., 1933. Pp. 82–128.

"Relación ó diario de la navegación que hizo Juan Rodríguez Cabrillo con dos navíos al descubrimiento del paso del Mar del Sur al Norte . . ." In H. R. Wagner, *Spanish Voyages to the Northwest Coast of America in the Sixteenth Century.* San Francisco, 1929. Pp. 450–63 (facsimile). Pp. 79–93 (English translation).

"Relación o diario muy circunstanciado del viaje que hizo el General Sebastián Vizcaíno." *Colección de diarios y relaciones para la historia de los viajes y descubrimientos* 4 (Madrid, 1944) : 41–68.

Revillagigedo, Juan Vicente de Güemes Pacheco de Padilla, Conde de. Letter to Manuel de Godoy, Mexico City, April 12, 1793. In Andrés Cavo. *Los Tres Siglos de México.* Vol. 3. Mexico City, 1836. Pp. 112–64.

Rodrigues Cermenho, Sebastião. "Derrotero y relación del descubrimiento que hizo el capitan y piloto mayor Sebastián Rz. Cermenho, por orden de su Magestad, hasta la Isla de Cedros." English translation in H. R. Wagner. "The Voyage to California of Sebastián Rodríguez Cermeño in 1595." *CHSQ* 3 (1924) : 10–20.

Servin, Manuel P., ed. "The Instructions of Viceroy Bucareli to Ensign Juan Perez." *CHSQ* 40 (1961) : 237–48.

"Short Account of Some Voyages Made by Order of the King of Spain, to Discover the State of the West American Coast From California Upward. Dated Madrid, 24 March, 1776." In *Summary Observations and Facts Collected From Late and Authentic Accounts of Russian and Other Navigators, to Show the Practicability and Good Prospect of Success in Enterprises to Discover a Northern Passage for Vessels by Sea, Between the Atlantic and Pacific Oceans . . .* London, 1776. Pp. 28–29.

Sierra, Fray Benito de la. "Diario, 1775." English translation in *CHSQ* 9 (1930): 209–42.

Suría, Tomás de. "Quaderno q. contiene el ramo de historia natural . . . 1791." CtY-BWA (Coe 464). English translation in *PHR* 5 (1936) : 240–76. Retranslated into Spanish. Mexico City, 1939.

Treat, John B. Letter to Samuel Breck, Nootka, July 14, 1789. In Robert L. Brunhouse, ed. "An American at Nootka Sound, 1789." *PNQ* 31 (1940) : 285–86.

Tobar y Tamáriz, José. [Informe,] September 18, 1789. In Fray Luís de Sales. *Noticias de la Provincia de California.* Valencia, 1794. Pp. 57–86.

"Viaje por las costas de las Californias de Juan Rodríguez Cabrillo." *Colección de diarios y relaciones para la historia de los viajes y descubrimientos* 1 (Madrid, 1943) : 29–42.

Viana, Francisco Xaxier de. *Diario del Teniente de Navío D. Francisco Xavier de Viana, trabajado en el viaje de las corbetas de S. M. C. "Descubierta" y*

*"Atrevida," en los años de 1789, 1790, 1791, 1792 y 1793.* Cerrito de la Victoria, Uruguay, 1849.

## Secondary Works

Alexander, William DeWitt. "The Relations Between the Hawaiian Islands and Spanish America in Early Times." *Hawaiian Historical Society Papers* 1 (1892) : 1–11.

Altamira y Crevea, Rafael. "The Share of Spain in the History of the Pacific Ocean." In *The Pacific Ocean in History: Papers and Addresses Presented at the Panama-Pacific Historical Congress, 1915*. New York, 1917. Pp. 34–54.

Bancroft, Hubert Howe. *History of the Northwest Coast*. 2 vols. San Francisco, 1886–88.

Barras de Aragón, Francisco de las. "Un Gran Marino Español del siglo XVIII: Don Francisco Antonio Maurelle," *Anales de la Asociación Española Para el Progreso de las Ciencias* 26, no. 1 (Madrid, 1951).

————. *D. Estéban José Martínez, el alumno del Colegio de San Telmo de Sevilla*. Madrid, 1953.

————. *Reconocimiento de las Islas Hawai (Sandwich) por el marino Español Quimper*. Madrid, 1954.

Barry, John Neilson. "Heceta's Chart Ends Long Dispute." Portland *Sunday Oregonian*, 20 September 1931.

————. "Spaniards in Early Oregon." *WHQ* 23 (1932) : 25–34.

————. "Who Discovered the Columbia River." *OHQ* 29 (1938) : 152–61.

Bolin, L. A. "Nombres Españoles en las costas de Alaska." *Revista General de Marina* 156 (Madrid, 1959) : 608–21.

Bolton, Herbert Eugene. *Fray Juan Crespi, Missionary Explorer on the Pacific Coast, 1769–1774*. Berkeley, 1927.

Bright, Verne. "Quivira, A Legendary City of the Northwest Coast [1540–1874]." *OHQ* 52 (1951) : 114–24.

Bulfinch, J. T. A. "Early Exploring Expeditions on the Northwest Coast." *The Washington Historian* 1 (1900) : 27–32.

Buño, Washington. "Escorbuto durante la exploración y conquista de América: Una epidemia de 1603 descrita por Torquemada." *Archivo Iberoamericano de historia de la medicina* 5 (1953) : 576–83.

Burpee, Lawrence Johnstone. *The Search for the Western Sea: The Story of the Exploration of North-western America*. 2 vols. Toronto, 1935.

Butterfield, Willshire. "Voyages and Explorations Leading to the Discovery of California." *Magazine of Western History* 5 (1886–87) : 624–30.

Carey, Charles H. "Some Early Maps and Myths." *OHQ* 30 (1929) : 14–32.

Carril, Bonifacio del. *La Expedición Malaspina en los mares Americanos del sur: La Colección Bauzá, 1789–1794*. Buenos Aires, 1961.

Caselli, Carlo. *Alessandro Malaspina e la Sua Spedizione Scientifica Intorno al Mondo, con Documenti Inediti*. Milan, 1929.

Caster, James G. "The Last Days of Don Juan Pérez, the Mallorcan Mariner." *JW* 2 (1963) : 15–21.

Chapman, Charles Edward. "The Alta California Supply Ships, 1773–76." *SHQ* 19 (1915) : 184–94.

———. "Gali and Rodriguez Cermenho: Exploration of California." *SHQ* 23 (1919–20) : 204–13.

———. "Sebastian Vizcaino: Exploration of California." *SHQ* 23 (1919–20) : 285–301.

*Compendio histórico de las navegaciones practicadas por oficiales y pilotos en buques de la Real Armada sobre las costas septe[n]trionales de California, con el objeto de descubrir y determinar la extensión y posición de sus distritos, e islas adyacentes. Ordenados por un oficial de la Marina Real Española. México: año de 1799.* Mexico City, 1948.

Cotton, S. J. *Stories of Nehalem.* Chicago, [1915].

Cutter, Donald C. *Malaspina in California.* San Francisco, 1960.

———. "California, Training Ground for Spanish Naval Heroes." *CHSQ* 49 (1961) : 109–22.

———. "Early Spanish Artists on the Northwest Coast." *PNQ* 54 (1963) : 150–57.

———. "Spanish Scientific Exploration Along the Pacific Coast." In *The American West—An Appraisal,* edited by Robert G. Ferris. Santa Fe, 1963.

———, ed. *The California Coast. A Bilingual Edition of Documents from the Sutro Collection.* Norman, Okla., 1969.

Davidson, George C. "An Examination of Some of the Early Voyages of Discovery and Exploration on the Northwest Coast of America, from 1539 to 1603." U.S. Coast and Geodetic Survey. *Report for 1886.* Appendix 7 (Washington, D.C., 1887).

———. "Early Voyages on the Northwestern Coast of America." *National Geographic Magazine* 5 (1893) : 235–56.

———. "Maps of the Northwest Coast of North America." In *The Alaska Boundary.* San Francisco, 1903. Pp. 49–53, 149–82.

DeLongchamp, Mildred K. "Explorations to the Northwest Coast of America Before 1800." Master's thesis, Adams State Teachers College, Alamosa, Colo., 1946.

Edwards, Clinton R. "Wandering Toponyms: El Puerto de la Bodega and Bodega Bay." *PHR* 33 (1964) : 253–72.

Espinosa y Tello, José. "Noticia de las principales expediciones hechas por nuestros pilotos del Departamento de San Blas al reconocimiento de la costa noroeste de América, desde el año de 1774 hasta el 1791, extractada de los diarios originales de aquellos navegantes." In Alejandro Malaspina. *Viaje político-científico alrededor del Mundo . . .* Madrid, 1885. Pp. 420–33.

Estrada, Rafael. *El Viaje de las corbetas Descubierta y Atrevida y los artistas de la expedición, 1789–1794.* Madrid, 1930.

[Evans, Elwood, et al.] *History of the Pacific Northwest: Oregon and Washington. Embracing an Account of the Original Discoveries on the Pacific Coast of North America.* 2 vols. Portland, Ore., 1889.

Fernández, Justino. *Tomás de Suría y su viaje con Malaspina.* Mexico City, 1939.

Fernández de Navarrete, Manuel. "Introducción," pp. i–clxvii in *Relación del viaje hecho por las goletas Sútil y Mexicana en el año de 1792,* by [José Cardero]. 1 vol. and alas. Madrid, 1802.

————, and Fernández de Navarrete, Eustaquio. "Examen histórico-crítico de los viajes y descubrimientos apócrifos del Capitán Lorenzo Ferrer Maldonado, de Juan de Fuca y del Almirante Bartolomé de Fonte." *Colección de documentos inéditos para la historia de España.* 112 vols. Madrid, 1842–95. Vol. 15 (1849) : 5–363.

Fleurieu, Charles Pierre Claret de. "Introduction historique," pp. i–cci in vol. 1 of *Voyage autour du Monde, pendent les années 1790, 1791 et 1792,* by Étienne Marchand. 6 vols. Paris, 1798–1800.

Furber, Holden. "An Abortive Attempt at Anglo-Spanish Commercial Cooperation in the Far East in 1793." *HAHR* 15 (1935) : 448–63.

Galbraith, Edith C. "Malaspina's Voyage Around the World." *CHSQ* 3 (1924): 215–37.

Giesecke, E. W. "The Case of the Shipwrecked Spaniard." Portland *Oregonian,* 11 February 1959, p. 20C.

González Ruíz, Felipe. *De la Florida a San Francisco: Los exploradores Españoles en los Estados Unidos (1492–1776).* Buenos Aires, 1949.

Greenhow, Robert. *Memoir, Historical and Political, on the Northwest Coast of North America, and the Adjacent Territories.* New York, 1840.

————. *The History of Oregon and California, and Other Territories on the North-west Coast of North America . . . .* Boston, 1844.

Harbron, John D. "Spaniards on the Coast." *Beaver* 288 (Winnipeg, Summer 1957) : 4–8.

Heizer, Robert Fleming. "The Introduction of Monterey Shells to the Indians of the Northwest Coast." *PNQ* 31 (1940) : 399–402.

————. *Archaeological Evidence of Sebastián Rodríguez Cermeño's California Visit in 1595.* San Francisco, 1942.

Hernández y Sánchez-Barba, Mario. "Españoles, Rusos e Ingleses en el Pacífico Norte, durante el siglo XVIII." *Información jurídica* 121 (Madrid, 1953) : 549–66.

————. *La Última Expansión Española en América.* Madrid, 1957.

Hidalgo Sereno, Jacinto. "Un Viaje de descubrimiento por la costa del Pacífico Noroeste." *Revista de Indias* 21 (Madrid, 1951) : 271–93.

Holmes, Maurice G. *From New Spain by Sea to the Californias 1519–1668.* Glendale, Calif., 1963.

Howay, Frederick William. "The Spanish Settlement at Nootka." *WHQ* 8 (1917): 163–71.

————. "The Spanish Discovery of British Columbia in 1774." *Canadian Historical Association Annual Report* 4 (1923) : 49–55.

————. "Presidential Address [concerning the discovery of the Strait of Juan de Fuca]." *BCHA Annual Report* 3 (1924) : 22–28.

Hult, Ruby El. *Lost Mines and Treasures of the Pacific Northwest.* Portland, Ore., 1957.

Johnson, Margaret Olive. "Spanish Exploration of the Pacific Coast by Juan Perez, 1774." Master's thesis, University of California, 1911.

Jordán de Urriés y Ruiz de Arana, Juan María, Marqués de Ayerbe de Llerta y de Rubí. "Sucesos ocurridos en Nootka en 1789." In *Tres Hechos memorables de la marina española en el siglo XVIII. Estudios históricos.* Madrid, 1907. Pp. 183–239.

Kingston, C. S. "Introduction of Cattle Into the Pacific Northwest." *WHQ* 10 (1919) : 141–49.

Lavender, David S. *Land of Giants: The Drive to the Pacific Northwest, 1750–1950.* New York, 1958.

Leonard, H. L. W. *Oregon Territory: Containing a Brief Account of Spanish, English, Russian and American Discoveries on the North-West Coast of America. Also, the Different Treaty Stipulations Confirming the Claim of the United States, and Overland Expeditions to the Columbia River . . . .* Cleveland, 1846.

Lummis, Charles F. *In Memory of Juan Rodríguez Cabrillo Who Gave the World California.* Chula Vista, Calif., 1913.

McDonald, Lucile. *Search for the Northwest Passage.* Portland, Ore., 1958.

Manjarres, Ramón de. "La Comunicación del Atlántico con el Pacífico; Ensayo sobre la parte de España en las investigaciones y proyectos." *Boletin del Centro de Estudios Americanistas de Sevilla* 1, no. 2 (1913) : 1–28.

Mathes, W. Michael. *Vizcaino and Spanish Expansion in the Pacific Ocean, 1580–1630.* San Francisco, 1968.

Novo y Colson, Pedro. *Historia de las exploraciones árticas hechas en busca del paso del nordeste.* Madrid, 1880.

————. *Sobre los Viages apócrifos de Juan de Fuca y de Lorenzo Ferrer Maldonado.* Madrid, 1881.

Nunn, George Emra. *Origin of the Strait of Anian Concept.* Philadelphia, 1929.

Ocaranza, Fernando. "Verdades, mentiras y fantasías, que fueron escritas por un fraile Carmelita, cuando formó parte del séquito de Sebastián Vizcaíno en su segunda entrada a las Californias (1596)." *Memorias de la Academia*

Priestly, Herbert Ingram. "The Log of the Princesa by Estévan José Martínez. *Mexicana de la Historia* 18 (1958) : 232–40.

"The Oregon Beeswax Mystery." *Shell News* 29, no. 12 (1961) : 20–21. What Does it Contribute to Our Knowledge of the Nootka Sound Controversy?" *OHQ* 21 (1920) : 21–31.

Ramos-Catalina y de Bardaxí, María Luisa. "Expediciones científicas á California en el siglo XVIII." *Anuario de estudios americanos* 8 (1956) : 217–310.

Rasmussen, Louise. "Artists with Explorations on the Northwest Coast." *OHQ* 42 (1941) : 311–16.

Raup, Hallock Floy. "The Delayed Discovery of San Francisco Bay." *CHSQ* 27 (1948) : 289–96.

Ratto, Héctor Raúl. *La Expedición de Malaspina (Siglo XVIII).* Buenos Aires, 1945.

Rickard, T. A. "The Strait of Anian." *BCHQ* 5 (1941) : 161–83.

Ruin, Ida Louise. "The Voyages of Vizcaíno." Master's thesis, University of California, 1926.

Sage, Walter N. "Spanish Explorers of the British Columbia Coast." *CHR* 12 (1931) : 390–406.

Schafer, Joseph. *The Acquisition of Oregon Territory*. Part 1: *Discovery and Exploration*. Eugene, Ore., 1908.

Scholefield, Ethelbert Olaf Stuart, ed. *British Columbia From the Earliest Times to the Present*. 4 vols. Vancouver, B.C., 1914. (Vol. 2 by Frederick W. Howay.)

Smith, Francis E. "The Nootka Sound Diplomatic Discussion, August 28 to September 26, 1792." *Americana* 19 (1925) : 133–45.

———. "Nootkaland; a Narrative of the Exploration and Survey of the Northwest Coast of North America." *Americana* 19 (1925) : 336–78.

Smith, Silas B. "Early Wrecks on the Oregon Coast." *Oregon Native Son* 1 (1899–1900) : 443–44.

Speck, Gordon. *Northwest Explorations*. Portland, Ore., ca.1954.

Stafford, Orin Fletcher. "Wax of Nehalem Beach." *OHQ* 9 (1908) : 24–41.

Stewart, Charles L. "Martínez and López de Haro on the Northwest Coast, 1788–1789." Ph.D. dissertation, University of California, 1936.

———. "Why Spaniards Temporarily Abandoned Nootka Sound in 1789." *CHR* 17 (1936) : 168–78.

Sykes, Godfrey. "The Mythical Straits of Anian." *Bulletin of the American Geographical Society* 47 (1915) : 161–72.

Tate, Vernon Dale. "The Juan Pérez Expedition to the Northwest Coast, 1774." Master's thesis, University of California, 1930.

Taylor, Alexander Smith. *Discovery of California and Northwest America. The First Voyage of the Coast of California; Made in the Years 1542 and 1543, by Juan Rodríguez Cabrillo and His Pilot, Bartolomé Ferrelo*. San Francisco, 1853.

———. "Memorials of Juan de Fuca." *Hutchings' Illustrated California Magazine* 4 (1859) : 116–22, 161–67.

Taylor, George P. "Spanish-Russian Rivalry in the Pacific, 1769–1820." *The Americas* 25 (1958) : 109–27.

Thurman, Michael E. "Juan Bodega y Quadra and the Spanish Retreat From Nootka, 1790–1794." In *Reflections of Western Historians: Papers of the 7th Annual Conference of the Western History Association . . . 1967*. Tucson, 1969, pp. 49–63.

Torre Revello, José. *Los Artistas pintores de la expedición Malaspina*. Buenos Aires, 1944.

Torres Campos, Rafael. *España en California y en el Noroeste de América: Conferencia . . . .* Madrid, 1892

Tucker, Ephraim. *A History of Oregon Containing a Condensed Account of the Most Important Voyages and Discoveries of the Spanish, American and English Navigators on the North West Coast of America; and of the Different Treaties Relative to the Same . . . .* Buffalo, N.Y., 1844.

Van Alstyne, Richard W. "International Rivalries in the Pacific Northwest." *OHQ* 46 (1945) : 185–218.

Vela, V. Vicente. "Expedición de Malaspina: Epistolario referente a su organización." *Revista de Indias* 11 (1951) : 193–218.

Wagner, Henry Raup. "The Discovery of California." *CHSQ* 1 (1922–23) : 36–56.

Wagner, Henry Raup. "The Voyage of Pedro de Unamuno to California in 1587." *CHSQ* 2 (1923–24) : 140–60.

———. "The Voyage to California of Sebastian Rodriguez Cermeño in 1595." *CHSQ* 3 (1924) : 3–24.

———. "Quivira, a Mythical California City." *CHSQ* 3 (1924) : 262–67.

———. "California Voyages, 1539–1541: Translations of Original Documents." *CHSQ* 3 (1924) : 307–97.

———. "Some Imaginary California Geography." *PAAS,* n.s. 36 (1926) : 83–129.

———. *Spanish Voyages to the Northwest Coast of America in the Sixteenth Century.* San Francisco, 1929.

———. "Fray Benito de la Sierra's Account of the Hezeta Expedition to the Northwest Coast in 1775." *CHSQ* 9 (1930) : 201–08.

———. "Apocryphal Voyages to the Northwest Coast of America." *PAAS,* n.s. 41 (1931) : 179–234.

———. "The Last Spanish Exploration of the Northwest Coast and the Attempt to Colonize Bodega Bay." *CHSQ* 9 (1931) : 313–45.

———. "A Map of Cabrillo's Discoveries." *CHSQ* 11 (1932) : 44–6.

———. "Biblio-Cartography." *PHR* 1 (1932) : 103–10.

———. *Spanish Explorations in the Strait of Juan de Fuca.* Santa Ana, Calif., 1933.

———. "Journal of Tomás de Suría of His Voyage With Malaspina to the Northwest Coast of America in 1791." *PHR* 5 (1936) : 234–39.

———. *The Cartography of the Northwest Coast of America to the Year 1800.* 2 vols. Berkeley, 1937.

———. "Creation of Rights of Sovereignty Through Symbolic Acts." *PHR* 7 (1938) : 297–326.

———. *Juan Rodríguez Cabrillo, Discoverer of California.* San Francisco, 1941.

———. "Francisco de Ulloa Returned." *CHSQ* 19 (1940) : 240–44.

———. "Early Franciscan Activities on the West Coast." *Historical Society of Southern California Quarterly* 23 (1941) : 115–26.

———. "Memorial of Pedro Calderón y Henríquez Recommending Monterey as a Port for the Philippine Galleons with a View to Preventing Russian Encroachment in California." *CHSQ* 23 (1944) : 219–25.

Wagner, Henry Raup, and Newcombe, W. A. "The Journal of Jacinto Caamaño." *BCHQ* 2 (1938) : 189–94.

Walbran, John T. *British Columbia Coast Names, 1592–1906.* Ottawa, 1909.

Waterman, Ivan R. *Juan Rodrigues Cabrillo, Discoverer of California.* Sacramento, 1935.

Whitebrook, Robert Ballard. *Coastal Exploration of Washington.* Palo Alto, Calif., 1959.

Wilson, Iris Higbie. "Scientific Aspects of Spanish Exploration in New Spain During the Late Eighteenth Century." Master's thesis, University of Southern California, Los Angeles, 1962.

———. "Spanish Scientists in the Pacific Northwest, 1790–1792." In *Reflections of Western Historians: Papers of the 7th Annual Conference of the Western History Association . . . 1967.* Tucson, 1969. Pp. 31–47.

Ybarra y Bergé, Javier de. *De California á Alaska. Historia de un descubrimiento.* Madrid, 1945.

OTHER NATIONALITIES ON THE NORTHWEST COAST

*Sources*

[Bell, Edward.] *A New Vancouver Journal on the Discovery of Puget Sound, By a Member of the Chatham's Crew.* Edited by E. S. Meany. Seattle, 1915.

[Beresford, William.] *A Voyage Round the World; But More Particularly to the North West Coast of America; Performed in 1785–88.* Edited by Captain George Dixon. London, 1789.

Boit, John. "Log of the Second Voyage of the *Columbia.*" In F. W. Howay, ed. *Voyages of the "Columbia."* Boston, 1941. pp. 363–431.

Bishop, Charles. "Journal of the *Ruby,* 1794–95." Edited by T. C. Elliott. *OHQ* 28 (1927) : 258–80; 29 (1928) : 337–46.

British Museum. Department of Printed Books. Map Room. *Sir Francis Drake's Voyage Round the World, 1577–1580: Two Contemporary Maps.* London, 1927.

Broughton, William Robert. *A Voyage of Discovery to the North Pacific Ocean . . . in the Years 1795, 1796, 1797, 1798.* London, 1804.

Colnett, James. *A Voyage to the South Atlantic and Round Cape Horn Into the Pacific Ocean.* London, 1798.

———. *The Journal of Captain James Colnett Aboard the Argonaut from April 26, 1789 to Nov. 3, 1791.* Edited by F. W. Howay. Toronto, 1940.

Cook, James. *A Voyage to the Pacific Ocean.* 3 vols. and atlas. London, 1784.

Cox, Ross. *Adventures on the Columbia River.* 2 vols. London, 1831.

Coxe, William. *Account of the Russian Discoveries Between Asia and America.* London, 1780.

Dalrymple, Alexander. *Plan for Promoting the Fur-Trade, and Securing it to This Country, by Uniting the Operations of the East-India and Hudson's-Bay Companys.* London, 1789.

Dixon, George. *Letter and Memorandum From Capt. George Dixon to Sir Joseph Banks Regarding the Fur Trade on the Northwest Coast, A.D. 1789.* San Francisco, 1941.

———. *Remarks on the Voyages of John Meares, Esq. in a Letter to That Gentleman.* London, 1790. Facsimile: F. W. Howay, ed. *The Dixon-Meares Controversy.* Toronto and New York, ca.1929.

———. *Further Remarks on the Voyages of John Meares, Esq. in Which Several Important Facts, Misrepresented in the Said Voyages, Relative to Geography and Commerce, are Fully Substantiated. To Which is Added, a Letter from Captain Duncan, Containing a Decisive Refutation of Several Unfounded Assertions of Mr. Meares, and a Final Reply to His Answer.* London, 1791. Facsimile: F. W. Howay, ed. *The Dixon-Meares Controversy.* Toronto and New York, ca.1929.

Douglas, William. "Extract of the Journal of the Iphigenia." [April 20–June 2, 1789.] In John Meares. *Memorial.* Portland, Ore., 1933. Pp. 56–76.

*Drake, the World Encompassed by Sir Francis Drake, Being His Next Voyage to*
    *That to Nombre de Dios Formerly Imprinted; Carefully Collected Out of the*
    *Notes of Master Francis Fletcher, Preacher in This Imployment, and Diuers*
    *Others His Followers in the Same* . . . . London, 1628.

Ellis, William. *An Authentic Narrative of a Voyage Performed by Captain Cook*
    . . . . 2 vols. London, 1782.

"Examination of the Russian Claims to the Northwest Coast of America." *North*
    *American Review* 15 (1822) : 370–401.

Felch, Alpheus. "Explorations of the Northwest Coast of the United States.
    Report on the Claims of the Heirs of Captains Kendrick and Gray." *HM,*
    2d ser. 8 (1870) : 155–75.

Franchère, Gabriel de la. *Rélation d'un voyage à la côte du Nord-ouest de*
    *l'Amérique Septentrionale, dans les annés 1810, 11, 12, 13 et 14* . . . .
    Montreal, 1820. English translation: *Narrative of a Voyage to the Northwest*
    *Coast of America in the Years 1811, 1812, 1813 and 1814 or the First American*
    *Settlement on the Pacific.* New York, 1854.

Haswell, Robert. "Log of the First Voyage of the *Columbia.*" In F. W. Howay,
    ed. *Voyages of the "Columbia."* Boston, 1941. Pp. 2–107.

———. Log of the Second Voyage of the *Columbia.* In ibid. Pp. 293–359.

Henry, Alexander, and Thompson, David. *The Manuscript Journals of Alexander*
    *Henry and of David Thompson, 1799–1814: New Light on the Early History*
    *of the Greater North-west.* Edited by Elliott Coues. 3 vols. New York, 1897.

Hill, Samuel. "Loss of the Boston." *Columbian Sentinel, Boston,* 20 May 1807.
    Reprinted in *WHQ* 27 (1926): 282–87.

Hoskins, John. "Narrative of the Second Voyage of the *Columbia.*" In F. W.
    Howay, ed. *Voyages of the "Columbia."* Boston, 1941, Pp. 161–289.

Howay, Frederick William. "Captains Gray and Kendrick: The Barrell Letters."
    *WHQ* 12 (1921) : 243–71.

———. *The Dixon-Meares Controversy.* Toronto and New York, ca.1929.

———. "Letters Concerning Voyages of British Vessels to the Northwest Coast
    of America, 1787–1809." *OHQ* 39 (1938) : 307–13.

———. *Voyages of the "Columbia" to the Northwest Coast, 1787–1790 and*
    *1790–1793.* Boston, 1941.

Hunter, W. *Letter From W. Hunter Regarding the Voyage of the Vessels "Captain*
    *Cook" and "Experiment" to the Northwest Coast in the Fur Trade.* San
    Francisco, 1940.

"Instructions to John Meares, 24 December 1787." In Vincent Todd Harlow,
    ed. *British Colonial Developments, 1774–1834: Select Documents.* Oxford,
    1953. Pp. 30–32.

Jewitt, John Rodgers. *Narrative of the Adventures and Sufferings of John R.*
    *Jewitt: Only Survivor of the Crew of the Ship Boston, During a Captivity of*
    *Nearly Three Years Among the Savages of Nootka Sound: With an Account*
    *of the Manners, Mode of Living, and Religious Opinions of the Natives* . . . .
    [Middletown, Conn., 1815.]

*A Journal of a Voyage Around the World.* London, 1781.

Kotzebue, Otto von. *A New Voyage Round the World, in the Years 1823, 24, 25, and 26.* London, 1830.

Kruzenshtern, Ivan Fedorovich. *Voyage Round the World in the Years 1803–1806, by Order of His Imperial Majesty Alexander the First, on Board the Ships "Nadeshda" and "Neva"* London, 1813.

[L. . . . , C. . . .] *A Voyage Round the World, in the Years 1785, 1786, 1787, and 1788. Performed in the King George, Commanded by Captain Portlock; and the Queen Charlotte, Commanded by Captain Dixon.* London, 1789.

Langsdorff, Georg Heinrich von. *Voyages and Travels in Various Parts of the World, During the Years 1803, 1804, 1805, 1806 and 1807.* 2 vols. London, 1813–14.

La Pérouse, Jean François Galaup de. *Voyage de La Pérouse Autour du Monde.* 4 vols. and atlas. Paris, 1797.

Ledyard, John. *A Journal of Captain Cook's Last Voyage to the Pacific Ocean.* Hartford, Conn., 1783. *John Ledyard's Journal of Captain Cook's Last Voyage.* James K. Munford, ed. Corvallis, Ore., 1963.

Lisianskii, Iurii Fedorovich. *A Voyage Round the World, in the Years 1803, 4, 5 & 6: Performed, by Order of His Imperial Majesty Alexander the First, Emperor of Russia, in the Ship "Neva."* London, 1814.

Lütke, Fedor Petrovich. *Voyage autour du Monde fait par ordre de Sa Majesté l'Empereur Nicolas I^er. sur la corvette le Séniavine pendant les annés 1826, 1827, 1828 et 1829.* 3 vols. and atlas. Paris, 1835–36.

Mackenzie, Alexander. *Voyages from Montreal, on the River St. Lawrence, Through the Continent of North America to the Frozen and Pacific Oceans, in the years 1789 and 1793.* London, 1801. Reprinted in American Explorer Series. 2 vols. New York, 1922.

Marshall, James Stirrat, and Marshall, Carrie, eds. *Pacific Voyages: Selections From Scots Magazine, 1771–1808.* Portland, Ore., 1960.

Meares, John. *Authentic Copy of the Memorial to the Right Honourable William Wyndham Grenville, One of His Majesty's Principal Secretaries of State, by Lieutenant John Mears, of the Royal Navy; Dated 30th April, 1790, and Presented to the House of Commons, May 13, 1790. Containing Every Particular Respecting the Capture of the Vessels in Nootka Sound.* London, 1760 [i.e., 1790]. 2d ed. by Nellie B. Pipes. Portland, Ore., 1933.

———. *Voyages Made in the Years 1788 and 1789, From China to the North West Coast of America.* London, 1790.

———. *An Answer to Mr. George Dixon, Late Commander of the Queen Charlotte in the Service of Messrs. Etches and Company . . . in Which the Remarks of Mr. Dixon on the Voyages to the North West Coast of America, & Lately Published, are Fully Considered and Refuted.* London, 1791. Facsimile: F. W. Howay, ed. *The Dixon-Meares Controversy.* Toronto and New York, ca.1929.

Menzies, Archibald. *Menzies' Journal of Vancouver's Voyage, April to October, 1792.* Victoria, B.C., 1923.

———. Journal, November 1792 to December 1793. *CHSQ* 2 (1924) : 265–340.

Morris, Grace Parker, ed. "Some Letters From 1792–1800 in the China Trade." *OHQ* 42 (1941) : 48–87.

Mortimer, George. *Observations and Remarks Made During a Voyage to the Islands of Teneriffe . . . Owyhee, the Fox Islands on the Northwest Coast of America . . . in the Brig Mercury Commanded by John Henry Cox.* London, 1791.

[Müller, Gerhard Friedrich.] *A Letter From a Russian Sea-Officer, to a Person of Distinction at the Court of St. Petersburgh; Containing His Remarks Upon Mr. de L'Isle's Chart and Memoir, Relative to the New Discoveries Northward and Eastward From Kamtschatka. Together With Some Observations on That Letter.* Edited by Arthur Dobbs. London, 1754.

———. *Voyages From Asia to America, for Completing the Discoveries of the North West Coast of America. To Which is Prefixed, a Summary of the Voyages Made by the Russians on the Frozen Sea, in Search of a North East Passage.* London, 1761.

Myers, John. *The Life, Voyages and Travels of Capt. John Myers, Detailing His Adventures During Four Voyages Round the World; and Exhibiting a Most Instructive Description of the North-West Trade.* London, 1817.

"New Fur Trade." *World,* 6 and 13 October 1788. Reprinted in *"New Fur Trade," an Article From the World . . . Describing the Earliest Voyage to the Northwest Coast of America.* San Francisco, 1941.

Nuttall, Zelia, ed. *New Light on Drake: A Collection of Documents Relating to His Voyage of Circumnavigation, 1577–1580.* London, 1914.

*On the Ambitious Projects of Russia in Regard to North West America, With Particular Reference to New Albion & New California.* London, 1830. 2d. ed., with an introduction by George P. Hammond. Kentfield, Calif., 1955.

Patterson, Samuel. *Narrative of the Adventures and Sufferings of Samuel Patterson.* Palmer, Mass., 1817. 2d ed. Providence, 1825.

Péron, François. *Mémoires du Capitain Péron, sur ses voyages aux côtes d'Afrique, en Arabie, . . . aux côtes nord-ouest de l'Amérique . . . etc.* 2 vols. Paris, 1824.

Pipes, Nellie B., ed. "Later Affairs of Kendrick; Barrell Letters." *OHQ* 30 (1929): 95–105.

Portlock, Nathaniel. *A Voyage Round the World; but More Particularly to the North West Coast of America; Performed in 1785, 1786, 1787, and 1788 in the King George and Queen Charlotte, Captains Portlock and Dixon.* London, 1789.

Puget, Peter. "The Vancouver Expedition: Peter Puget's Journal of the Exploration of Puget Sound, May 7–June 11, 1792." *PNQ* 30 (1939) : 177–217.

Rezanov, Nikolai Petrovich. *The Rezanov Voyage to Nueva California in 1806: the Report of Count Nikolai Petrovich Rezanov of His Voyage to That Provincia of Nueva España From New Archangel.* Edited by T. C. Russell. San Francisco, 1926.

[Rickman, John.] *Journal of Captain Cook's Last Voyage to the Pacific Ocean.* London, 1781.

Roquefeuil, Camille de. *A Voyage Round the World, 1816–19, in the ship "Borde-lais."* London, 1823.

Sarychev, Gabriil Andreevich. *Account of a Voyage of Discovery to the North-east of Siberia, the Frozen Ocean, and the North-east Sea.* 2 vols. in 1. London, 1806–07.

Sauer, Martin. *An Account of a Geographical and Astronomical Expedition to the Northern Parts of Russia.* London, 1802.

[David Scott & Co.] *Sailing Instructions Governing the Voyage of the Vessels "Captain Cook" and "Experiment" to the Northwest Coast in the Fur Trade.* San Francisco, 1941.

Strange, James. *James Strange's Journal and Narrative of the Commercial Expedition From Bombay to the North-west Coast of America.* Madras, 1928.

Stuart, Robert. *Discovery of the Oregon Trail; Narratives of His Overland Trip Eastward From Astoria in 1812–13; the Tonquin's Voyage and Events at Fort Astoria; and Wilson Hunt's Diary of His Overland Trip in 1811–12.* New York, 1935.

Tate, Vernon Dale, ed. "Spanish Documents Relating to the Voyage of the "Racoon" to Astoria and San Francisco." *HAHR* 18 (1938) : 183–91.

Vancouver, George. "A Narrative of My Proceedings in His Majesty's Sloop Discovery from 18th of August to the 26th. September 1792, Particularly Relative to Transactions with Sigr. Quadra, Respecting the Cession of Certain Territories on the N. W. Coast of America." In "Papers Relating to Nootka Sound and to Captain Vancouver's Expedition." *BCPAD Report, 1913* (1914): 11–30.

———. *A Voyage of Discovery to the North Pacific Ocean and Round the World.* 3 vols. and atlas. London, 1789.

Zimmermann, Heinrich. *Zimmermann's Captain Cook: An Account of the Third Voyage of Captain Cook Around the World, 1776–1780.* Toronto, ca.1930. Translated from the German edition of 1781.

### Secondary Works

Andrews, Clarence L. "The Wreck of the St. Nicholas." *WHQ* 13 (1922) : 27–31.

———. "Russian Plans for American Dominion." *WHQ* 18 (1927) : 83–92.

Andrews, K. R. "The Aims of Drake's Expedition of 1577–1580." *AHR* 73 (1968): 724–41.

Atherton, Gertrude. "Nicolai Petrovich Rezanov." *North American Review* 189 (1909) : 651–61.

Augur, Helen. *Passage to Glory: John Ledyard's America.* New York, 1946.

Barbeau, Charles Marius. *Pathfinders in the North Pacific.* Caldwell, Idaho, 1958.

Barras de Aragón, Francisco de las. "Los Rusos en el Noroeste de América." *Anales de la Asociación Española Para el Progreso de las Ciencias* 31 (Madrid, 1956) : 111–26.

Barry, John Neilson. "Broughton on the Columbia in 1792." *OHQ* 27 (1926): 397–411.

Barry, John Neilson. "A Valuable Manuscript Which May be Found." *WHQ* 19 (1928) : 112–16.

———. "Broughton's Reconnaissance of the San Juan Islands in 1792." *WHQ* 21 (1930) : 55–60.

———. "Broughton, Up Columbia River, 1792." *OHQ* 32 (1931) : 301–12.

———. "Columbia River Exploration, 1792." *OHQ* 33 (1932) : 31–42, 143–55.

Berkh, Vasilii Nikolaevich. *Khronologicheskaia istoriia otkrytiia Aleutskikh ostrovov* . . . . St. Petersburg, 1823. English edition: *The Chronological History of the Discovery of the Aleutian Islands or the Exploits of the Russian Merchants*. Seattle, 1938.

Bishop, R. P. "Drake's Course in the North Pacific." *BCHQ* 3 (1939) : 151–82.

Blok, T. "The Russian Colonies in California—A Russian Version." *CHSQ* 12 (1933) : 189–90.

Blue, George Verne. "Vessels Trading on the Northwest Coast of America, 1804–1814." *WHQ* 19 (1928) : 294–95.

———. "French Interest in Pacific America in the Eighteenth Century." *PHR* 4 (1935) : 246–66.

Boone, Lalla Rookh. "Vancouver on the Northwest Coast." *OHQ* 25 (1934) : 193–227.

Bowman, J. N. "Cook's Place in Northwest History." *WHQ* 1 (1906–07) : 113–21.

Brereton, Robert Maitland. *Question: Did Sir Francis Drake Land on Any Part Of the Oregon Coast?* Portland, Ore., [1907?].

Brunhouse, Robert L. "An American at Nootka Sound, 1789." *PNQ* 31 (1940) : 285–86.

Buache, Jean Nicolas. *Mémoire sur les pays l'Asie et de l'Amérique, situés au nord de la Mer du Sud*. Paris, 1775.

Buache, Philippe. *Considerations géographiques et physiques sur les nouvelles découvertes au nord . . . de la Mer du Sud . . . .* Paris, 1753.

Bullfinch, Thomas. *Oregon and Eldorado: Or Romance of the Rivers*. Boston, 1866.

Bushnell, David I. *Drawings by John Webber of Natives of the Northwest Coast of America, 1778*. Smithsonian Miscellaneous Collection. Vol. 80, no. 10. Washington, D.C., 1928.

California Historical Society. *Drake's Plate of Brass, Evidence of His Visit to California in 1579*. San Francisco, 1937.

———. *The Plate of Brass: Evidence of the Visit of Francis Drake to California in the Year 1579*. San Francisco, 1953.

Chevigny, Hector. *Lost Empire. The Life and Adventures of Nikolai Petrovich Rezanov*. New York, 1937.

———. *Lord of Alaska. The Story of Baranov and the Russian Adventure*. New York, 1942.

———. *Russian America: the Great Alaskan Venture, 1741–1867*. New York, 1965.

Chinard, Gilbert. *Le Voyage de Lapérouse sur les côtes de l'Alaska et de la Californie: 1786*. Baltimore, 1937.

Chittenden, Hiram Martin. *The American Fur Trade of the Far West.* New York, 1902.

Dahlgren, Erik Wilhelm. *Les Relations commerciales et maritimes entre la France et les côtes de l'Ocean Pacifique.* Paris, 1909.

Davidson, George C. *Identification of Sir Francis Drake's Anchorage on the Coast of California in the Year 1579.* San Francisco, 1890.

———. "The Tracks and Landfalls of Bering and Chirikof on the Northwest Coast of America." *Transactions and Proceedings of the Geographical Society of the Pacific,* 2d ser. 1 (1901) : 1–44.

———. "Francis Drake on the Northwest Coast of America in the Year 1579." *Transactions and Proceedings of the Geographical Society of the Pacific,* 2d ser. 5 (1908).

———. *Francis Drake on the Northwest Coast of America in the Year 1579: The Golden Hinde Did Not Anchor in the Bay of San Francisco.* San Francisco, 1908.

Delisle, Joseph Nicholas. *Explication de la carte des nouvelles découvertes au nord de la Mer du Sud.* Paris, 1752.

———. *Carte génerale des découvertes de l'Amiral de Fonte, et autres naviga-teurs Espagnoles, Anglois et Russes, pour le recherche du passage a la Mer du Sud.* Paris, 1752.

———. *Nouvelles Cartes de découvertes de l'Amiral de Fonte, et autres naviga-teurs Espagnols, Portugais, Anglois, Hollandois, François & Russes, dans les mers septentrionales, avec leur explication . . . .* Paris, 1753.

Dillon, Richard H. "Letters of Captain George Dixon in the Banks Collection." *BCHQ* 14 (1950) : 167–71.

———. "Archibald Menzies' Trophies." *BCHQ* 15 (1951) : 151–59.

Dufour, Clarence John. "The Russian Withdrawal from California." *CHSQ* 12 (1933) : 240–76.

Dulles, Foster Rhea. *The Old China Trade.* Boston, 1930.

Dunbabin, Thomas. "How British Columbia Nearly Became a Colony of Australia." *BCHQ* 15 (1951) : 35–46.

Dunmore, John. *French Explorers in the Pacific. The Eighteenth Century.* London and New York, 1965.

Elliott, Thompson Coit. "The Fur Trade in the Columbia River Basin Prior to 1811." *OHQ* 15 (1914) : 241–51. Reprinted in *WHQ* 6 (1915) : 3–10.

———. "The Log of H.M.S. 'Chatham.'" *OHQ* 18 (1917) : 231–43.

———. "Remnant of the Official Log of the Columbia, Captain Robert Gray, 1792." *OHQ* 22 (1921) : 352–56.

———. "Gray's First Visit to Oregon, Haswell's Log of the Sloop Washington." *OHQ* 29 (1928) : 162–88.

———. "Cook's Journal of His Approach to Oregon." *OHQ* 29 (1928) : 265–77.

———. "Journal of John Mears' Approach to Oregon." *OHQ* 29 (1928) : 278–87.

———. "The Oregon Coast as Seen by Vancouver in 1792." *OHQ* 30 (1929) : 33–42, 384–394.

———. "Bodega to Clayoquot in 1790 in a Long Boat." *OHQ* 42 (1941) : 125–32.

Elyea, Winifred. "The History of Tatoosh Island." *WHQ* 20 (1929) : 223–27.

Engel, Samuel. *Mémoires et observations géographiques et critiques sur la situation des pays septentrionaux de l'Asie et de l'Amérique.* Lausanne, 1765.

Essig, E. O. "The Russian Settlement at Ross." *CHSQ* 12 (1933) : 191–209.

Eyer, Marguerite. "French Expansion Into the Pacific in the 17th, 18th and 19th Centuries." *PHSSC* 11 (1918) : 5–23.

Farrar, Victor John. "The Reopening of the Russian-American Convention of 1824." *WHQ* 11 (1920) : 83–88.

Fink, Colin G., and Polushkin, E. P. *Drake's Plate of Brass Authenticated.* San Francisco, 1938.

Fleuriot de Langle, Paul. *La Tragique Expédition de Lapérouse et Langle.* Paris, 1954.

Forster, Georg. *Geschichte der Reisen, die Seit Cook an der Nordwest- und Nordost-küste von Amerika und in dem Nördlichsten Amerika Selbst von Meares, Dixon, Portlock, Coxe, Long u. a. m. Unternommen Worden Sind.* Berlin, 1792.

Golder, Frank Alfred. *Russian Expansion on the Pacific, 1641–1850: An Account of the Earliest and Later Expeditions Made by the Russians Along the Pacific Coast of Asia and North America; Including Some Related Expeditions to the Arctic Regions.* Cleveland, 1914.

———. *Bering's Voyages: An Account of the Efforts of the Russians to Determine the Relation of Asia and America.* 2 vols. New York, 1935.

Gronsky, P. "L'Établissement des Russes en California." *Révue d'histoire moderne* 4 (1929) : 401–15; 5 (1930) : 101–23.

Hague, James D. "The Drake Medal." *Bulletin of the American Geographical Society of New York* 40 (1908) : 449–69.

Halliday, E. M. "Captain Cook's American." *AH* 13, no. 1 (1961) : 60–72, 84–87.

Haselden, R. B. "Is the Drake Plate of Brass Genuine?" *CHSQ* 16 (1937) : 271–74.

Heizer, Robert Fleming. "Francis Drake and the California Indians, 1579." *University of California Publications in American Archaeology and Ethnology.* 42 (Berkeley and Los Angeles, 1947) : 3, 251–301.

———. and Elmendorf, William W. "Francis Drake's California Anchorage in the Light of the Indian Language Spoken There." *Pacific Historical Review* 11 (1942) : 213–17.

Hosie, John. "Thomas Muir, Scottish Political Martyr and His Connection With Vancouver Island." *BCHA Annual Report* 1 (Victoria, 1923) : 28–32.

Houghton, F. L. "Captain Vancouver: His Work on the Pacific Coast." *Canadian Defense Quarterly* 12 (Ottawa, 1935) : 174–82.

Howay, Frederick William. "Early Navigation of the Straits of Fuca." *OHQ* 12 (1911) : 1–32.

———. "The Fur Trade in Northwestern Development." In *The Pacific Ocean in History: Papers and Addresses Presented at the Panama-Pacific Historical Congress, 1915.* (New York, 1917). Pp. 276–86.

———. "The Voyage of the Hope: 1790–1792." *WHQ* 11 (1920) : 3–28.

———. "Authorship of the Anonymous Account of Captain Cook's Last Voyage." *WHQ* 12 (1921) : 51–58.

————. "John Kendrick and His Sons." *OHQ* 23 (1922) : 277–302.

————. The Loss of the Tonquin." *WHQ* 13 (1922) : 83–92.

————. "Early Days of the Maritime Fur-Trade on the Northwest Coast." *CHR* 4 (1923) : 26–44.

————. "Letters Relating to the Second Voyage of the Columbia." *OHQ* 24 (1923) : 132–51.

————. "Indian Attacks Upon Maritime Traders of the North-west Coast, 1785–1805." *CHR* 6 (1925) : 287–309.

————. "Some Additional Notes Upon Captain Colnett and the 'Princess Royal.'" *OHQ* 26 (1925) : 12–22.

————. "Captain Simon Metcalfe and the Brig 'Eleanora.'" *WHQ* 16 (1925) : 114–21.

————. "An Early Account of the Loss of the Boston in 1803." *WHQ* 17 (1926), 280–88.

————. "Early Followers of Captain Gray." *WHQ* 18 (1927) : 11–20.

————. "A Ballad of the Northwest Fur Trade." *New England Quarterly* 1 (1928) : 71–79.

————. "The Trading Voyages of the Atahualpa." *WHQ* 19 (1928) : 3–12.

————. "The Ballad of the Bold Northwestman: An Incident in the Life of Captain John Kendrick." *WHQ* 20 (1929) : 114–23.

————. "The Ship 'Margaret,'" *Hawaiian Historical Society Annual Report, 1929* (1930) : 34–40.

————. *The Hawaiian Islands: Early Relations With the Pacific Northwest.* Honolulu, 1930.

————. "A List of Trading Vessels in Maritime Fur Trade, 1785–1794." *Proceedings of the Royal Society of Canada,* 3d ser. 24 (1930) : 111–34; 25 (1931) : 117–49; 26 (1932) : 43–86; 27 (1933) : 119–47; 28 (1934) : 11–49.

————. "A Yankee Trader on the Northwest Coast, 1791–1795." *WHQ* 21 (1930) : 83–94.

————. "Some Notes on Cook's and Vancouver's Ships, 1776–80, 1791–95." *WHQ* 21 (1930) : 268–70.

————. "An Outline Sketch of the Maritime Fur Trade." *Canadian Historical Association Report of the Annual Meeting, 1932* (1932) : 5–14.

————. "The 'Resolution' on the Oregon Coast, 1793–4." *OHQ* 34 (1933) : 207–15.

————. "About That 'Valuable Manuscript.'" *WHQ* 24 (1933) : 25–27.

————. " A Short Account of Robert Haswell." *WHQ* 24 (1933) : 83–90.

————. "The Journal of Captain James Colnett, 1789. *Proceedings of the Royal Society of Canada,* 3d ser. 33 (1939) : 91–102.

Howay, Frederick William, and Elliott, Thompson Coit. "John Boit's Log of the Columbia, 1790–3." *OHQ* 21 (1921) : 257-351.

————. "Voyages of the 'Jenny' to Oregon, 1792–94. *OHQ* 30 (1929) : 197–206.

————. "Vancouver's Brig *Chatham* in the Columbia." *OHQ* 43 (1942) : 318–27.

Howay, Frederick William, and Matthews, Albert. "Some Notes Upon Captain Robert Gray (1755–1809)." *WHQ* 21 (1930) : 8–12.

Howe, George. "The Voyage of the Nor'west John." *AH* 10, no. 3 (1959) : 64–80.

Hunt, Morton M. "First by Land." *AH* 8, no. 6 (1957) : 42–47, 94–95.

Irving, Washington. *Astoria*. New York, 1849.

Kashevaroff, Rev. A. P. "Fort Ross: An Account of Russian Settlement." *Alaska Magazine* 1 (1927) : 235–42.

Kuykendall, Ralph S. "James Colnett and the 'Princess Royal.' " *OHQ* 25 (1924) : 36–52.

Lamb, W. Kaye. "The Mystery of Mrs. Barkley's Diary." *BCHQ* 6 (1942) : 31–59.

Laut, Agnes Christina. *Vikings of the Pacific: The Adventures of the Explorers Who Came From the West, Eastward*. New York and London, 1905.

———. *Pioneers of the Pacific Coast: A Chronicle of Sea Rovers and Fur Hunters*. Toronto and Glasgow, 1915.

Lyman, Horace S. "Early New England Exploration of Our North Pacific Coast —the Columbia River." *American Historical Magazine* [i.e., *Americana*] 1 (1906) : 52–67.

McCracken, Harold. *Hunters of the Stormy Sea*. Garden City, N.Y., 1957.

McDonald, Lucile. "Mystery of Famous Convict's Visit to Nootka is Clarified." *Seattle Times*, 4 March 1962, Sunday magazine section.

Manning, Clarence A. *Russian Influence on Early America*. New York, 1953.

Markoff, Alexander. *The Russians on the Pacific Ocean*. Los Angeles, 1955.

Masson, Marjorie, and Jameson, John Franklin. "The Odyssey of Thomas Muir." *AHR* 29 (1923) : 49–72.

Masterson, James R., and Brower, Helen. "Bering's Successors, 1745–1780: Contributions of Peter Simon Pallas to the History of Russian Exploration Toward Alaska." *PNQ* 38 (1947) : 35–83, 109–55.

Meany, Edmond S., Jr. "The Later Life of John R. Jewitt. *BCHQ* 4 (1940) : 143–61.

———. *Vancouver's Discovery of Puget Sound*. Portland, Ore., 1942.

Mazour, Anatole G. "Dimitry Zavalishin: Dreamer of a Russian-American Empire." *PHR* 5 (1936) : 26–37.

Morison, Samuel Eliot. *The Maritime History of Massachusetts, 1783–1860*. Boston and New York, 1921.

———. "The Columbia's Winter Quarters of 1791–1792 Located." *OHQ* 39

———. "Nova Albion and New England." *OHQ* 28 (1927) : 1–17.

(1938) : 3–7.

Neatby, Leslie H. *In Quest of the Northwest Passage*. New York, 1962.

Newcombe, Charles Frederic. *The First Circumnavigation of Vancouver Island*. Victoria, B.C., 1914.

Nuttall, Zelia. *New Light on Drake*. London, 1914.

Oko, Adolph S., "Francis Drake and Nova Albion." *CHSQ* 43 (1964) : 135–58.

Okun', Semen Bentsionovich. *The Russian-American Company*. Cambridge, Mass., 1951.

Pemberton, C. C. "Discovery and Naming of the 'Strait of Juan de Fuca.' " *BCHA Annual Report* 4 (1929) : 33–36.

Phillips, Paul Chrisler. *The Fur Trade*. Norman, Okla., 1961.

Poniatowski, Michel. *Histoire de la Russie d'Amérique et d'Alaska*. Paris, 1958.

Porter, Edward G. "The Discovery of the Columbia River." *New England Magazine,* n.s. 6 (1892) : 472–88. Reprinted in *Old South Leaflets,* p. 131.

Porter, Kenneth W. *John Jacob Astor, Business Man.* 2 vols. Cambridge, Mass., 1931.

Power, R. H. "Portus Novae Albionis Rediscovered?" *Pacific Discovery* 7 (1954) : 10–12.

Robertson, John W. *Francis Drake & Other Early Explorers Along the Pacific Coast.* San Francisco, 1927.

Ross, Frank E. "The Early Fur Trade of the Great Northwest." *OHQ* 39 (1938) : 389–409.

*The Russians in California.* San Francisco, 1933.

Shiels, Archibald Williamson. *Early Voyages of the Pacific: A Few Notes on the Days of Iron Men and Wooden Ships.* Bellingham, Wash., 1931.

Scheffer, Victor B. "The Sea Otter on the Washington Coast." *PNQ* 31 (1940) : 371–88.

Skinner, Constance Lindsay. *Adventurers of Oregon: A Chronicle of the Fur Trade,* New Haven, 1921.

Smith, Francis E. *Achievements and Experiences of Captain Robert Gray, 1788 to 1792.* 2d ed. Tacoma, Wash., 1923.

Sparks, Jared. *The Life of John Ledyard* . . . . Cambridge and New York, 1828.

Sperlin, O. B. "Washington Forts of the Fur Trade Regime." *WHQ* 8 (1917) : 102–13.

Sturgis, William. *The Northwest Fur Trade, and the Indians of the Oregon Country.* Boston, 1920.

Taylor, Eva G. R. "Master John Dee, Drake and the Straits of Anian." *Mariner's Mirror* 15 (1929) : 125–30.

———. "More Light on Drake." *Mariner's Mirror* 16 (1930) : 134–51.

———. "The Missing Draft Project of Drake's Voyage of 1577–80." *GJ* 75 (1930) : 44–47.

———. *Tudor Geography, 1485–1583.* London, 1930.

———. "Francis Drake and the Pacific: Two Fragments." *PHR* 1 (1932) : 360–69.

———. "Early Empire Building Projects in the Pacific Ocean, 1565–1585." *HAHR* 14 (1934) : 296–306.

Temko, Allan. "Russians in California." *AH* 11, no. 3 (1960) : 4–9, 81–85.

Tompkins, Stuart Ramsay. *Alaska, Promyshlennik and Sourdough.* Norman, Okla., 1945.

———, and Moorehead, Max L. "Russia's Approach to America. Part I, From Russian Sources, 1751–1761." *BCHQ* 13 (1949) : 55–66; "Part II, From Spanish Sources, 1761–1775." 13 (1949) : 231–55.

Torrubia, José. *I Moscoviti nella California, o sia dimostrazione della verita' del passo all' America Settentrionale nouvamente scoperto dai Russi, e di quello anticamente practicato dalli popolatori, che vi transmigrarono dall' Asia.* Rome, 1759. 2d ed. in *Nuova Raccolta d'opuscoli scientifici e filologici* 7 (Venice, 1760) : 471–536.

Vandiver, Clarence A. *The Fur Trade and Early Western Exploration.* Cleveland, 1929.

Vaugondy, Didier Robert de. *Mémoire sur les pays de l'Asie et de l'Amérique, situés au nord de la Mer du Sud: Accompagné d'une carte, intitulée: Nouveau système géographique, par lequel on concilie les anciennes connoissances sur le pays Nord-ouest de l'Amérique, avec les nouvelles découvertes des Russes.* Paris, 1774.

Wade, Mark S. *Mackenzie of Canada.* Edinburgh and London, 1927.

Wagner, Henry Raup. *Sir Francis Drake's Voyage Around the World: Its Aims and Achievements.* San Francisco, 1926.

Whitebrook, Robert B. "From Cape Flattery to Birch Bay: Vancouver's Anchorages on Puget Sound." *PNQ* 44 (1953) : 115–28.

Woollen, William Watson. *The Inside Passage to Alaska, 1792–1920, With an Account of the North Pacific Coast From Cape Mendocino to Cook Inlet, From the Accounts Left by Vancouver and Other Early Explorers, and From the Author's Journals of Exploration, and Travel in That Region.* 2 vols. Cleveland, 1924.

### THE NOOTKA CONTROVERSY

### *Sources*

*An Address to the Parliament of Great Britain on the Past and Present State of Affairs Between Spain and Great Britain, Respecting Their American Possessions.* London, 1790.

Burges, Sir James Bland. *Letters Lately Published in the Diary on the Subject of the Present Dispute With Spain Under the Signature of Verus.* London, 1790.

———. *A Narrative of the Negotiations Occasioned by the Dispute Between England and Spain in the year 1790.* London, [1791].

Calvo, Carlos, ed. *Colección completa de los tratados, convenciones, capitulaciones, armisticios . . . de todos los estados de la América Latina.* 11 vols. Paris, 1862–69.

Cantillo, Alejandro del, ed. *Tratados, convenciones y declaraciones de paz y de comercio que han hecho con las potencias extranjeras los monarcas Españoles de la casa de Borbón.* Madrid, 1843.

Cobbett, William, ed. *Cobbett's Parliamentary History of England.* 36 vols. London, 1806–20.

*Comments on the Convention With Spain.* London, 1790.

*Convención entre el Rey Nuestro Señor y el Rey de la Gran Bretaña, transigiendo varios puntos sobre pesca, navegación y comercio en el Océano Pacífico y los Mares del Sur, firmada en San Lorenzo el Real á 28 de octubre de 1790, cuyas ratificaciones se canjearon en el mismo sitio á 22 de noviembre siguiente.* Madrid, [1790?].

Dalrymple, Alexander. *The Spanish Memorial of 4th June Considered,* London, 1790.

———. *The Spanish Pretensions Fairly Discussed.* London, 1790.

*The Errors of the British Minister in the Negotiation With the Courts of Spain.* London, 1790.

[Etches, John], *An Authentic Statement of All the Facts Relative to Nootka Sound: Its Discovery, History, Settlement, Trade, and the Probable Advantages to be Derived from It. In an Address to the King.* London, 1790.

———. *A Continuation of an Authentic Statement of All the Facts Relative to Nootka Sound.* London, 1790.

*Official Papers Relative to the Dispute Between the Courts of Great Britain and Spain on the Subject of the Ships Captured in Nootka Sound, and the Negotiation that Followed Thereon.* London, 1790.

Petty, William, 1st marquis de Lansdowne. *The Substance of the Speech of the Marquis de Lansdown, in the House of Lords, on the 14th of December, 1790; on the Subject of the Convention With Spain, Which Was signed on the 28th of October, 1790. By One Present.* London, [1790].

"State Papers." *Annual Register, 1790* 32 (1793) : 285–306.

"Strictures on the Spanish Declaration." *General Advertiser.* London, 1. September 1790.

### Secondary Works

Blue, George Verne. "Anglo-French Diplomacy During the Critical Period of the Nootka Controversy." *OHQ* 39 (1938) : 162–179.

Caillet-Bois, Ricardo R. "La Controversia del 'Nootka Sound' y el Río de la Plata." *Humanidades* 20 (Buenos Aires, 1930) : 341–74.

Manning, William Ray. "The Nootka Sound Controversy." *AHA Annual Report, 1904* (1905) : 279–478.

Mills, Lennox. "The Real Significance of the Nootka Sound Incident." *CHR* 6 (1925) : 110–22.

Norris, J. M. "The Policy of the British Cabinet in the Nootka Crisis." *EHR* 70 (1955) : 562–80.

Young, Frederick George. "Spain and England's Quarrel Over the Oregon Country." *OHQ* 21 (1920) : 13–20.

### THE SPANISH AND OREGON'S EASTERN PERIMETER

### Sources

Abel-Henderson, Annie Heloise, ed. "Trudeau's Description of the Upper Missouri." *Mississippi Valley Historical Review* 8 (1921) : 149–79.

*An Account of the Red River in Louisiana, Drawn up from the Return of Messrs. Freeman and Custis to the War Office, in the United States, Who Explored the Same in the Year 1806.* n.p., 1807.

Coues, Elliott, ed. *The Expeditions of Zebulon Montgomery Pike.* 3 vols. New York, 1895.

Jackson, Donald, ed. *Letters of the Lewis and Clark Expedition, with Related Documents, 1783–1854.* Urbana, Ill., 1962.

———, ed. *The Journals of Zebulon Montgomery Pike, With Letters and Related Documents.* 2 vols. Norman, Okla., 1966.

Nasatir, Abraham P., ed. *Before Lewis and Clark: Documents Illustrating the History of the Missouri, 1785–1804.* 2 vols. St. Louis, 1952.

Pike, Zebulon Montgomery. *An Account of Expeditions to the Sources of the Mississippi, and Through the Western Parts of Louisiana.* 4 vols. Philadelphia, 1810.

Tabeau, Pierre Antoine. *Tabeau's Narrative of Loisel's Expedition to the Upper Missouri.* Edited by Annie Heloise Abel-Henderson. Norman, Okla., 1939.

Thomas, Alfred Barnaby, ed. "Documents Bearing Upon the Northern Frontier of New Mexico, 1818–1819." *NMHR* 4 (1929) : 146–64.

### Secondary Works

Bloom, Lansing B. "The Death of Jacques d'Eglise." *NMHR* 2 (1927) : 369–79.

Cox, Isaac Joslin. "The Exploration of the Louisiana Frontier, 1803–06." *AHA Annual Report, 1904* (1905) : 149–74.

———. *The Early Explorations of Louisiana.* Cincinnati, 1906.

Diller, Aubrey. "James Mackay's Journey in Nebraska in 1796." *Nebraska History* 36 (1955) : 123–28.

Ficklen, John R. "The Northwestern Boundary of Louisiana." *Louisiana Historical Society Publications* 2 (1899) : 26–29.

Goetzmann, William H. *Army Exploration in the American West.* New Haven, 1960.

———. *Exploration and Empire: The Explorer and the Scientist in the Winning of the American West.* New York, 1966.

Hill, Joseph J. "Spanish and Mexican Exploration and Trade Northwest from New Mexico Into the Great Basin, 1765–1853." *Utah Historical Quarterly* 3 (1930) : 3–23.

Hollon, William Eugene. *The Lost Pathfinder: Zebulon Montgomery Pike.* Norman, Okla., 1949.

Houck, Louis. *Spanish Régime in Missouri.* 2 vols. Chicago, 1908.

Jackson, Donald. "How Lost Was Zebulon Pike?" *AH* 16, no. 2 (1965) : 10–15, 75–80.

Kenner, Charles L. *A History of New Mexican-Plains Indian Relations.* Norman, Okla., 1968.

Loomis, Noel M., and Nasatir, Abraham P. *Pedro Vial and the Roads to Santa Fe.* Norman, Okla., 1967.

Marshall, Thomas Maitland. *A History of the Western Boundary of the Louisiana Purchase, 1819–1841.* Berkeley, 1914.

Nasatir, Abraham P. "Jacques D'Eglise on the Upper Missouri, 1791–1795." *Mississippi Valley Historical Review* 14 (1927) : 47–55.

———. "Spanish Exploration of the Upper Missouri." *Mississippi Valley Historical Review* 14 (1927) : 57–71.

———. "Anglo-Spanish Rivalry on the Upper Missouri." *Mississippi Valley Historical Review* 16 (1929–30) : 359–82, 507–28.

———. "Formation of the Missouri Company." *Missouri Historical Review* 25 (1930) : 10–22.

———. "John Evans: Explorer and Surveyor." *Missouri Historical Review* 25 (1930) : 219–39, 432–60, 585–608.

————. "Jacques Clamorgan: Colonial Promoter of the Northern Border of New Spain." *NMHR* 17 (1942) : 101–12.

————. "Jacques Clamorgan." In LeRoy R. Hafen, ed. *The Mountain Men and the Fur Trade of the Far West*. Glendale, Calif., 1965, 2 : 81–94.

————. "Jacques D'Eglise." In LeRoy R. Hafen, ed. *The Mountain Men . . . .* 2 : 123–34.

Robertson, James Alexander. *Louisiana Under the Rule of Spain, France, and the United States, 1785–1807*. 2 vols. Cleveland, 1911.

Solano Costa, Fernando. "Los Problemas diplomáticos de las fronteras de la Luisiana." *Historia diplomática* 3 (Zaragoza, 1956) : 51–95; 4 (1958) : 121–54.

Thomas, Alfred Barnaby. "The Yellowstone River, James Long, and Spanish Reaction to American Intrusion Into Spanish Dominions, 1818–1819." *NMHR* 4 (1929) : 164–77.

Wheat, Carl Irving. *Mapping the Transmississippi West, 1540–1861*. 2 vols. San Francisco, 1957–58.

Williams, David. "John Evans' Strange Journey." *AHR* 54 (1948–49) : 277–95, 508–29.

## OTHER WORKS UTILIZED

Abernethy, Thomas Perkins. *The Burr Conspiracy*. New York, 1954.

Adams, Ephraim Douglas. *The Influence of Grenville on Pitt's Foreign Policy, 1787–1798*. Washington, D.C., 1904.

Adams, Henry. *History of the United States of America*. 9 vols. New York, 1890–91.

Adams, John. *Works*. Edited by Charles Francis Adams. 10 vols. Boston, 1850–56.

Adams, John Quincy. *Memoirs*. Edited by Charles Francis Adams. 12 vols. Philadelphia, 1874–77.

————. *Writings*. Edited by Worthington C. Ford. 7 vols. New York, 1913–17.

Alexander, Philip Frederick. *The North-west and North-east Passages 1576–1611*. Cambridge, 1915.

*American State Papers: Foreign Relations*. 6 vols. Washington, D.C., 1834–61.

————: *Indian Affairs*. 2 vols. Washington, D.C., 1832–34.

————: *Miscellaneous*. 2 vols. Washington, D.C., 1834.

Amundsen, Roald. *The North West Passage*. 2 vols. London, 1908.

Andrews, Ralph W. *Indian Primitive*. Seattle, 1960.

Aspinall, Arthur, ed. *The Later Correspondence of George III*. Vol. 1. *December to January 1793*. Cambridge, 1962.

Bailey, Thomas A. *A Diplomatic History of the American People*. 7th ed. New York, 1964.

Bakeless, John. *Lewis and Clark, Partners in Discovery*. New York, 1947.

Barbé-Marbois, François. *Histoire de la Louisiane et de la Cession*. Paris, 1829. English translation: *The History of Louisiana, Particularly of the Cession of that Colony to the United States*. Philadelphia, 1830.

Barry, John Neilson. "Lieutenant Jeremy Pinch." *OHQ* 38 (1937) : 223–27.

Bemis, Samuel Flagg. "Relations Between the Vermont Separatists and Great Britain, 1789–1791." *AHR* 21 (1916) : 547–60.

———. *Jay's Treaty*. New York, 1924. Rev. ed. New Haven, 1962.

———. *Pinckney's Treaty: A Study of America's Advantage From Europe's Distress, 1783–1800*. Baltimore, 1926. Rev. ed. New Haven, 1960.

———. *The Diplomacy of the American Revolution*. New York, 1935. 2d ed. Bloomington, Ind., 1957.

———. *John Quincy Adams and the Foundations of American Foreign Policy*. New York, 1949.

———. *A Short History of American Foreign Policy and Diplomacy*. New York, 1959.

———. *A Diplomatic History of the United States*. 5th ed. New York, 1965.

Best, George. *The Three Voyages of Martin Frobisher in Search of a Passage to Cathay and India by the North-west*, A.D. *1576–8*. Edited by Vilhjalmer Stefansson. 2 vols. London, 1938.

Billington, Ray Allen. *Westward Espansion: A History of the American Frontier*. New York, 1949. 2d ed. New York, 1960.

Boas, Franz. *Chinook Texts*. Washington, D.C., 1894.

———. "The Social organization and secret societies of the Kwakiutl Indians." *U.S. National Museum Report . . . 1895* (1897) : 311–78.

Bolton, Herbert E. "General James Wilkinson as Advisor to Emperor Iturbide." *HAHR* 1 (1918) : 163–80.

Boyd, Julian P. *Number 7: Alexander Hamilton's Secret Attempt to Control American Foreign Policy*. Princeton, N.J., 1964.

Brabant, Rev. Augustin J. *Vancouver Island and Its Missions, 1874–1900: Reminiscences*. Hesquiat, B.C., 1900.

Brooks, Philip Coolidge. "The Pacific Coast's First International Boundary Delineation, 1816–1819." *PHR* 3 (1934) : 62–79.

———. "Pichardo's Treatise and the Adams-Onís Treaty." *HAHR* 15 (1935) : 94–99.

———. *Diplomacy and the Borderlands: The Adams-Onis Treaty of 1819*. Berkeley, 1939.

Brymner, Douglas. *Report on Canadian Archives . . . 1890*. Ottawa, 1891.

Buache de Neuville, Philippe. "Memoria sobre el descubrimiento del paso norte ó del mar Océano al del Sur por la parte septentrional de la América." In Alejandro Malaspina. *Viaje político-cientifico alrededor del Mundo . . . .* Madrid, 1885, Pp. 144–49.

Burt, Alfred L. *The United States, Great Britain and British North America From the Revolution to the Establishment of Peace After the War of 1812*. 2d ed. New York, 1961.

Carey, Charles Henry. *History of Oregon*. Chicago and Portland, Ore., 1922.

———. *A General History of Oregon Prior to 1861*. 2 vols. Portland, Ore., 1935–36.

Caughey, John W. *McGillivray of the Creeks*. Norman, Okla., 1938.

Ceballos, Ciriaco. *Disertación sobre la navegación á las Indias Occidentales por el norte de Europa*. Isla de León [Cádiz], 1789.

Clark, Dan Elbert. "Manifest Destiny and the Pacific." *PHR* 1 (1932) : 1–17.

Clark, Daniel. *Proofs of the Corruption of Gen. James Wilkinson, and of His Connexion with Aaron Burr.* Philadelphia, 1809.

Clark, Robert C. *History of the Willamette Valley.* Chicago, 1927.

Clark, George Rogers. *Papers.* Edited by J. A. James. *Illinois Historical Collection* 8 (1912); 19 (1926).

Clarke, Samuel Asahel. *Pioneer Days of Oregon History.* Portland, Ore., 1905.

Codere, Helen. *Fighting With Property: A Study of Kwakiutl Potlatching and Warfare 1792–1930.* New York, 1950.

Cooke, Edward. *A Voyage to the South Sea, and Round the World, Perform'd in the Years 1708, 1709, 1710, and 1711. Containing a Journal of All Memorable Transactions During the Said Voyage; the Winds, Currents, and Variation of the Compass; the Taking of the Towns of Puna and Guayaquil, and Several Prizes, One of Which a Rich Acapulco Ship. A Description of the American Coasts, From Tierra del Fuego to California . . . .* 2 vols. London, 1712.

Cox, Isaac Joslin. *The Early Explorations of Louisiana.* Cincinnati, 1906.

——. "The Louisiana-Texas Frontier." *SHQ* 17 (1913–14) : 1–42, 140–187.

——. "General Wilkinson and his Later Intrigues with the Spaniards." *AHR* 19 (1914) : 794–812.

——. "Wilkinson's First Break with the Spaniards." *Ohio Valley Historical Association Annual Report* 8 (1915) : 49–56.

——. *The West Florida Controversy, 1798–1813.* Baltimore, 1918.

——. "The Louisiana-Texas Frontier During the Burr Conspiracy." *Mississippi Valley Historical Review* 10 (1923) : 274–84.

——. "Opening the Santa Fe Trail." *Missouri Historical Review* 25 (1930) : 30–66.

——. "Hispanic-American Phases of the Burr Conspiracy." *HAHR* 12 (1932): 145–75.

Crouse, Nellis Maynard. *The Search for the Northwest Passage.* New York, 1934.

Dahlgren, Erik Wilhelm. *Les Relations commerciales et maritimes entre la France et les côtes de l'Océan Pacifique.* Paris, 1909.

Davis, Andrew McFarland. "The Journey of Moncacht-Apé." *PAAS,* n. s. 2 (1883): 321–48.

Davis, Matthew L. *Memoirs of Aaron Burr: With a Miscellaneous Selection from His Correspondence.* New York, 1852.

De Terra, Helmut. "Alexander von Humboldt's Correspondence With Jefferson, Madison, and Gallatin." *Proceedings of the American Philosophical Society* 103 (1959) : 783–806.

Dobbs, Arthur. *An Account of the Countries Adjoining to Hudson's Bay.* London, 1744.

Dodge, Ernest S. *Northwest by Sea.* New York, 1961.

Douglas, Jesse S. "Jeremy Pinch and the War Department." *OHQ* 39 (1938): 425–31.

Doylé, William. *Some Account of the British Dominions Beyond the Atlantic: Containing Chiefly What is Most Interesting and Least Known With Respect to Those Parts: Particularly, the Important Question About the North West Passage is Satisfactorily Discussed* . . . . London, 1770.

Drage, Theodore Swain. *A Voyage for the Discovery of a North-west Passage to the Western and Southern Ocean, 1746–47.* 2 vols. London, 1748–49.

———. [?] *The Great Probability of a North West Passage: Deduced from Observations on the Letter of Admiral de Fonte, Who Sailed From the Callao of Lima on the Discovery of a Communication Between the South Sea and the Atlantic Ocean* . . . . London, 1768.

Drucker, Philip. *Indians of the Northwest Coast.* New York, 1955.

———. *Cultures of the North Pacific Coast.* San Francisco, 1965.

Elliott, Thompson Coit. "The Strange Case of Jonathan Carver and the Name Oregon." *OHQ* 21 (1920) : 341–68.

———. "The Origin of the Name Oregon." *OHQ* 22 (1921) : 91–115.

———. "Jonathan Carver's Source of the Name Oregon." *OHQ* 23 (1922) : 52–69.

———. ed. "David Thompson: Narrative of the Expedition to the Kootanae and Flat Bow Indian Countries on the Sources of the Columbia River." *OHQ* 26 (1925) : 23–56.

———. "The Strange Case of David Thompson and Jeremy Pinch." *OHQ* 40 (1939) : 188–99.

Ellis, Henry. *A Voyage to Hudson's Bay, by the "Dobbs Galley" and "California," for Discovering a North West Passage, with an Accurate Survey of the Coast.* London, 1748.

Ford, Worthington Chauncey. *The United States and Spain in 1790. An Episode in Diplomacy Described from Hitherto Unpublished Sources.* Brooklyn, N.Y., 1890.

Franklin, Benjamin. *Writings.* Edited by Albert H. Smyth. 10 vols. New York and London, 1905–07.

Freeman, Lewis Ransome. *The Colorado River, Yesterday, To-day and Tomorrow.* New York, 1923.

Galvani, William H. "The Early Explorations and the Origin of the Name of the Oregon Country." *OHQ* 21 (1920) : 332–40.

Gershoy, Leo. *The French Revolution, 1789–1799.* New York, ca.1932.

———. *The Era of the French Revolution, 1789–1799.* Princeton, N.J. 1957.

———. *The French Revolution and Napoleon.* New York, [1964].

Ghent, W.J. " 'Jeremy Pinch' Again." *OHQ* 40 (1939) : 307–14.

Goldson, William. *Observations on the Passage Between the Atlantic and Pacific Oceans, in Two Memoirs on the Straits of Anian, and the Discoveries of De Fonte.* Portsmouth, Eng., 1793.

Green, Thomas Marshall. *The Spanish Conspiracy.* Cincinnati, 1891.

Guinness, Ralph B. "The Purpose of the Lewis and Clark Expedition." *Mississippi Valley Historical Review* 20 (1933) : 90–100.

Hafen, LeRoy. *Mountain Men and the Fur Trade.* 9 vols. to date. Glendale, Calif., 1965–69.

Hall, Hubert. "Pitt and General Miranda." *Athenaeum* 75 (London, 1902) : 498–99.

Hamilton, Alexander. *Papers*. Edited by Harold C. Syrett. 7 vols. to date. New York, 1961–63.

Hay, Thomas Robson. *The Admirable Trumpeter: A Biography of General James Wilkinson*. New York, 1941.

Hermann, Binger. *The Louisiana Purchase and Our Title West of the Rocky Mountains, with a Review of Annexation by the United States*. Washington, D.C., 1898.

Hill, Joseph J. "New Light on Pattie and the Southwestern Fur Trade." *SHQ* 26 (1922–23) : 243–54.

Hollon, William Eugene. *The Lost Pathfinder, Zebulon Montgomery Pike*. Norman, Okla., 1949.

Humphreys, F. L. *The Life and Times of David Humphreys*. 2 vols. New York, 1917.

Jacobs, James Ripley. *Tarnished Warrior, Major-General James Wilkinson*. New York, 1938.

Jane, Sister M., SHF. "Concepción Argüello." Master's thesis, University of San Francisco, 1962.

Jefferson, Thomas. *Writings*. Edited by H. A. Washington. 9 vols. Washington, D.C., 1853–54.

———. *Writings*. Edited by Paul L. Ford. 10 vols. New York, 1892–99.

———. *Papers*. Edited by Julian P. Boyd. 17 vols. to date. Princeton, N.J., 1950–65.

Josephy, Alvin M., Jr. "A Man to Match the Mountains [David Thompson]." *AH* 11, no. 6 (1960) : 60–63, 81–85.

———. *The Nez Perce and the Opening of the Northwest*. New Haven and London, 1965.

Keller, Arthur S.; Lissitzn, Oliver J.; and Mann, Frederick J. *Creation of Rights of Sovereignty Through Symbolic Acts, 1400–1800*. New York, 1938.

Kellner, [Charlotte] L. *Alexander von Humboldt*. London, 1963.

Larsell, Olaf. *The Doctor in Oregon*. Portland, Ore., 1937.

Lewis, William S. "Some Notes and Observations on the Origin and Evolution of the Name Oregon as Applied to the River of the West." *WHQ* 17 (1926) : 218–22.

Logan, John, Jr. *No Transfer: An American Security Principle*. New Haven, 1961.

McCaleb, Walter Flavius. *The Aaron Burr Conspiracy*. New York, 1903. Expanded edition, with introduction by Charles Beard. New York, 1936.

———. *New Light on Aaron Burr*. Austin, 1963.

Masson, L. R., ed. *Les Bourgeois de la Compagnie du Nord-Quest*. 2 vols. Quebec, 1899–90. Reprinted New York, 1960.

Mathiez, Albert. *The French Revolution*. New York, 1962.

Miller, David Hunter, ed. *Treaties and Other International Acts of the United States of America*. 8 vols. Washington, D.C., 1931–48.

Meyers, J. A. "Oregan—River of the Slaves or River of the West." *WHQ* 13 (1922) : 282–83.

Parton, James. *The Life and Times of Aaron Burr*. New York, 1858. Rev. ed. 2 vols. Boston and New York, 1892.

Pattie, James Ohio. *The Personal Narrative of James Ohio Pattie of Kentucky.* Cincinnati, 1831.

Peattie, Donald Culross. "Return of the Sea Otter." *Reader's Digest,* May 1961, pp. 121–24.

Perkins, Dexter. *A History of the Monroe Doctrine.* Boston, 1955.

Pettit, George A. *The Quileute of La Push: 1775–1945.* Berkeley, 1950.

Philbrick, Francis Samuel. *The Rise of the West, 1754–1830.* New York, 1965. Paperback ed. 1966.

Pickersgill, Richard. *A Concise Account of Voyages for the Discovery of a Northwest Passage, Undertaken for Finding a New Way to the East-Indies: With Reflections on the Practicability of Gaining Such a Passage.* London, 1782.

Pierce, Richard A. *Russia's Hawaiian Adventure, 1815–1817.* Berkeley and Los Angeles, 1965.

Plumb, John H. "Our Last King." *AH* 11 no. 4 (1960) : 4–23, 95–101.

Pratt, Julius W. *A History of United States Foreign Policy.* Englewood Cliffs, N.J., 1955.

Pullen, Captain Thomas C. RCN. "We Found a New Northwest Passage." *Saturday Evening Post,* 10 May 1958, pp. 23–25, 62–70.

Quinn, D. B., ed. *The Voyages and Colonizing Enterprises of Sir Humphrey Gilbert.* 2 vols. London, 1940.

Reed, V. B., and Williams, J. D., eds. *The Case of Aaron Burr.* Boston, 1960.

Rees, John E. "Oregon—Its Meaning, Origin and Application." *OHQ* 21 (1920): 317–31.

Robertson, David, ed. *Reports of the Trials of Aaron Burr.* 2 vols. Philadelphia, 1808. 2d ed. New York, 1875.

Rogers, Woodes. *A Cruising Voyage Round the World: First to the South-seas, Thence to the East-Indies, and Homewards by the Cape of Good Hope. Begun in 1708, and Finish'd in 1711.* London, 1712.

Rowse, A. L. *The Expansion of Elizabethan England.* London and New York, 1955. Paperback ed. New York, 1965.

Safford, William Harrison, ed. *The Blennerhasset Papers.* Cincinnati, 1861.

Santos, Angel, SJ. *Jesuitas en el Polo Norte. La Misión de Alaska.* Madrid, 1943.

Serrano y Sanz, Manuel. *El Brigadier Jaime Wilkinson y sus tratos con España para la independencia del Kentucky (años 1787 á 1797).* Madrid, 1915.

Shreve, Royal O. *The Finished Scoundrel: General James Wilkinson, Sometime Commander-in-chief of the Army of the United States, Who Made Intrigue a Trade and Treason a Profession.* Indianpolis, 1933.

Sorel, Albert. *L'Europe et la Révolution Française.* 8 vols. Paris, 1885–1904.

Sproat, G. M. *Scenes and Studies of Savage Life.* London, 1868.

Stenberg, Richard R. "The Boundaries of the Louisiana Purchase." *HAHR* 14 (1934) : 32–64.

*Summary Observations and Facts Collected From Late and Authentic Accounts of Russian and Other Navigators, to Show the Practicability and Good Prospect of Success in Enterprises to Discover a Northern Passage for Vessels by Sea, Between the Atlantic and Pacific Oceans.* London, 1776.

Swanson, Earl H. "Nootka and the California Gray Whale." *PNQ* 47 (1956) : 52–56.

Szászdi, Adam. "Governor Folch and the Burr Conspiracy." *Florida Historical Quarterly* 38 (1960) : 239–51.

Teggart, Frederick John. "Notes Supplementary to Any Edition of Lewis and Clark." *AHA Annual Report, 1908* (1909) : 183–95.

Thompson, James M. *The French Revolution.* 2d ed. Oxford, 1962.

Thwaites, Reuben Gold, ed. *Original Journals of the Lewis and Clark Expedition, 1804–1806.* 8 vols. New York, 1904–05.

Turner, Frederick Jackson. "English Policy Toward America in 1790–1791." *AHR* 7 (1901–02) : 706–35; 8 (1902–03) : 78–86.

Tyrell, Joseph B., ed. *David Thompson's Narrative of His Explorations in Western America, 1784–1812.* Toronto, 1916.

———. "Letter of Roseman and Perch, July 10, 1807." *OHQ* 38 (1937) : 391–97.

U.S. Congress, Senate, *Journal of the Executive Proceedings of Senate of the United States of America, 1789–1905.* 90 vols. Washington, D.C., 1828–1948.

"Unveiling of Memorial Tablet at Nootka Sound." *BCHA Annual Report* 2 (1924) : 17–36.

Washington, George. *Diaries . . . 1748–1799.* Edited by J. C. Fitzpartick. 4 vols. Boston and New York, 1925.

———. *Writings.* Edited by J. C. Fitzpatrick. 39 vols. Washington, D.C., 1931–44.

Wilkinson, James. *Memoirs of My Own Times.* 3 vols. Philadelphia, 1816.

## MANUSCRIPT MATERIALS

*Major Repositories for Spanish Material Related to the Pacific Northwest*

The repositories are listed alphabetically according to the abbreviations given on pages xv–xvi, above. The guides referred to may be found above, under Bibliographical Aids.

CaBViPA (Provincial Archives of British Columbia, Victoria, B.C., Canada). Has original material relating to Charles and Frances Barkley, Colnett, Kendrick, Bishop's journal of the *Ruby;* translations of Moziño and Tikhmenev; transcript of Caamaño's diary of 1792; many volumes of pertinent transcripts from SpAGI and MxAGN.

CClH (Honnold Library, Pomona College, Claremont, California). The "Henry R. Wagner Collection of History and Cartography of the North Pacific" includes forty-four bound volumes and fifty additional packages of photostats and transcripts, plus 629 maps, mostly in photostat, gathered by the late historian.

CLU-WAC (William Andrews Clark Memorial Library, University of California, Los Angeles, California). Original manuscript accounts of the Spanish expeditions of 1774 (anon.), 1775 (Mourelle), and 1788 (Narváez).

CSmH (Henry E. Huntington Library, San Marino, California). Papers of José de Gálvez (1,500 pieces); miscellaneous manuscripts on Spanish expeditions to Nootka, Pedro Alberni, and the Voluntarios de Cataluña; journals of Martínez (1789), López de Haro (1788), and Bodega (1792).

CtY-B (Beinecke Library, Yale University, New Haven, Connecticut). The Coe and Beinecke Collections include many unique items on Malaspina, other Spanish commanders and friars on the northwest coast, Viceroys Flores and Bucareli, Colnett; also to be found there are a table summarizing the Spanish fur trade (appendix C), journals from the fur trade, rare charts, and a Webber painting of Nootka. Most of the pertinent items have been acquired subsequent to the publication of Withington's *Catalogue* (1952).

CU-B (Bancroft Library, University of California, Berkeley, California). Numerous originals and extensive transcripts and microfilm holdings of material related to the northwest coast; Revillagigedo's personal archive (Robbins Collection). Guides: Fisher, 1955; Morgan and Hammond, 1963.

DLC (Manuscript Division, Library of Congress, Washington, D.C.). Ingraham's original log; Manning Transcripts from Spanish archives concerning Nootka Controversy; many volumes of photostats from MxAGN, SpAGI, and SpAHN concerning the northwest coast; hundreds of rolls of microfilm of selected *legajos* from these same archives, done under "Rockefeller Project A," pertaining to the subject, indexed three ways: chronologically, alphabetically, and by shelf order in original archive. The volumes copied from MxAGN are indexed in a desk copy of Bolton, 1913. Other guides: Jones, 1919; Martin, 1929 and 1930; Griffin, 1941.

FrBN (Bibliothèque Nationale, Paris, France). Manuscripts relating to the *San Francisco Xavier,* José de Gálvez, and Viceroy Revillagigedo. Guides: Paris. Bibliothèque, 1881–92; bid., 1899.

ICN (Newberry Library, Chicago, Illinois). The Ayer Collection holds many transcripts from Spanish and Mexican archives; originals of anonymous account of the 1774 expedition; José de Gálvez, "Informe"; García de León y Pizarro, "Compendio." Guides: Hussey, 1930; Butler, 1937.

MH-P (Peabody Museum, Harvard University, Cambridge, Massachusetts). Originals of Webber drawings of the northwest coast, 1778.

MxAGN (Archivo General de la Nación, Mexico City, Mexico). Diaries and reports, royal orders, etc., relating to the interior provinces and to the northwest coast. The most important archive for the present study. The portions of greatest interest are: Sec. Hist., vols. 24, 31, 61–71, 277, 324, 328–29, 397; Prov. Internas, 3, 4, 6, 23, 134, 153, 212; Californias, 8, 25, 28, 42, 61–62, 72, 78. Most useful guide: Bolton, 1913.

MxBN (Biblioteco Nacional, Mexico City, Mexico). A number of unique journals of Spanish expeditions, including the anonymous "Viaje" (1775), and a volume titled "Reconocimiento de los quatro establecimientos que el Imperio Ruso ha formado al Norte de la California," containing the essential documents of the 1788 expedition. Ph of the latter in DLC. Guide: Bolton, 1913.

MxMDN (Archivo de la Biblioteca, Ministerio de Defensa Nacional, Lomas de Chapultepec, Mexico City, Mexico). Manuscripts relating to the Spanish attempts to intercept Lewis and Clark. Formerly called the "Secretaría de Guerra y Marina" and housed in the Palacio Nacional, its pertinent contents are catalogued in Bolton, 1913.

NmSRC (State Record Center and Archives, Santa Fe, New Mexico). Material relating to the abortive attempts to intercept Lewis and Clark. Guide: Twitchell, 1914.

SpAGI (Archivo General de Indias, Seville, Spain). Vast and virtually unfathomable manuscripts from the ministry of Indies relating to the northwest coast. The most pertinent sections: V, Audiencias de México, Guadalajara, and Indiferente General; IX, Estado 20 through 43. Useful guides: Torres Lanzas, 1900 and 1919; Shepherd, 1907; Hill, 1916; Chapman, 1919; Paso y Troncoso, 1928–31; Bermúdez Plata, 1949.

SpAHN (Archivo Histórico Nacional, Madrid, Spain). Inexhaustible volume of papers from the ministry of state relating to the interior provinces, the northwest coast, and the Nootka Crisis. Although no adequate guide exists, see Shepherd, 1907; *Relaciones diplomáticas* . . . , 1944–46. The material of greatest value was found in Sec. Estado, *legajos* 919, 2848, 3370, 4243, 4258, 4285–91, 4631, 4639, 4669, 4819, 5542, and 5661–62. This is perhaps the most important repository for sources that have eluded examination for the present work, due to the difficulty of probing its depths for want of catalogues and indices, and because it closes annually during the month of August.

SpBP (Biblioteca de Palacio, Madrid, Spain). Bibliographical gems collected for the monarchs' perusal include manuscripts by Bodega, Mourelle, and Abad y La Serra. Guide: Domínguez Bordoña, 1935.

SpMA (Museo de América, Madrid, Spain). A collection of original drawings from the Malaspina expedition, formerly found in the Ministerio de Educación.

SpMN (Museo Naval, Madrid, Spain). Originals or certified copies of the instructions, logs, and reports of every one of the Spanish expeditions to the northwest coast; Malaspina papers, drawings, engravings, and charts. Card index by author, and printed giudes: Guillén y Tato, 1932; Vela, 1946.

UKLBM (British Museum, London, United Kingdom). Letters relating to the Nootka Sound controversy; an extract of the Cepeda account (1792); Russian and Spanish maps; Webber drawings of the northwest coast (1778). See London. British Museum. 1875–77.

*Extant Journals for Each Spanish Expedition, 1774–96*

Complete titles may be found in the first footnote in which a source is cited. Those that have been published are also listed on pages 561–65 of this bibliography.

1774 Of the first Spanish expedition to the northwest coast, four first-hand accounts of known authorship exist: those by Padres Crespi, SpAGI (Guad. 1), published in 1891 and 1969, and Peña Saravia, SpAGI (Guad. 515) and SpMN (331), published in 1891 and 1969; a Pérez diary, MxAGN (Hist. 61), MxMN (Lancaster-Jones Collection), and SpAGI (Estado 38–3 and Estado 20–11); and a Martínez diary, MxAGN (Hist. 61) and SpAGI (V, Guad. 516). There are anonymous accounts in SpMN (331), CtY-BWA (379) and ICN (Ayer Collection 1079).

1775 Of the Hezeta expedition a number of first-hand accounts are known: Mourelle's journal, published in English in 1781 and 1920, of which variant manuscript versions in Spanish exist, some of them richer in detail, in MxAGN (Hist. 324), SpBP (299–6), SpAGI (Estado 38–11), SpMN (331, 332, and 575), T in DLC (Conway transcripts); Hezeta's "Diario," MxAGN (Hist. 324), SpAGI (Estado 38–11), T in DLC (Conway Transcripts); an extract of the same in Mourelle's journal; Bodega, "Navegación," SpMN (622), published in 1943; Bodega, "Primer viaje," SpMN (618), published in 1865; Bodega, "Diario," SpMN (622); Bodega, "Extracto del Diario," SpMN (126); Bodega, "Comento," SpMN (618); Pérez account, MxAGN (Hist. 324); Sierra, "Diario," DLC (G. R. G. Conway Collection), published in 1930; Campa Cos, "Diario," MxAGN (Hist. 324), SpAGI (V, Guad. 515), ICN (Ayer Collection 1053), T in DLC (Conway Transcripts), published in English in 1964; Anon., "Diario," SpAGI (Estado 38–4); Anon., "Viaje," MxAGN (Hist. 24 and 44); Anon,. "Viaje," MxBN (MSS 2–29–7), Ph in DLC; Anon., resumé, CtY-BWA (379).

1779    Many first-hand accounts of the Arteaga expedition are known: Arteaga, "Diario," MxAGN (Hist. 63), SpAGI (Estado 38–13), and SpMN (622); an Arteaga report, MxAGN (Calif. 39), Ph in DLC; Bodega, "Segunda salida," SpMN (618), published in 1865; Bodega, "Navegación y descubrimientos," MxAGN (Hist. 64), SpAGI (Estado 38–15), SpMN (332), copy in CU–B; Bodega report to Viceroy Mayorga, MxAGN (Hist. 63); Bodega, "Comento" on expeditions of 1775 and 1779, SpMN (618), SpBP (324–8); Mourelle, "Navegación," SpMN (332 and 622) and CLU-WAC, of which an extract was published in La Pérouse, *Voyage* 1 (1797) : 324–42; Aguirre, "Diario," MxAGN (Hist. 64), SpAGI (Estado 38–18), copy in CU-B, Ph in DLC; Camacho, "Diario," MxAGN (Hist. 64), SpAGI (Estado 38–16), copy in CU–B, Ph in DLC; Cañizares, "Navegación," MxAGM (Hist. 64), SpAGI (Estado 38–17), copy in CU–B, Ph in DLC; García Riobó, "Relación," CtY-BWA (Coe 12, attributed erroneously to Arteaga), published in 1918–19; Pantoja, "Diario," MxAGN (Hist. 64), SpAGI (Estado 38–19), copy in CU–B, Ph in DLC; Pantoja, "Extracto," CtY-BWA (S–216); Quirós, "Diario," MxAGN (Hist. 64), SpAGI (Estado 38–14), copy in CU–B, Ph in DLC; Anon. "Diario," SpMN (622); Anon., "Tercera exploración," SpMN (331).

1788    None of the extant journals of the 1788 expedition have as yet been published: Martínez, "Diario," SpAGI (V, Aud. Mex. 1529); López de Haro, "Diario," CSmH; López de Haro account, SpAHN (Estado 4289), Mondofía, "Diario," SpAGI (V, Aud. Mex. 1529); Narváez journal, CLU-WAC; Palacios, "Diario," MxBN (MSS 30), Ph in DLC; Serantes journal, MxBN (MSS 30), Ph in DLC; Anon. "Diario," SpMN (331); Anon., "Noticia de lo acaecido," SpMN (330); Anon., "Razón de lo ocurrido," SpMN (332), SpAGI (Estado 43–11).

1789    In addition to the many letters from Martínez to the viceroy, cited in the text, the primary Spanish accounts of the expeditions of 1789 are: Martínez, "Diario," SpMN (732), published in 1964, extracts translated (from a copy in CU-B) in Colnett, *Journal,* 1940, pp. 308–18; Sánchez, "Historia," CtY-BWA (415); Tóbar, "Informe," September 18, 1789, MxAGN (Hist. 65), published in 1794; Tóbar, "Informe," October 7, 1789, MxAGN (Hist. 65); Tóbar, "Noticias," August 21, 1789, MxAGN (Hist. 65); Anon. Franciscan, "Noticias," MxAGN (Hist. 31).

1790   The first-hand accounts of Spanish expeditions of 1790 are: Fidalgo, "Diario," and letter to the viceroy, MxAGN (Hist. 68); Fidalgo, "Extracto . . . del Diario," SpMN (271); Fidalgo, "Relación," SpAHN (Estado 4286); Fidalgo, "Noticias," SpMN (575 bis); Mourelle extracts, SpMN (331); Quimper, "Diario," MxAGN (Hist. 68), SpAHN (Estado 4286), partly published in 1933; Anon., "Noticias de Fuca," SpMN (330), published with the foregoing, 1933; Caamaño, "Diario," 1790–91, MxAGN (Hist. 69) and SpMN (330), T in CaBViPA.

1791   For Spanish explorations in 1791 there exist: Eliza, "Extracto," SpMN (332), published in English in 1933; Pantoja, "Extracto," SpMN (331), with variants published in 1849 and in English in 1933; Viana, "Diario," published in 1849; Carrasco, "Extracto," MxAGN (Hist. 44), partly translated by Wagner, 1933, 200–2; Suría, "Quaderno," CtY-BWA (Coe 177), published in 1936 (English) and 1939 (Spanish); and the Malaspina documentation, SpMN (729, 749, 755, and 898) and CtY-BWA, much of which was published in 1885.

1792   The original journals of Spanish activities on the northwest coast in 1792 are: Bodega, "Viaje," CSmH (HM141); Alcalá Galiano, "Expedición," SpMN (143); Anon., "Noticias," UKLBM (Add. 13974); Caamaño, "Extracto del Diario," MxAGN (Hist. 71) and MxAGN (Prov. Int. 134), T in CaBViPA, published in 1849 and in English in 1938; Moziño, *Noticias de Nutka;* [Cardero,] *Relación del viaje hecho por las goletas Sútil y Mexicana;* and an anonymous account of the same voyage, SpMN (619).

1793   The explorations of Eliza and Martínez y Zayas in 1793 are described in: Anon., "Resultas," SpMN (575 bis): Martínez y Zayas, "Viaje," SpMN (331), published in English in 1931; Eliza, "Extracto," published in English in 1931; and Goycoechea, "Diario," published in English in 1931. For Nootka, there is Fidalgo's "Diario," MxAGN (Hist. 71), Ph in DLC.

1794   For 1794 there is solely Saavedra's "Diario," MxAGN (Hist. 71), Ph in DLC.

1795   There are no known Spanish journals from 1795.

1796   For 1796 there is Tóbar's "Extracto," SpAGI (Estado 25–45).

Other first-hand sources for the above expeditions exist, in the form of letters and instructions, but they are too numerous to list here. The most important are cited in footnotes to the text at the points where they document the narrative.

# Sources of Illustrations

Archivo General de Indias, Seville   17

Archivo General de la Nación, Mexico City   60

Archivo Histórico Nacional, Madrid   27, 29, 46, 61

Banco Urquijo, Madrid   26

Beinecke Rare Book and Manuscript Library, Yale University, New Haven
   1, 33

Biblioteca Nacional, Madrid   4

British Museum, London   10

Philippe Buache, *Considerations géographiques et physiques sur les nouvelles découvertes au nord de la Grande Mer, appellée vulgairement la
   Mer du Sud,* Paris, 1753   9

[José Cardero], *Relación del viaje hecho por las goletas* Sútil y Mexicana
   *en el año de 1792,* Madrid, 1802   40, 43

Charles E. Cook, Private Collection   2, 3, 44, 45

Warren L. Cook, Private Collection   5, 6, 8, 18, 35

Eusebio Gómez de la Puente, *Iconografía de gobernantes de la nueva España,*
   Mexico City, 1921   28

John Meares, *Voyages Made in the Years 1788 and 1789, from China to the
   North West Coast,* London, 1790   19, 20, 21

Junta de Iconografía Española, Madrid   12

Museo de América, Madrid   30, 32, 37, 38, 39, 41, 42, 48, 53, 54, 55, 56,
   57

Museo de Bellas Artes, Madrid   24

Museo del Prado, Madrid   11, 23

Museo Naval, Madrid   14, 15, 16, 31, 34, 36, 47, 49, 50, 51, 52, 58

Provincial Archives of British Columbia, Victoria   22, 62

Robbins Collection, Bancroft Library, University of California at Berkeley
   59

Sterling Memorial Library, Yale University, New Haven   25

Tillamook County Pioneer Museum, Tillamook, Oregon   7

# Index